DATE DUE

~~DE~~			
~~DE~~			
~~FE 5 '03~~			
~~JE 04~~			
~~MY 2 '05~~			
MY 13 '09			

DEMCO 38-296

Handbook of
Organized
Crime
in the United States

HANDBOOK OF
ORGANIZED CRIME
IN THE UNITED STATES

Edited by
ROBERT J. KELLY, KO-LIN CHIN,
and RUFUS SCHATZBERG

Foreword by Francis A. J. Ianni

GREENWOOD PRESS
Westport, Connecticut • London

Library of Congress Cataloging-in-Publication Data

Handbook of organized crime in the United States / edited by Robert J.
  Kelly, Ko-lin Chin, and Rufus Schatzberg ; foreword by Francis A. J.
  Ianni.
       p. cm.
    Includes bibliographical references (p.   ) and index.
    ISBN 0–313–28366–4 (alk. paper)
      1. Organized crime—United States—History.   2. Organized crime—
  United States—Prevention.   3. Organized crime investigation—
  United States.   I. Kelly, Robert J.   II. Chin, Ko-lin.
  III. Schatzberg, Rufus.
  HV6446.H345   1994
  364.1'06'0973—dc20   94–7428

British Library Cataloguing in Publication Data is available.

Library of Congress Catalog Card Number: 94–7428
ISBN: 0–313–28366–4

First published in 1994

Greenwood Press, 88 Post Road West, Westport, CT 06881
An imprint of Greenwood Publishing Group, Inc.

Printed in the United States of America

The paper used in this book complies with the
Permanent Paper Standard issued by the National
Information Standards Organization (Z39.48–1984).

10 9 8 7 6 5 4 3 2 1

Contents

Foreword

FRANCIS A. J. IANNI

Robert Redfield, the eminent American anthropologist, once remarked that the surest sign of the emergence of a new subdiscipline in science was analogous to what he had found to be characteristic of the establishment of small folk societies: a social structure organized by a kinship system made up of clans which shared a common folklore and mythology about the origins and values of the group. This timely and comprehensive volume of essays, demonstrates that by Redfield's definition, the study of organized crime has established itself at last as a coherent subdiscipline, if not yet as a functional community, of research interest.

When in the 1950s organized crime burst anew into the popular culture, questions of its character, structure, and dimensions were the exclusive province of government law-enforcement officials, some journalists, and a very few scholars such as Daniel Bell and Donald Cressey. This volume demonstrates how far we have come since then. Not only criminologists, but sociologists, anthropologists, historians, economists, political scientists, and legal scholars along with journalists and jurists have joined with criminal justice professionals to define, describe, analyze and recommend solutions to what is clearly a world-wide rather than peculiarly American social phenomenon. But despite decades of research, investigation, and any number of books and films—both documentary and dramatic—the study of organized crime remains a morass of conflicting claims and often spurious assertions held together more by controversy than by any consensus.

Within the loosely knit social structure of students and pundits of organized crime, we established a kinship system dividing ourselves into a number of clans: the academic scholars, whose totem is the cautious and contemplative owl; the journalists, whose totem is the clever and resourceful fox, sniffing about the forests for the dramatic "facts"; and, finally, the criminal justice professionals, whose totem is the beaver tirelessly building dams to hold back the floods. Like kinship systems everywhere, each of the clans developed its own folklore and mythology about organized crime, only some of which was shared by the other clans because we did not share a common set of values and often did not even speak the same language. And again, like kinship systems everywhere, our clans were further subdivided into families and lineages, each with its own agenda for itself, for the clan and, ultimately for society itself.

The relationships among the three clans has seldom been one of productive cooperation. To some extent, this has been the result of the natural competition which develops when groups with different professional interests view the same social phenomena. But to some extent it also develops because each group has its own role-based set of values and so its own ideology which influences its views on organized crime. Ideology in this sense is more than a preferred style of viewing the world; it molds and shapes the seeking of evidence about the world, the means for analyzing what one sees, and schemes for organizing and implementing change in society.

How different are these ideologies? The criminal justice system professional is the practitioner, the pragmatic professional who finds it impossible to divorce ideas and concepts from his responsibility to deal with what exists for him or her on a daily basis and so seeks his or her facts existentially in the real world. Lewis Feurer once described this process as one of direct confrontation with problems. On the other hand, the scholar is the man of ideas, usually without any direct responsibility for practical affairs and, practitioners often maintain, usually lacking the firsthand knowledge of them which comes from being "in the trenches." Edward Shils has described this style as based on a need to deal with ideas and symbols which are more general than immediate reality and so independent of a particular place or time. Finally, the journalist role is one where drama, color and newsworthiness are valued. Consequently, as Elizabeth Reuss-Ianni once pointed out about media coverage of police work, analytic statements, contravening cases, the development and testing of hypotheses, and the stringent assessment of reliability and validity are not concerns of the same order that they are for the scholar.

How one defines or even thinks about organized crime is of more than academic interest, since strategies for its control develop from an understanding of how and why it is organized. If one sees it as one aspect of professional crime, then a violation-response approach which is little different from attempts to control street crime seems appropriate. The criminal conspiracy view leads naturally to campaigns of "attrition" and "interdiction" that grow out of intelligence-based approach to political conspiracies. If, on the other hand, organized crime is viewed as a function of the market economy, then a different approach emerges—one of intervening in the production-distribution process, of reducing the spread between profits and expenses, and of providing competitive legitimate markets through decriminalization. If one sees organized crime as a social system that develops within the social fabric, another strategy based on social amelioration and reform to eliminate the social causes of organized crime seems appropriate.

While Redfield's tongue-in-cheek remark provides some intriguing folk wisdom about the establishment of a congruent field of research interest, there are some more structured notions that need to be considered if we are ever to develop a theory or set of theories which can present organized crime as what it is rather than what various interest groups would like it to be and provide the insights for public policy. The essays in this volume mark, I believe, a significant advance in the research-based study of organized crime and, even more importantly, the emergence of a new shared understanding which can lead to what I consider the essential steps needed to deal with the complex of problems, the nuances of interpretation, and adequacy of implementation schemes in organized crime control.

First, the development of a comprehensive theory or complementary theories of organized crime requires the prior development of a conceptual framework or picture of the social phenomenon and its ecological world of social action against which researchable questions can be posed. The early study of organized crime was, per se, the study of "Mafia" or "La Cosa Nostra" as an essentially alien conspiracy with its own Italian cultural ethos despite the evidence of the involvement of other ethnic minorities before and after the period of Italo-American dominance and its obvious utility for America's legislature and economic systems. This collection of essays convincingly and admirably demonstrates how far we have come in both expanding and refining the conceptual base for understanding organized crime. Essays on organized crime activity among Chinese, African Americans, and Russians in America are included along with the articles which focus on Italo-Americans. And the activities that can be included in the array of operations involved also expand beyond the vice and violence focus to include other organized criminal behavior such as racketeering within New York City school boards and money laundering.

Once the problems and questions that develop out of a comprehensive and consistent conceptual framework have been posed, research methodologies which are applicable to and compatible with the specific problems or questions under study are capable of producing data that advances our research and understanding and can eventually inform policy formulation for organized crime control. Here again this volume marks a significant departure over previous works. Particularly pertinent are chapters dealing with the development of models and the critical but constructive review of existing research which points out the need for new species of data as well as more rigorous methodology. At the same time it makes apparent the need for involving a wider array of scholars so that we might profit by expanding the scope of understanding by, for example, looking beyond the more traditional approaches for the culture history of this new expanded vision of organized crime and involving economists in the understanding of organized crime as an illicit part of the economic enterprise system.

I have always been convinced that the study of organized crime is (like the study of education or medicine) an applied professional field—what Herbert Simon once described as an artificial field—and that our research should always develop out of the field of professional practice rather than borrowing explanatory models from other sciences or fields. Thus, our research should always have the clear potential for stimulating further research (the development of knowledge) and informing the decisions and policy made by practitioners (the use of knowledge). Moreover, organized crime is a unique and complex field that cannot be studied as an analogue of business or industry or government, or even street crime. It is in this regard that this collection of essays seems particularly powerful in reorienting our thinking about organized crime control. Not only is there excellent descriptive and analytical treatment of such areas as intelligence development, the role of crime commissions, and the policing function, the essayists have been diligent in pointing out inadequacies and the need to seek out and utilize new methods as well as more accurate data.

Finally, if we are to develop a creative and productive science of the study of organized crime, it becomes essential that we must venture beyond existing theoretical models to seek new understandings, to replace the collective folklore of practitioners' war stories with hard data, rigorously gathered, and to venture beyond the files into the social field itself. If we are really to understand the nature of organized crime, we must first become engaged in a "search" strategy even before we propose problem defining and solving research methodologies. That is, we must first search for and develop ways of discovering how to think about organized crime and the environments within which it develops and operates. The essayists, and particularly the editors, of this collection, deserve our admiration and gratitude for providing the conceptual models which allow us to do just that.

Preface

We embarked on this project with the avowed intention of showing that there has been some progress in the study and control of organized crime. It may, however, occur to some that the opposite outcome has been achieved. If so many conflicting perspectives remain in the field, each with its own partisans, what issues can be said to have been even provisionally resolved? If none of the questions has been finally settled, what can progress consist of?

These chapters demonstrate not so much the disappearance of some nagging problems or the growing dominance of one or another perspective, but a significant change in the fashion in which the questions are posed and in the measure of agreement concerning the character of their solution. While *answers* as such have not been found, the area in which resolutions of problems reside has been narrowed. In part, this appears to be the result of intellectual deprovincialization where the contemporary currents of modern social science methods and criminal justice technologies fertilize each other and have begun to impinge upon what has been, and in some quarters still is, a snug and insular enterprise.

Over the past decade, the activities of government at all levels have reinforced our belief that there is a genuine need for an assessment of the various research and enforcement areas of organized crime. The volume is an attempt to satisfy this need. Though the book is intended as a report to scholars, practitioners, and students alike on current perspectives about organized crime in America, it is driven not by a conscious agenda but rather by a concern for understanding, with as few illusions as possible, the phenomenon. More specifically, our aim has been to provide a balanced account of the central issues and controversies that have developed in the field since the appearance of the landmark 1967 Task Force Report on Organized Crime.

In a sense a pioneer effort, the 1967 Task Force Report was written with more conviction than most scholars and practitioners allow themselves to show, and while this probably helped to secure it a larger and enduring audience, it seems now that much of the heat and validity of its argument would have been more sustainable and persuasive if it had been presented in a more tempered form.

This *Handbook* is organized topically. Occasionally this subdivision of chapters may appear to be violated. Instructors and others should not feel obliged to use the text material in the order of our arrangement. The sequence in which the selections are presented attempts to highlight the interrelationships among the various articles. The *Handbook*'s utility is primarily twofold: as a source of information and as a point of departure for the exploration of controversies in the literature on organized crime. We can conceive of equally plausible configurations in which the readings might be studied and consulted. Colleagues, students, and law enforcement practitioners will no doubt think of still other combinations.

Since many of the chapters deal with a variety of issues that are tangibly linked, it was by no means obvious where a given chapter should be placed. Our grouping, we hope, is sensitive to the fact that the compartments are not watertight. We hasten to add that we did not allocate chapters under preconceived part headings and then solicit work appropriate to each. Rather, headings emerged with the generation of the chapters through a process of mutual accommodation and feedback between editors and authors.

The *Handbook* is not designed to reflect the standpoint or advance the views of one perspective on organized crime. Since it is addressed to an audience of nonspecialists as well as academics and criminal justice professionals, the contributors have been asked to write in as untechnical a manner as their subjects allow, but they have not been expected to achieve simplicity at the cost of accuracy or completeness.

In the case of organized crime, there is a very wide field to cover. We do not suppose that the last word has been said upon any of the issues; we do hope that the book has fulfilled its tasks in charting the way for clearer understanding. Above all, the chapters try to present their views in a way that can be of interest to the general reader.

The *Handbook* should be of particular use to reference libraries and teachers in criminology and criminal justice courses and to law enforcement practitioners at all levels of government. There are both practical guidance and theoretical discussion throughout the book.

Our thanks are to Mildred Vasan and Penny Sippel, Greenwood Press, who aided and abetted in this enterprise. Their detailed suggestions and patience at all stages of the project have been invaluable and made the work an enriching experience. Also, we wish to express our deep appreciation to the chapter contributors for their sufferance, flexibility, and willingness to tolerate our sometimes capricious demands despite their inclinations or misgivings. Many thanks.

Introduction

One of the clearest statements about the general nature of organized crime can be found in *The Underworld as Servant*, written by Walter Lippmann more than sixty years ago.[1] In 1931, Prohibition was nearing its end. For a decade, gang wars had plagued New York City. Al Capone, who virtually ruled Chicago, was facing sentencing in the federal court on tax charges. Samuel Seabury's investigation in New York City revealed that corruption permeated city government from top to bottom: the popular Mayor James Walker resigned, several magistrates and judges were dismissed, and many police went to jail. Seabury pointed to underworld support from New York City political alliances. Reform movements in Chicago revealed criminal conspiracies linking gangsters, politicians, and police. This was the climate, according to Lippmann, in which organized crime "performs services for which there is some kind of public demand," and it satisfies certain "persistent and outlawed human appetites."

Today a medley of dynamic socioeconomic conditions encourages the existence of organized crime in American society. What these are and how they are conducive to criminal activity have changed somewhat over the past half century. Yet, hypocritical and ambivalent attitudes of the American public toward organized crime persist. In the 1930s contradictory public demands for illicit goods and services produced huge profits for gangsters and financed their entry into legitimate business, enabling them to gain some marginal degree of respectability. For Lippmann and many others at the time, Prohibition took hold of the public's imagination; it was the benchmark event giving birth to organized crime as we know it.

Consistent with ethnic xenophobia, the cities teeming with immigrant populations stimulated discussions of the emergence of organized crime. Within the burgeoning urban immigrant settlements in the northeastern, midwestern, and southern states, a complex set of ties among ethnicity, politics, and crime developed. Daniel Bell described this transfer from one wave of immigrants to another as a "queer ladder of social mobility" among the impoverished where organized criminal activity was a rung in the ladder of escape from the squalor of slum existence into the broad mainstream of middle-class life.[2]

ETHNIC SUCCESSION

From the nineteenth century onward, one can follow a pattern of ethnic succession in crime affecting different immigrant groups. Where the Irish dominated organized criminal activities at the turn of the century, Jewish immigrants gained a share through the depression, with Italians rising to prominence during Prohibition.[3] It would be simplistic to take these crude historical boundaries as absolute—Irish gangsters battled the Al Capone organization well into the 1930s; and Jews retained active involvement in vice activities through the 1960s. Still, with the possible exception of Italian Americans, a broad process of one ethnic group's supplanting and succeeding another in certain types of criminal activity appears discernible and seems generally plausible.

Consistent with this perspective has been the recent rise of increased criminal activity among African Americans, Asians, and new minorities, who are moving into vice activities in their ghettos and enclaves. In general, they have immersed themselves in drug trafficking—the modern equivalent of Prohibition. These new groups of Latino, Asian, Eastern European, and African American criminals operate mostly in the safety of their ethnic communities, which provide a cocoon of cultural insulation from police intervention. However, as with the minorities preceding them, until political influence is achieved through acculturation, the new ethnic criminal organizations are not able to mount a significant challenge to the dominance of La Cosa Nostra (LCN). Despite the feasibility of ethnic succession, widespread skepticism still persists in governmental agencies that ethnic succession accurately describes the dynamics of participation in organized crime.[4]

Doubts and suspicions about the explanatory viability of ethnic succession suggest several alternative possibilities, for example, that the organizational power of new minorities may actually be illusory, a consequence of LCN's leasing vice franchises in certain high-risk markets while retaining a comfortable profit margin for themselves. This point of view is scarcely far-fetched when other facts are taken into consideration. To begin with, it has been only over the past decade that determined prosecutions of crime bosses have occurred. Organized crime families have been the prime target of investigatory bodies, commissions, and federal agencies, which together have set a policy of vigorous law enforcement against them. With resources committed to the destruction of LCN, other organized criminal groups may be filling the vacuum. If that is the case, it remains to be seen how well organized and formidable they actually are. The chapters in this book take up these questions.

PUBLICIZING ORGANIZED CRIME

Efforts to eliminate Cosa Nostra have been mixed. Historic public outrage led to the end of Capone, but it did not destroy organized crime in Chicago; nor did the Thomas Dewey prosecutions in the 1930s and 1940s that sent major crime figures to jail or exile put a stop to syndicate crime in New York.[5] With all the vigorous activity against it, Cosa Nostra continues to persist as the most powerful criminal organization in the United States.

It is difficult to think of modern organized crime as something more than, or different from, La Cosa Nostra or Mafia. Before World War II, most writers referred to the *underworld* or *crime syndicates* and described the ethnic heterogeneity of racketeers, bootleggers, and gamblers in colorful terms. In 1891, eleven Italians, alleged to be mafiosi, were lynched in New Orleans after having been accused of assassinating the police chief. When the furor subsided, the press and public lost interest, but the haunting question remained: was there a secret, nationwide conspiracy of Italian criminals?

Not until the Kefauver Committee investigations in 1951 did this issue surface again. The Kefauver Committee hearings were televised, and the drama of gangsters taking the Fifth Amendment and top law enforcement officials discussing a national crime conspiracy shocked the public. The conclusions of the committee's report that "there is a nationwide crime syndicate known as the Mafia whose leaders are usually found in control of the most lucrative rackets in their cities" heightened interest and fears only for a short time. Then, in 1963, in testimony before the McClelland Committee, Joseph Valachi, a soldier in the Genovese crime family, described what he called La Cosa Nostra and Italian American criminal groups called families in many urban areas of the United States.[6]

Following Valachi's sensational revelations about bosses, underbosses, caporegimes, and soldiers, the 1967 task force report contained an influential discussion on the structure of La Cosa Nostra. In the report, prepared by Donald Cressey, the crime families were described as organizations, marked by a hierarchy of integrated positions arranged in a division of labor, with clear patterns of authority and centralized leadership, and with standardized methods of recruitment, apprenticeship, and control.[7] Mafia and Cosa Nostra become interchangeable as generic terms for organized crime. A confusing excess of labels such as the Mob, the syndicate, crime cartels, confederations, and the rackets was suddenly swept aside for the term that referred specifically to secret societies of Italian and Italian American criminals. Though the bewildering terminology was replaced with LCN/Mafia, the proliferation of terms and their etymological histories are relevant to definitions of organized crime in that each label and its variants refer to regional differences in criminal activity, specific types of criminality, and the formal structure of a criminal organization. Michael D. Maltz's chapter on defining organized crime is relevant here. He examines precisely why the phenomenon is so resistant to clear definitions not only from a legal perspective but from a scientific standpoint as well.

CRESSEY'S MODEL

Cressey's portrayal of a Mafia bureaucracy dominating organized crime in the United States has been challenged by academic scholars, social scientists, practitioners, and journalists. Early critics focused on some interrelated issues: first, the data supportive of the structure of Cosa Nostra crime families and, second, whether LCN exercised the power and control ascribed to it. Some concluded that the evidence for Cressey's version was far from reliable.[8]

The issue concerning structure and scope is not a trivial, scholarly debate. The testimony of Valachi and interpretation of major events (the Apalachin meeting in 1957; the *Sicilian Vespers* during the Castellammaresse War) became the cornerstone of government initiatives from which followed federal policy enabling a massive official effort against organized crime.

From the conceptualization of organized crime as virtually synonymous with Mafia, some predictable results followed. In thinking about Cosa Nostra or Mafia as a secret society composed of individuals of Italian ancestry held together by bonds rooted in a common cultural background, it is easy to imagine a cohesive force capable of dominating and overwhelming those who resist, whether they are criminal rivals, law enforcement, or victims.

Cressey's argument in its descriptive form is fairly easy to grasp. There is organized crime, and there is La Cosa Nostra. The latter dominates, which means, when it is stripped down to its cultural essence, we must be prepared to note how in its development and later history it deepened and hardened the distinctions between itself and other more tractable forms of criminal behavior. Cressey offered a significant departure from previous accounts. It was not a pure narrative, though it depended heavily upon Valachi's testimony and law enforcement files that were mainly anecdotal. Cressey is weakest in his failure to challenge the data made available to him. *Theft of the Nation*, based on government intelligence data, presents an articulate exposition of the law enforcement perspective on organized crime.

In view of the controversies surrounding Cressey's model, one must ask how valid it is. Recent prosecutions of major crime bosses in which electronic surveillance information and high-level criminal defectors provided testimony would seem to confirm Cressey's structural descriptions of LCN and the types of crime it organized. It is possible that after Mafia/LCN came to national attention with Estes Kefauver and Valachi, Cressey saw the evidence and his task as one designed to solidify and give intellectual respectability to the official discourse on it, to systematize its insights, and to show its organizational viability.

Has the Mafia orthodoxy sometimes been stretched to fit a simplified, xenophobic version of organized crime that is too conspiratorial and neat? Is the underworld solely an alien intrusion imposed by immigrants on a society otherwise free of organized crime? The exponents of alternatives to the Mafia model have been broadly attacked for raising these questions and for two propositions that are the basis of their analyses: first, that organized crime is an integral feature of American socioeconomic enterprises that goes well beyond ethnic and working-class criminality, and, second, that poor ethnic, working-class criminal groups tend to yield the underworld to newer, more recent immigrants on lower rungs of the social class ladder of opportunity and mobility. But given all the emerging evidence from the flood of information on organized crime that appeared since the early 1970s, who could deny that the Mafia existed and was the predominant force in the underworld? Concerning ethnic succession,[9] the predictions (lacking temporal parameters) did not happen. New immigrant groups did enter the underworld, but not with the dominance and clout of the Cosa Nostra.

LA COSA NOSTRA PERSISTS

Over the past four decades since the Apalachin meeting, crime families have diminished neither in size nor in influence. As for the structural forces that produce them, it may test the limits of credulity to imagine, as the concept of illicit enterprise more or less urges, that Mafia makes illegal, dynamic processes, activities, and markets such that, if properly understood, loan sharks are actually street bankers, fences are unregulated retailers, and drug smugglers are importers.[10] While it is not hard to conceive of gangster influence in trade unions activated by labor/management conflicts, their business tactics in general resemble few types of tactics in legitimate enterprise.

The issue is not that those opposed to the Mafia/LCN model are wrong or the parties to the dispute about Mafia dominance must already be agreed as to what will count as an empirical demonstration of their positions. They are not. Enthusiasts of the Cressey model appear to think that the wrongness of the critics is decided by evidentiary and logical procedures embedded in the structure of scientific methodology and, most important, that they are uninvolved in any agenda or position that takes a slant on the evidence. The disagreements about the data and their meanings and significance are not mere quibbles over minor details but go the heart of what constitutes a legitimate interpretation of the evidence. These issues are the substance of the chapters by Jay S. Albanese, Alan A. Block, Peter Reuter, Dwight C. Smith, Jr., and Mark H. Haller.

One argues only from a position (law enforcement compared with social science), and the argument one makes will be convincing to someone who shares, at least in part, that same position. Standards of right and wrong do not exist apart from assumptions but follow from them; they are the standards that are decided upon, not standards that decide—notions in dispute rather than notions that settle disputes. The evidence either contending party would be willing to admit would be a function of its assumptions and therefore could not be used to confirm or disconfirm them; and the evidence adduced by other parties could not be disinterested but would be a function of their assumptions, which those either pro- or con-LCN would have to share if they were to be at all swayed. Assumptions do not stand in an independent relationship to verification criteria; they determine the shape of such procedures, and if others are to be persuaded that they are wrong, they must first be persuaded to embrace the assumptions within which one's argument or analysis claims to be convincing. In short, the act of description is itself interpretive, and at no point is any observer or analyst within hailing distance of a fact that has been independently (objectively) specified.

Asserting that interpretive strategies rather than clear-cut conflicts define the difference between Cressey model defenders and its detractors may seem to confirm the concerns of those who argue for the need of determinate meanings; for, it might be argued, if, indeed, interpretation separates the protagonists in the debate about LCN's structure, organization, and predominance in American organized crime, there is nothing to constrain or prevent irresponsible claims that, for instance, the Mafia is a myth or the sinister fabrication of criminal justice elites, of xenophobic racists, or of those who find comfort in thinking of organized crime as an intrusive Italian American criminal force in American society.

A ROSE IS A ROSE IS A ROSE

Anticipating the objection to this claim that there really is no problem after all, no substantive debate between various views of the Cosa Nostra's pivotal role in organized crime, it is likely to take at least two different forms, according to the political disposition of the critics. From a law enforcement perspective (in this instance, for the sake of argument we assume a monolithic community), progress in understanding organized crime occurs when the machinery of description is refined, when its definitions, categories, levels, and so on have been brought into a closer correspondence with the facts; progress is impeded when that machinery is informed by the bias of an individual observer or partisan group with an ideological ax to grind. The check against interpretive bias is the facts, which are therefore objects to be described. Progress, then, is a function of a database's operation as a regulating and adjudicative principle, and in the best scenario, when the database has been completed, the correct description will have been achieved.

OTHER GROUPS—NONTRADITIONAL

The predominant models of organized crime officially endorsed by government agencies are no exception to the fact that, like people, ideas and theories travel from situation to situation and from one period to another. Whether it takes the form of acknowledged influence as wholesale appropriations, the movement of ideas from one place to another is both a fact of life and a usefully enabling condition of intellectual activity. Having said that, however, it is well to specify the kinds of movement that are possible and that occur and to ask whether by virtue of having moved from one place and time to another, an idea or theory gains or loses in strength and whether a theory in one historical period and ethnic culture becomes altogether different for another period or situation.

As a result of specific historical circumstances of government hearings, committee investigations, testimonies, and government intelligence data, the Cosa Nostra theory arose. What happens to it when it is used in different circumstances and for new reasons? What can this tell us about theory itself—its limits, its possibilities, its inherent problems—and what can it suggest about the relationship between theory and the social problems associated with the phenomenon of organized crime as it appears in different subcultural settings? Has the transplanted theory that drives government criminal justice programs yielded results and transformed itself to accommodate new realities? Obviously, any satisfactorily full account of these questions would have an enormous task. The work of Ko-lin Chin, James O. Finckenauer, Robert M. Lombardo, and Rufus Schatzberg offers some useful empirical evidence in addressing these questions.

Theorizing is a kinetic art, but as theories develop out of particular situations and begin to be used and gain acceptance, there is no reason it cannot become a reductionist schema. That is, if a theory can move down, so to speak, and become a dogmatic reduction of its original version, it can also move up to a sort of bad infinity. The risk has been that LCN as a theoretical overstatement of organized crime threatens to become something of a parody of itself that is too inclusive, too expansive, and too ceaselessly active as an explanatory mechanism. Theory is certainly needed. In fact, it is ever-present, even if not apparent. Accompanying it should be a critical recognition that there is no theory capable of covering, closing off, predicting all the situations in which it might be useful. This is another way of saying (as many critics have in this volume) that no intellectual system can be so dominant as to be unlimited in strength.

Nontraditional refers to the coming-of-age of post-Mafia/LCN criminal groups—racial and ethnic minorities that have emerged in the wake of Italian American decline in crime. There is some degree of terror induced by the overscaled images of Chinese triads, Jamaican posses, and Japanese yakuza. Official pronouncements and literature fuel public apprehension because they lack the discriminate contents and realistic definitions of these groups so that new, designated enemies bent on destroying our way of life help to incite a fearful public behind an overbearingly paranoid estimate of the actual threat these groups actually pose.[11]

The appearance of new groups raises questions as to what may be expected from them. What new law enforcement policies do these groups call for? It is useful to begin by acknowledging that the logic of criminal borders does not end with the LCN. The discussions in the chapters on Russian (Finckenauer),

Chinese (Chin), and African American (Rufus Schatzberg) organized crime make it clear that to pretend that these types of crime conform with LCN images would be a distortion. An implication running through the pieces that examine theory sociologically (Albanese, Smith, and Haller) and the officially sponsored views of organized crime that are subjected to historical analysis (Block, Patrick J. Ryan, and Lombardo) is that it is relatively easy to be insular with nontraditional crime by regarding it as merely marginal and inconsequential. A steadfast adherence to the Cosa Nostra model as the means of an official, public discourse is disaffiliative, sustaining an innocence and remoteness under the rubric of an ironclad narrative that has acquired almost fetishistic dominance over our thinking.

The new groups reveal a different criminal topography but not a different set of imperatives. As criminal organizations, their aim is familiar: profits and power through any means. What is also clear (and revelatory in retrospect about earlier ethnic/minority criminal groups) is that criminal organizations are protean; they are tied to circumstances large and small. New criminal groups operate in specific situations that they cannot escape and that shape the opportunities and constraints in their milieus. The external constraints have thickened over time: the Racketeer Influenced and Corrupt Organizations (Act) (RICO), specialized intelligence units, electronic surveillance, jury and witness protection, immunity for testimony, and so on. What this means is that the area for criminal action may not be as flexible as it was for earlier ethnic criminal groups that burst out of their enclaves and communities into the larger society when opportunities beckoned. On the other hand, the use of ethnicity (which the President's Commission on Organized Crime used in its reports) to characterize various types of criminal groups seems too narrow and limiting. Because of the evolving law enforcement strategies that have succeeded in penetrating the protective ethnic cocoon that insulated Cosa Nostra members for so long, there are good reasons for thinking that nontraditional groups will operate, if not out of need, then willingly and voluntarily in international and multiethnic contexts.

If one could identify one element that characterizes contemporary nontraditional groups, it would be drug trafficking, as Mark Kleiman's chapter illustrates. Drugs provide opportunities for expansion beyond the confines of the ethnic enclave and ghetto; moreover, the cultivation, manufacture, and importation of narcotics require criminal entrepreneurs in different countries and from different ethnic, linguistic, cultural, and racial backgrounds to interact and cooperate in order to conduct their business. Indeed, as historical research by Block has shown and as Prohibition demonstrates, no single criminal conspiracy dominates organized criminal operations.[12] Organized crime is often multiethnic, and interethnic cooperation, whether voluntary or compelled by more sophisticated law enforcement strategies, illustrates the increasingly constructed role that it plays in organized criminal activities.

The historical fear of immigrants, with the attendant deprivations they experience as a result of discrimination and prejudice, no doubt causes some to find illegal means of support. The "queer ladder of social mobility," or crime, which traced the interconnections among immigration, ethnicity/race, employment, and criminal activities in an earlier generation of new arrivals to the United States seem applicable today with regard to Asians, Eastern Europeans, and Latin Americans.

The significant prosecutions and effective implementation of the law in the last decade have undoubtedly hurt traditional organized crime. To the extent that nontraditional groups move into the vacuum, the prosecution and surveillance of these organizations may be more difficult at first despite the expertise law enforcement officials have gained with LCN.

There are interesting parallels today between traditional and nontraditional types of criminal enterprises concerning the prospects for law enforcement and prosecution. So far, prosecutions of Chinese, Russians, and African Americans have increased but are relatively few when compared with LCN, for many of the same reasons that enabled Italian, Jewish, and other early ethnic groups to evade the law. There are the language barrier and implicit distrust of the police in ethnic communities. Because of the lack of good understanding of the culture and only grudging community support, penetrating the neighborhoods and infiltrating criminal enterprises are an arduous process that usually fails. The significance of cultural differences should not be underestimated. A nationwide survey of law enforcement officials in 1989 reported that organized crime was no longer perceived as dominated by Italian Americans. Colombian drug cartels, Chinese groups, Jamaican *posses*, and, interestingly, Los Angeles African American street gangs (Crips and Bloods) were seen as of more immediate concern. The report went on to say that

many officials told us that language difference, coupled with a shortage of skilled interpreters, and difficulty in penetrating tightly knit ethnic communities hamper police use of traditional investigative tools such as wiretaps, informants, and undercover operatives.[13]

Controlling Organized Crime: Some Tools of the Trade

Over the past decade there have been many success stories against organized crime. To take a case closest to hand, the prosecution and conviction of John Gotti, head of the powerful Gambino crime family, illustrate effective employment of modern crime-fighting technologies, including the shrewd deployment and concentration of law enforcement personnel. We need not linger on the record of murder, intimidation, and other standard accompaniments of racketeering enterprises common to Cosa Nostra practices that occasioned his prosecution. It is enough to note that the federal government's efforts against Gotti and others in the leadership of the Gambino crime family had repeatedly failed before the successful trial of 1992. Until then, the cases mounted against Gotti were somewhat slapdash; they lacked the enthusiastic participation of the Federal Bureau of Investigation (FBI) and did not efficiently exploit the investigative work of New York State's Organized Crime Task Force, which had been probing racketeering in New York City's construction industries for some time.

The eleven-count RICO indictment was the weapon that set in motion the unraveling of the crime organization. Before the Gotti prosecution, successful offensives had been launched by the FBI and local law enforcement agencies in Los Angeles, Boston, Kansas City, Atlantic City, and Philadelphia. In 1988, the entire leadership of the Philadelphia family headed by Nicodemo Scarfo was successfully prosecuted. The convictions on racketeering and murder charges sent off to prison the boss, underboss, consigliere, and all the caporegimes. This coincided with the New York prosecution of the Mafia Commission and Pizza Connection cases in the southern district of New York. In this case, the Cosa Nostra's entire ruling body and the nationwide Sicilian heroin trafficking networks were put out of business. With the Colombo and Bonanno families crippled, the Lucchese family under attack, and the Genovese family virtually leaderless, the Gambino family remained.

In December 1990, the government moved against the leadership of the Gambino family. Gotti; Salvatore Gravano, consigliere/underboss; Frank Locascio, underboss; and Thomas Gambino, capo, were arrested and charged with murder, racketeering, bribery, extortion, tax fraud, illegal gambling, and the obstruction of justice.

The case against Gotti and his associates was mounted using electronic surveillance technologies, which yielded the evidence necessary to break the code of silence that had been the hallmark of the Cosa Nostra. Gravano, a man in his early forties, when faced with the evidence of the tapes linking him to murder conspiracies and racketeering, had but one way out of life in prison with no chance of parole: cooperating with the government against the boss and underboss of the Gambino family. Gravano had still another consideration: since it was a RICO case, he could forfeit most of his criminally generated wealth and resources. Because provisions of the RICO statute allowed forfeiture, the confiscation of illegally acquired property upon a conviction, it did not take much to realize that cooperation with the government was the only way of avoiding a life sentence without parole.

The tapes of conversations and the corroboration of Gravano were terribly damaging to Gotti and Locascio. The electronic evidence showed Gotti to be the boss of the crime family and showed that he routinely discussed criminal activities and that he admitted participation in several murders. The tapes and Gravano's devastating testimony led to the conviction of Gotti and Locascio on the principal counts of the indictment.

Behind the convictions of the Cosa Nostra leadership stands RICO. Under it, entire criminal organizations may be prosecuted. The law also provides for asset forfeiture of money, businesses, and property accumulated as a result of criminal activity. Further, under confiscation procedures and penalty enhancement for those convicted through RICO provisions, the very existence of a crime family is a crime. As G. Robert Blakey's chapter shows, RICO has had unanticipated applications quite apart from its intended targets of organized crime groups. Since 1970, there have been political corruption prosecutions and white-collar crime cases before RICO was effectively implemented against the groups for which it was crafted. The private bar brought civil RICO actions approximately five years after its passage into law.

HOOVER AND ORGANIZED CRIME

It may seem odd that the federal government did not move rapidly against organized crime until the 1980s. Certainly, since the 1950s, as Frederick Martens and Charles Rogovin show, federal commissions repeatedly pointed to the threat it posed. Yet until the Kennedy administration, the attitude toward organized crime in the highest law enforcement circles was reserved at best. A good deal of the blame for this can be laid on the peculiar mind-set of J. Edgar Hoover, who directed the FBI since 1924. It was not until the Valachi Senate hearings in 1963 that Hoover finally had to admit publicly that such a thing as organized crime did, in fact, exist.[14]

Hoover may have resisted involvement in organized crime investigation for a number of reasons. Information has come to light that the FBI director's reluctance to commit his agency to the investigation of organized criminal activities may have been connected with his personal habits and entanglements with racketeers. Hoover had to know that organized crime had grown powerful as a result of Prohibition and was able, therefore, to compromise law enforcement agencies through bribery and corruption. Perhaps, apart from his personal, incriminating peccadilloes, he did not want to subject his agents to the temptation gangsters could hold out. Above all, he apparently wished to maintain a public image of his agency as corruption-free crime fighters and, consequently, concentrated the agency's resources on hoodlums and criminals not affiliated with the powerful crime syndicates.[15]

The FBI was not the only government agency whose anticrime efforts were selective. In James D. Calder's words, a "state-sanctioned criminology of organized crime"[16] infected the Internal Revenue Service (IRS) concerning its records on Al Capone. Out of self-preservation of its bureaucratic prerogatives, the IRS controlled the flow of information to favored researchers. The impact of such policies is to jeopardize accurate and comprehensive accounts of major social events, including crime.

Apart from the politics of organized crime, contemporary law enforcement control strategies fall into several categories. Some approaches are complicated by the politicization and ethnic sensitivities of the issues involved. The political dimension is reflected in questions as to the effectiveness with which law enforcement operates and in the corruption of government. The ethnic and racial aspects combine with economic and social issues in ways that are difficult to disentangle. As noted by Lippmann and others, much organized crime activity involves the supplying of illicit goods and services desired by a substantial part of the population, with the consequent dilution of public support for enforcement.

The thrust of the chapters by Blakey, Ronald Goldstock, Marilyn B. Peterson, Ryan, Rogovin and Martens, William Cook, and John Dombrink and John Song focuses on objectives of organized crime enforcement policy, which is, and ought to remain, the destruction and operational impairment of organized crime groups rather than simply the conviction and imprisonment of their members, no matter how important the positions such individuals occupy in criminal hierarchies.

Since 1967, the criminal justice system has gone through a period of reassessment of its techniques and methodologies in order to develop approaches that would neutralize, diminish, or contain organized criminal activity. By establishing discrete prosecutorial and investigative units—e.g., strike forces and a unit within the Department of Justice specializing in organized crime—steady progress appears to have been made. The passage of legislation relating to electronic surveillance, witness immunity and security, RICO, and special grand juries and the provision of financial and logistical support for local and state intelligence operations have created more sophisticated prosecutions, and this success is owed, in part, to collective experience accumulated over the years, as Peterson suggests.

At least two major changes have vastly improved organized crime enforcement. First, there is a greater integration of strategic decision making with the implementation of modern investigation techniques, such as electronic surveillance, long-range undercover operations, stings, and the improved quality of analytical intelligence work. Over time, the distinctive roles of various law enforcement components have been sharpened and better devised, resulting in less suspicion and competition among agencies and more collective sharing of information and resources. The catalyst for interagency relationships was the Omnibus Crime Control Act of 1970, the Bank Secrecy Act of 1970, and the Money Laundering Control Act of 1986. For operational units, their roles are more clearly articulated as, among other things, information-generating groups useful to intelligence operations. Likewise, intelligence units are more likely to comprehend that their missions and functions are to provide data supportive of operations.

However, though it is acknowledged that intelligence data make possible the enforcement process, and most analysts stress the importance of intelligence units as vital to effective enforcement, the intelligence processes are not accorded the status commensurate with their indispensability for operations and prosecutions.[17] Organizational obstacles have tended to sustain the exclusion of intelligence units so that their full institutional integration into law enforcement agencies remains incomplete. There are, of course, the natural tensions between investigators involved in evidence gathering in the streets and desk-bound intelligence analysts.

More important, as Peterson notes, investigative and prosecutorial agencies mobilize their work on near-term horizons and deploy resources to support pending investigations and prosecutions, rather than fact gathering and analyses that will enable them to initiate future or long-term actions against organized crime enterprises.

Linked to intelligence innovations is prosecutorial modernization. Goldstock's discussions of the role of contemporary prosecutors describe new administrative and managerial dimensions that are revising traditional conceptions of the prosecutor as law enforcer. Prosecutors play a more vigorous role in case developments at their incipient stages; and organized crime task forces and coordinating committees have facilitated better working relationships among agencies at different levels of government and across different jurisdictions.[18]

RICO figures prominently in the prosecutorial repertoire. It is more than a set of laws around which a case is mounted; it is also an investigative instrument that assists planning and the formulation of enforcement work agendas as cases proceed. Here, too, interagency cooperation, including the cross-assignment of personnel from different enforcement areas that possess differential resources in terms of specialized technical staffs and capabilities, enables the prosecutor to strike directly at the heart of criminal enterprises.

The second significant reorientation in enforcement strategies and tactics has occurred within the planning and targeting process. Utilizing social scientific research and exploiting its findings in unprecedented ways, law enforcement agencies have come to recognize the value and relevance of examining organized criminal groups from a number of perspectives. The focus of the key prosecutions in recent years emphasizes a concentration not only on individuals as targets of investigation and prosecution but also on reducing the influence of groups themselves. The enterprise approach is based on the realization that the prosecution of high-level raketeers was not that effective in diminishing their power and harm.[19]

It would not be unreasonable to suggest that when law enforcement agency files and other sources of data had been collected and made available to research activity within and outside law enforcement groups, new strategies and new perspectives began to emerge to deal with the evolving complexities and new forms of organized criminality. The efforts of analysts and commentators have informed and guided enforcement policies. But as Peter Reuter points out, several obstacles frustrating the generation of data suitable for scientific analyses are identifiable. Even when access is gained, organized crime data are not maintained in agency files for research purposes and for that reason possess limited value. They are biased by law enforcement agency needs; access may itself be circumscribed and hindered by confidentiality mandated by law. A way around these barriers is difficult and may not succeed: if the process of freeing up agency files—since these are the most obvious and likely source of data—and influencing the character of data gathered by agencies is to occur, then researchers will have to demonstrate the value of their work for enforcement agency goals. It follows that research programs lacking clear, practical advantages for law enforcement, whatever their intrinsic scientific merits, may not materialize.

With the issue of data access and availability in mind, the new prosecutorial models attacking organized crime depart from the traditional focus of concentrating on bosses for discrete crimes because this in itself does not greatly diminish a crime organization's power to survive and flourish. Historical analyses demonstrate the regenerative power of organized crime when the object of investigations and prosecution was particular individuals. Removal of leaders from the street environment is most effective in dealing with predatory crime where the conviction of particular individuals directly involved in violence would be a deterrent, but combating racketeering enterprises in parasitic and symbiotic criminal situations where the primary activities are the provision of illegal goods and services and the infiltration of legitimate businesses demands different strategies. Thus, the RICO criminal and civil remedies, the criminal forfeitures, civil injunctive relief, and pretrial restraints cripple the capacity of criminal organizations to maintain their assets and enterprises intact.

Major stress is placed on the identification and clarification of issues in organized crime control by those writing from an enforcement perspective. At the same time, it is also widely recognized that the task of framing research operations and agendas is a prerogative of criminal justice practitioners but is informed by the work of scholars and academic researchers whose detachment and distance from the heat of enforcement activity afford a degree of objectivity that is all but a luxury to officials and officers. Cook, for example, identifies new areas where organized crime has surfaced: school boards and districts where the potential for corruption and illegal manipulation of services is most inviting. Smith asks that practitioners and scholars alike look beyond the hierarchical tables of organization of crime groups in order to see the relevance and value to law enforcement of examining criminal groups from the standpoint of illicit enterprises—criminal business firms. Using modern organizational theories and models can determine the assets and functions of criminal groups that are crucial to their continuity and profitability and, therefore, their ability to survive. Smith's approach offers diagnostic tools by which the tangible and intangible assets of a criminal group can be identified and analyzed, which then offers the possibility of shifting the focus from individual criminal activities to organizations, structures, and enterprises very much in line with RICO enforcement perspectives.

The chapters in this volume point to a number of issues in understanding the nature of organized crime activity in the United States. For law enforcement strategies to be effective against traditional and emerging nontraditional groups, criminal justice agencies must have accurate and comprehensive data and analysis. Support of policy and practice is then dependent not only on the intelligence resources of agencies but also on research conducted by scholars.

For the future, a number of questions emerge, each challenging the academic and criminal justice communities. Are the enforcement histories against traditional groups, such as the LCN, applicable to newer criminal organizations? In what kinds of environments does organized crime flourish? How can scientific research inform the law enforcement effort to affect these milieus? What social components in communities at risk from criminal groups can be mobilized to control and contain and inhibit crime? What are the vulnerabilities of organized crime groups? Do emerging nontraditional criminal groups evolve in ways that parallel LCN? What is the nature of criminal ties to the noncriminal sectors of communities? Are these accessible to law enforcement intervention opportunities? How do legitimate businesses and markets behave when confronted by criminal infiltrators or the threat thereof? What sectors in the public and private domains of communities encourage the emergence and growth of organized crime? Finally, is incarceration of criminal entrepreneurs and activists an effective tactic of law enforcement?

CONCLUSION

We are confident that this book will stimulate thinking about the ideas and methodologies involved in conceptualizing, measuring, controlling, and containing organized crime. Over the past two decades since the inception of the RICO laws, the conviction of major criminal leaders and the disruption of criminal enterprises have served as performance and success measures of the country's criminal justice approaches. These measures represent the basic goals of public policy; at the same time, however, incarceration of the top leadership of criminal enterprises is not the only or necessarily the best indications of what criminal justice agencies do. Few officials believe that their work alone determines the prevalence of crime activity. Experience and research show that the operations of criminal enterprises depend on factors much removed from law enforcement activities. Indeed, criminal justice practitioners can scarcely be expected to do what families, parents, schools, teachers, clergy, and economic opportunities may have failed to do.

While the chief aim of the *Handbook* is to provide a comprehensive overview of the problem, what also emerge—if only implicitly—are discussions on how partnerships between criminal justice practitioners and citizens may be forged. The active cooperation and support of the public are essential: to expect police and prosecutors alone to solve society's problem with organized crime is unrealistic. Though it is unrealistic to ask that only law enforcement groups aggressively suppress organized crime in drug trafficking, extortion, racketeering, and the vice industries, it is reasonable to demand that, with adequate resources and with the requisite support of other social institutions, the major purposes of criminal justice be avidly pursued. These include promoting secure communities and noncriminal options and making offenders fully accountable. These are the goals the criminal justice system must pursue if it wishes to retain legitimacy and enjoy the public's confidence.

NOTES

1. Walter Lippmann, "The Underworld as Servant," *Forum* (January/February 1931): 162–72.

2. Daniel Bell, "Crime as an American Way of Life," *Antioch Review* 13 (1953): 131–54.

3. Francis A. J. Ianni, with Elizabeth Reuss-Ianni, *A Family Business: Kinship and Social Control in Organized Crime* (New York: Russell Sage Foundation, 1972).

4. President's Commission on Organized Crime, *The Impact: Organized Crime Today* (Washington, DC: U.S. Government Printing Office, 1985); Hearings, Permanent Subcommittee of Investigations, *Organized Crime: Twenty-Five Years After Valachi* (Washington, DC: U.S. Government Printing Office, 1990).

5. Humbert Nelli, *The Business of Crime: Italians and Syndicate Crime in the United States* (New York: Oxford University Press, 1976); Alan Block, *East Side—West Side: Organizing Crime in New York, 1930–1950* (New Brunswick, NJ: Transaction Books, 1983).

6. Peter Maas, *The Valachi Papers* (New York: Bantam Books, 1969).

7. Donald Cressey, "The Functions and Structure of Criminal Syndicates," Appendix A, *Task Force Report: Organized Crime. President's Commission on Law Enforcement and Administration of Justice* (Washington, DC: U.S. Government Printing Office, 1967; Donald Cressey, *Theft of the Nation: The Structure and Operations of Organized Crime in America* (New York: Harper and Row, 1969).

8. Joseph Albini, *The American Mafia: Genesis of a Legend* (New York: Appleton Century-Crofts, 1971).

9. Francis A. J. Ianni, Suzy Fisher, and Jeffrey Lewis, "Ethnic Succession and Networks Formation Is Organized Crime," *National Institute of Law Enforcement and Criminal Justice* (Washington, DC: U.S. Government Printing Office, 1972).

10. Dwight C. Smith, Jr., "Paragons, Pariahs and Pirates: A Spectrum-Based Theory of Enterprise," *Crime and Delinquency* 26 (July 1982): 358–86; Dwight C. Smith, Jr., "Organized Crime and Entrepreneurship," *International Journal of Criminology and Penology* 6 (1978): 161–77.

11. Hearing before the Permanent Subcommittee on Investigations, *Asian Organized Crime* (Washington, DC: U.S. Government Printing Office, 1992); U.S. Department of Justice report on *Asian Organized Crime* (Criminal Division, Washington, DC; President's Commission on Organized Crime, 1988) *Organized Crime of Asian Origin: Record of Hearing 111—Oct. 23–25, New York* (Washington, DC: U.S. Government Printing Office, 1984).

12. Alan Block, "The Snowman Cometh: Coke in Progressive New York," *Criminology* 17 (May 1979): 75–99.

13. U.S. Comptroller General, *Non-Traditional Organized Crime* (Washington, DC: General Accounting Office, 1989); Jay S. Albanese and Robert D. Pursley, *Crime in America: Some Existing and Emerging Issues* (Englewood Cliffs, NJ: Regents/Prentice Hall, 1993), 53.

14. John H. Davis, *Mafia Dynasty* (New York: Harper Collins, 1993), 86–87.

15. Richard G. Powers, *Secrecy and Power: The Life of J. Edgar Hoover* (New York: Free Press, 1989).

16. James D. Calder, "Al Capone and the Internal Revenue Service: State-Sanctioned Criminology of Organized Crime," *Crime, Law and Social Change* 17 (1992): 1–23.

17. Frederick T. Martens, "The Intelligence Function," in *Major Issues in Organized Crime Control*, ed. Herbert Edelhertz (Washington, DC: Department of Justice, National Institute of Justice, 1987).

18. Ronald Goldstock, "Operational Issues in Organized Crime Control," in Edelhertz, *Major Issues*.

19. Statement of Oliver B. Revell, Senate Hearing, *Organized Crime 25 Years After Valachi*, Hearings before the Permanent Subcommittee on Investigation (Washington, DC: U.S. Government Printing Office, April 11, 1988), 430–44.

Part I

Background Issues

1

Defining Organized Crime

MICHAEL D. MALTZ

Crime was long concerned only with brutal, solitary and personal impulses. But nowadays the murderers and robbers are forming ranks; they obey discipline; they have given themselves a code and a morality; they work in gangs with well-devised schemes.

—Louis Blanc, 1840[1]

What do we mean by the term *organized crime*? It is more than merely a specific type of "crime," the way that a "violent crime" is a subset of all crimes. For example, we can talk about a violent crime and describe a particular incident to others; if the incident's description fits the legal definition of the crime and includes violent acts as a part of its commission, then we understand the incident to be a violent crime. But we cannot talk about "an organized crime" in the same manner, because we do not conceive of "an organized crime" as a similar subset of all crimes; rather, we conceive of a crime fitting into the category "organized crime" by virtue of other factors, such as whether the person committing the crime is affiliated with a criminal enterprise and the description of the circumstances surrounding the crime—these are needed for an understanding of "organized crime."

This is not to say that definitions of organized crime do not exist; this chapter describes some examples. Nor have they all been without merit; each of them adds some measure of understanding to the term. Unfortunately, however, none of them appear to me to hit the mark entirely. This chapter is yet another attempt to explore some of the characteristics of a definition of organized crime that would be of use to social scientists, criminologists, and legal scholars.

There are a number of reasons for wanting to define organized crime. One is to determine how resources should be allocated and how effectively they have been expended in attacking it. For example, the General Accounting Office (GAO),[2] while passing judgment on the Justice Department's organized crime strike forces, was critical of the fact that the Justice Department had not defined "organized crime." In fact, millions of dollars have been spent over the past fifteen years to combat organized crime. Congressional hearings and presidential commissions have addressed this topic, as have research programs. Yet, as the GAO pointed out, organized crime is still with us—unabated, as far as we can tell—and we cannot even define it, let alone measure it. How can we know if our attacks on organized crime are bearing fruit without specifying what it is?[3]

Another reason for defining it is for legal purposes. If a specific penalty, for example, obtains for a person convicted of an offense when the offense is considered an organized crime, there should be some means of distinguishing organized crime-related offenses from others. Somehow a prosecutor's appearing before the judge at sentencing and intoning, "This person is a member of organized crime," in order to justify an extended sentence does not appear to be just; there should be standards and criteria that can be incorporated into a statute. The case law that has developed around the Federal Racketeer Influenced and Corrupt Organizations Act (RICO) is replete with attempts to define such organizations. The definition is important not only at the trial stage but at the investigative stage as well: it may be used to justify the use of more intrusive means of investigating a case and the priority attached to (and agencies involved in) an investigation.

A third reason for defining organized crime is territorial. At one time there were fourteen federal organized crime strike forces; now they are merged with U.S. attorneys' offices.[4] All of them work in concert with criminal justice agencies at the state and local level. Are there any criteria for deciding whether a given case should be investigated and prosecuted by federal, state, or local agencies, if all agencies can rightfully claim jurisdiction?

A fourth reason for defining it is to understand it as a phenomenon. While some still maintain that the proof of its existence, like the proof that God exists, is a leap of faith best left to theologians,[5] others have traced its different manifestations over the past century and are interested in tracing its growth and evolution in this country and others. For example, the breakup of the Soviet Union has uncovered the extent to which organized crime groups have flourished under (or as a consequence of) this centrally planned economic system. It would be interesting to understand to what extent organized crime growth depends on governmental style or size or on other factors of this nature.

Obviously, no single definition is going to meet all of these needs, addressing resource allocation and evaluation problems, solving legal problems and jurisdictional problems, and furthering an understanding of its characteristics in one fell swoop. But it is useful to keep these needs in mind when attempting to define organized crime.

In this chapter I direct my attention to the fourth reason, defining it so that we can better understand it. I focus my attention on one particular manifestation of organized crime, the type that most people seem to have in mind when they use the term. I describe earlier definitions of organized crime; I then focus on what I see as the major defect in these definitions; then I discuss the characteristics that have been attributed to organized crime and explain why some appear to be necessary and others not.

EARLIER DEFINITIONS

To give some idea of the difficulty of defining "organized crime," we can consider some of the definitions that have been employed in statutes. The only definition of organized crime in federal statutes I found in Public Law 90-351, the Omnibus Crime Control and Safe Streets Act of 1968: "Organized crime means the unlawful activities of members of a highly organized, disciplined association engaged in supplying illegal goods and services, including but not limited to gambling, prostitution, loan sharking, narcotics, labor racketeering, and other unlawful activities of members of such associations."

The vagueness and circular reasoning in this definition are striking. First, it defines organized crime not so much in terms of unlawful activities as in terms of who is committing those unlawful activities. Thus it is an ad hominem definition (which may be inescapable). Second, it lists a number of unlawful activities, but these are not necessarily the ones that define "organized crime." According to this definition, to determine whether a given activity is an organized crime, one should:

- find an "association engaged in supplying illegal goods and services, including but not limited to gambling, prostitution, loan sharking, narcotics, labor racketeering, and other such unlawful activities"; then
- determine whether it is a "a highly organized, disciplined association"; then
- if the individual in question is a member of this association, and if he or she has committed an unlawful activity, that activity (it need not be one of the listed activities) is ipso facto an organized crime.

This definition is not used for legal, jurisdictional, or resource allocation purposes; few definitions are. For example, in 1975 the law creating New York State's organized crime task force was declared unconstitutional by the New York State Supreme Court because it did not define "organized crime."[6]

It is interesting to note that the Federal Organized Crime Control Act of 1970 (PL 91-352), which was passed two years after the Safe Streets Act, did not use the aforementioned—or any other—definition of "organized crime."

Since that time some states have developed definitions for their own purposes. Of particular interest is the definition used by Ohio: " 'Organized criminal activity' means any combination or conspiracy to engage in criminal activity as a significant source of income or livelihood, to violate or aid, abet, facilitate, conceal, or dispose of the proceeds of the violation of, criminal laws relating to prostitution, gambling, counterfeiting, obscenity, extortion, loan sharking, drug abuse or illegal drug distribution, or corruption of law enforcement officers or other public officers, officials, or employees.'' This definition no longer focuses solely on the substantive violation of the law; rather, it includes any activity that is related to the violation. However, it is very specific in the substantive offenses that are included; for example, arson, hijacking, murder, and labor racketeering are not included in the list.

Robert G. Blakey et al.[7] describe the different issues involved in defining organized crime, noting that the terms *white-collar crime, criminal enterprise, criminal cartel, criminal syndicate,* or *criminal venture* might also be used; or, in fact, the term *organized crime* might well be used to refer to the entire criminal underworld. They conclude that "it is probably best to avoid trying to use 'organized crime' as a legal concept," agreeing with the 1970 Pennsylvania Crime Commission that "criminal syndicates cannot be outlawed or punished *per se,* since they cannot be defined with sufficient exactness, but the substantive portions of our criminal law can be better molded to encompass their schemes and activities."

Mark Kleiman[8] is also reluctant to be pinned down to a specific definition, because "it can be somewhat misleading. Nevertheless we retain it as a convenient shorthand for the kinds of criminal enterprises we take to be the concern of policies designed to 'stop organized crime.' " He suggests that the following characteristics are found in organized crime: enforcement resistance, power and wealth, intangible criminal capital, reputational capital, provision of dispute resolution, economics of scale in law-breaking, corruption, and violence. Kleiman seems to be focusing more on well-established groups to the exclusion of emerging groups by inclusion of, for example, power and wealth as characteristic of organized crime.

My first attempt to define organized crime[9] strikes me, upon reconsideration, as somewhat off the mark. The focus then was on the fact that there are many "organized crimes" and that we corrupt the English language if we state that only certain types of organized crime are truly organized crime. The taxonomy of organized crimes that I developed is useful but limited. Most of the organized crimes listed require organization in the commission of the crime—stolen car rings, gambling, price-fixing, and so on—whereas many organized crimes are organized not so much in their commission as in subsequent actions: distribution of the stolen goods through retail outlets, a network of associates and colleagues to help in special circumstances, and financial and even psychological support systems. Organized criminal activity of this nature cannot be included in a taxonomy that focuses only on organized illegal acts, because it ignores those (organized) actions and processes that facilitate the commission of future crimes or improve the felon's situation after committing the crimes. That is, the connections of the crime to the organization, to other crimes, and to associated activities must also be comprehended. To understand organized crime in all its manifestations—especially in those manifestations of importance for nonenforcement purposes—the associated activities that take place well before or well after the crime must also be understood and included.

Of course, we could just define organized crime by characterizing it as "crime that is organized," which gets us nowhere.[10] I feel that it is more appropriate to distinguish within that classification the activity of those criminal enterprises that most observers agree are part of the more virulent type of "organized crime." To distinguish between the more general term *organized crime* and the more dangerous manifestation, the latter will be termed OC.

OC AND "CONNECTIVITY"

One characteristic of OC that, I believe, we would all agree with is that there is a connection among the crimes committed by criminal enterprises that makes them "organized crimes." That is, the hijacking of a truck is not by itself an organized crime, but the fact that a trucking firm employee was bribed to provide the information concerning cargo and route, that the truck was taken to a prearranged drop point, that the driver was (credibly) threatened with reprisals, and that the cargo made its way into a legitimate outlet makes it an OC-type organized crime. Thus, the whole is greater than the sum of its parts, due to the synergy inherent in the criminal organization in connecting the individual crimes to each other. It leads directly to some of the characteristics Kleiman notes— power and wealth, intangible criminal capital, and reputational capital.

An important factor in this description is "connectivity." The individual crimes of commercial bribery, armed robbery, assault, and receiving stolen property are all connected, making their combination so much more dangerous than the sum of the separate crimes. In a previous study[11] I demonstrated how connectivity among organized crime cases can be used to evaluate enforcement programs that target organized crime; in this study connectivity among different aspects of an operation is used to aid in defining organized crime.

This concern for connectivity is important in other areas of criminal justice as well. The fact that the police have been focusing on crimes as individual incidents rather than connected "problems" has led to the development of problem—or community—oriented policing. Similarly, OC-type organized crime should be seen as a "problem"—a process that generates individual crimes as well as other antisocial outputs (fear, distrust, corruptible officials). In other words, I aim not to attempt to fashion a definition that can be used as a legal standard for any individual crime but to fashion one that can be used to determine whether a pattern exists that appears to be OC.

Ronald Goldstock (personal communication 1991) has pointed out that connectivity leads directly to increase opportunism for criminality. A loan shark on his own can threaten a debtor with bodily harm, but a loan shark tied to an organized crime group can threaten a debtor employed, say, by a trucking firm into providing the cargo and route information. This can be used by the group because of its diversification into other enterprises. Similarly, a postal employee who steals stock certificates can make use of them only through such a diverse criminal firm. Thus, the enterprise as a whole is able to avail itself of these "targets of opportunity" that a less diverse criminal group could not.

Dealing with connected cases requires a concerted effort aimed not just at the actors through prosecution and not just at the criminal enterprise through RICO but at the conditions that permit the enterprise to thrive. Goldstock argues in this book that the role of the prosecutor be expanded to that of problem solver, "empowered to employ a wide variety of remedies in implementing innovative strategies to control 'criminal problems.' " It is clear that the nature of the problems requires a rethinking of the roles of all elements of the criminal justice system; this proposal should be seriously considered as a possible means of dealing with problems that require more than the standard law enforcement response.

CHARACTERISTICS OF OC

To approach the task of defining OC, we can first analyze the characteristics of earlier definitions. Among the characteristics they suggest are the following:

- corruption
- violence
- sophistication
- continuity
- structure
- discipline
- ideology (or lack thereof)
- multiple enterprises
- involvement in legitimate enterprises

In addition to these elements, another one to be considered is the "bonding" ritual, such as those rituals reported to have been used in "making" members of the Mafia, Cosa Nostra, La Nuestra Familia, and the Hell's Angels. These nine potential elements of a definition should be examined in the context of all types of OC, not just Mafia-like groups but newer and emerging groups as well. Some appear to be central to the concept of OC, while others either are peripheral or refer to only one manifestation of it.

Corruption

OC ordinarily involves corruption, although the more general organized crime may not.[12] For example, the Black Hand societies at the turn of the century—and the Blackstone Rangers more recently—were, inter alia, organized extortion rings, but corruption was not the means by which security was achieved. The other parties in the transactions, the victims of extortion, were told in no uncertain terms what would happen to them, their families, and their businesses if they assisted the police. The fact that the extorted businessmen were, for the most part, members of ethnic groups that at that time did not place much trust in the police also helped maintain the security of the scheme.[13] The businessmen should have wanted the police to learn of the scheme and help them, but they were afraid to cooperate with police.

As these groups evolved and matured, they developed enterprises that dealt in illegal goods and services, in which the other parties to the transactions, the purchasers of illegal goods and services, wanted to keep their involvement secret. In contrast with the previous example, these parties do not want the police to know, but if caught, they are often turned into informers who cooperate with the police. In the first case the parties are usually reputable businessmen who have much to lose if the extorters carry out their threats, while in the second case the parties are often addicts and petty criminals with little more to lose at the hands of those against whom they inform than from the police. Because of this greater exposure to arrest and conviction, OC groups dealing in these areas find it more expedient to make payoffs to police, prosecutors, and judges than to attempt to keep all their customers in line. Customers have little to lose by informing, but corrupt officials have a great deal to lose if their involvement becomes known.

It is usually implicitly assumed that the term *corruption* refers only to public officials who violate their oaths of office. However, corruption of nongovernmental employees is also used to protect schemes from exposure. Bank officials may use their discretionary authority to approve loans for which stolen securities are used as collateral. They may break the law by camouflaging or not recording transactions they are legally required to report, in order to protect OC schemes. Airport personnel may alter records of flights or may assist in the shipment of contraband. Buyers for department stores and discount houses may alter records of purchases to permit stolen merchandise to be commingled with legally purchased merchandise or may buy merchandise at a premium price from an OC business. In all of these cases the individuals are acting corruptly, in that they are being paid to violate the trust placed in them by their employers. Insofar as the corrupt individuals are concerned, there is no difference between public and private corruption: in both cases they are using their positions of authority within their organizations to make money at the expense of their employers. However, public corruption is truly of a different nature than private corruption.

When individuals working for a private business take payoffs in violation of the trust placed in them by their employer, the effects are felt primarily in that particular business, although competitors may also be affected. When an individual working for a public agency takes payoffs, it harms the integrity of government and affects every individual. Some years ago, the director of the Financial Crimes Bureau of the Illinois Attorney General's Office, during a college lecture on organized crime, was asked about immunity: why was the industrialist who bribed a half dozen legislators granted immunity in return for his testimony against them, when he was the one who initiated the bribes in the first place? Shouldn't he have been the one to be prosecuted? The director first gave a practical reason: when the industrialist's lawyer got wind of the investigation, he brought his client in to make a deal; there would have been no case against anyone had the industrialist not come forward.

But there were other strong reasons that this offer was acceptable to the prosecutors. Since the goal of private business is to make a profit, that some businessmen upon occasion resort to illegal practices would not be unexpected. The goal of governments is "to establish justice," to make sure that illegal practices do not go unpunished. If the integrity of government is threatened, then such illegal practices will become the norm.

Furthermore, money is frequently offered to public officials in return for votes, decisions, contracts, and so on. If officials are put on notice that bribers may be granted immunity from prosecution if they turn the officials in and that serious enforcement efforts are under way, even the most corrupt officials will hesitate before accepting a bribe. Prosecuting the officials thus was expected to have a greater deterrent effect than prosecuting the industrialist.

Because of its greater harm to society, only public corruption is here considered an element of OC. Whether it is a necessary element is still an open question.

Violence

While some types of crimes require violence or the threat of violence or their commission, others do not. But even when an OC group engages only in "victimless" crimes, even when it has a monopoly in its enterprises, and even when its employees, customers, and associates are docile and stable, violence may be required to keep down both competition and rebellion.

One might think an OC group can maintain itself without violence if the group's political or economic power is established; once it matures, it may not need to resort to physical power. Yet physical violence is almost always necessary. Disputes continually arise within and between organizations; if they cannot be settled peacefully by the disputants, then coercion must be used. In our society the legal system is used to settle disputes and is backed by the legal and overt use of nonviolent coercive force—judicial orders, injunction, judgments, sentences, and so on. But these are unavailable to OC groups; instead they use criminal and violent force—shootings, beatings, threats of violence, and the like. This suggests that the potential for violence is always present in an OC group.[14]

The coercion need not always be administered by the OC group itself. During the "beer wars" in Chicago, Al Capone found it quite useful to let the police know about his competitors' operations; this helped him to maintain his monopoly, while at the same time helping the police by improving their arrest statistics.

Sophistication

Many descriptions and definitions of OC imply that it is a "sophisticated" operation. Here the term means that illegal enterprises are not run blatantly and that the actors are familiar with the rules of criminal procedure and how to use them to their advantage. Thus, telephone conversations between participants are likely to be in code; illegal goods are rarely handled by the principals; dummy corporations are established, ostensibly by nominees; paper trails are lengthy and ambiguous. That many OC organizations engage in some criminal activity of this sort is very likely; however, sophistication is not always present. An OC group engaged in "traditional" activities—gambling, prostitution, loan-sharking, narcotics—may be very unsophisticated in its operation. Although many OC groups that come to the attention of the authorities engage in a number of sophisticated activities, this is not invariably the case.

Continuity

Many noncontinuous organized crime enterprises result from opportunities in a number of situations. For example, a businessman's gambling debts may force him to turn his business over to his organized crime debtors, who then pull a bankruptcy scam: they use credit to order merchandise, sell it below cost, keep the money, and then declare bankruptcy after all other assets have been sold. This is a one-shot, noncontinuous operation.

Can one envision an OC group that relies entirely on noncontinuous, separable operations like this, that works together only at those times? Such a group might join forces to plan and execute a major crime and then disband until another opportunity arises.

If such a group exists, it may be an organized crime group of a more general nature, but it is not an OC group. Even if it engages in different types of crimes—first a hijacking, then a bankruptcy scam, then securities theft—they are still separate crimes that for the most part can be investigated and prosecuted separately. The thread of connectivity among the crimes is missing, except for the fact that the same actors are involved in their execution. This suggests to me that one of the cohesive elements of an OC group may be a continuing enterprise, such as drug distribution, extortion, or gambling.

Structure

An OC group is, of course, organized. But how organized would one ordinarily expect it to be? For example, Donald R. Cressey's[15] definition of organized crime implies that the organization has a very formal structure. He specifies that it has "an established division of labor and" positions for, inter alia, a corrupter, a corruptee, and an enforcer. It seems highly unlikely that such roles are truly as formal as Cressey implies; although some OC groups may be this formal, with organization charts and the like, it is doubtful that this is common practice.[16] There may be individuals who corrupt, who are corrupted, and who enforce within a particular criminal enterprise, but their roles may change for other enterprises. Studies of particular criminal organizations[17] bear out the contention that relationships are often task-dependent and changeable.

Although it is questionable whether basing a definition of OC on a group's internal structure is useful, the structure nonetheless exists. It often has a well-defined hierarchy that is maintained by force or other means (see the later section on "bonding"). Yet predicating a definition on structure would create problems, since one would need to determine the nature of the structure (which may be quite fluid) in order to prove that a particular manifestation of organized crime was OC.

The presence of corruption may have an impact on whether there is a well-defined structure to the OC group. Many OC groups, especially the emerging groups, may consist of shifting networks of players, in some cases specifically because they feel that any crystallization of an organizational structure will invite concerted enforcement action against the upper echelons of the groups.[18] This suggests that one factor in the development of a hierarchical structure is the corrupter-corruptee dyad. A corrupt official may be loath to maintain ties to more than one or two individuals.[19] The corrupter, the person who does have the tie to the official, thus has a measure of control over the OC activity that can be protected by this tie. This can lead to a more structured OC group.

Mark H. Moore[20] describes four different structural models of organized crime "firms," ranging from the tightly organized hierarchical structure described by Cressey[21] to the professional association of criminals generally called "the underworld." He suggests that the possession of certain assets—corruption, violence, and control over capital—would tend to centralize the structure of an organized crime enterprise into an OC group.

Discipline

The reputation that OC groups have for discipline within their ranks has been eroded considerably over the past two decades. Joseph Valachi's testimony,[22] Vincent Teresa's disclosure,[23] Jimmy Fratianno's story,[24] Gay Talese's book on Bill Bonanno,[25] and the Gallo-Profaci "war" in the 1970s, among other confessions and events, have demonstrated that discipline within OC groups has been less than rigid.

One should not expect otherwise. When all individuals in a group are armed and have no compunction about using their weapons, which is one of the criteria for acceptance by the group, then the ability to govern them must depend to a great extent on the consent of the governed. Discipline of a group's members can be maintained only if it is in their own self-interest. Although there must be some discipline (just as there must be some structure) in order for a particular collection of individuals to become an organization, it may not play an important part in defining OC.

Ideology

Many observers draw a sharp distinction between ideologically based organizations such as the Ku Klux Klan, Weathermen, and Black Panthers and the profit-based organizations such as the Mafia, Cosa Nostra, and motorcycle gangs, with only the latter considered OC groups. The problem is that the distinction often gets blurred over time. According to some accounts, the Mafia started out as a resistance movement, as did other organized crime groups[26]; and the history of the drug trade in Southeast Asia is also replete with examples of politically oriented movements that lost their ideological purity as the money from drugs began to pour in.[27]

The fact that an organization has an ideology should not necessarily excuse it from consideration as an OC group. For the most part governmental agencies do the defining, and many of the ideological groups commit profit-oriented crimes to support themselves and their causes.

Furthermore, the "apolitical" OC organizations do have an impact on the established government: a businessman who pays protection or a bookie who pays a "street tax" to a member of an OC group is actually paying a nongovernmental organization for governmental services. Even in these situations, the OC group is competing with the established government.

Multiple Enterprises

There are many reasons that a criminal organization would diversify its activity beyond a single criminal enterprise. A business that is dependent on only one good or service faces greater risks than one that has a number of product lines:

- A pesticide or fungus could destroy a year's poppy, coca, or marijuana crop.
- Improved drug detectors or other enforcement action might close down the only supply route, making diversity in supply routes, as well as in enterprises, a necessity.
- If the profits are high, others will compete for a share of the market.

• A substitute product may steal most of the market for a product.

• By diversifying, a business hedges its bets; not all of its eggs are in one basket.

But there are advantages to concentrating on a single product. When all of a business's efforts are expended in making sure that the product meets the needs of its clients, it becomes a specialist. It becomes intimately familiar with enforcement mechanisms used to investigate that particular operation. It needs to monitor the efforts of only one or two enforcement units (e.g., gambling would be enforced by state and local vice units) instead of a dozen or more if a number of diverse activities are engaged in. It keeps a lower profile by restricting itself to only one enterprise.

Since a criminal organization engaged in only one enterprise has a lower profile, we might conclude that an OC group must normally be involved in many enterprises; any lesser operation would be only an organized crime group. But this conclusion is debatable, especially when the scale of an organization and the means used to maintain the enterprise are far-reaching. Consider the hypothetical case of a single organization engaged solely in controlling the distribution of an illegal drug, such as heroin, throughout the country or a major region. The scale of this organization clearly brands it as OC.

Of course, to control all distribution of an illegal commodity in a region requires a great deal of organizational ability—and a great deal of corruption. Expansion into other areas seems an inevitable result of such large-scale corruption. Having developed a profitable "connection," most groups would exploit it to the fullest. For example, in the city of "Wincanton"—Reading, Pennsylvania—John A. Gardiner[28] shows how the "Stern" syndicate, whose main business was gambling, used its corrupt connections to local government officials to branch out into fixing city contracts and zoning and licensing applications and into prostitution.

Another situation in which diversity is not necessary to make a crime an OC is the criminal running of a major legitimate organization. The most obvious example is the International Brotherhood of Teamsters. The prosecutorial effort waged against Jimmy Hoffa in the 1960s by the Justice Department's "get-Hoffa squad" was tantamount to a strike force operation.[29] Even when only union-related crimes are involved (e.g., sweetheart contracts, theft of pension funds, threatening rivals in union elections), such activities might well constitute OC merely because of the scale of the enterprise. A union as strong as the Teamsters exerts a powerful influence on day-to-day commerce; when officials of only one local are involved in union-related crimes, they can have a profound effect on the industry in the region because of their almost total control of trucking; "there is no industry today that can carry on its business if the Teamsters lay down their reins."[30]

"Multiple enterprises," therefore, may be inadequate as a unique descriptor of OC, as important as the number or diversity of enterprises is to the power and influence wielded by the group. By analogy, suppose one person owned a hospital, a nearby pharmacy, a ''free'' clinic, and a medical testing laboratory, and suppose a second person owned four hospitals in four different cities, four pharmacies in other cities, four clinics in yet other cities, and four labs in still other cities. The second person would be wealthier overall, but the first person's influence and control over the market for medical services in his or her area would be considerably greater. A large number of separate and distinct enterprises does not have the clout of a small number of enterprises that are tied to each other.

Legitimate Business

Many have decried Melvin K. Bers[31] for pointing out the deleterious effect that an OC group can have on its competitors and customers. It often does not play by the rules,[32] preferring to use force and violence instead of standard business practices to maximize profits.

Both business and nonbusiness pressures move OC groups to become involved in legitimate enterprises. For one, the group may have started out primarily in legitimate business,[33] gravitating to criminal activity because of the greater potential for profits. On the other hand, the OC group may enter legitimate business when it is offered a part or all of a business—as payment, for example, for gambling or loan shark debts.

In addition, legitimate business can be used to ''launder'' money by declaring more profits than the business actually earned. In that way individuals making most of their money illegally can attribute part of it to the business and spend it openly without running afoul of the Internal Revenue Service (IRS).

Legitimate businesses also serve as ''fronts'' in another way. Stolen merchandise can be ''laundered'' by commingling it with legally purchased merchandise; if the goods have no identifying marks (e.g., a truckload of meat or razors or cigarettes), there is no way of tracing the goods to a theft. This has the added advantage of cutting business cost, giving the business an unfair advantage over its competitors.

The desire to gain respectability sometimes motivates an OC group's entry into legitimate business. Organized crime has been called the ''queer ladder of social mobility,''[34] a shortcut to financial success for groups without access to legitimate means of power. Although social status in this country is based primarily on wealth, wealth from criminal activity does not bring the respectability that legally earned money does. Other family members, who often feel the social stigma more keenly than the member of the OC group, may exert pressure on the group member to assume a cloak of respectability.

Thus, there are many reasons for an OC group to diversify into legitimate business. In fact, there are so many that one is inclined to believe that an OC group will always have legitimate enterprises, but our collective experience does not necessarily bear this out. The Hell's Angels, Blackstone Rangers, and La

Nuestra Familia may have been OC groups before they became involved in legitimate business, but they would have been considered OC groups regardless of such involvement. Furthermore, by suggesting that involvement in legitimate business is a necessary characteristic, one runs the risk of overlooking emerging OC groups.

Bonding

Many OC groups have rituals that appear to combine mysticism, fraternity initiation rites, and the process of being made a partner in a law firm. The financial benefits of partnership are, of course, the driving force for wanting to become a "made man," but what role does the ritual itself play? Is it a necessary concomitant of an OC group?

First, let us consider the reasons that may underlie the rituals. To start, they may lend an air of legitimacy and romance to the group's criminal activity, by attempting to transform vicious people and acts into a revolt against society. The rituals reinforce the feeling of separateness: "It's us against them" or "We'll show them what happens when they exclude us."

The bonding ritual also probably gives those on the lower rungs of the organization a goal, which keeps them in line while they work their way up to membership. In addition, although lip service may be paid to the idea of brotherhood among the "made" members—an "all for one, one for all" feeling—the ritual may make it easier to accept that those at the top rule the roost. In other words, the bonding ritual may make people feel that they "belong." This attraction evidently aided one of the sting operations in Washington, D.C. The thieves who frequented the police-run fencing operation were arrested when they eagerly awaited the appearance of "the don" from New York.

That the bonding ritual exists in Mafia families has been amply documented. Nevertheless, it is not necessarily an attribute of all OC groups. Even if it had been proven that all such groups in the United States do have some form of ritual associated with them, it is possible to conceive of a group that does not need them.

CONCLUSION

In reviewing the attributes that have been considered potential indicators of OC—corruption, violence, sophistication, continuity, structure, discipline, ideology, multiple enterprises, legitimate business, and bonding—the chapter argues that corruption, violence, continuity, and involvement in multiple enterprises may be characteristic of essentially all OC groups; that all have, of necessity, some structure, although no particular structure characterizes all possible OC groups; that most, if not all, are engaged in legitimate businesses as well as in criminal enterprises, but this characteristic may not be essential; and that although sophistication, discipline, ideology, and bonding may be characteristic of some OC groups, they are neither necessary nor typical.

More time has been spent on determining the characteristics of OC groups than on determining the characteristics of OC. This reflects the ambivalence discussed elsewhere: is OC an act or a group?[35] This chapter concentrated on the acts, thus leaving out the connections that tie the acts together, the group. This discussion suggests that OC cannot be defined based on acts alone; it must also refer to the people who work together as a group to commit them.

A thread links the attributes that have been rejected as determinants of OC (discipline, sophistication, and bonding): they are all characteristics of the archetypical Mafia family. This image of OC is so powerful that it often blinds us to other potential forms. OC groups can start out as legitimate businessmen, as a collection of burglars, as a guerrilla or resistance unit, or even as a group of military or police personnel. For example, can we consider France's OAS (Secret Army Organization), which robbed banks as well as assassinated its enemies, an OC group? Perhaps. Even though its mission was to "save" France from the disgrace of granting independence to Algeria, its activities went far beyond political action. The SDECE, France's equivalent of the Central Intelligence Agency (CIA), was deeply implicated in heroin trafficking throughout the world,[36] especially in the French Connection.

In a recent paper, Mark H. Haller[37] describes three characteristics of illegal enterprises: corruption of both police and politicians; overlapping partnerships or interconnections among illegal entrepreneurs; and internal economic factors, such as specialization and horizontal and vertical diversification. His conclusion regarding the nature of illegal enterprises is similar to the characterization of OC discussed here.

Obviously, there is a continuum of organized crime enterprises, from the most nonviolent boiler room or black market operation to the most vicious and venal gang of assaulters and robbers. Even more to the point, organized crime enterprises can be considered to have different dimensions, and they are arrayed along these different dimensions according to their characteristics. I do not expect that the entire region of possibilities will be represented by some organized crime group. For example, this chapter suggests that those low in the "corruption" dimension would also be low in the "structure" dimension, and vice versa, and the type of enterprise this chapter focuses on when referring to OC is the violence-based criminal enterprise that has few scruples when it comes to committing crimes or maintaining its markets.

Nothing in this description is meant to suggest that we should revise or curtail statutes used for the prosecution of stock manipulators or other nonviolent organized criminal enterprises. The basis for their prosecution under the federal RICO Act and similar state statutes is that the enterprise was used for criminal purposes, and the enterprise itself should be subject to punishment: not using violence to carry out these criminal purposes should not immunize the enterprise from criminal penalties. Rather, the purpose of this chapter is to help us discriminate among the different types of organized crime that are found in the United States and elsewhere. Definitions that are too broad (e.g., "organized crime is crime that is organized") are not helpful because there is not enough discrimination; definitions that are too narrow (e.g., "organized crime=Mafia") are not helpful because they are merely ad hominem. What is needed is an approach somewhere in the middle, which is the goal of this chapter.

NOTES

1. Louis Chevalier, *Laboring Classes and Dangerous Classes in Paris During the First Half of the Nineteenth Century* (Princeton, NJ: Princeton University Press, 1973).

2. U.S. Government Accounting Office, *War on Organized Crime Faltering: Strike Forces Not Getting the Job Done*, Report No. GGD-82-2 (Washington, DC: U.S. Government Printing Office, 1977).

3. Michael D. Maltz, *Measuring the Effectiveness of Organized Crime Control Efforts* (Chicago, IL: Office of International Criminal Justice, 1990).

4. In fact, territorial disputes between U.S. attorneys' offices and independent strike forces led to the dissolution of the strike forces.

5. Gordon Hawking, "God and the Mafia," *The Public Interest* (1969): 24–51; Dwight Smith, *The Mafia Mystique* (New York: Basic Books), 1975. In fairness to these individuals, their doubt did not concern whether organized crime existed so much as whether the Mafia existed.

6. This was later reversed by the New York State Court of Appeals because the term was used only to determine whether the Organized Crime Task Force had jurisdiction in the case, not whether the acts that were committed constituted "organized crime." The court, however, recognized the inherent vagueness in the term, stating, "The phrase 'organized crime' is itself not susceptible to precise judicial definition."

7. Robert G. Blakey, Ronald Goldstock, and Charles H. Rogovin, *Rackets Bureaus: Investigation and Prosecution of Organized Crime* (Washington, DC: National Institute of Law Enforcement and Criminal Justice, 1978).

8. Mark Kleiman, *Marijuana: Costs of Abuse, Costs of Control* (Westport, CT: Greenwood Press, 1989).

9. Michael D. Maltz, "On Defining Organized Crime: The Development of a Definition and a Typology," *Crime and Delinquency* 26 (1976): 338–46.

10. Herbert Edelhertz, et al., *The Containment of Organized Crime: A Report to the Arizona Legislative Council* (Seattle, WA: Battelle Human Affairs Research Centers, 1981). They comment on the definition of organized crime used by Arizona: "Its defect is that it encompasses a very broad range of the criminal universe. Its virtue is that it permits flexibility of approach with respect to new and developing forms of criminal group activity and encourages attention to emerging groups."

11. Michael D. Maltz, *Measuring the Effectiveness of Organized Crime Control Efforts* (Chicago: Office of International Criminal Justice, 1990).

12. It also affects an OC group's structure; see the discussion of structure.

13. In fact, the United States is experiencing a resurgence of such organized crime in the newer immigrant communities from the Far East.

14. Justin J. Dintino and Frederick T. Martens, "The Process of Elimination: Understanding Organized Crime Violence," *Federal Probation Quarterly* 45 (1981): 26–31.

15. Donald R. Cressey, *Theft of the Nation: The Structure and Operation of Organized Crime in America* (New York: Harper and Row, 1969).

16. In fact, even in legitimate formal organizations, the organization chart may not represent the organization's actual structure.

17. Francis A. J. Ianni, *A Family Business: Kinship and Social Control in Organized Crime* (New York: Russell Sage Foundation, 1972); Annelise G. Anderson, *The Business of Organized Crime: A Cosa Nostra Family* (Stanford, CA: Hoover Institution Press, 1979); Peter Reuter, *Disorganized Crime: The Economics of the Visible Hand* (Cambridge: MIT Press, 1983).

18. This was pointed out by Ezra Stotland (personal communication, 1990).

19. This is not true for corruption at the "retail" level, for example, for judges who sell verdicts to defense attorneys in the lower courts. It is probably more valid for OC-related corruption, which is often at a higher level.

20. Mark H. Moore, "Organized Crime as a Business Enterprise," in *Major Issues in Organized Crime Control*, ed. Herbert Edelhertz (Washington, DC: National Institute of Justice, 1987).

21. Cressey, *Theft of the Nation.*

22. Peter Maas, *The Valachi Papers* (New York: G. P. Putnam's Sons, 1968).

23. Vincent Teresa, *My Life in the Mafia* (New York: Doubleday, 1973).

24. Ovid Demaris, *The Last Mafioso* (New York: Times Books, 1981).

25. Gay Talese, *Honor Thy Father* (Greenwich, CT: Fawcett, 1971).

26. Joseph L. Albini, *The American Mafia: Genesis of a Legend* (New York: Appleton-Century-Crofts, 1971).

27. Alfred W. McCoy, *The Politics of Heroin in Southeast Asia* (New York: Harper and Row, 1973).

28. John A. Gardiner, *The Politics of Corruption: Organized Crime in an American City* (New York: Russell Sage Foundation, 1970).

29. Steven Brill, *The Teamsters* (New York: Simon and Schuster, 1978).

30. Ibid., 13. This was stated by a union leader in 1902, and it is still true today.

31. Melvin K. Bers, *The Penetration of Legitimate Business by Organized Crime: An Analysis* (Washington, DC: Law Enforcement Assistance Administration, 1970).

32. This is not to say that legitimate businesspersons always play by the rules; Edwin H. Sutherland, *Principles of Criminology* (Philadelphia: J. B. Lippincott, 1949) pointed this out over forty years ago, and it is still true today; Marshall B. Clinard et al., *Illegal Corporate Behavior* (Washington, DC: National Institute of Law Enforcement and Criminal Justice, 1979).

33. We normally think of OC groups as starting out as criminal gangs and then "maturing" into OC syndicates. This is not always the case; see Albini, *The American Mafia*, for some examples.

34. Daniel Bell, "Crime as an American Way of Life," in *The End of Ideology* (New York: Collier, 1961).

35. Maltz, "On Defining Organized Crime."

36. McCoy, *The Politics of Heroin.*

37. Mark H. Haller, "Illegal Enterprise: A Theoretical and Historical Interpretation," *Criminology* 28 (1990): 207–36.

2

Organized Crime: History and Historiography

ALAN A. BLOCK

The alarmed response of older academics to multicultural intrusions into their curriculum would seem odd if it were not founded on a sound self-interest. The great books of the West are holy writ in literature departments not just for their inarguable merit but for having already been well enough learned to be taught without further struggle for something new to say. . . .

The inescapable marks of wither upon La Cosa Nostra present the same troubling challenge to us journalists, who are no less lazy and disinclined to new areas of research than academics. Make no mistake: once the federal prosecutors contrive to encase John Gotti, we shall have lost the last of the grand personages who had been our dependence for supporting the myth of the Mafia as a force in current history.

Organized crime will no longer be a crude euphemism for fascinatingly disreputable Italo-Americans. We shall have to flog ourselves studying the gangs of Chinese Americans, Vietnamese Americans, Korean Americans, Russo-Americans, Albanian Americans, Dominican Americans, etc., etc. We too must engulf ourselves in a tide of multicultural criminality.

Journalists find their audience, if seldom their code of personal conduct, among good citizens. And good citizens have always insisted upon being assured that crime is an un-American activity confined to alien sects. The Mafia was enormously serviceable to that illusion; and peddling its recondite lore required no more than airs of familiarity with scungilli, the Sicilian Vespers, the governments of Palermo suburbs, and the organizational table of the Roman legions.

—Murray Kempton, ''Another Case of Multiculturalism,''
The New York Review of Books (9 April 1992)

The history of the phenomena of organized crime in American society contains numerous pitfalls, although none quite so precarious as the presence of a standard historiography. The orthodox model states that organized crime's crucial history is the rise of Italian American organized crime.[1] This view is sustained, however, by several faulty assumptions, some historical, others sociological. Historically speaking, the most important goes something like this: Italian American criminals formed the nation's most powerful underworld society, and the historian's task primarily is to explain how this came to pass. The supposition rests primarily upon a law enforcement perspective, and endeavors to accomplish a fully found history based on this have not been very satisfactory.[2] This chapter is broadly divided into two sections: the first explores questions of historical evidence as well as the interplay between certain key sociological notions about organized crime and historical data all having to do with La Cosa Nostra; the second attempts to construct a history of organized crime within the broader context of American social and urban history.

RUMMAGING FOR A PAST: LA COSA NOSTRA HISTORIOGRAPHY

The 1980s witnessed the most impressive and sustained "war on organized crime" in the history of American law enforcement. Thousands of racketeers, including many of the most prominent leaders of long-established crime syndicates, were successfully prosecuted. This accomplishment is striking. But for historians and sociologists there should be a caution raised, for far too many presume these cases have also nailed down the issues of the history and sociology of organized crime. No matter how detailed they are, along with the material derived from them presented to congressional committees and other law enforcement-oriented, fact-finding bodies, they are often misleading guides for historical and sociological workers.

For instance, in the civil Racketeer Influenced and Corrupt Organizations (AcT) (RICO) suit pressed by the U.S. attorney in New York's southern district against the Teamsters' Union in an attempt to break "La Cosa Nostra's control over one of the largest labor unions in the nation," assistant U.S. attorney Randy M. Mastro stated, "The Government has established the existence of La Cosa Nostra, a/k/a the 'Mafia' or 'Our Thing' " partially "through the testimony of Angelo Lonardo, former Underboss of the Cleveland Organized Crime Family."[3] Mastro remarked that Lonardo established these items concerning La Cosa Nostra: (1) it operates throughout the United States; (2) it has a commission made up of the bosses of New York's five La Cosa Nostra families and "at various times, representatives of other La Cosa Nostra Families throughout the United States"; (3) the commission is a "national ruling council" of Mafia groups; and (4) the commission's function includes regulating, facilitating, and controlling relationships among Mafia groups.[4]

The historian's interest in these items concerns whether a fair reading of

Lonardo's statements supports the contentions. If not, they suffer in this instance from what historian David Hackett Fischer called "the fallacy of the pseudo proof."[5] This is not to doubt what Lonardo said at various trials, nor to call into question the convictions on many substantive crimes of the organized criminals tried. I do question, however, whether his testimony on particular historical issues corresponds with what he said to the Federal Bureau of Investigation (FBI) before the trials because historians must seek the best relevant evidence possible—in Lonardo's case, his recollections prior to his many trial appearances as a government witness.

Lonardo was interviewed about the "history of the Cleveland La Cosa Nostra (LCN) family" by Special Agents Richard B. Hoke and R. Gerald Personen on 28 October 1983.[6] At the very beginning of his story he noted that his Mafia boss through the mid-1970s, John Scalish, "was not familiar with the names and activities of his peers in other families around the country." When Scalish traveled, he would have to ask Lonardo for factual information about other bosses. Scalish died in May 1976 and had to be replaced. The successor was James Licavoli, who at first demurred, claiming he wasn't nearly as qualified as Lonardo was for the position. In fact, Lonardo stated to his FBI inquisitors that "Licavoli was completely ignorant of certain matters of protocol required by his new position and it was he [Lonardo] who advised Licavoli that he had to go to New York to advise the boss of the Genovese family of his new position and to pay his proper respects."

Later on Lonardo was asked about his own knowledge of "La Cosa Nostra (LCN) families in other cities." He answered that New York had five and there was one in each of the following American and Canadian cities: "Los Angeles, San Francisco, Denver, Milwaukee, Chicago, Kansas City, Detroit, Cleveland, St. Louis, Buffalo, Philadelphia, Boston, Providence, Pittsburgh, New Orleans, New Jersey [*sic*], Windsor, Ontario, Toronto, Ontario, Montreal, Quebec." Lonardo added that the Chicago Mafia was "responsible for settling certain disputes and making administrative type decisions that affect the various families in the Western half of the United States." The eastern region was the responsibility of New York's Genovese family, with certain important exceptions. Eastern waterfront organized crime, for example, was controlled by New York's Gambino family.

With the Chicago mob administering western Mafias and the Genovese gang doing much the same for eastern ones, it is a fair question to wonder precisely what the commission was empowered to do. This must have been on the interviewing agents' minds also for they next wrote, "Lonardo acknowledged the existence of a national commission of LCN bosses which meets on rare occasions to settle disputes or make high-level decisions involving national LCN matters." Although Lonardo was far and away the most knowledgeable Cleveland mafioso when it came to national LCN matters, it turned out he knew only two members of the commission. They were both from New York.

These statements cannot stand as confirmation of any of the general principles enunciated by the government about La Cosa Nostra in its case against the Teamsters. Indeed, when questioned about the Teamsters' involvement with LCN, Lonardo had this to say about his boss Licavoli's knowledge: "Licavoli asked Lonardo why the Cleveland LCN family cared who became head of the Teamsters since they were not getting any money from the Teamsters." Amusingly, Lonardo and an associate, Milton Rockman, couldn't find on their own a Chicago office where they were supposed to discuss Teamster politics with the Chicago LCN. They had to ask directions from someone at a dry cleaning shop, who warned them "they were in a bad neighborhood and would be lucky to get out alive." No matter what Lonardo said about these matters later, it seems that in October 1983 he wasn't very much more aware of the LCN commission than his two bosses. What made his memory improve later is anyone's guess.

This brief excursion into the claim of a smooth, imperious commission serves to introduce wider historical themes. Statements about La Cosa Nostra and the commission, at the commission trial in New York in testimony before President Ronald Reagan's Commission on Organized Crime and later in hearings held by the Senate's Permanent Subcommittee on Investigations, reveal serious historical (and conceptual) errors. Several key dates, for example, dominate the issue. The earliest was given by the Justice Department's Organized Crime Intelligence and Analysis Unit, which operates within the Criminal Investigative Division's Organized Crime Section. The unit presented to the Permanent Subcommittee on Investigations a "Chronological History of La Cosa Nostra in the United States," which began with the 1890 murder of David Hennessey, who was superintendent of police in New Orleans.

This murder and subsequent ones in New Orleans stimulated by it "created perhaps the first significant public awareness of the La Cosa Nostra (LCN)."[7] At the start of this discussion it is most important to point out that this statement is an example of the "fallacy of ambiguity which consists in the use of a word or an expression which has two or more possible meanings, without sufficient specification of which meaning is intended," mixed with the error or "prolepsis," which "describes an event as happening before it could have done so."[8] It is simply not true that the Hennessey murder made anyone aware of La Cosa Nostra as a term signifying organized crime, for it was probably not invented and certainly not popularized for another seventy-three years. Even the Intelligence and Analysis Unit knew the statement was factually incorrect, for it followed this preposterous claim by noting that this event triggered the introduction into American society of the term *Mafia*.

One may wish to argue at some point, such as the commission trial in the 1980s, that Mafia and La Cosa Nostra are synonymous, but one cannot argue that until both terms are invented. Of course, the Intelligence and Analysis Unit was merely looking for some starting point to present its "chronological history" of LCN, and I presume no one was to take the Hennessey murder as actually signifying anything very seriously.[9] The Intelligence and Analysis Unit itself had a later date in mind, which was really significant for the formation of

La Cosa Nostra. This penchant for reaching as far back into the past as possible to establish the first instance of the criminal conspiracy later called La Cosa Nostra was also an intriguing feature of the "commission" indictment, which charged that "from 1900 to the present there existed a nationwide criminal society known as La Cosa Nostra or the Mafia," and so on.[10] My criticism of the Intelligence and Analysis Unit's historical sense also holds for the "commission" indictment's use of the past.

LCN's important history, commented the unit, started thirty years later with Prohibition, "which enabled the small, but powerful LCN to capitalize upon its international contacts, its reputation for ruthlessness, and—above all—*its rigidly disciplined structure of cooperating gangs* to establish the position of unrivaled eminence it holds in the American underworld today" (emphasis added).[11] To prove this minithesis, the unit's history then rattles off murder after murder, beginning with the killing of "Big Jim" Colosimo on 11 May 1920 and ending with the April 1931 shooting of Giuseppe Masseria, "boss of all bosses." But this decade of reported mayhem cannot sustain that part of the thesis that holds the LCN was by 1920 small and composed of rigidly disciplined, cooperating gangs. If anything, the facts marshaled by the unit indicate the opposite or nothing at all. New terms are thrown in willy-nilly such as "Camorra," which is said to have merged with LCN in Chicago on 7 September 1928 following yet another killing.[12] No evidence is developed through this list of violence that the LCN had international contacts, another important part of its alleged development.[13]

By far the most egregious error lies in the unit's resurrection of perhaps the best-known false claim in the historiography of organized crime. This is the alleged transformation of LCN structure following the murders of Masseria and, on 10 September 1931, of Salvatore Maranzano.[14] This is the infamous example of the discredited "alien conspiracy myth," as Dwight Smith, Jr., called it.[15] A tale of murder and the reorganization of LCN in 1931, it never had credible sources, as several writers carefully noted years ago.[16]

The burden of establishing historical accuracy for the development of Italian American organized crime exceeded the grasp of the Intelligence and Analysis Unit. The same failure holds for the analysts in the Intelligence Division of the New York City Police Department, who presented the discredited story in attenuated form to the Permanent Subcommittee on Investigations.[17] The unit likely figured a "potpourri" of mob facts placed in chronological order would somehow reveal the actual essence of organized crime—La Cosa Nostra.

In these pseudohistories the writers also commit the "fallacy of essences," which emerges from the notion that everything (in this case, organized crime) contains, deep inside, an essence, "an inner core of reality" (in this case, La Cosa Nostra).[18] For those who subscribe to this, the facts about a culture, an ideology, or an institution (even a secret criminal order) are important only to the degree they demonstrate the essence of the subject. But this is an essentially fruitless endeavor, as philosopher Karl Popper remarked when noting that the "progress of empirical knowledge requires, not a search for essences, which cannot be found by any empirical method, but rather a search for patterns of external behavior."[19]

In addition to the mistaken historical claims mentioned so far, it is interesting that the search for sound historical material about an American Mafia by trained analysts with wide-ranging access to confidential sources and material has nonetheless missed a key document, which originated in 1940. Compiled by the Italian Treasury Police, the document was forwarded by Italian authorities to a U.S. Customs supervisor in New York, who sent it on to the supervising customs agent in Chicago. From there it finally made its way to the Federal Bureau of Narcotics.[20]

The communication states there is a Grand Council of the Sicilian Mafia in the United States composed of nine men who manage the affairs "carried on by this gang throughout the U.S. and Europe." The Mafia council was led by Vincent Mangano from Brooklyn and included his brother Philip from Brooklyn, Joe Bonanno from Brooklyn, Joe Profaci from Brooklyn, Joe Traina from Brooklyn, Paul Ricca (Paul DeLucia) from Chicago, Steve Magaddino from Niagara Falls, New York, and Al Polizzi and Frank Milano from Cleveland. Although there is nothing about what the council manages and how successfully it carries out its responsibilities, at least there is finally a historical document worth considering that speaks to the quest for a La Cosa Nostra commission.

But what does the message mean? The primary point appears to be Brooklyn's dominant position on the council—five representatives from the Borough of Churches and Trees out of nine members. Indeed, with two-thirds of the council representing New York State and with what we already know about Cleveland's distracted Mafia leadership,[21] the council as a governing body was obviously very limited in scope. Of course, it is possible that a larger, more inclusive Italian American underworld society grew from this Mafia council or that the council was subsumed later by a commission. But there are no data to determine these possibilities.

To speak about a governing body is usually to postulate something about decision making and dispute resolution, and of this there is nothing from the Italian police but the simple claim of management. The chronologists from the Intelligence and Analysis Unit mentioned Profaci, the Mangano brothers, Joe Bonanno, and Frank Milano in their account of social change in the LCN during the years of intense gang warfare in 1930–31.[22] What these men actually did and how they fit into the larger story told by the Intelligence and Analysis Unit are once again unknown. Thus, no data indicate how and if the council exerted control over Sicilian American racketeers, let alone over non-Sicilian ones.

The Romance of Mafia: Buscetta's Tale

In the 1988 Permanent Subcommittee hearings, which were provocatively titled *Organized Crime: 25 Years After Valachi*, a fairly recent Sicilian Mafia defector, Tomasso Buscetta, appeared as a principal government witness. In introducing him it was pointed out that Buscetta's 1986 testimony in Sicily "was instrumental in the conviction of 435 members of the Sicilian Mafia" and that the year before (1985), his testimony in the "famous Pizza Connection case in New York City helped to convict 35 members of the New York and Sicilian La Cosa Nostra." [23] He appeared before the Senate panel to relate what he knew about the history of the Sicilian Mafia La Cosa Nostra and, in particular, its relations with its American counterpart.

Buscetta, who came from Palermo, first stated his credentials, pointing out that he was "a member of the Mafia, or Cosa Nostra, in Sicily, known within the Cosa Nostra as a Man of Honor." His tenure in the Mafia began in 1948, and, most important, he was "part of this organization both in Sicily and later as a favored and protected guest in the United States." Among his announced American Mafia/Cosa Nostra associates were "Lucky" Luciano, Carlo and Paul Gambino, Paul Castellano, and Joe Bonanno. Buscetta added that he knew a great deal about Cosa Nostra violence, having "lost one brother, two sons, one brother-in-law, three nephews, and one son-in-law all at the hands of the Mafia." [24]

There are two historical issues to consider in the discussion of Buscetta: his account of the formation of a Sicilian Mafia/La Cosa Nostra commission and claims about more fundamental historical changes within the Sicilian Cosa Nostra itself. On the first issue Buscetta states that the inspiration for a Sicilian commission came from none other than Lucky Luciano. Buscetta reported that following Luciano's deportation from the United States to Italy, "*in the early 1950s,*" he and Luciano became fast friends. During this period Luciano supposedly told him "how and why he created the commission in America." The reason was to prevent the "killing of Men of Honor unjustly." With this in mind the commission was formed and "had the bosses of all the families in the United States as its membership," although this would have been news, as we already know, to Cleveland's "Men of Honor." As it was formed to stop indiscriminate killings, the American commission's essential function, Buscetta explained, was the organization of sanctioned mob murders.

It is taxing to consider seriously this history, for several reasons. Everyone familiar with Luciano's career knows, except his good friend Buscetta, that he was deported from the United States in the winter of 1946. [25] Moreover, he spent the greatest amount of his Italian exile in the Naples area, not Palermo, though this would not preclude his chatting with Buscetta when in Palermo. Nevertheless, not knowing the era of Luciano's deportation raises concern about the historical credibility of Buscetta's testimony about Luciano.

In addition, Buscetta's claim that rationalizing murder was the first cause in commission formation still lacks any convincing proof. While this could have been on Luciano's mind and even expressed at some point to Buscetta, there is still no evidence that this possible desire led to real organizational innovation. The previously mentioned "Chronology" presented by the Intelligence and

Analysis Unit lists murder after murder following the time when Luciano would have had to form the U.S. commission (before he was arrested, tried, convicted, and sent to prison in 1935–36). Although a few of the many listed killings were allegedly carried out after some form of consultation among gangsters, most appear not to have been. Consider these entries: "August 17, 1936: 'Big Nose' John Avena (also known as John Nazzone), boss of the Philadelphia Family, was shot to death while talking to a friend on a Philadelphia street corner"; "April 6, 1950: Charles Binaggio, boss of the Kansas City Family was found shot to death, along with his bodyguard, Charles Gargotta"; "June 5, 1950: James Lumia, boss of the Tampa Family, was shotgunned to death on a street corner."[26]

It is not possible to say that these killings were not approved by an American commission, but there is no evidence presented that this was so. Moreover, even if this was part of the original motivation for an organized crime commission and could be established as such, the obvious fact that bosses have not been protected and organized crime murder has not been rationalized through some thoughtful and structured sanctioning process should have ended this particular explanation long ago. U.S. law enforcement's favorite organized crime informant in years past was Joe Valachi. He stated that the rationalization of murder was the major function of a New York commission of crime bosses. Valachi came to know this, he related, when another New York gangster told him that no member of La Cosa Nostra could be killed without the permission of the New York council (or bosses). This more localized version of governance made sense to Valachi for several reasons, perhaps foremost because he believed La Cosa Nostra was pretty much a New York affair. When asked by FBI interrogators, for instance, about the extent of "Causa [*sic*] Nostra," he answered there were about two thousand active members, with "no more than a few hundred outside New York."[27]

But whether permission to murder was routinely sought or whether it was routinely given or denied, the sociological significance of La Cosa Nostra (on either a national or New York level) in controlling violence cannot be determined without structured study. The fact that grievances were often aired in mob "sit-downs" does not tell us much without an analysis of outcomes. Grievance hearings could just as well function as a method to determine the scope of a mobster's protection, thereby adding to the total of those to be killed, rather than as a methodology of restraint. So much appears to depend upon individual personalities and perhaps idiosyncratic circumstances.

Contemporary historical events in and around Philadelphia show that murderous rancor remains the heart of the matter. This is made clear by the following list of assassinated mobsters presented to the U.S. Senate Judiciary Committee in February 1983 by Justin J. Dintino of the New Jersey State Police.

The Bruno War[28]

1. Angelo Bruno	21 March 1980
2. Antonio Caponigro	18 April 1980
3. Alfred Salerno	18 April 1980
4. John Simone	12 September 1980
5. Frank Sindone	30 October 1980
6. John McCullough	18 December 1980
7. Philip Testa	15 March 1981
8. Harry Peetros	26 May 1981
9. Chelsais Bouras	27 May 1981
10. John Calabrese	6 October 1981
11. Frank Narducci	7 January 1982
12. Pietro Inzerillo	15 January 1982
13. Dominick De Vito	25 February 1982
14. Rocco Marinucci	15 March 1982
15. Frank Monte	13 May 1982
16. Robert Hornickel	27 January 1983

The sixteen reported dead represent a sort of midterm casualty list. The killing continued through at least 1985. When the violence subsided, the Bruno "family" was left in "tatters, with at least 28 dead, dozens in jail and six . . . full-fledged members as informants," reports the Philadelphia *Daily News.*[29]

What to make of this mayhem, given the theme being explored? Does it represent an organized crime aberration or not? Can it be compared with other gang wars, which may then shed light on the issue of violence within organized crime? The latter can be briefly explored by comparing Philadelphia's organized crime murders through the Dintino midterm report with organized crime murders in New York City's Chinatown carried out by members of three warring tongs[30] from 1902 to 1914. One important reason to select the latter lies in the common notion that Chinese American organized crime has been (and continues to be) highly structured and disciplined.

The Chinese American syndicates battling during the first decade and a half of the twentieth century were the On Leong, the Hip Sing, and the Four Brothers. Though the On Leong and Hip Sing were established as benevolent associations, the former as a business association, the latter as "a protective society for laborers and seamen," they also "functioned as operators of opium, prostitution and gambling dens."[31] Current concern at the federal level indicates a preoccupation with the tongs' role in heroin smuggling, although several scholars are concentrating on their activities in northeastern urban garment centers. Elizabeth Petras, for one, has found a recrudescence of gangsterism in Philadelphia's garment industry, which had moved to Hong Kong and Taiwan but had recently returned as labor conditions in the City of Brotherly Love matched those in Southeast Asia.[32]

On Leong gangsters murdered thirteen Hip Sing and three Four Brothers members; the Hip Sings, in turn, killed eight On Leong criminals and two likely unaffiliated Chinese American gangsters; lastly, the Four Brothers assassinated ten On Leong rivals. The remaining victims were either killed by individuals from the same tong or murdered by unknown assailants. The Chinese American organized crime murders were geographically concentrated on three Manhattan streets—Doyers, Mott, and Pell whose conjunction became known as the Bloody Angle. This murderous conjunction was only steps from the headquarters of On Leong on Mott Street and Hip Sing on Pell—both organizations remain in precisely the same spots, a record of spatial continuity approaching one hundred years.

A review based on newspaper accounts reveals forty-eight murders in the twelve years surveyed—four per year, precisely the same as in the Philadelphia slayings Dintino reported. The first few years of the Philadelphia killings were slightly more murderous than the following ones, ending, as mentioned, with a newspaper count of ''at least'' twenty-eight victims. Using this figure for the moment, the homicide rate derived from the Bruno War for ten years in Philadelphia is somewhat less than the Chinese American one of forty-eight slain in twelve years. There are any number of reasons to explore in attempting to account for this and any other differences and similarities, though none that are derived from the proposition that Italian American underworld governors were able to restrain violence.

The analytical issues to examine are the comparative insularity of the two underworlds; a comparison of the structure of law enforcement in progressive-era New York with contemporary Philadelphia; a search for the number of underworld partisans belonging to the tongs, on one hand, and the Bruno syndicate, on the other, in order to determine at least an approximate base figure of potential targets; a comparison of the social structures of the Chinese American syndicates with the Bruno syndicate; a comparison of the relationship between killers and the killed in both instances; a comparison of the origins of the violence; and so forth. In other words, the methods to pursue derive from comparative history and sociology.[33] There can be no systematic, intellectual progress in the study of organized crime assuming contentious governing structures beforehand.

Feuds and vendettas are endemic within underworld societies, though one cannot assume there are never any effective restraints. It makes perfectly good sense for mobsters of any ethnic or racial background in any era to realize that killing other mobsters is dangerous and for them to seek allies or determine the range of opponents when contemplating such action. Sometimes those they wish to kill are frightening enough to restrain violence; sometimes not. Reasonable fear aside, other factors either impede or stimulate organized crime's internal violence. Among the most important is whether or not there is a serious law enforcement investigation focusing on particular syndicates, for when organized criminals face potentially decisive prosecutions, they turn to killing one another with abandon, knowing that their closest allies pose an unacceptable risk.

Informing is often good for business, particularly when it eliminates competition in various illicit activities. Giving up other criminals thus helps to keep the police away from one's own door. Informing is also demanded by law enforcement for its own organizational needs, both for continuing general intelligence and to maintain a record of arrests and prosecutions—all this without mentioning corruption in the classic sense, where police figures are more deeply embedded members of criminal syndicates or those variants where police units are, in effect, criminal syndicates. In these variations, intelligence gathering through a flow of coerced underworld informants is constant.

In the complex web of relations between organized crime and law enforcement, informing on others is a crucially important activity. That organized criminals "grass" (inform) to police is more the rule than is the romantic notion of "omerta" (the code of silence). This naturally sets off a murderous cycle—those with critical information know they may well be killed by their closest confederates so they in turn either kill them, flee, or turn to law enforcement as informants. It is always a very precarious business, with treachery at every step.

Patron-client networks, which can be thought of as complex grids of constantly changing social power holding precariously together professional criminals, their clients and victims, criminal lawyers, police, and politicians, are the predominant form of association characteristic of underworlds. Obviously, crime bosses and others in these networks seek to achieve a situation in which they will be protected—bosses from ambitious underlings and rival bosses, underlings and associates from bosses either somewhat psychopathic or under pressure from law enforcement. But there are no methods for controlling violence once these networks begin to change, as they invariably do, except the traditional one of murdering actual and, more importantly, potential informers.

In the social world of organized crime, who can ever know with certainty what criminal with important knowledge will inform? The fluid structure of criminal syndicates and the turbulent world within which organized criminals operate always undermine loyalty and restraint despite what crime bosses anxious about their safety may wish. The most important variables of instability are the waxing and waning of law enforcement's needs, the pressures of political reform movements, and simple ambition. They all have a corrosive effect on the connective tissue between patron and clientage.

Nonetheless, the notion of contained violence still persists, as Buscetta's testimony makes clear, indicating it probably serves other purposes or represents an "idealization" of organized crime. In fact, an "idealized" version of organized crime's development may well aid the bureaucratic needs of state agencies. It also appears to fit with popular, though mistaken, social science paradigms, in this case, that of criminal modernization.[34] In the latter case this theme—

sanctioned murder leading to a more complex criminal organization or the other way round—gained a foothold among criminologists because it seemed so logical. Hence, it was not noticed that it reversed the link between data and interpretation. Underworld tattlers filled in the appropriate empirical slots in an already extant theoretical structure.

The most cogent criminological statement that reveals this backward development was given by Robert T. Anderson several decades ago. In his quite famous article, "From Mafia to Cosa Nostra," Anderson argued that the Sicilian Mafia was changing as Sicily itself underwent the process of modernization. Part of that process can be seen, Anderson noted, in the Mafia's adaptation and expansion of its "techniques of exploitation."[35] Quoting from a 1960 article by reporter Claire Sterling, Anderson found that the Mafia had become urbanized: " Today there is not only a Mafia of the *feudo* (agriculture) but also Mafias of truck gardens, wholesale fruit and vegetable markets, water supply, meat, fishing fleets, flowers, funerals, beer, *carrozze* (hacks), garages, and construction. Indeed, there is hardly a businessman in western Sicily who doesn't pay for the Mafia's 'protection' in the form of '*u pizzu.*' "[36] It is not certain what is urban about all these activities (fishing fleets, for instance), but it is plain that Mafia enterprises had widened from what earlier accounts had suggested.

When all was said and done, the dramatic point was that the Mafia "has bureaucratized," almost bureaucratized, or was on the road to bureaucratization. Anderson wrote that the old or traditional Mafia was "family-like," lacking at least three of the four necessary "characteristics of a bureaucracy." However, that was all changing as Sicily "poised for industrialization with its concomitant changes." But because Sicily was on the brink of modernization, the Sicilian Mafia was momentarily, at least, a mix of the old and the new. There was no doubt, however, where it was heading.

Remarkably enough, the American Mafia provided the example and model. It had achieved bureaucratization, remarked Anderson, "beyond that even of bureaucratized Sicilian groups." One of the key elements in this process involved a striking change in Mafia custom: "Modern *mafiosi* avoid the use of force as much as possible, and thus differ strikingly from old Sicilian practice."[37] Here, Anderson intimates that the contemporary Sicilian Mafia is also moving in the same direction—away from violence, toward other methods of dispute settlement. His discussion of the American Cosa Nostra holds that this overarching structure, which is both a proof and attribute of Mafia bureaucratization, serves to "adjudicate disputes . . . to minimize internecine strife, rather than to administer co-operative undertakings."

An derson said it; criminologist Donald Cressey said it; the Intelligence and Analysis Unit said it; Buscetta said it—the meaning of La Cosa Nostra, the function of the commission, the movement of organized crime history were to minimize violence, to rationalize murder, to routinize homicide. No matter how it was declared—the direction of criminal organization was tied to an interpretation of murder. Because the belief in La Cosa Nostra was so tenaciously developed and held, the characteristics of murders committed by organized crime had to fit the theory. Depending on who was speaking for these developments, certain twists were added. But they were of utterly no significance until someone looked at organized crime murders to see whether they really did conform to the claims made. But with one exception in Sicily, no one with any degree of analytical sophistication has done so.[38] Thus when Mafia wars erupted in Sicily, and dead bodies seemed to be falling everywhere, there was no change in the theoretical structure built upon serious historical errors.

To reiterate, the theory states that the high point in organized crime development in both the United States and Italy is La Cosa Nostra and/or the commission of La Cosa Nostra, and it came about first and foremost to rationalize murder. But for Sicily, the achievement came and went in a flicker of time. In Sicily, we know without the slightest doubt that La Cosa Nostra restrained nothing. Despite the road from feudality to bureaucracy, the Sicilians would not behave as Anderson and others so confidently predicted.

Buscetta's confession given in Palermo long before his appearance before the U.S. Senate's Permanent Subcommittee on Investigations establishes a radically different history from what theory demanded. "Now, however, the informer Tomasso Buscetta, a longtime Mafia member, well acquainted with facts, broke the wall of Omerta. He did so for the purpose of destroying an organization that had *degenerated* into one of wild and unscrupulous criminals."[39] The key point stressed in Buscetta's story as outlined in the Tribunale de Palermo's 1984 indictment of 366 Mafia figures was that as an "uomo d'onore" (a man of honor) it was all right to talk because the organization had lost honor.[40] Buscetta was most upset because the Mafia had perverted itself through violating certain organizational principles having to do with murder. As we know, Buscetta asserted that Mafia principles demanded the regulation of murder: particular syndicates were not allowed to murder people in another syndicate's territory, not without permission in all cases from the "Commission, known as Cosa Nostra." The Mafia lost honor in proportion to its involvement in indiscriminate, unregulated murder.

But if the Sicilian Mafia was changing in the way Anderson and others speculated, then the strongest sign, the most important indication, would be discriminating regulated murder. How could one square the development of La Cosa Nostra and an increase in unregulated Mafia warfare? The uncomplicated answer is that there never was much of a straight-line connection between the restraint of murder and criminal organization—organization did not reduce murder, and a diminution in violence at any particular time could be and was followed by violent outbreaks.

In Sicily the creation of La Cosa Nostra in 1963 was actually coterminous with the start of a war. It then became a cause for warfare that lasted for decades. The core of Buscetta's statements about the war centers on control of "the Commission of the Cosa Nostra."[41] In 1963 the Cosa Nostra commission "scattered'' in the wake of battles between Palmeritan gangsters, its ability to direct affairs a nullity.

There were several other Cosa Nostra commissions established in Sicily after 1963. Each was as ineffective in managing affairs and reducing violence as the first. In fact, control of the commission became a prize fought for by various Mafia groups. Cosa Nostra leadership, in particular, a significant place on the commission, conveyed status, hence it stimulated conflict.

The root of contemporary Mafia savagery lies in the competitive and treacherous relations among the major Mafia gangs both in Palermo and in the traditional Mafia towns of western Sicily. In 1984 Buscetta identified thirty-eight Mafia gangs, placing several in Palermo and locating others in towns such as Termini Imerese, Caccamo, Bagheria, Cinisi, Terrasini, Carini, Partinico, Borgetto, San Giuseppe Jato, Alcamo, Riesi, and Corleone, which have had a Mafia presence for about a century.[42] The Corleone Mafia's leadership was held by Luciano Leggio, his assistant, Salvatore Riina, Bernardo Provenzano, Leoluca and Salvatore Bagarella, and Michele Navarra.

Over the past three decades the Corleone Mafia has exerted and expanded its power and influence against Mafia rivals primarily from Palermo. No doubt part of the Corleone Mafia's appetite for power and violence stems from its own recent history. Corleone is a small, bitterly poor, violent mountain town south of Palermo. The 1977 census reported a population of 11,057, making it one of the smaller Mafia ''agro-towns.''[43] From 1953 to 1958 Corleone lost about 1/66th of its population to murder. If sustained decade in and decade out, Corleone would have had as many actual murders in five decades as New York City experienced from 1866 through 1929.[44]

In some ways the Corleone Mafia was just another band of thugs in the long and dreary nightmare of that town's history. Some idea of life in Corleone can be gleaned by turning to the work of reformer, writer, and poet Danilo Dolci, who interviewed peasants in Corleone and elicited a sort of reverie on murder. Killing was the context of their daily lives. Corleone natives measured the passage of time through the dates of different murders.[45] The peasants provided an encapsulated history of Corleone's Mafia. The first mafioso remembered was Mariano Cuddetta, ''a real cutthroat, stealing animals, killing people.'' He was followed by the ''orphan Piddu Uccedduzzu''; then came Cicci Figatellu and subsequently Vincenzo Crisciune. Each was overwhelmed by murder. Besides the people they killed, Figatellu lost two brothers to other Mafia murderers, while Crisciune had a son shot to death. Soon after Crisciune's son was murdered, he was too. The last Mafia boss the peasants mentioned to Dolci was Doctor Navarra—''He even made plans to have the president killed up there in Rome,'' they said. So it went, murder after murder, until one of the speakers turned to Dolci, commenting ''How the hell can I remember them all?''[46]

There are no historical reasons to believe in a new ''degenerate Mafia,'' a category discovered by Buscetta to justify informing. There is also no reason to accept the claimed correlation between violence and La Cosa Nostra, whether discussing the United States or Sicily. There is no credible historical evidence to sustain the thesis.[47]

An Alternate Explanation

There are some important issues raised in Buscetta's various statements, nonetheless. He recounted, for example, a meeting with American mobster Joe Bonanno, who told him "how the American commission was a good way to resolve family conflicts, and how if a Sicilian commission were [sic] created, this would be a way of renewing ties between the American and Sicilian Mafia. These ties had been broken in the early 1950s.''[48] Leaving aside commission talk for the moment (which in Bonanno's case was ironic, for in the 1960s Bonanno was chased from New York, allegedly by the commission, which found out he planned to assassinate key members), the most interesting part of this discussion turned on American-Sicilian relations.

Assuming Buscetta's recollection was accurate in this instance, the questions to ponder are, What soured relations in the first place, and what might have brought the parties back together? It would seem that cultural conflict is a potential explanation. The Mangano brothers were murdered in 1951, and they were, according to Italian authorities mentioned earlier, part of the small leadership cadre of the Sicilian American Mafia. There appears little doubt that they were done away with by Albert Anastasia, who was of Calabrian descent. Perhaps their murders were part of recurring southern Italian cultural rivalries.

Joe Valachi spoke of this general theme in an interrogation with FBI special agents at the Westchester County Jail on 14 December 1962. Valachi said it was his understanding " 'Causa [sic] Nostra' was originally an exclusively Sicilian organization, with very few exceptions just prior to 1930. . . . Neopolitans [sic] are numerous in 'Causa Nostra' today, as are Sicilians, and Calabrese. However, basic intolerance of Sicilians and Neopolitans [sic], one for the other, still exists in the hearts of each. Valachi remarked that he was once told that if he had a Sicilian friend and wronged another Sicilian, his Sicilian friend would join all Sicilians against him.''[49]

The Mangano murders could have served to sever ties between American gangsters of Neapolitan and Calabrian descent and Sicilian ones. In such a situation only traditional revenge could bring the parties back together. That may well have been the primary reason Anastasia was shot to death in October 1957, for it is certain that Sicilian-born Gambino and his gang were the major beneficiaries of this murder.[50]

Whether an understanding of cultural rivalries tells us more about violence within Italian American organized crime and something about relations between American criminals and those from abroad is naturally not settled. But it seems a more fruitful line of inquiry than the one chosen, which is to see all events, in some cases since 1890, in others 1900, 1930, 1931, or 1936, through commission-colored glasses.

Let me suggest that American organized crime would have been more or less the same had Sicilians, Neapolitans, and Calabrians never migrated to the United States. Though much of American organized crime is ethnically oriented, it never depended on the migration of criminally inclined southern Italians to prosper. In fact, as far as drug racketeering is concerned, the important entry of Italian American gangsters came after World War II, and their presence signaled a mostly disastrous reorientation of the American market, according to users.[51]

As many addicts attested, Jewish American racketeers were disproportionately represented in smuggling and distributing opium and opiates. Moreover, their dope was purer and cheaper than what came after they apparently left the scene. The accounts indicate that they were replaced, particularly after World War II, by Italian American racketeers who sold terrible heroin (cut far too many times with far too much toxic junk) for exorbitant prices. This ethnic change thus represented an era of increasing pain and desperation for users.

The transformation of notable drug racketeers from Jewish Americans to Italian Americans was at least partially the result of the Nazi interregnum, which destroyed everything Jewish in Europe, including overseas traders who supplied American drug distributors. In addition, the effects of chaos in Asia, particularly after Pearl Harbor, finished other Jewish American connections with European-born traders living in Chinese coastal cities such as Shanghai and Tientsin. The comparatively stable connections of the pre-Nazi, prewar decades, which had produced purer narcotics at affordable prices, were terminated. Italian American racketeers responded to the temporary shortage of narcotics and their new position on the line of production and supply in predictably capitalist ways—prices soared and quality plummeted. It was only the postwar U.S. drug world that was crafted on the distribution of bad heroin by Italian American racketeers to users who were overwhelmingly African American. It must also be added that for at least the two decades following the war, the overseas suppliers for the Italian American drug distributors were typically French, Greek, Lebanese, and Syrian traders.

The historical reasons for these factors are not difficult to ascertain. The vast majority of Italian American migrants to the United States came from impoverished rural, agricultural backgrounds. The history of the Mezzogiorno from the risorgimento (1860) through World War II reveals it as a backward, exploited agricultural zone deliberately maintained that way by northern Italian industrialists and their political cronies. Historian Jack Reece notes that Sicilians did not participate in post–World War I protest movements characteristic of northern Italy because social, political, and economic structures there were "retarded"—"there were no factory occupations in Sicily because there were virtually no factories."[52] The typical Mafia crimes of this period were "cattle rustling, robbery and extortion."[53] Politically astute Sicilians complained quite rightly that Sicily was far more like a colonial outpost than a "constituent part of the Italian Kingdom." Ceasare Mori, the prefect of police under the Fascist regime, argued that the Mafia was a consequence of illiteracy and pauperism, malaria and chronic economic exploitation brought about by an antediluvian "Latifundia" system, and the personal politics of "clientelism."[54] As so many historians and social scientists have found, the Mafia phenomenon emanated in the postrisorgimento movement of estate guards to rural power brokers largely caused by the landlords' endemic absenteeism. Southern Italians who migrated to the United States in the latter decades of the nineteenth and the early decades of the twentieth centuries unquestionably lacked entrepreneurial skills honed from a commercial environment. They were a world apart from any phase of international commerce, including the commerce of drugs. They were far different in this respect from many of the Eastern European migrants to the United States who had these skills and contacts with European, Middle East, and Far East contraband traders.

As common sense suggests, Americans who either shared a communal heritage with overseas criminals or otherwise were prepared to develop overseas contacts were far more successful than those without the heritage or contacts. The latter's primary recourse if they wished to enter the narcotics trade was to align themselves with key U.S. importers and wholesalers, which is precisely what was done. Italian American underworld figures who aligned with Jewish American ones were thus enabled to work in the more profitable spheres of drug trafficking.[55]

A USABLE PAST: URBAN AND SOCIAL HISTORY

Given the identified defaults of mainstream organized crime historiography, we can with confidence turn to the historical conditions that spawned and supported U.S. organized criminal syndicates. To start with, we can posit that organized crime is an urban phenomenon, rising from and with the evolving structures of local politics and industrial labor characteristic of post–Civil War American cities. Organized crime's particular ethnic bases were just a function of the changing population of certain American cities from the 1880s through the early 1920s.

The last third of the nineteenth century, along with the first two decades of this century, has long been characterized as the era of rapid urban and industrial development, both fueled by and supported by millions of southern Italians and Eastern European Jews (called the "new immigrants" by a generation of historians) migrating to U.S. cities. Both groups were positioned to supply the large electoral base needed by American urban politicians and the large laboring class demanded by urban industrialism.

From these new urban villages (as Herbert Gans called Italian American urban neighborhoods) and the tenement-house districts, those inclined to illicit activities, able to forge links with emerging political bosses and to patrol left-wing unionism, formed the first modern criminal syndicates. This history is, in one sense, indisputable; but, in another, it too can be abused, for the organization of crime is not directly a consequence of the processes of urbanization and industrialization, a concomitant of modern political machines. Criminal syndicates occur in premodern urban and rural societies. Of course, certain organized crime activities cannot exist outside the modern urban industrial context. They would include labor racketeering, bootlegging and drug distribution based on mass middle-class and working-class markets, and securities frauds and money laundering, which depend on cash credit, bearer bonds, Eurodollars, and stock certificates serviced by a myriad of financial institutions.[56] In premodern epochs, organized crimes such as highway robbery, counterfeiting, kidnapping, cattle rustling, horse stealing, and piracy were familiar. Some of these plainly survived into the modern era, but those that did, for the most part, acquired a modern technological base.

Professional criminals labor in any or all of the modern outlaw vineyards, though whatever draws individuals to a life of crime has nothing in particular to do with the ways in which crime is organized, nor has it anything to do with peculiarly modern circumstances. Modern organized crime is embedded within the institutions and professions with which it interacts—police forces at all levels whose modern design was itself a feature of nineteenth-century industrial culture, criminal lawyers, brokerage houses, labor unions, manufacturers associations, and the trucking, construction, rubbish, restaurant, and resort industries come to mind.

The historical roots of the relationship between police and organized crime, how they impacted one upon the other, are of prime importance. On this subject historian David R. Johnson is a reliable guide. Concentrating on street crime, professional theft, gambling, and prostitution, Johnson notes their significance "in shaping police behavior" and notes that each also "played a major role in defining the limitations of police reform."[57] Perhaps the most important cause of this lies with the structure of urban police forces in northern cities in place by 1855. The new police forces, with certain exceptions, were "tailored to respond to decentralized popular control by giving ward politicians control over appointments."[58] Ward politicians in general were protective of numerous vice enterprises, using their patronage power over the police and local judiciary as a shield for illicit enterprises.

Vice enterprises—prostitution and gambling—were among the more highly visible activities in growing urban underworlds. Growth and change were bywords of urbanization: as land use became more specialized, "districts offering specialized services" emerged, differentiating the core city by commercial, industrial, and entertainment areas and by class. Indeed, the dawn of mass transit had a revolutionary impact upon the distribution of urban social classes, producing that pulsive beat in which the affluent began their move to urban peripheries, their place taken in central city areas by waves of poor immigrants. Of course, following the Civil War and the failures of Reconstruction, foreign-born migrants were joined by internal, native-born African Americans in increasingly pauperized sections of inner cities, producing yet another pattern of urban differentiation, this one based on race.

A word of caution: although the pattern of ethnic and racial segregation in American cities has a long and often prominent historiography, this clustering does not seem to hold for medium-sized cities. Howard Chudacoff's study of Omaha, Nebraska, reveals a "dynamic phenomenon of residential mobility" that "catalyzed integration and limited the stay of an individual inside a relatively homogenous area." The only group for whom the pattern of ghettoization held was African Americans, who were forced to remain in one part of Omaha because they were unable to penetrate the white housing market.[59] The social experiences, the spatial density, and the residential mobility of immigrants seemed to differ according to city size. What that meant for the development of the nexus of illicit interests taking place in America's smaller cities such as Omaha remains vague, however.

Among those criminals who profited from urban growth and differentiation, Johnson adds, were "professional thieves and vice entrepreneurs."[60] The latter located their bordellos and gambling dens within close proximity to the emerging entertainment districts, drawing customers from hotels, rooming houses, restaurants, and theaters. Johnson argues that "specialized land use had concentrated the people interested in gambling and prostitution, thereby ensuring a high level of profits for vice entrepreneurs."[61]

Some scholars have raised objections to this scenario, finding this "sociology of territoriality" overstated when it comes to red-light districts.[62] Historian Timothy F. Gilfoyle contends that this model is too simplistic, obscuring "not only the flexible social structure of prostitution, but the way sexual behavior was commercialized and organized in American cities," and suffers from the "impression that a physical site controls a social process . . . a form of geographical determinism."[63] Nevertheless, Gilfoyle concedes in his study of New York that red-light districts contained the "most sophisticated and organized forms of the underground economy."[64] This meant, for example, that after 1850, on Broadway between Canal and Houston streets, where saloons, theaters, and hotels predominated, there were more than 200 whorehouses located in the immediately contiguous area. Gilfoyle's point, though, is that this represented only a little over 41 percent of New York's sporting houses.[65]

Naturally this particular cluster changed as the city enlarged ever northward on Manhattan island. Former entertainment areas were converted to industrial use as land values rose. The new entertainment centers, however, continued the association among theaters, restaurants, hotels, and brothels. Gilfoyle's argument for dispersal is based more on the ubiquitousness of prostitution, particularly in poor districts, rather than with the most heavily commercialized forms. In either instance, prostitution moved from place to place as the city itself transformed. Thus, he is correct in stating that "significant amounts of prostitution appeared throughout New York because it was an important part of the social structure of the nineteenth-century city," and that prostitution was fluid and flexible.[66]

Clearly, one should not expect to find part-time prostitutes working out of full-time brothels or be surprised when teeming immigrant districts were dotted

with bordellos utilized by working-class customers. So much of the differentiation hypotheses, it seems to me, depends on the cities and explicit time periods
examined and the types of prostitution studied. Thus in researching the origins
of that type of organized crime that expressed itself as commercialized vice, one
must be cognizant of both the development of red-light districts in highly dif-
ferentiated entertainment zones and vice establishments in other areas, such as
the growing immigrant tenement districts.

Urban differentiation does account for the development of "specialized entertainment districts" that drew many vice entrepreneurs to locate their brothels
and gambling dens there, but certainly not all of them. This conclusion is similar
to historian Barbara Meil Hobson's argument that the "process of demarcating
the social landscape of American cities" had variable effects on prostitution.
She confirms earlier opinions that there were manifest links between prostitution
and other urban entertainments. These included most gambling dens, many saloons, dance halls, and theaters, including vaudeville halls, many featuring ribald
shows with nude dancers.[67] Hobson remarks that illicit sexual commerce provided important employment for both external and internal migrants. It is not
surprising, then, to find in her study an affirmation of Daniel Bell's well-known
thesis that crime provides a queer ladder of social mobility. She writes that "for
immigrants and blacks denied access to legitimate commercial ventures, brothels, gambling and saloons were marginal businesses that allowed some movement up the economic ladder."[68]

Unfortunately, we know next to nothing about the history of African American organized crime, even though African Americans have almost always lived
on the most perilous of margins, and much of what passed for normal commerce
in white society was outlawed to them by racially motivated laws and racist
institutions. The legal and extralegal restrictions upon their economic and social
lives thrust them inevitably into a far wider world of illicit activities than probably any other group in American history. More or less contemporary studies
have indicated over and over again the pervasiveness and significance of illicit
activities in African American urban ghettos. For example, in 1977 Ivan Light
asserted that "numbers racketeers have been the largest investors in black-
owned business or ghetto real estate and the chief source of business capital in
the ghetto."[69] Given that mainstream financial institutions were unavailable to
the mass of Americans, gamblers and loan sharks were among the most important principals in shaping a vast informal economy that dominated the African
American experience.

The crux of the matter for the historical development of white criminal syndicates is the merging of the interests of vice entrepreneurs with those of urban
politicians. Over the course of the nineteenth century, the economy of prostitution, according to Hobson, became more rationalized and organized. By the
first decade of this century the division of labor in sexual commerce included
"proprietors, pimps, madams, runners, collectors (who paid off the police), doc-
tors, clothing dealers, and professional bondsmen."[70] Prostitution in cities with

burgeoning immigrant populations was a business managed by immigrants who were connected to urban machines and the police.[71] In other American cities, many of smaller size than the behemoths of the Northeast and Midwest, particularly in the South and portions of the West, the changes in the political economy of prostitution were similar, though without a similar immigrant cast.

Historian Johnson holds that "the symbiotic relationship between politics and vice developed at least by the 1840s,"[72] though it took some time before the full force of this was elaborated. Concentrating on gamblers at this juncture, Johnson notes that there are certain key figures whose careers epitomized the possibilities of cooperative exchange between professional gamblers and urban politicians. New Yorker John Morrissey was one. In fact, he was both an enormously successful gambler and politician.[73] The entrepreneurs of vice, especially gamblers, who had apparently far more social acceptability than bordello managers, provided both money and manpower for politicians at election time. In return, politicians aided them through their control of criminal justice.[74]

One of the important ways in which urban politics and policing were joined in New York was through the city's election process. The thousands of poll clerks and election inspectors needed to supervise elections were chosen from lists provided by the political parties to both Democrat and Republican police commissioners. The city paid the tab (which came to several hundreds of thousands of dollars by the late 1880s) for the work of registering voters and the recording and counting of votes. The lucrative jobs of printing and distributing ballots were controlled by district leaders.[75] It was a system designed for energizing patron-client networks binding the police, politicians, and thousands of political workers.

This does not imply that the complex world of urban politics was all of a kind. Graft may have been a staple, but there were gradations in it that were very important to some urban politicians. Charles Francis Murphy, who became the leader of New York's infamous Tammany Hall in 1902, "accepted the machine, played politics according to patronage-welfare rules, and saw his opportunities and took 'em." But Murphy had a strong "Irish puritanical distaste for commercial vice," making him stand out as something of a rarity.[76] Murphy's ethical code was explained in this fashion:

[Murphy] was terribly against the Kansas City kind of political organization, which got its supporting funds out of prostitution and crime. He believed it was perfectly all right to get it out of concessions on taxations, or contractor's fee, and things of that kind, but he would have nothing to do with what he considered immoral things. . . . He wouldn't protect a criminal and get the money for that, but he would take money from concessions on taxation. If your taxes should be five thousand, he'd make them three, and you'd put up one. That was all right.[77]

Of course Murphy's predecessors (and successors) were not necessarily as morally finicky; they also faced different problems than Murphy. Tammany leader Richard Croker, for example, had to manage the Hall through the problems of "middle-class tax revolts and the drying up of government revenue" during the tough times of the late 1880s. Croker thus constructed a "police graft system . . . filling Tammany's coffers with the payoffs from gambling, drinking, and prostitution." Croker had to deal with the dilemma caused by middle-class voters' antitax stance, while knowing that "conservative fiscal policies" produced working-class discontent. The choice was between retrenchment and patronage—the solution was a tax on vice.[78] This produced a quick backlash, however, when religious reformers and upstate Republicans exposed the police-graft-vice system through a state investigation in 1894. That year Tammany candidates were defeated.[79] Reform proved episodic, however, and the graft system continued, albeit with some moderation or less vigorous attention.

While hewing to basically the same structural lines, machine politicians were, as would be expected, a diverse lot and are viewed by scholars in distinct ways. New York's Timothy D. Sullivan is an example. He was first elected to the New York State Assembly representing the Five Points warren in 1886 when he was already an important Tammany leader.[80] Known as "Big Tim," Sullivan is credited by historian Daniel Czitrom with "creating a new metropolitan political style" by fusing "traditional machine politics, a close association with commercialized leisure," and "influence within New York's underworld."[81] What made "Big Tim" unique, according to Czitrom, was his blend of corrupt urban politics with actions that foreshadowed the New Deal's social welfare legislation. Sullivan had a strong commitment to women's suffrage and progressive labor legislation. Sullivan's gift was to socialize "portions of the vice economy, particularly gambling and the alcohol trade, to help support welfare activities in his district."[82]

Contrary to this interpretation, historian Steven P. Erie concludes Sullivan's largesse was neither so beneficent nor benignly motivated. Erie claims that Celtic party bosses worked hardest at protecting "the economic well-being and psychological security of the payroll Irish."[83] He cites Sullivan as a particular example, noting that by 1910 his district was 85 percent Jewish and Italian, 5 percent Irish. Nevertheless, Sullivan and the other Irish American sachems running Tammany steadfastly maintained ethnic control despite the overwhelming numbers of Jewish and Italian immigrants. "Between 1908 and 1933 every Tammany candidate for the Board of Aldermen, the State Assembly, and the Senate from the Lower East Side was Irish."[84] While Czitrom describes Sullivan's promotion of public entertainments through liberal state licensing laws for boxing and horse racing, gambling and saloons, and vaudeville and motion pictures as both creative and munificent, Erie contends they were part of a "minimal reward strategy."[85]

However motivated, there is no doubt that Sullivan was a key link among politics, organized crime, and popular culture. In 1892 Richard Croker turned over the leadership of the Third Assembly District to Sullivan, who promptly sold his saloons and ran for, and won, a New York State Senate seat the following year. This victory confirmed his stature within the party and made Sullivan's downtown clique (studded with relatives) the arbiter of New York's Lower East Side Bowery district, a polyglot of 300,000 people and New York's "center of working class social life and commercial entertainment."[86] Emerging from the potpourri of Bowery night life were several important entertainment entrepreneurs who brokered Sullivan's entrance into the theatrical world. Henry C. Miner, Sullivan's predecessor as leader of the former Bowery district and owner of five vaudeville theaters, became Sullivan's theatrical mentor. There was also George J. Kraus, a "musician, caterer, bookkeeper, law clerk, and theater manager."[87] In 1896, Kraus and Sullivan became partners, running both burlesque houses and music halls. Two years later they opened a 1,400-seat vaudeville theater, which featured new shows every week and matinee and evening performances every day.

Sullivan's interest in commercial entertainment continued through years of political battles and strife, which finally culminated in his withdrawal from direct political involvement, which had included two boring stints in the U.S. Congress in the first decade of the twentieth century. In 1904 Sullivan teamed up with John W. Considine, "an ambitious theater manager from Seattle," to purchase four vaudeville theaters in the Pacific Northwest.[88] In three years Sullivan and Considine had a highly successful booking agency and around forty theaters, most west of Chicago. They finally sold their venture to Loew Theatrical Enterprises in 1914 for a considerable sum. Several years before the sale to Loew, Sullivan began a working relationship with William Fox, characterized as "the archetypal Jewish immigrant movie mogul."[89] In 1908 Fox leased two of Sullivan's vaudeville theaters for $100,000 a year, turning them into combination vaudeville and movie theaters.[90]

Sullivan is an example of the ways in which many of the forms of modern popular entertainment were crafted by political entrepreneurs and their associates. Professional sports, including baseball, horse racing, and boxing, were created in the main by gamblers, while an assortment of vice entrepreneurs did the same for cabarets, music halls, burlesque houses, vaudeville, and movies. The reason is not difficult to ascertain. First of all, numerous successful urban politicians like Sullivan, intimately linked to full-time professional vice criminals, came from a working-class culture in which athleticism and drinking were important attributes. Many had been athletes as young men and saloon owners after. Saloons were spawning grounds both for singers, dancers, and comedians and for commercial sex. Urban politicians were usually adept at crafting large-scale urban entertainments to ensure their popularity with working-class voters. Professional sports were an expression of this as well as an opportunity structure for gamblers. Urban politicians and their criminal associates were, in a sense, always in the mass entertainment business. Whether baseball, boxing, vaudeville, saloons, gambling casinos, or bordellos, success depended on a large number of consumers. Urbanization certainly provided the numbers, and industrialization apparently provided enough money for workers to begin to play. The sense of time was changing with these processes: leisure was inexorably moving down the social scale. What to do with that free time was, at least partially, the gift of criminal entrepreneurs.

Urban politicians like Sullivan who led the way in many modern ventures crossed ethnic lines with hardly a thought. Though he presided over an Irish American political machine, Sullivan cultivated both upperworld and underworld figures from among the American Jewish Lower East Side. One of his important underworld associates was Martin Engel, the "omnipotent political boss of the local eighth ward in the Tammany Hall democratic empire."[91] Engel, who headed one of the most powerful families in the illicit vice industry, started out as a chicken flicker (plucker) and by 1894 was said to be worth $200,000 from illicit activities. At the turn of the century, Engel was thought to control numerous brothels on Allen Street, which historian Edward J. Bristow contends was "the centre of New York's red-light district, the place in fact where red lights displayed in the vestibules of bordellos first gave currency to the popular term."[92] Engel enjoyed a fearsome reputation as a powerful vice lord, which was sufficient to silence unhappy local residents living close by his noisy and noxious brothels. He was also powerful enough to seriously threaten investigators from a citywide reform organization called the Committee of Fifteen, whose mandate was the eradication of prostitution.[93] Another Lower East Side American Jewish racketeer who worked with Sullivan was Jack Wolf. A district captain who worked hard at ballot stuffing and other political jobs as well as a bagman for the local police, Wolf's primary business was running a notorious saloon where, among other criminal activities, immigrant thugs were taught New York methods.[94]

The networks within which vice entrepreneurs labored are but part of the history of the emergence of modern criminal syndicates. Organized criminals also worked in the vineyard of industrialization. Hired as "labor padrones" to organize construction gangs, as strikebreakers during the years of nascent unionism, or as general mediators between labor and industry, criminals took advantage of their reputation for violence and insinuated themselves into strategic roles within the constant of labor and management strife. These developments naturally took place within ethnic communities to begin with: Italian immigrant workers were managed by Italian American labor bosses; Jewish American ones found *shtarkers* (bosses and hustlers) a miserable fact of life.

But the American Jewish industrial experience was different from the Italian American one in several important respects. New immigrant Jews brought city skills, historian Thomas Kessner reports, while southern Italians, as commented on earlier, coming from a rural peasant background, did not.[95] It may seem curious at first glance that Italians did not seek to become farmers in America. The best explanation is that they were never farmers but instead farm laborers unacquainted with the tools of modern American farming and familiar only with the wooden plow, the mattock, and the ax. In the United States the toil that came closest to their experience was neither farming nor farm laboring but "excavation work."[96] Moreover, Jewish workers came from a European environment in which various brands of socialism were common coin. In general they, unlike their Italian counterparts, had experience with radical politics and the organization of workers.

Because of their divergent backgrounds, Italian immigrants, much more than Eastern European Jews, congregated in unskilled trades, particularly manual labor. Digging tunnels, hauling cement, and working as garbage haulers[97] or laborers on the waterfront were typical first-, second-, and perhaps in certain instances third-generation jobs for southern Italians. Given that difference, along with the American Jewish familiarity with trade unionism and the principles of socialism, and given that industrial and labor racketeers prey first and foremost on members of their own ethnic or national group, it is not surprising that American Jewish racketeers infiltrated the needle trades and Italian American ones the waterfront, construction trades, and the rubbish industry. Historian Mark Haller once described the development in this manner: racketeers followed the traditional patterns of ethnic acculturation.

These patterns were not written in stone, of course, and over time many trades, trade unions, and industries employed or represented people from a variety of ethnic or national groups. As diverse groups came together in employment and in management, predatory racketeers from several backgrounds found a variety of ways to deal with one another: some formed multiethnic syndicates, others occupied particular niches in a larger entity, hardly bothering one another, and still others violently displaced one another. Some contemporary industries dominated by racketeers, such as the private sanitation industry on Long Island, still reveal patterns of ethnic racketeer accommodation. A Jewish American criminal has been running the haulers' union for decades while Italian American racketeers have been in control of much of the rest of the unions.

In the early decades of urban unionism, the essence of racketeer activity lay in utilizing violent skills to control locals in order to hold down labor costs for employers. Commanding membership monies became another benefit. Once locals were seized by gangsters, they sold out the rank and file with sweetheart contracts for bribes and/or used the threat of strikes and unionization to extort monies from industry bosses. That sort of criminality lasted a long time but was eventually merged with, and then supplanted, in the decades after World War II, by the lure of welfare and pension funds piling up in union coffers. Nothing better illustrates this than the International Brotherhood of Teamsters, whose contracts became stronger and stronger and whose pension funds acted as banks for organized crime.[98] The better the benefits, the more there was to steal or embezzle. This gave racketeers an incentive to leave behind old-fashioned sweetheart contracts. Most of this went on in craft and industrial unions, which are fast becoming the relics of a bygone manufacturing era. The most important contemporary questions are whether, to what degree, and in what manner service unions whose employers are hospitals and municipal and state governments are prone to racketeering.

Underworlds have an ebb and flow. Criminals are on top one moment, out of power a moment later; some return when conditions are again favorable, while others spend their time in prison or penury. There were many factors capable of affecting criminal careers, including seemingly endless reform movements seeking to eradicate vice, to eliminate gambling, to destroy political machines, to end alcohol consumption, to restore unions to democratic ways, and so forth. For criminals whose protection was dependent on a particular political patron or who were committed to a vice activity under attack, firestorms of reform, some based on moral outrage and others on the ambitions of political outsiders, could and did end careers. But the successful reform impulse also laid the foundation for new criminal careers as well. Pushing desired commodities, such as narcotics and alcohol, deep underground had a profoundly uplifting effect for some organized criminals. The more illicit an activity became, the greater the profit margin for its vendors. Consumers had to pay more not only because of the sliding availability but also as a kind of value-added tax based on risk.

In the history of organized crime no reform movement (until the contemporary war on drugs) has quite the reputation for accomplishing this as does Prohibition. Whether in standard accounts or "Mafiologies," Prohibition has stood as a historical gateway, the supposed time when mobs first made really big money on a national scale. With an enormous consumer base in place, with little opprobrium attached to drinking, outside fundamentalist religious groups, bootlegging did provide a vital new enterprise for those inclined to organized criminality. Though it energized older syndicates that controlled saloons and criminal entrepreneurs familiar with the routines of trading contraband and created new opportunities for ambitious young urban toughs, it also had quite an impact on rural criminality. According to historian Robert Smith Bader, rural producers of whiskey in Kansas during the tenure of the Volstead Act, some operating in abandoned mines, were able "to establish markets not only in Kansas and the adjacent sections of Missouri and Oklahoma but also in Kansas City, Missouri, and other urban centers to the east."[99]

Urban bootlegging acted in some of the same ways that higher-level illegal gambling had in the past. Mark Haller writes that "bootleggers rose rapidly to wealth and influence against a background of long tradition of syndicate gambling."[100] Bookmaking in the years before Prohibition presented a somewhat similar opportunity structure—huge demand coupled with increasing technological sophistication, a regional and potential national sales territory, and vastly increased contact with criminals from around the nation. One would assume that some gamblers became bootleggers while some bootleggers became gamblers. Interestingly enough, Haller argues that the latter was a more likely outcome than the former: "Established underworld figures did not generally become bootlegging leaders."[101] This conclusion is sensibly based in part on an analysis of the age of those who became leading bootleggers as well as their past experience in crime and their ethnic backgrounds: "Prohibition arrived just as the first generation of Eastern European Jewish and Italian young people raised in America were reaching maturity.''[102] Bootlegging for many of these young men was their initial entry into sophisticated organized crime after preparation in juvenile gang work.

Still, it is not clear why already established underworld figures did not attain the leadership level in bootlegging, should they have wanted to. Haller's answer comes down to this: pre-Prohibition illicit enterprises were relatively violence-free.[103] Leadership went to a new generation more prone to shoot their way to the top of a criminal cartel. Already established racketeers were less likely to enter or dominate a new enterprise in which violence was so important. There was brutality associated with endemic hijacking, which brought on violent responses. There was also much gunplay stemming from competition for territorial supremacy. There is little doubt of the overall importance of savagery during the bootlegging era, but is it certain that this actually differentiates bootleggers from pre-Prohibition organized criminals?

Information about the Jewish American underworld on the Lower East Side during the two decades before Prohibition indicates what appears to be a high degree of violence among organized criminals.[104] This particular underworld is important to consider because, according to Haller, it was one of the main springboards for very successful bootleggers. Some of the known causes of violence prior to Prohibition include competition among mobs working in labor racketeering, control of prostitutes, and ethnic rivalries between Jewish and Italian gangsters who lived in very close proximity. Investigators for the Jewish self-defense organization, the Bureau of Social Morals, routinely paid a great deal of attention to "gunmen" involved in illicit activities. Usually the investigators excoriated them, though not in the case of Jack Zelig. The poorly written report of Zelig states the following: "Outlaw he maybe classed but he had done one thing and that is, he has rid the EASTSIDE of ITALIAN PIMPS AND THIEVES." It was believed that Italian American pimps were robbing Jewish American bordellos and then adding ethnic insult to economic injury, using Jewish American prostitutes in their brothels. Zelig and his gang of gunmen, who were known to take protection money from gamblers, became ethnic vice protectors. In short order Zelig gunned down two well-known Italian American racketeers and went to war with the Sullivan clan, previously mentioned, in an attempt to break their political power downtown. Several gunfights followed, including one in which Zelig was wounded by a gunshot in the neck. Within a fairly short period of time after Zelig's recovery, he was murdered.[105] The admiration for Zelig as a defender of Jewish criminals by the investigator is certainly unique. Perhaps he was a defender of the criminally weak from predatory outsiders. But there is abundant evidence that he was not unique among the organized criminals in his neighborhood for his reliance on violence. Gunmen were plentiful, as were gunfights. Shoot-outs in the streets, in saloons, and in whorehouses were not uncommon.[106] Another important Lower East Side racketeer known for his violence before Prohibition was Louis " 'Dutch' Goldberg" Shomberg, known as one of the area's premier strong-arm men. Following Prohibition he was considered the top liquor smuggler in New York. His career was temporarily halted in 1926, when he was sentenced to seven years in prison on a charge of homicide. After his release, Shomberg's reputation and influence in the New York underworld soared once again. A tireless traveler, his power soon extended to underworlds "in practically every section of the country."[107]

For urban bootleggers a willingness to engage in violence was no doubt important. Whether that distinguishes them in any important sense from already established organized criminals is not clear. Perhaps, though, Haller has in mind a difference in temperament between those who spent their entire criminal lives in bookmaking or running illegal casinos and those who reached avaricious hands into numerous types of illicit operations—sort of mobile marauders extorting from more stable, more enterprise-oriented criminals as well as renting themselves out for labor-management disputes. There do seem to me potentially important differences between these types of organized criminals. It is still an area needing much more exploration, however.

FINAL THOUGHTS

Whether or not Haller's explanation is on the mark, his data do show the emergence of new criminals from older, established underworlds rife with large-scale gambling enterprises, rising to become the leaders of large, complex bootlegging operations, many of whom later moved into large, complex gambling operations. It is also apparent that the greatest success in either major gambling or bootlegging syndicates depended on the ability to forge regional and national alliances in order to expand markets and sources of supply and the savvy to understand technological innovations. Neither the running of a successful neighborhood handbook nor the zeal in terrorizing local merchants was sufficient to demonstrate the potential for future sophisticated criminal accomplishments. What did indicate this capacity was quite the opposite—a propensity for geographical mobility and the formation of new partnerships with criminal groups similarly inclined. Expanding illicit enterprises from one's home base, say, from Boston, Cleveland, Minneapolis, Detroit, Chicago, or New York, to Newport and Covington, Kentucky, Hot Springs, Arkansas, Havana, Miami Beach, Los Angeles, New Orleans, Las Vegas, Reno, the Bahamas, and so forth made all the difference, though these were not necessarily strife-free expansions. Often disgruntled local syndicates had to be dealt with in one fashion or another—co-option, elimination, and cooperation were all tried. The road of expansion was recurrently bumpy.[108] Some of these expansion-minded syndicates left stay-behinds to tend to hometown illicit interests; however, their success was always contingent. Nonetheless, this wider world of action brought with it scores of new customers, more and more politicians, land developers, corporate and tax attorneys, banks, brokerage houses, and bond salesmen, all anxious to participate in a variety of projects with the new criminal confraternities.

The history of the phenomena of organized crime is but a part of the social history of the United States, in which the patterns of immigration, the rise and fall of the reform impulse, the organization of labor, the rise of a middle-class with a yen for travel and entertainment, the organization of policing and politics, and the expansion of financial institutions are the mix and mingle within which criminal syndicates, criminal confraternities, and cartels emerge and operate.

Surely those illicit enterprises based on the insuppressible desire to taste the forbidden fruit, whether sexual, potable, smokeable, or injectable, the need for risk, hence, to gamble, and the ambition to control prices and economic competition spring from some metahistorical condition. Yet their particular expression is what interests us, and for that we need explicit historical accounts based on familiar methods, not ones based on any ''community's legends about itself,'' however derived.

NOTES

1. The academic work that set the standard tone and many of the orthodox categories is Donald Cressey's ''The Structure and Functions of Criminal Syndicates,'' in *Task Force Reports: Organized Crime*, President's Commission on Law Enforcement and Administration of Justice (Washington, DC: U.S. Government Printing Office, 1976). Cressey later expanded this work in *Theft of the Nation: The Structure of Organized Crime in America* (New York: Harper and Row, 1969).

A thoughtful scholarly response in opposition to Cressey's history and sociology launched during the 1970s was particularly at odds with his ethnic demarcation of organized crime. It was led by sociologist Joseph Albini in his work *The American Mafia: Genesis of a Legend* (New York: Appleton-Century-Crofts, 1917). Other scholars, such as Dwight C. Smith, Jr., *The Mafia Mystique* (New York: Basic Books, 1975) and William J. Chambliss, *On the Take: From Petty Crooks to Presidents* (Bloomington: Indiana University Press, 1978), also made exceptionally insightful contributions to the revisionist cause.

2. This viewpoint stems from the wide-ranging employment of Title IX of the Organized Crime Control Act passed in 1970 (and amended since then), commonly known as RICO, standing for Racketeer Influenced and Corrupt Organizations (Act). RICO is a conspiracy statute, and its use compels the government to establish particular, discrete conspiracies. Thus prosecutors are searching for patterns of linked criminal activities, linked not at a particular time but in meaningful ways over time. Duration is quite important, and that is fine in those cases and statements where it is appropriately supported by reasonable evidence. But conspiracy thinking is often too expansive, casting a wider historical net than data can support. When prosecutors and their colleagues, including some academic researchers, whether in case presentation, public statements before congressional committees, or academic works based on these sources, talk about Italian American organized crime, their sense of history and conspiracy often is excessive and extreme.

The literature on RICO is voluminous, and I will make no attempt to mention more than a few examples. One of the fairly current articles worth consulting is Patrick J. Ryan and Robert J. Kelly, ''Analysis of RICO and OCCA: Federal and State Legislative Instruments Against Crime,'' *Violence Aggression and Terrorism* 3 (1989); see also G.

Robert Blakey and Brian Gettings, "Racketeer Influenced and Corrupt Organizations (RICO): Basic Concepts—Criminal and Civil Remedies," *Temple Law Review Quarterly* 53 (1980); Whitney Lawrence Schmidt, "The Racketeer Influenced and Corrupt Organizations Act: An Analysis of the Confusion in Its Application and a Proposal for Reform," *Vanderbilt Law Review* 33 (1980); Andrew R. Bridges, "RICO Litigation," *Georgia Law Review* 18 (1983); Robert P. Rhodes, *Organized Crime: Crime Control vs. Civil Liberties* (New York: Random House, 1984), particularly Chapter 8, "From Rico to Mail Fraud: Criminal Law Designed to Control Organized Crime"; G. Richard Strafer, Ronald R. Massumi, and Holly R. Skolnick, "Civil RICO in the Public Interest: 'Everybody's Darling,'" *American Criminal Law Review* 19 (1982); Denis Binder, "The Potential Application of RICO in the Natural Resources/Environmental Law Context," *Denver University Law Review* 63 (1986). A most interesting review of RICO can be found in the long statement "Additional Views of Commissioner Eugene H. Methvin," in *The Edge: Organized Crime, Business, and Labor Unions Appendix,* President's Commission on Organized Crime (Washington, DC: U.S. Government Printing Office, October 1985).

3. United States District Court, Southern District of New York, *United States of America, Plaintiff, against International Brotherhood of Teamsters, Chauffeurs, Warehousemen and Helpers of America, AFL-CIO, et al., Defendants,* "Declaration of *Randy M. Mastro,*" 88 Civ., 9.

4. Ibid., 9–10.

5. David Hackett Fischer, *Historians' Fallacies: Toward a Logic of Historical Thought* (New York: Harper and Row, 1970), 43.

Fischer's work was aimed at professional historians who committed logical and other philosophical errors time and again. It seemed that no historian, however prominent, escaped Fischer's attention. Of course, historians are not the only ones to either write or invoke history to explain current phenomena, nor are they the only ones who must be called to account for mistakes.

6. Lonardo Interview by Special Agents Richard B. Hoke and R. Gerald Personen, CV 183A-1129 Sub H—10/28/83, FD-302.

7. U.S. Department of Justice, Criminal Investigative Division, Organized Crime Section, Organized Crime Intelligence and Analysis Unit, "Chronological History of La Cosa Nostra in the United States, January 1920–August 1987" (October 1987), included in *Hearings, Organized Crime: 25 Years After Valachi,* U.S. Senate, Committee on Governmental Affairs, Permanent Subcommittee on Investigations (Washington, DC: U.S. Government Printing Office, 1988), 294.

8. Fischer, *Historians' Fallacies,* 267, 270.

9. U.S. Department of Justice, Criminal Investigative Division, Organized Crime Section, Organized Crime Intelligence and Analysis Unit, 295.

10. New York City Police Department, "Statement," in *Hearings, Organized Crime; 25 Years After Valachi,* U.S. Senate, Committee on Governmental Affairs, Permanent Subcommittee on Investigations, 950.

11. Intelligence and Analysis Unit, 296.

12. Ibid., 297.

13. Without wishing to beat unnecessarily a dead historical horse, there are still other interpretive errors accompanied by curious "non sequiturs" that need comment, such as the following, datelined 17 June 1933: "FBI Agent, Raymond J. Caffrey, 3 police officers, and hoodlum Frank Nash were killed in the Union Station parking lot during the

infamous 'Kansas City Massacre.' Reportedly the Kansas City LCN Family declined a request that it participate in the operation'' (Intelligence and Analysis Unit, 301). This factoid cannot establish anything about the LCN, even if it was true (which is not actually claimed) that someone asked it to participate in several murders. It is a variant of the ''prodigious fallacy,'' which ''mistakes sensation for significance,'' and an example of ''negative evidence,'' which is really no evidence at all. See Fischer, 62, 70. To the best of its knowledge, the unit had nothing positive to say connecting the LCN to the ''Kansas City Massacre.'' It wasn't involved, and it didn't participate; thus, what could the event possibly tell about LCN? The answer is, Nothing.

14. Intelligence and Analysis Unit, 299–300.

15. Smith, Jr., *Mafia Mystique*, 242, 324–27. See also Dwight C. Smith, Jr., ''Mafia: The Prototypical Alien Conspiracy,'' *Annals* 423 (January 1976).

16. I discussed this fourteen years ago in ''History and the Study of Organized Crime,'' *Urban Life: A Journal of Ethnographic Research* 6.4 (January 1978), which pointed out in some detail the absence of any credible historical sources for this claim. The debunking of this pseudohistory was standard fare among revisionists (see note 1, second paragraph). In the years since it was proven wrong, there have been no new sources identified that could conceivably have validated the issue.

17. New York City Police Department, ''Statement,'' 900.

18. On the ''fallacy of essences,'' see Fischer, *Historians' Fallacies*, 68.

19. Karl Popper's extended discussions on the philosophy of history are in *The Open Society and Its Enemies* (New York: Oxford University Press, 1945), 2 vols. and *The Poverty of Historicism* (New York: Harper Torchbooks, 1961). My remarks on Popper were taken from Fischer, *Historians' Fallacies*, 68–69.

20. The document is in the George White papers held by the Perham Electronics Museum on the campus of Foothill College in Los Gatos, California.

21. To reiterate, the Cleveland Mafia line goes from Polizzi to Milano to Scalish, and, as Lonardo stated, he seemed to know nothing much about either the Mafia or La Cosa Nostra outside his own patch.

22. Intelligence and Analysis Unit, 299–301.

23. PSI (U.S. Senate Permanent Subcommittee on Investigation); *Hearings,* 49.

24. Ibid.

25. Luciano sailed to Italy on 9 February 1946 aboard the SS *Laura Keene*.

26. Intelligence and Analysis Unit, 12, 17.

27. See U.S. Department of Justice, Federal Bureau of Investigation, Report of James P. Flynn, ''Joseph Valachi: Anti-Racketeering,'' Bureau File No.: 94–4282; Field Office File No.: 92–1459, 11 December 1962, 25.

For an extended discussion of the thesis that murder was routinized in New York during the depression decade, see my *East Side–West Side: Organizing Crime in New York, 1930–1950* (New Brunswick, NJ: Transaction Books, 1983), 201–36.

28. Lieutenant Colonel Justin J. Dintino, New Jersey State Police, ''The Structure of Organized Crime in New Jersey,'' presented to U.S. Senate Judiciary Committee (16 February 1983), 8.

29. Kitty Caparella and Joe O'Dowd, ''Stanfa Family Eyed in Hit Try,'' Philadelphia *Daily News*, 5 March 1992.

30. In a package on Asian Organized Crime put together by the New York State Assembly Committee on Conservation, which included material from U.S. Senate, Permanent Subcommittee on Investigations, *Hearings on Asian Organized Crime*, Part II, 5

November 1991, there is a distinction between triad societies, described as "ancient secret criminal societies which trace their roots to 17th century China," with "an estimated 80,000 members in 60 societies," and Chinese tongs, described as "Chinese fraternal and business organizations with chapters in major U.S. cities" whose "memberships . . . are composed largely of non-criminals," though "criminal investigations have determined that some members have ties to organized crime."

31. Senator Sam Nunn, "Opening Statement," *Hearings on Asians Organized Crime*, Part II, 5 November 1991, 5.

32. See Elizabeth McLean Petras, "Third World Workers in U.S. Cities: Asian Women in the Philadelphia Apparel and Textile Industry," paper presented at the American Sociological Association annual meeting, August 1990.

33. On comparative history as a method, see Theda Skocpol and Margaret Somers, "The Uses of Comparative History in Macrosocial Inquiry," *Comparative Studies in Society and History* (April 1980).

34. See Dean C. Tipps, "Modernization Theory and the Comparative Study of Societies: A Critical Perspective," *Comparative Studies in Society and History*, (1973). Tipps noted, "Many processes of change may be incompatible with others, and that because of differences in timing and initial setting, processes of institutional change associated with modernization in one context need not be recapitulated in others" (221).

35. Robert T. Anderson, "From Mafia to Cosa Nostra," *American Journal of Sociology* 71.3 (November 1965): 307.

36. Ibid.

37. Ibid., 309.

38. See Umberto Santino and Giorgio Chinnici, *La Violenza Programmata. Omicidi e Gueer di Mafia a Palermo dagli anni '60 ad oggio* (Milano: FrancoAngeli, 1989).

39. Tribunale di Palermo, Ufficio Istruzione Dei Process Penali, *Mandato Dicattura*, Palermo, Sicilia, 29 Settembre 1984, 116 (emphasis added).

40. Buscetta conceived of himself as standing for what was artfully phrased the "Permanencc of Archaic Values." His confession ends with the assertion that he's just an old-fashioned guy operating in a world turned upside down by rapacity and venality.

41. Tribunale di Palermo, 131. As reported by the Palermo Court, Cosa Nostra is a ruling clique composed of certain Mafia leaders trying to control the overall affairs of Mafia gangs in western Sicily.

42. Ibid., 121–28.

43. The census figures used are in Hammond Inc., *Medallion World Atlas* (1977), 35–36.

44. See the data in Haven Emerson and Harriet E. Hughes, eds., *Population, Births, Notifiable Diseases and Deaths, Assembled for New York City, 1866–1938* (The Delamar Institute of Public Health, Columbia University, 1941).

45." The first contract they put out right after the war was on a guy named Cianciana. They got him on the square, maybe for political reasons. Michele Randisio and Zu Matteo Capra's son, the one with the bad hand, they disappeared. The bones were found when everybody was looking for Placido Rizzotto's body. It was in the same pit where they threw Donna Calorina Saporita's son. We could've loaded up a whole cart with all the bones from that hole. Angelo Gulotta's and Ciccio Navarra's brothers. . . . Here the criminals are protected by the government. Even when they catch your killer, ten days later he's out of jail. See, it's the government that's crazy. It's awful how many murders there've been since the war. Here it never stops. . . . It's habit. It comes natural, like killing a goat'' (Danilo Dolci, *Sicilian Lives,* trans. Justin Vitiello [New York: Pantheon Books, 1981], 177–79).

46. Ibid., 188.

47. The most important historical question to emerge from Buscetta's statement is not that of a commission or of Luciano's influence and conversations with Joe Bonanno; it is, instead, organizational change associated with vastly increased financial power. The Mafia controlled so much money its relationship with politicians was radically altered as well as its ability to "negotiate with the national and international financial world." See Ezio Mauro, "A New Mafia," in *Notizie Dall'Italia,* no. 8, November 1982, 5.

The Mafia faced the problem of "allocating this large 'surplus value' from heroin, sums of money vast enough to upset the economy of one of our Regions," journalist Mauro wrote. This brought about new and extremely dangerous connections between the Mafia and the Sicilian banking world. Mauro cites the rapid growth of Sicilian banking in comparison to Italian banking in general during the critical years of Mafia drug trafficking and quotes part of a recent report by the Sicilian branch of Magistura Democratica (a judges' and magistrates' association), which stated this proposition: "The growing weight of banks in the Sicilian economy, the common interests shared by Banks and Mafia businesses, the selection banks make in granting credits or in financing the strangest and unknown organizations, places the Banking System itself at the centre of financial manoeuvres, making them the load bearing pillar of the entrepreneurial activities of political-Mafia groups," 6.

48. PSI, *Hearings,* 52.

49. U.S. Department of Justice, Federal Bureau of Investigation, File # NY 92–1459, "Interrogation of Joe Valachi," by Special Agents Patrick J. Moynihan and James P. Flynn at Westchester County Jail, 14 December 1962.

50. See my " 'On the Waterfront' Revisited: The Criminology of Waterfront Organized Crime," *Contemporary Crises* 6 (1982): 385.

51. The following is based on David Courtwright et al., *Addicts Who Survived: An Oral History of Narcotic Use in America, 1923–1965* (Knoxville: University of Tennessee Press, 1989).

52. Jack E. Reece, "Fascism, the Mafia and the Emergence of Sicilian Separatism (1919–1943)," *Journal of Modern History* 45 (June 1973): 263.

53. Ibid., 269.

54. Ibid., 270.

55. One might well wonder just what it was that blasted open the postwar trade to Italian Americans in addition to the destruction of Jewish underworlds. A brief outline should suffice. The Far East market was demolished, of course, by the war and its revolutionary aftermath (not to return until the 1950s and 1960s with the emergence of Southeast Asia's infamous Golden Triangle). The dearth of Asian narcotics correspondingly reinvigorated the Middle East and the Mediterranean trading area. At the same time, U.S. military and political interest in that area increased enormously. In particular, the U.S. desire to prevent indigenous Communist party victories in France and Italy (not to mention the horrific Greek civil war) meant what racketeers in both southern France and Italy had new and powerful patrons. See Ronald L. Filippelli, "Luigi Antonini, the Italian-American Labor Council, and Cold-War Politics in Italy, 1943–1949," *Labor History* (Fall 1992).

The politics of professional criminals are notoriously reactionary, certainly anti-Communist to the core. With both important clandestine political jobs to do for the

United States and vast American reconstruction funds available to rebuild ports and harbors in southern Italy, for example, Sicilian mafiosi and Corsican-born racketeers found themselves in unusual strategic positions. One perhaps unforeseen result of this new postwar milieu was the expansion of drug production in the Middle East by Turkey and Syria and the resumption of significant trafficking throughout the Mediterranean area. Sicilians as well as Corsicans were catapulted into a far larger world than previously. This produced major changes for Sicilian gangsters, not the desire for a La Cosa Nostra. As far as the Corsicans went, the fact that France had been the center of European illicit trafficking during the 1920s, along with their contacts in Turkey and French Middle East colonial nations, helped them run a corner on much of the postwar narcotics trade. Their natural North American market was French Canada, which by then had solidly entrenched Corsican and Sicilian crime syndicates, which worked closely together. See Alfred W. McCoy, *The Politics of Heroin: CIA Complicity in the Global Drug Trade* (New York: Lawrence Hill Books, 1991).

56. On money laundering, see my *Masters of Paradise: Organized Crime and the Internal Revenue Service in the Bahamas* (New Brunswick, NJ: Transaction Books, 1991).

57. David R. Johnson, *Policing the Urban Underworld: The Impact of Crime on the Development of the American Police, 1800–1887* (Philadelphia: Temple University Press, 1979), 3–4.

58. Ibid., 38.

59. Howard P. Chudacoff, "A New Look at Ethnic Neighborhoods: Residential Dispersion and the Concept of Visibility in a Medium-Sized City," *Journal of American History* 60.1 (June 1973): 91.

60. Ibid., 5.

61. Ibid., 6.

62. Timothy J. Gilfoyle, "Strumpets and Sporting Men: The Geography of Commercial Sex in New York City, 1790–1920," paper presented at the annual American Studies Conference, New Orleans, 1990, 3.

63. Ibid., 6.

64. Ibid.

65. Ibid., 12–13.

66. Ibid., 21–22.

67. Barbara Meil Hobson, *Uneasy Virtue: The Politics of Prostitution and the American Reform Tradition* (New York: Basic Books, 1987), 25, 29.

68. Ibid., 44.

69. Ivan Light, "Numbers Gambling Among Blacks: A Financial Institution," *American Sociological Review* (December 1977): 898.

70. Hobson, *Uneasy Virtue*, 141.

71. Ibid., 141.

72. Johnson, *Policing the Urban Underworld*, 172.

73. My introduction to Morrissey came by way of historian Mark Haller's manuscript "The Rise of Urban Crime Syndicates, 1865–1905."

74. Johnson, *Policing the Urban Underworld*, 176–77.

75. Daniel Czitrom, "Underworlds and Underdogs: Big Tim Sullivan and the Politics of Vice in New York, 1886–1913," paper presented to the annual American Studies Association meeting, New Orleans, 1990, 22–23.

76. Nancy Joan Weiss, *Charles Francis Murphy, 1858–1924: Respectability and Responsibility in Tammany Politics* (Northampton, MA: Smith College, 1968), 24.

77. Ibid., 60.

78. Steven P. Erie, *Rainbow's End: Irish-Americans and the Dilemmas of Urban Machine Politics, 1840–1985* (Berkeley: University of California Press, 1988), 56–57.

79. Ibid., 57.

80. Czitrom, "Underworlds," 1.

81. Ibid., 3.

82. Ibid., 7.

83. Erie, *Rainbow's End*, 100–101.

84. Ibid., 101.

85. Ibid., 102.

86. Czitrom, "Underworlds," 19.

87. Ibid., 28.

88. Ibid., 45.

89. Ibid., 47.

90. Ibid., 47.

91. Edward J. Bristow, *Prostitution and Prejudice: The Jewish Fight Against White Slavery, 1870–1939.* (New York: Schocken Books, 1983), 146–47.

92. Ibid., 146.

93. Ibid., 148.

94. Ibid., 152.

95. Thomas Kessner, *The Golden Door: Italian and Jewish Immigrant Mobility in New York City, 1880–1915* (New York: Oxford University Press, 1977), 38–39.

96. Ibid., 38.

97. Erie, *Rainbow's End*, 12.

98. See my *The Business of Crime: A Documentary Study of Organized Crime in the American Economy* (Boulder, CO: Westview Press, 1991), particularly Part III.

99. Robert Smith Bader, *Prohibition in Kansas: A History* (Lawrence: University Press of Kansas, 1986), 199.

100. Mark H. Haller, "Bootleggers and American Gambling, 1920–1950," in Commission on the Review of the National Policy Toward Gambling (Washington, DC, October 1976), Staff and Consultant Papers, Appendix 1, 102.

101. Ibid., 108.

102. Ibid., 109.

103. Ibid., 115.

104. The information on Jewish American crime comes from the files of the Bureau of Social Morals part of the New York Kehillah files, which are in the Judah L. Magnes Archives, housed in the Central Archives for the History of the Jewish People, Jerusalem, Israel.

105. Bureau of Social Morals, "*Jack Zelig*," Story # 14, October 1912.

106. An interesting case that indicates the endemic gunplay on the Lower East Side can be found in the details of the murder of Frederick Strauss, an innocent caught in the cross fire of rival mobs involved in strikebreaking and other illicit activities. See *New York Times*, 10, 11, 12, 13, 14, 15, 16, 18 January 1914; 1, 4, 6 June 1914; 27 November 1916; 4 December 1916; 17 February 1917; 28 March 1917.

107. U.S. Department of Justice, Federal Bureau of Investigation, "The Furdress Case," File No. I. C. 60–1501, 7 November 1939, 59.

108. See, for example, Lisa Ann Vardzel, ''Newport, Kentucky: A Study of Organized Crime, 1920–1952,'' master's thesis, Administration of Justice Department, Pennsylvania State University, 1989, in which she details the strife between local gamblers such as Peter Schmidt and Buck Brady and a syndicate from Cleveland composed of Moe Dalitz, Samuel Tucker, Morris Kleinman, Louis Rothkopf, Samuel Miller, Thomas J. McGinty, Alvin Giesey, and attorney Samuel T. Haas, 26–34.

Part II

Perspectives on Organized Crime: Theory and Research

3

Models of Organized Crime

JAY S. ALBANESE

WHAT IS A MODEL OF ORGANIZED CRIME?

Everyone knows the story of the blind men asked to identify an object that was actually an elephant. One grabbed the tail and guessed the animal was a snake. Another touched its tusks and thought it was a smooth stone. A third held its ear and surmised it was a large piece of leather. In each case, the perception was based on logical deductions, but the conclusion was wrong.

Models of organized crime have developed in much the same way. Government investigators, researchers, and scholars have examined various manifestations of organized crime, using informants, electronic surveillance, court records, participant-observation, interviews with convicted offenders, economic analyses, and historical accounts. By and large, these investigations have been conducted with integrity and true interest in discovering the actual nature of organized crime. Often the perceptions of these individuals have been correct, but the conclusions drawn have been misleading. Why?

A model is an effort to make a picture of a piece of reality in order to understand it better. We make physical models of the structure of the solar system in order to see how it is organized at a level difficult to observe otherwise, due to its immense size. We have modeled distinct stages of child development to illustrate the maturation process that is difficult to observe otherwise, due to its slow, gradual process. In each case, we simplify and "freeze" a model in time and space, even though the objects we are modeling are constantly moving and changing. As a result, models are limited but still useful. They make visible the physical objects too large (or too small) to observe, and they make understandable the objects too fast or too slow to capture. This ability to capture the essence of an object, system, or process without actually witnessing it makes models the most useful of all educational tools.

What U.S. Supreme Court Justice Potter Stewart said about obscene material holds equally true for organized crime: I might not know precisely what it is, but "I know it when I see it."[1] Everyone has perceptions of what organized crime is, even when it is difficult to explain in a comprehensive or systematic way. There have been a large number of efforts to model organized crime, most occurring during the last three decades. In every case the goal has been to capture the essence of organized crime in the form of a model because it is so difficult to observe otherwise.

THREE MODELS OF ORGANIZED CRIME

Like the blind men who attempted to identify the elephant, the outcome of efforts to model organized crime invariably reflects the perspective of the investigator. Economists model it in terms of economic factors. Government investigators model organized crime as a hierarchical, government-like enterprise. Social scientists view it as a social phenomenon. In too many cases the perceptions are based in reality, but the conclusions drawn are either inaccurate or overgeneralized. Just as in the case of the blind men who disagreed in their conclusions, the elephant still existed in a distinct form. They simply did not identify it correctly. Even though investigators may model organized crime inaccurately, organized crime continues to exist. The failure of a model to capture the true nature of organized crime should not be construed as proof, one way or the other, about its existence. Too often in the past a model shown to have shortcomings in its depiction of organized crime is rejected in its entirety. This overlooks the fact that the investigator's perceptions may have been correct, but the conclusions wrong. As a result, it is important to distinguish between the *facts and perceptions* on which models are based and the *conclusions drawn* from those perceptions and facts. The deduction of wrong conclusions does not mean necessarily that the facts and perceptions on which they are based are also inaccurate.[2]

Models of organized crime can be grouped into three general types: those that focus on hierarchical structure, those that emphasize local ethnic or cultural connections, and those that emphasize the economic nature of organized crime. As we will see, none of these models exclude consideration of the others, as some overlap clearly exists. Nevertheless, the development and structure of these models are distinct and will be treated separately.

HIERARCHICAL MODELS OF ORGANIZED CRIME

"Hierarchical" is defined in the dictionary as "a group of persons or things arranged in order of rank or grade." Various authors over the years have termed this the "bureaucratic," "national conspiracy," or "corporate" model of organized crime. Stated most simply, this model of organized crime characterizes it as a government-like structure, where organized illegal activities are conducted with the approval of superiors, "policy" is set by higher-ups, and illicit activities are "protec ted" through the influence of the hierarchy.

This model of organized crime was put forth first in these terms by Estes Kefauver, a U.S. senator who conducted hearings on the subject of organized crime in 1950. His committee concluded that "there is a sinister criminal organization known as the Mafia operating throughout the country with ties in other nations in the opinion of this committee."[3] Unfortunately, Kefauver had little more than the opinions of law enforcement officials to support his contention. The fact that he drew such sweeping conclusions without independent corroboration has been pointed out in several serious critiques of the Kefauver Committee.[4]

It was not until 1963 that evidence was produced that supported the notion that organized crime operated as a hierarchical structure. Senator John McClellan held public hearings during this period at which the government introduced the first "insider" in organized crime. His name was Joseph Valachi, then serving a prison sentence, who agreed to testify as part of a deal to avoid a possible death sentence for a murder he committed while in prison. Valachi's testimony became the basis for the hierarchical model of organized crime.

Valachi testified that a nationwide criminal organization did exist, as Kefauver had argued in 1950. Unlike Kefauver, Valachi said the organization's name was "Cosa Nostra," rather than Mafia. Valachi claimed he had never heard of the term *Mafia*, while no law enforcement official who testified had heard of Cosa Nostra. The Senate committee treated the two names for this apparently identical organization interchangeably.[5] Valachi claimed this organization arose out of a gangland war in New York City during the early 1930s. The main stake in this so-called Castellammaresse War, which was said to have lasted fourteen months, was "absolute control of the large segment of the underworld then in the hands of gang leaders of Italian nativity or lineage."[6]

Valachi described the organizational structure, established after this gangland war, as consisting of "the individual bosses of the individual families, and then we had an underboss, and then we had what we call a caporegime which is a lieutenant, and then we have what we call soldiers."[7] In this way territory and criminal enterprises were divided among "families" of men of Italian descent. According to Valachi, membership was restricted by Lucky Luciano, after the Castellammaresse War, to "Sicilians from the turn of the century through the 1920's," and then it was confined to "full Italians," requiring Italian parentage on both sides of a man's family. This restriction lasted until 1954, when membership was opened to others not meeting these requirements.[8]

Based primarily on Valachi's testimony and the statements of law enforcement officials from some large cities, the McClellan Committee concluded that "there exists . . . today a criminal organization that is directly descended from

Table 3.1
Hierarchical Model of Organized Crime

Structure (That Forms the Basis for Criminal Activity)
1. "Family" structure with graded ranks of authority from boss down to soldiers.
2. Bosses oversee the activities of family members.
3. A "commission" of bosses handles inter-family relations and disputes.

and is patterned upon the centuries-old Sicilian terrorist society, the Mafia. This organization, also known as Cosa Nostra, operates vast illegal enterprises that produce an annual income of many billions of dollars. This combine has so much power and influence that it may be described as a private government of organized crime.''[9] This characterization of organized crime as a large, centrally controlled, highly organized entity forms the basis for the hierarchical model of organized crime. The major attributes of organized crime according to this model are highlighted in Table 3.1.

As the table indicates, the hierarchical model posits a ''family'' structure with several military-style ranks from the boss down to soldiers. The bosses control the activities of the family. Valachi also testified that there exists a ''commission'' of bosses from approximately twelve families in large cities around the country.[10] This commission handles interfamily relations and disputes, according to the McClellan Committee's conclusions. The source of this information was largely Valachi and other criminal informants used by police agencies who also provided testimony at the McClellan hearings.

Over the last twenty-five years, the hierarchical model has been criticized for its imprecision. Inaccuracies in several important factors to the hierarchical model were believed by some to render the model useless. Problems with the hierarchical model included (1) the inability to confirm historically that any type of gangland war occurred during the early 1930s,[11] (2) information provided by Valachi himself and others after him that the ''family'' actually plays very little role in directing the lives and activities of its members,[12] and (3) subsequent informants, such as Jimmy Fratianno, who differed widely in their testimony about the size and structure of Cosa Nostra.[13] Most investigations that produced findings that contradicted parts of the hierarchical model were historical in nature, relying on court records, testimony, interviews, and archival data. The number, method, and similarity in conclusions of these investigations suggest that they raise valid criticisms of parts of the hierarchical model. What they failed to establish, and perhaps were not intended to prove, is that the hierarchical model is valid as a description of at least some parts of organized crime.[14]

It is true that Valachi's history was faulty, and it is unfortunate that the Senate and subsequent investigators for the President's Crime Commission in 1967 did not assess Valachi's statements more carefully. The President's Commission Task Force on Organized Crime essentially repeated Valachi's testimony and added little new insight.[15] Nevertheless, the most important question remains unanswered: are the errors arising from the McClellan hearings incidental, or do they warrant an abandonment of the hierarchical model altogether?

The decade of the 1970s witnessed a growing body of scholarly research into the nature of organized crime. It began with sociologist Joseph Albini in 1971, continued with anthropologists Francis Ianni and Elizabeth Reuss-Ianni in 1972, and was followed by others. In every case the researchers were unable to find any connection between the individuals and groups they studied and a larger, controlling hierarchy. This led to growing doubts about the existence of a national crime syndicate and led to the emergence of a second model of organized crime, discussed later.

Not until the 1980s was information available that showed conclusively that the hierarchical model accurately portrayed at least some manifestations of organized crime. The "Mob trials" of the 1980s and 1990s were the most significant organized crime prosecution efforts in the history of the United States. Several hundred high-level organized crime figures were convicted, based on electronic surveillance and protected witnesses that provided documentary evidence of how organized crime operates in some areas. The "Commission" trial of 1986 was perhaps the most notable Mob trial because it involved the alleged "bosses" of the five New York City "families" of the Cosa Nostra as defendants. The defense conceded that the "Mafia exists and has members" and that "there is a commission," which was mentioned in the wiretapped conversations of the defendants. The defendants tried to argue that their membership was not synonymous with criminal activity, but they were each convicted and sentenced to 100 years in prison for various crimes.[16] Interestingly, the defendants argued that the purpose of the "commission" was to resolve disputes, rather than to plan crimes, an argument not unlike that made by Valachi in the 1960s, who characterized the commission as a mechanism for dispute resolution between families. The defense stipulations, wiretap evidence, and jury findings in the commission trial and in the successful prosecution of John Gotti in 1992 make it clear that the hierarchical model clearly characterizes at least some part of organized crime in the United States.[17] Consider the testimony of Salvatore, "Sammy the Bull," Gravano in the trial of Gotti:

Assistant U.S. Attorney Gleeson: Have you ever heard the term "administration"?

Gravano: Yes.

Gleeson: To you what does that mean?

Gravano: There is the boss, the underboss, and the *consigliere*, it's the higher up in the family. The administration.

Gleeson: Were you part of the administration?

Gravano: Yes.

Gleeson: Who was the rest of the administration?

Gravano: John (Gotti) was the boss, I was the underboss, and Frank—and Joe Piney was the *consigliere*, Frankie was acting *consigliere* . . .

Gleeson: What's below the administration?

Gravano: Captains.

This testimony from Gravano, a criminal informant of higher "rank" than Valachi, is remarkably similar to Valachi's testimony nearly thirty years earlier.[18] Gravano's description of his "induction" ceremony into the Cosa Nostra and of the "commission" made up of leaders of various "families" is quite similar to Valachi's version in 1963.[19] There is no apparent cause or reason for Gravano or the other criminal informants from the decade of the 1980s to model their testimony after that of Valachi, so it reasonably can be said that the structure of Cosa Nostra (at least within New York City) is based on the same hierarchical model described by Valachi in the early 1960s.

Given the available evidence to date, it is clear the hierarchical model characterizes organized crime among Italian Americans in the New York City area who are connected to the Cosa Nostra. There is also evidence from other cities in New England and elsewhere that *at least within* those cities a significant part of organized crime is controlled by organized criminals of Italian American roots. The hierarchical model fits best in its description of how the group functions in accord with respect for position and in partnerships and deference to other "connected" individuals in organized crime.

The hierarchical model is weakest, given the evidence to date, in describing whether there exists a true connection among organized crime groups in different cities and in specifying the role of Cosa Nostra in the lives of its members. The commission trial in New York City established how the various "families" operate and divide their criminal activities there. The trial sheds little light, however, on (1) the existence and nature of connections among organized crime groups in different cities, (2) the extent of the connections between Italian and non-Italian groups in the same cities, or (3) whether organized crime *not* connected with Cosa Nostra is structured in similar fashion. Contemporary investigations suggest that organized crime activities, both within and outside the Cosa Nostra, might be becoming less hierarchical and more entrepreneurial in nature.[20]

LOCAL, ETHNIC MODELS OF ORGANIZED CRIME

Some said during the 1980s that once free-market competition was introduced into the U.S. telephone system, the price of making a telephone call would drop considerably. The government was ultimately successful in adding competition to the long-distance telephone marketplace, but the results were far from dramatic. A similar logical, but incorrect, prediction often arises from the hierarchical model of organized crime.

Perhaps the biggest problem with the hierarchical model of organized crime is that it leads to the conclusion that prosecution of the "bosses" and others in control will make organized crime less prevalent and less threatening. The successful prosecutions of the 1980s and 1990s illustrate that this is not necessarily the case, in that the demand for drugs, gambling, and stolen property and a weak regulatory system provoke the emergence of illicit entrepreneurs to cater to the illegal markets or to exploit the legal marketplace. Once these entrepreneurs are removed by arrest or incarceration, others emerge because the demand remains, as do the opportunities for criminal exploitation of the legitimate marketplace.[21]

Social scientists became involved in the study of organized crime in a significant way in the 1970s. For the first time a series of independent studies appeared that relied on information from sources outside the government. The first was conducted by sociologist Albini, who found that individuals involved in organized crime "do not belong to an organization." Rather than a "criminal secret society, a criminal syndicate consists of a system of loosely structured relationships" that develops so each person can maximize profits.[22] The following year anthropologists Ianni and Reuss-Ianni conducted a two-year study of one specific organized crime "family" in Brooklyn. Francis Ianni became a participant-observer, and based on his observations of this group and those of two other criminal groups he studied, he found these groups not to be "bureaucratic." In fact, he found them to have "no structure . . . independent of their current 'personnel.' "[23]

Unlike the prevailing view at the time that organized crime operated as "a private government," both Albini, and Ianni and Reuss-Ianni found little organization and found that friendships based on cultural (i.e., Italian) and economic ties formed the basis for organized crime activities. These authors' findings are limited, of course, by the areas and groups they studied, much in the same way that Valachi was limited in his knowledge about organized crime outside the New York area. The primary difference between Valachi's model of organized crime and the newer local, ethnic model developed by social scientists centers on the degree of organization within and between organized criminal groups.

The body of social science evidence continued to grow from the 1970s to the present. Now numerous studies of organized crime groups in various locales around the country have all found that (1) cultural and ethnic ties link organized criminals together, rather than a hierarchy, and (2) the groups studied appear to be local in nature without apparent connections to a national crime syndicate.[24]

This model, outlined in Table 3.2, has obvious differences from the hierarchical model first detailed by Valachi, but there are similarities as well. All these studies highlight the importance of heritage (i.e., racial, ethnic, or other cultural ties) in forming the basis for working relationships, and from Valachi forward

Table 3.2
Local, Ethnic Model of Organized Crime

Structure (That Forms the Context for Criminal Activity)
1. Cultural and ethnic ties bind the group together, rather than a hierarchical structure.
2. Individuals control their own activities and take partners as they wish.
3. No evidence of connection of these groups with a national crime syndicate in most cases.

it has been clear that even those organized crime members who are part of Cosa Nostra obtain relatively little direction in their day-to-day activities. Consider Valachi's statement at the McClellan hearings in 1963:

Senator Javits: That is the function of the family . . . that is mutual protection?

Mr. Valachi: Right.

Senator Javits: Otherwise, everybody operates by himself. They may take partners but that is their option.

Mr. Valachi: Right.

This exchange shows that the organization of organized crime, even as a member of the Genovese crime family, as Valachi claimed, is rather loose.[25] Therefore, the differences between the hierarchical and local, ethnic models appear to lie entirely in *how* illicit relationships are structured, rather than in the nature or extent of the criminal activity itself.

A third model of organized crime developed in the late 1970s, when the economics of organized crime drew interest among researchers and policymakers. Rather than focusing on the personal relationships that form the basis for organized crime, this group of investigations focused on the economic relationships that drive the business of organized crime.

ORGANIZED CRIME AS A BUSINESS ENTERPRISE

The enterprise model of organized crime grew out of dissatisfaction with both the hierarchical and local ethnic models. A growing number of investigations had found that relationships between individuals (hierarchical, ethnic, racial, or friendship) were the genesis of organized crime activity (as opposed to individual, less organized forms of criminal behavior). The view was that if the factors causing these illicit relationships to form (i.e., conspiracies) could be isolated, a determination might be made about the true causes of organized crime. The conspiratorial nature of organized crime makes it serious. The individual drug dealer and illegal casino operator does not cause public concern, as much as how these individuals organize their customers, suppliers, and functionaries to provide illicit goods and services for a profit.

The realization that organized crime operates as a business spurred a series of studies in an effort to isolate those factors that contribute most significantly to the formation of criminal enterprises. Dwight Smith was among the first to attempt to explain the economic origins of organized crime in a systematic manner. In his book *The Mafia Mystique* and in his subsequent publications he developed a "spectrum-based theory of enterprise."[26] Applying general organization theory to criminal activity, Smith found that organized crime stems from "the same fundamental assumptions that govern entrepreneurship in the legitimate marketplace: a necessity to maintain and extend one's share of the market." According to this view, organized crime groups form and thrive in the same way that legitimate businesses do: they respond to the needs and demands of suppliers, customers, regulators, and competitors. The only difference between organized crime and legitimate business, according to Smith, is that organized criminals deal in illegal products, where legitimate businesses generally do not.

The business enterprise model of organized crime focuses on how economic considerations, rather than hierarchical or ethnic considerations, lie at the base of the formation and success of organized crime groups. Regardless of ethnicity or hierarchy, the enterprise model labels economic concerns as the primary cause of organized criminal behavior. A number of empirical studies of specific organized crime operations support this perspective. Patricia Adler's participant-observer study of illicit drug sales in the Southwest found that "dealers and smugglers I studied operated within an illicit market that was largely competitive, or disorganized, rather than visibly structured." Disputes were settled in "a spontaneous and unrestricted manner."[27] She concluded that the drug markets she observed consisted of "individual entrepreneurs and small organizations rather than massive, centralized bureaucracies," which were "competitive" rather than "monopolistic" in nature.[28] In a study of bookmaking, loan-sharking, and numbers gambling in New York City, Peter Reuter found them "not monopolies in the classic sense or subject to control by some external organization." Instead, he observed that "economic forces arising from the illegality of the product tend to fragment the market," making it difficult to control or centralize these illegal activities on a large scale.[29]

Studies like these typify the enterprise model of organized crime. Rather than the product of illicit relationships based on hierarchical or ethnic relationships, this model sees organized crime as the product of market forces, similar to those that cause legitimate businesses to flourish or die in the legal sector of the economy. The major characteristics of the enterprise model are summarized in Table 3.3. This table shows that economic relationships, rather than personal

Table 3.3
Enterprise Model of Organized Crime

Structure (Incidental to the Criminal Opportunities)
1. Organized crime and legitimate business involve similar activities on different ends of "spectrum of legitimacy" of business enterprise.
2. Operations not ethnically exclusive or very violent in order to enhance profit.
3. Rarely centrally organized due to the nature of the markets and activities involved.

relationships (based either on hierarchy or ethnicity), form the basis for organized crime activity. Organized crime activity is seen as a deviant variation of legitimate business activity that is often interethnic and nonviolent, because these latter two factors enhance profit maximization.

Several studies have found that organized crime can be interethnic in nature and also less violent than is commonly believed. Historian Alan Block saw that, although Jews dominated the cocaine trade in New York City during the early 1900s, there was also notable "evidence of interethnic cooperation" involving Italians, Greeks, Irish, and black participants.[30] A contemporary account of the Irish mob the Westies on Manhattan's West Side saw that they cooperate occasionally with Cosa Nostra groups to further mutual interests.[31] Annelise Anderson's analysis of a single organized crime "family" indicated that there was "no strong evidence" of violence in its legitimate businesses, and the use of force to encourage payments from loan shark customers was "almost nonexistent."[32] An investigation of organized crime infiltration of the New York City construction industry showed that "actual violence is only rarely necessary."[33] Reuter, Jonathan Rubinstein, and Simon Wynn noted that vending machine and waste collection industries in the New York City area had "outgrown the racketeers," inasmuch as "there is no point in a racketeer using force to control machine placement in a bar or restaurant unless he is also able to provide the patrons with the games they desire. If he cannot, the patrons will just move to another bar."[34] Each study demonstrates that organized crime activity operates according to economic factors faced by any business enterprise (i.e., the pressures of suppliers, customers, regulators, and competitors). The enterprise model clearly places these business-related concerns as more significant than hierarchical obligations or ethnic links in the genesis and continuation of organized crime.

FITTING THE MODELS TOGETHER

Thus, there is evidence to support each of the three models of organized crime in certain respects. Clear evidence from criminal informants, electronic surveillance, and jury findings indicate that the hierarchical model characterizes relationships among the New York City Cosa Nostra families and some groups in other cities. The mob trials of the 1980s and 1990s removed any doubt that existed after the Valachi testimony in the 1960s. Yet there is clear evidence that much organized crime remains unconnected to Cosa Nostra activity. This evidence has been derived largely from independent case studies (cited earlier) of organized crime groups in a number of different cities. In many cases these groups are locally based and bound by ethnic or cultural ties, groups that are often non-Italian. Finally, there is clear evidence that economic considerations are a significant factor in the development and maintenance of criminal enterprises. These findings stem largely from economic analyses of organized crime markets (cited earlier) in different regions of the country.

To what extent do these three models overlap? There are three distinct ways in which these models merge. Cosa Nostra groups are hierarchical (if loosely so), ethnically bound, and perhaps also maintained by market forces. Ethnically bound organized crime groups exist that are not hierarchical in structure but driven by economic concerns. There are also organized crime groups not hierarchical or ethnically bound that engage in criminal activities corresponding to the nature of the available market. These three possibilities point out the major similarities and differences in the three models of organized crime and suggest how organized crime might be addressed more effectively in the future.

Both the hierarchical and local ethnic models focus on how organized crime *groups are organized*; the enterprise model focuses on how organized crime *activities are organized*. This is why the three models do not conflict in any significant way. While it is important to understand how a criminal group is organized, if one is to develop a criminal conspiracy case, it is not always necessary to understand the group structure to understand how and why it engages in the activities it does. Perhaps Mark Haller said it best: ''It makes little sense, for instance, to compare an Italian-American crime family to a Jamaican cocaine distribution group. One is largely a social group that serves its members' business interests; the other is a business group distributing illegal drugs.''[35] The Jamaican group, in Haller's view, exists simply as a mechanism to engage in the drug business with little in the way of structure or cultural ties beyond the drug business itself. On the other hand, the Cosa Nostra group has both preexisting hierarchical and cultural ties that form the basis for launching illicit enterprises. As Haller puts it, it's like ''comparing a Rotary Club and a department store. It is more appropriate to compare stores with stores, and Rotary Clubs with other social organizations.''[36]

The perceived inconsistencies among the hierarchical, ethnic, and enterprise models of organized crime are incidental for the purposes of both study and crime control. Once one recognizes, as the organized crime literature clearly indicates, (1) that some organized crime is hierarchical in nature, and much is not; (2) that some is locally based and ethnically bound in nature, and much is not; and (3) that all organized crime activity is entrepreneurial in nature, then the differences among the models become less significant.

Organized crime is studied most fruitfully as an economic activity and is prosecuted most effectively on the basis of the relationship among its participants. For the scholar, the economic activity is paramount inasmuch as it provides more leads to understanding the genesis and maintenance of the illegal acts. For the law enforcement official, the structure of the group is paramount inasmuch as it provides more leads for prosecution purposes. Hopefully, an appreciation of each of these models will enable both scholars and the law enforcement community to understand that the apparent tension among the various models of organized crime is inconsequential, rather than contentious.

The enterprise model characterizes all organized crime activity, whereas the precise structure of particular organized crime groups becomes more or less important depending on the group in question (especially whether it predated the current illicit activity, or whether it merely arose in response to the criminal opportunity). Future investigations should take greater care to appreciate the dynamic and better distinguish between organized crime activities and organized crime group characteristics as recognized in the three models of organized crime. Just as the three blind men who examined various parts of the elephant had good instincts and made logical judgments, their conclusions were still wrong. When it comes to understanding the true nature of organized crime, it is equally important not to lose sight of the "elephant" as one studies its various structures and activities.

NOTES

1. *Jacobellis v. Ohio*, 84 S. Ct. 1676 (1964).
2. Charles H. Rogovin and Frederick T. Martens, "The Evil That Men Do," *Journal of Contemporary Criminal Justice* 8 (February 1992): 62–79.
3. U.S. Senate Special Committee to Investigate Organized Crime in Interstate Commerce, *Third Interim Report* (Washington, DC: U.S. Government Printing Office, 1951), 2.
4. Daniel Bell, "Crime as an American Way of Life," *The Antioch Review* 13 (June 1953): 131–54; William H. Moore, *The Kefauver Committee and the Politics of Crime, 1950–1952* (Columbia: University of Missouri Press, 1974).
5. U.S. Senate Committee on Government Operations Permanent Subcommittee on Investigations, *Report on Organized Crime and Illicit Traffic in Narcotics* (Washington, DC: U.S. Government Printing Office, 1965), 117.
6. Ibid., 12.
7. U.S. Senate Committee on Government Operations Permanent Subcommittee on Investigations, *Organized Crime and Illicit Traffic in Narcotics: Hearings Part I* (Washington, DC: U.S. Government Printing Office), 80, 215.

8. Ibid., 13.

9. U.S. Senate, *Report on Organized Crime and Illicit Traffic in Narcotics*, 117.

10. Ibid.

11. Alan A. Block, "History and the Study of Organized Crime," *Urban Life* 6 (1978): 455–74; Humbert S. Nelli, *The Business of Crime: Italians and Syndicate Crime in the United States* (Chicago: University of Chicago Press, 1981).

12. Jay S. Albanese, *Organized Crime in America*, 2d ed. (Cincinnati: Anderson, 1989), 45; Annelise G. Anderson, *The Business of Organized Crime* (Stanford, CA: Hoover Institution Press, 1979), 44; Mark H. Haller, *Life Under Bruno: The Economics of an Organized Crime Family* (Conshohocken: Pennsylvania Crime Commission, 1991).

13. Albanese, *Organized Crime in America*, 46–62; Ovid Demaris, *The Last Mafioso* (New York: Bantam, 1981), 20–22; U.S. Senate Committee on Governmental Affairs Permanent Subcommittee on Investigations, *Organized Crime and Violence: Hearings Part I* (Washington, DC: U.S. Government Printing Office, 1980), 88.

14. Robert J. Kelly, "Trapped in the Folds of Discourse: Theorizing About the Underworld," *Journal of Contemporary Criminal Justice* 8 (February 1992): 11–35.

15. President's Commission on Law Enforcement and Administration of Justice, *Task Force Report: Organized Crime* (Washington, DC: U.S. Government Printing Office, 1967); Donald R. Cressey, *Theft of the Nation* (New York: Harper and Row, 1969).

16. Albanese, *Organized Crime in America*, 62–69.

17. John Gotti, *The Gotti Tapes* (New York: Times Books, 1992).

18. Ibid., 134–35.

19. Ibid., 146–49.

20. Peter Reuter, *Disorganized Crime: The Economics of the Visible Hand* (Cambridge: MIT Press, 1983); Patricia A. Adler, *Wheeling and Dealing: An Ethnography of an Upper-Level Drug Dealing and Smuggling Community* (New York: Columbia University Press, 1985); Pino Arlacchi, *Mafia Business: The Mafia Ethic and the Spirit of Capitalism* (London: Verso, 1986).

21. Howard Abadinsky, *The Mafia in America: An Oral History* (New York: Praeger, 1981); Joseph L. Albini, *The American Mafia: Genesis of a Legend* (New York: Irvington, 1971), 289; Peter Reuter, Jonathan Rubinstein, and Simon Wynn, *Racketeering in Legitimate Industries: Two Case Studies* (Washington, DC: National Institute of Justice, 1983); Dwight C. Smith, "Organized Crime and Entrepreneurship," *International Journal of Criminology and Penology* 6 (1978): 161–77.

22. Albini, *The American Mafia*, 288.

23. Francis A. J. Ianni, with Elizabeth Reuss-Ianni, *A Family Business: Kinship and Social Control in Organized Crime* (New York: New American Library, 1972), 20.

24. Abadinsky, *The Mafia in America*; Albini, *The American Mafia*; Anderson, *The Business of Organized Crime*; Ianni and Reuss-Ianni, *A Family Business*; Adler, *Wheeling and Dealing*.

25. U.S. Senate, *Organized Crime and Illicit Traffic in Narcotics: Hearings Part I*, 116, 194.

26. Smith, "Organized Crime and Entrepreneurship," 161–77; Dwight C. Smith, "Paragons, Pariahs, and Pirates: A Spectrum-Based Theory of Enterprise," *Crime & Delinquency* 26 (July 1980): 358–86; Dwight C. Smith, *The Mafia Mystique*, rev. ed. (Lanham, MD: University Press of America, 1990).

27. Adler, *Wheeling and Dealing*, 80.

28. Ibid., 82.

29. Reuter, *Disorganized Crime*, 176.

30. Alan A. Block, "The Snowman Cometh: Coke in Progressive New York," *Criminology* 17 (May 1979): 75–99.

31. T. J. English, *The Westies* (New York: St. Martin's, 1991), 136–78.

32. Anderson, *The Business of Organized Crime*, 66, 117.

33. Ronald Goldstock et al., *Corruption and Racketeering in the New York City Construction Industry* (New York: New York University Press, 1990), 31.

34. Reuter, Rubinstein, and Wynn, *Racketeering in Legitimate Industries*, 33.

35. Haller, "Bureaucracy and the Mafia," 7.

36. Haller, "Bureaucracy and the Mafia," 8; Haller, *Life Under Bruno*, 227.

4

Research on American Organized Crime

PETER REUTER

Organized crime in America is a subject that fascinates the populace in both America and Europe. A continuing flow of popular novels and films depicts various forms of the Mafia and similar groups; network television rarely lacks a series dealing with either organized crime or its pursuit. Newspapers, from the *New York Times* and *Wall Street Journal* to the yellowest of dailies, provide a steady diet of stories on organized crime in many forms. Organized crime also gets a great deal of attention from politicians. Estes Kefauver became a presidential candidate on the basis of his hearings on organized crime. Thomas Dewey began his rise to national political prominence with a series of widely reported organized crime prosecutions. Even now it has served a number of prosecutors well in getting them political prominence: former governors James Thompson of Illinois and Richard Thornberg of Pennsylvania owe their start to success in prosecuting organized crime.

Despite this, this phenomenon has not attracted much scholarly attention. It would be difficult to identify as many as half a dozen books that report major research findings, or even that many significant articles. This probably reflects the extreme difficulty of obtaining acccess to relevant official records, which inevitably involves more sensitive private information than is needed for most criminological research. Field research also faces substantially more serious obstacles than it does for other forms of criminal activity. The increasingly quantitative bent of modern criminology has further limited research on organized crime in recent years, since statistical data are almost impossible to develop.

The literature that does exist is highly descriptive. Theoretical writing, which might attempt to embed analysis of organized crime in a broader theory of criminal organization, is almost nonexistent. Indeed, it is interesting to note that there is little literature on criminal organization at all. The dominant concern of criminological research has been with the individual and his interaction with family, victims, and the agencies of social control. There has been little concern with interaction among criminals outside juvenile gangs.

A substantial, nonscholarly literature, however, contributes significantly to our understanding of organized crime. Some investigative materials of a very detailed nature have been released in the course of trials. Investigators and prosecutors have written a number of memoirs with a great deal of useful description. Some members of organized crime have written, usually with the aid of a reporter, accounts of their careers. The latter two groups of books have to be treated with a great deal of care, given the difficulty of verifying their rather sensational detail. But it may be argued that we can learn as much from these sources as from the published scholarly literature.

A very important limitation of the existing materials is that they deal almost exclusively with the most prominent instance of organized crime, namely, the Mafia. A rather sterile debate concerning the very existence of this group seems to have ended, to be replaced instead by a somewhat more productive one concerning its strength, durability, and uniqueness. Clearly, other groups ought to be called "organized crime," though that already presumes that an agreement on definition can be reached; but we lack here either a scholarly literature or the kind of official and anecdotal literature that has yielded an understanding of the Mafia.

Let me suggest now what we should seek from research on organized crime: a description of what it does and is, an explanation of why it occurs and when and where it does, and a suggestion as to what might be done to control it. The existing literature takes the first task seriously, the second rather lightly, and the third one rhetorically at best.

A review article dealing only with the existing literature would spend most of its time on a colorful but not very helpful set of descriptive studies, for the theoretical literature can be summarized very briefly. In this chapter, I propose to detour from review and synthesis to speculation. An effort will be made to sketch out a theoretical framework for organized crime research. It is not a very tightly specified theory; rather, it is a method for organizing a variety of scattered observations and setting out a possible empirical research agenda that might permit cumulation of knowledge in a systematic fashion.

There is one other preliminary to be noted before describing the outline of this chapter. We restrict the domain of the survey to studies and materials concerned with organized crime in the United States. A modest scholarly literature deals with the same subject in other countries; only in Italy has it been apparently a major area of study, for rather obvious reasons. Two widely cited works, available in English, on the Mafia in Italy are Henner Hess[1] and Anton Blok;[2] the phenomenon they describe has such vastly different origins and setting, being primarily rural and small-town, that it really does seem to require a different research approach. John Mack[3] suggests that this may be true for Europe generally. The available English-language materials simply do not permit generalization.

This chapter begins with a discussion of definition, for there is substantial confusion about what we should label organized crime. Definition ought to lead to theory, but in this instance it is more appropriate to summarize the descriptive material first, for that will provide the reader with a basis for understanding the extraordinary thinness of the existing literature. After a brief foray into problems of data collection, we then turn to theoretical matters. The existing literature is summarized briefly, followed by a rather longer presentation of an alternative approach to the problem. The final section then presents some pessimistic prognostications concerning the future of organized crime research.

DEFINITION

The statute books of this nation contain many definitions of organized crime, distinguished by their variety and inconsistency. The research literature presents relatively few (Howard Abadinsky;[4] Joseph Albini[5]), generally of a descriptive nature. While definitional discussions are inevitably tedious, it is useful to give some bounds to our review by distinguishing those kinds of criminal organization with which we are concerned from those many others with which we are not.

Statutory definitions cover the full range of possible entities. At one extreme, we have that of the state of Mississippi: "Two or more persons conspiring together to commit crimes for profit on a continuing basis."[6] By this definition, two bank robbers who planned and executed robberies together would qualify. While this would constitute an elementary form of criminal organization, it does not seem to describe a very distinctive phenomenon, worthy of particular statutory or investigative attention.

Many states use definitions that emphasize fear, discipline, and corruption. For example, Kansas refers to "a continuing criminal conspiracy organized for power and profit utilizing fear and corruption to obtain immunity from the law." Some become more specific, delineating the likely set of criminal activities of organized crime. For example, Pennsylvania's immunity law says, " 'Organized crime' and 'racketeering' shall include, but not be limited to, conspiracy to commit murder, bribery or extortion, narcotics or dangerous drug violations, prostitution, usury, subordination or perjury and lottery, bookmaking or other forms of organized gambling." Most statutes clearly encompass a much wider variety of entities than those referred to as organized crime outside legal settings. Not all conspiracies to commit perjury or sell LSD meet common perceptions of organized crime.

Organized crime is not an appropriate label to apply to *all* illegal market enterprises, such as brothels and heroin distribution operations. Yet it is often assumed that these enterprises, if of any size, must be under the control of organized crime. It follows that it is appropriate to define larger enterprises themselves as organized crime. Indeed, that is quite explicitly the basis for federal intervention into enforcement against large intrastate gambling operations, embodied in 18 USC 1955. Congress argued that organized crime affected interstate commerce. Any large gambling enterprise (defined as involving five or more persons and operating for thirty days or grossing $2,000 per day in wagers[7]) was presumed to be a part of organized crime. Hence, it was appropriate to give the Department of Justice jurisdiction over such enterprises, even if they did not directly participate in interstate commerce.[8]

This assertion may have been true at the time of the Kefauver Committee hearings on organized crime in 1951[9] or the later McClellan Committee hearings on the same subject.[10] But it is implausible that it was truly universal or timeless. Peter Reuter has argued that there was always a good deal of evidence against the proposition, outside of a few cities where political and police corruption was particularly rife.[11] Nonetheless, it is probably the explanation for many of the statutory definitions adopted by the various states.

The scholar who has most persistently dealt with the issue of definition is Michael Maltz.[12] In his first paper, Maltz focused on acts that might be called organized crime. His later effort reframed the question and asked about attributes of groups that made them organized crime. He identified nine, drawing mostly on the definitions offered by other scholars and institutions: corruption, violence, sophistication, continuity, structure, discipline, multiple enterprises, involvement in legitimate enterprises, and bonding rituals.

This kind of definition, a listing of organizational attributes, is fairly standard. Reuter and Jonathan Rubinstein follow the same path.[13] In their case, the list has five elements: multiple enterprises, durability, hierarchy, nonviolent dispute settlement procedures, and use of violence and/or corruption to protect the criminal enterprises.

One can reasonably ask whether these are definitions or descriptions. No author offers a statement of the method by which the definition is to be developed. Implicitly, all represent listings of those qualities of gangs that have historically been given the label "organized crime" and that seem plausibly to be important to their success in achieving that status; other gangs presumably have tried and failed. Though occasionally it is asserted that the definition is intended for other purposes, it appears that the actual function of the definitions is to provide guidelines for law enforcement agencies.

One justification for this approach is contained in comments by G. Robert Blakey,[14] who, as counsel to Senator McClellan, was the primary author of the 1970 Organized Crime Control Act. He suggests that "organized crime," like "crime" itself, is an essentially political term. We apply it to those entities that permit criminal conspiracy against which we believe it is appropriate to use particularly severe instruments (either investigative or punitive) because of the peculiar dangers that they present to society. Listing the distinctive characteristics of gangs that have posed that threat in the past is then an admissible method for defining the gangs against which we should employ those instruments.

My own preference is to adopt Blakey's suggestion and inquire as to what qualities permit a certain set of gangs to pose a "peculiar threat" to society. The threat is that of coercion, the capacity to force others, criminal and non-criminal, to follow illicit commands without actual physical violence. I call that capacity "reputation" since it arises from the reputation that these gangs have for the control of great violence; whether they actually have such control is, at least in the short run, irrelevant to the efficacy of the threat.

Members of the Mafia have that capacity. The threat of a Mafia member to have a person beaten up, even if that person follows reasonable precautions, or to prevent that person from carrying out normal business transactions is an instantly credible one. Individuals threatened may believe that they can find effective counterforce, but the gang member's threat is one to take seriously. This enables members of the Mafia to undertake what Thomas Schelling[15] suggested may be the central activity of organized crime, namely, extortion. Persons who are not members of gangs with this reputation will find it much more expensive, if possible at all, to force others to carry out their wishes.

Reputation is not a binary quality. It has breadth and power. Breadth refers to the size of the community in which the reputation is held. The Mafia may be the only national organized crime group, since it is the only one whose name is feared throughout the nation. But within particular communities, certainly immigrant ethnic communities in major cities, other gangs may also have this capacity or reputation.

Power refers to how strong the reputation is within those communities in which it is recognized at all. The threats may be completely believed or merely assigned a reasonable probability. Their credibility may be dependent on the existence of competing organized crime groups. If those threatened can find protection with another, more powerful, gang, then we must consider the possibility that a community can have only one organized crime group.

To make the threat of contingent violence fully effective, it is also necessary that those threatened believe that the gang can either corrupt legitimate authority or in some other way ensure that they avoid apprehension. Otherwise, the victim may, if a law-abiding citizen, turn to the police for protection.

This additional element of reputation, for neutralizing law enforcement, enables us to distinguish between organized crime and gangs possessed of what one might call a "bubble" reputation for violence. The latter set of gangs emerges in urban neighborhoods from time to time. They use violence frequently and openly for the purpose of rapidly building up the capacity to extort other members of the community. They tend to be short-lived for precisely that reason, since demonstrative use of violence is most likely to trigger effective police intervention.

Durability may then be a second defining characteristic for organized crime. Durability of a reputation makes it more credible, since it enhances belief in the ability of the gang to withstand either efforts to suppress it or the loss of members from time to time.

For the remainder of this chapter, we shall use this rather parsimonious definition of organized crime: gangs that have maintained a capacity for credible threats of violence over a long period of time. How long a period is obviously a matter of judgment. My own inclination is to stress the ability to handle a generational change of leadership, since that suggests that the gang itself has acquired a value independent of that associated with the reputation of its most prominent member.

DESCRIPTIVE STUDIES

The empirical research literature on organized crime has a very short history. Prior to the work sponsored by the 1967 President's Commission on Law Enforcement and the Administration of Justice, there were only two works of any significance. John Landesco[16] carried out a study of organized crime in Chicago as part of the Illinois Crime Survey. Much praised as that work has been in the last fifteen years, it was essentially unknown until its reissue in 1968. William Foot Whyte[17] carried out a classic participant-observation study of an Italian ghetto in Boston in the late 1930s that also provided a great deal of information about the operation of a higher-level structure of organized crime. That study is generally cited for its observational work rather than its implications concerning organized crime.

The President's Crime Commission published a number of consultant papers that became widely cited and resulted in two books, by Donald Cressey[18] and John Gardiner.[19] This began a continuing, if thin, line of research that has produced five original, book-length studies. A.F.J. Ianni[20] provides a detailed description of the relationships within an Italian organized crime family (whose ties to the Mafia he is unsure of) in New York. William Chambliss[21] carried out fieldwork in Seattle to develop a description of a complex set of relationships among politicians, businessmen, officials, and criminals that he believes deserves the label organized crime. Annelies Anderson[22] used federal agency files to describe the activities of a Mafia family in an unnamed northeastern city. Alan Block[23] provides a history of organized crime in New York, based on a very rich set of investigative agency files. Reuter[24] used police files, informants, and materials seized from gambling operations to provide a description of major illegal markets in New York and the relationship of organized crime to these markets.

There is, as previously suggested, a second literature on organized crime. Where the first is academic, written by university scholars, the other is sensationalistic, written generally by gangsters, journalists, or former law enforcement officials. The difference in motivation is reasonably clear, but the true sources and the final products are surprisingly similar. There is some claim to completeness with respect to the modest academic literature. The sensationalistic literature is, on the other hand, vast; a comprehensive review is neither feasible nor probably desirable. I have selected for inclusion those accounts that seem to me most plausible, a highly subjective test. Perhaps the degree of elaboration and melodrama is the most obvious criterion; I place more faith in the less dramatic and polished expositions, particularly among the large library of gangster autobiographies.[25]

A general point should be mentioned before wading into this material. It deals almost exclusively with the Mafia and a few early ethnic gangs and mostly with Chicago and New York. There are simple explanations for both these observations in the sensationalist literature. The public is intensely aware of the Mafia and not much interested in other groups; there is a ready market for memoirs and derring-do tales about the Mafia and the gangs associated with it in the first thirty years following Prohibition. Chicago and New York, the two largest cities, have also been the center of public fascination; the names of Al Capone and John Gotti are probably as well known in Detroit and Philadelphia as those of Joseph Zerilli and Angelo Bruno, the longtime leaders of the Mafia in those two cities. The research literature, so much derived from law enforcement activity, is also Mafia-oriented, though not so strongly focused on the two cities.

Whatever the explanation, it is clear that the available literatures are far from comprehensive. We have almost nothing on the contemporary non-Mafia gangs that might be organized crime, such as motorcycle gangs in California[26] and the larger drug distribution groups in the Southwest. If in many states there are structures of officials, businessmen, and illicit entrepreneurs such as that described by Chambliss in Washington state, we lack any description of them. What we can learn from the available material is a good deal about the operation of the Mafia in a few big cities. I shall occasionally remind the reader of this fact but shall generally refer to the phenomenon being described as organized crime.

This review is organized around the major descriptive questions:

1. What does organized crime do? In particular, what generates income for members of organized crime?
2. What is the method of recruitment into organized crime?
3. What are the internal relationships of organized crime? In particular, to what extent does formal hierarchy translate into command and control?
4. What are the relationships between organized crime and other participants in the criminal world?
5. What is the relationship of organized crime to legitimate institutions, including government and business?

Activities

There is substantial consensus about the major activities of organized crime: provision of illegal goods and services, such as gambling and narcotics, and the use of capacities for violence and corrupt political power to extort unions and businesses. There is even a good deal of consensus about the particular illegal markets and legitimate industries in which organized crime plays an important role.

Landesco, writing during the Prohibition era, understandably emphasized the importance of the production and distribution of illicit alcohol. But he also provided an interesting history of organized crime involvement in prostitution and illegal gambling of all forms, prior to Prohibition; he also listed a number of industries from which organized crime extorted payments through employer associations and/or unions. Landesco even provided a few financial details, particularly concerning the gambling operations of Mont Tennes, the dominant figure in illicit gambling during the period 1900–20. Those figures, though, show considerable inconsistency[27] and require a contextual interpretation that Landesco did not provide.

Forty years later, Cressey described a similar array of activities, though illicit liquor had disappeared as a major activity. Gambling was now the most important activity. "The profits are huge enough to make understandable the fact that any given member of Cosa Nostra is more likely to be a millionaire than not."[28] Loan-sharking, barely mentioned by Landesco, was now prominent. This is consistent with the view of Mark Haller and John Alviti,[29] who believe that there was little organized extortionate lending by organized crime until the 1930s in Chicago and the 1940s in New York. Cressey also laid more stress on union corruption as the source of control of legitimate industries, where Landesco had seen employers' associations, often formed precisely to resist unionization, as the central source of their power. This probably reflected changes in the powers of unions in the economy generally and, more speculatively, the greater stringency of post–World War II antitrust activity.

Ianni, using contracts with members of a Mafia[30] family in New York, reported numbers banking and loan-sharking as the major illegal market activities. The family had extensive investments in legitimate firms, which seemed to be increasingly important to the family's economic well-being; these firms covered a wide range of industries from travel services to garbage collection. There was little implication that the firms were run in an illegitimate way, though the leading figures in the family were particularly well connected politically. There was no reference to control of corrupt unions.

Block's description of the major activities of organized crime in New York from 1920 to 1950 is also consistent with this. Gambling and prostitution are the enduring illegal market activities, with bootlegging as the dominant activity during Prohibition. From organizing employer associations during the depression, there was a shift to direct union corruption in the post–World War II era; the waterfront provided a particularly significant focus for that activity. It is perhaps of some interest that the narcotics trade receives scant mention.

The most quantitative study is that of Anderson,[31] dealing with a major northeastern city. Using documents provided by a federal law enforcement agency covering the 1960s, she concluded that the two major illegal market activities for the Mafia group in the city were numbers betting and loan-sharking. Narcotics, at that time, was apparently not significant. Of more interest was the apparent lack of involvement of the Mafia family in bookmaking, asserted to be handled by another criminal group. Anderson carefully classified the legitimate businesses in which members of the family had an interest, finding that they were mostly in the retail food and drink sectors, though the largest enterprises were in manufacturing. She did not find any evidence to suggest that corrupt labor unions were a significant source of income.

For smaller cities, we have the work of Chambliss and Gardiner. Chambliss, describing the functions of a rather ill-defined criminal organization in Washington state from 1960 to 1967, found that its major illicit activities were card games and related gambling and prostitution; legitimate businesses were extorted by corrupt police. No mention was made of corrupt labor unions as a source of funds. Gardiner, in reviewing the workings of organized crime in Reading, Pennsylvania, found illicit gambling and the corrupt allocation of government contracts to be the most significant source of revenue. Again, labor racketeering was not mentioned.

The gangster biographies provide the same picture. Joe Valachi, the Mafia member whose testimony in front of the McClellan Committee provided the first public enunciation of what came to be the official view of the Mafia, spent most of his early criminal career involved in burglary and robbery.[32] A typical tough guy, he graduated to control of a few illegal slot machines, given to him by "Lucky" Luciano, when he was about thirty. That industry was terminated by an aggressive New York City administration (Fiorello LaGuardia's), and he then became involved in numbers, bookmaking, and loan-sharking. Never an important figure within his family, Valachi does not seem to have moved beyond a minor role in these illegal market activities, except for the operation of a bar.

Vincent Teresa[33] was a more significant figure, close to the Mafia underboss in Boston. He claims not to have been actually a member but was so intimately involved as to make dubious that claim, necessary perhaps to avoid suspicion of homicide, an alleged condition of membership. His specialty was confidence games (e.g., inducing businessmen to invest in nonexistent schemes), but he was also very active as a loan shark and casino operator or tout.

The most detailed and credible information about Mafia activities comes from two electronic surveillances carried out in New Jersey in the early 1960s. Partial transcripts of these surveillances were released in the course of trial proceedings. The first deals with the activities of a minor New Jersey family headed by Sam De Cavalcante; Henry Zeiger[34] provides a chronological account of these transcripts. The second surveillance was on a New Jersey branch of the powerful Genovese family, headed by Angelo de Carlo; Zeiger[35] contains a set of these transcripts organized by major activities.[36]

In both cases, minor gambling operations occupy a great deal of the time of the leaders of the gangs; neither seems to have much power or to gain large sums from the gambling. Zeiger provides an insightful summary of the material's implications concerning the sources of income: "The men in the higher echelons of organized crime served principally as brokers between those who actually conducted illegal transactions and the cops and politicians who stayed out of their way."[37] De Carlo was active as principal of a loan-sharking operation; his involvement in the killing of a loan shark victim led to the trial that triggered the release of the documents. De Cavalcante's main illegal interest seems to be various forms of illegal gambling. But it is noteworthy that some members are said to be unable to make a living with these traditional illegal market activities and have been forced to undertake riskier activities, such as safecracking.[38]

It is difficult to draw very definite conclusions from this material. Illegal gambling is prominent in all accounts of the money-making activities of organized crime, but the more recent sources suggest that it may not be a major source of income. Narcotics and loan-sharking are also frequently mentioned, but it seems likely that not all members even of the Mafia have significant involvement with these activities.

There is similar confusion with respect to the legitimate business interests of organized crime. Landesco and Ianni make clear that members of organized crime have had extensive legitimate business enterprises since powerful gangs first formed. But where some, such as Anderson, see these as essentially passive investments, others, such as Cressey and Block, view them as adjuncts to their control of various union activities.

Recruitment

The methods by which gangs maintain themselves, namely, the selection of new members, are obviously critical for entities whose powers are so dependent on continuity. Most of the available studies provide no information on selection. The few that do provide sharply contrasting views. The anecdotal literature adds only slightly to our knowledge.

Cressey and Ianni provide the extreme accounts. Cressey stresses formal recruitment procedures:

Some recruits are deliberately sought out and trained on the assumption, implicit or explicit, that without the induction of youngsters the organization will founder. Other recruits, usually mature college graduates, are sought out because they possess the expert skills needed for modern large-scale business operations.[39]

He goes on to approvingly quote Raymond Martin,[40] who has an even more formalistic notion of the recruitment process, at least in Brooklyn:

From a safe distance the mob instructors observe the operation (of a burglary) and prepare for a subsequent critique of the job. . . . A team that shows capacity for avoiding trouble is eventually allowed to operate on its own, though it must still get mob clearance on each job. Frightened kids are weeded out, tougher ones move closer to the day when they join the syndicate and achieve the good life.[41]

Within the Lupollo family, Ianni saw two different types of recruitment. The first was operative within the extended blood family. Many eligible family members self-selected out of family operations, choosing more respectable occupations or organizations or moving out of the New York area altogether. Others were offered minor positions and moved up if they performed well. At the lower level of the organization, recruitment was from a much broader pool, namely, youths in neighborhood gangs. Some fulfilled minor tasks that were offered to them; others showed a lack of judgment that disqualified them for further opportunities. But Ianni is clear that recruitment is not into some formal family; that is restricted to relatives by blood or marriage.

Teresa provides only one detail about recruitment, an oft-asserted claim that initiation into the Mafia requires that the person have committed a murder. I think it important in this respect to note the value to the organization arising from such a belief. First, it establishes the toughness of the organization, and, second, it suggests that, since other members must know about the murder, the individual member has to be cautious about being an informant, since he exposes himself to a charge for which there is no statute of limitations.

That does not enable us to determine whether the claim is true. Given the number of different gangs in the Mafia (twenty-four) and the difficulty of effective central administration, it seems most plausible to assume that there is variation over time and gangs. Some component gangs may have imposed this requirement for membership during some periods. Others probably did not.

Recruitment is clearly restricted by location and, for the most part, ethnicity. There seems to be no mention of any intercity mobility at the point of entry in recent years. There has been movement of established members from older cities to newer ones. For example, Joe Bonanno, a leading figure in the New York Mafia in the early 1960s, moved to Tucson in 1966, as Capone moved from New York to Chicago in 1919. But initial recruitment appears to be only among the local toughs.

In discussing recruitment, we are handicapped by a lack of knowledge concerning leaders' incentives for expanding gang membership. Subject to a concern about loyalty, surely gang leaders want larger rather than smaller gangs. Yet it has been credibly asserted (e.g., Ralph Salerno and John Tompkins[42]) that the Mafia has prohibited the constituent gangs from adding to their membership from time to time. The explanation offered by Cressey is that this was required to ensure that no one gang became so powerful as to threaten the others. If so, it is a curiously inefficient rule. Allowing each gang the same rate of growth would surely accomplish the same purpose and at the same time permit the growth of the Mafia's powers generally.

It might be argued that individual gang leaders dilute the prestige of membership if they make it too freely available. The difficulty of entry might spur competition among candidates, in terms of both performance and the amounts they are willing to pay their superiors in order to remain members. However, there is nothing to suggest that such competition exists either at or after the point of entry.

Internal Relationships

Such controversy as exists in the literature on organized crime concerns the appropriate organizational analogy to apply to organized crime, at least in the case of the Mafia. Cressey uses a corporate analogy, though his hierarchy and command/control mechanisms are far more rigid than is the case in most legitimate corporations. At the other extreme lies Ianni's model, in which the gang is an extension of complex family ties, and the organizational values are the opposite of bureaucratic.

Ianni is able to present fairly compelling evidence for his proposition within the context of the Lupollo (pseudonymous) family. The blood ties between senior members of the gang are strong, and there is clearly an expectation that leadership within the gang will remain within the small set of families that founded the gang. Incidents of conflict are resolved within the framework of family relationships. Ianni points to the extremely complex set of intermarriages within and between Mafia gangs to suggest the centrality of clanship generally.

Cressey again presents a very different picture of relations within the hierarchy of the Mafia. He refers to a posture of silent awe and unthinking acceptance that permits the leaders of criminal organizations to trust their subordinates and to ensure that these subordinates are willing to incur substantial penalties on behalf of the organization. He ascribes bureaucratic procedures to the families. Though Cressey is careful to allow that the organization, like that of a corporation, does not work perfectly, he does attribute to it an unusual degree of success in maintaining discipline. Rule infractions are asserted to be punished severely and hence to be few.

Teresa, describing the New England Mafia gang run by Raymond Patriarca, gives no emphasis to family relationships within the gang. Many members, including Teresa himself, come from families with many males involved in crime (Teresa's uncle was a small-time swindler), but their membership and status seem dependent on their individual performance rather than any ascribed characteristics. This is consistent with the account of Barboza[43] concerning the same gang. Teresa asserts that the hierarchy of control is absolute within the gang; indeed, he ascribes his own reluctance to join the gang to his unwillingness to accept such control.

Anderson analyzes the De Cavalcante tapes with respect to the internal relations of the Mafia. She concludes that the transcripts "do not support statements about organized crime that it is totalitarian in organization, that its structure is as complex as that of any large corporation, or that its laws are more rigidly enforced than those of legitimate governments."[44] This sentence refers to a set of assertions by the President's Commission on Law Enforcement and the Administration of Justice.[45] On the other hand, the transcripts do indicate a set of well-defined functional roles and a capacity for higher-level discipline.

One distinctive characteristic of the Mafia, as compared with any other set of gangs about which we have information, is that there is an established mechanism for dealing with intergang difficulties. The exact power of the national commission, a group of family leaders from various cities, is a matter of controversy. Cressey attributes considerable powers to it; Anderson suggests that it serves only to deal with matters that cause interfamily dispute, relatively rare events. But it appears to have intervened successfully in a number of such matters.

Relationships with Other Criminals

The ability of members of organized crime to coerce other criminals is the most distinctive asset acquired through membership. In theory, it should add to members' earning power and enable them to control certain activities.

The official view is that members of organized crime control illegal markets—that operators in such markets either are agents for organized crime or pay some rent for the right to operate. For example, the Department of Justice stated in 1976 that "it is convinced that illegal gambling operations are under the control of organized crime."[46] Cressey made the same claim with respect to a variety of illegal markets in the late 1960s.

The little research that has been done on illegal markets contradicts this view. Anderson finds no evidence that the Mafia family she studied had any control over the markets in which they participated. Block, in describing the events surrounding the entry of "Dutch" Schultz into the black numbers business in Manhattan, finds documentary evidence in Dewey's files that Schultz, a prominent white bootlegger, was unable to coerce the numbers operators into accepting terms more favorable to him. He was able to play an important role in the business because of superior police protection and access to capital, but his power was restricted to preventing other high-level bankers from entering the market.

Reuter and Rubinstein report details of the operation of three markets in New York: numbers, loan-sharking, and bookmaking. In each case, they find significant evidence of competition and nothing to suggest that organized crime is able to restrict entry or tax all operators. The evidence is clearest for bookmaking, where efforts to form a cartel have been unsuccessful.

The evidence from the de Cavalcante and de Carlo tapes also points to the limited powers that Mafia members have over other criminals.

All this merely points to the limits of power. It does not mean that member-ship does not provide organized crime members with some ability to intimidate others. But not all will be intimidated, and even those who are will resist some gross demands.

Relationship with Government

The ability to corrupt government, in particular, law enforcement agencies, is arguably as important for organized crime as the ability to intimidate. The belief that complaint is useless lowers the probability that victims of intimidation will attempt to resist. The major illegal markets of previous eras, bootlegging, pros-titution, and certain forms of gambling, all share the characteristic that they are difficult to conceal, so that efficient operation required the co-option of whole agencies. Whyte provides a particularly thorough description of the workings of such corruption; Reuter[47] analyzes the consequences of this for the relationship between organized crime and gambling in the period 1930 to 1970.

There is evidence that at times organized crime has been a central influence in the politics of major cities. Most notorious is Chicago during Prohibition. For example, in 1927, Capone supported a candidate in the suburban town of Cicero, other bootlegging groups supporting the rival candidate. A great deal of violence marked the election, in which Capone's candidate won. The result was control of vice in the town, which became a center for such traffic in the Chicago area.

Gardiner found that the "Stern" gang was a major figure in the politics of Reading. In this case, the gang itself became a major issue, with some elections being fought around reform, that is, the removal of the gang. However, in most cases, the gang was able to come to terms with the reform administration.

In recent years, the evidence that organized crime has significant political power has been scant. Block and Chambliss[48] infer such power from the con-tinued success of various organized crime groups, but this is an appeal to our intuition rather than a showing of cause and effect.

The only known organized crime figure to maintain political visibility in re-cent years has been Anthony Scotto, reputedly a member of the Gambino family, who was a prominent figure in New York politics until his conviction on rack-eteering charges in 1980. Block notes that his character witnesses at his trial included two former mayors of New York as well as the secretary-treasurer of the American Federation of Labor and Congress of Industrial Organizations (AFL-CIO). Scotto's political connections were undoubtedly an important sources of his power to extort on the waterfront.

Scotto appears to be an isolated figure. In recent years, the numerous trials of major Mafia figures, such as Frank Tieri, Carmine Galante, Jack Brooklier, and Antonio Corallo, have been notable for the lack of any evidence that these men had any particular capacity to reach high government officials for protec-tion. Though it is clear that corruption of police is still an important factor in the operation of various illegal market enterprises, there is nothing to suggest that organized crime has, as in the past, gained control of police agencies so as to provide themselves with a tool for the extortion of other operators. This, of course, contrasts sharply with the situation that seems to have existed at the time of the Kefauver Committee's deliberations.[49]

This absence of evidence for centralized corruption at the local level is quite striking, for it hits at the basis for federal intervention into organized crime control, a process that began in the 1960s and expanded in the 1970s. That effort, as described by Blakey,[50] asserted, not unreasonably, that local government had shown a propensity to corruption that required a higher level of government to intervene.

Getting Data

The barriers to empirical research in this area are obviously very substantial and do a great deal to explain the limited accomplishments. It is not likely that much can be done to reduce them in the near future.

The paucity of data on organized crime has been the subject of comment before. John Galliher and James Cain analyzed the sources cited in twenty criminology textbooks written over the previous two decades. They conclude that "authors of criminology textbooks have purveyed the common belief in the conspiratorial threat by organized crime usually without indicating the limitations of their sources."[51] Their explanation for this was simple: "Since social scientists have largely limited themselves to secondary sources of data, particularly government documents, in their analysis of organized crime, they could not be expected to give an independent challenge to such sources."[52]

Perhaps the most fundamental problem is that organized crime is not an activity but a structure. Official agencies that have devoted a good deal of effort to improving their measures of the extent of particular criminal activities can scarcely be faulted for having less systematic data on such a nebulous concept as structure. A similar point is made by Cressey.[53] Nor, indeed, is there any obvious meaning to the notion of the "amount" of organized crime, precisely because it is a structure.

Agencies do keep files on the behavior of individuals in certain groups that they have labeled organized crime. Precisely because these files report on *individual* behavior, and even members of organized crime do a great deal that is not necessarily part of their role as members, they provide unsystematic data on organized crime itself. Moreover, there is a great deal of question as to whether the agencies have much knowledge of organized crime outside of a few well-known groups, mostly the Mafia, and a few activities by those groups. Intelligence follows, rather than leads, strategy in this area.

Nonetheless, there may well be a great deal of relevant information scattered in the files of official agencies, though much intelligence information is not recorded.[54] But access even to that imperfect information is exceedingly hard to obtain. Much of the interesting material concerns events that did not trigger official action, in particular, arrest. It is almost invariably protected from public scrutiny by state privacy acts. The researcher is unlikely to be able to make a request for the data in such a way as to obtain that information unless someone within the agency has already provided a good guide to where it is and what form it takes. Cressey seems to have had considerable access to the Federal Bureau of Investigation's (FBI) materials; he was in the unique position of being a consultant to a very prestigious presidential commission. Others have had little access.

Of course, official files are not the only possible source of data. Field research has contributed a great deal in the study of organized crime. Official agency records and fieldwork involve very different trade-offs between breadth and depth. Official records, except for wiretaps, tend to be very synoptic; a little detail is provided about many activities. Fieldwork provides the opposite mix; the researcher obtains a great deal of information about certain matters and perhaps none about others.

The work of Ianni and Anderson presents the contrast nicely. Ianni gives a great deal of information about internal relationships and about the licit and less opprobrious of the Lupollo illegal activities. However, he has little to say about their more serious illegal activities. It is implausible that the family had no involvement in heroin distribution or the use of violence for discipline and competition. It is understandable, in dealing with a respectable observer such as Ianni, that these activities might get little mention. The result is that our picture of the Lupollo family activities and style is very partial.

Anderson's work presents the other extreme. It appears that she relied almost entirely on records made available to her by a federal law enforcement agency. She had access to no informant herself and made only one field trip to the city itself, where she observed some of the legitimate businesses. Her analysis reflects this. She is most comfortable dealing with the kind of issue for which detail is either not essential or is readily obtained, like the industrial classification of businesses in which the agency knew of family member interests or the size of numbers banks (probably raided by a law enforcement agency). The internal relationships, about which law enforcement records contain little, were not discussed. There is correspondingly a very distant feeling to her description; one has little sense of what the gang members do with themselves.

A major problem in all the empirical studies is the credibility of sources. The nature of the subject matter inevitably leads the researcher to rely on private information, whose source can be only very roughly described and certainly not verified by anyone else. The reader can only rely on his own intuition, perhaps reflecting the consistency of the level of detail offered, to evaluate the veracity of the sources used by each researcher.

Similar comments can be made about Cressey's comments on the scale of the Mafia's activities. How can he know that any given member of the Mafia is more likely to be a millionaire than not unless he or his sources conduct a systematic analysis of financial statements, which are very unlikely to be available? The statement is certainly plausible, but it is highly speculative and requires a careful description of its source to have any credibility.

THEORY—SO TO SPEAK

The theoretical literature is slight, both in quantity and quality. Most of the contributions seem to be the result of a few days' musing, perhaps spurred by a particularly interesting newspaper series on organized crime activity or a conference invitation to consider a novel topic. None have exerted any noticeable influence on empirical research.

The most cited article is that of Schelling, sponsored by the 1967 Crime Commission. Schelling focused on why some criminal activities lent themselves to organization and others not. He suggested that, at least for illegal markets, the principles of economics developed to explain the organization of legal markets would apply here also. Beyond that he made two important observations. First, it was plausible that organized crime was not so much the provider of illegal goods and services as an extortionist of providers. The source of their extortionate power could be any one of a number of factors; their control of corrupt police in some cities, such as Miami in the 1940s, was simply one possible source. Second, where extortion could be made into a uniform tax, as with raising the price of a purchased input such as laundry services, the subjects of the extortion were not likely to be very adversely affected, since they could pass the tax on to the final customers.

James Buchanan[55] and Paul Rubin[56] have further developed an economic approach to the sources and consequences of organized crime, treated as a monopolist in illegal markets. Buchanan pointed to the fact that monopolists raised prices and lowered output; in the production of a prohibited good, that was surely a socially desirable outcome. He then presented some arguments concerning the social costs of organized crime that might counteract this effect, finding none of them persuasive. For example, he considered the argument that criminal monopolists, perhaps tapping economies of scale, are able to produce a given output more cheaply. At first sight this would seem to be undesirable, yielding higher profits to the criminal world. But Buchanan argued that this also implied that more resources were freed for noncriminal uses, a desirable outcome.

This is, characteristic of an economist, a highly schematized, indeed skeletal, account. Consequences of criminal monopoly not considered by Buchanan seem to constitute more powerful arguments against it. For example, criminal monopoly may provide concentrations of capital that enable the more efficient execution of other criminal acts, such as the corruption of city administration. Given the imperfections of illegal capital markets, that is, the difficulty of borrowing funds at a competitive rate of return, only market monopolies permit the aggregation of large pools of capital. At a minimum, one could say that Buchanan ignored any dynamic effects arising from criminal monopoly.

Rubin concerned himself with the sources of criminal monopoly. He suggested that three were likely to be important: risk pooling, internalizing the costs of violence, and increasing returns to corruption expenditures. Risk pooling was likely to be most important for gambling, where the larger the number of bets taken by an individual operator, the lower the uncertainty faced. The argument about violence was more general and had already been noted by Schelling: a monopolist would take into account police response to an act of violence. If one assumed that acts of violence in a particular market led to increased enforcement against that market, this made the monopolist more efficient than a group of small businesses, none of which would bear a large share of the increased cost of enforcement.[57] The arguments concerning corruption were also perfectly general: an official bribed to ignore one act would charge less to ignore a second. Rubin also suggested that it could lead to multimarket monopolies; the official who accepted a bribe from a gambling operator would also have a lower price for overlooking a drug violation.

The last of the economic analyses of organized crime is that of Jurgen Backhaus,[58] extending arguments of Buchanan. Backhaus focused on the issue of contractual uncertainty in markets without court enforceable contracts. He suggested that organized crime was a device for providing contractual insurance for which it was likely that there were economies of scale since such insurance had a large fixed cost element in it. He also enunciated a dynamic argument about the costs of criminal monopoly: monopoly profits provided the capital for larger criminal ventures that otherwise could not obtain external finance.

Somewhat along the same lines are the arguments of Reuter[59] concerning dispute settlement in illegal markets. He suggests that the participants in illegal markets are motivated to seek third-party settlement of disputes that arise in criminal commerce, the courts being unavailable for such disputes. To use violence, another alternative, would be to acquire a reputation as a dangerous transactor, thus reducing the set of customers, suppliers, and agents willing to enter into commercial relations. The gang with the strongest reputation for command of contingent violence (the capacity to deliver violence against someone who fails to perform a particular act) will be the low-cost provider of such settlement services. The Mafia seem to be the sole provider of dispute settlement services in New York, and it is plausible that they are the gang with the strongest reputation. However, it is argued that the control of the dispute settlement market does not provide a base for extorting the underlying illegal markets since it is possible, by adopting cautious routines in choice of transacting partners, to minimize use of the service.

Economists have generally associated organized crime with criminal monopoly. The implicit argument is that there must be some element of market power for any factor of production, including management or organization itself, to earn incomes persistently greater than could be earned in other activities. It seems to be believed that members of organized crime earn much larger incomes than other criminals with comparable skills. If that is the case, then we must find the source of market power and the market that permit this.

Oddly enough, criminologists share this market-oriented view. A fairly standard textbook statement is that of Gresham Sykes: "The existence of a strong and persistent demand for such illegal goods and services as illicit sex, drugs, and gambling presents an opportunity to make enormous profits. The cost of providing such goods and services is low, and the price can be set high by those able and willing to circumvent the law in the creation of a monopoly based on the intimidation of small operators and competitors. It is this situation that allows organized crime to flourish in the United States in an illegal parody of American business enterprise."[60]

Sykes assumes that the cost of establishing a monopoly based on violence (more accurately, intimidation) is small.[61] It is not, in fact, clear that this is so for many illegal markets. There is, for example, no evidence that any component of the marijuana market, the second largest illegal market by official accounts, is subject to monopoly control.[62] It may well be that mass illegal markets are a necessary precondition for the development of organized crime but that is not to say that all such markets are controlled by organized crime.

The most famous sociological essay on the sources of American organized crime is that of Daniel Bell, written in response to the Kefauver Committee. In a phrase that has been quoted many times, Bell referred to organized crime as providing the "queer ladder of social mobility" in America. He argued that for the Italian immigrants who arrived in major American cities in the first quarter of this century, the legitimate paths to success were blocked. City administration, particularly the police and the church, were dominated by other ethnic groups, concerned to keep the new group out. Gangs provided both the path for individual accumulation and the instrument by which urban Italians could acquire political and economic power in those cities.

The theory may have some historical validity but leaves unanswered the current question of most interest, namely, the continued dominance of Italians in organized crime. Bell predicted that, in fact, the Italian community would in succeeding generations find new paths to success, and it obviously is true that the Mafia members are a trivial fraction of the Italian-descent male community in this nation. But it is not clear, despite Ianni's prognostications, that there has been significant progression by newer immigrant groups. They may have acquired more control of their own illegal market enterprises, but that could be seen as a return to the condition that apparently existed prior to about 1930. Certainly there is little to suggest that they have acquired the more general criminal powers of the Mafia.

The thinness of the theoretical literature is, I speculate, a consequence of the murkiness of the existing descriptive work. It is simply not clear what one should be theorizing about. Economists focus on markets, which they are trained to analyze. An anthropologist such as Ianni focuses on organized crime not as a market phenomenon but as a cultural response to certain social, political, and economic conditions. A sociologist such as Bell views it as a source of social mobility.

It is probably possible to create unified theory that encompasses all these elements. No one has done so. I believe that the task is not likely to be a productive one, for these may well be theories about different phenomena. But the simple truth is that the contributions are of such a scattered nature, and the researchers are so briefly involved in the subject that it is scarcely surprising that what we have presently is a patchwork of ideas, only loosely related to each other and having little consequence for empirical research.

Theory: An Alternative

I now sketch the outline of a theory of organized crime; only the outline exists. Its purpose is to suggest the possibility of a research program, both conceptual and empirical, for the study of organized crime. As such, it is intended to have operational content and permit testing.

First I should state what it is a theory *of*. It attempts to explain under what circumstances some gangs acquire the defining characteristic of organized crime, namely, broad and durable reputation, and to determine the consequences of the existence of such gangs. As such, it could attempt to be completely general in time and space. Realistically, given that it is based only on a knowledge of the literature concerning the phenomenon in twentieth-century urban America, it should be assumed to have at least those limitations.

We begin with the notion that the adult gang is an efficient method for executing certain kinds of criminal transactions. Such gangs are assumed to differ from juvenile gangs in that the basic motivation for their formation is not expressive.[63] Juvenile gangs may commit many crimes for profit, but that is not their prime purpose. The adult gang is seen as predominantly instrumental, a means to better one's economic situation, and only secondarily expressive. A gang is efficient for some transactions (e.g., extortion) and not for others (e.g., mugging).

We further assume that, in large American cities, there always exist adult criminal gangs. Whether they acquire the distinctive capabilities of organized crime is determined by both demand and supply conditions. By demand conditions we mean the extent of a demand for the kinds of services that only organized crime can offer, such as dispute settlement and mediation with hostile, dominant political authority. By supply conditions, we mean those factors that facilitate the acquisition of the distinctive capabilities. The distinction is not always clear; we shall illustrate the problem after consideration of some candidate variables.

The first issue is to develop an operational measure for the existence and extent of organized crime. The defining characteristics—durability and reputation—suggest the possibility of measurement. Durability might be determined by identification of a generational change in leadership without loss of continuity. This is a fairly stringent test; if the American Mafia can be said to have originated with the gangs of Prohibition, many of the individual gangs had the same leadership for thirty or even forty years. For example, Frank Costello was a prominent figure by the late 1920s and was still active into the 1960s, though not actually the leader of his family at the end. But some indicator of durability can be developed, using newspaper and/or police reports; in this matter they are often the same documents.

Reputation is an extrinsic variable. It is a knowledge of the existence and a belief in the powers of the gang held by others. Newspaper reports are certainly one possible measure; for example, one could use the frequency with which a newspaper reports certain kinds of criminal acts by the gang. One might even consider using the number of times that the district attorney announces each year the beginning of the end for the gang.

Community is, of course, not coterminous with media market. A more direct measure is a survey of residents of the relevant community, also to determine knowledge and perceptions about the gang. Names of the gang leaders as well as the gang itself might be presented for recognition and for ascription of powers. Gardiner was able to describe community knowledge of the workings of the "Stern" syndicate in Reading, Pennsylvania, through such a survey.

These are clearly very rough measures of reputation. Defining the relevant community is not a simple matter. In a city as large and heterogeneous as Los Angeles, for example, we might allow that reputation could be specific to a particular population within it. There might well be durable, powerful gangs whose reputations are confined to the more than 1 million Hispanics and unknown by any of the other major population groups.

Now let us turn to identification of the factors that affect the extent of organized crime. We begin by listing some sets of variables, together with a brief discussion of how they impact on organized crime. The description of each variable is intentionally discursive, since many subvariables are potential candidates.

1. Illegal market opportunities. Illegal markets, such as gambling, narcotics distribution, and loan-sharking, require the existence of enterprises, or coordinated, ongoing groups of individuals involved in frequent interactions with each other. Such groups will require and may themselves generate gangs that can provide certain services that facilitate commerce in the absence of state-protected contracts and property rights.

The enterprises themselves are not necessarily organized crime. Durability and reputation may provide no advantage to a bookmaker, though they ease debt collection somewhat. A bookmaker may find it more efficient to purchase debt collection services in the market rather than to invest in development of these resources himself. But the demand from illegal markets for various kinds of services most efficiently provided by organized crime is likely to be a major factor in the development of organized crime.

Illegal markets differ in the extent of their demand for these services. The frequency of interactions among the enterprises in the market may be highly significant. Bookmakers have frequent dealings with each other, which may generate a demand for dispute settlement services. Heroin dealers, concerned about revelation of their participation in the market, may deal with only a very small number of other dealers, thus having little need for organized crime services. It may be necessary to break down illegal market activities into some broad groups, according to such characteristics.

It is a difficult task to provide a measure of the size of individual illegal markets within a community. For gambling and certain drugs in wide use, there are some crude measures available through household surveys. For other activities, such as loan-sharking and the fencing of stolen goods, a survey is not likely to provide even a crude measure, simply because such a small percentage of the general population participates. Reliance on police knowledge in these matters is often a questionable practice.

2. *The extent of recent migration of important ethnic groups within the community.* The historical record strongly suggests, as does casual theorizing, that newer ethnic groups with weak ties to the dominant political culture of the city provide the base for organized crime.[64] There are at least two senses in which this statement appears to be true. First, young males are more likely to find other avenues of economic progress blocked in such communities. Gangs have a broader base of recruitment as a result, including some individuals of talent. Second, the community is more likely to be supportive of at least some gang activities. The historical record points to organized crime's providing critical links to the political system in at least some of these ethnic communities. Haller suggests that during the period 1880 to 1905 "gambling syndicates *were* the local political organization."[65]

Recent migration is important since there is a history of upward mobility in ethnic communities. The constant flow of young males from poorer regions of Italy has certainly been critical in providing a continuing base for Mafia recruitment, since so much of the second- and third-generation Italian migrant community has moved out of the concentrated urban ghettos, such as Little Italy in New York and the North End in Boston, over the last quarter century. The diminution of such flows from Eastern Europe after 1950 may be important in accounting for the decline of the Jewish gangs in New York and Chicago.[66]

3. *The strength and corruptness of local political authority.* A uniquely powerful instrument for organized crime is availability of powerful, corrupt political authority at the local (occasionally, state) level. Chicago's dismal record with respect to organized crime corresponds also to a long history of machine control of the city. The repetitive scandals revealing relationships between senior gangsters and major party figures are the direct indicators of the source of the problem.

The focus on local political authority is arguable. Some aspects of organized crime power clearly go to national politics, most notably, labor racketeering. The power of the Mafia over the leadership of the Teamsters' union, as well as the laborers and restaurant workers' unions, is the most obvious and important expression of this. But it can be argued that this is simply the agglomeration of local gang powers. The cities from which the leadership of the Teamsters has come are indicative of this: Detroit (James Hoffa and James Fitzsimmons), Chicago (Gus Williams), and Cleveland (Jackie Presser). The capacity of local gangs, member groups of the Mafia, to control the locals in those cities provides the basis for the power of the set of gangs collectively over the national union.[67]

It may also be argued that the growth of recent groups, such as the prison gangs in California and the motorcycle gangs in the Southwest, points to the lack of need for corrupt political authority for the acquisition of durable power. Though these gangs may have acquired some political power in small communities, this is clearly not the basis for their power in general. But it should be noted here that we are not identifying the necessary conditions for the existence of organized crime, merely the conditions that promote its growth.

Undoubtedly, many other variables may have some influence. If economic opportunity is important, then time and location indicators of employment should obviously be included. But I am inclined to stress long-term characteristics of community; cyclical fluctuations, except for the depression, are unlikely to make a great difference to the recruitment or criminal opportunity patterns of gangs.

The three major sets of variables we have identified are not independent of each other. Political authority is affected, in many dimensions, by the flow of new immigrants into the community. The same can be said for the scale of illegal markets; new immigrants often bring their own peculiar vices (such as distinctive forms of gambling) with them.[68] Nor is it clear that these variables are unaffected by organized crime. It could be argued that the power of organized crime affects the scale of illegal markets, the extent of new immigration of the same ethnic groups, and the extent of corruption and centralization of political power. However, I believe that the links in those directions are very weak relative to those going in the other direction.

This discussion has focused on the conditions that bring about organized crime. We have so far said nothing about how organized crime uses its powers. What will members of organized crime do as a consequence of their membership that they would not do as members of some other gang? Presumably, they will make use of the unique capacity that membership provides for extortion and intimidation.

In legal markets, that turns out to be a powerful hypothesis. The capacity to intimidate provides an important asset for the organization of cartels involving large numbers of firms. Reuter[69] illustrates this, using material concerning the solid waste collection market in New York City. He argues that the power to make credible threats of continuing violence, supported by a historically corrupt union, permits members of organized crime to organize a customer allocation agreement with over 300 member firms. Defection from the cartel rule is minimized by the threat of physical retaliation, thus solving the problem traditionally faced by large cartels.[70] This seems also to be the role that organized crime played in a variety of industries during the depression.

Cartel organization is by no means the only method for using reputation, even in legal industries. Many businesses are susceptible to threats of various kinds. Any bar can be closed because of a few fights within in, leading to license authority sanction. Small stores generally may be willing to make modest payments to ensure that there is no physical damage to their premises. Certainly, police officers routinely comment on the fact that otherwise law-abiding store owners make such payments rather than bring complaints because they doubt the credibility of police promises to ensure that no damage is inflicted. We may treat this as generalized extortion, separate from the more widely reported extortion related to corrupt control of a union.

In illegal markets, we have already mentioned Schelling's hypothesis that organized crime serves to tax (extort) entrepreneurs providing goods and services. But it can also be argued that organized crime provides services as well; dispute settlement is the most obvious, or at least best explored, of these services. The stability of organized crime groups may also enable them to accumulate capital, though it is unlikely that capital is ever jointly owned; these are highly individualistic enterprises. The gang probably serves as a network, too; one may go to organized crime members when looking for a specialist capable of performing particular services, knowing that most underworld figures come into contact with organized crime.

Finding a method for estimating the importance of these hypothesized effects is obviously exceedingly difficult. There are apparently countervailing effects of increased organized crime activity, for example, on the price of bookmaking. If organized crime extorts bookmakers, then we would expect to find a higher price, ceteris paribus, for bookmaking services in cities with stronger organized crime. However, if organized crime sells services, such as dispute settlement and debt collection, that reduce uncertainty for bookmakers, then its existence may lower the price. Indeed, there could be both elements present in the same market, with ambiguous net effect on the price.

Implicit in these speculations is the hypothesis that organized crime performs the same functions in different settings, except as there are differences in the set of opportunities, exogenously determined. That is not obviously true. The vision and talent of the gang leader can lead to important differences in the gang's scope and performance. For example, Teresa comments on perceived differences among Mafia families: while the Detroit family is ''a very solid close group and very dedicated to old man Joe Zerilli,'' he observes that ''Chicago is an eat-'em-up-alive outfit . . . they don't give a damn who gets it in the back.'' The sources and consequences of these differences remain to be explored.

As stated in the beginning of this section, this is merely the sketch of a theory. It will be successful not to the extent that any of the hypotheses or suggested measurements turn out to be correct, but inasmuch as it persuades readers of the need (and possibility) to move beyond descriptive studies of actual organizations and embed empirical research in a broader theoretical framework.

CONCLUSION AND PROGNOSIS

The accomplishments of research on organized crime to date have clearly been meager. Few have ventured into the area, fewer have persisted, and not very much useful knowledge has been accumulated. Unfortunately, there is little reason to believe that the future prospects are any brighter.

The explanations for the failure of research in this area have already been alluded to at various points. Most important has been the difficulty of obtaining good-quality data on any of the important characteristics of organized crime. The major studies have mostly involved extended fieldwork, usually arising from unique opportunities not under the control of the researcher. The supply of researchers willing to engage in the time-consuming and potentially somewhat hazardous endeavors involved in acquiring such data is understandably limited. Given the lack of data, it is also understandable that there is little theoretical writing on the subject, for it is not clear about what one should, indeed, be theorizing.

One factor that might lead to increased research activity in this area is the perception that organized crime is becoming a more serious social problem. Given the lack of any agreed upon measure of the extent of organized crime, it is obviously difficult to make that determination. Here I suggest a few indicators that seem relevant but that are not easily knit together into a single measure of the direction of change.

The Department of Justice is devoting increased resources to its organized crime control programs. There has also been a substantial increase in organized crime enforcement programs of other agencies, such as the Drug Enforcement Administration and the Labor Department. We have no data on state and local programs, but, impressionistically, these have not been a significant share of total expenditures on organized crime control for at least a decade.

The Department of Justice has reported significant successes in its continuing efforts against the Mafia. In New York, Chicago, Cleveland, Kansas City, and a number of other cities, the department has obtained convictions against the leading figures in the Mafia families, often with long sentences. While there are no claims of final victory, official claims that the Mafia may be less capable of carrying out its wishes seem to have some credibility.

With respect to other organized crime groups, such statements cannot be made. Impressionistically, little seems to have happened to the leadership of the major motorcycle gangs. Whether the successful drug gangs in the Colombian and Mexican communities will shortly expand into other spheres of criminal activity and thus start to acquire the characteristics of organized crime groups is simply indeterminable.

It is difficult to find any evidence that the problem is becoming more serious.

This suggests that there is unlikely to be a surge of research on organized crime. In addition, criminology is becoming increasingly quantitative. The methodologically ambitious are unlikely to find organized crime an interesting area to explore. While the field of organizational studies continues to grow, none of its exponents have made a serious foray into the study of criminal organization. Given the difficulties of obtaining detailed and credible data, this is understandable.

Is there any reason to care much about the dismal prospects for organized crime research? My own view is that the phenomenon was far more important three decades ago than it is now. In terms of social problems, it now deserves a rather meager share of the research attention devoted to crime and justice. On the other hand, it is a social phenomenon of great intellectual interest. We may be able to give plausible, casual accounts of its decline (improved social conditions for most migrant groups, less political corruption, more professional and overlapping policing), but the centrality of large-scale criminal organizations in the politics of many American cities during the first half of this century is not something for which we have even first-order accounts.

There is, moreover, the continued love affair that the American people have conducted with organized crime. The great attention devoted in England to the Krays, a family of moderately successful vice entrepreneurs in London, is suggestive of a more general public fascination with this kind of crime.[71] It is not uncharitable to suggest that a major reason to study organized crime is precisely to show how limited and specific are its powers. While the mass market publishers continue to turn out such highly dramatized accounts as that of Ovid Demaris[72] and the president refers to "a syndicate of organized criminals whose power is now reaching unparalleled heights," as well as asserting that "today the power of organized crime reaches into every segment of our society,"[73] a modest scholarly effort to demonstrate the more sober realities seems worthwhile. If it is also methodologically sound, so much the better.

NOTES

1. Henner Hess, *Mafia and Mafiosi: The Structure of Power* (Lexington, MA: Lexington Books, 1973).

2. Anton Blok, *The Mafia of a Sicilian Village* (New York: Harper and Row, 1974).

3. John Mack, *The Crime Industry* (Westmead, England: Saxon House, 1975).

4. Howard Abadinsky, *Organized Crime* (Boston: Allyn and Bacon, 1981).

5. Joseph Albini, *The American Mafia: Genesis of a Legend* (New York: Appleton-Century-Crofts, 1971).

6. Howard Abadinsky, *The Mafia in America: An Oral History* (New York: Praeger, 1981).

7. The statute uses nominal dollars, thus, in an inflationary world, making the threshold of decreasing stringency. The same $2,000 requirement in 1970 would have been $5,500 in 1984, if adjusted for inflation.

8. G. Robert Blakey, *The Development of the Law of Gambling: 1776–1976* (Washington, DC: National Institute of Law Enforcement and Criminal Justice, 1977), 600.

9. U.S. Congress, Senate Special Committee to Investigate Organized Crime in Interstate Commerce (Kefauver Committee), *Report* (Washington, DC: U.S. Government Printing Office, 1951).

10. U.S. Congress, Permanent Subcommittee on Investigations of Senate Committee on Government Operations (McClellan Committee), *Gambling and Organized Crime* (Washington, DC: U.S. Government Printing Office, 1962).

11. Peter Reuter, *Disorganized Crime* (Cambridge: MIT Press, 1983), Chapters 1–3.

12. Michael Maltz, "On Defining Organized Crime," *Crime and Delinquency* 22 (July 1976); Herbert Alexander and Gerald Caiden (eds.), *Political and Economic Perspectives on Organized Crime* (Lexington, MA: D. C. Heath, 1984).

13. Peter Reuter and Jonathan Rubinstein, *Illegal Gambling in New York* (Washington, DC: National Institute of Justice, 1982).

14. G. Robert Blakey, "Remarks," paper presented Second National Conference on Organized Crime at the University of Southern California, 11 November 1983.

15. Thomas Schelling, "Economic Analysis of Organized Crime," in President's Commission on Law Enforcement and the Administration of Justice, *Task Force Report: Organized Crime* (Washington, DC: U.S. Government Printing Office, 1967).

16. John Landesco, *Organized Crime in Chicago* (Chicago: University of Chicago Press, 1929; reissued in 1986).

17. William Foot Whyte, *Street Corner Society* (Chicago: University of Chicago Press, 1943).

18. Donald Cressey, *Theft of the Nation* (New York: Harper and Row, 1969).

19. John Gardiner, *The Politics of Organized Crime in an American City* (New York: Russell Sage Foundation, 1970).

20. A.F.J. Ianni with Elizabeth Reuss-Ianni, *A Family Business* (New York: Russell Sage Foundation, 1972).

21. William Chambliss, *On the Take* (Bloomington: University of Indiana Press, 1978).

22. Annelise Anderson, *The Business of Organized Crime* (Stanford, CA: Hoover Institute Press, 1979).

23. Alan Block, *East Side-West Side* (New Brunswick, NJ: Transaction Press, 1983).

24. Reuter, *Disorganized Crime.*

25. I have excluded fictional accounts, though some of them, such as Jimmy Breslin's *The Gang That Couldn't Shoot Straight* (New York: Viking Press, 1971), clearly describe real people and events. The task of separating fact from fiction is simply too difficult. However, it is often noted that mafiosi read, applaud, and imitate some of this fiction.

26. Hunter Thompson's *Hells Angels: A Strange and Terrible Saga* (New York: Random House, 1966) about the Hell's Angels is the one semiserious study of the bike gangs. Like all of his writings, it contains a great deal of insight about the motivations and relationships of individuals. But Thompson was more concerned with public and media reactions to the Angels than with the bikers' organization itself. He stressed the strong sense of loyalty to the life-style of the gang and their sense of separateness from the rest of the world. Though the gangs intimidated police and the public, Thompson did not see this as an effort to create an asset for income-generating purposes but simply a consequence of their high level of rage. The study is, of course, seriously dated; at that time, the gang seems to have had fairly marginal involvement in the drug trades, whereas now it has a

well-documented central role in the trafficking of methamphetamines and other stimulants. For example, the 1983 report of the Organized Crime Drug Enforcement Task Forces asserts that a significant percent of their cases involved bike gangs.

27. For example, at one point, Tennes is asserted to have received payments from bookmakers in other cities of $12,000 per month (John Landesco, *Organized Crime in Chicago,* Chicago: University of Chicago Press, 1968, p. 71). Yet reference is made on the previous page to non-Chicago monthly revenues of $20,000. A few individual city figures offered on the same two pages are also quite contradictory.

28. Cressey, *Theft of the Nation*, 75.

29. Mark Haller and John Alviti, "Loansharking in American Cities: Historical Analysis of a Marginal Enterprise," *American Journal of Legal History* 21 (1977).

30. Ianni claims in *A Family Business* (New York: Russell Sage Foundation, 1972), to know of no connection between the Lupollo (pseudonymous) family and the Mafia: "We have no evidence that would indicate that the family is part of any national or international syndicate. Neither, of course, do we have any conclusive evidence that they are not" (p. 89). However, the family is constantly referred to as an example, possibly atypical, of Italian organized crime in America, and comparisons are made with Mafia families.

31. Anderson, *The Business of Organized Crime.*

32. Peter Maas, *The Valachi Papers* (New York: Bantam Books, 1967).

33. Vincent Teresa, with Thomas Renner, *My Life in the Mafia* (Greenwich, CT: Fawcett, 1973).

34. Henry Zeiger, *Sam the Plumber* (Bergenfield, NJ: New American Library, 1973).

35. Henry Zeiger, *The Jersey Mob* (Bergenfield, NJ: New American Library, 1975).

36. A highly critical analysis of these materials is given in Dwight C. Smith, *The Mafia Mystique* (New York: Basic Books, 1975, 293–97). The fact that members of the Mafia were overheard giving contradictory accounts of the same events, a matter that Smith felt threw these materials into doubt, might just as reasonably be seen to add to their credibility.

37. Zeiger, *The Jersey Mob*, 2.

38. Anderson, *The Business of Organized Crime*, 29–30.

39. Cressey, *Theft of the Nation*, 236.

40. Raymond Martin, *Revolt in the Mafia* (New York: Duell, Sloan, and Pearce, 1963).

41. Cressey, *Theft of the Nation*, 242.

42. Ralph Salerno and John Tompkins, *The Crime Confederation* (Garden City, NY: Doubleday, 1969).

43. Joe Barboza and Henry Messick, *Barboza* (New York: Dell Books, 1975).

44. Anderson, *The Business of Organized Crime*, 33.

45. President's Commission on Law Enforcement and the Administration of Justice, *Task Force Report: Organized Crime* (Washington, DC: U.S. Government Printing Office, 1967), 1.

46. Commission on the Review of the National Policy Toward Gambling, *Hearings* (Springfield, VA: National Technical Information Service, 1977).

47. Peter Reuter, "Regulating Rackets," *Regulation* (September/October 1984).

48. Allan Block and William Chambliss, *Organizing Crime* (New York: Elsevier, 1981).

49. Daniel Bell, "Crime as an American Way of Life," in *The End of Ideology* (Glencoe, IL: Free Press, 1964).

50. Blakey, *The Development of the Law of Gambling*, Chapter 6.

51. John Galliher and James Cain, "Citation Support for the Mafia Myth in Criminology Textbooks," *The American Sociologist* (May 1974): 74.

52. Galiher and Cain, "Citation Support," 73.

53. Donald Cressey, *Criminal Organization: Its Elementary Forms* (New York: Harper and Row, 1973), Chapter 5.

54. Reuter and Rubinstein, *Illegal Gambling*, 153.

55. James Buchanan, "A Defense of Organized Crime?" in *The Economics of Crime and Punishment*, ed. Simon Rottenberg (Washington, DC: The American Enterprise Institute, 1973).

56. Paul Rubin, "The Economic Theory of the Criminal Firm," in *The Economics of Crime and Punishment*, ed. Simon Rottenberg (Washington, DC: American Enterprise Institute, 1973).

57. Mark Furstenburg made a stronger argument that organized crime, by internalizing disputes, reduced the incidence of violence in illegal markets. The argument rests on the assumption, not borne out by data, that illegal market participants are all members of organized crime ("Violence in Organized Crime," Staff Report to the National Commission on the Causes and Prevention of Violence [Washington, DC: U.S. Govt. Pub. Office, 1969]).

58. Jurgen Backhaus, "Defending Organized Crime? A Note," *Journal of Legal Studies* 8 (June 1979).

59. Peter Reuter, "Social Control in Illegal Markets," in Donald Black, ed., *Toward a General Theory of Social Control* (New York: Academic Press, 1984).

60. Gresham Sykes, *Criminology* (New York: Harcourt Brace Jovanovich, 1978), 194–203.

61. Herbert Packer in his classic discussion of the "crime tariff" goes further. He asserts that "when we make it illegal to traffic in commodities for which there is an inelastic demand, the effect is to secure a kind of monopoly profit to the entrepreneur who is willing to break the law" (279). This assumes, implausibly, that the supply of criminal entrepreneurship and labor is restricted. Herbert Packer, *The Limits of the Criminal Sanction* (Stanford, CA: Stanford University Press, 1968).

62. Ken Carlson, *Unreported Taxable Income from Selected Illegal Activities* (Cambridge, MA: Abt Associates, 1983).

63. Albert Cohen, *Delinquent Boys* (New York: Free Press, 1955).

64. Mark Haller, "Bootlegging in Chicago: The Structure of an Illegal Enterprise," paper presented at American Historical Association Convention, 28 December 1974.

65. Mark Haller, "The Changing Structure of American Gambling in the Twentieth Century," *Journal of Social Issues* 35.3 (1979): 88.

66. Migration from Eastern Europe (Russia and satellites) accounted for only about 8 percent of European migration from 1950 to 1970, fewer than two hundred thousand persons.

67. Daniel Brill, *The Teamsters* (New York: Simon and Schuster, 1978).

68. Ivan Light, "Numbers as a Black Financial Institution," *American Sociological Review* 42 (August 1977).

69. Reuter, "Social Control in Illegal Markets."

70. Bjorn Fog, "How Are Cartel Prices Determined?" *Journal of Industrial Economics* 5 (1956).

71. Norman Lucas, *Britain's Gangland* (London: W. H. Allen, 1969).

72. Ovid DeMaris, *The Last Mafioso* (New York: Bantam Books, 1981).

73. Organized Crime Drug Enforcement Task Force Program, *Annual Report* (U.S. Government Printing Office, Dept. of Justice, Washington, DC, 1984), 11.

5

Illicit Enterprise: An Organized Crime Paradigm for the Nineties

DWIGHT C. SMITH, JR.

INTRODUCTION

How does one go about defining an organization? What are its boundaries? The answers are not simple. Assuming that the existence of organization requires some pattern of roles and relationships, we can ask the following:[1]

1. Are the patterns defining an organization determined by the persons occupying certain roles and enjoying certain relationships?
2. Are they determined by the activities undertaken by those persons?
3. Are they determined by constraining or facilitating environmental circumstances?
4. Are they determined by stakeholders within the organization exclusively or unilaterally, or do stakeholders external to the organization help define it; and if so, who are they?
5. Does an organization determine its actions, or do actions determine an organization?
6. How does one distinguish an organization from its environment; that is, where does the organization end?

Classical organization theory focused on the first two of these six starting points. In retrospect, the significance of these two approaches is the assumption that organizations are created by the interaction of their members and not by anyone (or anything) else. That other premises could lead to different ways of defining organizations did not enter the organizational debate until systems and contingency theories appeared in the mid-1960s and early 1970s.

Systems theory showed that organizations are never self-sufficient or self-contained.[2] They depend on outside forces as sources of inputs and receivers of outputs. Organization patterns reflect that dependency. Contingency theory showed that organizations do not always control outside influences and must adapt to them.[3] The concepts of uncertainty, limited information, and bounded rationality then became permanent attributes of the theoretical landscape and significant organizational determinants.

Systems theory and contingency theory were the opening wedges for what has become an array of perspectives from which to think about how organizations are defined and modeled. Questions 3–6 in my opening list lead to some of them. Classical concepts remain viable but generally subordinate in their significance to newer constructs. The new constructs have much to offer the organized crime debate.

The heart of any theory is a model that depicts how the components of the theory fit together. As Jay S. Albanese suggests elsewhere in this *Handbook*, contemporary organized crime theories use models that can be grouped into three general types: "those that focus on hierarchical structure, those that emphasize local ethnic or cultural connections, and those that emphasize the economic nature of organized crime."[4] All three types took shape in the late 1960s and early 1970s. They were continuations of, or responses to, discussions that gained initial momentum from congressional hearings associated with the testimony of Joseph Valachi[5] and ended with *Task Force Report: Organized Crime*.[6] As will be evident in this chapter, my perspective is that of the third model, which emphasizes an entrepreneurial view of organized crime under the label of "illicit enterprise."

In essence those discussions concerned a number of individuals, most of whom had criminal reputations, if not records, and who were distinguished by having some association with one another. They were deemed by that association to be organized. The subsequent question is, How can their organized association and its apparent activities, behaviors, and consequences be explained?

The three models created to answer that question are distinctive. As Albanese suggests, the first two focus on how organized crime *groups* are organized, whereas the third focuses on how organized crime *activities* are organized. Both are appropriate responses from a classical point of view. The two decades since they first appeared have been marked by a continuing debate as to which should be accepted as the single, all-encompassing paradigm. But the debate may have been wrongly focused. The models "do not conflict in any significant way. . . . [Their] perceived inconsistencies . . . are incidental for the purposes of both study and crime control." Albanese concludes—wisely and correctly—that "when it comes to understanding the true nature of organized crime, it is . . . important not to lose sight of the 'elephant,' as one studies its various structures and activities."

From today's perspective, it seems to me that our efforts have been limited by their starting point. We should have begun with a theory and then tried to determine whether the facts supported it. Instead, we started with relationships needing to be explained and interpreted. As we have seen, available theories were also limited then. If we were to start the process anew, with theory as the point of departure, we would enjoy a significant advantage by using theories about organizations that simply did not exist when the debate over models began. The result should be a new model with greater theoretical power and scope.

My primary purpose in this chapter is to discuss two avenues of post-1975 thought that appear to be most promising for future research.[7] I begin, however, with a brief look at definitions of organized crime as they evolved in two time periods conveniently separated by World War II. This review, culminating with comments concerning Michael D. Maltz's discussion of definitions elsewhere in this volume, leads to several questions and suggestions that will be useful as the definitional discussion continues. I then look at the three models and some of the theoretical and definitional problems inherent in them. I conclude by discussing multiple-constituency theory and neoinstitutionalism, two theoretical approaches that usefully inform the modeling process.

THE PROBLEM OF DEFINING ORGANIZED CRIME

Students of organized crime history will recall that "organized crime" first appeared in the 1920s, through the work of F. M. Thrasher[8] and J. Landesco.[9] Neither of them defined organized crime, but it is clear that as they used it, neither intended it to be synonymous with *gangster* or *racketeer*, other criminal labels then in vogue. Those labels "referred to people, whereas 'organized crime' referred to a social condition."[10] Organized crime meant both a general organization of the underworld and groups within that economy that planned and executed elaborate and sustained criminal activities. Organization of and within the underworld was fluid, with new alliances and alignments possible on short notice. Thus, the earliest use of the term included connectivity and continuity, two characteristics that, as Maltz has shown elsewhere in this volume, remain important elements of any definition.

The new term was taken by the Wickersham Commission of 1929–31 and expanded in scope to cover two criminal areas. The first and most significant from the standpoint of monetary loss was commercialized fraud, "organized scheming carried on as a regular business, and, in many of the most serious cases, masquerading as legitimate business enterprises." The second area was extortion and racketeering, "the forcing of persons to pay voluntary tribute to the perpetrators of the crime as a result of fear for life, liberty, bodily safety, reputation, or property."[11] That definition did not survive, and its demise can be attributed to two circumstances. First, when the featured recommendations of the Wickersham Commission concerning Prohibition were rejected, all of its reports were relegated to back shelves in library stacks.[12] Second, when E. O. Sutherland later coined the concept of "white-collar crime,"[13] he defined a research territory that preempted the businessman-gone-wrong from the Wickersham definition.

Interest in organized crime was rekindled following World War II. Its proponents now were led by federal law enforcement agencies that introduced an ethnic dimension to the definition. Though the propriety of that linkage had been debated in some law enforcement circles,[14] the president's commission made it official by stating that the core of organized crime consisted of twenty-four groups whose "membership is exclusively men of Italian descent."[15] The link was reinforced by D. R. Cressey's assertion that "if one understands Cosa Nostra he understands organized crime in the United States."[16] The structural model of organized crime is a direct outgrowth of this definition.

A major portion of the subsequent debate has concerned this definition's ethnic dimension. Is ethnicity an unnecessary, perhaps inaccurate, even misleading restriction? As Maltz's analysis in this book suggests, responses to such questions will depend on one's reason for a definition in the first place. Maltz identifies four reasons. The first three are of particular concern to various elements within the law enforcement community: those responsible for the planning and evaluation aspects of program management; those responsible for the operational aspects of investigation and prosecution; and those responsible for the executive oversight of case management. The structural model of organized crime was intended originally to meet the definitional needs of those in law enforcement responsible for investigations and prosecutions in technologically complex urban environments.[17]

Maltz's fourth reason, understanding organized crime as a social phenomenon, is of particular interest to researchers. The kinship and enterprise models of organized crime were created by researchers to meet perceived difficulties accompanying an ethnically focused definition. Much pertinent history about organized criminal behavior and illicit enterprises in this country and elsewhere lacked an Italian ethnic dimension and thus was not congruent with the structural model. Furthermore, despite a frequent disclaimer that there were non-Italian entities properly called "organized crime," its revival was so identified with traditional Italian American criminal networks that the new definition and its structural model were never transferred effectively to non-Italian criminal settings.

Several recent commentaries explicitly illustrate the problem of fit. I note, in particular, the analysis by G. W. Potter and L. K. Gaines[18] of rural vice and corruption in America and the analysis elsewhere in this volume by Alan A. Block concerning narcotics trading in Europe and Asia before World War II. In this context, Maltz's newest contribution to the definitional discussion is timely for its analysis of the attributes that define organized crime (OC, as he refers to the "more dangerous manifestation" of organized crime); and for his conclusions concerning "a continuum of organized crime enterprises."

Consider first the attributes of OC. Maltz discusses ten characteristics of "earlier" (i.e., since 1967) definitions of organized crime. He concludes that four of them are characteristic of "essentially all OC groups"; that two others are often present, though perhaps not essential; and that the remaining four "may be characteristic of some OC groups [but] are neither necessary nor typical.'' Most important, he then adds that there ''appears to be a thread linking the attributes that have been rejected as determinants of OC. . . . They are all characteristics of the archetypical Mafia family.'' Maltz continues: ''This image of OC is so powerful that it often blinds us to other potential forms,'' of which he describes several possible OC candidates from this country and abroad.

This is a powerful commentary on the predominant definition and its structural model. The rejected attributes became part of organized crime in its post–World War II revival. If they are not essential to the definition and their blinding power is removed, then perhaps the attributes and examples of organized crime from the pre–World War II literature may regain saliency for at least two of Maltz's purposes, research and program management.

Even if the definition is restated, however, is it useful to pursue it, especially since it is aimed exclusively at the OC subset of organized crime? I put this question with some hesitancy because I appreciate and respect Maltz's efforts here and elsewhere. But recalling C. Perrow's observation that ''theorizing is not a 'neutral' activity, but one guided by strong interests and values that need to be explicated,''[19] we may ask, If organized crime has other manifestations, some of which Maltz names in discussing the prospect of a ''continuum of organized crime enterprises,'' why focus solely on the ''violence-based enterprises'' encompassed by OC? The apparent answer: these enterprises are the greatest threat on the organized crime horizon and should therefore be at the definitional center. This is a respectable response, but the question it answers implies alternatives that reflect other values. Is the collusive racket, defined in the pre–World War II period by G. L. Hostetter and T. Q. Beesley,[20] a more important threat to the body politic because it contributes to (and reflects) ethical ambiguity? Or is entrepreneurial behavior, at the edge of legality, where ambiguity and controversy are common attributes, more important because it reflects the constant pressure with which honestly intentioned but marginal businesses must contend?

As these questions suggest, the researcher has a clear choice of focus. One may choose to look only at behavior classified as OC, or one may choose to look at the spectrum of enterprises that includes OC as a special case. My choice is the latter. The continuum that Maltz recognizes as an ''obvious'' condition and then puts aside in order to focus on a more discriminatory definition of OC may be more important both for researchers and for law enforcement specialists. It has several potential advantages, the most important of which is that it does not require development of new theory. Instead, it provides a natural bridge by which to extend existing and tested theories and research methodologies that were developed to explain and explore the legitimate portion of the market spectrum.

My preference for the continuum focus reflects my earlier writings[21] about a ''spectrum of legitimacy.'' Its roots extend to the pre–World War II period of organized crime studies, when the Wickersham Commission described criminal frauds ("the more important" branch of organized crime) in the following terms:

Such criminal schemes shade off by imperceptible degrees into enterprises which are so conducted as to avoid criminal liability although employing unethical or even illegal methods of doing business; and the line between criminal and noncriminal activity is thus frequently a rather arbitrary one. Commercialized fraud is more often business run amuck than an offshoot of ordinary crimes against property, and the typical criminal of this class is not the bandit or the recidivist, but the business man gone wrong.[22]

The problems of entrepreneurship at the boundaries of legality and the special case of the pariah entrepreneur[23] may be targets for research and investigation of equal (or greater) interest and importance than OC, given Maltz's listing of its essential characteristics.[24]

MODELS OF ORGANIZED CRIME AND THEIR THEORETICAL UNDERPINNINGS

Past definitional debates had the unfortunate consequence of stopping the process of model building in its tracks. Whether one chooses OC or the continuum of illicit enterprise as the focal problem, we need an infusion of new theory. As a starting point for considering some theoretical options, we will look first at the three models, their theoretical underpinnings, and some of their apparent limits.

The Structural Model

When Cressey wrote *Theft of the Nation* in 1969, his principal objectives were to draw attention to the social problem of organized crime and to explain it in a logical way. He did not intend to enhance or advance organization theory, but he could not avoid theoretical questions about organizations because " 'organized crime' obviously involves organization."[25] The structural model of organized crime was the result of his explanation.

From Cressey's perspective, organized crime was authoritarian and bureaucratic, "rationally designed"[26] to maximize profits and grounded in a code of behavior with rules and procedures carried out by persons occupying functional roles in a division of labor. It had permanence of form extending beyond individuals. "Organization, or 'structure,' not persons, gives Cosa Nostra its self-perpetuating character";[27] the authority structure "constitutes the 'organization chart' of Cosa Nostra."[28] Behind the structure was the "fictitious 'family,' . . . an important integrating mechanism"[29] needed to maintain an organization dominated from the top. The code of conduct embedded in the "family" culture functioned to protect the personal power of leaders: "The code . . . is the code of a despot bent on securing conformity to his demand that he be left alone to enrich himself at the expense of men who shower him with honor and respect."[30]

From a theoretical standpoint, the structural model was thus based on classical concepts concerning the division of labor, scientific management and bureaucratic attributes of precedence, rules, procedures and functional roles. Rationality and certainty were still the predominant determinants of organization theory when Cressey wrote, despite rebellious protests from neoclassicists who pointed to the nonrational aspects of organizations, the limits of bounded rationality, and the importance of coalition management as a way to "satisfice" competing objectives. Nevertheless, Cressey anticipated change as authority of rank gave way to authority of expertise. As a consequence of power and respectability, the need for secrecy would be reduced and the need for expertise would increase. "(T)he pattern of extreme totalitarian control will change."[31] There might be a new wave of violence; "membership" lines might become blurred; patterns of authority and recruitment would shift; and lower participants might begin to demand more rights for themselves. With these suggestions Cressey partially satisfied the researcher's criterion that a model have predictive power. But his predictions of change reflected the politics of civil rights, not organization theory. "If these men begin demanding their rights we will witness in the ranks of organized crime rebellions comparable in principle to the current rebellions of Negroes."[32]

The text is silent as to whether Cresscy attached theoretical importance to his predictions. The chapters of *Theft of the Nation* that follow concern the problem of corruption of law enforcement and politics and, in the light of corruption, the strategic possibilities for dealing with organized crime. Nothing further is said about the structural model or the possibility of change. No one has tried to operationalize and test his predictions. We are left, then, with the initial model of a continuing, formal, rationally designed, top-down authority system in which coercive power might be replaced by the bosses' power to reward.

The structural model is not a totally closed system. It indirectly recognizes the environment through the relationship between "corrupter" and "corruptee." But the relationship is not interactive. The corruptee is created as part of the organized crime structure, not its environment, to respond to certain actions.[33] The model also ignores market dynamics, focusing instead on internal organization as the unilateral creation of its participants.[34]

The Kinship-Based, Patron-Client Model

This model is associated primarily with the work of J. L. Albini[35] and F.A.J. Ianni,[36] both of whom wrote in response to the ethnic perspective of organized crime that the president's commission had set in 1967. Their work was intended specifically as an alternative to the structural model. Their searches took them (as it had Cressey) to social conditions in Sicily, but their interpretations focused on behavioral dynamics rather than organizational structure.

Albini took a structural-functionalist approach, viewing organized crime as an indigenous phenomenon that, "irrespective of whether [its] participants were of foreign or native birth, [has] always functioned within the American political and economic system."[37] The particular contribution of Italians was the use of patron-client relationships as they had developed in the stratified society of Sicily.

Patronage can be viewed as a way of life, a pattern of power interaction, and a system whereby the powerless are able to feel some sense of power. . . . Often the patron may serve . . . as a "mediator" between the community and the outside world; as such he may serve as the link between the government or urban center and the rural village. . . . [The] *mafia* in Sicily . . . is not an association as such but rather a system of patron-client relationships which weaves itself through both the legitimate and illegitimate segments of Sicilian society.[38]

The patron-client system was integral to the culture that Sicilian Italians brought to the United States. In that setting the term *mafioso* could refer to one capable of using violence to enforce his will, but more specifically the title was public recognition "of the power [the mafioso] can command through effective patrons and clients."[39]

Ianni undertook a participant-observation field study of a particular group of Italian Americans and their forebears. From his observations he elaborated the patron-client concept by distinguishing between cooperative relationships that could be called "organized" and the role of Mafia values in personal relationships. His distinction was fundamental to the interpretation of patterns of relationships. To describe links between individuals as a formal structure was analogous to interpreting the sociogram of a grade school class as evidence of organization and an authority structure. Italian Mafia families, he argued,

are traditional social systems, organized by action and by cultural values which have nothing to do with modern bureaucratic virtues. Like all social systems, they have no structure apart from their functioning; nor . . . do they have structure independent of their current "personnel." And when the cultural values which underlie the social system weaken, the families also weaken and die.[40]

The kin-centered system of social control had its roots in the Italian Mezzogiorno (south of Italy), where the family was the "first source of power."[41] It provided the mediation structure for a patron-client milieu. To reinforce the bonds of kinship, Sicilian mafioso behavior emphasized the practice of dealing in personal terms. The individual needing help should sense a personal influence at work on his behalf; the benefactor should be seen as a patron, not the representative of an impersonal organization. Dependence on such personal influences "describes the exchange relationship of *mafia* which finds its persistence in the patterns of obligations and responsibilities established through favors and services."[42]

Italian American criminals might operate in a seemingly organized way, but authority and a division of labor reflected a network of family relationships and loyalties, not bureaucratic organization. Kinship was as important in criminal affairs as it is in any other business. Members of a kinship group "are sustained in action by the force of kinship rather than driven by fear or motivated by crime"; "[the] roles . . . within the organization . . . seem to be a function of kin relationship."[43] They

are rightly called families because the relationships established within them produce kinship-like ties among members. . . . Every family member knows that every other member has some duties toward him and some claims on him. . . . Like clans everywhere, these crime families enter into exchange relationships with one another and form alliances which are perpetuated. . . . This clan pattern . . . also provides a common system of roles, norms, and values which not only regulate the behavior within the family but also structure relationships among families. . . . [The] universality of this clan organization and the strength of its shared behavior system . . . makes Italian-American criminal syndicates seem so similar. . . . [It] is this similarity which has inclined observers to maintain that the different crime families constitute some sort of highly organized national or even international crime conspiracy.[44]

Ianni predicted that kinship ties would weaken as future generations achieved respectable roles in American society, rather than being recruited into criminal syndicates of the future. Eventually, "ethnic succession in organized crime will force them out,"[45] a possibility that Ianni later explored in his work on black ethnic succession in organized crime.[46] His prediction was hedged by an apparent obstacle: "With public interest in organized-crime infiltration of business and politics at its height, the *Mafia* stigma will act, temporarily at least, as a brake on this natural movement.[47] This prediction and hedge have also never been tested directly, though the data behind M. H. Haller's initial analysis of succession within the "Bruno" family of Philadelphia might support a partial analysis.[48]

The model focuses on the kinship network and on the role of the patron. Because it is less structured, its environmental interdependence is not fully developed. Mutual dependencies are recognized but not elaborated. Roles are described within the kinship network but not beyond it.

Nevertheless, the kinship-based, patron-client model is theoretically attractive because of its parsimony. It has been accepted by some as a valid alternative to Cressey's structuralist interpretation. It has been troublesome to others who see obvious (to them) signs of organization being treated as something less than that. The result is a model seemingly without structure. How can that be? How can anyone consider it as a viable alternative to the description of a formal structure? Are genealogies substitutes for organization charts? In part, the apparent paradox reflects ambiguity in common speech and in specialized uses of the terms *organization* and *structure*. If the paradox can be put aside for the moment, both models are touched by Maltz's analysis of the essential attributes of organized crime. They remain equally vulnerable to the ''blinding'' power of ethnicity that prevents one from seeing other potential forms of organized crime.

The Enterprise Model

The final model, based originally on my work,[49] has a different and wider focus. It looks at the marketplace environment of criminal organizations and at organizational imperatives that are dictated by the necessity of maintaining entrepreneurial domain in the face of uncertainty. From that perspective, dubbed ''illicit enterprise,''[50] the marketplace is a continuum from ''the very saintly to the most sinful,'' to use Leslie Wilkins's phrasing.[51] The arbitrary (from a marketplace view) definition of legality intersects that continuum but does not alter the essential domain imperative. Thus, organizing principles governing the legal side of the continuum apply on the illegal side as well. The market writes the rules, not a conspiracy with structural formality and alien origins or a kinship-based, patron-client network.

In contrast to the structural model, which looks at what people do (or how they behave) according to formal organizational roles and rules, and in contrast to the kinship-based, patron-client model, which looks at how people handle mutual obligations in a kinship network, the enterprise model focuses on core technologies and task environments as impersonal components of entrepreneurial behavior. The shift in focus is a deliberative move from the static structure of classical organizational theory. Its theoretical base is J. D. Thompson's systems-based contingency theory.[52] His approach links the closed system approach of classical theorists with open systems theory.

To Thompson, organizations were simultaneously open systems required to cope with uncertainty and closed systems subject to criteria of rationality and needing certainty.[53] The task environment was the source of uncertainty; the core of technology's need for efficiency demanded certainty. Work might have a variety of structures or employ different technologies, but it always contained a mix of determinateness and uncertainty that organizations were designed to meet.

The spectrum of legitimacy opens a new way of viewing organized crime by showing that different kinds of crimes have organizational needs based on core technologies whose definitions are independent of legality. That is, a loan shark will be organized more like a banker than a bookie. The underlying structure of the enterprise model can be summarized in four propositions that apply, regardless of whether the enterprise is legal or illegal.

1. The heart of any enterprise is its core technology, the technical functions by which it is able to create and dispose of its end product or services.

2. That core technology exists in a task environment, a set of external conditions that enable it to function but simultaneously offer hazards to its continuance.

3. The core technology of an enterprise works most efficiently when it is protected by some form of buffering from the uncertainties of the task environment.

4. The result of activity aimed at protection of the enterprise's technology is the creation of a territory, or domain: a set of claims staked out in terms of a range of products, population served, or services rendered.[54]

Enterprise may be the principal characteristic of this model, but it is not assumed to be the only characteristic. A complete explanation incorporates the conspiracy elements of the structural model and the kinship elements of the kinship-based, patron-client model.

An entrepreneur's task environment . . . is markedly different on the illegal side of the spectrum, primarily because of the absence of regulation to ensure order and protect property rights. An operating strategy is required, as is a mechanism through which order and stability can be maintained. The former is explained in part by conspiracy theory, since the device of conspiracy may be the best way to further outlawed economic activity. The latter is best explained by kinship, since kinship ties[55] provide the strongest possibility of ensuring trust among persons who cannot rely on the law to protect their rights and obligations within cooperative but outlawed economic activity.[56]

Earlier formulations of the enterprise model contain potentially testable predictions. One set concerns a practical and potentially observable phenomenon: the transformation process by which a pariah entrepreneur gains social legitimacy and, consequently, standing and reputation.[57] A second set concerns implications that follow further theory development.[58] They also remain to be tested, along with the predictions of Cressey and Ianni.

The principal advantage of the enterprise model is its wider scope. It recognizes an organization-environment interdependence and accommodates the concepts of kinship and conspiracy as significant components of entrepreneurship. That is, modified structural and kinship models can be embedded or "nested" in the enterprise model. It is not a closed model focused exclusively on its structural participants; but it still focuses on the entrepreneur as having primary responsibility for initiating action while the environment takes a more passive, responsive role. Most important, it has not been fully developed.

In particular, there is a need to identify the determinants of the spectrum (or continuum) of legitimacy. That it exists is intuitively appealing, but how is it operationalized? Maltz in this book suggests that there are several dimensions to the continuum of organized crime enterprises, including corruption, structure, and violence. My earlier suggestion[59] was that its dimensions may be product-specific and that each market would therefore follow its own requirements. Probably, both general and specific characteristics are present, but specifying them is a task that lies ahead.

CONTEMPORARY ORGANIZATION THEORY
AND ILLICIT ENTERPRISE

Intentionally or otherwise, theorists follow their perceptual underpinnings. They are products of their respective surroundings; they think about what they perceive. From early classicists to the structuralists, organizations were the centerpiece: rational institutions, purposefully designed to accomplish established objectives through defined rules, formal authority, organizational control, and coordination.[60] The human relations school accepted that focus but perceived both a new dimension of people in organizational situations and the reciprocal influence between organizations and people in work and goal achievement. The systems and contingency schools saw yet another dimension, arguing that organizations could not be understood in isolation from the environments within which they functioned. These later theories simply enlarged the organizational venue, however, while retaining it as the principal frame of reference. Two other perspectives pertinent to illicit enterprise have broken through that frame: multiple-constituencies theory, an unexpected way of examining the people associated with organizations, and transaction cost economics, a part of the new institutional economics revival[61] that provides a fresh way of looking at organizations and the marketplace.

Most readers will not be familiar with these perspectives. In the absence of a grounding in tangible illustrations, the theoretical abstractions that follow can be uncertain and frustrating. I focus specifically on theory in this section, however. The next section is intended to show by example how these theories can be used in the illicit enterprise context.

Multiple-Constituencies Theory (M-C)

The M-C approach departs radically from the classical goal-centered, organization-focused perspective. "An organization . . . is simply a legal fiction, an 'artificial construct under the law which allows certain organizations to be treated as individuals.' "[62]

Organizations exist, but they are not defined solely by formal structure. They are the results, not the initiators, of action. They are formed when constituencies or stakeholders meet around their shared interests in a group of activities.[63] Their "organization" is not a particular structure but the locus of incentive exchanges.[64]

Stakeholders include external constituencies (clients or customers, competitors, suppliers, regulatory agencies) and quasi insiders (boards of directors, commercial associations, public relations consultants), as well as internal participants and groups (owners, managers, workers). Each constituency shares goals with others while holding unique interests and expectations. Each tries to move the center of its interactions—the organization—in its direction. They collaborate and compete in establishing priorities, and conflict is virtually inevitable. Structure reflects that interaction and conflict.

Contrary to traditional expectations, goals do not determine structure in the M-C perspective. Rather, each organization is a site for the distribution of satisfactions, a process governed by power relationships acting through the intersections of multiple influence loops.[65] An organization is located not by the tangible geography of its assets but by the location (more conceptual than physical) of currently powerful constituencies. That location and the structure accompanying it can change. Satisfactions can be distributed sequentially in a "time-share" process that periodically redefines who the powerful constituencies are.

The M-C perspective turns the "legal fiction" of organization inside out, like a glove. A major premise behind that shift is that stability—a governing assumption of the structuralist view—has less impact on the shape and behavior of legitimate organizations than uncertainty, a concept introduced by systems theory. As the M-C viewpoint provides insights into legitimate organizations, it can also bring new understanding to the study of illicit enterprise, where there is no "legal fiction" to distract us. The principal question, addressed in the next section, is, Who are the stakeholders who influence the organization of illicit enterprise?

Transaction Cost Economics (TCE)

Like M-C theory, TCE assumes that organizations come into being only because they are needed. Firms (the economist's term for organizations) exist because of certain costs that accompany transactions.[66] Without those costs, transactions occur naturally in the market without the need for organization.

The principal transaction costs are those of learning and haggling over the terms of a trade. Classical economic theory assumed that parties to that process would be rational, have full knowledge of conditions underlying the trade, and try to minimize costs and maximize profit through production efficiency and product desirability. In simple face-to-face exchanges between buyer and seller, simple market mechanisms suffice. But most transactions are more complex. Product reliability and warranties, for example, entail extended learning and haggling that prolong the life of a transaction beyond the point of initial exchange. Or, learning and haggling may have to be undertaken repeatedly as different components of production, valuation, and exchange satisfaction are played out.

Cost estimates that reflect uncertain or unknown conditions may become so unnegotiable that a marketplace contract cannot be reached. The costs of learning and haggling can be controlled or reduced, however, if one party is given authority over the terms of trade by incorporating it into an organizational setting. To R. Coase, a firm is thus defined when the price mechanism governing exchange is replaced by instructions or orders issued by a boss. A firm has come into being to economize on transaction costs.

But organization has costs, as a result of errors, inefficiencies, and administrative rigidity. The boundaries of the firm are determined not by the balance between power and dependency in decision making, but by the marginal point where cost savings from internal transactions and internal costs of rigidity and error are equal.

Prior to TCE, decision-making authority and the power over it were central to theories about internal organization and to relations between the organization and its environment. In neoclassical economic theory, for example, a firm is understood to be "a collection or set of feasible production plans, presided over by a manager who, buying and selling inputs in a spot market, chooses the plan that maximizes owners' welfare."[67] In contingency theory (as described earlier in this chapter), the boundary of an organization is its domain: a set of claims staked out in terms of a range of products, population served, or services rendered. Domain thus "identifies the points at which the organization is dependent on inputs from the environment."[68]

TCE looks behind the distribution of power and decision making to focus on key components of the decision: factors that add or subtract cost in a transaction. They are the ultimate organization building blocks, not production structures or bureaucracies. The central question shifts from, What is an organization? to, What are the transaction costs that require organization? As Oliver Williamson, the principal, theorist, and advocate for TCE has put it, "Transaction cost analysis supplants the usual preoccupation with technology and steady-state production (or distribution) expenses with an examination of the *comparative costs of planning, adapting, and monitoring task completion under alternative governance structures.*"[69]

From the TCE perspective, the critical dimension of any transaction is a condition known as asset specificity, or investments that are necessary for a contract to be carried out over time. The skills of a worker, the capabilities of a machine, or the characteristics of a raw material are asset-specific to the extent that they are used for a limited number of products and cannot be redeployed easily to something else. Outside the TCE perspective, they are often referred to as "sunk costs."

When a buyer wants a product whose assets are thus specific, and none other, and the supplier wants to provide it to that buyer, the resulting mutual dependency narrows contract options. Over time, market-based transactions involving assets that are specific to the deal become bilateral arrangements that develop into mutually acceptable organizational arrangements.

The buyer and seller could operate without friction except for two potential behavioral conditions. First, humans are subject to bounded rationality, a concept first articulated by H. A. Simon in 1949.[70] The capacity of the human mind is small in comparison to the size of problems to be solved, and it is limited in knowledge, foresight, skill, and time.[71] As a result, behavior is "*intendedly* rational, but *limitedly* so."[72] Second, humans are prone to opportunism, "a condition of self-interest seeking with guile."[73] When uncertainty is added to the mix, the contracting process becomes complex, but manageable through different arrangements.

Assume, for example, that both parties are opportunistic and assets are specific, but there are no limits to knowledge and rationality. The parties may not trust each other, and they may each have sunk costs, but they can write a contract in which all relevant issues are settled in advance, and all contingencies are fully anticipated and appropriately met. The key to their success is planning, made possible because they are not limited by bounded rationality.

Or, assume that both parties are subject to bounded rationality and that their transactions are supported by specific assets, but both believe the other's word. They write a contract that is incomplete because they cannot anticipate all contingencies, but they agree in advance to seek only fair returns and to resolve any future problems in a joint profit-maximizing manner. The key to their success is trust, made possible because opportunism is absent.

Finally, assume that both parties are subject to bounded rationality and given to opportunism, but there are no specific assets in the transaction. Neither buyer nor seller has a sunk cost that would be lost if the contract did not continue. Contracts are then written for what each party believes to be the best terms for that transaction. The key to success is market competition, because any supplier is as good as any other.

When bounded rationality, opportunism, and asset specificity are all contained in the transaction, however, none of these arrangements suffice. Planning is incomplete because of bounded rationality; trust breaks down because of opportunism; and the continuing identification between buyer and seller now matters because of asset specificity. Some form of organization is inevitable.

The simplest example is an organization in which a human resource function replaces daily spot hiring of labor. The owner needs continuity of employment to protect a wage investment in skill and experience; the worker seeks the security of employment continuity.[74] More complex examples: to reduce transaction costs associated with buffering the production process, a business may grow vertically by buying, co-opting, or contracting with a favored supplier or distributor; to reduce costs of sales transactions, a business may grow laterally by buying a competitor or by joining with competitors to establish a self-regulating association; or to protect buyers in general and to reduce uncertainty for all competitors, the state may impose a regulatory agency to oversee operations and sales. In each of these instances, the interplay of asset specificity, opportunism, and bounded rationality under conditions of uncertainty is obvious. Equally apparent is the importance of opportunism as a driving force for shrewd contracting, unethical behavior—or worse. The critical distinction for our purposes is the presence of a law being violated, turning an unethical situation into illicit enterprise.[75]

MULTIPLE CONSTITUENCIES, TCE, ILLICIT
ENTERPRISE, AND OC

For those accustomed to the excitement and derring-do of conventional organized crime literature, organization theory may be boring. Nevertheless, when
the chase shifts from villains and victims to ideas, the conclusions can be equally
stimulating. Haller's continuing efforts[76] to reinterpret the Philadelphia story of
Angelo Bruno show that the shift pays off. What additional reinterpretation and
theory development for illicit enterprise lie within M-C theory and TCE?

The application of contemporary organization theory to illicit enterprise is
premised on a mutual recognition that the spectrum of legitimacy joins two
previously independent frames of reference. Organization theorists will then discover that the concept of organization is not bounded by the politics of legality.[77]
Similarly, those concerned with illicit enterprise, particularly its OC component,
will discover that contemporary theories about organizations and about the behavior of people within the dynamics of organized action provide solid grounds
for research.

The essence of illicit enterprise is a bilateral relationship between customers
and suppliers that occurs in a range of circumstances.[78] Customers in the relationship can be classified initially into three groups: those with legitimate needs
for whom the legitimate market is unresponsive; those with illicit needs who
cannot risk dealing with legitimate entrepreneurs who keep business records that
could be subpoenaed; and, ultimately, the extortionist (or pirate) who is intent
simply upon exploiting the domains of other entrepreneurs. They interact with
suppliers whose motives may have multiple stimuli: a fear of failure greater than
a fear of illegality, contempt for the law and/or its minions, a high tolerance for
rationalizing questionable behavior, a desire for profit at any cost, or a principled
disagreement with certain legal restrictions.

Motives are hard to classify and measure when they are not well regarded and
therefore seldom articulated. Nevertheless, these rough approximations set the
stage for Williamson's basic TCE question. When does the market cease to be a
viable arena for contracting? When do the costs of asset specificity and/or uncertainty and/or opportunism require organizational control mechanisms? Bearing in
mind the perspective of multiple constituencies, who, besides the customer and
supplier, influences that organization's structure? Let me suggest some answers,
using four disparate examples from the enterprise spectrum: the Towers Financial
Corporation; the electrical price-fixing conspiracy of 1959; rural crime networks
in eastern Kentucky; and the Angelo Bruno family (or network) of Philadelphia.

I want to emphasize at the outset that my observations are intended to be
illustrative, not definitive. They reflect a preliminary review of secondary
sources. My intentions are to demonstrate how the TCE and M-C perspectives
can be applied to illicit enterprise, not to assert and prove particular conclusions;
and to invite a dialogue through which other theoretical insights can be applied
to illicit enterprise.

According to D. B. Henriques,[79] the Towers Financial Corporation is the outgrowth of a series of corporate shells begun in 1980 with the formation of Professional Business Brokers (PBB). In 1986, PBB bought a publicly traded shell company that allowed Towers to become a public company without submitting a formal prospectus to the Securities and Exchange Commission (SEC). Between 1987 and 1993 Towers sold at least $250 million in notes through private placements limited to wealthy, sophisticated investors. The advantage of private placement was that Towers did not have to meet state registration requirements. On 8 February 1993, the SEC filed a civil suit accusing Towers and its chief executive, Steven Hoffenberg, "of defrauding nearly 3,000 investors through the use of false and 'grossly exaggerated' financial statements."[80] The following month Towers filed for bankruptcy court protection, and Hoffenberg was removed as chairman of the corporation. A court-appointed trustee subsequently reported that Towers had insufficient collateral and could not account for "scores of millions of dollars" it had borrowed. However the case turns out,

it is clear from evidence already made public that Mr. Hoffenberg has played loose with the facts about his business life over the years. In countless annual reports, contracts and court settlements, he has made promises to investors and others that he did not keep. Confronted with a number of examples in an interview last week, Mr. Hoffenberg disputed key details or blamed others, denying that he was in any way untrustworthy.[81]

Ostensibly legal, Towers engaged in questionable activities that reflect both connectivity and continuity, as Maltz uses the terms in this book. Its actions illustrate the ambiguities that surround an enterprise at the margin of legitimacy. When an enterprise can be "merely" unethical but still legal, does the difference affect the utility of the firm as a supplier? How does a single firm's behavior affect the reputation and credibility of the industry of which it is a part? Towers is part of the securities industry, and the firm's actions illuminate the combination of bounded rationality, opportunism, and asset specificity with which the industry must contend in its transactions. The SEC was the "organizational imperative" (as Williamson puts it)[82] that emerged to protect industry stakeholders when these three conditions were joined.

The principle constituencies responsible for its creation, structure, and operations are the public (acting through national political mechanisms, complexities in themselves) and the securities industry whose members, being prone themselves to opportunism, may advocate self-interested and conflicting goals for the structure and operations of public oversight.

The case also illustrates the problem of controlling opportunism, or "self-interest seeking *with guile*." Towers manipulated two loopholes in the regulatory process: the ability to become a publicly traded company without submitting to SEC review, and the ability to engage in direct securities sales without state regulatory review. The SEC may win its suit against Towers, but investors have incurred losses they are unlikely to recover, and—most important—the loopholes that Towers manipulated will remain for other opportunists to use.

As Williamson notes, "The assumption that court ordering is efficacious in a regime of bounded rationality and opportunism is plainly gratuitous, but it is the maintained assumption nonetheless."[83] To assume that humans are opportunistic does not mean that they are all opportunistic all the time. Rather, "the assumption is that *some* individuals are opportunistic *some* of the time and that it is costly to ascertain differential trustworthiness."[84] Control of opportunism requires advance safeguards. They may not always work; but as H.L.A. Hart has observed, " 'Sanctions' are . . . required not as the normal motive for obedience, but as a *guarantee* that those who would voluntarily obey shall not be sacrificed by those who would not."[85]

The electrical price-fixing conspiracy of 1959 was in its time the largest action brought under the Sherman Anti-Trust Act. Between February and July of 1960 a total of twenty indictments handed up by four Philadelphia grand juries accused executives of twenty-nine electrical manufacturing companies, led by General Electric and Westinghouse, of having actively conspired for several years to fix prices in competitive bidding worth at least $7 billion.

What happened was this: forty-five leading executives . . . got together over a long period of years in conspiratorial meetings. They set the meetings up from public phone booths, or by letters on blank stationery signed by coded names. They never permitted themselves to be seen together in public dining rooms or hotel lobbies. They often registered in hotels as individuals, rather than as company representatives. They made their expense accounts out for one city, and showed up in another an equivalent distance away. They developed complex and unique systems to work out their conspiracies, utilizing the moon, of all things, to act as a signal lamp for their plans. . . . The purpose of these . . . meetings . . . was simple: To milk Federal, State, public utility, and private industrial purchasing departments of every extra cent possible. . . . The method was equally simple: Split the pie up in proportion to the weight of each company; squash any outsiders who tried to compete; decide on who gets the contracts; fake other bids to make them look legitimate, push the prices up as high as possible—and there you are. As F. F. Loock, president, general manager, and sales manager of the Allen-Bradley Company said: "No one attending the gatherings was so stupid he didn't know the meetings were in violation of the law. But it is the only way a business can be run. It is free enterprise."[86]

When the defendants were arraigned, they expected to enter responses of nolo contendere, which, if accepted, would have kept the evidence from the public domain (and from subsequent use as evidence for civil damages by defrauded customers). But federal district judge J. Cullen Ganey rejected them, forcing each company to respond directly to the indictments. In the face of overwhelming evidence, they all eventually entered guilty pleas.

The electrical conspiracy was a case of opportunism for the purpose of managing the risks of asset specificity. Though all twenty-nine codefendant firms were legal entities, some of their senior managers created a thirtieth and illegal entity when they met around their shared interests in connected and continuous bid-rigging transactions. These managers were accountable for profits, which required that they work out a way of protecting their sunk costs. If they all had to bid seriously on every job, they would each assume unacceptable risks that their machinery, factories, material, and personnel would be committed to contracts that were never completed.

The bid-rigging entity was clearly an illicit enterprise. Whether the conspirators acted as independent agents or on behalf of their employers was never fully resolved,[87] and we cannot fully specify the constituency they represented. Their entity was influenced also by a second constituency, the Anti-Trust Division of the Justice Department. In accepting nolo contendere pleas in other Sherman Act cases, the department had sent a clear signal regarding the amount of risk the conspirators would be undertaking, and their procedures reflected that level of risk. When Judge Ganey insisted on direct pleas, their organization turned out to be maladapted, and seven individual defendants went to jail.

Rural crime networks in eastern Kentucky are described by Potter and Gaines[88] as falling into two categories: wholesale production and supply (marijuana growing and processing and transshipment of cocaine) and retail sales and service (the traditional vice occupations of liquor, drugs, prostitution, and gambling). The networks provide a database that is the pathway to the primary purpose of their study: "to describe the types and modes of corruption in rural settings and to explore the relationship between organizations providing illicit goods and services in rural settings and public officials."[89] The authors are unequivocal in their conclusion:

To argue, as most traditional accounts of organized crime have, that it cannot exist long without corrupting trusted officials is to tell only half the story. Many social contradictions are resolved by, and many "legitimate" social functions are in fact sustained by, organized crime groups. Organized criminals and public officials form a close, symbiotic bond that usually places the latter in the center of the illicit enterprise. Public officials are not just the minions of organized crime; they are part of its fabric, albeit the part found in society's legitimate and respected institutions.[90]

The twenty-eight networks are the "organizations" in this study. Corruption is ancillary to them. From the perspective of organization analysis, however, corruption itself is the organization of interest. A bond that "usually places" public officials "in the center of the illicit enterprise" has structural implications worth pursuing. We may ask, Does the Potter and Gaines analysis support the assumption of centrality?

Three networks showed no evidence of corruption,[91] but the other twenty-five "have ongoing relationships with elected public officeholders and law enforcement officials in their home counties,"[92] categorized unidimensionally by "modes of corruption": official acquiescence (eleven networks), familial rela-

Figure 5.1
**Distribution of Organized Crime Networks by Characteristics Governing
Nonenforcement of Vice Laws**

		Monetary Exchange	
		Yes	No
Family	Yes	5	5
Relationship	No	4	11

Adapted from Potter and Gaines, 1992, 44.

tions (five networks), bribery and extortion (four networks), and active participation (five networks).[93]

"Official acquiescence" describes knowing nonenforcement in the absence
of a monetary exchange. I assume that, given the importance of family relations
in rural enterprise, "active participation" describes familial relations that are
distinctive because officials profit from the network.[94] These being the case, the
data might more usefully be categorized on two dimensions that provide a better
foundation for structural analysis. Given knowledge that a network exists that
engages in illegal activity, is there a family relationship between local officials
and the network? Is there monetary exchange that would support an economist's
presumption of contract?

When the data are rearranged, we see different relationships from those emphasized by Potter and Gaines (see Figure 5.1). In nearly two-thirds of the
sample there is no monetary exchange between a network and local officials. Is
"corruption" the appropriate organizing condition for describing them?

In calling knowing nonenforcement "official acquiescence" and in catego-
rizing it as "corruption," Potter and Gaines follow a standard criminological
approach to selective enforcement or nonenforcement.[95] But using their analysis
and commentary, a theorist from the multiple constituencies perspective would
describe it differently. The actors in this situation include various factions within
the voting public: elected officials and law enforcement personnel; illicit entrepreneurs; and their patrons. Obviously, many individuals play multiple roles. As
Potter and Gaines point out,[96] the voting public has elected and influenced public
officials to pass vice laws. The public has also influenced those officials to
operate within limited funds for public services, including law enforcement, thus
mandating severe resource allocation restrictions. Meanwhile, patrons want illicit
goods and services to remain available despite the law; and local businesses
(whose owners may or may not be patrons as well) find their businesses are
indirectly supported through the cash flow associated with vice. They encourage

public officials not to enforce the vice laws. Given the political and financial costs of investigation and prosecution, officials put their money and interests elsewhere. The laws thus become "virtually unenforceable" because non-enforcement without exchange is the equilibrium point among the multiple constituencies that have created the local sociopolitical scene.[97] The absence of monetary exchange thus signals the absence of organization in this segment of the data. To refer to it as corruption is to prejudge the data through the ideological stance of the moral entrepreneur.

In the remaining nine cases, however, a connected and continuous monetary exchange accompanies the transaction as a cost of nonenforcement. An observer from the TCE perspective would ask, What conditions of the transactions require the additional cost of organized nonenforcement?

The data provided by Potter and Gaines are not a sufficient base from which to answer this question. Even though asset specificity, uncertainty, and opportunism are potential reasons for using payments as an organizing mechanism, in both the retail and wholesale trade, conditions for nonenforcement are not uniform in either sector. Nonenforcement is accompanied by monetary exchange in some instances; in others it is not. The most likely condition, however, is opportunism, particularly in the retail trade.

It can work both ways. The enforcement officer may be opportunistic, seeking payoffs from networks with insufficient social or political influence. Or the network may encourage organized payments as a means of controlling opportunism within the local industry. Customers have a recourse if a retailer tries to back out of an implied contract (i.e., failing to pay gambling winnings or selling bad liquor), and networks have a mechanism for regulating competition in the market. As Potter and Gaines observe, "Selective enforcement serves a vital control function. The reduction of competition by the criminal justice system limits organizational strain and reduces the potential for violence."[98]

Until the spring of 1980,[99] the Angelo Bruno crime family (or network) of Philadelphia was the urban equivalent of the rural organized crime networks described by Potter and Gaines. The principal difference between them appears to have been a function of size. The Bruno network had approximately fifty-eight active members in the late 1960s, according to Haller (this book), whereas Potter and Gaines report that the largest network in their study had seven "related individuals in management positions."[100]

Despite its greater size, however, the Bruno network limited its entrepreneurial focus to two primary activities, loan-sharking and numbers gambling. "There were other illegal markets in the Delaware Valley [but] in most, members of the Bruno [network] were of minor importance. . . . There were, in short, important areas of illegal enterprise in which members of the Bruno [network] played, at best, a marginal role" (Haller, this book).

Haller describes Bruno's organization as a system of partnerships and commission agents. Operations were decentralized, and overhead was minimized. There was no central obligation to support unprofitable enterprises. Risks of oversight were minimized; market entry and exit were simplified. Its classical model appears to be the internal contract system, which was "widely used by organizations in the nineteenth century, and into the twentieth century, in the major capitalist nations of Britain, Japan and the United States."[101] In this system an employer and owner of capital hired internal subcontractors who negotiated a lump sum payment in exchange for specific goods. "It was left up to the internal contractor to determine how, by whom, at what profit or loss to the contractor and in what way the transaction was accomplished."[102]

In Bruno's case, however, the cash exchange was reversed, and the subcontractor paid the capitalist. What prompted the difference? In TCE terms the reversal is an exchange of asset specificity protection for the control of opportunism. In classic internal contracting, the owner had fixed assets that were "rented" to subcontractors, and the internal contract was the owner's asset protection. Organization was prompted primarily by the owner's needs. With the Bruno network, however, organization was prompted by the subcontractor's needs for regulatory control. As Haller in this book correctly points out, "For this world of small business to operate with a minimum of conflict and with reasonable cooperation, it was necessary to have a set of norms or rules and a rudimentary system of dispute settlement." Why was it necessary? To control opportunism by entrepreneurs themselves, their competitors,[103] or their customers.

Haller's analysis is a valuable elaboration of my earlier suggestion of a "service technology of security and enforcement."[104] But it is constrained by the conventional organized crime assumption that the process of controlling opportunism represents "a sort of shadow government." The assumption has dramatic inferences, but we may be better served by seeing it as the illicit equivalent of shared regulation, by which public and private organizations in legitimate industries and the professions share this responsibility.

In these systems of shared regulation—more commonly known as "self-regulation"—private organizations play central roles in surveillance, investigation, and control, usually under governmental oversight; government generally defers to private regulatory efforts in the absence of conspicuous regulatory failures.[105]

The parallel among Bruno's organizational response, the organization of corruption in rural Kentucky, and SEC oversight of the Towers Financial Corporation is inescapable. In the first case, small networks were brought into a single framework; in the second, illicit networks contracted upward as independent agents; in the third, public oversight of the securities industry was mandated by Congress. The organizing motive, controlling opportunism, was the same in all three cases, but situational constraints led to different solutions.

CONCLUSIONS

In broad terms, the enterprise model of the 1990s will retain a primary identification with its 1975 predecessor, supplemented (as suggested earlier) by appropriate components from the structural and kinship-based, patron-client models and buttressed by contributions from contemporary organization theory. As we have seen, transaction cost economics and multiple-constituencies theory are two substantial building blocks, and I conclude with final observations about them.

The principal challenge from the TCE perspective is clear: "Beware Opportunists!" Who can gain by guileful behavior? Before answering, it is critical to bear in mind that economists distinguish between simple self-interest seeking and self-interest seeking with guile. An illegal transaction is not by definition "guileful" when all parties with interest in the transaction know that it is illegal and have taken into account the risks incurred by dealing where there is no legal recourse.

We need also to remember that opportunism is not limited to illegal behavior. An agent who arranges special but legal perks (e.g., a golden parachute) acts opportunistically at the expense of both owner profit and job security of other employees.

As Williamson points out, "Problems of economic organization are compounded if the propensity to behave opportunistically is known to vary among members of the contracting population."[106] The Machiavellian remedy is preemptive opportunism: "A prudent ruler ought not to keep faith when by so doing it would be against his interest, and when the reasons which made him bind himself no longer exist."[107] But Williamson suggests a "more important" alternative:

Transactions that are subject to *ex post* opportunism will benefit if appropriate safeguards can be devised *ex ante*. Rather than reply to opportunism in kind, therefore, the wise prince is one who seeks both to give and to receive "credible commitments." Incentives may be realigned, and/or superior governance structures within which to organize transactions may be devised.[108]

The TCE lesson: provision for credible commitments is an inevitable and critical part of any structure for continuing and connected illicit enterprises.

The principal challenge from the M-C perspective is also clear: "*cherchez les depositaires d'enjoux!*" But who will be the stakeholders? The primary external parties affecting illicit enterprises are their suppliers, customers, competitors, and regulators.[109] They are familiar groups, having been identified previously as the environmental sources of "crucial contingencies" for the original enterprise model.[110] But when the M-C perspective shifts our focus away from the organization as initiator of action (for which those four groups are the pertinent environmental forces) and toward constituencies as the active shapers of organizations, a fifth external constituency comes in view: the media.[111]

Naming the media as a shaper of illicit enterprise might be surprising to one not familiar with the public debate about "Mafia" over the past century. Anyone familiar with that history is aware of the influence of news reports and fiction over public expectations about organized crime.[112]

I do not mean to suggest that entities within the media promote organized crime. Rather, they have their own goals, to write and publish stories and reports that fill a knowledge or entertainment need of their customers. Their goals, combined with those of other interested constituencies, create multiple constraints on the structure of organizations at the center of those interests that can verge on self-fulfilling prophecies. To the contemporary analyst, these constraints are what R. A. Cloward and L. E. Ohlin meant by "illegitimate opportunity structures."[113]

The M-C lesson: the constituencies affecting the structures of illicit enterprises are not limited to those who stand to gain directly from them.

T. J. Kuhn suggests that a shift from the pre- to the postparadigm period in the development of a scientific field comes with the adoption of a paradigm "that identifies challenging puzzles, supplies clues to their solution, and guarantees that the truly clever practitioner will succeed."[114] With the appropriate infusion of ideas and findings from multiple-constituency theory, transaction cost economics, and other tested organization theories, the enterprise perspective of the 1990s promises to provide such a paradigm. The four examples discussed here are but a taste of the research and theory-building possibilities that lie ahead.

NOTES

1. Theorists and researchers today ask these questions about legitimate organizations. They come to different conclusions, and they argue among themselves. Their arguments can be useful when the participants respect varying theoretical premises as to how an organization can be defined.

2. "Systems theory views an organization as a complex set of dynamically intertwined and interconnected elements, including its inputs, processes, outputs, feedback loops, and the environment in which it operates and with which it continuously interacts. A change in any element of the system causes changes in other elements" (J. M. Shafritz and J. S. Ott, *Classics of Organization Theory*, 3d ed. [Pacific Grove, CA: Brooks/Cole, 1992], 263).

3. In contingency theory, "the effectiveness of an organizational action (for example, a decision) is viewed as dependent upon the relationship between the element in question and all other aspects of the system—at the particular moment. Everything is situational; there are no absolutes or universals. Thus, contingency views of organizations place high importance on rapid, accurate information systems" (Shafritz and Ott, *Classics*, 267. See also F. E. Kast and J. E. Rosenzweig, "General Systems Theory: Appli-

cations for Organization and Management," *Academy of Management Journal* 1972 (December): 447–65).

4. Since the word *hierarchy* has a particular meaning in contemporary organization theory, I refer to the first model as the "structural" model. For simplicity, I refer to the second as the "kinship" model, though this reference omits the equally important patron-client dimension. I refer to the third as the "enterprise" model.

5. U.S. Senate Committee on Government Operations, Organized Crime and Illicit Traffic in Narcotics; Hearings Before the Permanent Subcommittee on Investigations of the Committee on Government Operations, U.S. Senate, 88th Congress, Parts 1–5 (Washington, DC: U.S. Government Printing Office, 1963–64).

6. President's Commission on Law Enforcement and Administration of Justice, *Task Force Report: Organized Crime* (Washington, DC: U.S. Government Printing Office, 1967).

7. Peter Reuter correctly observes elsewhere in this volume that "while the field of organizational studies continues to grow, none of its exponents have made a serious foray into the study of criminal organizations." My intent is to address this deficiency.

8. F. M. Thrasher, *The Gang* (Chicago: University of Chicago Press, 1927).

9. J. Landesco, *Organized Crime in Chicago, Part III of the Illinois Crime Survey of 1929*; reprint, with a new introduction by Mark H. Haller (Chicago: University of Chicago Press, 1968).

10. D. C. Smith, Jr., *The Mafia Mystique* (New York: Basic Books, 1975; reprint, Lanham, MD: University Press of America, 1990), 78–79.

11. National Commission on Law Observance and Enforcement, *Report on the Cost of Crime* (Washington, DC: National Commission, 1931), 405–6.

12. For a review of the Wickersham Commission and its findings and recommendations concerning organized crime, see D. C. Smith, Jr., "Wickersham to Sutherland to Katzenbach: Evolving an 'Official' Definition for Organized Crime," *Crime, Law and Social Change* 16 (1991): 135–54.

13. E. O. Sutherland, "White-Collar Criminality," *American Sociological Review* 5 (1940): 1–12.

14. Smith, *The Mafia Mystique*, 243–50.

15. President's Commission, *Task Force Report*, 6.

16. D. R. Cressey, *Theft of the Nation: The Structure and Operations of Organized Crime in America* (New York: Harper and Row, 1969), 21.

17. Like any other professional community, law enforcement is affected by environmental constraints and need not present a monolithic point of view about organized crime. Thus, the operating perspectives of different segments of the community could well lead to different nuances of definition. An analysis of those perspectives would be an interesting and useful research project within organizational studies.

18. G. W. Potter and L. K. Gaines, "Country Comfort: Vice and Corruption in Rural Settings," *Journal of Contemporary Criminal Justice* 8.1 (1992): 36–61.

19. C. Perrow, *Complex Organizations: A Critical Essay*, 3d ed. (New York: McGraw-Hill, 1972), 146.

20. G. L. Hostetter and T. Q. Beesley, *It's a Racket!* (Chicago: Les Quin, 1929).

21. Smith, *The Mafia Mystique*, 335–36; D. C. Smith, Jr., "Paragons, Pariahs, and Pirates: A Spectrum-Based Theory of Enterprise," *Crime & Delinquency* 26 (1980): 358–86; D. C. Smith, Jr., "White-Collar Crime, Organized Crime, and the Business Establishment:

Resolving a Crisis in Criminological Theory," in *White Collar and Economic Crime*, ed. P. Wickman and T. Dailey (Lexington, MA: D. C. Heath, 1982), 23–38, esp. 24–25.

22. National Commission, *Report*, 406.

23. Smith, "Paragons," 376–81.

24. Elsewhere in this volume, Reuter concludes that while there is a public perception "that organized crime is becoming a more serious social problem. . . . The phenomenon was far more important three decades ago than it is now. . . . It is not uncharitable to suggest that a major reason to study organized crime is precisely to show how limited and specific are its powers. . . . [A] modest scholarly effort to demonstrate the more sober realities seems worthwhile." I infer that he means Michael D. Maltz's OC subset of illicit enterprise.

25. Cressey, *Theft of the Nation*, 300.

26. Ibid., 72.

27. Ibid., 110.

28. Ibid., 126.

29. Ibid., 159.

30. Ibid., 213.

31. Ibid., 246.

32. Ibid., 247.

33. Ibid., 252–53.

34. Haller's observation under the heading of "Illegal Enterprise" is to the point: "Members of crime families . . . are generally independent entrepreneurs who have carved out a world of opportunistic ventures and informal illegal enterprises within the interstices of a larger and more bureaucratic society. . . . To see them as cogs in a bureaucracy misses a central characteristic of their economic endeavors" M. H. Haller, "Bureaucracy and the Mafia: An Alternative View," *Journal of Contemporary Criminal Justice* 8.1 (1992): 6.

35. J. L. Albini, *The American Mafia: Genesis of a Legend* (New York: Appleton-Century-Crofts, 1971).

36. F.A.J. Ianni, with E. Reuss-Ianni, *A Family Business* (New York: Russell Sage Foundation, 1972).

37. Albini, *The American Mafia*, 14.

38. Ibid., 111–12.

39. Ibid., 136.

40. Ianni, *A Family Business*, 108.

41. Ibid., 17.

42. Ibid., 40.

43. Ibid., 161.

44. Ibid., 169–73.

45. Ibid., 194.

46. F.A.J. Ianni, *Black Mafia: Ethnic Succession in Organized Crime* (New York: Simon and Schuster, 1974).

47. Ianni, *A Family Business*, 193.

48. M. H. Haller, *Life Under Bruno: The Economics of an Organized Crime Family* (Conshohocken: Pennsylvania Crime Commission, 1991). This chapter is not the place for such an analysis; but the circumstances Haller describes in the ultimate succession of Nicholas Scarfo over Angelo Bruno in the 1980s suggest an intriguing parallel with the succession of Vito Genovese over Frank Costello in the 1950s.

49. Smith, *The Mafia Mystique*; D. C. Smith, Jr., "Organized Crime and Entrepreneurship," *International Journal of Criminology and Penology* 6 (1978): 161–77; Smith, "Paragon"; Smith, "White-Collar Crime."

50. "Illicit enterprise is the extension of legitimate market activities into areas normally proscribed—i.e., beyond existing limits of the law—for the pursuit of profit and in response to latent illicit demand" (Smith, *The Mafia Mystique*, 335).

51. L. T. Wilkins, *Social Deviance* (Englewood Cliffs, NJ: Prentice-Hall, 1965), 46–47.

52. J. D. Thompson, *Organizations in Action* (New York: McGraw-Hill, 1967).

53. Ibid., 10.

54. Smith, "Organized Crime," 164–65.

55. The 1980 text referred to "ethnicity" and "ethnic ties." For consistency with this chapter I have substituted the term *kinship*. I believe the substitution improves the original text.

56. Smith, "Paragons," 375.

57. Ibid., 381–86.

58. Smith, "White-Collar Crime," 34–37.

59. Smith, *The Mafia Mystique*, 343–45.

60. Shafritz and Ott, *Classics*, 343.

61. O. E. Williamson, *The Economic Institutions of Capitalism* (New York: Free Press, 1985).

62. M. C. Jensen and W. H. Meckling, "Agency Costs and the Theory of the Firm," *Journal of Financial Economics* 3 (1976): 310. The passage is quoted by Shafritz and Ott, *Classics*, 344.

63. Shafritz and Ott, *Classics*, 345.

64. P. Georgiou, "The Goal Paradigm and Notes Toward a Counter Paradigm," *Administrative Science Quarterly* 18 (1973): 291–310.

65. T. Connolly, E. J. Condon, and S. J. Deutsch, "Organizational Effectiveness: A Multiple-Constituency Approach," *Academy of Management Review* 5 (1980): 211–17.

66. R. Coase, "The Nature of the Firm," *Economica* 4 (1937): 386–405.

67. O. Hart, "An Economist's Perspective on the Theory of the Firm," in *Organization Theory from Chester Barnard to the Present and Beyond*, ed. O. E. Williamson (New York: Oxford University Press, 1990), 155.

68. Thompson, *Organizations*, 27.

69. Williamson, *The Economic Institutions*, 2.

70. In the original edition of *Administrative Behavior* Simon discusses "limits of rationality" that are derived "from the inability of the human mind to bring to bear upon a single decision all the aspects of value, knowledge, and behavior that would be relevant. . . . Human rationality operates, then, within the limits of a psychological environment [that] imposes on the individual as 'givens' a selection of factors upon which he must base his decisions" (H. A. Simon, *Administrative Behavior,* New York: Macmillan, 1949). All the elements are present, but calling it "bounded rationality" did not occur until later.

71. H. A. Simon, *Models of Man* (New York: John Wiley, 1957), 198–99.

72. H. A. Simon, *Administrative Behavior*, 2d ed. (New York: Macmillan, 1961), xxiv.

73. Williamson, *The Economic Institutions*, 30. Note that in this discussion "opportunism" has a different meaning from that assumed by Ronald Goldstock in this book

in his use of the word as a substitute for "opportunity"; see the discussion of OC and "connectivity" in Maltz in this book.

74. The farm labor market illustrates an alternative response to spot hiring: the use of a "crew chief" as the intermediary who organizes a group of migratory workers and arranges a schedule with farm owners for moving the group as needs for cultivation and harvesting change.

75. The continuing threat for the migrant farm worker is that the crew chief and farm owner will take advantage of their bounded rationality and opportunistically conspire to reduce the wages they receive from what the farmer pays the crew chief. If the arrangement does not break a law, it may be considered unethical by some (although others may argue that getting the best deal for oneself is the essence of competitive contracting). If the arrangement is illegal and not simply unethical, it is an illicit enterprise.

76. Haller, *Life Under Bruno*; Haller, "Bureaucracy"; Haller in this book.

77. As an illustration of the problem to be surmounted, see my comments on the conceptual limits of the Standard Industrial Classification (SIC) Manual in Smith, "Paragons," 363–65.

78. Smith, "Paragons," 379.

79. D. B. Henriques, "How a Country Boy Snared a Money Man from the Big City," *New York Times*, 4 April 1993, Sec. 3, 1, 6.

80. Ibid., 1.

81. Ibid., 6.

82. Williamson, *The Economic Institutions*, 32.

83. Ibid.

84. O. E. Williamson, "Chester Barnard and the Incipient Science of Organization," in *Organization Theory from Chester Barnard to the Present and Beyond*, ed. O. E. Williamson (New York: Oxford University Press, 1991), 190.

85. H.L.A. Hart, *The Concept of Law* (Oxford: Oxford University Press, 1961), 193. Quoted by Williamson, "Chester Barnard," 191.

86. J. G. Fuller, *The Gentlemen Conspirators: The Story of Price-Fixers in the Electrical Industry* (New York: Grove Press, 1962), 13–14.

87. Westinghouse acknowledged responsibility for the actions of its managers, but General Electric (GE) did not, using as its shield "Directive 20.5," which stated that no employee was permitted to indulge in practices forbidden by the antitrust laws. In response, individual GE defendants claimed that their actions were governed by a "corporate way of life" in which 20.5 was simply a sheet of paper that top management expected them to ignore. They could not prove their claim, however, and GE held to its official position of corporate noninvolvement. Fuller, *The Gentlemen*, 87.

88. Potter and Gaines, "Country Comfort," 40.

89. Ibid., 37.

90. Ibid., 58.

91. As Potter and Gaines note, the three are headed by women and are engaged primarily in wholesale marijuana production and distribution. Their comments on this circumstance invite further study.

92. Ibid., 56.

93. Ibid., 43–45.

94. Ibid., 44.

95. M. Johnston, *Police Corruption and Public Policy* (Monterey, CA: Brooks/Cole, 1982), 75. Quoted by Potter and Gaines, "Country Comfort," 43.

96. Potter and Gaines, "Country Comfort," 54–58.

97. Potter and Gaines note that four of the nine networks engaged in bootlegging are beneficiaries of nonenforcement as a result of familial relations to public officials or law enforcement officers (Ibid., 52). The relation is only one factor in calculating multiple-constituency equilibrium, however; the relative who tried to "protect" a network in the absence of nonenforcement equilibrium would most likely not remain in office.

98. Ibid., 55.

99. In March 1980 Bruno was shot and killed outside his home in South Philadelphia. His murder was followed by a struggle for succession that lasted for a year. After the murders of two interim leaders, Nicholas Scarfo assumed Bruno's mantle (readers not familiar with this history should consult Haller, *Life Under Bruno*). Family fortunes declined rapidly, in part because Scarfo imposed a different style of leadership and organization structure (indeed, much like that theorized by Cressey in 1969, *Theft of the Nation*) on the old Bruno network. Within a decade Scarfo was in prison, and the network that he inherited was in shambles. The styles of Bruno and Scarfo are contrasting illustrations of strategic-contingency leadership theory. See D. J. Hickson et al., "A Strategic Contingencies Theory of Intra-Organizational Power," *Administrative Science Quarterly* 16 (1971): 216–29; G. R. Salancik and J. Pfeffer, "Who Gets Power—And How They Hold On to It: A Strategic-Contingency Model of Power," *Organizational Dynamics* (1977), 417–29.

100. Potter and Gaines, "Country Comfort," 47.

101. S. R. Clegg, *Modern Organizations* (London: Sage, 1990), 65.

102. Ibid.

103. "Among those who accepted the legitimacy of the family—whether members or not—a central principle was that the businesses of members or their associates were protected from raids by other members or by outsiders. This was, in fact, one of the advantages of membership" (Haller, in this book).

104. Smith, *The Mafia Mystique*, 344.

105. S. R. Faerman and D. P. McCaffrey, "Shared Regulation in the United States Securities Industry," Unpublished paper (Albany, NY: University at Albany, 1993).

106. Williamson, *The Economic Institutions*, 48.

107. N. Machiavelli, *The Prince* (New York: New American Library, 1952) 92.

108. Williamson, *The Economic Institutions*, 48–49.

109. Elsewhere in this volume, John Dombrink and John Song, and James O. Finckenauer remind us that crimes with ethnic (Chinese and Russian, respectively) implications also entail foreign and international law enforcement constituencies.

110. Smith, *The Mafia Mystique*, 340.

111. I use *media* as a shorthand expression covering the communication of news, entertainment and fiction.

112. See Smith, *The Mafia Mystique*, Chapters 4, 9, 298–305. Among other tidbits, the history shows that some elements in law enforcement and the media have at times (but not always: see ibid., 245) worked in parallel to create a public image of organized crime consistent with the structural model. See also Finckenauer's comments elsewhere in this volume concerning media "romanticism" surrounding Russian organized criminal groups in this country. Some observers have challenged that image and the structural model on the grounds that it was a self-fulfilling prophecy. R. J. Kelly's comments in

this regard are useful; see R. J. Kelly, "Trapped in the Folds of Discourse: Theorizing About the Underworld," *Journal of Contemporary Criminal Justice* 8.1 (1992): 11–35.

113. R. A. Cloward and L. E. Ohlin, *Delinquency and Opportunity: A Theory of Delinquent Gangs* (Glencoe, IL: Free Press, 1960), 150.

114. T. J. Kuhn, *The Structure of Scientific Revolutions*, 2d ed. (Chicago: University of Chicago Press), 179.

Part III

Organized Crime Groups and Operations

6

The Bruno Family of Philadelphia: Organized Crime as a Regulatory Agency

MARK H. HALLER

In 1959 Angelo Bruno Annalore—known during most of his life as Angelo Bruno, or "Ange" to his friends—became the boss of the South Philadelphia Italian American crime family. Born in the town of Villalba, Sicily, in 1910, he was raised in South Philadelphia, where his father owned a small grocery store. By the late 1930s, he had become a successful operator of numbers gambling and took pride in his skill and reliability as a criminal entrepreneur. His success as an entrepreneur and his political skills enabled him to assume the position of boss during a leadership crisis of the late 1950s. During his twenty-one-year leadership of what became known as the Bruno family, he was a careful, secretive boss, who even looked like a stodgy and conservative accountant.[1] As boss, he continued drawing profits from numbers gambling and loan-sharking, while expanding his investments in numerous legitimate businesses in the Philadelphia region, Florida, and elsewhere. His leadership abruptly ended on 21 March 1980, when he was shot and killed in front of his home in South Philadelphia. The existence of the Bruno family and of allied families in other American cities raises the obvious question, Why do men involved in a range of illegal and legal money-making activities find it useful to join and support such groups? What functions do the groups perform for members? One answer is that the families function as a sort of shadow government or regulating agency that brings some predictability and structure to their part of the urban underworld. Because the Bruno family enjoyed a remarkable stability and held a recognized place in the underworld of Philadelphia and of several surrounding cities, it provides a good case study. An examination of the role of the family in the late

1970s, in the years before Bruno's death, can clarify the family's regulatory functions.

INTRODUCTION

In order to understand the regulatory functions of the Bruno family, it is necessary to examine two different types of structures. One is the structure of the illegal (and legal) businesses operated by the members. These businesses were owned and directed by the members and their partners and were not operated on behalf of the family. As owners, the members and their associates pocketed the profits, when there were profits; they suffered the losses, when there were losses.

The other structure was the family. The family was not a business or money-making operation, nor did it control any businesses. As one longtime member declared with reference to money-making activities: "The family don't run anything."[2] The family, instead, was like a fraternal organization. In the world in which the members operated, there was prestige in belonging to the family, with its powerful reputation and its secret ways. In the restaurants and nightspots where they hung out, they enjoyed the special attention that they received. Many members took seriously the social bonds that were forged among members and were displayed at marriages, funerals, and other occasions where they exchanged gifts and acknowledged their loyalties to each other.

Under Bruno, the family had a normal structure, which may have existed since the 1930s. There were a boss and underboss. There was also a consigliere, who was supposed to be a wise and neutral figure to advise the boss and mediate disputes among members. The family also had capos (often referred to in Philadelphia as "capis"). In theory, at least, each member reported to a capo.

The family, while not involved in money-making schemes, aided the economic interests of its members and their associates. One function was to provide a group within which members could make useful contacts, learn about business opportunities, and exchange mutual favors. But there was also a second function. The family was a sort of shadow government, providing a set of rules and expectations that facilitated the members' legal and illegal activities. A willingness of underworld wheelers and dealers to risk money in chancy enterprises and to trust others as partners or agents required that they feel confidence that commitments would be honored. For legal businessmen, regulatory structure is provided by the law and by ethical standards enforced formally and informally through bar associations or better business bureaus. The Bruno family, then, was like a bar association or better business bureau in providing a structure of rules for those who accepted its legitimacy.

It is necessary first to understand the problems and the risks faced by the members in their business activities. Then it will be possible to understand the ways in which the Bruno family provided rules that gave structure to the world in which members operated.

ILLEGAL BUSINESSES

In the late 1960s, the Bruno family had approximately fifty-eight active members. Of these, a few pursued only legal sources of income; some had only illegal sources of income; and others, generally those best known to the public and to law enforcement, combined legal and illegal sources of income.[3] By the late 1970s, the number of active members—as estimated by the Pennsylvania Crime Commission in 1980—had declined by about ten. The distribution of their involvement in legal and illegal activities, however, generally followed the same pattern.

The members structured their illegal businesses in order to share profits and spread the risks. There were two patterns by which this was done. Although sometimes a loan-sharking operation or numbers bank was owned by a single individual, typically the ownership was by two or more partners. The partners could include both family members and nonmembers. Usually all of the partners invested money in the enterprise, but one member was responsible for day-to-day oversight of the business. By forming partnerships, the owners spread the risks and combined their resources and expertise.[4]

While an illegal business was generally established and controlled by partners, the next level of participants was often commission agents—a system in which persons received a share of the profits from that part of the business in which they participated. In numbers gambling, for instance, a numbers writer in a barbershop or saloon received a percentage of the money that was bet at his or her retail outlet. Similarly, loan sharks made arrangements with agents by which agents shared in the profits that they generated from loans. In effect, agents were uninvested partners in that phase of the loan shark business for which they had responsibility.[5]

There were a number of implications from the system of partnerships and commission agents. First of all, such a system meant that each person's income was tied directly to how well the activities turned a profit. This minimized the necessity for oversight since each person had a stake in doing well. Second and connected to this, the system provided for considerable decentralization of operation and therefore minimized central oversight. Each person in a numbers bank, loan shark operation, or sports book had wide discretion in carrying out his end of the enterprise. Finally, the system meant that most illegal enterprises had minimal overhead expenses or ongoing financial commitments. As an example, numbers writers sold numbers from their own bars, barbershops, or newspaper kiosks, so that the numbers bank had many outlets without the necessity of paying rent. Furthermore, since income was tied to profits, if the enterprise lost money or went out of business, there was no obligation to continue paying salaries or other expenses. This minimized risks of those overseeing the enterprise and simplified entry and exit.

The system also fit the life-style of the people in the rackets. While they often faced periods of intense activity, in general they were free of bureaucratic supervision and controlled their own time while carrying on business by cryptic telephone conversations, meetings on street corners, and exchanges of information in bars or restaurants. Written records, while important, were few and kept informally—often written by hand. These were people who spoke of their world as being "on the street." They enjoyed the life of deals, negotiations, whispered conversations; and they escaped the bureaucratic responsibilities of overseeing formal organizations.

The major illegal business engaged in by members of the Bruno family was loan-sharking[6]; however, probably the members were only a minority of loan sharks in the Philadelphia region. Nevertheless, loan-sharking was significant not only because of the money earned by those who operated as loan sharks but also because, as lenders who financed various illegal activities, the loan sharks sometimes exercised a broad economic influence on the underworld of the Delaware Valley. The loans to legal businessmen, at the same time, made them important players in the small businesses of South Philadelphia.

Because some borrowers were chronically delinquent in their payments, the attempt to collect from those in default was a loan shark's most difficult and time-consuming activity. The ultimate collection tool was violence—or, more accurately, the threat of violence. For those who were members of the Bruno family, the fact of their membership increased the credibility of their threats. Regular borrowers, though, were often aware that threats were seldom followed by actual violence. In Philadelphia, loan-sharking was largely nonviolent. Unreliable borrowers, of course, lost their access to future loans—a genuine threat for those who regularly relied on loan sharks. In general, however, defaulters were threatened as a means to induce them to recognize their obligation and agree to a new payment schedule.

Important loan sharks operated within a structure in which most of the loans were, in fact, made and collected by others. One pattern was for a leading loan shark to make arrangements for others to handle the contact with customers. In this case, the loan shark and the agent would split equally the profits from those loans managed by the agent. The agent had some independence in making loans and in managing repayment. But he was typically expected to operate within guidelines laid down by the loan shark and to seek prior approval for large or risky loans. A second pattern was for the chief loan shark to lend money to other loan sharks, who, in turn, would lend to customers. In theory, the subsidiary loan shark was an independent businessman whose income, if he managed the loans skillfully, was the difference between what was collected and what was paid for the money. In reality, though, the loan could not be repaid if those to whom the money was lent reneged on their payments. As a result, the chief loan shark was consulted concerning large or risky loans and also consulted with regard to strategies for collection when borrowers were in arrears. This created complex relations of debt among loan sharks as well as with the ultimate customers.

The second most important illegal activity was numbers gambling. Most of the numbers banks in South Philadelphia were owned by members of the Bruno family and their associates. Some of the numbers banks in Northeast Philadelphia, while independently operated, were owned by persons who had friends and associates within the Bruno family. Bruno family members also had numbers banks in Trenton and Bristol. Numbers banks in the African American neighborhoods of Philadelphia were largely independent, as were many white-operated numbers banks outside South Philadelphia.

Numbers banks have existed in Philadelphia since numbers gambling was first introduced into the city in the early 1920s.[7] It is a gambling game popular in many neighborhoods. In the most common method of playing the game, bettors place their money on any three-digit number from 000 to 999. While the payoff odds have varied from time to time and from bank to bank, the standard payoff in the late 1970s was 650 to 1. Since the odds of winning were 1,000 to 1, the persons involved in the numbers game would, in the long run, earn $350 out of every $1,000 that was bet. Numbers have traditionally been sold in barbershops, bars, newspaper kiosks, and other neighborhood outlets. There are also walking writers who go door-to-door in the neighborhood. The problem for those running the business, though, is that bettors believe in lucky numbers; and, on any given day, many bettors may select the same number. If that number wins, then the seller will be unable to make payments from the money bet on losing numbers.[8] What is profitable in the long run may lead to bankruptcy in the short run.

This is the reason for numbers banks. The bank assumes the risk by agreeing to pay off winning bettors. As a result, the numbers writers take bets in the neighborhoods. They keep a fixed percent of the money bet with them (often 20 percent) and pass on the rest of the money and the betting records. They are assured a steady income based on the amount bet with them. The bank, then, assumes the risk of paying winners and is responsible for providing the writers with enough money to cover the winning bets. The bank takes on the risks in the expectation of making a profit from the bets placed with a large number of writers. Often a pickup person collects from the writers, handles payments to writers on his route, and settles with the bank every week or two.

Those who ran numbers banks, as a result, were at the center of an elaborate system for managing risk. They had to prescribe policies to the pickup men concerning "cut" numbers and betting limits and maintained daily contact with the operations that might involve dozens of numbers writers. In turn, the banker often had regular contact with an "edge-off" house as well as with a loan shark. The system operated on credit. Periodically, the pickup person settled with writers and with the banker; the banker had to settle with the edge-off house and, perhaps, with a loan shark. It was a system run on the assumption that people would meet their obligations and pay their debts.

A few members of the Bruno family operated zignetti games in South Philadelphia and floating crap games at various locations in the Delaware Valley. While these games were few in number, they constituted a significant proportion of the zignetti and crap games in the region. Almost always they were run as partnerships. It was necessary to have a bankroll present at the game in case the players had a run of good luck. (The bankroll for a high stakes craps game might run as high as $100,000.) Few entrepreneurs had that sort of money— and even fewer were willing to risk losing that much on a bad night. As a result, they pooled their investments to spread the risks. But it was standard that one partner was present at the game to hire and oversee the lookouts and operators, to make significant decisions concerning such matters as extending credit to players, and to guard against embezzlement in what was largely a cash enterprise.

There were other illegal markets in the Delaware Valley. In most, members of the Bruno family were of minor importance. A few members ran sports bookmaking—and others became involved because, as loan sharks, they made loans to bookmakers. Members of the family, though, operated a small proportion of the sports betting in the region. With regard to drugs, a handful of members had been wholesalers of heroin in an earlier period; by the late 1970s, however, they were largely absent from the dealing in heroin, cocaine, and marijuana. By the end of the decade a few trafficked in P2P, used in the manufacture of methamphetamine. Nevertheless, in drug dealing, the most lucrative (and risky) underworld market, members of the Bruno family were notable chiefly for their relative nonparticipation.[9] There were, in short, important areas of illegal enterprise in which members of the Bruno family played, at best, a marginal role.

LEGAL BUSINESSES

The members of the Bruno family, their relatives, and their associates also controlled a range of small businesses in the Delaware Valley. Probably the most numerous were bars, nightclubs, and restaurants. Given a life-style that involved socializing and conducting business at restaurants and nightspots and given the traditional use of such places as centers for loan-sharking and gambling, they felt comfortable in ownership of such businesses. Probably a majority of successful members had an ownership interest in at least one restaurant or nightspot. Other businesses owned by members and associates provided services to nightspots, such as food services, vending machine companies, and financial services such as insurance and real estate. One associate ran a talent agency that placed entertainers in nightspots in the Delaware Valley. Even in the control of labor unions, the chief influence of Bruno family members was within locals of the Hotel, Restaurant and Bartenders Union.

Because so many of their businesses were connected to restaurants and nightspots, there was a great deal of mutual dealing among members and associates in legitimate businesses. They bought from each other and recommended each other's businesses to others. On the whole, their businesses were small. Often close relatives were officers in the businesses and oversaw day-to-day operations.

FUNCTIONS OF THE BRUNO FAMILY

Members of the Bruno family and their business associates, then, were involved in numerous independent legal and illegal business enterprises. They invested money together in risky ventures, bought and sold on credit, borrowed from each other, and owed each other favors for services rendered. For this world of small business to operate with a minimum of conflict and with reasonable cooperation, it was necessary to have a set of norms or rules and a rudimentary system of dispute settlement. The Bruno family provided such regulatory functions for those who recognized its legitimacy.

Much of the underworld in the Delaware Valley did not recognize the legitimacy of the family and operated outside its framework. Although there were some ties between a few Bruno family members and some African American criminals, on the whole, the African American underworld was independent. The same was true of the small underworld of Asian Americans. Finally, substantial portions of the white underworld—especially drug dealers and many sports bookmakers—maintained a complex but generally independent position. Nevertheless, in Philadelphia, Chester, Atlantic City, Trenton, and even Newark there were significant networks of persons in illegal and legal businesses who recognized the legitimacy of the family's norms and often operated within its framework.

An example will show how the family could provide the structure of predictability that facilitated business activities. In the mid-1970s, a Bruno nephew and an insurance dealer in northeast Pennsylvania were involved in a surety bond fraud. At one point, they decided that their scheme might be helped by a bribe of $100,000 to state regulators. Of this amount, the insurance dealer was to contribute $25,000. He was worried, though, that, if he put up the money and the bribe fell through, he might not get his money back. Consequently, he explained his problem to Albert Scalleat, whose brother Joseph was a longtime and respected member of the Bruno family operating from the Hazelton, Pennsylvania, area. Scalleat contacted Bruno and obtained his assurance that there was nothing to fear. Later the bribe scheme failed, and the insurance dealer's money was returned to him.

In this instance, Scalleat and Bruno provided the framework that made the scheme possible for two associates who accepted the family's legitimacy. The many daily transactions of members and associates would not be possible, however, if every transaction required the personal intercession of a family leader. Instead, then, the members recognized and operated within a set of formal and informal rules that had evolved over time to guide them in their business behavior.

At the initiation ceremony, new members swore their loyalty to the family and its leadership. For those who took the oath seriously, this represented a commitment to a group of men and a pattern of behavior. For most new members, having already proven themselves through business partnerships with members, admittance to the family represented formal recognition that they had proven their adherence to a code of "honorable" criminal behavior.

At the initiation ceremony, in addition, new members were solemnly informed that some criminal activities were forbidden. These included kidnapping, prostitution, counterfeiting of money, and drug dealing. There was a mixture of reasons for the bans: to maintain order within the underworld, to avoid crimes that would result in heavy penalties, and to sustain their concept of themselves as "honorable" men who disdained dishonorable activities. The mandate to shun prostitution represented a view that living off the money of a prostitute was dishonorable. Probably the mandate against kidnapping reflected the fact that in the late 1920s and early 1930s, in a number of cities such as Chicago and New York, the underworld was disrupted by gangs that kidnapped other criminals and held them for ransom. The creation of a stable underworld required stamping out such behavior.[10] The origin of the ban on drugs, probably dating from the 1950s, reflected the perception that, because drug trafficking was a federal offense, such activity presented a danger of vigorous enforcement and stiff sentences. But the ban also gave members an image of themselves as good citizens in their neighborhood and also meant that many people in South Philadelphia tolerated the family because it was seen as a group that protected the area from drug dealers.

There were other explicit elements of the code designed to maintain stability and order. As in crime families elsewhere, no member was to kill anyone without the permission of the boss. It was further understood that members were to inform their capo of their illegal ventures, so that the capo could determine whether the venture would be upsetting to another member.[11] In practice, however, this rule was not taken seriously. Another rule, according to one mob defector, was that members were not supposed to place bets with bookmakers who were members, thereby avoiding the types of quarrels that could arise if either the bettor or the bookmaker failed to make payment afterward.[12] All of these rules were intended to keep peace and stability among the members and associates.

To avoid attracting the attention of the public or authorities, Bruno pressured members to shun ostentation. Even Frank Sindone, Bruno's longtime associate and his partner in a major loan-sharking operation, found Bruno's rules stultifying. As he once exclaimed to Salvatore Merlino: "He [Bruno] don't want nobody that drinks around him, and nobody that gambles! He wants all priests around him!" When Merlino remarked, "What's the good having it [money] if you can't spend it," Sindone complained: "I've got plenty of f--ing money! What am I going to do? Die and leave it to my family? I don't want to leave it to my family! I want to live, too!" He made clear: "I love this guy [Bruno]! This guy, this guy has been good to me!" Yet he added in exasperation: "But he's got them old f--ing ways! He ain't getting out of them, you know what I mean?''[13]

Most of the code was not stated explicitly but can be inferred from the numerous conversations that were recorded by law enforcement agencies over the years. Of central concern was a set of informal rules that defined "unfair" competition. Anyone was allowed to start or expand an illegal business; but he should do so by recruiting his own agents and customers and not by trying to recruit agents or customers already attached to the business of another member or associate.

This was clear, for instance, in a June 1978 conversation in which Charles ("Chickie," or "Noodle," or "Chicken Noodle") Warrington, a respected family associate, spoke with an unidentified numbers banker named Busco. Busco came to Chickie to complain that someone was trying to steal his numbers writers. Chickie's response was that anyone had a right to start a numbers bank: "See, I don't, I don't mind anybody, ah, you know, you can't stop a guy from makin' a livin.' '' Busco agreed but added:

Busco: But, . . . don't f-- with my books. Now, how many times I come to you. And you tell that motherf--in' Pat . . .

Chick: Yeah.

Busco: To stay away from my f--in' writers. . . . And, ah, I know right, damn right well, if I'm f--in' with your books, you're gonna come, "Hey, Busco, what the f-- are you doin'?" You know.[14]

Not only was it wrong to recruit someone's agents but also to entice away customers. Harry Riccobene, who joined the Philadelphia family in 1931 and was regarded by many as a repository of family lore, explained the rules to Louis "Babe" Marchetti in an October 1977 conversation. Using the example of a loan-shark customer, Harry explained: "Knowing that somebody is doing business with somebody else, you shouldn't do business with them. That is all." He elucidated later: "Say I got a customer. 'Joe Blow' is my customer. He comes to you and says, 'Hey, Babe, I'm in a jam, I need a hundred dollars.' Right? Now you know he's my customer. You know he's doing business with me. Not only money, maybe other things. Your place to him is: 'Oh, geez, you're doing business with Harry. Why are you coming to me?' Now he'll give you another cock and bull story. And you say, 'I can't give it to you until, unless Harry okays it.' You follow, you understand what I'm saying?"[15]

Among those who accepted the legitimacy of the family—whether members or not—a central principle was that the business of members or their associates were protected from raids by other members or by outsiders. This was, in fact, one of the advantages of membership. Nonmembers frequently sought out members as partners because their illegal businesses would then be protected from unfair competition.

There were, however, obligations, as well as opportunities, for those who chose to do business with a family member. If, for instance, a numbers banker borrowed from a member loan shark who also took edge-off bets, then the numbers banker was also expected to provide his edge-off business to the loan shark. Some persons went beyond being occasional customers and dealt regularly with one or more members. They were regarded as being "with" the member who was their closest associate. Although they were not expected to make payments to the member, they were expected to cooperate in a range of business activities. In 1977, for instance, a Center City bookmaker who was known to be "with" Harry Riccobene was not giving his edge-off work to Harry. Another associate of Harry's approached the bookmaker and admonished him, in his words: "Everybody around here knows you are with Harry . . . and you are giving f--ing edge to somebody else."[16]

On another occasion Harry explained the rules of the relationship to an associate named Babe:

Harry: If you want to work under my wing?

Babe: Right, right, right.

Harry: I want to know what you're doing!

Babe: Okay.

Harry: Now, I don't want nothing! I don't need, I don't want nothing from you. I'm not looking for anybody to give me anything! You understand what I'm saying?

Babe: You're helping me?[17]

At any rate, members, their associates, and their customers constituted a complicated system of mutual obligations and exchange of favors.

Another quasi-governmental function of the family was an informal system for handling a member's businesses if the member died or went to prison. With regard to legal businesses, they remained with the member's partners or relatives, much as the businesses would for any legal small-business man. With regard to an illegal business, the business generally remained with the partners if the business had been operated by partners. If there were no partners, however, the family might redistribute ownership. This was often a complicated process. For a loan-shark operation, for instance, it would be necessary to find the scattered and incomplete records in order to reconstruct a list of loans and payments. There was, furthermore, a responsibility to take care of the member's family and to return the business to the member when the member returned to the street.[18]

Finally, the Philadelphia family was part of a national network of families. This meant that Philadelphia family members had the advantage that they could call upon contacts in other cities in their legal and illegal businesses. There was, furthermore, a complicated protocol by which members from one city could open businesses in another city. If a member of a family from another city wished to open a business in an area where Bruno family members operated, there had to be consultation and generally an offer to share in the profits. Phil Testa, then the underboss in the Bruno family, explained an agreement between New York and Philadelphia with regard to Trenton, New Jersey: "In other words, they have an agreement for card games and crap games. Say like you're from New York and I want to open up this game. I say, 'Look, I want to open up. You've got fifty percent." He went on to state that Carl "Pappy" Ippolito, a Bruno family member in Trenton, had a half interest in a local crap game run by two New Yorkers.[19]

In the late 1970s, several Gambinos opened a series of businesses in the Delaware Valley; these included a restaurant in Cherry Hill, New Jersey, a disco in Atlantic City, and a number of pizza parlors in South Jersey and Philadelphia. (Later it would be learned that the pizza parlors were fronts for the distribution of heroin.) While the Gambinos who were active in these businesses had been born in Sicily and presumably became Mafia members there, they operated in the Delaware Valley under the aegis of the Gambino family of New York. Angelo Bruno was a longtime friend of Carlo Gambino, the head of the New York family; indeed, Bruno's wife, Sue, owned property in Florida jointly with Carlo. Bruno met with the Gambinos at their Cherry Hill restaurant. Out of these contacts evolved a set of mutual favors. The pizza parlor owners sought Bruno's advice concerning cigarette vending companies to service their parlors, used an attorney who was also attorney for John's Vending (in which Bruno had an interest), and bought insurance from Bruno's son-in-law Ralph Puppo.[20] The opening of the business, in short, involved a fairly elaborate negotiation of mutual favors and assistance.

Members and associates of the Bruno family, then, carried on their legal and illegal businesses within a complicated informal framework of rules and obligations. The quasi-governmental functions of the family constituted the most important way that association with the family impacted upon the business activities of those within the family's influence.

CONCLUSION

During the 1970s, under the leadership of Bruno, the economic activities of the members exhibited a number of characteristics.

Most important, perhaps, each of the active members carried on his money-making activities within a relatively independent cluster of business partners and associates who cooperated in a variety of enterprises. Sometimes only one participant in the cluster was a member of the family. In the group around Scalleat in Hazleton, for instance, only Scalleat was a member; he formed partnerships with various relatives and outside businessmen to run the garment factories and beer distributorship that were a central part of his business operations. Riccobene, similarly, was the only Bruno family member in the cluster of legal and illegal activities operated by him and his stepbrothers in South Philadelphia. In the cluster of businesses coordinated by Sindone from a headquarters in South

Philadelphia, by contrast, there were at least half a dozen members, along with a number of associates, who formed shifting partnerships to operate in a variety of illegal activities.

While different participants in each cluster might specialize in particular types of businesses, the central figures in each cluster were involved in a range of legal and illegal ventures. Sometimes an enterprise was owned by one man, but more commonly enterprises were owned by two or more partners. Typically one of the partners took responsibility for day-to-day oversight of the enterprise, either by becoming the manager or by keeping in regular contact with the manager. If the enterprise was illegal, like a numbers bank or loan-sharking operation, then generally persons working on commission reported to the manager. Examples were the runners who collected from the numbers writers or loan-shark agents who placed loans and oversaw collection. In the case of a legal venture, like a restaurant or bar, the structure would parallel the structure of similar legal businesses owned by legitimate businessmen.

Members carried on their money-making activities chiefly with their partners and associates. Their partners and associates, not the family, were the focus of their daily rounds: discussing a loan-shark deal with an agent, tallying the daily reports from numbers runners, and stopping in at the bar or restaurant in the evening to see how business was going. These were ventures that they had established or purchased and from which they derived their illegal and legal income.

At the same time, as members of the Bruno family, they had a number of expectations and informal obligations. Particularly in places like Hazleton, Pennsylvania, or Newark and Trenton, New Jersey, where members of several families were active in the same region, they were expected to observe the protocol that defined the ways that members of different families did mutual favors and avoided disruptive competitive activities. Sometimes members of different families formed partnerships. At other times, they used each other's contacts for mutual advantage.

More important, of course, the Bruno family provided a quasi government within which members and associates operated. Sometimes persons in one cluster of enterprises did business with someone in another cluster. Commonly, for instance, a numbers banker would edge off with the numbers bank of another member. Beyond this, members and their associates were aware that they should carry on their businesses in keeping with the informal rules of the family. In short, members and associates recognized they were part of a larger network of legal and illegal businessmen who were expected to do favors for each other, avoid acts of unfair competition, and not cheat those who ran businesses that were "connected" to other members.

NOTES

1. In the fall of 1962, Bruno explained that his success in numbers gambling derived from his honesty in running the business: "If I wanted business, I can get all the business

I want. I turn it down every day. They come to me because they know I'm solid. . . . They know if they got $50 going [on a numbers bet], they are going to get paid. They are not sure of a lot of guys. That's why I get all the business I want'' (*The F.B.I. Transcripts* on Exhibit in *U.S.A. v. DeCavalcante, Vastola, and Annunziata*, Lemma, 1970, VI, 13:39).

After Bruno's assassination, his old friend and attorney Jacob Kossman reminisced about Bruno for a reporter: "I've known him 40 years. . . . I like his wife's cooking, which is the best. And then I have known his children and his grandchildren." Kossman added: "He's a great reader; he's a philosopher. In terms of government, he sees our government sinking with inflation. He sees the government sinking with communism" (Philadelphia *Bulletin*, 23 March 1980).

2. Confidential interview, 27–28 July 1989.

3. Annelise G. Anderson, *The Business of Crime: A Cosa Nostra Family* (Hoover Institution, 1979), 2–3.

4. Mark H. Haller, "Illegal Enterprise: A Theoretical and Historical Interpretation," *Criminology* (May 1990): 207–35.

5. Ibid.; Peter Reuter, *Disorganized Crime: The Economics of the Visible Hand* (Cambridge: MIT Press, 1983), Chap. 4; John M. Siedl, " 'Upon the Hip,' —A Study of the Criminal Loan-Shark Industry," Ph.D. diss., Harvard University, 1968.

6. Anderson, *Business of Crime*, Chapter 4.

7. Mark H. Haller, "Bootleggers and American Gambling, 1920–1950," in Commission on Review of National Policy Toward Gambling, *Gambling in America* (G.P.O.), Appendix I, 117–21.

8. Another risk was that writers or pickup men would try to cheat the bank by waiting until after the winning number was known and then slip winning numbers into the daily bets. Because of this danger, those operating numbers banks had to maintain a small headquarters and oversee the daily responsibility of collecting a record of all bets each day before the winning number could be known.

9. For a summary of involvement of Bruno family members and associates in various drug trafficking, see Pennsylvania Crime Commission, *A Decade of Organized Crime: 1980 Report*, Chapter 6.

10. Ralph Salerno and John Tompkins, *The Crime Confederation* (Garden City, NY: Doubleday, 1969), 119–20. This development paralleled warfare in the Middle Ages when fighting often involved an attempt to capture the enemy and hold him for ransom. Eventually, there was mutual agreement among nobles to ban the practice. This parallel was pointed out to me by my colleague, Russell F. Wrigley; Wrigley, *The Age of Battles: The Quest for Decisive Warfare from Breitenfeld to Waterloo* (Indiana University, Press, 1991), 18.

11. Interview, 27–28 July 1989.

12. From the federal RICO indictment, 81–00049, 20 February 1981. The rule forbidding betting with member bookmakers did not, of course, protect independent bookmakers. There were examples of members who bet with independents and, when they lost, refused to pay. According to one informant, Nicholas Caramandi once bet with Joseph Mastronardo, former mayor Frank Rizzo's son-in-law, the largest sports bookmaker in the Delaware Valley, and then refused to pay after losing. Allegedly Mastronardo was stuck with a $50,000 loss.

13. Referring to Bruno's generation, Sindone added: "Those guys, I don't know. I don't understand them! It's just get the money! Get the money! Get the money! . . .

Don't spend it! What the f-- good is it?'' See FBI transcript, 2 April 1976, at Frank's cabana.

14. FBI transcripts, 2 October 1977, at Tyrone DeNittis Agency.

15. FBI transcripts, 2 October 1978, at Tyrone DeNittis Agency.

16. FBI transcripts, 28 September 1977, at Tyrone DeNittis Agency.

17. FBI transcripts, 28 September 1977, at Tyrone DeNittis Agency.

18. Interview, 27 July 1989.

19. FBI transcript, 4 November 1977, at Tyrone DeNittis Agency, recording conversation among Harry Riccobene, Philip Testa, Frank Narducci, and Nicky Scarfo.

20. Based chiefly on testimony of Angelo Bruno, Emmanuel Gambino, and Domenico Adamita before New Jersey State Commission of Investigation. The later highly publicized Pizza Connection trials concerning heroin smuggling have been chronicled in several books; see Shana Alexander, *The Pizza Connection* (New York: Weidenfeld and Nicolson, 1988).

7

The Organized Crime Neighborhoods of Chicago

ROBERT M. LOMBARDO

Despite law enforcement efforts, traditional organized crime has continued to flourish in the Chicago metropolitan area. Since Al Capone was arrested in 1931 for income tax violations, those guilty of racketeering in Chicago have continually been prosecuted, yet traditional organized crime continues to exist. Ronald Goldstock points out that the incarceration of an underworld figure may disrupt an individual enterprise until new leadership is established, but the disruption, if any, is often minimal.[1] The death or incarceration of a major organized crime figure results in someone within the hierarchy moving to take his place, and the vacancy in the ranks is filled by a recruit.

Referring to organized crime, Donald R. Cressey notes that in some neighborhoods all three of the essential ingredients of an effective recruiting process are in operation, namely, inspiring aspiration for membership, training for membership, and selection for membership.[2] Evidence of neighborhood areas' providing support for recruitment into organized crime has been found by Irving Spergel and William F. Whyte in their community studies and by Francis A. J. Ianni in his study of a New York crime family.[3] According to Spergel, the presence of a well-organized criminal system in the "Racketville" neighborhood that he studied offered a learning environment that eventuated in certain types of behavior in preparation for later careers in the rackets.[4]

Do the "racket neighborhoods" that were studied by Spergel, Whyte, Ianni, and others still exist today despite changing social and economic conditions? Richard A. Cloward and Lloyd E. Ohlin state that important structural changes have taken place in large urban areas.[5] Suburbanization, the end of machine politics, the large influx of black populations, and the rationalization (movement toward syndicated gambling) of organized crime have all altered the social structure of racket areas. This position is supported by Selwyn Rabb, who maintains that organized crime is in decline because of increased law enforcement pressure by the U.S. Justice Department and the impact of demographic changes, including the dispersal of Italian American populations away from urban neighborhoods.[6]

This chapter investigates whether neighborhood areas are still relevant to organized crime recruitment today. In the Chicago metropolitan area, five communities have a history of being associated with organized crime. These communities are the homes of the five original "street crews" of the Chicago "Outfit," as traditional organized crime is referred to in Chicago. Street crews are organizational groupings in which organized crime activities are carried out. Do these areas provide new recruits for organized crime in Chicago, as suggested by past research, or are there other mechanisms that continue to provide recruits for the Chicago Outfit?

This discussion begins with a review of the relevant sociological literature linking recruitment into organized crime to the social structure of community areas. The discussion then moves on to a review of the history of organized crime in Chicago and a reconsideration of the sociocultural factors that have contributed to its development. An analysis of nativity and residency data is then conducted in order to determine the communities of origin of the members of the Chicago Outfit. The chapter also reviews the history of each of the five street crew neighborhoods in order to explicate the relationship between these communities and organized crime.

DELINQUENT AREAS, RACKET SUBCULTURES, AND DEFENDED NEIGHBORHOODS

In 1929, John Landesco conducted research into organized crime as part of the Illinois Crime Survey. The main theme of Landesco's book was that organized crime had its roots in the social structure of the neighborhoods in which its members had been raised.[7] He found that the members of the crime syndicate came from neighborhoods "where the gang tradition is old" and where the residents could absorb the attitudes and skills necessary to enter into the world of organized crime.

Landesco was part of the "Chicago school" of sociologists who, like Frederic Thrasher and Clifford Shaw and Henry D. McKay, recognized the existence of certain communities in which attitudes and values are conducive to delinquency and organized crime in particular. Shaw and McKay found that the presence of large numbers of adult criminals in certain neighborhood areas meant that children there are in contact with crime as a career and with organized crime as a way of life.[8]

Other evidence of social structural support for organized crime can be found in the work of Whyte. In his study of Cornerville, a name given to an undisclosed Boston neighborhood, Whyte found that the "problem" in this "slum" district was not a lack of social organization but the failure of the community's own organization to mesh with that of the society around it.[9] The differential organization of the community became apparent when one examined the channels through which the Cornerville person gained advancement and recognition in their neighborhood and the larger society. To get ahead, a Cornerville resident must move either in the world of business and Republican politics or in the world of Democratic politics and the rackets. Other avenues of social mobility were closed to community residents because of their immigrant status and association with the Cornerville area.

Additional evidence of societal structures that support the pursuit of a career in organized crime can be found in the delinquency literature. Cloward and Ohlin state that the form of delinquency that is adopted in a particular area is conditioned by the social organization of that area.[10] As such, their study uncovered three types of "criminal subcultures": the criminal, the conflict, and the retreatist. Among the various "criminal subcultures" was one that tied delinquency to organized crime in select neighborhood areas.

Spergel proposed a major modification to the Cloward and Ohlin formulation by dividing the criminal subculture into racket and theft adaptations. The central hypothesis of Spergel's work was that "delinquent subcultures" resulted from the varying nature and extent of illicit opportunities available to youth in lower-class neighborhoods.[11] According to Spergel, each neighborhood provided different opportunities for the development of distinctive and characteristic types of delinquent subcultures. The racket subculture was seen as arising within an area where the presence of an integrated and well-organized criminal system offered learning environments that eventuated in certain types of behavior in preparation for later careers in the rackets.

The existence of community structures that support organized crime was also found by Gerald Suttles in his study of the Addams area of Chicago and by Donald Tricarico in his study of Greenwich Village.[12] Suttles found that many of the adolescent street corner groups in the Addams area were building blocks out of which the older, more powerful social athletic clubs (SACs) originated. Some of these SACs had members who belonged to the Chicago Outfit and as such provided a mechanism for the association of youth gangs and street corner groups with traditional organized crime. In the South Village area of New York, Tricarico also found that street corner boys interacted with Mafia clubs, which functioned as outposts for syndicate activity. These clubs served as centers for the consumption of syndicate services, such as gambling, and for the recruitment and socialization of competent personnel.

Both the Addams area of Chicago and the South Village area of New York have been described as defended neighborhoods. The defended neighborhood is classically portrayed by Tricarico as a safe, moral world that kept the city at arm's length.[13] Tricarico notes that while the city may have been threatening and noted for crime, the defended neighborhood was a different place. Although there were exceptions, people were trustworthy, and crime was infrequent within its boundaries. Doors and windows were left open, and there was no fear of the streets, even at night. Neighbors were watchful and solicitous and closely monitored the movements of strangers. A careful scrutiny of outsiders and a toughness with interlopers earned such neighborhoods a reputation that residents believed would frighten predators away.

The defended neighborhood, just like criminality itself, is the result of weak societal control. Suttles maintains that given the inability of formal procedures of social control to detect and forestall all or even most forms of urban disorder, a set of rules has developed in the form of a cognitive map that is used to regulate spatial movement in order to avoid conflict between antagonistic groups.[14] These cognitive maps give birth to the defended neighborhood as an additional basis for social differentiation and social cohesion. Suttles states that the necessity for this additional basis of social organization lies in the very nature of urban areas, since cities inevitably bring together populations that are too large and composed of too many conflicting elements for their residents to find cultural solutions to the problems of social control.

The roots of the defended neighborhood lie in social disorganization theory. Along with immigration, population diversity, and individual variability, industrialization and urbanization have brought about a change in mechanisms of social control. Robert E. Park, Ernest W. Burgess and Roderick D. McKenzie, state that the general nature of this change is indicated by the fact that the growth of the city has been accompanied by the substitution of indirect, secondary relations for direct, face-to-face, primary relations in the association of individuals in the community.[15] This is caused by the fact that the city is too diversified and heterogeneous to provide a single normative order that is shared sufficiently by its citizens to maintain order. The shift of social control to the formal sections of society has not been entirely successful, as evidenced by the persistence of organized criminality and other forms of aberrant conduct.

What is unique about organized crime is the societal efforts at social control, in the form of the establishment of the defended neighborhood, have actually acted to support deviant phenomena. For example, in the area of Greenwich Village studied by Tricarico, a substantial portion of neighborhood life was organized in defense against strangers.[16] Male street corner groups were the self-appointed enforcers of local order. Their job was to make sure that the streets were safe. This control function was reinforced by the "Mafia," which supported corner boys with a reputation for total violence. This reputation was a valuable resource for the residents of the defended neighborhood, who reciprocated by providing a safe haven for "Mafia" activities.

Roderick D. McKenzie states that in its traditional application, the term *neighborhood* stood for rather definite group sentiments, which were the products of the intimate personal relations among the members of small, isolated communities of which society was formerly composed.[17] Though this definition suggests that the urban neighborhood is a remnant of an earlier rural community, McKenzie maintains that neighborhood sentiment can take on the characteristics and qualities of the current inhabitants. Just as this sentiment reflects lines of religion, language, and ethnic tradition, it may also reflect cultural and normative acceptance of criminal or deviant values. Suttles found this to be true in the Addams area of Chicago. There residents shared collective representations and moral sentiments that allowed them to be privileged to a diversity of knowledge regarding organized crime.[18]

In the Addams area, many residents valued the fact that they shared or believed they shared associations with members of the Outfit. Within the Addams area is a section called Taylor Street. Above anything else, Suttles found that residence in this area implied a connection with organized crime. Even though the public stereotypes applied to the Taylor Street area did not identify a lifestyle acceptable to the larger society, they did offer for some neighborhood residents a certain honor and for others a way of defining people.[19] Thus, persons embraced the images of "gangster," "hood," and "tough guy" that were provided because the images gave them an image of power that few were willing to question. Suttles even found that those who rejected these labels themselves assumed their truth for the wider community. To show how far the residents carried their belief in the crime syndicate, Suttles gave an example of young boys referring to Frank "the Enforcer" Nitti (of Al Capone fame) as casually as other boys might mention current baseball heroes.

Similarly, Spergel found that the racketeer was more than a person who shared a residential identity and knowledge of the underworld.[20] The racketeer was actually the standard bearer of the neighborhood and the acknowledged source of norms and values. These racketeers were sought out to settle family and neighborhood arguments. They were even used as a shroud of protection, for those who claimed their association, against threatening groups from outside the community.

The studies of both Suttles and Spergel indicate that the concerned communities developed values sympathetic to the criminal underworld, which the residents drew upon in orienting themselves to the community. Albert J. Reiss contends that a major source of a person's norms lies in the social controls of the community and its institutions.[21] Criminality results when there is a relative absence of, or conflict in, social rules or techniques for enforcing behavior in the social groups or institutions of which the person is a member. There is obviously a conflict in normative values in any community that embraces the gangster image or acknowledges the racketeer as a source of norms and values. Such conflict may be viewed as a consequence of the failure of the primary group to properly define organized criminal activity as deviant or aberrant conduct. Once such a failure occurs, a specialized social structure is created that will support the pursuit of a life in organized crime.

THE HISTORICAL ANTECEDENTS OF ORGANIZED CRIME IN CHICAGO

The city of Chicago, population 4,000, was incorporated on 4 March 1837. Chicago's growth as a city began in 1848 with the completion of the Illinois and Michigan Canal.[22] This canal, connecting the Illinois River and the south branch of the Chicago River, provided midwest farmers with access to Great Lakes shipping and eastern markets. Chicago's first railroad, the Galena and Chicago Union, also began operating in 1848. By the late 1850s, Chicago was the rail crossroads of the nation. In 1860, Chicago's population reached over 112,000 people, making it the largest city in Illinois.

Chicago's ecological position as the gateway to the unsettled lands of the West is also said to have contributed to its involvement in crime. Many young bachelors spent their last nights in Chicago before heading out to make their fortunes in the vast western wilderness. Chicago was often their last chance for supplies and other needed items. Saloons, gambling parlors, and brothels quickly sprang up to make these pioneers' last night in "civilization" memorable. Commenting on the times, Dwight Moody, founder of Chicago's Moody Bible Institute, once remarked: "If the Angel Gabriel came to Chicago, he would lose his character within a week."[23]

Organized crime in Chicago had its beginning in the 1870s with the activities of Michael Cassius McDonald.[24] McDonald owned a tavern known as the Store, which was reportedly the largest liquor and gambling house in downtown Chicago. So extensive was gambling in Chicago's center that the two-block stretch on Randolph between Clark and State streets was known as "Hairtrigger Block," named so because of the large number of shootings that occurred there stemming from disagreements in the gambling houses.[25] McDonald was also active in politics. In an effort to frustrate the reform activities of then mayor Joseph Medill, McDonald organized Chicago's saloon and gambling interests and elected their candidate, Harvey Colvin, as mayor of Chicago. The year was 1873. With Colvin in office, McDonald organized the first criminal syndicate in Chicago, composed of both gamblers and compliant politicians.

With McDonald's death in 1907, control of gambling in Chicago passed to a number of different people, the most prominent of whom were Mont Tennes and First Ward aldermen Michael Kenna and John Coughlin. Tennes, as the proprietor of the General News Bureau, controlled the telegraph wire services that carried race results to Chicago from throughout the United States. Tennes's ownership of the General News Bureau led to his ultimate control of all racetrack gambling in Chicago.[26]

The Levee

"Hinky Dink" Kenna and "Bathhouse" John Coughlin, as they were called, controlled politics and vice in Chicago's downtown area and the near South

Side, which was commonly referred to as the Levee. The name "Levee," according to Emmett Dedmon, came about as the result of the influx of southern gamblers to the area.[27] During the 1890s, the Levee occupied the blocks between Van Buren and Roosevelt, from State Street to the river.[28] Dominic A. Pacyga attributes the growth of the Levee, and in particular its red-light district prostitution trade, to the fact that four of Chicago's six railroad depots were centered in the area.[29] By 1910, because of the growth of Chicago's downtown business district, the Levee was eventually relocated to the area between 19th and 22d streets, from State to Clark. The "New Levee," as it was called, became home to many of Chicago's taverns and brothels, including the infamous Everleigh Club at 2131 South Dearborn, which was reportedly frequented by Chicago's elite.

Working in the First Ward as a precinct captain at this time was James Colosimo. Colosimo had earned his position as a precinct captain by organizing fellow street sweepers into a voting bloc.[30] Through his control of the vote in the Italian settlement centered around Polk and Clark streets within the First Ward, Colosimo's political power soon eclipsed that of his sponsors.[31] "Big Jim" Colosimo, as he was referred to, was also involved in prostitution and other vice activities in the near south side Levee district.[32]

Colosimo and his associates built the first Italian crime syndicate in Chicago. Like many other successful Italians of the time, Colosimo became the target of Black Hand extortionists. The Black Hand was not an organization, but a practice by which businessmen and other wealthy Italians were extorted for money. Intended victims were simply sent a note stating that they would come to violence if they did not pay a particular sum of money. Colosimo sent for a New York relative, Johnny Torrio, to help him deal with this threat. Torrio had been a member of New York's Five Points Gang and had dabbled in Black Hand extortion himself.[33] Torrio's usefulness soon extended to overseeing prostitution and gambling for Colosimo.

Prohibition

Upon the death of Colosimo in 1920, Torrio took full control of their crime syndicate, which was now beginning to expand because of the passage that year of the National Prohibition Enforcement Act. Commonly referred to as the Volstead Act, this law ended the sale of alcoholic beverages in the United States. This unpopular law created a strong demand for illegal alcohol, which the Colosimo vice syndicate and other similar groups around the city were in a position to supply. They were organized and had the political connections to prevent interference from local government. According to Landesco, all the experience gained by years of struggle against reformers and secret agreements with corrupt politicians was brought into service in the production and distribution of beer and whiskey.[34]

Torrio ran his criminal organization with the help of his trusted lieutenant,

Alphonse Capone, from the Four Deuces Cafe at 2222 South Wabash. Torrio is widely believed to have been a no-nonsense businessman who truly "organized" crime. Humbert Nelli states that he excelled as a master strategist and organizer and quickly built an empire that far exceeded Colosimo's.[35] However, in 1923 Chicago elected reform mayor William Dever, and one year later Chicago police arrested and convicted Torrio on bootlegging charges. Torrio was shot, probably by members of the rival O'Banion gang, shortly before entering jail to serve out his sentence. After his release, he returned to New York, where he worked as a bail bondsman for organized crime figures there.[36]

Dever's reforms forced Capone to move many of the Torrio organization's operations to nearby Cicero, Illinois. As a result, people still associate Cicero with organized crime, even though there is no organized crime group currently centered there today. The Capone syndicate also set up shop in a number of south suburban areas. The widespread use of the automobile ushered in the era of the "roadhouse." Located in the nearby towns of Chicago Heights, Blue Island, Burnham, Stickney, and others, these roadhouses provided all the comforts of the Levee—prostitution, gambling, and liquor.

Reform also caused Capone to support the return of William Hale Thompson to the mayor's office. "Big Bill," as he was fondly referred to, had been Chicago's mayor prior to the reform-minded Dever. Promising that he "was as wet as the Atlantic Ocean," Thompson was returned to the mayor's office in 1927 with strong public support.[37] The retirement of Torrio and the election of Thompson placed Capone firmly in control of Chicago's First Ward and the Near South Side of Chicago.

Capone reportedly donated $260,000 to Thompson's campaign fund.[38] Such support made it clear that the manipulation of the political apparatus was essential to the operation of organized crime in Chicago. Police and judicial corruption was so widespread that a group of prominent businessmen formed an organization known as the Secret Six. Working in cooperation with the Chicago Crime Commission, the Secret Six donated $1 million to fight organized crime. This money was used to hire private investigators who developed informants, tapped telephones, paid witnesses, and generally collected information on mob activity that was passed on to a group of Justice Department investigators under the supervision of Eliot Ness.

Outside the area of the First Ward and Capone's organization, other gangs were also working in collusion with local politicians and police to promote vice activities and violate prohibition laws. Dion O'Banion and his followers controlled Chicago's Near North Side.[39] Klondike O'Donnell and his brothers controlled the Near Northwest Side. Roger Toughy, who claimed to be only a bootlegger and not involved in vice, controlled the Far Northwest Side.[40] The "Terrible" Genna brothers controlled the Near West Side Taylor Street area. The Far West Side was controlled by Terry Druggan and Frankie Lake and their Valley Gang. On the Southwest Side both the Irish O'Donnell brothers and the Saltis-McErland Gang were active in bootlegging.

Chief among the Capone organization's rivals were O'Banion and the six Genna brothers. O'Banion was raised in the Irish shantytown of Kilgubbin on Chicago's Near North Side.[41] His ability to deliver the Irish vote made him an important political figure in ward politics. O'Banion and his followers, George "Bugs" Moran and Earl "Hymie" Weiss, were known to the police as hijackers, burglars, and safecrackers. With the advent of Prohibition, the O'Banion gang quickly moved into the illegal liquor business.

The Genna brothers, Angelo, Sam, Jim, Pete, Tony, and Mike, were reportedly under the political protection of Republican ward committeeman "Diamond Joe" Esposito. Diamond Joe operated the Bella Napoli, a well-known Italian restaurant, at 850 South Halsted Street.[42] Esposito had also established himself as a "padrone," or boss, in the Taylor Street Italian neighborhood, utilizing old-country mafiosi tactics.[43] The Gennas had a government license for processing industrial alcohol at their plant, located at 1022 West Taylor, where they also produced illegal whiskey.[44] The Genna brothers were in direct competition with O'Banion for control of bootlegging territories. This struggle led to the deaths of four of the six Genna brothers. The remaining two fled Chicago. Their bootlegging activities were taken over by Joseph Aiello and his family. Both Angelo Genna and Aiello were active in the "Unione Siciliana."

The Unione Siciliana originally emerged as a lawful fraternal society designed to advance the interests of Sicilian immigrants.[45] The Italian American National Union, as it later became known, provided life insurance and was active in Italian American civic affairs. The union was also a major supporter of the White Hand Society. The White Hand was established by Italian Americans to fight Black Hand extortion in the Italian community.[46] The respectability of the union, however, declined with the advent of Prohibition, when the union organized large numbers of Italian immigrants, on Chicago's Near West Side, in the home production of alcohol.

So extensive was bootlegging on Chicago's Near West Side that the intersection of Roosevelt and Halsted streets was referred to as Bootleggers Square. The very fact that the "Unione Siciliana" was involved in bootlegging placed it in direct competition with the Capone syndicate. As a result, Capone tried to take over the organization by electing one of his own followers president. The competition for control of the union led to a number of deaths and the eventual takeover by the Capone organization.

The intense competition among these groups led to Chicago's famous "beer wars" during the 1920s. The gangs mainly aligned themselves according to ethnic ties. For example, the Aiellos, the successors to the Genna brothers, eventually sided with the Capone syndicate. In the end, the Capone organization emerged victorious. Through such violent acts as the "St. Valentine's Day Massacre," which resulted in the deaths of seven men, the Capone organization emerged as the dominant force in Chicago's underworld. When Prohibition ended in 1933, Al Capone was in jail for income tax violations. The organization that he had created turned its attention once again to the control of gambling, prostitution, and other illegal activities.

During the years that followed Prohibition, it became increasingly clear that organized crime in Chicago was now dominated by the Italians. There is no evidence, as commonly believed, that these Italians were members of an "alien conspiracy" that brought organized crime, in the form of the Sicilian Mafia, to America's urban centers. As a matter of fact, recent research has shown that the Mafia, as the term is commonly understood, never did exist. Pino Arlacchi maintains that "Mafia," as it existed in Italy at the time of the massive Italian immigrations to the United States, was actually a form of behavior, a mechanism of social control, and not a criminal organization as such.[47]

Italian Immigration

Between 1820 and 1930, an estimated 4.7 million Italians immigrated to the United States.[48] This was the largest and longest European exodus in modern times. Driven by the hope of employment and a better life, many of these Italians began migrating to Chicago during the 1850s.[49] The first Italian immigrants came mainly from the more advanced regions of the north, where they had gained experience as merchants, shopkeepers, and businessmen. During the 1880s emigration began to shift to southern Italy, the Mezzogiorno, or land of the midday sun, where living conditions were among the worst of all of Italy.

Rudolph J. Vecoli observes that the causes that initiated and sustained the mass emigrations of Italians from the south of Italy were rooted in the defects of its agricultural system.[50] Most southern Italian farmers were landless peasants tied to the estates of absentee landowners. These landlords paid poorly and made few improvements to their lands. In addition, pestilence, recurring drought, and burdensome taxation plagued the people of the Mezzogiorno. A dramatic increase in the Italian population also contributed to emigration. The island of Sicily alone added over 1 million people to its population during the years between 1871 and 1901.

The harsh conditions of life in the south of Italy led to the development of a fatalistic, alienated view of life—"La Miseria"—in which a people conceive themselves as having little, if any, control over their lives.[51] Such a view prevented a man from cooperating with his neighbors because in so doing he jeopardized his position in a competitive world where goods were scarce. Instead, he used whatever means, fair or unfair, to gain his share of worldly possessions.

The southern Italian's distrust of government and other individuals who lie outside the bounds of family and kinship groups can be traced to the area's history of foreign domination. Since the fall of the Roman Empire, southern Italy has had a succession of foreign rulers, including the Arabs, Normans, French, and Spanish. Howard Abadinsky states that the history of southern Italy is a history of 1,000 years of political, social, and economic repression.[52] As a result, a culture developed in the south of Italy that stressed values necessary for survival in a hostile environment. Absolute loyalty to the family and distrust of government became the custom of the Mezzogiorno.

Not recognizing the authority of foreign rule, the people of the Mezzogiorno developed their own code of conduct, which stressed suspicion and resentment of government. Omerta, the quality of remaining silent and of being a man with honor and dignity, demanded that a man resolve his own problems without recourse to the law. Joseph L. Albini states that such a custom is common to many societies that have been the victim of government persecution.[53] The code of omerta allowed the people of the Mezzogiorno to cooperate individually to frustrate the efforts of a government that sought only to exploit them.

In Sicily the code of omerta found its most sophisticated expression in the development of the Mafia. Historically, the Mafia was not a secret criminal organization but a form of social organization that developed in Sicily and Calabria, where it is known as the *'ndrangheta*, under very specific social and cultural conditions. The Mafia exploited the gap in Sicilian society left by an ineffective state government. Its main function was to impose some form of rudimentary order on the anarchy of Sicilian life. The Mafia developed as a method of social control in an area where the official political structure was unable to impose its will on the populace.

The typical mafioso was *uomo di respetto* (a man of respect) "who kept faith with his friends, knew how to repay a favor, held honor and gratitude in high esteem, and was ready to use violence to ensure that these values were respected."[54] Such a man was highly respected in the Sicilian village, where the formal mechanisms of government were in a constant state of disarray. Those who were willing to use violence to protect their honor and the honor of their family were sought out by others who were less capable of protecting themselves from the hardships of life in the Mezzogiorno. The eventual competition among the various mafiosi in each town led to conflict and finally dominance by one individual who now had the entire area under his patronage. Because of their position of dominance and willingness to use violence such *un'uomo d'onore* (men of honor) were entrusted with a series of important functions that were normally the prerogative of the state. These included protection, repression of nonconformist behavior, and the mediation of disputes.

The sociocultural background of the southern Italian and, in particular, the Sicilian immigrant contributed to their entrance and success in organized crime. Their fierce loyalty to the family and suspicion of government allowed these immigrants to rationalize their entrance into the rackets. The ethos of amoral familism justified law violation if it was in the interest of supporting the nuclear family. If jobs were not available in the legitimate sector, one could always turn to the gangster in the underworld to find employment.

The unpopularity of national Prohibition and the southern Italian's distrust of government worked to rationalize the illegal production of alcohol. Prohibition was forced upon the urban working class by social reformers and agrarian America. Corruption was widespread, and the government did little to suppress bootlegging. As a result, Prohibition was viewed by the Italian immigrant as just one more example of government suppression of the common man.

Many of the southern Italian and Sicilian immigrants who were attracted to organized crime at the time of its inception had subscribed to the code of omerta and had lived under a Mafia-dominated social order prior to emigrating to the United States. Combining the traditions of omerta and those of the Mafia with the illegal opportunities made available by Prohibition, these Italian gangsters became a dominant force in organized crime. These new inheritors of the urban rackets turned to their own communities for recruits. There were large Italian communities immediately adjacent to the Levee and on the West and North sides of Chicago where vice activities were now dominated by the Capone syndicate.

THE ORGANIZED CRIME NEIGHBORHOODS OF CHICAGO

The first Italians who came to Chicago settled within walking distance of the Dearborn Street Station—Polk and Dearborn streets.[55] This area was known among the Italians as the "Polk Depot" and served as an area of transition for newly arriving immigrants. By the 1880s many of Chicago's northern Italians had resettled in the area centered around Franklin and Orleans streets, where they had founded Chicago's first Italian Catholic parish, the Assumption of the Blessed Virgin Mary.

According to Vecoli, the establishment of Italian and other immigrant colonies was not haphazard but was determined by the "socio-economic ecology" of the city.[56] The Chicago River with its north and south branches provided the basis for the industrial topography of Chicago. The river's twenty-four miles of shoreline provided access to both water transportation and waste disposal for the city's emerging industries. As a result, an industrial belt developed hugging the course of the river.

Leaving the Polk Depot, Italian immigrants began settling in the River Wards along Taylor Street and Grand Avenue and in the Near North and Armour Square community areas. These four communities and the suburb of Chicago Heights became the major southern Italian enclaves in the Chicagoland area. They also became home to the five street crews of the Chicago Outfit. There are other Italian communities in Chicago as well as other communities that have had a reputation of being associated with organized crime. These communities differ, however, in that they did not contain indigenous organized crime groups. The organized crime groups that have been present in these other Chicago areas began because people from the five original street crew neighborhoods relocated there.

Taylor Street

The most famous street crew neighborhood in Chicago is Taylor Street. Taylor Street was annexed to the city of Chicago in 1851, when the boundaries of

the city were extended to Western Avenue. Taylor Street is contained within
the Near West Side community area of Chicago.[57] This area was first settled by
German, Irish, and Scandinavian immigrants. In the decades that followed the
great Chicago Fire of 1871, new immigrants arrived, including Italians and Russian and Polish Jews.

Taylor Street's involvement with organized crime can be traced to the 1920s
and the adolescent street corner group known as the 42 Gang. The 42 Gang
derived its name from the legend of Ali Baba and the Forty Thieves.[58] The gang
had forty plus two members, hence the name 42 Gang. They frequented Mary's
Restaurant, which was located on the corner of Taylor and Bishop. The gang
specialized in truck hijacking and auto theft.[59] Many members of the 42 Gang
were recruited by the Capone mob. For example, Sam Battaglia, William Dad-
ano, and Felix Alderiso, all former members of the 42 Gang, became important
members of the Outfit.

Sam Giancana states that the 42 Gang was recruited by Al Capone to help
him gain control of bootlegging activities on Chicago's Near West Side.[60] One
member of the 42 Gang, Sam Giancana, rose through the ranks to head organized crime in Chicago during the 1950s. Giancana had gone to jail in 1939 on
bootlegging charges. While in the federal prison at Terre Haute, Indiana, he met
Edward Jones, the policy racket king of Chicago's South Side.[61] After his release
from jail, Giancana quickly took over the policy rackets through violence and
extortion. The increased revenue that he brought to organized crime greatly
increased his stature in the Outfit.

Grand Avenue

Grand Avenue is contained within the West Town Community Area of Chicago.[62] Anthony Accardo, the longtime senior statesman of the Chicago crime
syndicate, was born in 1906 at 1353 West Grand Avenue. Accardo had once
been a bodyguard and enforcer for Al Capone. Accardo began his criminal
career as a member of the Circus Cafe Gang, led by Vincenzo DeMora, aka
"Machine Gun" Jack McGurn. The Circus Cafe Gang was a group of young
toughs that frequented a tavern called the Circus Cafe on West North Avenue
in Chicago. McGurn and Accardo are believed to have been two of the men
who actually took part in the St. Valentine's Day Massacre. Accardo's involvement with Capone is believed to have been the beginning of the Grand Avenue
street crew and this community's involvement with the Chicago Outfit.

Crime syndicate activities continue in the Grand Avenue community today.
There are restaurants in the area where bookmakers regularly meet and a social
club at Grand and May where organized crime figures gather. One man interviewed about the neighborhood stated that you could go into a certain restaurant
on a Friday night and find twenty bookmakers present and a half dozen more
in local social clubs.

Twenty-Sixth Street

Crime syndicate activities are also visible in the Twenty-Sixth Street area. Twenty-Sixth Street is contained within the Armour Square Community Area of Chicago.[63] It is named after the nearby Armour Institute of Technology (original name of the Illinois Institute of Technology). Armour Square was first settled in the mid-1800s by Irish, German, and Swedish laborers. The northern half of Armour Square was annexed to the city of Chicago in 1853.[64] The southern half of the area was settled after the opening of the Union Stockyards in 1865. By 1895, all of the vacant land in the area had been built upon. In 1908, Charles Comiskey bought land from Chicago mayor "Long John" Wentworth and erected the White Sox ballpark at Thirty-Fifth and Shields.

Italians, Yugoslavians, and Chinese began moving into the community during the early 1900s. In 1912 a group of Chinese, who had lived on the south edge of the Loop, moved en masse to the area of Twenty-Second and Wentworth.[65] This was the beginning of Chicago's Chinatown. The Twenty-Sixth Street crew, in fact, is often referred to as the Chinatown crew because of the large numbers of Chinese who settled in the Armour Square area. Blacks next began to move into the community during the time of World War I. By 1940, nearly one-half of Armour Square's population was black; however, much of the black population was displaced with the building of the Dan Ryan and Stevenson expressways, beginning in the 1950s. Today, the Armour Square community is made up largely of black, Chinese, and Italian residents, each group occupying their own segment of the community.

The Twenty-Sixth Street area is called the "Patch." The term *patch* is increasingly being applied by both the police and those knowledgeable about underworld activities to the other organized crime-connected areas as well. An oral history respondent told the Chicago Historical Society in 1927 that his father had established a successful cabbage farm in the area of Thirty-Fifth and Wells during the late 1800s. As a result, the area became known as the Patch. Local tradition holds that this cabbage patch was the setting for Kate Douglas Wiggins's book, *Mrs. Wiggins and the Cabbage Patch.*

Located between Fourteenth and Indiana and the Twenty-Sixth Street neighborhood is the site where the New Levee, the birthplace of the Capone syndicate, once stood. As a matter of fact, the New Michigan Hotel, which was Al Capone's headquarters, can still be seen on the corner of Twenty-Second and Michigan. The Twenty-Sixth Street crew is considered to be the direct offspring of the original Torrio-Capone syndicate, which is the forerunner of today's Outfit.

The Twenty-Sixth Street neighborhood continues to be a racket area today. This neighborhood is probably the strongest street crew neighborhood in metropolitan Chicago. Unlike the Taylor Street area, there have been no major urban renewal efforts in this community. The housing stock has remained good, and the neighborhood has remained racially stable. While people from other neighborhoods have moved to the suburbs, people from Twenty-Sixth Street have remained in the neighborhood. According to an experienced organized crime investigator, the Outfit has a very real base in this area. Many of the members of the Twenty-Sixth Street crew continue to live in the neighborhood, and there is a social club located in the community where they can regularly be seen.

The North Side

Unlike the Grand Avenue and Taylor Street areas, there is no organized crime activity in the North Side community today. The North Side is located within the Near North Side community area of Chicago.[66]

The turn of the century also brought large numbers of Italians, in particular, Sicilians, to the area who eventually replaced earlier immigrant groups. By 1910, the Italian community extended across Chicago Avenue to Division Street and by 1920 across North Avenue into the Lincoln Park Community Area.[67] Little Sicily or Little Hell, as the Italian community was known, was centered along Sedgwick Street from Division to North Avenue.[68] The name Little Hell pre-dated Sicilian immigration and was derived from the gasworks that were located there near the river whose belching flames lit the sky at night. According to Vecoli, the name Little Hell also began being applied to the area because of extensive Black Hand extortion.[69] The intersection of Oak and Cambridge, in Little Sicily, soon became known as Death Corner because of the large number of shootings, stabbings, and murders that were committed there.

The natural clash between the well-to-do families of the east and the immigrant families of the western portion of the Near North Side resulted in the central area's becoming progressively less desirable as a residential district.[70] Consequently, many of the wealthier families and businesses moved from the area. The residential hotels and large homes that were left behind were soon transformed into profitable boardinghouses, which brought a large transient element to the area as well as a population of lower economic status. Soon, the once-fashionable district became a center for dance halls, prostitution, nightclubs, and other forms of illegal activity and the beginning of the Clark Street and later Rush Street vice districts in Chicago.

Vice activities in these areas were strictly controlled by the Chicago Outfit. This dominance can be traced to Prohibition. The control of illegal liquor also facilitated the control of prostitution and gambling, which was centered in the nightclubs and taverns that dotted the area. Once the Capone organization had taken control of bootlegging activities in the North Side area, it was a simple matter for them to also dominate vice activities. The connection between the North Side Italian community and the Chicago Outfit can also be traced to Prohibition and vice activity in the Clark Street and Rush Street areas. The proximity of Little Hell to these areas provided the Capone organization with access to recruits for its criminal syndicate.

The North Side, as a street crew neighborhood, no longer exists today. The old Sicilian neighborhood in which "North Side" organized crime activity was previously centered has been replaced. Much of the area was razed between 1942 and 1962 during the successive stages of the construction of the Dabrini-Green housing complex. This community has completely changed as a result of social and economic development and is no longer viewed as an organized crime area.

Chicago Heights

Another area in which organized crime activity is in decline is the suburb Chicago Heights. The development of organized crime in Chicago Heights parallels the development of organized crime in Chicago. By 1908, this newly established city had a reputation for being overrun with gamblers, and many of the saloons were also supporting prostitution.[71] As a matter of fact, Mayor Lee H. Hooks was arrested with five other people that year on gambling charges. Crime became a recurrent theme in Chicago Heights politics. On 8 April 1915, the Chicago Heights *Star* newspaper reported that mayoral candidate Craig Hood promised to crush commercialized vice and clean out the police department if elected. John Thomas promised in 1929 that, if elected, he would see the commercial gambling and vice of all descriptions did not exist in Chicago Heights while he was mayor.[72]

During Prohibition, Chicago Heights became famous for its bootlegging activities in violation of the Volstead Act. George Golding of the Treasury Department stated in 1928 that Chicago Heights was one huge distillery and that there was nothing in the United States equal to it. Prohibition brought the influence of the Capone mob into Chicago Heights. Prohibition also brought an increase in violent crime as mobsters fought for control of the illegal liquor business. In February 1929, the Shanghai (China) *Times* reported that there were sixty-five murders in a two-year period in Chicago Heights, calling it the most lawless community in the United States.

Today, organized crime activity in the Chicago Heights community is on the decline. The 1989 conviction of Chicago Heights mob boss Albert Caesar Tocco was devastating to the Chicago Heights crew. According to a federal law enforcement officer who had participated in the Tocco investigation, the card rooms and social clubs that the members of the Chicago Heights crew frequented are gone, and it is now difficult to locate organized crime figures in the Chicago Heights area.

ORGANIZED CRIME AND HUMAN ECOLOGY

The records of the Chicago Police Department indicate that there are currently 191 members of the Chicago Outfit. The communities of origin of ninety-eight, or 51 percent, have been identified (Table 7.1). Of these, fifty-nine (60 percent) were born in one of the five street crew communities. Forty (41 percent) still

Table 7.1
Street Crew Residence, Chicago Crime Syndicate

	Total Members			Community Nativity		Current Residence	
	No.	I.D.	%	No.	%	No.	%
Talyor Street	49	25	51	6	24	2	8
Grand Avenue	33	27	82	23	85	17	63
26th Street	40	27	67	24	89	15	55
The North Side	35	11	31	3	27	3	27
Chicago Heights	29	8	28	3	37	3	37
Bosses	4						
Unidentified	1						
TOTAL	191	98	51	59	60	40	41

reside there today. These data are consistent with earlier findings that members of organized crime come from select neighborhood areas. A review of the data for each of the individual communities, however, indicates that rates of nativity and residence vary among the different neighborhoods examined.

The majority of the members of the Grand Avenue and Twenty-Sixth Street crews were raised in these two areas. Of the thirty-three current members of the Grand Avenue crew, the communities of origin of twenty-seven (82 percent) have been determined. Of these, twenty-three (85 percent) were raised in the Grand Avenue area. Of the forty members of the Twenty-Sixth Street crew, the communities of origin of twenty-seven (67 percent) have been identified. Of these, twenty-four (89 percent) have been identified as having been raised in this area.

There are also large numbers of organized crime figures still living in both the Grand Avenue and the Twenty-Sixth Street neighborhoods. Seventeen (63 percent) of the identified members of the Grand Avenue crew still reside in the Grand Avenue neighborhood. Fifteen (55 percent) of the twenty-seven identified members of the Twenty-Sixth Street crew still reside there today. The fact that a large number of crime syndicate members were born in street crew areas and that many still reside there lends support to the conclusion that racket-prone areas exist today.

Qualitative data also support the position that racket areas still exist. Informants state that street crew activities are still visible in both the Grand Avenue and Twenty-Sixth Street areas, where organized crime figures can be seen frequenting social clubs and spending large portions of their time in the communities.

Taylor Street and the North Side, however, report different findings. There are currently forty-nine members of the Taylor Street crew. I have been able to identify the community of origin of twenty-five (51 percent). Of these, only six were raised in the Taylor Street community. Only two still reside there today. The remaining nineteen identified members come from various other Chicago communities. Of the thirty-five current members of the North Side crew, the communities of origin of eleven (31 percent) have been identified. Of these only three were raised in the area, and three continue to reside there today. Both of these neighborhoods have undergone extensive social and economic change, which could explain why they no longer produce recruits for organized crime. Few crime syndicate members reside in either area, and those that are part of both street crews were probably recruited from outside the neighborhood.

Of the twenty-nine members of the Chicago Heights crew, the communities of origin of eight (28 percent) have been determined. Of these, three have been identified as having been raised in the Chicago Heights community. Three continue to live there today. It should be noted that community nativity and residence data concerning the Chicago Heights crew has been particularly difficult to obtain due to the fact that, because of its suburban location, the Chicago Police Department does not keep extensive records on the Chicago Heights crew's activity, and the Illinois State Police no longer have an organized crime unit.

The fact that most of the members of the Grand Avenue and Twenty-Sixth Street crews were raised in these two areas and that a significant number still reside there supports the conclusion that racket-prone areas still exist. These data are particularly significant when one considers that there are a total of 207 community and suburban areas in metropolitan Chicago from which these people could have come. These findings suggest that neighborhood areas are still important to organized crime recruitment today.

The thesis that organized crime in America is in decline because of demographic changes in urban neighborhoods cannot be totally supported by the findings presented here. Though the Taylor Street community is no longer producing new recruits, the Taylor Street crew still exists. In fact, the Taylor Street crew is considered to be the largest and most powerful of the Chicago Street crews, even though the data indicate that most of its members were recruited from outside the area.

These findings suggest that factors other than community contexts explain how organized crime continues to successfully recruit new members. If neighborhood areas are no longer relevant to recruitment, as in the case of the Taylor Street crew, the question becomes, What is? What are the mechanisms that allow organized crime groups to recruit new members despite changing social and economic conditions?

NOTES

1. Ronald Goldstock, "Operational Issues in Organized Crime Control," in *Major Issues in Organized Crime Control*, ed. Herbert Edelhertz (Washington, DC: U.S. Government Printing Office, 1987), 82.

2. Donald R. Cressey, "The Functions and Structures of Criminal Syndicates," *Task Force Report: Organized Crime* (Washington, DC: U.S. Government Printing Office, 1967), 4.

3. Irving Spergel, *Racketville, Slumtown, Haulburg* (Chicago: University of Chicago Press, 1964); William F. Whyte, *Street Corner Society* (Chicago: University of Chicago Press, 1943); Francis A. J. Ianni, *A Family Business* (New York: Russell Sage Foundation, 1972).

4. Spergel, *Racketville, Slumtown, Haulburg*, 44.

5. Richard A. Cloward and Lloyd E. Ohlin, *Delinquency and Opportunity* (New York: Free Press, 1968), 202.

6. Selwyn Raab, "A Battered and Ailing Mafia Is Losing Its Grip on America," *New York Times*, 22 October 1990, 1.

7. John Landesco, *Organized Crime in Chicago* (Chicago: University of Chicago Press, 1968), 207.

8. Cliford R. Shaw and Henry D. McKay, *Juvenile Delinquency and Urban Areas* (Chicago: University of Chicago Press, 1969), 73.

9. Whyte, *Street Corner Society*, 273.

10. Cloward and Ohlin, *Delinquency and Opportunity*, 153.

11. Spergel, *Racketville, Slumtown, Haulburg*, 44.

12. Gerald Suttles, *The Social Order of the Slum* (Chicago: University of Chicago Press, 1968), 31–32; Donald Tricarico, *The Italians of Greenwich Village* (Staten Island: Center for Migration Studies of New York), 41.

13. Ibid., 41.

14. Gerald Suttles, *The Social Construction of Communities* (Chicago: University of Chicago Press, 1972), 31–32.

15. Robert E. Park, Ernest W. Burgess, and Roderick D. McKenzie, *The City* (Chicago: University of Chicago Press, 1967), 23.

16. Tricarico, *The Italians of Greenwich Village*, 43.

17. Roderick D. McKenzie, *The Neighborhood* (New York: Arno Press, 1970), 348.

18. Suttles, *The Social Order of the Slum*, 25–26.

19. Ibid., 25–26.

20. Spergel, *Racketville, Slumtown, Haulburg*, 19.

21. Albert J. Reis, "Delinquency as the Failure of Personal and Social Controls," *American Sociological Review* 16 (1951): 196–207.

22. World Book Encyclopedia, 1969 ed., S. V. "Chicago."

23. Jack McPhaul, *Johnny Torrio* (New Rochelle, NY: Arlington House, 1970), 64.

24. Humbert Nelli, *The Italians in Chicago* (New York: Oxford Press, 1970), 148.

25. John H. Lyle, *The Dry and Lawless Years* (Englewood Cliffs, NJ: Prentice Hall, 1960), 25.

26. Landesco, *Organized Crime in Chicago*, 59.

27. Emmett Dedmon, *Fabulous Chicago* (New York: Random House, 1953), 251.

28. Lloyd Wendt and Herman Kogan, *The Lords of the Levee* (New York: Garden City, 1944), 194.

29. Dominic A. Pacyga, *Chicago, City of Neighborhoods* (Chicago: Loyola University Press, 1986), 214.

30. Howard Abadinsky, *Organized Crime* (Chicago: Nelson Hall, 1990), 169.

31. Wendt and Kogan, *The Lords of the Levee*, 329.

32. Herbert Asbury, *The Gem of the Prairie* (DeKalb: Northern Illinois University Press, 1986), 314.

33. McPhaul, *Johnny Torrio*, 51.

34. Landesco, *Organized Crime in Chicago*, 43.

35. Nelli, *The Italians in Chicago*, 148.

36. McPhaul, *Johnny Torrio*, 224–38.

37. Nelli, *The Italians in Chicago*, 232.

38. Dennis E. Hoffman, *Business vs. Organized Crime* (Chicago: Chicago Crime Commission, 1989), 2.

39. Lyle, *The Dry and Lawless Years*, 171.

40. Roger Toughy, *The Stolen Years* (Cleveland: Pennington Press, 1959).

41. John Kobler, *Capone* (New York: Collier Books, 1971), 84–86.

42. Nelli, *The Italians in Chicago*, 225–26.

43. Samuel M. Giancana and Chuck Giancana, *Double Cross* (New York: Warner Books, 1992), 14.

44. Dedmon, *Fabulous Chicago*, 292; Kobler, *Capone*, 90.

45. James Inciardi, *Careers in Crime* (Chicago: Rand McNally, 1975), 115.

46. Nelli, *The Italians in Chicago*, 220.

47. Pino Arlacchi, *Mafia Business* (London: Verso Books, 1986), 3–4.

48. Ianni, *A Family Business*, 43.

49. Nelli, *The Italians in Chicago*, 22.

50. Rudolph J. Vecoli, *Chicago's Italians Prior to World War I* (Ann Arbor, MI: University Microfilms, 1963), 81.

51. Joseph L. Albini, *The American Mafia* (New York: Appleton-Century-Crofts, 1971), 108.

52. Abadinsky, *Organized Crime*, 9.

53. Albini, *The American Mafia*, 108.

54. Arlacchi, *Mafia Business*, 23.

55. Nelli, *The Italians in Chicago*, 24.

56. Vecoli, *Chicago's Italians Prior to World War I*, 127.

57. Local Community Fact Book Consortium, *Local Community Fact Book for Chicago* (Chicago: Local Community Fact Book Consortium, 1984) , 75.

58. William Brashler, *The Don* (New York: Harper and Row, 1977), 27.

59. John Landesco, "The Life History of a Member of the '42' Gang," *Journal of Criminal Law, Criminology, and Police Science* 23 (1933): 964–98.

60. Giancana and Giancana, *Double Cross*, 18.

61. Brashler, *The Don*, 29.

62. Local Community Fact Book Consortium, *Local Community Fact Book for Chicago*, 62.

63. Ibid., 94.

64. Glen E. Holt and Dominic A. Pacyga, *Chicago: A Historical Guide to the Neighborhoods* (Chicago: Chicago Historical Society, 1979), 84.

65. Vecoli, *Chicago's Italians Prior to World War I*, 172.

66. Harvey W. Zorbaugh, *The Gold Coast and the Slum* (Chicago: University of Chicago Press, 1929), 160.

67. Vecoli, *Chicago's Italians Prior to World War I*, 174.

68. Zorbaugh, *The Gold Coast and the Slum*, 35.

69. Marian Lanfranchi, "A Political History of Chicago Heights," Unpublished Paper (Chicago: Governors State University, 1976), 9.

70. Lanfranchi, *A Political History of Chicago Heights*, 29.

71. Charles Liebman, "Some Political Effects of the Functional Differentiation of Suburbs," Ph.D. diss., University of Illinois, 2.

72. Lanfranchi, *A Political History of Chicago Heights*, 29.

8

African American Organized Crime

RUFUS SCHATZBERG

This chapter examines past and present African American organized crime patterns in three different time frames: first, the early policy numbers gambling operations that surfaced in New York City between 1920 and 1930; second, the criminal groups that operated in the ghettos between 1930 and 1970; and finally, the status of their activities from 1970 to the present day (they are now firmly embedded in their communities, and some are national in scope).

African Americans were not visible in nineteenth-century organized criminal enterprises. Indeed, they entered the twentieth century with no history of a leadership role or an active affiliation in any organized criminal gang.[1] In the first two decades of the twentieth century—when Caribbean and native-born African Americans migrated in large numbers into large northeastern and midwestern cities—illegal gambling, illegal alcohol-drinking establishments, and other illegal vice activities evolved in these newly settled African American communities. Many of these businesses were owned and operated by African Americans. While there continues to be lively debate about the degree to which African American criminal organizations are independently run and the extent of their threat in the years ahead, historically, African American involvement in organized crime has been greatest in the traditional vices such as gambling, drugs, prostitution, and, to a lesser degree, loan-sharking, theft, and fencing.

Models of African American organized gangs refer to a broad grouping that includes criminals made up of African Americans, Jamaicans, West Indians,[2] Nigerians, Haitians, and others. Two principal types of organized crime networks among African Americans are identified as based on social and cultural bonds. The first, a domestic kinship network, is generally headed by a dominant male and includes close relatives. The second is an associational network that is based on friendships developed in street gangs, prison, or neighborhood peer groups. Research shows that African American organized crime groups prey almost exclusively on each other and that this occurs mostly in their own areas, particularly within the inner cities.[3]

The recent exodus of businesses and jobs out of cities to overseas, combined with the transformations of the American occupational system to a service-oriented economy, has led to an increase in the number of subpoverty wage-level jobs for the lower strata workforce. The abandonment of the cities by both affluent whites and African Americans has left behind an underclass that is increasingly minority and poor in composition. Municipal tax bases have eroded in large cities, making it difficult for city officials to meet the needs of their citizens. Governmental policy changes and cutbacks in social programs in the 1980s have also widened the income gap between the poor and the affluent, quickening the instability of the inner-city African American family, already fragile and traumatized by neglect and racism. The effects on children have been devastating: by the early 1990s half of all African American children lived in female-headed households, and a similar proportion lived in poverty.[4] These enervating factors impinge on African American family life in ways that make crime attractive as an alternative to the squalor and misery of the impoverished ghettos. Although some African Americans have moved successfully into the mainstream in recent decades, the inner-city poor are worse off today than at any time since the Great Depression.

GOVERNMENTAL RESPONSE TO AFRICAN AMERICAN ORGANIZED CRIME

Some law enforcement organizations have suggested that African Americans are not disposed to creating an organized criminal enterprise, and many public officials either shy away from this topic as politically too sensitive or exaggerate the seriousness of the minority organized crime threat. Neither view is warranted. The New Jersey Commission of Investigation reports:

Law enforcement has long been reluctant to accept the existence of Afro-lineal organized crime, based primarily on an opinion that such ethnic groups were incapable of structuring syndicates of any consequence ... despite the existence of major organized criminal groups. ... In New York City ... drug lord Leroy "Nicky" Barnes. ... in Philadelphia ... the late "black Mafia" member Tyrone Palmer.[5]

In 1986 the President's Commission on Organized Crime gave scant attention to African American organized criminality, referring only fleetingly to radical political prison groups such as the Black Guerrilla Army, which existed in California's prison system more than twenty years ago, is presumably active today, and is possibly linked to the Black Liberation Army, which carried out armed robberies and the murders of policemen.[6] This is indeed puzzling since the hearings conducted by the President's Commission in 1985 sought testimony from representatives of federal and local law enforcement agencies that have been significantly involved in combating heroin trafficking, as well as from private persons who provided firsthand information on African Americans' participation as leaders or couriers in large-scale heroin trafficking networks. The testimony presented at the hearings suggested a level of organization that is fairly sophisticated and highly structured.[7]

The problem of ignoring African American organized crime is not unique to the President's Commission. During a symposium on organized crime control the Federal Bureau of Investigation (FBI) assistant director of investigation referred to "Nontraditional" organized crime groups, including "the outlaw motorcycle gangs, Mexican and Colombian narcotics cartels and oriental organized crime gangs," with no mention of African American organized crime.[8] Despite vigorous prosecutions against the Mafia throughout the United States and mounting evidence that organized crime is not limited to the operation of La Cosa Nostra and its crime families, "Italian geography"[9] still seems to dominate official and public thinking. The commission's *Final Report* did note that Asian and Central and South American groups play significant roles in drug trafficking and minor extortion rackets in their ethnic communities.[10] For some time official agencies have publicly stated that organized crime is not limited to La Cosa Nostra but is an integral part of the social system. Still, the fixation with Mafia persists—a legacy perhaps from the Estes Kefauver days and the emphasis placed on it by many officials and academic studies.[11]

Scholarly treatment of organized crime has ignored the role of African Americans involved in organized crime before World War II (U.S. involvement, 1941–45). In a widely used text Howard Abadinsky claims:

Heroin provided the vehicle by which black criminal operators were able to enter the ranks of organized crime. Resistance from already established Mafia enterpreneurs proved futile; emerging black criminal organizations revealed a willingness to use violence on a scale that neutralized otherwise formidable opposition.[12]

Abadinsky overlooks the data that show the existence of African American organized gangs long before World War II. They were bankers in the numbers racket in New York City and other large cities located in Northeast and north-central sections of the United States since the 1920s.

NUMBERS GAMBLING, 1920–30

African Americans in New York City controlled numbers banks during the 1920s and 1930s. Kinship networks were the common organizational bonds, but they were not always headed by males. One popular African American female policy banker, Stephanie Saint Clair, known in Harlem as "Madam Queen of

Policy,'' testified in 1930 before the Seabury Committee that she operated a policy bank from 1923 to 1928 and that the police took her money and kept arresting her runners. Outraged by the unscrupulous behavior and male chauvinism of the police department, she placed several paid advertisements in local Harlem newspapers and made serious charges of graft and corruption against it. Almost immediately she was arrested on what she termed a "framed charge" and was sent to jail for eight months.[13]

Before 1920 there were no arrests for policy numbers in New York City.[14] Perhaps policy numbers (not to be confused with lottery policy numbers) were unknown outside the African American community.[15] In 1920, there were seven arrests for violations of the policy laws in New York City,[16] and by 1935 the police reported 13,692 policy law violations for that year alone. Over this period, from 1920 to 1927, the Twelfth District Magistrate Court, located in Harlem, recorded 3,504 policy arrests, 93 percent of which involved African Americans,[17] New York City in the same period reported a total of 7,465 policy arrests.[18] At least 47 percent of the policy arrests in New York City during the 1920–27 period were made in the Twelfth District Magistrate Court. As the policy racket spread throughout the city, the Twelfth District Magistrate Court accounted for a smaller percentage of the entire city's total policy arrests. Still, this court processed approximately 37 percent of New York City's total policy arrests between 1920 and 1930.[19]

The economic fixation of the African American community with numbers may be explained by viewing numbers gambling groups as a substitute for the legitimate financial institutions that were conspicuously absent in impoverished communities. Ivan Light observes:

Mainstream financial institutions have never been able to provide generally prevailing service levels in poor communities. In the resulting partial-service vacuum, blacks invented numbers gambling. Numbers-gambling banks became sources of capital and a major savings device of urban black communities. With the usury industry, numbers banks framed an alternative institutional system for the saving-investment cycle in the slum. Number banking illustrates the conjoint contribution of institutional and cultural causes in an analysis of poverty.[20]

Numbers players typically placed a small amount of money with a runner (an agent who takes the bets from players) whom they trusted, hoping to receive a generous return if they "hit" a winning number. The numbers game or policy rackets may be seen as a substitute for financial institutions that were virtually nonexistent in African American communities. The fact that career criminals were not integral to the African American gambling enterprises and organizations and their management suggests that numbers were an indigenous response to the absence of legitimate organization that could provide jobs, ready capital, and financial resources to a hard-pressed community.

This parallels the genesis of the Mafia in southern Italy, where government had all but abandoned the peasantry and where corrupt police, an ambivalent church, and an aloof aristocratic elite exploited the local population. The Mafia provided rough justice, jobs, finances for grain, and help to those who could turn nowhere else. Similarly, in America's African American ghettos, policy operators were not perceived as "criminals" in the usual sense but rather as informal entrepreneurs prepared to respond to expediencies and meet needs.

Light's[21] comparative studies of African American and Chinese vice in the first half of the twentieth century illustrate the relevance of cultural factors in an illicit industry. (In fact, an examination of legitimate commercial activities operated by different cultural groups would show distinctive styles. Why, then, cultural overlays should not be apparent and relevant in illicit activities is a bit bewildering.) Light's research reveals that both African Americans and Chinese had strong motives for compensatory illicit income, since legitimate opportunities were sharply circumscribed by social prejudice and xenophobia. Thus, the Chinese and African Americans were indirectly encouraged into illegal activity. As Light puts it:

The black vice industry and the Chinese vice industry were internally different. The black vice industry consisted of streetwalkers and pimps who settled quarrels with fights. The Chinese vice industry consisted of syndicated brothels which resolved severe business rivalries by gang wars, but adjudicated individual quarrels. . . .

Black pimps relied upon their reputation for violent prowess to intimidate workers and rival pimps. . . . The black enclaves had high homicide rates, but no gang wars. Streetwalkers and their confederates frequently robbed their customers and, occasionally, robberies eventuated in killings. Chinatowns had low homicide rates, rampant gang wars, but no record of street robberies of visiting men. The implication is that the syndication of vice in Chinatown prevented petty robberies and unregulated conflicts among individuals, but encouraged collective struggles for business advantage. On the other hand, the free market organization of vice in black enclaves permitted individualistic killings and petty crime, but eliminated gang warfare.[22]

Light argues that the Chinese organized prostitution through their tongs, which licensed illegal businesses, coordinated their operation, and resolved conflicts. African Americans did not have available a similar cultural and historic tradition of "organized criminality." Consequently, the rough-and-tumble individual entrepreneurial style of the pimp or vice agent encouraged a free and open market competition generated by cadres of street pimps, and when the public demand for prostitution declined, the transition to alternative income-generating opportunities reflected their cultural and ethnic differences. The transformation to legitimate tourist industries among Chinese (restaurants, novelty shops, and entertainment) was accomplished without much loss of earnings because the Chinatowns did not pose the threat to visitors that African American ghettos did. The tongs that had organized the brothels and opium dens facilitated the growth and operation of restaurants. On the other hand, in the African American communities, the tourist trade for nightclubs and entertainment, even though these were owned by white racketeers with affiliations in powerful crime syndicates, was stymied by the high volume of street violence and the threat of street thugs.

While the demand for illicit goods and services encouraged minorities to respond, their particular method of meeting the demand is more clearly understood when the provider and supplier's cultural and social characteristics are appreciated. These seem to shape and mold the manner in which illicit activity is organized and predict its durability.

Light's studies on the ethnic and social organization of the vice industry suggest that sociocultural characteristics of provider subgroups are important factors affecting the manner in which responses are structured to meet consumer demands. Similarly, fieldwork on marijuana distribution networks in Brooklyn, New York, indicated that retail-level traffickers were sensitive to the real or imagined racial and cultural backgrounds of those with whom they chose to do business and how they conducted their illicit transactions.[23]

However, these issues do not address the internal organization of illicit activity within ethnic enclaves or ghettos that cater not only to outsiders but to coethnics and ghetto dwellers. It would be mistaken to suppose that the collapse of quasi-legitimate tourist industries in the African American ghettos and the decline of its vice industry meant that organized crime in the ghetto was under the shadowy stewardship of white criminals. Larger issues involving racism and alternative sources of vice services undoubtedly played a role in frustrating traditional organized criminal growth in African American ghettos.

Harlem Invents Numbers

Casper Holstein, a West Indian African American, is said to have started the first use of "clearinghouse bank" totals in the numbers game in Harlem about 1920.[24] Holstein arrived in New York just before the old policy game (the numbers game based on lottery numbers) was wiped out. A Fifth Avenue store porter with an eye for stock market reports who saw that clearinghouse bank totals differed each day, he devised the scheme of selecting three digits, two from the first and one from the second total, with bets placed upon the final number. He offered odds of 600 to 1.

In the first year of operation Holstein owned three of the finest apartment buildings in Harlem, a fleet of expensive cars, a home on Long Island, and several thousand acres of farmland in Virginia. During the 1920s, he operated the Turf Club, at 111 West 136th Street, the rendezvous of Harlem's fast set and headquarters for his policy operation. Holstein was known as Harlem's only African American philanthropist, providing college scholarships and helping the poor. He collaborated with the magazine *Opportunity* and set up a fund for literary prizes to aspiring writers and artists. Holstein "was renowned for his reliability" in paying his players on their winning bets.[25]

On 23 September 1928, Holstein was reported to have been kidnapped by white gangsters. He was released three days later. Holstein failed to identify the five men who were arrested for his kidnapping. The case sparked national attention; it was the first time a wealthy African American was kidnapped and held for $50,000 ransom. The *New York Times* reported that Holstein, one of Harlem's wealthiest African Americans, had bet more than $30,000 on the races at Belmont Park in the week before his abduction.[26] His notoriety depicted a Harlem engulfed not in wretched poverty but in affluence and deviance. A year later in Chicago, Walter Kelly, an African American policy banker, was also kidnapped by white gangsters and held for $25,000 ransom.[27]

In the early 1930s, when the Seabury Commission investigated Harlem policy operators and corruption in the magistrate's court, Holstein dropped out of the policy racket. He was arrested for the first time in 1935 for a policy violation. His aggressive involvement in Virgin Island politics led law enforcement authorities to investigate his gambling activities, for which he received a penitentiary term of nearly a year.

Although he may have ended ignominiously, Holstein was one of many criminal enterpreneurs who operated a large-scale policy bank in the Harlem ghetto employing hundreds of policy workers.[28] Apart from their chief purpose of generating money, numbers gambling banks created jobs and were a source of ready capital in the African American community.[29] In addition, a usury industry sprang up to serve the clientele of the numbers game. This species of an illegal appended enterprise may have broadened its scope beyond the gambling needs of the minority community and taken on a life of its own.[30] The extent to which numbers became an integral part of the economy in African American communities is suggested by J. Saunders Redding, who characterized the pervasiveness of numbers gambling as "the fever that has struck all classes and conditions of men."[31]

Before "Dutch" Schultz's gang, a white criminal organization, seized much of the Harlem policy racket and consolidated its control, numbers were not a criminal monopoly or cartel operation. It consisted of many independent bankers (mostly African Americans) who conducted the game, each for themselves, each providing the requisite operating capital and each taking the profits.[32] Early Harlem policy rackets were led by gambling "kings" and "queens" who were unsettled by the intrusions of white gangs that freely employed violence and cunning. The influence on corrupted political officials was the major tool employed by white competitors in the confrontation between community-based African American operators and alien white gangs. Schultz reportedly murdered forty people in his takeover of the policy kingdom.[33]

The Internal Revenue Service prosecuted several of Harlem's African American policy bankers when Samuel Seabury's investigations uncovered large bank accounts[34] belonging to Wilfred Brunder, who deposited $1,753,342 between 1925 and 1930, and Jose Enrique Miro, who deposited $1,251,556 from 1927 to 1930. Both were convicted for tax evasion.[35]

The political protection Schultz was able to muster through his Tammany

Hall links with Jimmy Hines, a powerful Democratic party boss in Manhattan, coupled with the firepower of his hoodlums, forced African American policy operators to capitulate. By 1932, Schultz, controlled a centralized policy racket in Harlem. He drained the profits out of the community, whereas previously, African Americans and Hispanic policy entrepreneurs had reinvested their profits back into the community.

Schultz's syndicate dissolved after his murder in 1935, but the lucrative profits and violence would not permit the policy racket to revert to its origins. Policy operators were susceptible to extortion and expropriation. The police had been prodded to action against Harlem policy operators so that if the game was to remain viable, it needed to reach out for white protection. When African American policy bankers had to pay off large "hits" with ready capital, wealthy white gangsters supplied loans for a percentage of the business plus repayment at a high rate of interest. Policy as an autonomous African American criminal enterprise was compromised from then on.

AFRICAN AMERICAN ORGANIZED CRIME: 1930 TO 1970

In 1944, black organized crime appeared to have a "class" structure:

There is a Negro "underworld." To it belong not only petty thieves and racketeers, prostitutes and pimps, bootleggers, dope addicts, and so on, but also a number of "big shots" organizing and controlling crime, vice, and racketeering, as well as other more innocent forms of illegal activity such as gambling—particularly the "policy," or the "numbers," game. The underworld has, therefore, an upper class and a middle class as well as a lower class.

The shady upper class is composed mainly of the "policy kings." They are the most important members of the underworld from the point of view of their numbers, their wealth and their power. The policy game started in the Negro Community has a long history. This game caught on quickly among Negroes because one may bet as little as a penny, and the rewards are high if one wins (as much as 600 to 1). In a community where most of the people are either on relief or in the lowest income brackets such rewards must appear exceptionally alluring.... During most of its history the policy racket in the Negro community has been monopolized by Negroes.[36]

The rise of African American organized criminal groups in the post–World War II era seems to have coincided with the rise of African American political consciousness and the awakening of political and social militancy. Major African American traffickers in drugs surfaced at approximately the same time, in the early and mid-1960s, when pressures mounted by African Americans for jobs, educational reform, fair housing, and a greater share of political power. Apparently, a combination of factors coalesced, some with unanticipated consequences, that produced legitimate and illegitimate opportunity structures for African Americans. In the wake of sweeping reforms, African Americans gained greater control over their communities, and as their political strength grew, criminal elements were able to take advantage of the correlative declines of white power and African American influence within the ghetto crime scene. They were able more than at any other time to wrest the ghetto's lucrative rackets away from white syndicates. They became less dependent on La Cosa Nostra's political and police clout and could bargain independently with white gangsters, who were no longer able to operate as freely in the ghettos.

The civil rights movement set in motion African American social and economic mobility and may have inadvertently diminished the power of white crime groups that had dominated these communities until then. As the ghettos developed their newfound strength and accumulated political punch, the political agent, the operator, and the machine functionary, not unfamiliar in white communities, who had connections in the ''administration'' or city hall, appeared on the scene. As the ghettos became more politically assertive and economically more viable, a host of new actors arose: the ''minority middlemen,'' the power brokers, those who were equally comfortable in the official world of government and business and in the shadows of opportunism and crime, where favors are arranged, deals are made, and money, when properly placed, can shield and immunize its possessors from the criminal justice system.

The African American underworld is not a homogeneous, monolithic structure of power and influence wielded only by America's blacks. Since the late 1960s in New York City, New Jersey, Baltimore, Washington, D.C., cities in Florida and California, and Toronto, Canada, the Rastafarians have engaged principally in marijuana and cocaine smuggling on a comparatively large scale.[37] The Rastafarian movement originated in Jamaica in the early 1930s. It centered on the belief that the coronation of Prince Ras Tafari Makonnen as Emperor Haile Selassie I of Ethiopia was the prophesied black king and that the time of deliverance for blacks would be near. *Ganja* (marijuana) is used as a religious sacrament among the members. A close-knit group centered in a religious ideology with political overtones that deify Ethiopia's former emperor, Haile Selassie, the ''Rastas'' have achieved something of a detente with white organized crime families and other African American criminal groups. The ''Rastas'' have gained territorial control over the criminal economy (temporarily, at least) in the West Indian and Jamaican communities in many cities of the United States. Whether they are hierarchically organized with descending positions from boss downward to the street worker is not known. It is probable that, as with other ghetto-bound criminal groups, a flexible system of patron and client relations exists.

AFRICAN AMERICAN ORGANIZED CRIME: 1970 TO PRESENT DAY

A puzzling question concerns why African Americans did not organize themselves much earlier into powerful criminal groups as others have done when their poverty and oppression were acute and painful. The early African American criminal organizations that did emerge in policy numbers, prostitution, and drug peddling were feeble by comparison with today's groups and were easily overwhelmed by powerful white gangsters.[38]

Crack is to ghetto entrepreneurial gangsters as booze was to the white ethnic gangsters during the Prohibition era. Prohibition made the alcohol gangsters rich; similarly, crack is the lucrative modus vivendi of today's drug dealers. Crack is more available to small-time ghetto gangsters than heroin, mainly because the initial investment is within the reach of small-time traffickers. A puzzling thing about crack cocaine is that it did not begin rotting American's urban landscape sooner. References to the recipe that used heat and baking soda to turn cocaine into hydrochloride, or powder, and into the smokable form of freebase called crack appeared throughout the 1970s in underground literature, media interviews, and congressional testimony. What turned crack into a craze was mass marketing. Cocaine power required an investment of at least seventy-five dollars for a gram, but a "hit" of crack cost as little as five dollars. Enormous profits may be made by converting cocaine into crack.

Three classes of criminals created the crack epidemic. One was composed of anonymous kitchen chemists and drug traffickers in the United States who used rudimentary science and marketing savvy to help hundreds of small-time criminals set up operations. Another group consisted of indigenous crime organizations, common in most medium-sized and large American cities, who seized local markets from the smaller operators. The third group was gangs on both coasts who franchised crack operations into every corner of the country, using African Americans and Latinos as their subordinates.

In 1974, a landmark study of organized criminal networks in Harlem found that "while there are characteristic patterns of organization with the various networks we observed there is no overall pattern that ties the networks together."[39] No "Mafia" or syndicate structures were apparent among these groups, which exhibited no common code of behavior or rules governing their relationships. Protection was not paid to operate in illicit goods and services of a magnitude that might reveal significant levels of political influence with law enforcement. There were no examples of networks influencing an election, delivering a vote, funding a political candidate, or dabbling in union affairs. The scale of corruption was modest and tied only to a particular local criminal activity. The structure of African American organized criminality may vary from its white counterparts, and its scale may be modest by Cosa Nostra standards, but these aspects, found in Francis A. J. Ianni's study, suggest a continuum of organized criminality ranging along several axes of size, division of labor, normative operating procedures, and power to influence the external constraints likely to impinge on their operations.

Ethnic succession theory proposes that illegal enterprises are domestic in origin rather than imported. The form and shape they take may be related to the cultural styles and taste of the participants. While the details were not worked out by Joseph Albini,[40] he advanced the same idea by emphasizing the spectrum of ethnic and racial minorities in the United States engaged in organized crime at one time or another. Ianni[41] and Albini[42] would describe the ethnic diversity of criminals as a response to structurally engendered poverty and disadvantages affecting these groups, not as a cultural proclivity or natural criminal predisposition.

Both Ianni's and Albini's arguments rest upon the anomie theory of deviance, which holds that when legitimate avenues of social mobility are blocked, the obstacles encourage the frustrated to seek out deviant or criminal ways to advance themselves socially and economically.[43] While such considerations are necessary to an explanation of the genesis of organized criminality, they are not sufficient. Over the past twenty years, the predominance of Italian Americans in organized crime has produced a blurring between the specific features of Italo-American criminal enterprises and the general problem of organized crime. The one has been made to appear synonymous with the other. At the other extreme, some critics of organized crime see it primarily as an Italian American phenomenon.[44]

Ianni's ethnographic study of African Americans and Cubans organized in crime networks sought to show that the phenomenon is not unique to Italian American experience but that it has a logic of its own, manifesting itself among other groups poised to exploit the criminal opportunities American society thrusts upon them.[45] What seems clear is that the styles of illegal activities are affected by the cultural and ethnic characteristics of the participants.

Ianni described the conditions in Harlem that produced the bases for a black Mafia.[46] For African Americans and Hispanic ghetto dwellers, one of their most important problems, one that confronted white ethnic immigrants decades earlier, was how to escape poverty through socially approved means when these means were virtually closed. This problem is resolved to some extent by indulging in criminal activities.

For most ghetto dwellers the provision of illegal goods and services or the illegal provision of licit goods and services is tolerated widely because it is not seen as morally evil or socially disruptive. Poverty provides the moral climate for organized criminality in the ghetto, with the exception, perhaps, of drug peddling. But even here, escape from the bondage of poverty provides the context for widespread drug use. The pervasive poverty of the ghetto is also at the basis of recruitment into criminal networks.

African Americans involved in ghetto criminal networks are driven by aims similar to those that motivated the Irish, Jewish, and Italian criminals who preceded them: assimilation in, and toleration and acceptance by, the larger American society. Apart from pervasive, cruel poverty, the cultural and structural forces that shaped the growth and evolution of white ethnic organized criminality may not yet be present among African Americans and Hispanics. There appear to be no cultural ethos and cohesive kinship system among African Americans that lead to a high degree of organizational development in criminal syndicates, as has been characteristic of Italians. Certainly, African American criminal networks can be expected to respond to their own subcultural imperatives, and for kinship and extended family solidarity they may find analogous substitutes in peer relationships formed in street gangs and friendship ties forged in prison. These social bonds may be strengthened by a common sense of racial victimization that together may form the catalyst necessary to generate and sustain an enduring criminal enterprise.

A decade after Ianni's field studies in the ghettos of New York City and New Jersey, testimony was presented to the Senate Judiciary Committee in 1983 by the New York City Police Department that described African American organized crime in the city as divisible into two main groups: American native-born and Jamaican-based Rastafarian religious cultists. Traditionally, African Americans have been confined mostly to roles within La Cosa Nostra that dominated rackets in ghetto gambling and drug dealing for decades. Sometime in the 1970s there seems to have been a rupture between African American criminals and their former La Cosa Nostra patrons and employers. In the 1970s major narcotics groups, established and operated exclusively by African Americans, appeared in the ghettos.[47] Eventually they either dissolved or were broken up by drug enforcement task forces and the police. Gambling profits and revenues derived from other enterprises, such as loan-sharking and the fencing of stolen goods, provided the capitalization for autonomous drug ventures by African American criminals. These drug rings developed their own international source of supply, importing methods, processing, and distribution outlets. As with their white counterparts, the huge profits earned in narcotics seem to have been funneled into lawful businesses in the ghettos and African American communities of the metropolitan New York region.[48] But they could not sustain the links that kept together the Italian American crime families.

Not all "legitimate" businesses are run honestly by their mobster owners or investors. Often they are just fronts for drug money or wedges to infiltrate an industry and destroy competitors. These businesses—retail food stores, bars, restaurants, livery services, and entertainment places—serve as contact and distribution locales for drug dealing.[49]

Every large, urban African American ghetto has criminal organizations operating in its midst. Some of these gangs are large; some, small. These criminal enterprises are usually led by a local (homey) African American. This study does not set out to identify each African American-led criminal organization throughout the country. The following operations display complex organizational structures.

New York's Drug Groups

Large powerful drug syndicates, like those of Frank Lucas and Leroy "Nicky" Barnes, spread beyond the ghetto in the 1960s and 1970s. The level of sophistication and scope of trafficking in the Lucas organization show that it was planned carefully. Frank Lucas and his brothers (Vernon Lee, Lee Van, Larry, and Ezell) employed relatives as a hedge against security breaches in their international narcotics smuggling operations.[50] Their group was known as the "Country Boys." Lucas did not restrict his trafficking to wholesaling but sought to control a network from Indochina to street-level sales in America's ghettos. All the trademarks of an astute organization that resemble La Cosa Nostra operations were apparent in the Lucas group: personnel were selected because they were trustworthy and reliable blood relatives, not because of some sentimental friendship or childhood attachment[51]; a division of labor was constructed whereby participants knew only what was necessary for them to function; and state-of-the-art technologies in transportation, processing, and packaging were vigorously exploited in the drug business.

Barnes (once known as "Mr. Untouchable" because of his seeming invincibility from prosecution) helped form a murderous drug syndicate in 1973 that brought together the heads of the seven largest drug rings in New York City. The syndicate, called the Council, employed hundreds of mill workers, distributors, and street dealers. In testifying before the 1985 President's Crime Commission, Barnes revealed that he had taken an "oath of brotherhood" to his Council, which was formed to assure cooperation between its member narcotics dealers in their distribution of thousands of pounds of heroin.[52] The Council was alleged to have ordered the murders of at least five suspected informants and killed several drug dealers for "mere larcenies or insubordination." There is further evidence that African Americans were highly organized in other illicit activities that resembled La Cosa Nostra operations.

Since his conviction Barnes has become a state witness, resulting in the indictment and conviction of numerous defendants. The seven leaders of the largest New York City drug rings were convicted of drug charges and received long prison terms based on his testimony.

In the Washington Heights section of Manhattan, New York (the scene of riots in the summer of 1992), Dominican drug gangs employed up to 100 people in the city's first big crack market.[53] The Renkers posse operated a huge portion of the crack trade in Brooklyn, New York. The Renkers employed fifty workers selling crack in the Bedford-Stuyvesant, Crown Heights, and Flatbush sections of Brooklyn. The Renkers branched out to Philadelphia, Baltimore, and the District of Columbia.

In many minority urban ghettos, crack cocaine is the currency of the informal economy. The gangs that developed around it reflect the dynamics of the trafficking systems that have emerged. In these respects modern minority criminal groups, African American organized crime in particular, have little structural resemblance to La Cosa Nostra crime families. Still, these groups are no less dangerous, nor are they likely to be short-lived or only drug-dependent since the gangs may thrive beyond the demand for crack and transform themselves to meet the illegal market conditions of other commodities in demand. Crack enables minority groups to generate essential criminogenic assets (the use of violence and the availability and distribution of illegal commodities). Once established, these groups can explore other criminal opportunities as did the criminal groups that emerged to serve the demand of illicit alcohol.

The Chambers Brothers of Detroit

A Detroit crack cocaine network operation founded in 1983 by the four Chambers brothers evolved in just a few years to some 200 crack houses that employed up to 500 people, mostly teenagers recruited from their hometown, Marianna, Arkansas. In 1988, during a drug conspiracy case against fourteen members of the Chambers brothers gang, authorities say that the Chambers network "once supplied half the city's crack."[54] Police allege that the Chambers's drug profits amounted to $1 million a week. A rigid set of rules often posted on crack house walls governed behavior. The gang leaders warned that crack and money were not to be carried simultaneously, prohibited speeding while driving, and prevented the use of lavish automobiles for business purposes. Quality-control managers posed as crack buyers to keep an eye on the product. Rule breakers were disciplined by a so-called wrecking crew.[55]

El Rukns of Chicago

In Chicago, where African Americans are at the bottom of the economic ladder, organized criminal groups are active in the ghettos. One, known as the Royal family, consisting of former inmates from the Statesville Penitentiary, modeled itself deliberately on the fictitious Corleone family in Mario Puzo's novel, *The Godfather*.[56] The Royal family did not challenge the white Chicago syndicate (the Outfit) but allied with it, working as enforcers.

The largest and most powerful African American organized criminal group in the Chicago area has been the El Rukns, a group that openly and contemptuously defied the Outfit.[57] El Rukns has been accused of narcotics dealing and assorted extortions and shakedowns in its communities. It evolved out of a street gang, the Blackstone Rangers, and has participated actively in local political campaigns. The group has even petitioned for status as a nonprofit charity organization while its key leaders are under indictment or imprisoned. This gang of toughened street youths, now adult, although engaging in serious crime, also works within the ghetto to help the indigent. Mafia organizations have done the same thing; they simultaneously exploit and help, always to their personal advantage.

Jamaican Posse Groups

The term *posse* was adapted by Jamaican gangs from Hollywood westerns. The gangs evolved as an informal mechanism in gaining local community control. Posse maturation in Jamaica has its underpinning in both political nationalism and the Rastafarian movement, which emerged in the late 1950s and

1960s. Neighborhood street gangs aligned themselves with either of the two leading political parties, the Jamaica Labor Party (JLP) and the People's National Party (PNP). These groups interacted closely with activist Rastafarians in various violent endeavors, drug and weapons trafficking. What have become known as criminal ''posses'' in the United States originated with Jamaican street gangs, and many active organizations in the United States still bear the names of streets or neighborhoods in Jamaica's cities. The first U.S. posses were the Untouchables from Tecks Lane in the Racetown section of Kingston and the Dunkirk Boys from the Franklin town area of Kingston. The Shower and the Spangler posses are two of the largest and the best organized of the posses operating in the United States.

Jamaican criminals use several methods to infiltrate a community. A common tactic is to select an African American female and lavish her with gifts, money, cocaine, or crack. She, in return, permits the Jamaican criminals to use her home for their drug trafficking operation. Another method is to pay selected individuals rent for apartments from which the posse operates. The Jamaican posses also establish ''gatehouses'' for their drug distribution. Gatehouses are usually vacant or abandoned buildings that are fortified to make their operation less vulnerable to police raids and robberies by competitors. Their illicit drug organizations are composed of individuals who serve as wholesalers, packagers of drugs, retailers, lookouts, and carpenters, whose jobs are to operate and protect the gatehouses.

Although Jamaican organized crime activity in the United States dates back to the 1970s, Jamaican posses emerged in the 1980s as a significant criminal threat in the United States. These groups are primarily involved in drug trafficking, especially cocaine and marijuana, and increasingly in illegal arms traffic and other weapons violations. Jamaicans have been successful at organizing and competing against other drug groups. A strong vertical structure enables Jamaican posses to control costs and offer lower prices than existing local criminal groups. Their aggressive marketing strategies have enabled them to expand rapidly. The posses have a strong propensity for violence and use it to acquire and maintain territories. Some have a multilayered structure; however, other less-structured Jamaican groups also exist, including some with family-based associations. In 1991 an estimated forty Jamaican posses, with 20,000 members, were alleged to be involved in illicit operations in the United States.

The two largest posses, the Spangles and Showers . . . have been whittled away by successful prosecutions in New York and Florida. But their street operations have quickly been taken over by new groups: the Dunkirk Boys in Queens (N.Y.) has some 2,000 members, Jungle Posse of Brooklyn's East New York section has 2,500 members, Samokan Posse also of Brooklyn, has 1,000 members.[58]

The *New York Times* reported that seventeen people were arrested by federal agents.[59] This gang of illegal aliens from Jamaica, known as the Gulleymen, operated a network of crack houses, and heroin dealerships and transported illegal handguns purchased in southern states and transported to the North. Federal agents allege that the gang made $60,000 a day in profits and believe that the Gulleymen take their name from a neighborhood in Kingston, Jamaica, called McGregor's Gully. Agents allege also that the gang has sold franchises to street-level dealers, supplying them with crack and protection for a set fee. Most of their murder victims were rival drug dealers and former gang members. Profits from drug and arms dealing have gone into real estate in Brooklyn and Long Island or have been returned to Jamaica to boost the campaign war chests of Jamaican politicians.

The Crips and Bloods of Los Angeles: The Black-Lash

During the spread of minority gangs in the mid-1980s, the United States was caught in a pincer movement: the Los Angeles street gangs moved east, and the Jamaican posses moved west from the East Coast and between them by the end of the decade they had introduced much of the rest of the country to crack.

The chief Los Angeles gangs are the Crips (approximately 30,000 strong now) and the Bloods (about 9,000), composed of Latinos and African Americans. Their expansion to other parts of the country took off in 1986. The Crips Gang expanded into Seattle and Oklahoma City in 1988.[60] In 1991 the Justice Department placed the Crips and Bloods in thirty-two states and 113 cities. Some experts think that Los Angeles-based gangs now control up to 30 percent of the crack trade.[61] Neither gang is rigidly hierarchical. Both are broken into loosely affiliated neighborhood groups called ''sets,'' each with 30 to 100 members. Many gang members initially left Southern California to evade police. Others simply expanded to other areas as the crack epidemic exploded by setting up branch operations in places where friends or family were located.

Compared with Los Angeles, other cities have been easy pickings, especially for ''rollers'' or ''Ogs'' (original gangsters) and others in their twenties with a thirst for more serious cash who have established a connection with Colombian suppliers. Crips and Bloods are reflections of a demographic bulge where its members tend to be in the most criminally prone age cohorts—adolescence to adulthood. Coupled with the exceedingly high unemployment rate among young males (36 percent), the conditions for the rapid expansion of minority crime are present.

In communities that are severely economically depressed, crime is often seen as an attractive alternative, if not the only one, to prolonged deprivation. The crime that emerges is not in the least beneficial to these communities. Generally, illicitly earned income among gang members, primarily drug money, is not recirculated in the community, banked, invested in commercial enterprises, or used to capitalize commercial activities that benefit the community as a whole. Instead, income is usually used for personal luxury items or reabsorbed by the drug economy, whose infrastructure lies outside the community of the users it exploits. Unlike the policy rackets, illicitly generated drug moneys flow out of the community and are drained off by large noncommunity-based syndicates.[62]

Los Angeles Gangs as a Revolutionary Lumpen-Proletariat

Although the study of street gangs is emerging now as a vast cottage industry, virtually little has been written about Los Angeles's sociologically destructive gang culture. The first generation of African American street gangs emerged as a defensive response to white confrontations in the schools and streets during the late 1940s. Until the 1970s these gangs tended to be defined mainly by school-based turf rather than by microscopically drawn neighborhood territories. Besides defending African American teenagers from racist attacks, these early gangs were also the architects of social space in new and usually hostile settings.

The decimation of the Black Panthers led directly to a recrudescence of gangs two decades ago. "Crippin," the most extraordinary gang phenomenon, was a bastard offspring of the Panthers' former charisma, which filled the void when the Panthers were crushed by law enforcement groups across the country. The legends about the Crips agree on certain particulars: The first "set" incubated in the social wasteland caused by the clearance for the Century Freeway, the traumatic removal of housing, and the destruction of neighborhood ties in Los Angeles. One legend has it that Crips stands for "continuous revolution in progress." However apocryphal this may be, it best describes the phenomenal spread of Crip sets across the ghetto between 1970 and 1972. Under incessant pressure, independent gangs federated as the red-handkerchief Bloods. The Bloods have been primarily a defensive reaction formation to the aggressive emergence of the Crips.

This was not merely a gang revival but instead a radical permutation of gang culture. The Crips inherited the Panther aura of fearlessness and transmitted the idealogy of armed vanguardism, and "Crippin" often represents an escalation of intraghetto violence to "Clockwork Orange" levels (murder as a status symbol). The Crips have also blended a penchant for ultraviolence with an overweening ambition to dominate the entire ghetto. The Crips achieved, like the El Rukns in Chicago, a "managerial revolution" in gang existence. If they began as a teenage substitute for the fallen Panthers, they evolved through the 1970s into a hybrid of teen cult and proto-Mafia.

In 1972 at the height of Crip mania hysteria, a conference gave a platform to the gangs, which produced a document of their grievances. To the astonishment of officials, the "mad dogs" outlined an eloquent and coherent set of demands: jobs, housing, better schools, recreation facilities, and community control of local institutions. It was a bravura demonstration that gang youth, however trapped in their own delusionary spirals of vendetta and self-destruction, clearly understood that they were the children of deferred dreams and defeated ambitions. Young African Americans have seen their labor market options virtually collapse as the factory and truck-driving jobs that gave their fathers and older brothers a modicum of dignity were replaced by imports or relocated to white areas far out of the galactic spiral-arms of the Los Angeles Megalopolis. The deteriorating labor market for these young males is a major reason the countereconomy of drug dealing and youth crime has burgeoned.

The tacit expendability of African American and Hispanic youths can be directly measured by the steady drainage of resources, with minimum outcry from elected officials, from the programs that served their most urgent needs. Job alternatives for gang members have been almost nonexistent, despite widespread recognition that jobs are the most potent deterrents to youth crime. The school system meanwhile has been traveling backward at high speed. At the state level the educational system has been in steep decline.

The specific genius of the Crips has been their ability to insert themselves into a leading circuit of the international drug trade. Through crack they have discovered a vocation for the ghetto in the ghetto's new world city economies. Peddling the imported, high-profit rock to a bipolar market of final consumers, including rich whites and poor street people, the Crips have become as much lumpen capitalists as outlaw proletarians.

In an age of narco-imperialism they have become modern analogues to the "gunpowder states" of West Africa, those selfish, rogue chieftains who were middlemen in the eighteenth-century slave trade, prospering while the rest of Africa bled. The contemporary cocaine or crack trade is a stunning example of what some economists call "flexible accumulation." The rules of the game are to combine maximum financial control with interchangeable deployment of producers and sellers across variable markets.

The appearance of crack has given the Crips subculture a terrible, almost irresistible allure. There is little reason to believe that the crack economy of the new gang culture will stop growing, whatever the scales of repression, or stay confined to African American ghettos. Although the epicenters remain in the Watts-like ghetto zones of hard-core youth unemployment, the gang mystique has spread into middle-class African American areas where parents are close to panic or vigilantism.

CONCLUSION

Several factors affect the development and persistence of organized crime. The comparative evaluation of these variables, which together form the constituent building blocks or organized criminality, will be summarized here from the descriptive studies reviewed in this chapter. It seems clear that corruption of public officials and law enforcement was a primary prerequisite for organized criminal activities prior to the explosion of crack street gangs in the ghettos. Political bosses and leaders of political machines, to be successful, must be able to guarantee police protection to those who provide both licit and illicit goods and services on demand. In other respects, the power brokers in political machines must be able to arrange variances and liquor licenses for the right people. They must be able to close their eyes to all kinds of infractions and illegalities.[63]

As Ianni[64] points out, within some segments of the economically depressed communities, acceptance and patronage of African American crime activists define the attitudes of many residents. For organized criminals, corruption is a tool to protect their operations. Corruption works at various levels and may be as complicated an interaction as the organization of gambling, loan-sharking, drug distribution, or dealing in stolen goods. Along with other ghetto residents, the nonpredatory criminal providing goods and services is often perceived as a victim of the white power structure. Furthermore, many activities, except for internal drug dealing, are not considered particularly harmful by many ghetto residents. The success of African American criminal activists also feeds into an image that many may emulate rather than despise because of the wealth and glamor it produces. The malfunctioning of the larger social system and the inadequate operation of the mainstream economic system that has failed to absorb and assimilate African Americans have contributed to organized criminal operations in the ghetto.

Corruption may still be rudimentary and minor compared with that of white criminals. Several factors—some historical, others structural—may account for the putative absence of African American organized criminals in large-scale corruption. With ghetto-bound vice activities, corruption may be limited to small street payoffs. Scattered and independent, certain vice activities have flourished, but, when they aroused public attention because of their profitability (as numbers gambling did fifty years ago), the pressures from police have increased to such an extent that they reorganized and eventually were subsumed into more powerful white crime syndicates against which they were helpless. Where criminal activities were capable of expanding beyond the confines of the African American community, and extra-ghetto illicit profits were realizable, as with drugs, compromises and coordination with nonblack crime activists occurred. Similarly, when white and nonblack criminals infiltrate the ghetto, they seem to require the coordination and participation of the African American crime activists who predominate in the area.

Although the avenues of corruption have been sustained assiduously by whites, the growing political and economic autonomy of the African American community suggests that rackets and political organization are, or will be, major continuing elements of slum life. While African American criminals may find it difficult to ingratiate themselves into the kinds of social relationships with white politicians that offer protection, it is not difficult to imagine how African American politicians operating from machines will provide services and favors for those on the periphery between the legal and the illegal.

There are parallels in the economic roles of "legitimate" and "illegitimate" business in the ghetto. Both forms are concerned with the provision of goods and services for which there is an economic demand. The relevant difference between the provision of licit and illicit goods and services is small, as shown in gambling and the traffic in consumer goods. In terms of social status, the legitimate business groups in the ghetto and the criminal groups are poles apart. Yet status does not fully determine behavior and the interrelation between groups. Functions modify these relationships in social settings where the informal economy is as large as the formal economy.

"Just as the political machine performs services for legitimate business, so it operates to perform not dissimilar services for illegitimate business: vice, crime and rackets."[65] Minority politicians asserting themselves in the ghetto are likely to organize in terms of their perceptions of their functions and their own survival needs. For both the legitimate and illegitimate sectors within the ghetto, the political machine has a similar function. Above all, it must satisfy the needs of its clientele and constituencies for an operating environment that enables criminal and noncriminal alike, in some cases, to meet economic demands without due interference from the government. Whether a political machine turns a blind eye to crime or vigorously attacks depends on the relative economic and political strength of the client or the protagonist. Finally, as far as market demands for goods and services are inadequately met by the legitimate sector, an alternative illegal sector will emerge and persist to fulfill them.

NOTES

1. Rufus Schatzberg, *Black Organized Crime: 1920–1930* (New York: Garland, 1993).

2. The term *West Indian organized crime* refers to those groups whose participants originated from the Bahamas, the British or U.S. Virgin Islands, Trinidad, the Greater Antilles, the Lesser Antilles, Belize, Barbados, Grenada, and the Cayman Islands (State of New Jersey Commission of Investigation, *21st Annual Report*, 1989).

3. The Bureau of Justice Statistics and the National Crime Survey report the black Americans suffer relatively more violent crime than other Americans and that crimes against them caused greater injury than similar crimes committed against persons of other races (U.S. Department of Justice, Office of Justice Programs, Bureau of Justice Statistics, *Black Victims* [Washington, DC: U.S. Government Printing Office, April 1990]).

4. U.S. Department of Commerce, Economics and Statistics Administration, Bureau of Census, *Statistical Abstract of the United States 1991* (Washington, DC: U.S. Government Printing Office, 1991).

5. State of New Jersey; Commission of Investigation, *21st Annual Report*, 1989.

6. President's Commission of Organized Crime, *The Impact: Organized Crime Today* (Washington, DC: U.S. Government Printing Office, April 1986), 79.

7. President's Commission on Organized Crime, *Organized Crime and Heroin Trafficking*, Record of Hearing V (20–27 February 1985), Miami, FL (Washington, DC: U.S. Government Printing Office, February 1985), 194–245. According to the testimony of Leroy "Nicky" Barnes, a "Council" of narcotics traffickers was formed in Harlem in the 1970s. Its prime purpose was to pool their capital for more lucrative wholesale buys. The Council also provided other services to its members. It made available other economic instruments that could be collectively shared: money launderers, attorneys, loans, and pharmaceutical supplies. While each Council member retained control over his own

organization, each had access to automobiles for transporting drugs and cash; numerous milling houses for processing and packaging; safe drops for street dealers; and more enforcement muscle, otherwise unavailable in the absence of syndication.

8. Oliver B. Revell, "The Many Faces of Organized Crime," papers presented at *Major Issues in Organized Crime Control: Symposium Proceedings*, National Institute of Justice, Langley, VA, 25–26 September 1986.

9. The term is Jimmy Breslin's. It refers to the practice of gathering information with no discernible purpose other than the information itself. According to Breslin: "This is practiced by the FBI, and many police intelligence units and newspapers and magazines. Italian geography is the keeping of information on gangsters: the price they pay for clothes, the restaurants in which they eat, the news of all relatives out to the fifth cousins, their home address and their visible daily movements. All this information is neatly filed and continually added to. This data is never used for anything, still the process goes on until the death of the individual concerned. But Italian geography keeps many people busy and collecting salaries, and is considered a commendable occupation" (Jimmy Breslin, *The Gang That Couldn't Shoot Straight* [New York: Viking Press, 1968], 171). Another devastating critique of a preoccupation with the Mafia may be found in Frederick Martens, "Media Magic, Mafia Mania," *Federal Probation* (June 1985): 60–68.

10. Jay S. Albanese, "Government Perceptions of Organized Crime: The Presidential Commission, 1967 and 1987," Paper presented to the thirty-ninth Annual Meeting of American Society of Criminology, Montreal, Canada, 13 November 1987.

11. Mafia is not a secret society in the ordinary sense of the phrase. Unlike the Masons, the Knights of Columbus, or the Knights of Pythias, it has no President, general initiation (there is some question as to induction rituals), dues, election, or bylaws, except unwritten ones. Its cohesiveness is guaranteed by family relationships that go back over generations and an uncodified ideology captured in the phrase "honore e famiglia" (J. Albini, *The American Mafia: Genesis of a Legend* [New York: Appleton-Century-Crofts, 1971] ; F.A.J. Ianni, "The Mafia and the Web of Kinship," *The Public Interest*, no. 22 [Winter 1971]), 1–22.

12. Howard Abadinsky, *Organized Crime*, 2d ed. (Chicago: Nelson-Hall, 1985).

13. Schatzberg, *Black Organized Crime, New York Age* (13 December 1930), 1.

14. The New York City's police commissioner's *Annual Report* does not show any arrest for policy before 1920.

15. "Policy numbers" referred to here is a numbers game that is based on a three-digit number selected from the clearing house bank's totals. This method of choosing policy numbers started around 1920. Later, in the early 1930s, racehorse pari-mutuel results were used instead of the Clearing House Bank totals to determine winning policy numbers.

16. Reported in the New York City's police commissioner's 1920 *Annual Report.*

17. The Twelfth District Magistrate Court is one of two courts that processed all arrests made in the Harlem area. During this period the area became the home for most of New York City's African Americans.

18. These arrest totals were published in the police commissioner's *Annual Report* for the period 1920–27.

19. This is an approximate average because it does not include the thirteen months of missing Twelfth District Magistrate Court docket book arrest data.

20. Ivan Light, "Numbers Gambling Among Blacks: A Financial Institution," *American Sociological Review* 42 (December 1977): 892–904.

21. Ibid.

22. Ibid., 469, 471.

23. Robert J. Kelly, "Field Research Among Deviants: A Consideration of Some Methodological Recommendations," *Deviant Behavior*, 3 (1982): 219–28.

24. J. Saunders Redding, "Playing the Numbers," *North American Review* (December 1934): 533–42.

25. Claude McKay, *Harlem: Negro Metropolis* (New York: E. P. Dutton, 1940).

26. *New York Times*, 23 September 1928, section 1:2.

27. *The New York Age*, 12 December 1929. Walter Kelly, reputed "King of Policy Operators" in Chicago, operated a 75,000 to 1 lottery wheel to determine winning numbers. Clearinghouse numbers were not used in Chicago at the time.

28. Schatzberg, *Black Organized Crime*; Marcellina Cardena, Joseph Matthias Ison, Wilfred Adolphus Brunder, Jose Enrique Miro, Masjoe Ison, Alexander Pompez, Stephanie Saint Clair, John Diamond, Fred Buchanan, Charles Durant, Marshal Flores, Edward and Elmer Maloney, Moe Levy, and Hyman and Pauline Kassell were several of the larger policy bankers operating in the Harlem area during the 1920s.

29. Light, "Numbers Gambling."

30. Henry R. Lesieur and Joseph R. Shelley, "Illegal Appended Enterprises: Selling the Lives," *Social Problems* 34.3 (June 1987): 249–60.

31. Redding, "Playing the Numbers," 542.

32. Humbert S. Nelli, *The Business of Crime: Italians and Syndicate Crime in the United States* (New York: Oxford University Press, 1976), Chapter 8.

33. Herbert Mitgang, *The Man Who Rode the Tiger: The Life and Times of Judge Samuel Seabury* (New York: J. B. Lippincott, 1963).

34. Thomas E. Dewey, *Twenty Against the World*, ed. R. Campbell (New York: Doubleday, 1974), 98–101.

35. Samuel Seabury, In the Matter of the Investigation of the Magistrates Courts in the First Judicial Department and the Magistrates Thereof, and of Attorney-at-Law Practicing in Said Courts, Supreme Court, Appellate Division, First Judicial Department, *Final Report*, 1932.

36. Gunnar Myrdal, *An American Dilemma* (New York: E. P. Dutton, 1940), 330.

37. "Report on Organized Crime in New York City," Testimony of the Police Department, City of New York (11 July) before United States Senate Committee on Judiciary, 1983.

38. John Kobler, *Capone: The Life and World of Al Capone* (Greenwich, CT: Fawcett 1971); Virgil Peterson, *The Mob: 200 Years of Organized Crime in New York* (Ottawa, IL: Green Hill, 1983); Schatzberg, *Black Organized Crime*.

39. Francis A. J. Ianni, *Black Mafia: Ethnic Succession in Organized Crime* (New York: Simon and Schuster, 1974).

40. Albini, *The American Mafia*.

41. Ianni, *Black Mafia*.

42. Albini, *The American Mafia*.

43. Robert K. Merton, *Social Theory and Social Structure*, enlarged ed. (New York: Free Press, 1968).

44. Gary S. Becker, "Crime and Punishment: An Economic Approach," *Journal of Political Economy* 76 (1968): 169–217; Thomas C. Schelling, "What Is the Business of

Organized Crime?'' *Journal of Public Law* 20 (1971): 71–84; Paul E. Rubin, ''The Economic Theory of the Criminal Firm,'' in *The Economies of Crime and Punishment*, ed. S. Rottenberg (Washington, DC: Cesseicen Enterprises Institute, 1973).

45. Ianni, *Black Mafia*.

46. Ibid.

47. President's Commission of Organized Crime, *Organized Crime and Heroin Trafficking*, Record of Hearing V (20–27 February 1985), Miami, FL (Washington, DC: U.S. Government Printing Office, February 1985).

48. *New York Times*. 2 December 1977, 1. During the narcotics trial of Leroy Barnes, Fiske, U.S. prosecutor, informed the jury that Barnes had reported $250,000 a year as ''miscellaneous'' income on his tax returns despite the fact that he used real estate tax shelters to avoid paying taxes on his high income. Barnes was heavily invested in real estate. The prosecutor contended that Barnes's income came from narcotics trafficking. It was alleged that Barnes wholesaled $1 million a month in heroin sales.

49. Peter A. Lupsha, ''Organized Crime in the United States,'' in *Organized Crime: A Global Perspective*, ed. Robert J. Kelly (Totowa,, NJ: Rowman and Littlefield, 1986).

50. C. R. Taplin, ''Lucas Family Troubles,'' *Sunday Bergen Record*, 1975, 1.

51. Ibid.

52. President's Commission, *Organized Crime*.

53. Selwyn Raab, ''Brutal Drug Gang War of Terror in Upper Manhattan,'' *New York Times*, 15 March 1988, B 1.

54. *Detroit News*, 13 October 1988, B 3.

55. Gordon Witkin et al., ''The Men Who Created Crack,'' *U.S. News and World Report*, 19 August 1991.

56. Abadinsky, *Organized Crime*.

57. Reuter may be correct in his estimate that the Mafia may be no more than a ''paper tiger'' with a fierce reputation when it comes to defending some of its criminal prerogatives. Not everyone is easily intimidated by its daunting name and legend. When some of Frank Matthews's drug dealers were threatened by New York crime families, he sneered. ''Touch one of my people,'' Matthews is alleged have said, ''and I'll load my men into cars and we'll drive down to Mulberry Street . . . and shoot every wop we see'' (Ibid.). Similarly, in Chicago, the leader of the El Rukns, an African American gang, was summoned before the leadership of ''the Outfit'' (the Cosa Nostra family in Chicago) and was warned to confine his drug operations to certain areas, or else. Jeff Forte, the head of the African American syndicate, was not intimidated and decisively countered by burning down the restaurant where the meeting took place the very next day. The Outfit was then told to get out of the South Side of Chicago or be carried out (Ibid.).

58. *New York Daily News*, 17 November 1991, 33; Charles M. Sennott et al. compiled an account of efforts by Jamaican, Russian, and Asian syndicates in related coverage of mob wars.

59. *New York Times*, 8 December 1990, 1.

60. Witkin, ''The Men Who Created Crack.''

61. Ibid., 51.

62. Harold D. Lasswell and Jeremiah McKenna, *The Impact of Organized Crime on an Inner City Community* (U.S. Department of Commerce. Springfield, Virginia, 1972). Their project was designed to gauge the effects of how organized crime interacts with the social process of the inner-city community of Bedford-Stuyvesant in New York City.

The research also analyzed the economic impact that drugs and the numbers racket had upon that Brooklyn community. The authors report that drugs and the numbers racket impact the community negatively.

63. Jerome Krase and Charles La Cerra, *Ethnicity and Machine Politics* (Lanham, MD: University Press of America, 1991).

64. Ianni, *Black Mafia*.

65. Merton, *Social Theory*, 132.

9

Chinese Organized Crime in America

KO-LIN CHIN, ROBERT J. KELLY, AND
JEFFREY FAGAN

INTRODUCTION

With the growth of the Chinese population in the United States after the enactment of the Immigration and Naturalization Act in 1965,[1] Chinese gangs began to appear in the Chinese communities of New York City, San Francisco, Los Angeles, Boston, and Chicago.[2] These gangs were alleged to have been involved in illegal gambling, extortion, promoting of prostitution, burglary, and robbery.[3] Gang shootouts often erupted in Chinese communities, resulting in the injury or death of innocent bystanders.[4]

The gangs are alleged to be closely associated with Chinese community organizations known as "tongs."[5] Tongs are fraternal associations first formed by Chinese immigrants in the United States in the 1850s as self-help groups. Owing to their pervasive and consistent involvement in illegal gambling, prostitution, opium trafficking, and violence, the tongs are considered by American law enforcement authorities as criminal enterprises. These associations, however, are registered with the American government as nonprofit organizations.[6]

Chinese tongs and gangs are also believed to be increasingly tied to organized criminal groups in Taiwan and China. Britain will cede Hong Kong to China in 1997. American law enforcement agencies predict that organized crime members from Hong Kong will seek new "havens" abroad because the Chinese government punishes criminal organizations harshly. The United States, Canada, and Australia are thought to be the prime targets of relocation.[7] It is believed that some criminal groups from Hong Kong are already active in the United States and are collaborating with local Chinese criminals.

Since the early 1980s, the activities of Chinese gangs and tongs have been the subject of great concern and scrutiny by officials in the United States and Canada.[8] Public hearings were convened to discuss the emergence of the so-called nontraditional organized crime groups.[9] Asian or Chinese gang task forces have been established in San Francisco; Los Angeles; Monterey Park, California; New York; Vancouver; and Toronto to cope with Asian crime groups. The Drug Enforcement Administration in New York City also has an Asian Heroin Group (also known as Group 41) which deals mainly with drug trafficking among the Chinese.[10] Other cities such as Oakland, Chicago, Boston, Dallas, Houston, and Arlington, Virginia, have also devoted law enforcement resources to Chinese gangs. The Immigration and Naturalization Service has established special task forces in Washington, New York, Boston, Houston, San Francisco, and Los Angeles to deal exclusively with Chinese offenders.[11] In order to more effectively attack the internationally active Chinese crime groups, federal agents in the United States have begun to work closely with law enforcement agencies abroad. Chinese crime groups are now considered by law enforcement authorities as the second most serious organized crime problem in America. It is speculated that Chinese criminal groups may surpass Italian organized crime groups in the near future.[12]

Despite official apprehension and fear, systematic research conducted on Chinese organized crime is limited. Most reports on Chinese crime groups are prepared by journalists, law enforcement authorities, and prosecutors. This information may poorly reflect the actual criminal behaviors or conditions prevailing in the Chinese community. Although some researchers have been able to interview small numbers of neighborhood leaders, gang members, and victims,[13] no meaningful study has collected systematic information from Chinese gang members or their victims.

This chapter offers a sociological description of Chinese organized crime, including (1) an overview of the history, structure, and activities of Chinese crime groups; (2) a theoretical explanation of the development of Chinese criminality; and (3) a discussion of community reactions to crime in the community. The goal is to provide the reader with a general picture of Chinese organized crime in American, especially in the East Coast of the United States.

The authors have conducted three research projects to study the activities of Chinese tongs and gangs. One was an exploratory study of various Chinese crime groups active in the United States and Asia. Another study focused on the problem of extortion in New York City's Chinese community, and a third research project explored the structure and activity of Chinese gangs.[14] The results of these projects are reported where deemed appropriate to provide a vivid illustration of gangs' and tongs' activities. Books, articles, and reports prepared by other researchers, journalists, law enforcement agencies, and prosecutors are also utilized to supplement our primary data.

THE EMERGENCE OF TONGS AND GANGS

Tongs

The word *tong* simply means "hall" or "gathering place." Tongs were first established in San Francisco in the 1850s by the first wave of Chinese immigrants.[15] Prior to the emergence of tongs, Chinese communities in the United States were controlled by the dominant family or district associations. Immigrants whose last name was shared by few or who came from a small district were not accepted by the established associations and were left unprotected. In order to fend for themselves, they banded together and established the tongs.[16] Because recruitment by the tongs was without restrictions, they expanded rapidly. Rival tongs were soon drawn into street battles known as the "tong wars."[17] The secretive nature of the tongs and the strong alliances among themselves when they fought with family and district associations enabled them to become the more powerful associations in the Chinese communities, prompting members of family and district associations to join a tong for additional protection.[18]

The tongs, like the family and district associations, provided many needed services to immigrants who could not otherwise obtain the help they needed. The tongs also acted as power brokers mediating individual and group conflicts within the community. More than thirty tongs were formed in the United States.[19] The Chih Kung, Bing Kung, Hop Sing, On Leong, and Hip Sing are some of the most active tongs in America.

In 1850, the Chih Kung was first established. Its major political goal was to overthrow the Ch'ing dynasty (1644–1911) and restore the Ming emperor. This goal was initiated by the Chinese secret societies.[20] Later, the Chih Kung and Sun Yat-sen's[21] revolutionary organization in Tokyo worked together to establish a financial support center that collected money from overseas Chinese to aid the revolutionary army in China. The center's ability to provide desperately needed financial aid to Chinese soldiers played a pivotal role in Sun's victory over the Ch'ing government.[22]

The On Leong Merchant Association was formed in 1894 in Boston by a Chih King member.[23] Ten years later, the On Leong headquarters was moved to New York City. In the mid-1970s, Eddie T. C. Chan, a sergeant with the Hong Kong Police Department, arrived in New York City. Chan was alleged to have been involved in extensive corruption while he was in Hong Kong. Soon after his arrival, Chan became a businessman and was elected president of the On Leong. During his tenure with the organization, he also became the vice-president of a Chinatown bank and the president of the Chinese American Welfare Association (a nationwide advocate group located in Washington, D.C.). Through his connection with the then Queens borough president, Chan came into contact with local and federal politicians.[24]

Law enforcement authorities charged that the On Leong leader had links with

Chinese gang members. Chan was alleged to be the man behind the shootings of the disgruntled Ghost Shadows in Chicago by gang members from New York City. He was also accused of ordering the killing of a gang leader who was extorting money from him. Chan was implicated in the fraudulent activities carried out by the Continental King Lung Group, an investment company he established. A triad member[25] in Hong Kong had identified Chan as the "dragon head" (crime boss) of New York Chinatown's underworld.[26] When subpoenaed by the President's Commission on Organized Crime in 1984 to testify at the commission's hearings, Chan fled the United States.

In 1990, leaders of the On Leong in New York, Chicago, and Houston were indicted in Chicago for racketeering activities.[27] Twenty-nine core members of the On Leong were arrested, close to half a million dollars of gambling cash was confiscated, and the building owned by the Chicago On Leong was forfeited. The case, however, ended in a hung jury, and the On Leong remains a powerful organization in the Chinese community.

Another powerful tong is the Hip Sing Association, which was formed in 1855. The headquarters of Hip Sing is located in New York City's Chinatown. Benny Eng is the permanent chief adviser of the Hip Sing. He also is the leader of the Chih Kung Tong. Little is known about Eng, except that he was imprisoned for murder in 1936 and was paroled eighteen years later. He had been arrested for assault, robbery, gambling, and drug offenses before his 1936 conviction for murder. In 1976, he was sentenced to prison for bribery.[28]

Other associations in New York City resemble the tongs in terms of their affiliation with Chinese gangs and extensive involvement in gambling operations. They are the Tung On Association, the Tsung Tsin Association, and the Fukien American District Association.[29] Immigrants from two areas of Canton province, Tung Kwong and Po On, formed the Tung On Association. Federal agents believe that the association is active in running gambling operations in Chinatown and that it is well connected with the Sun Yee On Triad Society in Hong Kong.

The Tsung Tsin was established in 1918. Members of the association are predominantly Hakka (meaning "guest"), an ethnic group that migrated to the southern part of China from midwest China during a period of war and famine. The Tsung Tsin's headquarters is only a few buildings away from the Tung On, and like the Tung On, it is heavily involved in gambling activities. The physical proximity between the two associations had enabled the Tung On Gang to provide protection to gambling operations of both associations.

The Fukien American District Association is probably the fastest growing community association in New York City's Chinatown. With the dramatic influx of both legal and illegal Fukienese migrants in the past decade, the association, which was established in 1942, is now in control of the newly expanded areas east and north of Chinatown. Members of the association are alleged to be active in illegal alien smuggling, promoting gambling and prostitution, and heroin trafficking.

Chinese Gangs

The West Coast/California

Chinese street gangs first appeared in San Francisco in the late 1950s. The first juvenile gang was known as the "Bugs" and was formed by American-born Chinese. The Bugs were heavily involved in burglary and were easily identified by their mode of dress, which included high-heeled, "Beatle"-type boots.[30]

In 1964, young immigrants organized the first foreign-born Chinese gang in San Francisco, which was known as the Wah Ching (Youth of China). The main goal of the gang was to protect members from American-born Chinese.[31] After the immigration laws were changed a year later, the Wah Ching rapidly evolved into a powerful gang by recruiting its members from new immigrants. Later, the Hop Sing Tong hired Wah Ching members as lookouts for its gambling establishments. As members of the Wah Ching became familiar with the gambling operations, they demanded and received higher salaries from the Hop Sing. The Suey Sing Tong in San Francisco also formed a youth group that they called the Young Suey Sing, or Tom Tom Gang. The rivalry between the two tongs resulted in street fights between the gangs.[32] One of the Wah Ching leaders, unhappy with Hop Sing's control over the gang, left the gang in 1969 to form the Yau Lai (or Yo Le), which later became the Joe Fong Boys.

Besides working as lookouts for the gambling casinos, members of Wah Ching and Joe Fong Boys began to prey upon retail businesses in their community. Most store operators paid extortion money to the gangs regularly to avoid being disturbed. The stores of those businessmen who refused to pay the gangs were often vandalized or destroyed.[33]

As the Wah Ching and Joe Fong Boys proceeded to become the most dominant gangs in San Francisco's Chinatown, street violence broke out. Between 1969 and 1973, eighteen murders in San Francisco were associated with Chinese gangs.[34] Between 1974 and 1977, there were about twenty-seven gang-related murders in San Francisco's Chinatown. One of the most vicious incidents took place in September 1977, at the Golden Dragon Restaurant in San Francisco's Chinatown. In order to avenge a shootout, three Joe Fong Boys armed with guns entered the restaurant to attack the Wah Ching. The gunmen recklessly opened fire on the customers. Five people were killed and eleven seriously wounded.

In addition to the Wah Ching, Joe Fong Boys, and Young Suey Sing, other Chinese gangs, such as the Hop Sing Boys, Kit Jais, Asian Invasion, Eddy Boys, Chinese Playground Boys, and Ping Boys are active in the San Francisco area.[35] Currently, the single largest Chinese gang in California is the Wah Ching. In the early 1980s, the California Bureau of Organized Crime and Criminal Intelligence (BOCCI) upgraded the gang from a street gang to an organized criminal group. BOCCI estimates that the Wah Ching has 600–700 members and associates, about 200 of whom are "hard-core." The Wah Ching is considered the foremost organized crime group in California.[36]

In Los Angeles, the most powerful Asian street gangs are the Wah Ching, Bamboo United, Four Seas, and Vietnamese gangs. When some of the Wah Ching members from San Francisco moved to Los Angeles in 1965, they established the Los Angeles Wah Ching by recruiting immigrant students who needed protection from Mexican gangs. Following the developmental pattern in San Francisco, some Los Angeles Wah Ching split to form the Los Angeles chapter of the Yau Lai (now extinct) in 1969. Since then, the Wah Ching and Yau Lai became perennial rivals. The Wah Ching was recruited by the Hop Sing Tong, and the Yau Lia is aligned with the Bing Kung Tong.[37]

In the Los Angeles area, Chinese gangs are also active in Monterey Park, which is known as "Little Taipei."[38] According to a former police chief, "The Asian gangs are struggling for control of the lucrative criminal enterprises in the Los Angeles and San Gabriel Valley, including gambling, illegal alien-smuggling, extortion, protection, and narcotic distribution rackets."[39]

Because law enforcement authorities in Taiwan made massive arrests of underworld figures in the late 1970s and early 1980s, hundreds of criminals from Taiwan sought refuge in the United States at that time. Most of them came to Monterey Park because the Chinese in that area were predominantly Taiwanese immigrants. Two Taiwan-based gangs, the Four Seas and the United Bamboo, are in control of criminal activities with that community.[40]

The East Coast/New York City

The number of Chinese gangs in New York City surpasses that in any other American city.[41] The city is now considered the power base of Chinese organized crime in the United States. The first Chinese street gang, the Continentals, was formed in 1961 by native-born Chinese high school students for self-protection. It had as many as 100 members and fought not only the Puerto Ricans and African Americans but also the Italians and other whites. Unlike Chinese gangs that emerged later, the Continentals was not affiliated with any tongs.[42]

In 1964, an On Leong leader organized a youth group made up of foreign-born teenagers. The group was called the On Leong Youth Club. Its major activity was practicing martial arts under the leadership of a tong member. The club later transformed itself into the first foreign-born Chinese youth gang, known as the White Eagles.

In the same year that the White Eagles was formed, Chung Yee was also established. Unlike the Continentals, who had difficulty recruiting new members because of the small number of native-born Chinese, both the White Eagles and Chung Yee were able to attract members from new Hong Kong immigrants. By 1965, the White Eagles and the Chung Yee had become the two dominant powers on the streets of Chinatown. These two groups not only fought non-

Chinese who caused trouble within the community but also drove the American-born Chinese off the streets.

In the following few years, new gangs appeared. By 1966, Quen Ying, the predecessor of Ghost Shadows, had emerged on the outskirts of Chinatown. In 1968, Quen Ying changed its name to Liang Shan. The year after Quen Ying was formed, the Flying Dragons came into existence under the auspices of the Hip Sing. In the meantime, some of the younger members of the White Eagles left the group to form the Black Eagles.

During their emergence stage, Chinese gangs were, in essence, martial arts clubs headed by Kung Fu masters who were tong members. Gang members were mainly involved in martial arts, driving away American-born young Chinese from Chinatown and protecting the community from rowdy visitors.

During the late 1960s and early 1970s, the gangs transformed themselves completely from self-help groups to predatory groups. They terrorized the community by demanding food and money from businesses and robbed illegal gambling establishments. When the youth gangs started to shake down merchants and gamblers who were tong members, the tongs finally decided to hire the gangs as their street soldiers to protect themselves from robbery and extortion and to solidify their position within the community.[43]

By the mid-1970s some gangs in Chinatown became inseparable from certain tongs. Gang members lived in apartments rented to them by the tongs and ate in restaurants owned by the tongs. Gang membership became a full-time occupation for the youths, who detached themselves almost completely from school and family. Despite all the security provided by gang membership, members still had to protect themselves, not only from rival gangs but also from rival factions within the same gang as gang conflicts reached an all-time high. Although gang members were offered membership and jobs by the tongs, they were too powerful to be fully controlled by the tongs. As a result, the community continued to experience an increase in extortion and robbery.[44]

The most violent year in the history of New York City's Chinatown was 1976. The violence reached an explosive stage when Man Bun Lee, a former president of the Chinese Consolidated Benevolent Association (CCBA)[45] who publicly requested that law enforcement officials get tough with Chinese gangs, was stabbed five times by a hired assassin. Although Lee survived, the incident brought a clear message to the community: no one who antagonizes the gangs is safe. Intergang and intragang wars often erupted in the streets of Manhattan's Chinatown. Merchants were terrorized by gang members who were heavily involved in theft, robbery, and extortion. Merchants who refused to pay put their lives in jeopardy. Official statistics also showed that the complaint rates for violent crimes within the Fifth Precinct reached an all-time high in 1976.[46]

By the end of 1976, Chinese gangs were not only "rumbling" in Chinatown but also spreading their operations to other parts of Manhattan. The police became aware that Chinese restaurant owners outside Chinatown were being victimized by Chinese gang members. After many fierce power struggles that crystallized power relationships, the gangs settled down in their respective territories or turfs. The least powerful gangs either dissolved or left the Chinatown area to find new territories of their own.

In the 1980s, new gangs, such as the Fook Ching, White Tigers, Tung On, Green Dragons, and Golden Star, emerged in the peripherals of Chinatown and in the outer boroughs of Queens and Brooklyn, following the emigration patterns of Chinese businesses and residents.

A considerable number of Fukienese came to the United States from southern China and Hong Kong in the early 1980s. The Fook Ching (Fukien Youth) Gang consisted predominantly of adolescents of Fukienese origin. The gang is alleged to be closely affiliated with the Fukien American District Association. Since 1983, the Fook Ching was involved in a series of crimes.

The White Tigers became the dominant gang in the newly established Asian community in Flushing, Queens, in the early 1980s. Local police officers and community leaders indicate that most Chinese businesses in the area are often extorted or robbed by the gang. Besides Queens, the northern area of Manhattan's Chinatown is also the scene of White Tigers' activity.

The Tung On is a relatively new but rapidly growing Chinese gang. It was formed by former Ching Yee members and controls the new commercial areas on Division Street and East Broadway, the territory of the Tung On Association. In 1983, when the gang was developing, its members were in constant conflict with the Kam Lum, a gang also active on East Broadway. In May 1985, the notoriety of the Tung On reached its peak when two factions of the gang were involved in a major shoot-out. Seven were wounded, including a four-year-old Chinese boy who was shot in the head as he walked along the street with his uncle.

The Golden Star, established by former Kam Lum members, has been constantly attempting to encroach on the Tung On's territory. Later on, the gang became closely affiliated with Vietnamese youths active on Canal Street between Lafayette and Centre streets. The activities of the Golden Star are now mainly found in the Sunset Park area of Brooklyn.

The Green Dragons, a Queens-based gang composed of former Fook Ching members, is considered by law enforcement authorities and Chinese business owners to be a very violent gang. The gang is not affiliated with any adult organization. However, it is alleged to be well connected with criminals in China and active in heroin trafficking. The leaders and core members of the Green Dragons were convicted in 1992 for a series of murders. Many Chinese store owners in Queens were heavily victimized by members of the Green Dragons in the early 1990s. Unlike gangs in Manhattan Chinatown, the gang does not hesitate to use violence against resistant victims.[47]

The Born-to-Kill (or the Canal Boys) was developed by former members of the Ghost Shadows and Flying Dragons. Members of the gang were predominantly Vietnamese or Vietnamese Chinese. The gang occupies an area at the outskirts of Manhattan Chinatown, where many Vietnamese or Vietnamese Chinese retail shops are located. The Born-to-Kill, like the Green Dragons, is not affiliated with an adult group and has a violent reputation. In the early 1990s, the gang was involved in a series of violent confrontations with other Chinese gangs. For a while, the Born-to-Kill was the most feared Asian gang in New York City. However, the gang's second-in-command was killed by rival gang members in the summer of 1991, and mourners, while attending his funeral in Linden, New Jersey, were shot at by three gunmen. Later, the leader of the gang and several members were convicted of murder, extortion, and other racketeering activities. Currently, the gang is on the verge of dissolution.

Other Chinese gangs active in New York City include the Freemasons, the Taiwanese Brotherhood, the White Dragons, and the Black Shadows (a female gang).

Beyond the cities of San Francisco, Los Angeles, and New York City, where Chinese gangs were first established, Chinese gangs are also reported to be active in Oakland, Dallas, Houston, Falls Church, Virginia, Arlington, Philadelphia, Chicago, and Boston. Media and law enforcement agencies in Southern California, Louisiana, Texas, Florida, Massachusetts, Virginia, Illinois, and Pennsylvania have also reported the existence of Vietnamese gangs in their jurisdictions.[48]

THE ORGANIZATIONAL STRUCTURE OF CHINESE CRIME GROUPS

Tongs

Most tong headquarters have a president, a vice-president, a secretary, a treasurer, an auditor, and several elders and public relations administrators.[49] Branches may be found in cities where there is a large number of Chinese. The On Leong and Hip Sing have chapters in Boston, Philadelphia, Pittsburgh, Providence, Cleveland, St. Louis, Detroit, Minneapolis, Washington, D.C., Baltimore, Miami, Houston, New Orleans, Richmond, Atlanta, Chicago, Oakland, Kansas City, San Francisco, Denver, San Diego, and Seattle. Each branch has a ruling body resembling its headquarters organization and including the president, secretary, treasurer, auditor, and several staff members.

Most tong members are gainfully employed or have their own businesses. Nationwide, there are 30,000 to 40,000 On Leong members. Members of the Hip Sing also range in the tens of thousands. These members pay their dues regularly, visit the associations occasionally to meet people or to gamble, and attend the associations' banquets and picnics a few times a year. They are not involved in the tongs' daily affairs or in decision making. Only a tong's officers and employees are involved in the organization's operations. Tong officers control internal and external affairs, and some are intermediaries between the tongs and street gangs.

Tong officers and staff members are elected by members. Elections are held either annually or every two years. Senior officers often continued to become "elders" or "advisers" on a permanent basis after they served their terms. Since most members have little interest in the tong's daily affairs, only a handful of members run for office. However, competition among this limited number of candidates is fierce, and election-related confrontations or violence is common in the Chinese community.

Gangs

Most Chinese gangs in New York City, especially the tong-affiliated gangs, have more than one leader or faction and are active in more than one location. For example, the Flying Dragons has two or more Dai Dai Lo (Big Big Brother) who are very close to certain officers or members of the Hip Sing. These Dai Dai Los control six factions of the gang, three in Manhattan and three in Queens. Each faction has about fifteen members and its own factional Dai Lo (Big Brother). More often than not, the factions are at odds with one another. Each street-level Dai Lo is in charge of several Ma Jais (Little Horses) or Lian Jais (Little Kids).[50]

The Dai Dai Los take orders from one or more tong officers or members, who are known as Ah Kung (Grandpa) or Sook Fu (Uncle) among the gang members. The Dai Dai Los then convey the orders to the Dai Los, who then relay them to the Yee Los or Sam Los, and the street-level leader eventually gives the orders to the Ma Jais. Most directives from the tong relate to gambling debt collection or protection of tong-supported gambling and prostitution houses.

The Mai Jais seems to have no idea of who their factional Dai Los are, not to mention the Dai Dai Los and the Ah Kungs or Sook Fus. They take orders only from their immediate leader, that is, the street-level Dai Lo. They are taught by the gang not to ask questions about the leadership structure. Likewise, the street-level Dai Los are familiar only with the immediate leaders—the Dai Los—and rarely talk to their Dai Dai Los or Ah Kungs directly. Thus, there is evidence that tong-affiliated Chinese gangs are highly hierarchical. Young gang members may see those above their immediate leaders only once—at the initiation ceremony for induction.

In sum, the gangs and the tongs are linked through certain tong members and gang leaders. If a tong needs help from its affiliated gang, the message will be conveyed to the Dai Dai Lo by the Ah Kung. Some Dai Dai Los are also officers of the affiliated tong. For example, before his arrest for heroin trafficking, a Dai Dai Lo of the Flying Dragons was elected as the national manager of the Hip Sing, as important position within the organization. Likewise, the highest leaders of the Ghost Shadows and the Tung On have, at times, served as officers of their affiliated adult organizations.

MAJOR CRIMINAL ACTIVITIES

According to reports prepared by government agencies, illegal businesses operated by the tongs ranged from operating illegal gambling operations, promoting prostitution, and importing heroin, to smuggling illegal aliens and other racketeering activities. Official reports also indicate that Chinese gangs are active in protection rackets, extortion, commercial or residential robbery, heroin trafficking, murder, assault, and other street crimes.

Gambling

Like other community associations in American Chinatowns, tongs have a long history of being involved in promoting gambling.[51] There are two types of gambling clubs in the Chinese community. Low-stakes gambling clubs are operated by small family or district associations. These clubs are open only to members and their friends and relatives. The gamblers know each other well, and most of them are employed. Gambling activities do not begin until late in the afternoon and slow down after midnight. Winnings or losses for the average gambler are a few hundred dollars. The most popular games are mahjong and thirteen-card poker. The association takes a 5 percent commission on all bets. Except for occasional minor conflicts among players, these clubs are normally tranquil and do not attract the attention of the street gangs.

High-stakes gambling clubs located in Chinatown are heavily guarded by Chinese gang members. While low-stakes gambling is a way for members to socialize with one another, high-stakes gambling is not. These clubs are open seven days a week and around the clock. Gambling activities in these clubs reach their peak after midnight. In addition to mahjong and poker games, pai gow and fan tan games run by professional dealers are available. A 5 percent commission of the bets goes to the shareholders of the house. More often than not, the shareholders are members of the tong that controls the area where the gambling club is located. Robbery, extortion, and murder occur often in these gambling locations because so much money is involved. The customers are mostly heavy gamblers, illegal aliens, or gang members.

If it has a basement or hall for rent, a tong will place an announcement in the organization bulletin. Tong members who want to rent it confer with the senior officers. There are usually no restrictions on how the place can be used. If the tong members who rent it want to set up a gambling operation, the tong may provide support. In order to operate smoothly, well-established Chinatown gambling clubs rely on a friendly gang to protect the club and its customers from the police, intruders, and other gangs.[52]

A legal gambling industry in nearby Atlantic City, New Jersey, was established in the late 1970s. Since then, many Chinese gamblers go there to gamble.[53] Consequently, the gambling industry in Chinatown has declined substantially since the 1980s.

Gambling activities in the Chinese communities in California are also controlled by tongs and Chinese gangs. According to law enforcement authorities, these gambling operations are beginning to expand beyond Chinatowns. Many legal gambling clubs in the suburban areas of California are allegedly owned and operated by Chinese gang members. These clubs not only offer high-stakes

Chinese gambling games (such as pai gow and fan tan) to their customers but are also involved in other illegal operations, such as money laundering.[54]

Extortion

Extortion is considered one of the most prevalent forms of crime in American Chinese communities. Police in New York City estimate that at least 80 to 90 percent of Asian businesses have been extorted by one or more gangs.[55] A business may be vandalized, burglarized, robbed, or set on fire if the owner refuses to pay extortion money. In some instances, businessmen and retail store owners have been beaten, shot at, or killed for resisting the gang.

Through extortion, the gangs establish and strengthen their control on certain territories. When two or more gangs decide to claim control of a specific territory, not only are store owners within that territory pressured to pay more than one gang, but street violence may also erupt during rival gang warfare for control.

There are four types of gang intimidation.[56] The first type is "protection." "Protection" denotes the demand for a fixed amount of money from the owner by gang members to ensure that the business will not be disturbed either by themselves or by other gangs. The amount of protection money is negotiated between the owner and the gang members. The money will be paid on a regular basis or on major holidays. Business owners are sometimes asked to make one large payment of protection money. This practice is closely related to territorial rights because, theoretically, only members of a gang that control the area where the victim operates his or her business are sanctioned to ask for protection money.

The second type of intimidation is "extortion." Extortion describes the sporadic and spontaneous demand for money from business owners by gang members.[57] The amount of payment is negotiated on each occasion, and the perpetrators do not promise to provide any service in return. This type of victimization is a manifestation of the underlying parasitic relationship between the offender and the victim that transcends gang turf. Gang members, like parasites, are free to approach any member of the business community for "help."

The third type of victimization involves gang members' selling items such as plants, cakes, or firecrackers to business owners on certain major holidays at exorbitant prices. The Chinese custom of consuming or displaying certain items on major holidays, coupled with the norms of ensuring "harmony" at all costs during these holidays, provides gang members with culturally reinforced criminal opportunities.

The last type of victimization is the practice of refusing to pay or asking for heavy discounts for food and services. Although this type of behavior could be legally called "theft of goods or services," it is culturally considered "reciprocal face-giving" behavior between the offender and the victim. That is, the material gain is only secondary to the symbolic meanings it conveys.[58]

Table 9.1

Patterns and Extent of Gang Victimization of Chinese Business Owners (N=603)

	Approached (%)	Victimized (%)	Average Annual Frequency (times)	Average Monetary Loss per Incident ($)	Average Monetary Loss per Year ($)
All 4 types of Victimization	69.0	54.7	10		615
Protection	21.6	11.4	14	129	1,140
Extortion	40.8	26.5	5	75	251
Forced Sales	51.1	40.8	2	51	117
Theft of Goods or Services	17.1	15.7	17	119	1,440

Source: Ko-lin Chin et al., "Patterns of Chinese Gang Extortion," *Justice Quarterly* 9.4 (1992).

In a victimization survey of Chinese businesses in New York City, the authors examined the extent of the four types of gang victimization.[59] We found that 416 (69 percent) of the 603 respondents had been approached by Chinese gang members, and 330 (54.7 percent) were victimized (i.e., they yielded to the gang demand). The victims were exploited on an average of ten times a year, costing them an average of $615 a year (see Table 9.1).

The rates of victimization vary by the type of extortion. For example, 130 respondents (21.65 percent) had been approached by gang members for protection money, and 69 respondents (11.4 percent) paid. Among those who paid, the average annual frequency of payment was fourteen times. Most paid once a month or three to four times a year. The average payment was $129, and the average annual monetary loss for each store for this type of crime was about $1,140. Two hundred forty-six subjects (40.8 percent) were extorted, and 158 (26.5 percent) were victimized. The victims were extorted about five times a year. On each occasion, each victim paid the gang an average of $75. Most victims were approached only two to three times a year and paid about $50 in each incident.

Forced sales were the most pervasive type of gang exploitation. Among the 603 respondents, 308 (51.15 percent) had been approached by gang members with items for sale, and 246 (40.8 percent) bought items at exorbitant prices from gang members. On an average, this happened twice a year, and the average financial loss was $51 per occasion and $117 annually. Meanwhile, 103 (17.1 percent) respondents had been approached by members of Chinese gangs for free or discounted foods or services. Ninety-four respondents (15.7 percent) had been victimized this way. These incidents occurred on an average of seventeen times a year and cost each victim $119 on each occasion and $1,440 annually.

We also found that although extortion is not encouraged, it is tolerated by the tongs. Most of the extortion activities are directed by gang leaders and carried out by gang members. Gang members turn the proceeds from extortion to their leader, who distributes the money to his followers at will.

Robbery

Unlike extortion activities, which are sanctioned by the gang as a group, robberies are often committed by a small number of members independent of their gang. Robbery targets can be categorized into three types: vice businesses, such as gambling clubs and massage parlors; legitimate businesses, such as jewelry stores and restaurants; and residential houses.

Gambling establishments in Chinatown are often robbed by Chinese gang members. Because most gamblers carry a considerable amount of cash, a successful robbery will normally net several thousands of dollars. Gang members invariably choose the hours between midnight and dawn for robberies because this is the time of peak activity at high-stakes gamblers clubs. Gang members sneak into the club posing as gamblers. If they learn that the street thugs guarding the establishment are not around, they pull out their weapons and announce a robbery. Gamblers who are slow to respond to the robbers' demands may be ruthlessly pistol-whipped or killed.[60]

As Chinese or Korean-owned massage parlors opened in Manhattan and Queens in the 1980s, New York City's Chinese gangs have turned their attention to these businesses. In 1985, masked Chinese gunmen robbed several massage parlors and in some instances wounded or killed the operators, guards, and customers.

Among legitimate businesses, restaurants are the most popular target for robbery. Since the mid-1970s, Chinese restaurants have been robbed frequently. Because most of these restaurants accept only cash, they carry a substantial amount of money. Robberies are usually carried out when the restaurants are about to close, a time when they have the most cash.

Jewelry stores are the next most popular target. Most jewelry stores in Chinatown are equipped with security doors and are tightly guarded, but well-dressed youths are able to gain entry, posing as customers to commit the robbery.

Chinese gangs, especially the Born-to-Kill, are alleged to be very active in residential robbery. Heavily armed gang members follow their victim home, enter the home, tie up all victims, and then ransack the place for cash and valuable items. On some occasions, young female victims are sexually assaulted by the offenders.[61]

Prostitution

Prostitution has long been one of the illegal enterprises of Chinese criminals, especially during the period between 1880 and 1924. At that time, Chinatowns in America were vice centers frequented by both white and Chinese patrons.[62] When the demand by white patrons for commercial sex diminished and the sex ratio among Chinese immigrants became more balanced, Chinatowns changed from vice districts to tourist attractions.[63]

However, the influx of single Chinese immigrants and Vietnamese refugees in the 1970s increased the demand for Asian prostitutes. This demand was first met by Korean women, who worked as prostitutes in massage parlors owned and managed by Koreans. However, since the patrons are mainly Chinese, the Chinese became increasingly active in the prostitution business. In 1985, there were at least twenty massage parlors in New York City, and new parlors opened in other cities with large Chinese populations. In addition to massage parlors, many nightclubs operated by Chinese and Koreans have commercial sex available in a more subtle way. For instance, nightclubs hire young Asian women as bar girls to drink or dance with the customers. If a customer wishes to take a girl out, he can do so after business hours.

Although women who work in massage parlors are predominantly Korean, women from Taiwan are also being imported to work in them. The manager of a massage parlor arranges with travel agents in Taiwan to find women willing to work as prostitutes. They then provide the women with visas and air tickets and about $7,500 to $12,500 as a bonus for signing a contract to work for one year in the United States. The women come into the country with a tourist visa that enables them to stay for six months, with an option to extend it for another six months. Once they arrive, the manager of the parlor withholds their travel documents. In the past decade, young women from Malaysia and China were also lured into the sex trade in the Chinese communities.

Chinese gangs also provide protection to the massage parlors. Some massage parlors in New York City are owned by Chinese gang leaders. However, the business is not considered a gang business. Not much is known at this time about the relationship between prostitution and the tongs.

Heroin Trafficking

Before 1980, Chinese criminals were importing small quantities of heroin. After 1983, the amount of heroin imported from Southeast Asia (known as "China White") increased dramatically. In 1984, law enforcement officials estimated that Chinese criminal groups were responsible for about 20 percent of the heroin imported into this country, and 40 percent of the heroin in New York City was found to be of Southeast Asian origin.[64] Chinese involvement in heroin trafficking continued to increase rapidly in the late 1980s.[65] During 1987, law enforcement authorities solved more than twenty major drug trafficking cases involving Chinese and seized 200 kilograms of high-quality heroin.

Apart from the tongs, Chinese gang leaders are becoming involved in the heroin trade. There was evidence that gang leaders of Ghost Shadows, Black Eagles, and Wah Ching had been involved in heroin trafficking and distribution.[66] The arrest of gang leaders for heroin trafficking began in 1987. Gang leaders of the Ghost Shadows and Flying Dragons were arrested for heroin trafficking.[67] In addition, leaders of the Tung On, Fook Ching, and Green Dragons were also implicated in heroin trafficking.[68] These gangs are believed to have good connections with heroin producers and dealers in Southeast Asia.

According to media reports, Chinese gang leaders are now playing an important role in the heroin business. These gang leaders hire nongang members to work for them. They travel frequently between the United States and Hong Kong to establish their network with drug producers and dealers in Southeast Asia. It is not clear, however, what role gang members play in their gang leaders' drug businesses. Drug enforcement authorities assume that the gang leaders' involvement in heroin trafficking is not related to their gangs.

To date, no tong as an organization has been indicted for heroin trafficking. However, tong members have been arrested for trafficking. A senior member of the New York City On Leong was convicted for working as a broker between heroin importers and buyers. When he was arrested along with thirty other defendants, drug enforcement authorities seized more than 800 pounds of heroin and approximately $3 million in cash.

Based on the number of arrests and the huge amount of heroin seized over the past five years, it can be concluded that Chinese traffickers are now one of the most active groups in international heroin trafficking. If the Chinese continue to dominate the heroin business, law enforcement officials predict that tongs and Chinese gangs will expand their illegal operations and penetrate mainstream American society through the heroin business. These tongs and gangs will be involved in money laundering and corruption and will infiltrate legitimate businesses by investing drug money in real estate and restaurants.

However, research found no evidence to sustain the allegation that tongs and Chinese gangs play a dominant role in heroin trafficking in the United States.[69] According to his study, a new generation of Chinese criminals is emerging on the American crime scene. These criminals belong neither to the tongs nor to the gangs. These criminals are responsible for the bulk of the heroin imported into the United States, and they are more likely than tong and gang members to infiltrate the larger society through drug trafficking, alien smuggling, money laundering, and other types of white-collar crime. They are wealthier, more sophisticated, and better connected with their associates outside the United States. Besides, they are not committed to the rigid triad subcultural norms and values and thus can assemble quickly when a criminal opportunity arises and dissolve the illicit operation upon completion of the criminal conspiracy.

Illegal Aliens Smuggling

The numbers of Chinese illegal aliens in America increased dramatically after the Chinese government's crackdown on the student movement in June 1989. One source indicates at least 80,000 Chinese illegal immigrants, predominantly from Fukien (or Fujian) province, in New York City.[70] Each illegal immigrant is believed to have paid approximately $35,000 to the smugglers, making the alien smuggling operation a lucrative business.[71]

Although Chinese tongs and gangs are alleged to be involved in the illegal alien smuggling business, little is known about the nature of their involvement. It is not known whether the highly organized international smuggling operations are sponsored by the tongs and the gangs as a group or are simply individual endeavors engaged in by certain members. Although new illegal immigrants are likely to seek help from community associations upon their arrival, this does not imply that the organizations are behind the smuggling operation.

One aspect of the connection between alien smuggling and Chinese gangs, especially the Fook Ching, is debt collection. Over the past three years, a number of Fukienese illegal immigrants have been kidnapped and tortured by Fukienese gang members when the former failed to pay the smuggling fee.[72] Because the crimes were committed in broad daylight in the crowded streets of Chinatown, and the victims were handcuffed and brutally punished by their captors, law enforcement authorities expressed concern over the debt-collecting role of Chinese gang members in the alien smuggling business.

Street Violence

Tong Violence

As mentioned earlier, one aspect of tong culture that has received much attention is the power struggles and street fights that have come to be known as "tong wars."[73] The fiercest of these occurred between 1894 and 1913 in San Francisco and later in New York City.

Most of the tong conflicts were provoked by individual members and later escalated into group conflicts. The reasons for the conflicts were many, ranging from interference before membership recruitment, turf invasion, and fights over so-called sing song girls (Chinese prostitutes), to disrespect from other tongs. According to a Chinese ambassador's report prepared in the 1930s, competition over the narcotics and gambling businesses was the major reason behind the tong wars.[74]

When two tongs were in conflict, they would announce their intention to go to war by posting a *chun hung* (declaration of war) on the walls of the community. Soon after the *chun hung* was displayed, the associations would mobilize their salaried soldiers, known as "hatchetmen" or "highbinders," to kill the rival's street soldiers. Ordinary members of the tongs, however, were not targeted. Meanwhile, officials of the rival tongs would disappear from the public scene, and the leader of the hatchetmen and his followers would take over the tong's affairs. An incident might last for weeks, months, or even years, spreading from the West Coast to the East Coast or vice versa.

After 1913, tong conflicts were arbitrated by the Wo Ping Woey, a peace association formed by leaders of various tongs and large family and clan associations to alleviate the murderous rivalries. Despite efforts to reconcile, conflicts sometimes got out of hand, and tong wars continued. In 1930, community leaders in New York City's Chinatown formed a Peace Committee. The CCBA, the umbrella organization of Chinatown, and the Kuomintang became actively involved in settling disputes. After the Communist takeover of China in 1949, the tongs, instead of fighting among themselves, banded together to prevent Chinese Communists from infiltrating the communities. In 1960, the On Leong and Hip Sing formally signed a treaty announcing that the two tongs would coexist peacefully. Since then, they have never been involved in open disputes. As a sign of courtesy, the two organizations send delegates to each other's annual conventions and celebrations.

Nevertheless, fatal confrontations may still erupt when a new tong encroaches on the territory of another. The formation of a new tong invariably creates tension among the existing ones. If the new tong is also involved in illegal activities, such as gambling and loan-sharking, the other tongs may consider it a serious threat. The 1982 Golden Star massacre in New York City is a good example.[75] Thus, tong conflict is by no means over. The elders of the elite tongs may settle disputes among themselves peacefully, but certain tong members who are in command of the street gangs may prefer to solve their problems through violence.

Gang Violence

Although tong violence is rare nowadays, gang violence is pervasive. Since the late 1960s, deadly gang assaults occurred almost weekly in San Francisco and New York City Chinatowns. Chinese gang conflicts can be categorized as intergang, intragang, or instrumental violence. Intergang violence is defined as violent behavior directed by one gang toward the members of another gang. The motivation for intergang violence can be further categorized into three types. First, violence is employed for status maintenance purposes. Violence between members of two different gangs is often caused by members' of one gang feeling that they were not respected or that they were sneered at by members of another gang. This type of violence is usually unplanned and spontaneous. Although it does not bring about tangible monetary rewards, it is important in maintaining the tough image of a gang.

Intergang violence is also motivated by instrumental/utilitarian purposes. Violence is often sparked by turf wars when one gang seeks to acquire part or all of the territory of another gang or when two different gangs want to take over the same piece of territory. This type of violence is often planned by the aggressor. The ultimate goal of turf expansion is for economic reasons. Since one source of income for gangs is receiving protection money from store owners, a larger turf, especially when situated on busy streets, is lucrative.

Third, intergang violence is instigated by motives of revenge. This type of intergang violence is usually provoked by another gang, as when a gang member has been assaulted or killed by another gang or when the turf of one gang has been taken over by another.

Intragang violence is defined as violent behavior between members of the same gang. There are also three types of intragang violence. First, gang members sometimes fight among themselves because of disputes about money or girlfriends; these fights are usually not serious, and weapons are not used. The second type is disciplinary violence. This type of violence is administered to punish those who violate the rules. Third, fights among members of the same gang may break out when members cannot agree about the operation or direction the gang is pursuing. Consequently, the gang may split into different factions.

The third type of gang violence is instrumental. It is directed against nongang members. Business owners who refuse to comply with the gangs may be assaulted or killed. In addition, gang members commit street and residential robberies. Gang members who are debt collectors often attack gamblers and illegal immigrants who fail to repay their debts. Violence is also used to intimidate witnesses to deter them from testifying in court.

COMMUNITY REACTION TO TONGS AND GANGS

Community reaction to tong and gang activities, especially extortion, may be described along three dimensions: (1) complying with (or resisting) gang demands for money and goods; (2) crime reporting; and (3) precautionary measures taken to prevent or reduce gang victimization.[76]

Complying with or Resisting Gang Demands

The rationales and justifications employed by Chinese business owners when complying with gang demands may be understood in terms of three main aspects: sociocultural, utilitarian, and folkloric. Some businesses construed extortion demands not as criminal per se but as consistent with Chinese customs and social traditions. As long as gang members are polite and deferential when making demands during Chinese holidays, many merchants seemed willing to comply. When gang members attempt to sell items at exorbitant prices on Chinese New Year, it is almost culturally improbable for merchants to refuse.

Giving money to the gangs is also rationalized as "reciprocal face-giving behavior" on the part of the business owners. Among the Chinese, it is expected to "give face" (or respect) to others, especially to those who deserve it or are in a position to demand it. Refusing to "give face" to a person, especially when that person has made an overt request for it, is a serious gesture of humiliation.

When "face" is given, the person who receives it has to reciprocate. Gang members normally demand that they be given "face."

Some businessmen yielded to extortion demands because they saw it not as an acceptable sociocultural custom, but as a more practical way to deal with the problem. They did it for purely economic reasons. Realizing that the police could not protect them or their businesses twenty-four hours a day and believing that they might be physically assaulted or their businesses would be disrupted by the gang if they refused to comply with gang demands, some business owners decided that it was cheaper, in the long run, to pay.

A third reason for giving in to gang members' demands rested on superstition or folklore. Many Chinese follow the folkloric custom of "resolving big problems into smaller problems, and small problems into no problem." Accordingly, no one should create a big problem out of a small problem, such as going to the police when a gang is demanding a small amount of money. Others believe that though disaster in life is inevitable for everyone, money could be spent to avoid calamities. Many owners see the gangs as ominous to their businesses and so are willing to spend a small amount of money to send them away.

There was little resistance from Chinese business owners against gangs. Only about one in five (20.1 percent) subjects approached by Chinese gang members resisted their demand.[77] Chinese business owners were least likely to refuse gang demands for free food or services, followed by forced sales, extortion, and protection. Respondents were more reluctant to satisfy gang demands for protection money because, unlike other types of victimization, once the victim agrees to pay, the victimization is likely to continue for a prolonged period of time. Overall, restaurants and service-oriented stores were less resistant to gangs than professional offices or garment factories. More-educated business owners were more likely to resist than the less-educated ones.

Crime Reporting

Law enforcement authorities have often attributed the rise in Chinese gang activities to the reluctance of Chinese victims to report crime. According to a survey conducted by the authors, only 4 percent of the victims reported to the police about forced sales from gang members. When respondents were approached for protection money, they were more likely to contact the police. Still, only one out of four victims approached for protection money contacted authorities. Their report rate is consistent with their resistance rate to gang victimization. That is, the more resistant merchants were more likely to report the crime to the police. In comparison, most victims called the police when their businesses were robbed (72 percent) or burglarized (82 percent).

It has been hypothesized by the police that one reason so many Chinese business owners hesitate to contact the police when victimized may be that many of these merchants came from Asian countries and experienced abuse by the police in their own countries. Therefore, they tend to distrust the police in the United States. Chinese customs also emphasize dispute solutions without involving the police.

Our survey found that many Chinese victims were disinclined to report their victimization to police because they considered the crime insignificant. They saw gang practices of soliciting for money or free food more as an annoyance than as a serious threat. Also, many respondents thought it was useless to report because they believed that the police placed a low priority on gang extortion compared with drugs and homicide. Some respondents indicated that contact with authorities did not necessarily result in police action. Others did not report to the police because they did not pay the gang, so they thought no crime was committed. Contrary to police suggestions, only a few respondents did not report the crime because of their distrust of the police based on unpleasant experiences in their homeland. Also, fear of retaliation was not a major factor deterring the report of crime by Chinese.

Our study also found that the major incentive for reporting incidents of extortion to police was that the victims anticipated help. Moreover, many respondents made clear that they also expected police to protect them from further incidents. One of the best predictive variables for reporting crime is the gang member's use of intimidation or threats while demanding money. If victims were threatened, regardless of the form or seriousness of extortion, they were more likely to contact the authorities. Also, Chinese merchants who spoke fluent English have a higher rate than those who spoke little English. Moreover, respondents whose businesses were outside the Chinese communities were more likely to report than store owners within the Chinese communities.

Precautionary Measures

The impact of gang victimization may also be measured by precautionary measures taken by the merchants. According to our survey of Chinese business owners, 22 percent of the respondents indicated they changed their life-styles to avoid gang victimization. Among the adjustments most often mentioned were dressing in casual clothes, wearing no jewelry, carrying little money, and driving inexpensive automobiles. In short, the common stratagem was to maintain a low profile and avoid being noticed as a prosperous businessperson.

Our study also found that 29 percent of the respondents altered their business practices to avoid victimization. These practices included closing earlier than usual, hiring only acquaintances or friends, keeping only a small amount of cash in the store, and doing business only with regular customers.

Almost six out of ten of the respondents claimed that they increased crime prevention measures in order to enhance security. Many stores have installed alarm systems, video cameras, or iron gates on their premises. In order to discourage young teenagers with beepers (which is one characteristic of gang members) from hanging around, some stores removed public phones from their premises. To avoid the possibility of gang members' robbing customers in rest rooms, business owners either locked rest rooms or reconstructed them so they could not hold more than one occupant at a time.

Other measures adopted by store owners included (1) hiring workers who spoke fluent English and instructing them to communicate with gang members in English, thereby frustrating and deterring offenders who may not speak English well; (2) hiring managers who can deal with gang members; (3) leaving the business premises in groups after closing; (4) carrying a gun; and (5) hiring non-Chinese employees.

THE SUBCULTURE OF CHINESE ORGANIZED CRIME

Most books and articles on Chinese organized crime have focused on the groups' history, initiation ceremony, structure, and criminal activities. Little attention is paid to social, political, and economic factors conducive to the formation and persistence of Chinese criminal organizations. As a result, there are few theoretical explanations on the development of Chinese organized crime.

Following Marion Wolfgang and Franco Ferracuti's work on the subculture of violence,[78] it appears that triad societies in Hong Kong, along with the Chinese tongs and street gangs in the United States, are a manifestation of a Chinese subculture initiated by the warriors of ancient China, crystallized by the vagabonds of the Sung dynasty (960–1127), and secularized by secret societies during the Ch'ing era. That is, triad subculture often thrived in a social milieu where the dominant culture was perceived as alien and foreign.

When the Ch'ing dynasty was overthrown and the Republic of China was established in 1912, triad subculture blossomed in politically chaotic and economically deprived Shanghai and its French and British concessions. Secret society leaders were able to recruit unemployed and the unskilled laborers. With the support of corrupt Kuomintang officials and foreigners who needed secret society members to maintain law and order within their territories, secret society members dominated the rampant drug importation and distribution, gambling, and prostitution operations in Shanghai.[79]

After the victory of the Communists in 1949, triad subculture again flourished in Hong Kong, a British colony. Peddlers and workers who tried to survive in an anomic environment ruled by a foreign government formed many triad societies. Since many Hong Kong residents were refugees who fled China during and after the civil war between the Kuomintang and the Communists, they were attracted to the triad societies, which could protect them away from their homelands.[80]

When Chinese migrated to Southeast Asia, Europe, and North America, they appealed to the triad subculture to protect themselves against a foreign culture.[81] In the United States, tongs mainly comprised people who were discriminated against by both the host society and Chinese elite groups such as the family and district associations who were already well established in America. The gangs were made up of young immigrants who were alienated from American society and ostracized by other ethnic groups and native-born Chinese. Through the gang, which is inspired by triad principles, these marginal newcomers found their own identity and place in society.[82]

In short, those who are unable or unwilling to become assimilated into either the dominant culture or the elite culture of overseas Chinese societies found triad norms and values attractive. Triads, tongs, and gangs became the convenient organizational settings for the marginalized and the disaffected to express their discontent and to achieve either political or economic goals. In fact, the social milieu in which triad subculture flourished was strikingly similar to milieus where the Mafia subculture emerged in Italy and the United States.[83]

Historically, because of the ineffectiveness or corruption of government agencies, many voluntary mutual-aid associations were developed by disaffected Chinese for self-protection.[84] Thus, the Chinese have a tradition of relying on their own primary organizations for support or as substitutes for ineffective government agencies. The popular Chinese motto "The heaven is high, and the emperor is far away" describes the cynicism local citizens had for the central government and its oppressive local bureaucrats who were concerned only with tax collection. The moral bankruptcy of the government led some of its citizens to completely disregard the government's rules and develop their own norms and values. These became "tolerated concordant values" for the disenchanted.[85]

Among the Chinese, members of the triad subculture are also called Dark Society members. The shady world in which they dwell is called the Dark Society or Jiang Hu (literally, "rivers and lakes," which denotes the members' rootlessness). Once persons are initiated into the world of Jiang Hu, they have to internalize, cherish, and observe triad norms. In the romantic world of Jiang Hu, members view themselves as patriotic, heroic, righteous, and loyal. Chinese conventional norms and values, such as filial piety, attachment to family and village, and nonradical philosophy, are replaced by loyalty to the organization and its members, rootlessness, and radicalism. Within this world, a powerless and detached person can become connected to a legendary and honorable society.

A Jiang Hu person is someone with a different way of life and a different set of values. Once initiated into the triad subculture, a person can justify his infraction of the laws as inevitable because one of the most famous maxims of the subculture is, "I am a Jiang Hu man; I do not have control over my fate." In other words, being a member of the subculture, he observes a very different set of values and norms. He has to seek revenge if someone attacks him or his "brother"; he has to help his "brother" even if the "brother" has committed a heinous crime; and he can never dissociate himself from his group's illegal activities. In sum, triad subcultural norms and values are such that a "good" member of the subculture will break the laws of the conventional society, even though he has no intention of committing a crime for personal gain. The more a person is committed to the norms and values of Jiang Hu, the less likely he is to be able to avoid defying the laws of larger society.

Jiang Hu people are often involved in the exploitation and intimidation of the rich and powerful and in the provision of illegal services, such as extortion and protection rackets, gambling, and prostitution. Members of the subculture believe that they are simply making a living in an alternative way—a way that is justifiable because it redistributes wealth in an imperfect society.

In sum, secret societies such as the Hung and the Ching, triad societies in Hong Kong, and tongs and street gangs in the United States, are all, in effect, members of the triad subculture. These groups share the same norms and values, worship the same god, memorize the same triad poems and slang, and adopt the same initiating ceremony, using similar triad paraphernalia.

DISCUSSION

Francis Ianni proposed that different immigrant ethnic groups in the United States have used and continue to use organized criminal activity as a means of social mobility.[86] Before the Italian Mafia, organized crime groups formed by the Irish and Jews preyed on their own communities through various protection and racketeering activities. When these early immigrants became part of the mainstream of American society, other ethnic groups lower on the social scale, such as the Hispanics and African Americans, began to move into organized street crime and vice activities. As mentioned earlier, law enforcement authorities in the United States propose that the "Chinese Mafia" is already a formidable criminal group. They tend to compare tongs and Chinese gangs with Italian crime organizations, emphasizing that the Chinese, as they follow the paths of the Italian gangs, will ultimately emerge as the number one organized crime group.

When comparing Chinese groups with the Italian groups within the context of ethnic succession in organized crime, we believe that the differences between them are more pronounced than their similarities. Tongs have been in the United States for almost 150 years. Although tong members are responsible for various racketeering activities within the Chinese communities, they have neither infiltrated the larger American society nor victimized people who are not Chinese. In comparison with the Italian crime families, the tongs' role in American crime is, up to this stage, relatively marginal. It is hard to imagine how the tongs will be able to surpass the Italian crime groups or how such a move by the tongs would provoke fierce competition from criminal organizations of other ethnic origins.

Language and cultural barriers, rather than competition, are the main factors that compel tong members to confine their activities to their own communities and to victimize only their own people. Because Chinese criminals in the United States normally do not, and could not, relate to the larger American society, they have little desire to expand their activities to a society that is so alien to them. Even if they were willing to do so, it is unlikely that they would be able to establish close relationships with public officials through corruption. Unlike

Italian crime groups, other ethnic crime groups, such as the African Americans and Hispanics, have not been successful so far in bribing the predominantly white officials for protection of their illegal activities.[87] Because of their unique cultural background, Chinese criminals are not in a better position than African Americans or Hispanics to corrupt public officials. Without protection from the police and politicians, the Chinese ability to expand their criminal networks outside their communities is seriously hampered. Thus, it is very unlikely that tongs and Chinese gangs will be able to get involved in activities like controlling labor unions, the waste industry, and other criminal activities that victimize non-Chinese people.

Also, most members of the tongs are law-abiding workers or businessmen who have nothing to do with the core members' criminal activities. Furthermore, tong activities are checked closely by government officials from China and Taiwan who are in the United States. Even though some core members are shady and corrupt, they cannot become overtly involved in illegal activities. After all, the tongs as organizations are not purely criminal organizations; they have many other civic and legitimate political responsibilities.

Finally, for the tongs to emerge as organized crime groups, they must control the gangs, without whose full support the tongs may never be able to impose their authority at the street level. Mutual mistrust and misunderstanding between the tongs and the street gangs are rampant. Just as the tongs do not always feel obliged to provide the gangs with all the support they want, the gangs do not feel compelled to follow the instructions of the tongs.

In view of these problems, we conclude that it is inappropriate to propose that the Chinese groups are now at the stage where the Italian groups were during the 1930s and will proceed to become the preeminent criminal organization in the United States. In fact, other than heroin trafficking, Chinese crime groups have not been able to expand their traditional criminal activities from their own communities to the mainstream society of America. Undoubtedly, what concerns law enforcement authorities the most and leads scholars of organized crime to propose that Chinese crime groups will become prominent is the assumption that Chinese tongs and gangs are importing the bulk of Southeast Asian heroin into the United States. However, the discussion of Chinese involvement in heroin trade already suggests that tongs and Chinese gangs are not the dominant players in the trade.[88]

The authors are not maintaining that tongs and Chinese gangs will not expand. Since the development of many new Chinese communities in the United States in the past two decades, tongs and Chinese gangs have expanded their influence to these new Chinatowns. In fact, our survey found that merchants in the newly established Chinatowns were as vulnerable to gang victimization as their counterparts in the traditional Chinese community.[89] Also, as the more successful and affluent Chinese begin to move into the suburban areas of America, Chinese gang members are following their prey into these areas, which are considered American mainstream society.

Nevertheless, it is more likely that Chinese crime groups will continue to expand their criminal operations by collaborating with criminals in Asia. That is, instead of confining their activities within the United States, they may exploit the increased social and commercial interactions between Chinese societies in North America and Asia. Since China adopted the open-door policy in the late 1970s, and Taiwan and other Asian countries became more democratic in the 1980s, the interactions between Chinese in North America and Asia have reached an all-time high. Under this new geopolitical condition, tongs and Chinese gangs may seize the opportunity to establish their strongholds in Chinese communities in the Pacific Rim and globalize their criminal operations.

NOTES

Support for this research was provided by Grant 89-IJ-CX-0021 from the National Institute of Justice. The opinions are those of the authors and do not reflect the policies or views of the United States Department of Justice.

1. Felicity Barringer, "Immigration Brings New Diversity to Asian Population in the U.S.," *New York Times*, 12 June 1992, A1.

2. Ko-lin Chin, *Chinese Subculture and Criminality: Nontraditional Crime Groups in America* (Westport, CT: Greenwood Press, 1990).

3. U.S. Department of Justice, *Oriental Organized Crime: A Report of a Research Project Conducted by the Organized Crime Section* (Washington, DC: U.S. Government Printing Office, 1985); Gerald Posner, *Warlords of Crimes* (New York: McGraw-Hill, 1988); U.S. Department of Justice, *Report on Asian Organized Crime* (Washington, DC: U.S. Government Printing Office, 1988); U.S. Senate, *Asian Organized Crime* (Washington, DC: U.S. Government Printing Office, 1992).

4. Tom Emch, "The Chinatown Murders," *San Francisco Sunday Examiner and Chronicle*, 9 September 1973, 6–14; Michael Daly, "The War for Chinatown," *New York Magazine*, 14 February 1983, 31–38; Paul Meskil, "In the Eye of the Storm," *New York Daily News Magazine*, 5 February 1989, 10–16; Fox Butterfield, "Killing of 5 in Boston's Chinatown Raises Fears of Asian Gang Wars," *New York Times*, 15 January 1991, B6; Frederic Dannen, "Revenge of the Green Dragons," *New Yorker*, 16 November 1992, 76–99.

5. Attorney general of California, *Proceedings of the Conference on Chinese Gang Problems* (Sacramento: California Organized Crime and Criminal Intelligence Branch, 1972).

6. The definition of "organized crime" has been a controversial issue in the study of organized criminality in the United States. Law enforcement authorities have loosely used the term *Chinese organized crime* to relate to *all* Chinese organizations or groups in America and Asia that are involved in illegal activities as a group or whose members are implicated in crime. This includes secret societies, triad societies, tongs, street gangs, and other Chinese crime groups such as heroin trafficking and alien smuggling rings. In this chapter, we consider tongs and Chinese gangs "Chinese organized crime" in America.

7. Michael Grace and John Guido, *Hong Kong 1997: Its Impact on Chinese Organized Crime in the United States* (Washington, DC: U.S. Department of State, Foreign

Service Institute, 1988); Ian Dobinson, "The Chinese Connection: Heroin Trafficking Between Australia and South-East Asia," *Criminal Organizations* 7 (May 1992): 1–7.

8. Fox Butterfield, "Chinese Crime Network Reported Moving into Areas of U.S., *New York Times*, 30 November 1986, A30.

9. President's Commission on Organized Crime, *Organized Crime of Asian Origin: Record of Hearing III—October 23–25, 1984, New York, New York* (Washington, DC: U.S. Government Printing Office, 1984); U.S. Senate, *Emerging Criminal Groups; Hearings Before the Permanent Subcommittee on Investigations of the Committee on Governmental Affairs* (Washington, DC: U.S. Government Printing Office, 1986); US. Senate, *Asian Organized Crime.*

10. Peter Kerr, "Chasing the Heroin from Plush Hotel to Mean Streets," *New York Times*, 11 August 1987, B1.

121. Immigration and Naturalization Service, *The INS Enforcement Approach to Chinese Organized Crime* (Washington, DC: Immigration and Naturalization Service, 1989).

12. U.S. Senate, *Asian Organized Crime.*

13. Betty Lee Sung, *Gangs in New York's Chinatown* (New York: Department of Asian Studies, City College of New York, 1977); Norman Robinson and Delbert Joe, "Gangs in Chinatown: The New Young Warrior Class," *McGill Journal of Education* 15 (1980): 149–62; Ko-lin Chin, "Chinese Triad Societies, Tong, Organized Crime, and Street Gangs in Asia and the United States"(Ph.D. diss., University of Pennsylvania, 1986); Calvin Toy, "Coming Out to Play: Reasons to Join and Participate in Asian Gangs," *The Gang Journal* 1 (1992): 13–29.

14. The first study was conducted by Ko-lin Chin between 1984 and 1986 in New York City. Based on interview data, official statistics, and field observations, the study examined the history, structure, and activity of four types of Chinese criminal organizations in Asia and the United States. The second research was conducted by Jeffrey Fagan, Robert J. Kelly, and Chin in 1989–91. Six hundred and three Chinese business owners in New York City were randomly selected and asked about the processes and extent of gang extortion and their reactions to their victimization. Fagan, Kelly, and Chin completed another study in 1991–92 by interviewing active and former members of Chinese gangs (N=70). The project focused on the background characteristics of Chinese gang members, the processes of joining gangs, and the structure and activity of gangs.

15. The first wave of Chinese immigrants, mostly laborers from Guangdong (Kwantung) province in China, arrived in California in the mid-nineteenth century to work in the gold mines. After the gold rush, these workers were hired to build the transcontinental railroads. During that period, most Chinese laborers congregated in San Francisco's Chinatown. Since then, the community has expanded into one of the largest ethnic enclaves in the United States.

16. Ying Eng Gong and Bruce Grant, *Tong War!* (New York: N. L. Brown, 1930).

17. C. Y. Lee, *Days of the Tong Wars* (New York: Ballantine Books, 1974).

18. Unlike family or district associations, tong members were hard to identify by surname or place of birth. Therefore, if a tong member commits a crime, authorities would be unable to immediately identify the offender with a particular tong.

19. U.S. Department of Justice, *Report on Asian Organized Crime.*

20. Chinese secret societies were formed during the Ming era (1368–1644) by patriotic Chinese for political purposes. These societies, especially the Hung societies and the Ching societies, played a pivotal role in the overthrow of the Ch'ing dynasty and the establishment of the Republic of China. Secret societies continued to be very active in

the political arena thereafter, but some societies or members also increasingly engaged in criminal activities. After the Communists took over China in 1949, some branches were reestablished in Hong Kong and Taiwan. Although the societies have maintained a low profile in the past forty years, they are now making a comeback in Taiwan, publicly recruiting new members and vowing to become more active in the political arena.

21. Sun is hailed as the founding father of the Republic of China by both the Communists and the nationalists because he was the architect of the revolution that ousted the Ch'ing dynasty.

22. L. Eve Armentrout Ma, *Revolutionaries, Monarchists, and Chinatowns* (Honolulu: University of Hawaii Press, 1990).

23. Since the 1960s, both the On Leong and the Hip Sing have abandoned the name *tong* and have renamed their associations because the word *tong* evokes unpleasant memories of the infamous tong wars.

24. Meskil, "In the Eye of the Storm."

25. *Triad* means a "triangle of heaven, earth, and man." Triad societies began as secret societies formed by patriotic Chinese three centuries ago to fight the oppressive and corrupt Ch'ing dynasty. When the Ch'ing government collapsed and the Republic of China was established in 1912, some societies degenerated into crime groups. Most triad societies now have their headquarters in Hong Kong, but their criminal operations have no national boundaries.

26. President's Commission on Organized Crime, *Organized Crime of Asian Origin.*

27. Gwen Kinkead, *Chinatown* (New York: Harper Collins, 1992).

28. Daly, "The War for Chinatown;" Meskil, "In the Eye of the Storm."

29. U.S. Senate, *Asian Organized Crime.*

30. Christopher Loo, "The Emergence of San Francisco Chinese Juvenile Gangs from the 1950s to the Present," M.A. thesis, San Jose State University, 1976.

31. Jennifer Thompson, "Are Chinatown Gang Wars a Cover-Up?" *San Francisco Magazine*, February 1976.

32. Attorney general of California, *Proceedings of the Conference on Chinese Gang Problems.*

33. Loo, "The Emergence of San Francisco Chinese Juvenile Gangs from the 1950s to the Present."

34. Emch, "The Chinatown Murders."

35. Toy, "Coming Out to Play."

36. David Kaplan, Donald Goldberg, and Linda Jue, "Enter the Dragon: How Hong Kong Notorious Underworld Syndicates Are Becoming the Number One Organized Crime Problem in California," *San Francisco Focus*, December 1986, 68–84.

37. Attorney general of California, *Proceedings of the Conference on Chinese Gang Problems.*

38. Fox Butterfield, "Chinese Organized Crime Said to Rise in U.S.," *New York Times*, 13 January 1985, A1.

39. President's Commission on Organized Crime, *Organized Crime of Asian Origin,* 465–66.

40. David Kaplan, *Fires of the Dragon* (New York: Atheneum, 1992).

41. Chin, *Chinese Subculture and Criminality.*

42. Henri Chang, "Die Today, Die Tomorrow: The Rise and Fall of Chinatown Gangs," *Bridge Magazine* 2 (1972): 10–15.

43. Michael Spataro, "Report on International Chinese Street Gangs and Triad Or-

ganized Criminal Activities,'' paper presented at the First Annual Meeting on Chinese Triad Societies, New York Police Academy, 1978.

44. Frank Ching, ''Street Crime Cast a Pall of Fear over Chinatown,'' *New York Times*, 19 January 1974, A1.

45. CCBA is the umbrella organization of American Chinatowns. In New York City, members of the CCBA include the majority of the most powerful community associations. Thus, CCBA's president is known as the ''mayor'' of Chinatown.

46. Chin, *Chinese Triad Societies, Tong, Organized Crime, and Street Gangs in Asia and the United States.*

47. Dannen, ''Revenge of the Green Dragons.''

48. James Badey, *Dragons and Tigers* (Loomis, CA: Palmer Enterprises, 1988); Diego Vigil and Steve Yun, ''Vietnamese Youth Gangs in Southern California,'' in *Gangs in America*, ed. Ronald Huff (Newbury, CA: Sage, 1990).

49. U.S. Senate, *Asian Organized Crime.*

50. The analysis in this section is based on data collected from a study conducted by the authors in 1991–92.

51. U.S. Senate, *Report of the Joint Special Committee to Investigate Chinese Immigration* (Washington, DC: U.S. Government Printing Office, 1877; reprinted New York: Arno Press, 1978).

52. To perform these jobs, a few members are dispersed on the streets outside the gambling den. Three or four members will guard the entrance while others stay inside. Street leaders who are in the gang's nearby apartments oversee the entire operation.

53. Casino operators have employed many aggressive and innovative marketing tactics to expand their Asian customer market. Extraordinary bonuses are offered to gamblers from Chinatown; famous entertainers from Hong Kong are invited to perform for the Chinese audiences on major holidays; and limousines are available to pick up heavy gamblers from the Chinese community. See Joel Millman, ''Casinos Luring Chinese,'' *New York Times*, 24 February 1985.

54. John Emshwiller, ''California Card Casinos Are Suspected as Fronts for Rising Asian Mafia,'' *Wall Street Journal*, 1 June 1992, A1.

55. Fenton Bresler, *The Chinese Mafia* (New York: Stein and Day, 1981).

56. Ko-lin Chin, Jeffrey Fagan, and Robert Kelly, ''Patterns of Chinese Gang Extortion,'' *Justice Quarterly* (forthcoming).

57. Chinese business owners make a distinction between ''extortion'' and ''protection'' that the New York State Penal Code does not.

58. ''Face'' is the equivalent of overt respect given and accepted in social intercourse. In this instance, business owners give ''face'' to gang members by not insisting that they pay for services in full; conversely, gang members provide owners with ''face'' by behaving in an acceptable or friendly manner with the business owners.

59. Chin, Fagan, and Kelly, ''Patterns of Chinese Gang Extortion.''

60. In one incident, a gambling club in Seattle's Chinatown was robbed by three gunmen, and all fourteen gamblers were tied and shot at close range. Only one survived. Likewise, five gamblers were shot dead inside a gambling den in Boston's Chinatown after they were robbed.

61. DeNee Brown and Patricia Davis, ''Home-Invasion Victim Tells of Threats,'' *Washington Post*, 9 October 1990, B1; Todd Burke and Charles O'Rear, ''Home Invaders: Asian Gangs in America,'' *Police Studies* 13 (Winter 1990): 154–56.

62. Mildred Crowl Martin, *Chinatown Angry Angel* (Palo Alto, CA: Pacific Books, 1977).

63. Ivan Light, "From Vice District to Tourist Attraction: The Moral Career of American Chinatowns, 1880–1940," *Pacific Historical Review* 43 (1974): 367–94.

64. President's Commission on Organized Crime, *Organized Crime of Asian Origin.*

65. Steven Erlanger, "Southeast Asia Is Now No. 1 Source of U.S. Heroin," *New York Times*, 11 February 1990, A26; Peter Kerr, "Chinese Now Dominate New York Heroin Trade," *New York Times*, 9 August 1987, A1.

66. For example, a twenty-two-year-old Ghost Shadow member and his girlfriend were executed in their apartment in July 1987. The couple were suspected of being major heroin traffickers, and the killings were believed to be the result of their mishandling of the drug. The former leader of the now extinct Black Eagles is believed to be a major heroin importer in the New York area. Police have charged that he is using his occupation in a nightclub in downtown Manhattan as a cover-up for his heroin business. A former leader of the Wah Ching, shot to death by unknown assailants, was a major cocaine trafficker in the San Francisco area. In order to stay ahead of his competitors, the gang leaders sold his drug well below market price, and his unorthodox way of marketing may have offended his rival dealers.

67. Paul Tang was arrested for selling several pounds of heroin to undercover drug agents. Tang was closely associated with the On Leong and served as the mentor of the Ghost Shadows for many years. Michael Yu, a leader of the Flying Dragons, was arrested, along with thirty-nine young men and women, for importing 100 pounds of heroin. None of the other arrestees were members of the Flying Dragons. A year later, Johnny Eng, the thirty-four-year-old top leader of the Flying Dragons, was arrested in Hong Kong for heroin smuggling. Drug enforcement authorities in New York also indicted him for two major drug-related crimes. The first case has to do with the importation of approximately 160 pounds of heroin into the United States, hidden in Chinese tea boxes and mixed with Chinese herbal medicine to dilute the smell of the drug. In the second case, the gang leader was charged when 180 pounds of heroin were seized by authorities in Boston. This time, the drug was concealed inside a bean sprout washer. Both Yu and Eng are now being prosecuted in New York City.

68. A Tung On gang leader whose elder brother is the leader of the Tung On Association was accused of operating a heroin smuggling ring that had close ties to traffickers in Hong Kong.

69. Chin, *Chinese Subculture and Criminality.*

70. Donatella Lorch, "Immigrants from China Pay Dearly to Be Slaves," *New York Times*, 3 January 1991, B1.

71. Al Kamen, "A Dark Road from China to Chinatown," *Washington Post*, 17 June 1991, A1.

72. John Kifner, "Abducted Chinese Illegal Aliens Rescued," *New York Times*, 8 January 1991, B3.

73. Richard Dillon, *The Hatchet Men: The Story of the Tong Wars in San Francisco's Chinatown* (New York: Coward-McCann, 1962).

74. Liu Pei-chi, *A History of the Chinese in the United States of America II* (in Chinese) (Taipei: Li Min, 1981).

75. Daly, "The War for Chinatown."

76. See the chapter by John Dombrink and John Song in this volume for the examination of law enforcement responses to Chinese organized crime.

77. Chin, Fagan, and Kelly, ''Patterns of Chinese Gang Extortion.''

78. Wolfgang and Ferracuti propose that in some subcultures people feel compelled by a value system that demands the overt use of force or violence in response to provocations and conflicts. See Marvin Wolfgang and Franco Ferracuti, *The Subculture of Violence* (Beverly Hills, CA: Sage, 1982).

79. Sterling Seagrave, *The Soong Dynasty* (New York: Harper and Row, 1985).

80. Zhang Sheng, *The Activities of Hong Kong Organized Crime Groups* (in Chinese) (Hong Kong: Tien Ti Books, 1984).

81. Carl Trocki, *Opium and Empire: Chinese Society in Colonial Singapore, 1800–1910* (Ithaca, NY: Cornell University Press, 1990).

82. Joseph Morici, ''Chinatown Youth Gangs–Past, Present and Future,'' *Youth Authority Quarterly* 32 (1979): 19–24.

83. Anton Blok, *The Mafia of a Sicilian Village 1860–1960* (New York: Harper and Row, 1975); Pino Arlacchi, *Mafia Business: The Mafia Ethic and the Spirit of Capitalism* (New York: Verso, 1987).

84. Jean Chesneaux, *Popular Movements and Secret Societies in China, 1840–1950* (Stanford, CA: Stanford University Press, 1972).

85. Wolfgang and Ferracuti, *The Subculture of Violence.*

86. Francis Ianni, *Black Mafia: Ethnic Succession in Organized Crime* (New York: Simon and Schuster, 1974).

87. Francis Ianni and Elizabeth Reuss-Ianni, eds., *The Crime Society* (New York: New American Library, 1976).

88. Chin, *Chinese Subculture and Criminality.*

89. Chin, Fagan, and Kelly, ''Patterns of Chinese Gang Extortion.''

10

Russian Organized Crime in America

JAMES O. FINCKENAUER

The purpose of this chapter is to lay out what is known about "organized crime" among Russian (Soviet) immigrants and émigrés in the United States. Since the vast majority of the persons with whom we are concerned in this discussion are émigrés, that is, persons immigrating for political reasons, this term will be used for the sake of simplicity. The focus is principally on the largest such Russian community—in Brighton Beach, Brooklyn—and to a lesser extent on émigrés elsewhere in the United States. The alleged Russian émigré organized crime problem is considered to be centered in Brighton Beach. The term *alleged* is used here because it is not crystal clear that what we are talking about is honest-to-goodness, full-fledged organized crime as such. This is one of the important questions that need to be addressed in future investigations. Information for the immediate discussion is drawn from available sources—some primary, but most secondary—and from a review of contemporary and historical literature.

The chapter is, of necessity, mainly descriptive, with some historical comparisons and some comparisons within and between the United States and the former USSR. The intent of this work is mainly to provide the conceptualization and framework for a possible research agenda—and to stimulate interest in future investigation—which would enable us to move from description and comparison to a higher order of explanation and fuller understanding.

CONCEPTUAL PERSPECTIVES

As indicated or at least alluded to elsewhere in this volume, organized crime theory is variously subject to criticism and controversy. Notwithstanding the charge that there really is no coherent theory of organized crime, there is some consensus that three dimensions seem to consistently play an important role in describing and helping to explain American organized crime. These dimensions are ethnicity, conspiracy, and enterprise.

Ethnicity is a defining element of organized crime that reflects in part the pluralistic, "melting pot" nature of American society itself. Organized crime in the United States has had, and continues to have, a peculiarly (although by no means exclusively) ethnic character: Italian and Sicilian, Chinese, Cuban, Colombian, Vietnamese, Nigerian, Japanese, and so on. A number of factors associated with ethnicity create an environment out of which crime in general and organized crime in particular can grow. Some of these are tied to the link that most often exists between ethnicity and being an immigrant. Ethnicity-related factors include the greater sense of trust and kinship that characterize fellow members of the same ethnic group; the special vulnerability of new immigrants, which makes them inviting targets for victimization, especially by their fellow ethnics, who are best positioned to exploit these vulnerabilities; the difficulties immigrants have in finding legitimate socioeconomic opportunities, which may force them into crime as an alternative opportunity, for example, the "queer ladder of mobility" thesis;[1] and the immigrant's general ignorance of the U.S. "system."

Along with these general elements, which operate to greater or lesser degree with all ethnic immigrant groups, some may be found only in certain situations or with certain groups. These include a distrust of, and/or a lack of respect for, the American system of law and criminal justice; an importation of criminal techniques and criminal values from the society of origin; and a view[2] that making it in America through honest work is for "suckers." These latter factors are especially pertinent to our understanding of Russian émigré organized crime.

The various ethnicity-related factors can be grouped into two constellations of possible contributing "causes" of organized crime. Trust and kinship with each other, distrust and disrespect for host institutions, imported deviant values, and a willingness to take advantage of criminal opportunities are offender-based explanations or individual factors. They help explain why particular individuals may choose to become involved in organized crime. Availability of peculiarly vulnerable target victims, opportunities for crime, and a lack of legitimate avenues for success, on the other hand, are social factors. They are characteristic of particular socioeconomic environments. These distinctions are important both in explaining organized crime and in considering various means for its prevention and control.

Criminal conspiracy is by definition the only way that crime can be "organized." Defined as an agreement between two or more persons to commit a criminal act or to commit by illegal means an act not in itself criminal, conspiracy is one of the critical elements distinguishing organized crime from all other crime. Conspiracy addresses the issue of how a particular criminal activity is planned. It is the operating strategy. It accounts for the methodical, systematic, highly disciplined, and secret actions (not accidental), of sophisticated criminal groups. Conspiracies are not always successful and well implemented, but, clearly, conspiratorial planning is the antithesis to what some claim is simply the random actions of poorly self-controlled, impulsive, purely hedonistic individuals who just happen to occasionally drift together to commit crimes.[3]

Because engaging in a criminal conspiracy puts one at risk, there must be an element of trust among the coconspirators. Ethnic ties may provide the strongest possibility for ensuring trust among persons who have nothing else to rely on. Peter A. Lupsha makes this argument:

> What one can note about ethnicity is that like family or blood tie, it is a useful trust variable. If a group all speaks the same language, has the same village roots, possesses the same myth and culture norms, then it can function as a unit with greater trust and understanding . . . it is the organizational need for trust, loyalty, intimate knowledge of character, security, sense of courage, prowess, honesty, ease of understanding, communication and control, that makes ethnicity, kinship, blood-tie, language, and race important variables for group bonding, organization and identification.[4]

The third dimension to be considered is *illicit enterprise*. Dwight C. Smith[5] was one of the first to describe illicit enterprise as the extension of legitimate market activities into the illegitimate demand/supply market. Illicit enterprises satisfy either legitimate or illegitimate demands, but in both cases they do so illegally. In the first instance, controlled market conditions, proscribing or rationing supplies, and limiting competition by regulations, licensing requirements, taxes, and so on may give rise to a black market that meets the resulting unmet demand. In the second instance, illicit enterprises respond to demands for illegal goods and services, for example, drugs, prostitution, and gambling.

Enterprise theory addresses questions pertinent to the business or businesses of organized crime. It is not in itself a theory of crime, but rather a theory of business and markets. The same questions thus can be asked of illegal enterprises as are asked of analogous legal businesses.[6] These refer to source of capital, where to locate, advertising, setting prices, and so on. Peter Reuter[7] points out that violence for economic purposes is also a distinct feature of illegal markets. Violence facilitates monopoly control and substitutes for the lack of legally enforceable contracts—both of which are critical distinctions between legal and illegal business enterprises.

Exploring the possible linking of ethnicity, conspiracy, and enterprise, Smith[8] wrote that "each contains some truth, and that a complete explanation for organized crime must call on each theory in some integrated way." Admittedly, only an elementary form of such an integrated framework guides this examination of Russian organized crime in the United States. This requires understanding who (ethnicity) the Russian émigrés are—their roots, their cultural heritage, their traditions; how and when they came to the United States; and the possible role of their past socialization into corruption and criminality in the former USSR. Second, it is also necessary to understand how (conspiracy) they are engaging in organized crime here and whether they may have been engaged in similar criminality prior to their emigration. What are their prior criminal histories? Who were and are their coconspirators? Do they have continuing criminal connections in the former Soviet Union? At this point, we know something about their criminal conspiracies here, but we know little about their prior criminal history.

Third is the issue or question of what (enterprise) they do. What are the particular criminal enterprises in which they have been involved? How do these enterprises operate? Gerald E. Caiden and Herbert E. Alexander[9] posed a set of issues to be considered in this regard, like the incentives and disincentives operating in illegal markets, the costs and losses in illegal businesses, the peculiar characteristics of specific illegal markets, and the internal regulation of such markets. Some of these issues are addressed here.

The goals of this discussion roughly follow the ideas of Menachem Amir,[10] who looked at the organized criminality of Soviet Georgian Jews who had immigrated to Israel. He spelled out four conditions that favored their continued criminality in Israel: (1) cultural customs and traditions, including a prior history of economic criminality in Soviet Georgia; (2) discrimination in the host society (Israel) that impeded their integration; (3) the existence of a criminal underworld structure in Israel that encouraged easy entry and participation in crime; and (4) a perception that law enforcement and criminal justice were weak and therefore not deserving of fear and respect.[11]

BACKGROUND

Our task is to explore the Russian version of American organized crime. In order to do that, it seems appropriate to begin with the Russian connection. The term *Russian* will be used here in the generic sense to describe all Soviet émigrés. This not only reflects how Soviet émigrés to the United States generally characterize themselves but also avoid the confusion of trying to sort out the various nationalities that actually make up the Russian émigré community.

We begin back in the former Soviet Union. The fact that it is the "former" Soviet Union is not a problem for our purposes, because most, if not all, of the persons with whom we are concerned had already left the USSR and established themselves in the United States before climactic events resulted in the collapse of that country at the end of 1991.

Organized Crime

During most of the seventy-four years of Soviet history, information about crime and criminals in the USSR was a closely guarded national secret. It was not until former Soviet president Mikhail Gorbachev instituted the policy of *glasnost* (openness) in the mid-1980s that crime data were generally publicized.

Taking account of all the usual limitations of reporting, accuracy, completeness, and so on, these data showed that the USSR had relatively far less common crime being reported than did the United States. But the figures also demonstrated that crime was increasing very rapidly at the end of the 1980s.

Along with the information about crime in general, there also began to appear in the newly enfranchised Soviet media sensationalistic reports of gangsters, racketeers, and a so-called Mafia. These reports were picked up and highlighted by the Western press. The *New York Times*, for example, reported in 1989 that "Western-style cooperative enterprises [in the Soviet Union] [were] being harassed by protection racketeers and organized criminals looking for ways to launder their money" and that the police were concerned about losing their struggle against organized crime.[12] Some of the more popular publications carried stories about a proliferation of gangsters and racketeers who were, as one reported, "into every imaginable racket—from smalltime shakedowns, drugs, prostitution, and even murder for hire to infiltration of legitimate new businesses, especially restaurants and construction firms."[13] Some 4,000–5,000 criminal groups were reported to be operating.[14] Soviet scholars simultaneously describe the evolving Soviet organized crime phenomenon as a menacing danger that developed because of the corruption of the Communist Party and the state apparatus.[15]

As sensational and frightening as these disclosures were for the average Soviet citizen, they were not taken (by knowledgeable insiders) to mean that a new phenomenon, called organized crime, was arising in the Soviet Union for the very first time. Although it is true that there were some new forms of organized crime, they were neither the first nor the only forms.

In the old USSR, the most elite type of organized criminals engaged in mass corruption and illegal trafficking in what were otherwise mostly legal goods and services—goods and services, however, that were subject to the chronic shortages produced by the inefficient, centrally planned economy. The top tier of Soviet organized crime was occupied by Communist party officials and top-level government bureaucrats. From their positions of power, these *apparatchiks* (bureaucrats) and *nomenklatura* (Communist Party officials) enriched themselves and controlled the dispensed goods and services that were in great demand. The "partocracy" abused and exploited its party and state positions in the form of white-collar crime, which was the most sophisticated Soviet manifestation of organized crime.[16] This organized crime bore no relationship to American organized crime. "Organized crime [of the state kind] bears a resemblance only in its muscle, power, and corruption of the use of legal procedures."[17] As a Russian colleague described it, it was as if La Cosa Nostra had taken over the government of the United States at every level.

Below this elite tier, clans of professional criminals operated in many cities in Russia and the other former Soviet republics. These organized criminal groups continue to operate and even to thrive under the present political and economic turmoil. Some, called "thieves in law" (*vory v zakone*), manage, organize, and maintain an ideology of professional crime—bribes and payoffs, financial and moral support for imprisoned clan members and their families, resolving clan conflicts, and so on.[18] These clans of sophisticated professional criminals are most akin to La Cosa Nostra in the United States. They maintain strict discipline, have certain bonding rituals, employ hired killers, and have international connections, which they are currently seeking to expand. "Racketeers [in the USSR] operate nationwide networks," said a *Newsweek* special report, "trading in scarce luxury goods, icons, even narcotics, and many of them do an international business with Soviet émigré gangs in the United States."[19]

Below the thieves in law are numerous clans of other more or less sophisticated criminal groups engaging in burglary, drug trafficking, weapons trafficking, murder for hire, pornography, prostitution, black market profiteering, trafficking in stolen cars, and so on. Protection rackets are run by various clans in which money is extorted either from common criminals as a form of street tax (a fee paid to be permitted to pursue their criminal activities) or from private cooperative businesses. The umbrella term *mafia* is loosely used to refer to all of these criminal groups.

The Corrupt Society

Organized crime and its Soviet accompaniments—corruption, the shadow economy, and the black market—arose and flourished because of the peculiarities of the Soviet economy and Soviet politics. Both the economy and the politics have changed dramatically in recent years, and even as this is being written changes are rapidly evolving. Again, however, this turbulent atmosphere does not present a problem because the foundation stones for the export of the seeds of Russian organized crime to the United States, as we currently know it, were set under the old system. Thus, that system is relevant.

Because of the unique confluence of circumstances and characteristics, we need to ask whether it is possible that the USSR produced a people uniquely socialized to facilitate their involvement (both as clients and victims) in organized crime. Lydia S. Rosner, for one, reached just such a conclusion:

The new Russian immigrant [to the United States] arrived on these shores already steeped in a criminal system . . . and with certain skills already in place. It is the conclusion of this study that these immigrants did not change their behavior to ascend the American social ladder. Rather, they continued patterns of behavior that were ingrained after a lifetime in a social system where extralegal values were stressed.[20]

Rosner divides Russian émigrés into survivors and connivers, then further subdivides them into necessary criminals, criminals, and system beaters.[21] Necessary criminals were forced by circumstances in the USSR into criminal behavior there. System beaters violate U.S. law in dealing with bureaucratic agencies here. Under this scheme, all Russian émigrés seemingly are law violators. But this may be a too limited and misleading explanation. Or, at least, it may be tarring too many of these émigrés with the same brush. Coercion into an illegal system does not always and necessarily lead to an acceptance and an internalization of that illegality. Soviet citizens did have to participate in illegal and nonlegal systems of self-help and free enterprise. To do otherwise, as Rosner argues, was to suffer the consequence of honesty, which was deprivation. It is also reasonable, on the other hand, to suppose that many Soviets begrudged their own behavior, that, as Arkady Vaksberg argues, they suffered [and hate] "the total corruption which riddled every level of the administration and every stratum of society."[22] If so, it means the possible explanation is more complicated.

Some ex-Soviets may, in fact, arrive here steeped in criminal methods and values, and they may use these to continue their criminality and even to become sophisticated, organized criminals—victimizers. Necessary criminals and possibly the criminals there may, however, become noncriminals here because they have other, noncriminal opportunities. Still others, similarly socialized, are more likely to become victims as a consequence of their own intimidation and vulnerability, which get magnified in the United States. A fourth group, seemingly rejected by Rosner, may become staunch and active opponents of crime and corruption. They may want to totally reject the old system and aspire to become simply honest, upright American citizens. We are not particularly concerned with the latter group, but I do want to acknowledge its possible existence.

No matter to which group they may now belong, all these émigrés nevertheless share a common heritage. This heritage includes the state-run, centrally planned Soviet command economy that produced massive shortages as well as widespread bribery and thievery. No area of life in the Soviet Union was exempt from pervasive, universal corruption. Scarce goods and services that were unavailable through normal channels could usually be gotten through *blat*, or connections, or *na levo*, on the left. An illegal second or shadow economy arose to operate in tandem with the official economy.

The notorious Soviet black market was a component of the shadow economy. It marketed a wide variety of products: Western consumer goods, such as perfume, jeans, and electronic equipment, as well as stolen goods, drugs, bootleg liquor, cigarettes, and so on. Because goods were priced much higher on the black market, there was also incentive to siphon off goods from the official market for sale on the black market. That this practice may be far from ended is evident in the "disappearance" of large amounts of Western aid shipped to Russia in the winter of 1991–92.

The Soviet political and socioeconomic system bred illegality and corruption on a scale matched by few countries.[23] It is interesting to contemplate whether this situation is historically comparable to that of any other country that has been a major source of immigrants to the United States. In his book, *USSR: The Corrupt Society*, Konstantine Simis described the pervasiveness of Soviet corruption and its links to the shadow economy:

Underground enterprise is a positive tumor of corruption. Like a drop of water, it reflects the whole world of Soviet improbability. Just as the human body cannot live without air, underground enterprise could not survive except for the fact that the Soviet state and society alike are rotten with corruption from the top to bottom.[24]

The relationships among culture, immigration, and crime have generally been assumed to operate in several possible ways. The strength of the traditional culture of origin may, at least initially, protect some newcomers from ''contamination'' by those elements of American society that tend to foster crime. Chinese Americans are an example of this kind of cultural insulation. Alternatively, culture conflict in which there is a clash of norms and values may actually lead to crime,[25] or discrimination against immigrants and/or an absence of socioeconomic opportunities may force them into illegal activities.[26] As suggested by Rosner, what we may be seeing with the soviet émigrés is a separate, perhaps fourth variation on the cultural theme or at least a different form of the culture conflict explanation. Under this variation and with the caveat that it is obviously not equally true for all Soviet émigrés, the culture of origin—with its criminals and necessary criminals, survivors and connivers, and its socialization into deviant attitudes and values—may stimulate and facilitate criminal behavior in the new setting.

By way of further background, let us turn to the recent history of how, from where, and under what circumstances Soviet émigrés (predominantly Soviet Jews) came to the United States and to an analogous earlier period of Russian Jewish immigration to America.

THE HISTORICAL BACKGROUND

As already indicated, Brighton Beach in Brooklyn contains the largest Russian immigrant community in the United States. Most of the members of this community are Jewish émigrés who were able to leave the Soviet Union and come to the United States under a grant of refugee status as politically oppressed peoples. Since 1988, when the Kremlin began to relax emigration restrictions, larger and larger numbers of Soviet have sought entry. Some 61,000 people, for example, (most of them Soviet Jews) were offered entry to the United States in 1991.

These latest émigrés are considered the fourth wave of Soviet emigrants— the first wave being those who came after the Russian Revolution in 1917, the second those who came after World War II, and the third those who came in the 1970s, when liberalized emigration policies regarding Soviet Jews were linked to American trade with the Soviet Union. The largest proportion of all these émigrés settled in Brighton Beach. The exact size of the émigré population in Brighton Beach—for that matter, elsewhere in the United States—is impossible to discern. This is because large numbers of illegal immigrants either entered the United States or have overstayed their visas. The illegals are estimated to number as many as 30,000. The U.S. Immigration and Naturalization Service believes, however, that most Russian criminals in the United States are legal aliens, having entered under refugee status (personal communication from an INS employee, 1992).

The post-1917 Soviet Jews were not the first Jews to come in large numbers from that part of the world. On the contrary, the first great immigration of Russian Jews to America began in the 1870s and reached its peak in the 1890s, followed by another influx after the 1905 Russian Revolution.[27] These periods predated the Soviet experience. Thus, it is informative to look at these earlier immigrations as a possible source of historical insight into the current situation.

Just as generations of other immigrants in the nineteenth century often turned to crime as the "major avenue for quick material success in America," so too "[y]oung Jews, children of immigrants, followed the pattern."[28] Irving Howe describes how "[c]rime befouled the life of the East Side [of Manhattan]" during the 1880s and 1890s, and later, "as immigrants learned the devices of native enterprise, the neighborhood would export some notable graduates to New York's underworld."[29] These notables included Arnold Rothstein, the son of Eastern European immigrants, who was considered to be the czar of the New York underworld in the 1920s; Isaac Zuker, who headed a Jewish arson ring; "Mother" Marm Mandelbaum, who was the "queen of the fences"; and, the members of the infamous Murder, Inc. Howe makes clear, however, that in the life of the Jewish immigrant community as a whole, "crime was a marginal phenomenon . . . it was never at the center of Jewish immigrant life."[30] The same is certainly true of the vast majority of Soviet Jews who have come in recent years.

Jenna Joselit similarly concludes that Jewish crime was mainly an immigrant phenomenon, turned to as a vehicle of upward mobility. "[F]or New York Jews," she writes, "crime was a one-generation phenomenon, a social and economic consequence of the immigrant experience. As they left the physical boundaries of that experience behind, second-generation Jews left as well its social pathologists [sic] and economic dislocations."[31] Joselit also points out that Jews, in fact, found it easier than some other immigrant groups to ascend the ladder of legitimate social mobility. "In comparison to other ethnic groups like the Italians who . . . found 'the more obvious big-city paths from rags to riches pre-empted,' Jews historically had greater latitude in climbing the ladder."[32]

The one-generation limitation was, of course, not true of gangsters like Rothstein, who really professionalized the underworld and in a major way laid the groundwork for modern organized crime. Rothstein was second-generation, and his ladder of success was organized crime. The same was true of such Jewish gangsters as "Lepke" Buchalter and "Gurrah" Shapiro and, later, Meyer Lansky.

Acculturation of some Jewish immigrants in the first half of the twentieth century seemed to be a two-edged sword in a way that may have implications

for the present experience. The economic and social acculturation of New York
Jews reduced the number of Jews turning to crime by providing them with the
alternative of other, legitimate opportunities, yet it also influenced Jewish crime
rates in a second, rather subtle fashion: the more acculturated the Jewish offender, the more sophisticated and less easily detected his offense. Thus, the
Jew who committed a crime was less prone to arrest—detection—if his appearance was less distinctly "green." By the same token, second-generation
Jewish criminals probably knew enough about the American criminal justice
system to concentrate on committing certain crimes (those with less risk of
detection) and to avoid others. Even if caught, second-generation, acculturated
Jews knew how "to work" with the system.[33]

For some, a belief that honest toil is for suckers was combined with a concentration on crimes of deceit and fraud and with the utilization of their particular skills at getting around the system. Each of these is purported to be
characteristic of the modern Russian gangsters as well, thus, for example, the
characterization of them as "survivors." The Immigration and Naturalization
Service (INS) believes Russian organized crime in the United States is generally
involved in what INS calls the "quieter" aspects of criminal activity, for example, prostitution and fraud, especially document fraud.

A final Joselit conclusion seems pertinent to the issue of whether Russian
organized crime represents imported or indigenous criminality and whether the
criminals here were possibly also criminals there. She suggests that the more
sophisticated, organized criminality of Murder, Inc., for example, was not a
Jewish problem but was rather an American product of "American conditions,
from American soil."

Few European Jews brought a tradition of illicit enterprise with them to the New World.
With the exception of the "Odessa Thieves," a group of Russian-born pickpockets and
master thieves whose specialty was robbing guests at Jewish weddings, and a number of
white slave traders from much the same region, most Jews then branded as criminals
apparently had become so in the New World, not the Old.[34]

Practically no one believes that the present crime problem is a "Jewish problem" either. The Jewish connection is rather one of the accidents of history and
politics. One difference between the modern Jewish émigrés and their ancestors,
which may or may not be incidental, is that the recent émigrés are secular Jews.
They are the products of more than three generations who were largely cut off
from the religion of their parents and grandparents by the atheist Soviet state.
Some other Jews resent these newcomers and their criminal connections, saying
they are Russians, not Jews!

Regarding the imported versus indigenous issue, or Old World versus New
World issue, on the other hand, many people, for example, Rosner, believe that
the present crime problem is very much a product of the old world and not the
new. One of the bases for that belief lies in the city of Odessa.

Odessa

The Odessa connection, mentioned by Joselit, is yet another interesting piece of the culture/crime mosaic. Odessa is a seaport in Ukraine, located on the Black Sea. Many of the residents of Brighton Beach came from Odessa, and consequently, many of the Soviet refugees suspected of involvement in criminal activity in the United States are believed to have come from Odessa. Like other great seaports, Odessa has large numbers of foreigners and a very diverse population—Russians, Ukrainians, Armenians, Rumanians, Tatars, Gypsies, and Jews, among others.

Odessa has its own folklore, jokes and songs, and a peculiar language of thieves' lexicon or slang. It also has long had a thriving black market. Not unlike many other seaports, it has a well-developed criminal subculture, going back to the times of the pirates. The Odessukuya Vory, or Odessa Thieves, were, in fact, the most notorious of all the thieves in Russia, both before and after the revolution.

The possibility is raised not only that have Soviet émigrés come generally from a society heavily imbued with crime and corruption but that many of them have come specifically from what is perhaps the most criminally sophisticated city in the former Soviet Union—a city considered to have a major organized crime problem. The Federal Bureau of Investigation (FBI) said to believe that former members of the Odessa underworld (referred to by some as the Malina, which in Russian means "raspberry" but is also a slang term for "underground" or "underworld") are trying to reestablish themselves in New York, Atlantic City, Philadelphia, Los Angeles, and so on, having brought crime as a trade from home.[35] Many sources further believe that a considerable number of the Soviet émigrés involved in crime here came out of Soviet prisons. But these are all hypotheses that need to be systematically examined.

RUSSIAN ORGANIZED CRIME IN AMERICA: MYTH OR REALITY?

What Is Organized Crime?

This is a controversial question for criminologists, law enforcement authorities, and lawmakers alike. As mentioned earlier, it must be raised in considering the current Russian crime situation in the United States. For purposes of this discussion, characteristics identified by Frank E. Hagan[36] and Michael D. Maltz[37] are particularly appropriate for creating a classification schema that could be applied to the Soviet émigré target group of criminals. Maltz distinguished between "the generic or general [notion of] organized crime and the brand name or specific organized crime group."[38] This distinction is useful in helping to determine whether any particular criminal group is or is not a "true" form of organized crime. The latter is not only theoretically but also practically important, because organized crime cannot be effectively dealt with by the traditional "one crime, one offender" approach used with "regular" crime. Organized crime means criminal enterprises, which require special legal tools, such as the Racketeer Influenced and Corrupt Organizations (RICO) statute, in order to target the enterprise itself as the criminal entity.

According to Maltz, corruption, violence, continuity, and involvement in multiple enterprises are characteristics associated with virtually all organized crime (OC) groups. OC groups use corruption to nullify and to immunize themselves from law enforcement. They also use it to gain an unfair edge in the competition for contracts. The potential for violence, or at least the threat of violence, is also always present in an organized crime group. Because they lack feasible access to the legal system, it is through the use of threatened use of violence that OC groups keep competition and rebellion down. Continuity means that the group is self-perpetuating. It continues beyond the life or participation of any particular individuals. Maltz suggests, in addition, that involvement in continuing enterprises (drug distribution, extortion, or gambling), is one of the cohesive elements of a true organized crime group. True OC groups almost always have multiple criminal enterprises. They engage in more than one kind of crime and have more than one source of illegal income.

Then there are the characteristics of structure and involvement in legitimate business. Structure refers to a division of labor into roles and positions. OC groups, according to Hagan, usually have a fairly well structured organized hierarchy with leaders or bosses, with followers in some rank order of authority, and with varied jobs and responsibilities. OC groups also almost always have legitimate enterprises in addition to their illegitimate enterprises. These provide a way of gaining respectable social status and of laundering illegal money.

Finally, Maltz delineates the characteristics of sophistication, discipline, and bonding. Sophistication refers to how well the OC group runs its criminal business. Does it have accountants, lawyers, and so on? Does it create dummy corporations, paper trials, and so on? Discipline is the degree of internal control and the enforcement of rules. Finally, bonding relates to ethnicity, restricted membership, and codes of secrecy. These last three characteristics, according to Maltz, may be present but are neither necessary nor typical of organized crime. Ethnicity may not be absolutely necessary, but as explained earlier, it has been fairly typical of American organized crime groups.

All of these definitional criteria are tied to the integrated—ethnicity, conspiracy, enterprise—framework described at the outset.

The Incipient Russian Mafia

Because of its relative newness and an absence of reliable and valid information, it is now impossible to completely classify and define Russian organized crime according to the above criteria. This problem is compounded because of the mystery, the romanticism, and the sensationalistic reporting surrounding it. There is something particularly exotic about new gangsters' coming directly from the former "evil empire." This mystique, of course, is not a situation unique to the Russians. What one finds in investigating the problem is that a great deal of the information that is available comes from the popular media. The media, in turn, seem to get their stories from each other or from a few law enforcement sources, who in turn often cite stories in the media or from each other. Thus, it is difficult to judge the accuracy of what is known about this purportedly emergent form of organized crime. Further, because arrests and convictions of Russian émigré criminals have been rare, there has not been available the type of information that normally comes from such actions. With those caveats, there are nevertheless indications—and it is certainly the belief of those who have examined the problem—that the Russians demonstrate in incipient form many of the characteristics historically associated with the growth and development of organized crime in America.

There is limited and somewhat sketchy evidence of the presence of a number of organized crime groups—made up of ex-Soviets—principally in the Brighton Beach community, but also in the Los Angeles and Philadelphia areas. Other cities, such as Baltimore, Chicago, Cleveland, Dallas, Phoenix, and Toronto, report such a presence as well. The tristate area of New Jersey, New York, and Pennsylvania ranks in the top ten areas in the country in terms of Soviet relocations. In these areas, not surprisingly, Russian organized crime is believed by law enforcement authorities to be most prevalent.

The exact number and size of the suspect groups are unknown. California authorities estimated that there were 150 hard-core members and another 200–300 associates nationwide.[39] Federal agents, on the other hand, have reported that there are approximately a dozen Russian organized crime groups in New York alone, with an estimated membership of 400–500 members. Similarly, the New York City Police Department lists about 500 suspected Soviet gang members. They are said to merge in shifting, rather unstructured groups who know each other and who use each other. Some sources refer to them as a confederacy of groups—ruthless, totally lacking in loyalty, and greedy—willing to do anything and everything for a dollar. Their sole purpose is to make money. Sources indicate that they appear to be without the codes of conduct and secrecy or the hierarchical, family structures of La Cosa Nostra. Members range from street corner thugs to educated professionals. A number of sources refer to them as educated and smart, even as perhaps the most intelligent and sophisticated form of organized crime currently in the United States. One popular publication, drawing upon law enforcement descriptions that are admittedly anecdotal and limited, described the Russians this way:

The Russian Malina today is almost a case study of where the Mafia was then [a century ago]. There's only one significant difference—most members of the Malina, far from being poor, ignorant immigrants, are highly educated survivors, skilled in all sorts of hi-tech gadgetry, familiar with outwitting the KGB itself. A number of them are veterans of the Soviet Army, and many are already involved in sophisticated white-collar criminal stings.[40]

The criminal activities attributed to these groups include extortion, forgery, counterfeiting, confidence schemes, and fraud, but also low-level narcotics trafficking, murder, burglary, theft, and arson. One group in particular, the Potato Bag Gang, was reported to prey on the New York Soviet expatriate community through the use of a con game in which victims who believed they had bought a sack of gold coins actually received only a bag of potatoes.[41] There is also a belief that Russian criminals have been infiltrating legitimate businesses. Consistent with historical patterns of organized crime development in immigrant communities, the principal victims so far have been their own. In this case, fellow Russian or Soviet émigrés are being victimized.

In one of the few serious studies of Russian organized crime in the United States—possibly the only such study—Rosner examined what was going on in Brighton Beach. Based on interviews with Russian émigrés and with the police, she concluded that there were groups of "interconnected criminals acting both in organized and in informal conjunction with others" and that "a vast amount of at least informally organized crime" existed there.[42] She quoted a Philadelphia Police Department report as saying: "It is evident that an organized criminal group exists within the Russian immigrant community. Members of this group refer to themselves as the 'Russian Mafia.' It is a present and growing threat to our nation. Their obvious sophistication far exceeds that of La Cosa Nostra in its infant state. The 'Russian Mafia' has perpetrated a series of crimes rivaling any of those perpetrated by existing organized criminal groups."[43]

Rosner's main implications were particularly dramatic but still remain to be tested and either confirmed or refuted:

It remains to be determined whether this particular Russian criminal, i.e., the one who is involved in major criminal activities on an international scale, or even just on a national scale, is part of a structured network. Additionally, it remains to be determined whether this criminal is controlled from within the USSR. These are two separate concepts: one suggests a Mafia-like structure based on previous association but uncontrolled by the political motives of another nation; the other suggests that there exists an overall control from a foreign power, which motivates a criminal element to serve, in part, its purposes ... we have before us a criminal element with great mobility, with a national and international scope, involved in a multiplicity of criminal activities, with a possible KGB connection.[44]

This is certainly a most interesting speculation, but again it must yet be pursued. It also has a different implication today, given the recent demise of the Soviet Union in general and the KGB in particular.

Recent preliminary research suggests that various criminal justice agencies and independent experts and researchers believe in the existence of a Russian organized criminal entity, variously known as the Malina, the Soviet-Jewish Mafia, and the Russian Mafia, as a nontraditional organized crime enterprise. Some of the agencies that hold this view include the FBI, Customs, the New

York State Police, the Pennsylvania Crime Commission, and the Philadelphia, Los Angeles, and New York City police departments.

Despite the concerns expressed in the media and elsewhere, however, there are said to be very few law enforcement agencies with intelligence units actively monitoring this Russian activity. A 1990 *Washington Post* article concluded that "[s]ince the Justice Department does not consider the Russian mob to be organized crime, it doesn't treat it with the seriousness that it reserves for more VIP criminals."[45] The author of this article, James Rosenthal, who is an investigative reporter and freelance writer, argues that the federal government does not view the Russian criminal activity as meeting the RICO criteria for defining a criminal enterprise. Therefore, he says, federal agencies are not aggressively pursuing the problem. Neither the FBI nor the New York City Police Department is doing anything about it (personal communication, 1992).

Law enforcement sources offer two explanations for the emergence of this alleged Russian organized crime in the United States. One is that during the latter 1970s, the Soviet government released criminals from its prisons and commingled them with émigrés leaving the USSR. A second explanation is that members of organized criminal groups in Odessa smuggled themselves out of the country with legitimate émigrés, concealed themselves in Israel or various European cities, and later emigrated to the United States. If the latter is true, it could mean that international underground networks were, and possibly still are, accessible to these criminals.

As indicated earlier, most suspected members of Russian organized crime are of Russian-Jewish backgrounds. Rosenthal, among whose sources are present and former prison inmates, says they are all Jews. Other Soviet criminals, some of whom are not Jewish, are said to have acquired the identities of either dead or jailed Russian Jews in the Soviet Union. Some agents involved with foreign intelligence suggested the possibility that the KGB had placed agents or cooperatives in the U.S. crime operation for both criminal and political purposes. Rosner was speculating about this view.

There are also two general views about the possible organizational structure of Russian organized crime. One, which, for example, is held by the intelligence unit of the Philadelphia police, is that under the umbrella known as Russian organized crime is a loose-knit organization without divisions. Other authorities believe that it is a confederation of gangs based on geographic origins in the former USSR. Thus, there are the Odessa Gang, the Kiev Gang, the Moscow Gang, the Leningrad Gang, and the more widely dispersed, so-called Gypsy Gangs.

Recent criminal activities attributed to the Russians include relatively unsophisticated larcenies, robberies, prostitution, complex and sophisticated extortions, counterfeiting, tax and insurance frauds, murder, jewelry and gold coin switches, arson, narcotics trafficking, and the infiltration of legitimate businesses. The victims include other Soviet immigrants, but also Jewish merchants and various insurance companies and government agencies.

Suspected members of Russian organized crime have demonstrated mobility in their criminal pursuits. For example, police documents indicate that various crimes that have occurred in the northeast section of Philadelphia have been committed by Russian residents of Brighton Beach. Suspected Russian criminals from Philadelphia have been involved in credit card and insurance frauds in Los Angeles. U.S. Customs has noted that casinos in Atlantic City, New Jersey, have been the targets of Russian criminal activity, for example, passing counterfeit money and stolen travelers' checks and laundering money, by Soviet émigrés residing in Toronto, Canada.

In yet another twist, members of alleged Russian organized crime are believed to have allied themselves with the Scarfo, Colombo, and Genovese crime families of La Cosa Nostra (LCN). In Philadelphia, Russians were said to have enlisted the aid of a Scarfo associate (Joseph Kahana) to commit arson on several businesses. In New York and New Jersey, the Russians and the Colombo and Genovese groups have combined to control "no brand" fuel distribution and retail sales. Circumvention of taxes by these enterprises has resulted in the evasion of hundreds of millions of dollars in state and federal excise taxes. Criminal convictions in New York and Florida also provide strong evidence that suspect Russians have associated and conspired with traditional LCN organized crime. The bootleg motor fuel enterprise, which has been the principal collaboration, is analyzed in detail in the next section.

POLICY ISSUES

The FBI, or at least the Washington-based organized crime unit of the FBI, admits to knowing relatively little about the Russian organized crime problem in the United States. It does, however, have a great interest in learning more. A 1991 strategic assessment by the INS consists mostly of information gleaned from the *New York Times*. But several indications contradict assertions, such as that mentioned earlier, that law enforcement is not moving against Russian émigré organized crime. One is the 1991 RICO prosecution of a defendant named Boris Goldberg. Goldberg was indicted in the U.S. District Court for the Eastern District of New York as the head of a criminal enterprise called the "Goldberg Crime Group." This racketeering enterprise was charged with trafficking in cocaine, attempted murder, armed robbery and extortion, fraud, illegal dealings with weapons and explosives, and using violence. Goldberg pleaded guilty to these charges in early 1992.

Among the racketeering counts in the indictment was one charging conspiracy to murder one Evsei Agron. The indictment alleged that in early 1983, Goldberg and other members of the Goldberg Crime Group discussed murdering Agron and then carried out a surveillance to that end. On 24 January 1984, Agron was shot and seriously wounded. But this was not the end of the matter.

Agron is said to have been a sort of self-styled "godfather" of Russian organized crime in New York in the early 1980s. One account by an independent journalist describes Agron and his activities as follows:

> He [Agron] made his reputation through several years spent in Soviet jails, and claimed to be an experienced killer. . . . [According to one source] ''Agron was supposedly one of the top people. When he came to this country he must have picked up with some of his old cronies.''
>
> Like most real-life mobsters, Agron was a low-life thug . . . he kept an electric cattle-prod in his car, and specialized in extortion and blackmail. . . . In his prime, he opened up the gasoline racket that would net millions, possibly billions of dollars for the Russians. He made contacts with émigré criminals in Europe. . . .
>
> In May 1985, as he left home for his daily Turkish bath, Agron was shot dead by two assassins posing as joggers. Like most mob murders, this one remains unsolved years later. An Agron lieutenant may have ordered the killing. Other suspects include one of the five crime families in New York's Mafia.[46]

Whether Agron, Goldberg, and some others who have been labeled as leaders give evidence to the existence of a structured hierarchy in the Russian operation is open to question. What is not to be doubted, however, is the obvious willingness to use violence. Further, the indictment suggests multiple and sophisticated criminal enterprises operated through a substantial conspiracy. By far the most sophisticated and the most lucrative enterprise of the Russians is the gasoline tax fraud, and its investigation indicates law enforcement has not been dormant.

A Case Study: The Bootleg Motor Fuel Enterprise

In 1991, the New Jersey State Commission of Investigation (SCI) undertook an investigation of motor fuel tax evasion. This investigation built upon previous investigations by law enforcement agencies in New York and by the U.S. Department of Justice. The SCI investigation culminated in public hearings in October 1991 and a report in February 1992. This discussion draws heavily on those sources.

The nature of the criminal enterprise here involves federal and state tax evasion. The estimated tax loss nationally is more than $1 billion annually, and the estimate of annual tax loss for New Jersey is approximately $40 million. This is thus a huge money-making operation. It exploits the fact that diesel fuel (which is taxable as motor fuel) and home heating oil (which is not taxed) are basically the same product. The tax in this instance acts as a market control that creates the opportunity to illegally market an otherwise legal commodity.

The typical scam for the tax evader is to buy No. 2 fuel oil and sell it as diesel with some markup for taxes but without remitting those taxes to the state or federal government. Often this scam is accomplished by the creation of a convoluted paper trail that includes dummy companies that cease operating before authorities are even aware that a crime has been committed. These firms usually issue invoices to purchasers of diesel fuel that are marked "all taxes included," regardless of whether or not ("not" usually being the case) a single penny of tax, has, in fact, been remitted.[47]

The dummy companies combine in what is termed a daisy chain. A daisy chain of bogus companies is a series of companies with very short life spans. These companies use fictitious identification and often are registered under the same people using different names; they are usually only mail drops and/or telephones with answering machines; they move frequently, changing names in the process; they use couriers for cash collections or wire transfers of cash; and they open bank accounts, again using phony names, through which are moved large sums of money but which are open for only very short periods of time. States like New York and New Jersey are particularly vulnerable to this kind of motor fuel tax evasion because they have many refineries and fuel distributors. The various investigations of the scheme have disclosed that many of those involved are ex-Soviets—most now living in Brooklyn (Brighton Beach). One witness in the hearings, the head of criminal investigations for New Jersey's Division of Taxation, was asked about this Soviet involvement by one of the New Jersey commissioners:

Mr. [Barry] Evenchick: Lastly, I'm curious, how is it that this seems—this situation seems tied to Russian immigrants? Anything in particular that makes this attractive to them, or how did this come about, do you know?

Mr. [Harvey] Borak: The only thing I can say of those that we've looked into, what we find is that many of them back in their home country had been involved in black market and white-collar crimes, like one has said to me on occasion this is a country club, we are a very, very, open country, we are a very open society, and for people who were able to survive doing these type of things in their very closed and very closely monitored society, it's kind of easy for them to do it.

One individual who served a jail term, unlike their prisons, ours was a country club compared to what he was used to. So for some people, there's gold on the streets.[48]

A New Jersey detective investigating the bootleg motor fuel business made inquiries of Interpol, using names from vehicle registrations. He described the results: "There were two names that I submitted to Interpol, I received information back . . . that they had been checked through the country of Israel and [they] had a birthplace of the USSR, and . . . had immigrated to Israel and from Israel into the United States."[49] "They" also turned out to be one and the same person.

Borak was asked whether INS, or anyone else, was reviewing these émigrés coming into the country. He indicated that, indeed, some reviews had been done at the state level and that these had determined that "most of them are legal." How this is to be reconciled with their having prior criminal histories and having been imprisoned was not explained. The issue of screening these émigrés by

INS seems to be an area where either there is no policy, the policy is ambiguous, or it is not enforced. This is something that clearly needs to be investigated.

Raymond Jermyn, the chief of the Rackets Bureau for the Suffolk County (New York) district attorney, also testified at the SCI hearings. He echoed the finding of a major presence of "eastern block immigrants" in the tax scam. Jermyn described the difficulties law enforcement had in investigating these individuals. "There was great difficulty. There was a language barrier to begin with. Conspiratorial conversations were often in a foreign language, there weren't many agents that could speak Rumanian, unfortunately, or Russian. There was inability to infiltrate these closely-knit groups by way of informants or police agents, and in addition to that, these individuals were well-educated and oftentimes smarter than law enforcement agencies."[50]

This testimony speaks to the conspiracy involved in the enterprise, to the structure of the groups, and to their criminal sophistication. The latter is also apparent from this testimony from the same investigator: "One of the abilities of the organizational skills of the principals involved in these schemes was that they were able to forge a very close working relationship. It became almost like a cartel between the traditional organized crime families and the eastern block people, and they were able to monopolize and control the price of unbranded gasoline in the Long Island area for many, many years."[51]

On links to La Cosa Nostra in the tax evasion scheme, there was this colloquy with Jermyn:

Q: Did you find evidence that traditional organized crime families received a set amount of money from the operations or scams for allowing them to occur?

A: Yes . . . the immigrants who became involved in business were bright enough to realize that they had to pay tribute to traditional organized crime families in order to operate in certain areas, and there was usually a one or two cents per gallon levy by the mob families imposed upon the sale of bootlegged gasoline.

Q: Is that called the mob tax?

A: Yes . . . [it] amounted to millions and millions of dollars.[52]

Jermyn testified that, in addition to the tax evasion, these same individuals were involved in a host of other crimes: bank fraud, embezzlement, commercial bribery of loan officers, and money laundering. He and other witnesses also described the role of violence in this marketplace—estimating that as many as a dozen murders had been committed over a seven-year period. One of the murder victims, a Rumanian named Michel Markowitz, is believed by other sources to have been an associate of Agron and to have been a key person in negotiating the gas deal with LCN families. Markowitz came to the United States in 1979 with virtually no money, according to Jermyn; but at the time of his murder in 1989, his estimated worth was $30 million to $50 million. Markowitz was shot to death in Brooklyn, after he had been convicted of bootleg-ging and was cooperating with the government. The murder is still unsolved.

The New Jersey SCI report concluded that the perpetrators of the tax evasion schemes, a "loosely knit group of immigrants from the Soviet Union and other eastern European countries," are "brazen, creative and, in some cases, danger-ous."[53] They are also well connected to La Cosa Nostra. The New Jersey state treasurer described them this way: "To these shrewd fly-by-night tax evaders, some of whom are said to have years of white collar experience in the Russian black market, America has become their playground. They are indeed becoming a national problem."[54]

CONCLUSIONS AND IMPLICATIONS

What do we know, then, about Russian organized crime? What, on the other hand, are the unanswered or only partially answered questions? We know that "it" is probably not a homogeneous entity. At least some groups making up that entity can be very sophisticated, use violence, have multiple criminal en-terprises, have some degree of structure, and many employ corruption. We do not know much about the continuity of the various groups or about their internal structures, that is, whether they are hierarchical, their size, how members become members, if membership is restricted and if so to whom, what kinds of internal discipline are employed, or whether there are codes of behavior and secrecy.

Looking back at Amir's conditions that he said favored Soviet émigré in-volvement in organized crime in Israel, there is evidence that some of these conditions may also be present in the United States. All of these émigrés came from a society in which they had been socialized into a system in which cor-ruption and deviance were practically the norm. How this affects their potential for, and active involvement in, organized crime, as they become acculturated into American society, is not clear. Based upon limited information, the relia-bility of which is unknown, some of the criminals identified here may have also been criminals, even organized criminals, in the Soviet Union. They may have been in prisons there. What is needed to really test this assumption is an ar-rangement (perhaps through Interpol) with the various ministries of internal affairs in the former Soviet republics that would permit checking the criminal histories of Soviet émigrés who are suspected of organized crime involvement here.

We do not know to what extent Russian émigrés are experiencing unemploy-ment and severe socioeconomic problems here that may be "forcing" them into crime as an alternate route to success. Are legitimate avenues of mobility and advancement blocked? Are youths in the various Russian émigré communities involved in juvenile delinquency? Are such youth being recruited into adult organized crime? A review of Russian émigrés who have been arrested would shed light on who they are: how long they have been in the country, whether they are employed and if so, as what, their education, skills, and training levels and so on.

It seems that for some of these émigrés, at least, as in Israel, entry into, and participation in, the American underworld have been comparatively easy. Beyond the gasoline tax scam, however, there is no evidence of other collaborative criminal ventures. Are there any?

Finally, again except for some very sketchy information, we do not know the perception that Soviet émigrés have of the American law enforcement and criminal justice system. Especially pertinent would be the perceptions of those involved in organized crime. We cannot, nor do we want to, replicate the Soviet police state. But perhaps other steps could be taken to counter misperceptions and to improve effectiveness.

Joseph Serio's recent published survey of the effects of Soviet organized crime on the international community made some thought-provoking observations:

As Aeroflot, the Soviet airline, increases direct flights from the USSR to the United States, and immigration increases dramatically in 1993 after the implementation of the new Soviet immigration law, we should expect a significant increase of Soviet crime in America. Indeed, law enforcement agencies predict that a wave of Soviet crime will sweep across Europe and America within five years. Many of these crimes will be committed by organized groups, some of whom will develop criminal networks all over the world.[55]

Circumstances and conditions in the former USSR have changed drastically since the Serio article was prepared in early 1991, but nevertheless his observations should still give reason for concern. The questions and unknowns that I have delineated here furnish the foundation of an agenda for research and investigation. Now is an opportune time for spelling out and implementing that agenda.

NOTES

1. Daniel Bell, "Crime as an American Way of Life," *The Antioch Review* 13 (1953): 172–91.

2. Peter A. Lupsha, "Individual Choice, Material Culture, and Organized Crime," *Criminology* 19 (1981): 3–24.

3. Michael Gottfredson and Travis Hirshi, *A General Theory of Crime* (Palo Alto, CA: Stanford University Press, 1990).

4. Peter A. Lupsha, "Organized Crime in the United States," in *Organized Crime: A Global Perspective,* ed. R. J. Kelly (Totowa, NJ: Rowman and Littlefield, 1986), 34.

5. Dwight C. Smith, *The Mafia Mystique* (New York: Basic Books, 1975).

6. Mark H. Haller, "Illegal Enterprise: A Theoretical and Historical Interpretation," *Criminology* 28 (1990): 208.

7. Peter Reuter, *The Organization of Illegal Markets: An Economic Analysis* (Washington, DC: National Institute of Justice, U.S. Department of Justice, 1985).

8. Dwight C. Smith, "Paragons, Pariahs, and Pirates: A Spectrum-Based Theory of Enterprise," *Crime and Delinquency* 26(3) (1980): 375.

9. Gerald E. Caiden and Herbert E. Alexander, "Introduction: Perspectives on Organized Crime," in *The Politics and Economics of Organized Crime*, ed. H. E. Alexander and G. E. Caiden (Lexington, MA: D. C. Heath, 1985), 10.

10. Menachem Amir, "Organized Crime and Organized Criminality Among Georgian Jews in Israel," in *Organized Crime: A Global Perspective*, ed. R. J. Kelly (Totowa, NJ: Rowman and Littlefield, 1986), 172–91.

11. Amir, "Organized Crime," 188.

12. Francis X. Clines, "There's a Crime Wave, or a Perception Wave, in the Soviet Union," *New York Times* 17 September 1989, E2.

13. Daniel Gurevich, "Moscow Gangland," *Details* (October 1990): 24.

14. Joseph Serio, "The Soviet Union: Disorganization and Organized Crime," *Criminal Organizations* 6 (1992): 3, 4, 5, 6, 7, 13, 14, 23.

15. I. I. Karpets, "The Reality of Crime," *Soviet Sociology* (May–June 1990): 63–80; Boris Z. Rumer, *Soviet Central Asia* (Boston: Unwin Hyman, 1990).

16. Arkady Vaksberg, *The Soviet Mafia* (New York: St. Martin's Press, 1991).

17. Konstantin M. Simis, *USSR—The Corrupt Society* (New York: Simon and Schuster, 1982), 7.

18. Yuri Shchekochikhin, "Where the Mafia Reigns," *The Literary Gazette International* 2 (February 1990): 18–19.

19. "On Reform: Prime Time for Crime," *Newsweek*, 4 June 1990, 24, 25.

20. Lydia S. Rosner, *The Soviet Way of Crime* (South Hadley, MA: Bergin and Garvey, 1986): 132–33.

21. Ibid., 83.

22. Vaksberg, *The Soviet Mafia*, 69.

23. Simis, *USSR*.

24. Ibid., 179.

25. Thorsten Sellin, *Culture Conflict and Crime* (New York: Social Science Research Council, 1938).

26. Bell, "Crime;" Francis A. J. Ianni, *A Family Business* (New York: Russell Sage, 1972).

27. Arthur Hertzberg, *The Jews in America* (New York: Touchstone, 1989).

28. Ibid., 204.

29. Irving Howe, *World of Our Fathers* (New York: Harcourt Brace Jovanovich, 1976), 101.

30. Ibid., 101.

31. Jenna W. Joselit, *Our Gang: Jewish Crime and the New York Jewish Community, 1900–1940* (Bloomington: Indiana University Press, 1983), 159.

32. Ibid., 161.

33. Ibid., 161–62.

34. Ibid., 19.

35. Daniel Burstein, "Death of a Hustler," *New York Magazine*, 2 May 1983, 28.

36. Frank E. Hagan, "The Organized Crime Continuum: A Further Specification of a New Conceptual Model," *Criminal Justice Review* 8 (1983): 52–57.

37. Michael D. Maltz, "Toward Defining Organized Crime," in *The Politics and*

Economics of Organized Crime, ed. H. E. Alexander and G. Caiden (Lexington, MA: D. C. Heath, 1985), 21–35; Michael D. Maltz, *Measuring the Effectiveness of Organized Crime Control Efforts* (Chicago: Office of International Criminal Justice, University of Illinois at Chicago, 1990).

38. Maltz, "Toward Defining Organized Crime," 24.

39. Bureau of Organized Crime and Criminal Intelligence, *Organized Crime in California* (Sacramento: Department of Justice, State of California, 1987).

40. Mike Mallewe, "From Russia with Guns," *Philadelphia Magazine* (May 1983): 147.

41. President's Commission on Organized Crime, *The Impact: Organized Crime Today* (Washington, DC: U.S. Government Printing Office): 122.

42. Rosner, *The Soviet Way*, 113, 116.

43. Ibid., 116.

44. Ibid., 122.

45. James Rosenthal, "Russia's New Export: The Mob—How a Bunch of Emigre Gangsters Found a Home in Brooklyn," *Washington Post*, 24 June 1990.

46. Tim Cornwell, "Russian Mafia," 1992, unpublished.

47. State of New Jersey Commission of Investigation, *Motor Fuel Tax Evasion* (Trenton, NJ: Author), February 1992: 1.

48. Ibid., 37–38.

49. Ibid., 196.

50. Ibid., 56.

51. Ibid., 58.

52. Ibid., 57.

53. Ibid., 12.

54. Ibid., 377.

55. Serio, "The Soviet Union," 7.

11

Corruption and Racketeering in the New York City School Boards

WILLIAM J. COOK, JR.

INTRODUCTION

The year 1988 was difficult for New York City government. The Edward Koch administration was still haunted by a series of scandals that had been exposed a few years earlier. Names such as Donald R. Manes, Stanley Friedman, and Bess Myerson had been powerful in city politics but were now sullied by accusations of corruption.[1] A new cynicism emerged as ever-jaded New Yorkers began to lose faith in their government. Then, another maelstrom of scandal broke when a principal in the Bronx was arrested on drug charges.

As the story of that principal came to light, questions were asked about the school system in which he served. Within days, it became apparent that the problem with this principal was not an isolated matter but, rather, the symptom of a far more invasive disease—political corruption—that was ravaging the entire school system. This chapter recounts the story of the New York City school system corruption scandal that unfolded in 1988. Beginning with a history of the school system, it covers the major corruption cases that involved community school boards.

The goal of the chapter is to introduce the reader to the circumstances under which corrupt organizations developed in the school boards. School board membership allowed criminals and other opportunists to become part of an organization that enabled them to plunder the resources allotted for the schooling of a city's children. Though the activities of corrupt school board members were different from that of traditional organized criminal or "Mafia" groups, it is argued that the board members engaged in another "species" of organized crime.

BACKGROUND

The ethnic and racial complexion of New York City began to change noticeably during the decade of the 1960s. The black and Hispanic populations expanded at the same time that whites fled to the suburbs. Minority leaders asserted that the government of the city was not responsive to the needs of its constituents. Soon, the rallying cry was "community control of politics"; the immediate goal was to wrest control of services from the powerful white bureaucrats through the decentralization of government. According to David Rogers, the two major goals of the decentralization movement were, first, to make the bureaucracies more responsive to the needs of minorities and, second, to create employment opportunities for minorities in city government.[2]

The earliest target of the decentralization movement was the school system. The New York City school system is a vast enterprise. In 1982, for example, it had a budget of approximately $3 billion, which has more than doubled today. The Board of Education operates approximately 1,000 buildings and employs more than 100,000 persons. It educates nearly 1 million students, while feeding about 500,000 of them lunch each day.

During the 1960s, a massive centralized bureaucracy characterized the Board of Education headquarters. In this imposing system of administration and management, the leaders of the school system had become a Brahmin caste of public servants insulated from the community. The proponents of the board decentralization argued that there would be more accountability of educators to their local communities, more parental involvement and control in educational decision making, and more jobs in the schools for district residents.[3]

Bowing to significant political pressures, the Central Board of Education tested community control of the schools on a limited basis in 1967. One of the places chosen for the decentralization experiment was the Ocean Hill-Brownsville area of Brooklyn, a mostly black and Hispanic community.

In May 1968, the new Community School Board in Ocean Hill-Brownsville decided to remove nineteen white teachers whom it had identified as antagonistic toward community control. Following this controversial decision by the Ocean Hill-Brownsville board, there were citywide strikes called by the teachers' union to protect teachers from being fired unfairly or illegally. The first ten weeks of the fall school term in 1968 were lost to a strike by approximately 50,000 teachers. The growing tensions in the city forced the state legislature into action. New legislation was effected in 1969 that created a decentralized city school system; the new law was tailored, however, to meet the demands of the city teachers' union.

Under the decentralization law, thirty-one (later changed to thirty-two) districts were formed. Each district was to be governed by a locally elected school

board consisting of nine members for whom there were no professional requirements. School board members were to be unsalaried but were entitled to a
monthly stipend.

The boards were to have the power to "choose their own district superinten-
dents and would appoint principals." The local school boards were given the
power to hire nonprofessional personnel, as well as to oversee many of the
purchases and other business transactions in a school district. As a check to
the local school boards' powers, the chancellor of the Central Board, who is its
primary executive, was authorized to "suspend, supersede, or remove a community school board or its members" if they were found to have violated laws
or regulations of the Central Board of Education.[4]

Upon its implementation, decentralization displayed certain disturbing flaws.
First, the majority of students' parents simply did not participate in the elections
of school board members. By the 1989 school board election, only 6 percent of
the eligible parents voted. The upshot was that, in some districts, one could
easily be elected with only a few hundred votes.

Second, it became evident that school board members were being drawn into
corrupt activities. Joseph P. Viteritti has observed that six of the thirty-two
school boards were being investigated for corruption within the first decade after
the decentralization law took effect. Three community school board members
from Harlem were "convicted of conspiracy to misuse public funds in school
board election campaigns . . . [and] . . . in Ocean Hill-Brownsville, a school
board president and former state assemblyman was convicted of soliciting bribes
from a producer of educational materials."[5]

It has been claimed that the quality of school board membership rapidly de-
teriorated during the 1970s. The earliest community school board members were
idealistic and professional; they were interested in parental concerns and sought
to represent and advocate these. However, these original members soon discovered that they did not have much power over policy decisions as they had
hoped—this power had been retained by the Central Board. Rogers asserts that,
as a consequence, these idealistic school board members abandoned the school
boards; he maintains that, by 1980, they were all gone. The vacuum was quickly
filled by persons who were agents of various interest groups. He says that "several [board members] became increasingly involved in district management, particularly in the allocation of jobs and patronage." The result was that "what
has emerged in some districts has been community school board control by local
'power brokers' who represent organizational interests that do not include parents, and are not oriented toward educational considerations."[6]

That special interest groups had usurped control of the school boards escaped
the general attention of the public for nearly twenty years. Then, in 1988, the
arrest of a principal led to the exposure of the unimaginable corruption that was
concomitant with the changes in school board leadership that are a legacy of a
policy two decades old.

THE SCHOOL BOARD CORRUPTION SCANDAL OF 1988

On the afternoon of Wednesday, 9 November 1988, Matthew Barnwell, the principal of Public School No. 53 in the Bronx, was arrested by narcotics officers after he bought two vials of "crack" cocaine on a Harlem street corner. Charged with the criminal possession of a controlled substance, he identified himself to police as a school aide.[7]

A few days after the incident, more about Barnwell, who was the first principal ever to be arrested on drug charges, was revealed. Though they denied it, members of Community School Board No. 9 denied there were continuing reports of Barnwell's latenesses, unpredictable behavior, and slovenly personal appearance. Yet, according to Robert F. Wagner, Jr., then president of the Central Board of Education, the community school board had not attempted to discipline him by filing charges.[8]

Richard R. Green, chancellor of the New York City school system, instituted an inquiry into the actions of Community School Board No. 9 because of its "failure to deal with a problem principal over time."[9] But, within three weeks of the Barnwell arrest, concerns about the operations of School Board No. 9 were extending beyond the chancellor's office to that of the Bronx County district attorney. On 23 November 1988, news broke that a grand jury was investigating complaints that members of the local school board were using drugs and stealing school property. It was reported that "Bronx law enforcement officials said a number of allegations were being investigated, including an accusation that some school board members stole computers and furniture from schools to buy drugs."[10] The incident involving Barnwell had opened the gates so that the district attorney's office was deluged with complaints about the district. Curiously, School Board No. 9 members, when asked about the complaints, stated that they, for the most part, knew nothing about them.

Paul T. Gentile, district attorney of the Bronx, announced at a news conference that he had subpoenaed the financial records of Community School District No. 9. He outlined the areas of his investigation as focusing on (1) fund-raising for District No. 9 board members' election campaigns; (2) the possible connection between one's political contributions of fund-raising activity and appointment to positions as principals and assistant principals or to other types of openings; (3) the purchases of expensive equipment by the district; (4) an allegation that Community School Board No. 9 members received payments in order to keep school buildings open (i.e., buildings are sometimes opened for private use for basketball games or parties); and (5) allegations that community school board members had distributed and used drugs with their subordinates. Further, it was announced that a grand jury had begun investigating a second Bronx district.[11]

After the news release about the Bronx district attorney's probe of complaints about Community School Board No. 9, Chancellor Green suspended the members of that school board. He appointed two Bronx lawyers, as well as two Central Board employees to administer the district.

By the end of November 1988, no more than two weeks after the arrest of Barnwell, an unbridled scandal was beginning to wrench the entire school system. The focus remained on School Board No. 9, which had a budget of more than $100 million and control of thirty-three elementary and middle schools in a predominantly black and Hispanic area.

Gentile, the prosecutor, observed, "You basically have a framework and atmosphere that is fertile ground for corruption."

Indications that the difficulties present in this Bronx school district were not unique surfaced quickly. Soon, the press reported that accusations were being leveled at other school boards. The district attorneys' offices in Queens, Brooklyn, Manhattan, and the Bronx all began to investigate complaints about their school boards. Allegations ranged from sexual harassment to misappropriation of funds.

The district attorney's office in the Bronx announced that it had received about sixty complaints, while the district attorney's office in Queens reported that it had received about twelve complaints. Investigators stated that "many of the complaints are difficult to evaluate because they are simply one person's word against another's."[12]

Another complaint, which was being investigated by the Office of the Inspector General of the Board of Education, was that two East Harlem school officials, one a former city councilman and member of Community School Board No. 4 in Manhattan and a superintendent of the same district, had misappropriated funds donated for school use (i.e., to benefit the children of the district's schools). It was claimed that they had spent the money for travel and personal expenses.

The school board officials were dismissed by Chancellor Green after an inspector general's office report concluded that money from the school donations fund had been used to finance a "sweet sixteen" party for the daughter of one of the district's officials and to purchase a bracelet from Tiffany's. The school board member apparently used about $1,800 from the fund to pay for damages from a lawsuit that was unrelated to Board of Education business. Another $8,000 went to school district employees as loans; the "loans" were generally not repaid. Other expenditures paid for with money drawn from the fund included a catering firm's bill for $3,644 and thousands of dollars in purchases from a liquor store. There was also evidence that money from the fund was used to pay for a trip to a conference in Puerto Rico that was attended by both officials. The inspector general, Michael P. Sofarelli, observed that, even though there had been at least $60,000 in the fund at one point, "the funds were never properly accounted for. And by that, I mean both the receipts and the disbursements. We just aren't sure where some of it went."[13]

The district superintendent was not repentant. In fact, he insisted that he "was the victim of a sloppy investigation." Having acknowledged buying the bracelet at Tiffany's, he explained that it was a retirement gift. He also claimed that the caterer who had told investigators that "he was paid with school money for the party will now say he was mistaken."[14]

In addition to allegations of criminal wrongdoing, other information was revealed about political infighting and interconnections between some of the districts being investigated. Community School Board No. 19 members in Brooklyn gained notoriety for their political "dogfights" concerning the hiring of personnel for the district. This board had hiring authority over thirty principalships and assistant principalships, fifty school aides, and fifty-five paraprofessionals, as well as fifty other nonprofessional positions (e.g., security guards). Principals earn a yearly salary of approximately $69,000, while assistant principals are paid $65,000. Staff workers have an annual salary of $23,690, while guards and aides are paid $9.74 per hour and $8.61 per hour, respectively. Community school board members in District 19 were so divided about which candidate to hire that seven of the openings for principals and assistant principals, as well as an assistant superintendent's position (which commanded a yearly salary of at least $85,000), were not filled.

The primary candidate for the deputy superintendent's position was a principal from Community School District No. 32. His sister was a member of Community School Board No. 32 and also a fund-raiser for a Democrat congressman from Brooklyn. It was reported that some members of Community School Board No. 19 had stated that the congressman "had pressed for [the principal] to be appointed" to the position of deputy superintendent. Thus, it became apparent that two different school boards had established political connections "with members of different boards, trading jobs" with each other.[15]

The allegations of extensive corruption in the city's school boards led to a crisis for the Koch administration. In mid-December 1988, the mayor announced that he believed that "corruption is almost certainly rampant throughout the city's school system." In a letter to Governor Mario Cuomo, he formally requested that an independent panel, which would be modeled on the Knapp Commission, be instituted in order to investigate the corrupt activities of the school boards. Koch noted that Cuomo could form the investigative panel under the authority of the Moreland Act. This law, enacted in 1907, "allows the governor to investigate departments or agencies and use the conclusions for legislative recommendations." The Moreland Act had previously been invoked to authorize investigations of alcohol-beverage control, nursing homes, and the New York Parking Violations Bureau, all of which had been tinged by corruption scandals.[16]

Cuomo refused to form the investigative panel. Though he agreed with the mayor about the seriousness of the problems plaguing the Board of Education, he decided not to establish a special investigative panel because "the district attorneys in the city were aggressively investigating the allegations of misconduct by members of some of the 32 community school boards." Koch responded by saying that he would explore the possibility of creating a locally authorized investigative panel.[17]

Even as Koch wrestled with the issue of how the scandal should be investigated, more waves of allegations about corruption in the Bronx buffeted the school system. The focus now turned toward District No. 12, located in the south-central Bronx. It had been ranked as the lowest performer in reading and math scores of all of the school districts. The *New York Times* reported the following allegations about the school board members: (1) during a search for a new superintendent, a forged letter was used to ensure that the "preferred" candidate would be hired, while other, more qualified candidates were excluded; (2) relatives of some school board members were placed on the payroll with the agreement of five other members (this is permitted by Board of Education policy); (3) two or more board members were believed to have taken expensive equipment (e.g., computer equipment) that had been purchased for use by the schoolchildren; and (4) board members used district funds to pay for trips to professional conferences in such places as Las Vegas and South Hampton.

At the heart of the *Times* report was a description of the community school board's patronage system, which controlled "millions of dollars a year worth of district jobs." One board member explained that there was a secret list of hires that was kept so that "when a new coalition took power, the [board] members knew who had been hired by previous coalitions and could be dismissed." The former executive secretary of that local school board revealed that she would tell people that no jobs with the district were available unless the person knew to mention a school board member's name. Then, he or she would be given an application. No one without a "padrino," or patron, was ever hired. Many of the successful applicants were not even literate but "were often those who had collected signatures for school board members when they ran for election."[18]

This pattern of shameless patronage was uncovered in a different borough in a grand jury investigation of Community School District No. 32 led by a tough, streetwise special prosecutor, Roger Adler. In a grand jury report, Adler related that testimony before a Brooklyn grand jury "revealed that over the course of time, the District Personnel Directors became increasingly drawn into the political ambitions of various School Board members." The personnel directors were required not only to work in political campaigns but also to solicit campaign contributions. The pressure exerted by school board members "escalated to the point that the Personnel Office did not process applications for non-professional positions, absent a referral from a politically active member."

The Brooklyn grand jury report provided a unique glimpse into the operations of the patronage system. Regardless of whether a person was qualified or not, sponsorship by a school board member determined whether or not one would be hired. There was a list kept in the personnel office by a secretary so as to "insure that applicants who claimed Board member referral could be checked out to verify the claim and to demonstrate that board recommendations were being followed." The initials of the sponsoring board member were entered next to the name of an applicant on the secretary's list. The report concluded that "jobs have become perceived as rewards for political activity."[19]

Persons in other districts related that jobs and promotions could be "attained by other means, including payoffs." A former assistant principal in District No. 12 in the Bronx complained that "a Board member asked her for $5,000 to keep her job after she failed a qualifying examination." Another person said that a different Community School Board No. 12 member solicited a seventy-dollar payment, along with her application for a cafeteria job.

Another member of the board in District No. 12 acknowledged that she was "involved with drugs." She was homeless, having been evicted from her apartment. A former associate on the school board was asked about how a drug addict could be allowed to serve with the school board and commented that "they wanted to use her, but no one wanted to help her."[20]

On 17 December 1988, just five weeks after the arrest of Barnwell, it was reported that no fewer than eleven of the thirty-two school boards were now under investigation. The investigations were being pursued by the district attorneys' offices of the boroughs of Manhattan, the Bronx, Brooklyn, and Queens, as well as by the Inspector General's Office of the Board of Education.[21] One effect of these investigations was that the New York State legislature approved three of Governor Cuomo's Board of Education proposals. One of the approved items was the creation of a "School Construction Authority" to oversee the construction of new school buildings. The second sought to prohibit political officeholders, party officials, or employees of the school system from being elected to the community school boards. The third measure was designed to evaluate results of the decentralization of the New York City Board of Education.[22]

Part of the fallout from the investigations of the school boards was an initiative of Mayor Koch, who decided to name a commission to investigate corruption in the school system. The commission would consist of a five-member panel and have a budget of $1 million. The panel was given the task of not only investigating corruption but also searching for methods of improving school decentralization. The staff that would serve under the commissioners included lawyers, police officers, investigators, and accountants.

Koch explained that the commission was to be patterned after the well-known Knapp Commission, which had probed corruption in the New York City Police Department in the 1970s. The new panel, known as the Joint Commission for Integrity in Schools and informally called the "Gill Commission," would "cooperate with district attorneys who are already pursuing criminal investigations of school boards and would not usurp their role." The commission would be given subpoena power under the authority of the New York City Department of Investigation. It would conduct public hearings and possibly seek immunity from prosecution for some witnesses. It was anticipated that the new commission would release its first report within three months of commencing its operations.[23]

CORRUPTION CASES OF 1989

Subsequent to the Koch move and the continuing investigations of the district attorneys, the administrators of the New York City school system searched for reasons as to why the educational system could be so engulfed in corruption. Some believed that the Central Board of Education had failed in its supervision of the local school districts, allowing them to mismanage their budgets and to substitute political concerns for educational goals. There seemed to be some truth in this criticism. For example, the records maintained by the Central Board's Office of Community School District Affairs were, at best, often inadequate or incomplete. Other critics suggested that part of the problem resulted from the ineffective work of the Inspector General's Office of the Board of Education. Between June 1987 and June 1988, the Inspector General's Office received 1,582 complaints related to wrongdoing in the school system. Sofarelli, a former assistant district attorney in Brooklyn who served as inspector general since 1981, stated that "all allegations are given attention and that 17 of every 100 lead to a finding of wrongdoing or a recommendation of some sort." Most complaints were unfounded or "impossible to substantiate."

Staff of the Inspector General's Office numbered about sixty investigators. The office did not have subpoena or arrest powers, and it could not discipline an employee when wrongdoing was uncovered. When administrative violations (e.g., attendance problems) were found, they were referred to Central Board or to the local districts for disciplinary action. When investigative findings indicated criminal activity (violations), then the cases were referred to the various district attorneys' offices for contemplation for prosecution.

Though some critics argued that the inspector general was ineffective—"neither diligent nor responsive"—Sofarelli defended his office. He pointed out that in 1986 and 1987, twenty-six Board of Education building inspectors were indicted for bribery after a long investigation by his office.[24]

The problem may have been that no one seemed to be looking at the "big picture"; various facets of the local school district operations were monitored, but no one was attempting to view the composite picture of local school board activity.

One telling criticism of the school boards had to do with insufficient parental involvement in school activities. The laws regulating decentralization had specified that local school boards should regularly consult with parent groups. In many cases, the parents were bypassed or simply ignored; most of the members of the school boards did not even have children in school. In one group studied, only 25 percent of the community school board members had children in the schools in the districts that they governed.[25] Thus, one of the intended counterbalances for the decentralized system had not become operational.

By the end of January 1989, just four months after the Barnwell incident, a Bronx grand jury returned indictments against four school board members and one superintendent from Community School District No. 9.[26]

More about the inner workings of other districts was soon revealed. District No. 21, which covers the area of South Brooklyn, had been found to have "often subordinated the educational interests of school children, particularly minority-group pupils, to a broad political agenda." Neil A. Lewis and Ralph Blumenthal reported in the *Times* that an inquiry into misconduct in District No. 21 produced these observations: (1) the wives of three board members, as well as the wife of the Brooklyn borough president, were among the highest paid employees in the district; (2) black and Hispanic schools in the district received a smaller portion of the resources of the district; (3) teachers of the district claimed to have been coerced into writing letters of support for a "hotly contested" $300 million housing complex in which the school board's president had an interest (i.e., he was vice-president of the company that wanted to build the project); (4) a District No. 21 school principal who had been indicted in 1986 on charges of grand larceny, falsification of business records, and tampering with a witness, all of which charges stemmed from an investigation of a summer camp program that he ran, was now said to be having fund-raising activities at his school for which there was no accounting; and (5) a school principal was also reported to have pressured teachers to spend their personal time gathering signatures for a nominating petition for an individual who was running for reelection to the board.

Members of the Community School Board No. 21 also held other public offices. For example, of the nine-member board, two were Democratic district leaders, one was a Republican district leader, and four members were also on Local Community Planning Boards. In addition, some members of the board were employees of the Board of Education. It was said that board members engaged in nepotism and job trading. A board member from another district was promoted to principal in 1984 in Community School District No. 21; during that year, a Community School District No. 21 board member was then promoted to principal in that other district. Thus, Lewis and Blumenthal observed that members of the District No. 21 board "formed an *interlocking power base* to secure jobs and promotions for relatives and friends and advance a major private development project" (emphasis added).[27]

Barnwell went to trial in Manhattan Criminal Court on Wednesday, 3 May 1989. He had been offered a plea-bargain agreement under which he would have been given a sentence of probation. Had he accepted the plea, he more than likely would have been discharged from employment with the Board of Education.

The jury in Barnwell's trial became deadlocked. His defense lawyer, Ronald Kuby, had argued that the police had fabricated the story of his buying cocaine. According to one juror, Steven Panitz, some jurors did not believe the police. After the jurors informed the judge on several occasions that they "were having irreconcilable differences" during a weekend of deliberations, he declared a mistrial and released the jurors. Barnwell was finally convicted nearly one and one-half years later in another trial and sentenced to three years' probation.[28]

The effect of the first mistrial in Barnwell's case was short-lived. Three days later, on 11 May 1989, Chancellor Green died suddenly of an asthma attack. This left the school system in a turbulent state as the system absorbed the shock of the loss and began a search for a new leader.[29]

The public's interest in the corruption scandal had begun to ebb. Investigations continued, but not much about them was reported in the news.

The Joint Commission on Integrity in the schools, otherwise known as the Gill Commission, had been in operation for several months without drawing much attention to the investigation of the corruption plaguing the Board of Education. Finally, on 7 June 1989, the results of its work were seen when a Brooklyn teacher was arrested for buying drugs by police officers assigned to the Gill Commission.

Gill explained that his investigators had initiated a surveillance of the teacher's activities after they had received information that he had been "nodding off" in class. Gill criticized the Board of Education, saying that its investigatory and disciplinary process had failed. He said this because this teacher's drug problem had been known to his superiors, who sent him to the medical department of the Board of Education on more than one occasion; he was once found to be unfit by the medical examiners and placed on leave. His supervisors were not informed of the reason for the leave ("because it was confidential"), and he was eventually returned to work.

The Gill Commission investigation of the drug-abusing teacher did not impinge on the corruption in the local school boards, but it did point to the lack of control that seemed to be characteristic of the Central Board.[30]

A salvo was soon fired against the Central Board by auditors from the Department of Education of New York State. These auditors examined a sample of complaints received during the 1987–88 school year and concluded that there was "no way to document the extent of the Board's inquiries into most of the allegations they sampled." The commissioner of education of New York State, Thomas Sobol, argued that the audit showed that "if the Board had a more effective system of investigation, many cases of corruption in school boards could have been 'deterred or discovered' " before the crisis emerged in 1988.

The audit report concluded that employees of the Board of Education were either unaware or unwilling to follow procedures in reporting malfeasance to the Central Board for investigation.[31]

During the summer of 1989, Jean O. Lee, member of Community School Board No. 9, pleaded guilty to a count of petit larceny, a misdemeanor. The new district attorney for the Bronx, Robert T. Johnson, said that Lee had been charged because she had used Board of Education paper, ink, and presses to print materials for her election campaign. Robert Geiger, a political consultant, was also convicted of petit larceny for having assisted Lee in printing the campaign literature. Lee and Geiger were sentenced to probation for three years, and they were required to each pay $1,000 restitution. Lee resigned from the board immediately after her conviction.[32] Though the conviction of Lee was not a watershed in the investigation of the political corruption scandal afflicting the school system, it was a vindication of the efforts of corruption investigators.

On the heels of the Lee conviction, prosecutor Johnson announced that he had filed other charges against three other members of Community School District No. 9. Two of these board members had been previously indicted on felony charges about six months earlier; they were now awaiting trial on the first charges. The new indictments against the three included charges of grand larceny and official misconduct and specified "instances of fraud, theft of property, and the misuse of equipment and employees on the city's payroll during working hours."[33]

Eventually, Curtis Johnson and Jerome Greene, District No. 9 board members, would be convicted. Johnson pleaded guilty to grand larceny, defrauding the government, receiving bribes, and official misconduct. He had collected more than $18,000 in kickbacks from vendors. He was sentenced to six months in jail and four and one-half years' probation.[34] Later, Greene also pleaded guilty to larceny charges. He admitted that "he had used his position to have the city pay for cameras, television equipment, and other merchandise that he had ordered for his personal use." Within slightly more than one year of the original charges surfacing in District No. 9, nine persons from that district, including Greene, were convicted of crimes that included "the signing of phony invoices, bribery, and defrauding the government."[35]

The next major event in the unfolding of the corruption scandal occurred in October 1989. A Queens school superintendent became a cooperating witness for the Gill Commission and agreed to secretly tape-record conversations with school board members. The superintendent, Coleman Genn, then testified before the Gill Commission that "dozens of unnecessary jobs in his district were awarded to friends and supporters of these board members at an annual cost of about $1 million."

Genn had been the superintendent of his district, Community School District No. 17, since July 1987. The district serves approximately 29,000 students from areas of Queens that border Kennedy Airport. The annual budget for the district was $96 million. Genn, angered by some of the community school board members' actions, which he believed would usurp his authority, decided to approach the Gill Commission. This was the first time that someone in a key position who also had direct knowledge of the patronage system was willing to publicly discuss it.

The Gill Commission learned that Superintendent Genn felt obliged to defer to the wishes of the board members about hiring decisions; otherwise, his job would be in jeopardy. He told the commission that, during a business trip to California, he was pressured one evening during dinner by four of the school board members. They told him that if he "would be a good boy and allow them to take charge of appointments and personnel issues, I [Genn] would have a nice long career as a superintendent." Among the board members present at that dinner were a former Republican district leader of the twenty-third Assembly District and the vice-president of the school board. The result of the patronage system in the district was that there were more than forty-five professionals and school aides who "don't have a *real assignment* and are costing the taxpayers $80,000 a month" (emphasis added).

During one of Genn's recorded conversations with James C. Sullivan, he (Genn) was told that eleven jobs had to be filled "if Mr. Genn wanted a one-year extension of his contract." In another conversation with Sullivan, Genn was asked to arrange for an office job paying $42,000 per year for William Sampol, a Republican politician. Sampol, secretary of the Queens County Republican Committee, had not worked in education "except for a year in the early 1970's when he helped set up a drug prevention program." Sullivan wanted Sampol to be put in charge of a satellite school board office.

In a third recorded conversation, Sullivan and Genn discussed the school board's decision not to hire some black assistant principals. Genn supported the hiring of the blacks, whom Sullivan had opposed. As they talked, Sullivan said, "And a year from now, your contract is going to be up." He later asked, "O.K., do you understand what the considerations become then? And how the ante becomes a little higher under those new guidelines?" The conversation progressed, and Genn said, "I understand that I would not get another contract." To which Sullivan replied, "It's possible." The issue that they discussed was that Genn had supported the hiring of too many blacks; Sullivan explained that not hiring persons whom the board had selected would cost him his job.[36]

Action against the board members of District No. 27 was swift once Genn's testimony was publicly revealed. The school board was suspended, and indictments against two of the board members were announced on 1 December 1989. Sullivan and another school board member "were indicted on federal and state charges of illegally using their positions to try to force the District Superintendent to place their relatives, political cronies, and friends in school jobs."

In the federal indictments, Sullivan and the other board member were accused of extortion "for trying to force Mr. Genn to allow them to control the hiring of personnel in the district" and of mail fraud "because job applications and other papers connected with their activities were sent by mail." The threat used against Genn was that his contract would not be renewed, so he would therefore lose his job.

The New York State court indictments accused the two board members of "bribery, coercion, and conspiracy." The bribery charge was based on the allegation that Genn was offered an extension of his contract if he cooperated with the board members in their schemes.

Sullivan pleaded guilty at his federal arraignment, admitting that he had pressured Genn. He was allowed to plead guilty to one charge, mail fraud, following an agreement that he made with prosecutors. The maximum sentence for conviction of that one count of mail fraud was five years in prison and a fine of $250,000. Sullivan also pleaded guilty to the charge of coercion in New York Supreme Court in Queens. In accordance with the plea agreement, which was arranged by Queens district attorney John Santucci, all other charges were dropped, and it was agreed that "any jail term imposed by the state cannot exceed that given on the Federal Charge."

The other board member pleaded not guilty at both of his arraignments in federal and state courts. He was allowed to go free without bail. Conviction of the charges against him could bring stiff penalties. The maximum federal sentence was twenty-five years in prison and a fine of up to $250,000; in state court, he could be sentenced to fifteen years in prison.[37]

By the end of the first year after the corruption scandal had broken at the Board of Education, seven board members from around the city were under indictment. The investigations continued, and more indictments followed. Though only a fraction of the actual cases of wrongdoing could actually be prosecuted, there was no doubt that many of the community school boards were deeply immersed in corruption.

The most common types of crimes in which school board members engaged were theft, fraud, extortion, and bribe receiving. They were accused of stealing Board of Education property such as furniture and computers, submitting fraudulent vouchers for reimbursement, and soliciting bribes from vendors. Charges of extortion against school board members were based on their ability to threaten Board of Education employees with losing their jobs if they did not comply with the wishes of the board members.

School board members were also accused of soliciting payments from school employees in exchange for promotions. These payments might range between $5,000 and $10,000; one method of payment might be to contribute to the sponsoring board member's election campaign fund. For those who sought lower-level jobs, the requirements would be to serve in the board member's reelection campaign. The job seeker might be asked to collect voters' signatures on a nominating petition or even commit fraud by falsely signing voters' names.

COMMUNITY SCHOOL BOARD CORRUPTION—IS IT ORGANIZED CRIME?

The term *organized crime* has evolved in its meaning so that, to most persons, it represents a very specific type of criminal activity—usually that of Italian American crime families or LCN. However useful the LCN model has been, it has created a certain myopia, blinding us to other forms of organized criminal activity. As Robert J. Kelly has noted, "As a self-fulfilling prophecy, it [i.e., Cressey's LCN model] could function as a mechanism whereby researchers and criminal justice practitioners selectively attend to information and discard that which does not fit the LCN matrix."[38]

Mark H. Haller has suggested that when the "lens of criminal enterprise" is used to analyze the activities of racketeers, "we find that it is held together—or divided—by economic ties . . . and various informal systems of cooperation and competition emerge as crucial factors that structure criminal enterprise."[39]

Thus, one should look beyond the traditional "Mafia" or "LCN" image when attempting to identify occurrences of organized crime.

In examining the activities of the community school board members, can one properly assert that their illegal activities should be labeled organized crime? In the terms of the LCN model, it would obviously require a procrustean effort to do so; the corrupt activities of the school board members were much different from those of the "Mafia." Nevertheless, as one explores the illicit actions of the community school board members from other perspectives, it is certainly reasonable to propose that it represents a different "species" of organized crime—or a "Mafia."

School board members, using the inherent advantage of the structure of the school board system, conspired to commit theft, fraud, and bribe receiving. As David J. Bellis has noted when describing political corruption in "machine-run cities," "Corruption among local elected officials and their subordinate administrative employees is *sui generis*; they conspire among themselves, perhaps in collusion with powerful private interests, to break the law." He concludes that this activity of elected officials is organized crime "because in many cases there is actual conspiracy to engage in criminal acts, and it is highly organized, though such conspiracies are extremely difficult to prove."[40]

One method of adducing a generic and objective definition of organized criminal activity would be to refer to the Organized Crime Control Act, which is part of the United States Code (USC). Among the predicate acts listed in section 1961 of Title 18 of the USC that constitute "racketeering activity," one finds extortion, dealing in narcotics, bribery, embezzlement, fraud, and theft. During the emergence of the school system's corruption scandal, it became apparent that some school board members were banding together to extort money or compliance with their wishes, receive bribes, embezzle, steal, and commit fraud. Much of their criminality was similar to that proscribed by the Organized Crime Control Act.[41]

Though the crimes of the school board members were primarily "white-collar" offenses, one could still find patterns of racketeering; in fact, these patterns were essential to the continuing nature of the school board members' activities. Edwin H. Sutherland observed that "white collar crimes are not only deliberate; they are organized. Organization may be formal or informal." He concluded that formal organization was evidenced in such things as gentleman's agreements, practices of trade associations, and cartels. The informal organization for criminality was manifested in the occurrence of a "consensus among businessmen."[42]

School board members joined together to create systems of patronage. They ensured that their base of power would be firmly supported by those for whom they found jobs. In such difficult economic times, the ability to employ someone is a powerful motivational tool. Those who were the beneficiaries of patronage could be counted upon to help get votes or take part in other schemes that board members designed. These schemes ranged, theoretically speaking, from theft of equipment, to bribes, kickbacks, fraud, and extortion.

The power of the local board members was reflected in a remark by special prosecutor Roger Adler who said, "There are inbred loyalties to the system . . . the prosecutor comes and goes . . . the forces on the school boards stay."[43] Speaking about the same issue, a criminal investigator who had probed school board corruption commented that she was "surprised how they covered for each other and lied to protect each other."[44]

White-collar criminals do appear to observe an informal "code of silence." Similar observations were made by law enforcement officials who investigated insider trading on Wall Street. One federal prosecutor of securities fraud, Bruce Baird, was said to have been "immediately struck by the similarities between insider trading investigations and Mafia cases he'd worked on." He noticed that, in a fashion similar to "organized crime, the Wall Street suspects prized silence and loyalty over any duty to tell the truth and root out corruption."[45]

One might ask, How did it come to be that community school boards became the focal point for organized criminality? First, the opportunity was created by the vacuum that occurred with the exodus of the earliest, concerned school board members during the 1970s. Second, this is one of the places "where the money was" in poor neighborhoods—the budgets of the various school districts were enormous. The local school board members were involved in decisions that controlled the spending of approximately $100 million each year for a district. Third, community school boards were not tightly controlled by the Central Board of Education. Regardless of how outrageous the choices or actions of the board members, frequently no Central Board administrators had done anything to stop them. Thus, there existed an opportunity and a structure for individuals to utilize in fostering their corrupt activities. The bureaucratic structure of the school board enabled criminally disposed individuals to form conspiracies to take illicit advantage of the inherent power of their positions.

Other reasons relate to the attitudes toward white-collar crime and the victimization of bureaucracies. School board members who broke the law did not see themselves as criminals; their constituents seemed rather tolerant or indifferent to their activity. For example, some incumbent board members who had served on two scandal-ridden boards in the Bronx in 1988 were reelected when they ran again. When speaking about businessmen who were criminals, Sutherland touched upon this point: "White collar criminals do not conceive of themselves as conforming to the stereotype of 'criminal' . . . the public, likewise, does not think of the businessman as a criminal; that is, the businessman does not fit the stereotype of criminal."[46] Though some school board members did engage in criminal activity, one could easily imagine how they might justify it to themselves. In the case of kickbacks, for example, they might feel that they deserved to get "something on the side" because they had served on the board without pay. The attitude that a bureaucracy is a "fair" target may be another reason the corruption occurred among school board members. Pillaging a bureaucracy appeals to a kind of "Robin Hood" attitude that is not uncommon. Erwin O. Smigel and H. Laurence Ross have argued that the "size, wealth, and impersonality of big business and governments are attributes which make it seem excusable, according to many people, to steal from these victims." They also suggest that the crimes against bureaucracy tend to be "low visibility" and, thus, in conjunction with general antipathy toward bureaucracies, lead "to a failure of the public to stigmatize the perpetrators of these crimes."

Another consideration when discussing the occurrence of political corruption, or white-collar crime in general, as a species of organized crime, is that it is extremely difficult to detect. One explanation for this is that "the more blatant forms of crimes against bureaucracy may be difficult to discover because they may be completely or partially legitimized by the subgroup."[47] Further, even when these crimes are discovered, there is a tendency not to prosecute them.

Thus, one might make a case that school board members were drawn to commit crimes against the bureaucracy of the school system because of an implicit support of their activities by their peers. Then, because chances of corrupt individuals being caught are so slim, hardly any external deterrent might counterbalance peer acceptance of their illicit endeavors. Further, if one were caught, the likelihood of facing prosecution was minimal; if prosecuted and convicted, penalties were usually not severe. The upshot is that, given such a hospitable substrate for the genesis of criminal activity, it is not difficult to visualize how corruption became rampant within the decentralized school board system. Finally, the structure and inherent power of the school boards provided an incipient infrastructure for organized criminal activity.

CONCLUSION

This chapter explored the development of the corruption scandal that tore the New York City school system in 1988. It is argued that the corruption found among various school boards was actually a form of organized crime, though obviously not in the traditional and popular understanding of it. Members of the school boards coalesced into conspiracies, sometimes across district lines, and engaged in patronage, extortion, bribery, theft, and fraud. Though not violent, the crimes committed by those who were publicly accused caused untold personal suffering for Board of Education employees and students, as well as great financial loss for the school system in general.

One may wonder how this extensive corruption developed within the school boards. The answer may lie in a story once told by Lincoln Steffens, the early twentieth-century journalist, who often described urban corruption. An Episcopal bishop at a meeting in Seattle once, when touching upon the issue of explaining corruption, rhetorically stated, "What we want to know is who founded the system, who started it, not only in San Francisco and Los Angeles . . . but way back, in the beginning." Most people said it was Adam who was at fault; but then, Adam blamed Eve, who in turn, accused the Serpent. In actuality,

Steffens thought that the blame lay otherwise. He said, "Now I come and I'm trying to show you that it was, it is, the apple."[48]

NOTES

1. The corruption scandal involving Donald R. Manes, deceased ex-borough president of Queens, and Stanley Friedman, former Bronx Democratic leader, is described in Michael Oreskes, "A Yearlong Look at Government's Underside," *New York Times*, 4 January 1987, Sec. 4:6. Bess Myerson, former commissioner, is described in *Facts on File Yearbook 1988*, 3 June 1988, 408.

2. David Rogers, "Community Control and Decentralization," in *Urban Politics, New York Style*, ed. J. Bellush and D. Netzer (Armonk, NY: M. E. Sharpe, 1990), 147.

3. Leonard Buder, "Decentralization of Schools Provides Painful Lessons," *New York Times*, 11 December 1988, Sec. E8.

4. Joseph P. Viteritti, *Across the River, Politics and Education in the City* (New York: New York University Press, 1983), 216–17.

5. Ibid., 10.

6. David Rogers and Norman Chung, *110 Livingston Street Revisited* (New York: New York University Press, 1983), 216–17.

7. Neil A. Lewis, *New York Times*, 10 November 1988, B1.

8. Neil A. Lewis, "Arrest of Principal Rekindles a Debate Over School Tenure," *New York Times*, 12 November 1988, B1.

9. James A. Barron, "Arrest of a Principal Prompts Bronx District Inquiry," *New York Times*, 15 November 1988: B4.

10. Sam Howe Verhovek, "Bronx School Board Members Investigated," *New York Times*, 23 November 1988, B1-2.

11. Neil A. Lewis, "Green Suspends the School Board in Bronx District," *New York Times*, 24 November 1988, A1, B4.

12. Information about school board corruption complaints is from Neil A. Lewis, "Complaints About School Boards Pour In," *New York Times*, 1 December 1988, B1, B14.

13. Quotation and information are from Neil A. Lewis, "School Officials Being Ousted over Funds," *New York Times*, 8 December 1988, B1, B13.

14. "Accused Schools Chief Says He's a Victim of Investigation," *New York Times*, 10 December 1988, 30.

15. Neil A. Lewis, "School Boards Found Failing to Meet Goals," *New York Times*, 5 December 1988, B1, B6.

16. Neil A. Lewis, "Koch Urges Cuomo to Name Panel to Investigate School Corruption," *New York Times*, 15 December 1988, A1, B18.

17. Richard Levine, "Cuomo Denies Koch's Request for School Inquiry," *New York Times*, 16 December 1988, B4.

18. Quotation and information about District No. 12 are from Ralph Blumenthal and Sam Howe Verhovek, "Patronage and Profit in Schools: A Tale of a Bronx District Board," *New York Times*, 10 December 1988, A1, B4.

19. All quotations and information about District No. 32 are from Roger Bennet Adler, "An Inquiry into the Detrimental Effects of Politics on the Education of Our Children," *Report of the Term 4, 1990 Extended Kings County Grand Jury* (n.d.) 7-17.

20. Ralph Blumenthal and Anthony Levine, *New York Times*, 8 June 1989, A1, B3, B4.

21. "11 of 32 Boards Under Investigation," *New York Times*, 17 December 1988, 30.

22. Philip S. Gutis, "Bronx Schools Inquiry Influenced Vote in Albany," *New York Times*, 18 December 1988, 59.

23. Quotations and information about Gill Commission are from Todd S. Purdum, "Koch Panel with Broad Powers to Investigate 32 School Boards," *New York Times*, 23 December 1988, A1, B3.

24. Leonard Buder, "New York School Board Faulted for the Disarray of Local Districts," *New York Times*, 7 January 1989, Sec. 1:30.

25. Sarah Lyall, "In New York, Parents Lack Say in Schools," *New York Times*, 16 January 1988, A1, B2.

26. Sarah Lyall, "5 in Bronx Indicted in First Cases in Inquiry on City's School Boards," *New York Times*, 27 January 1989, A1, B3.

27. Quotations and information about Community School District No. 21 are from Neil A. Lewis and Ralph Blumenthal, "Powerbase vs. Schools in Brooklyn District," *New York Times*, 10 February 1989, A1, B4.

28. Ronald Sullivan, "Drug Trial Starts for a Principal from the Bronx," *New York Times*, 4 May 1989, B5; and "Jury Deadlock Brings Mistrial in Principal's Case," *New York Times*, 8 May 1989, B1, B5.

29. Neil A. Lewis, "Schools Chancellor Green Is Dead; New York School System Faces Disarray," *New York Times*, 11 May 1989, A1, B4.

30. Information and quotations are from Leonard Buder, "Brooklyn Teacher Arrested on Drug Charges in Inquiry," *New York Times*, 8 June 1989, B3.

31. Sam Howe Verhovek, "School Pursuit of Corruption Is Put in Doubt," *New York Times*, 16 June 1989, B1.

32. Neil A. Lewis, "Bronx School Board Member Pleads Guilty to Theft Count," *New York Times*, 12 July 1989, B3.

33. "Two School Leaders Face New Charges," *New York Times*, 22 July 1989, 30.

34. Joseph Berger, "School Graft: One Man's Abuse of Power," *New York Times*, 10 February 1990, A1, B3.

35. John T. McQuiston, "A Guilty Plea Ends Bronx Prosecution of School Officials," *New York Times*, 12 February 1991, B3.

36. Quotations and information about Coleman Genn are from Joseph Berger, "School Superintendent in Queens Tells of Costly Patronage Scheme," *New York Times*, 24 October 1989, A1, B4.

37. Quotations and information about James C. Sullivan and Samuel Granirer are from Leonard Buder, "Two on Board Face Charges About Hiring," *New York Times*, 2 December 1989, 29.

38. Robert J. Kelly, "Trapped in the Folds of Discourse: Theorizing About the Underworld," *Journal of Contemporary Criminal Justice* 3.1 (1992): 23.

39. Mark H. Haller, "Bureaucracy and the Mafia: An Alternative View," *Journal of Contemporary Criminal Justice* 8.1 (1992): 7.

40. David J. Bellis, "Political Corruption in Small, Machine-Run Cities," in *The Politics and Economics of Organized Crime*, ed. H. E. Alexander and G. E. Caiden (Lexington, MA: Lexington Books, 1985), 102.

41. *Federal Criminal Codes and Rules* (St. Paul, MN: West, 1990), 643–44.

42. Edwin H. Sutherland, *White Collar Crime* (New Haven, CT: Yale University Press, 1983), 231–32.

43. Roger Bennet Adler, personal interview, 30 June 1992.

44. Elsy Farfan-Rocco, personal interview, 2 July 1992.

45. James B. Stewart, *Den of Thieves* (New York: Simon and Schuster, 1991), 346.

46. Sutherland, *White Collar Crime*, 231–32.

47. Erwin O. Smigel and H. Laurence Ross, *Crimes Against Bureaucracy* (New York: Van Nostrand Reinhold, 1970), 5–7.

48. Lincoln Steffens, "Los Angeles and the Apple," in *Theft of the City*, ed. John A. Gardiner and David Olson (Bloomington: Indiana University Press, 1974), 287.

12

Organized Crime and Commercial Sex

CHARLES WINICK

This chapter deals with the role of organized crime in commercial sex, which includes prostitution and production and distribution of sex-oriented media. Both activities have been regarded as offensive and been subject to criminal prohibition, as well as controls such as regulation in terms of geographical restrictions and minimum age of consumers.[1]

In some communities, like the Tenderloin District of San Francisco, the same geographic area is the site for both prostitution and sex-oriented bookstores and movies. In other jurisdictions, there have been efforts to use the prostitution laws to prosecute actors who are photographed engaging in sexual activity for movies and videotapes on the grounds that they are being paid to have sex. In recent years, the injunction and abatement laws of the early twentieth century that permitted a citizen or prosecutor to seek an injunction against a brothel as a public nuisance have been used against premises where sexually explicit films were being made.

PROSTITUTION

During the first several decades of the twentieth century, prostitution was a substantial source for organized crime profits, because it provided an illegal service for which there was a continuing demand. The United States was one of the few countries where prostitution was illegal and the only country where the customer, in some states, could be tried for a criminal offense.

Organized crime has had a range of relationships to prostitution in the United States, reflecting the circumstances, formats, and degree of acceptance and law enforcement enjoyed by prostitution at different epochs. Prostitution can be defined as the granting of nonmarital sexual access for remuneration that provides all or part of the prostitute's livelihood. We can examine the changing relationships of prostitution to organized crime in terms of the white slave traffic, the brothel, prostitution in Nevada, and recent trends.

The White Slave Traffic

The activities of criminal organizations in prostitution have long been tied to the white slave traffic, or the transport of children and women for immoral purposes from one country to another or from one part of the United States to another. From the turn of the century until the strict 1924 immigration laws made the importation of children and women by procurers in this country less financially rewarding, a number of criminal rings regularly brought in young women for purposes of prostitution, usually via misrepresentation, false promises of marriage, and other forms of deceit, drugs, and violence. Such a traffic required a complex level of organization, arrangements, financing, and marketing.

National interest in white slavery surged in 1909, when George Kibbe Turner published a widely discussed article on "The Daughters of the Poor" in *McClure*'s, the muckraking magazine.[2] He argued that a number of Jewish men were organized in what was ostensibly a burial society (the Independent Benevolent Association) but actually a cover for an organization to procure, manage, and move prostitutes from one country and location to another. Turner claimed that the New York Democratic organization, Tammany Hall, protected the prostitution racket.

The Turner article had numerous consequences, one of which was the impaneling of a special grand jury chaired by billionaire John D. Rockefeller, Jr.[3] The grand jury, which handed down fifty-four indictments, could not confirm the existence of one central organized ring but found that there were several syndicates exploiting women. In 1911, when Rockefeller established the Bureau of Social Hygiene as a voluntary agency to study prostitution, one of its first activities was the support of George J. Kneeland's study of prostitution in New York City.[4] Kneeland reported that a typical syndicate of thirty-eight men owned thirty brothels. The men bought and sold shares in the business among themselves and controlled all the activities of the brothels. Other syndicates controlled other brothels.

From 1910 to 1914, Stanley Finch, head of the Bureau of Investigation, later called the Federal Bureau of Investigation (FBI), led the crusade against the white slave traffic. The bureau enforced the 1920 Mann Act, which prohibited interstate transport of women for immoral purposes. Among the celebrities arrested for violation of the act, with much attendant publicity, were the black boxing champion Jack Johnson and the architect Frank Lloyd Wright. Chief

Finch told Congress that "no one could tell when his daughter or his wife or his mother would be selected as a victim."[5]

The FBI has periodically continued to direct its attention to white slave matters. In the 1930s, director J. Edgar Hoover implemented major initiatives directed at the traffic in women and children. The FBI won 296 Mann Act convictions in 1936, 523 in 1937, and 595 in 1938. Hoover personally led vice raids in Baltimore and Atlantic City in 1936.[6]

The white slave traffic, which has always involved significant proportions of non-Caucasian women and children, attracted more international attention as it became less politically salient in this country. The League of Nations in 1934, the United Nations in 1949, and Interpol in 1965 proposed international agreements to outlaw the traffic in women and children. The United States, which has long had the world's most restrictive laws against prostitution, has not signed any of these agreements, presumably because of their interference with states' rights. In recent decades, prosecutions have been scarce in this country under either the Mann Act or the Bennet Act, which prohibits importing women from other countries for immoral purposes.

In the late 1970s, there was a revival of interest in the worldwide white slave traffic. A 1979 book by Kathleen Barry reformulated the problem as an example of the larger issue of female sexual slavery.[7] A few years earlier, there was national interest in the Minnesota Connection, said to be a highly organized syndicate of New York procurers and pimps recruiting some 400 young women annually from small farm towns throughout the upper Midwest.[8] The women, said to be blue-eyed and blonde, supposedly worked in the Times Square area on a section of Eighth Avenue that was called the Minnesota Strip. According to one of the two Minneapolis officials in charge of the investigation, the women had become eager to abandon their lives of enforced prostitution.

In trips to New York in November and December 1977, the officers were unable to find even one juvenile Minnesota prostitute. Early in 1978, one officer was removed from the investigation. The other officer concluded that there was no organized traffic in young women, became a born-again Christian minister, and the widely publicized crusade was abandoned. The heavy publicity surrounding the Minnesota Connection helped to revive the notion of teams of pimps and organized crime representatives recruiting prostitutes to order. However, the crusade's failure and the difficulty of confirming the existence of national or international trafficking in girls and women have led, up to recently, to a loss of follow-up on the part of United States government and international agencies.

Since the 1970s, first Korean, and more recently, Chinese criminal groups have been importing their countrywomen into the United States to work as prostitutes in massage parlors, modeling studios, hair salons, and other settings. The women service both the large numbers of male Asian immigrants as well as other American men. Taiwanese women are also imported to work as prostitutes, arriving either in Houston to go on a seven-state circuit of massage parlors or in Chicago to travel on a six-state circuit. The women stay in each city for a few weeks before being rotated to the next site.[9]

More recently, young Chinese women have been illegally brought into the United States by organized gangs of Chinese smugglers who charge them approximately $30,000 to get into this country. The women work in massage parlors and other settings here in order to pay off the money for their passage. Chinatown in New York City has more than twenty houses of prostitution that are staffed by such illegal immigrants.[10]

A separate network of houses, in a number of cities, is still run by Koreans. South Korean entrepreneurs typically pay up to $5,000 to American soldiers to marry Korean women and return with their new wives to Texas, where the soldiers divorce the women for an equal sum. The women, who do not speak English, are placed in massage parlors and brothels in Houston, Detroit, and other cities in order to pay back the marriage and transportation fees.

For decades, American women have been attracted to Japan for work as fashion models, dancers, or singers, from various West Coast cities. When they arrive, many find that they have no contractual protection and are coerced into prostitution. The books of photographs that they had expected to go to theatrical producers, fashion organizations, and catalogs are used to get bookings at brothels for the women.

The breakup of the Soviet bloc, dislocations of population because of ethnic wars, and the international development of what Pope John Paul called in 1992 "the degrading practice of sex tourism" have combined to produce a worldwide expansion of the traffic in women and children in recent years. Since the American Social Health Association (formerly the American Social Hygiene Association) terminated its systematic reports on prostitution in the 1970s, there has been no monitoring of this traffic. As a result, sensationalistic journalistic reports—for example, that 30 million women have been sold for prostitution worldwide in the last twenty years—represent the major sources of information on the traffic.[11] One thorough journalistic report by an English investigator gives convincing details of the international slave trade and the efforts of some American police and other agencies to combat it.[12] But without the backing of the United Nations or the power to subpoena witnesses, confirmation of such reports is very difficult. Emerging social problems such as acquired immunodeficiency syndrome (AIDS) and homelessness are more likely to get support than programs against prostitution.

The Brothel

The brothel, which is a house or apartment where a number of women are available for customers and which is typically managed by a madam, is the prostitution format that has been of greatest interest to organized crime. The availability of a choice of women attracts customers, and the madam's collection of the house's income facilitates the pickup of money by a syndicate overseer and payoffs to police authorities. In many brothels prior to World War II, the women lived and worked on the premises. Since then, most women live elsewhere and report to the brothel only to work. The brothel, which used to occupy a house and was called a parlor house or resort before World War II, is more likely to be an apartment in recent decades.

From the turn of the century until 1917, every sizable American city had a red-light district with brothels.[13] The bigger cities had several such districts. At around the same time, many nationally important political and civic figures such as Theodore Roosevelt, Jane Addams, Emma Goldman, Abraham Flexner, and Raymond Fosdick spoke and wrote about the negative consequences of prostitution, which was so centrally important at the time that it was called "the social evil" or "the master problem."[14] Edwin R. A. Seligman, the noted economist who later became the editor of the *Encyclopedia of Social Sciences,* called his 1902 book on prostitution *The Social Evil.*[15]

The antiprostitution movement got a firm institutional base with the formation of the American Social Hygiene Association (ASHA) in 1913. President Charles W. Eliot of Harvard, former president Herbert Hoover, and philanthropist John D. Rockefeller, Jr., were among the prominent Americans associated with ASHA. Between 1911 and 1916, twenty-seven cities launched major investigations of what was sometimes called "commercialized vice." Thus, during the Progressive Era, from 1900 to 1918, organized brothel prostitution was both very profitable and illegal, highly visible, and the subject of a major but unsuccessful campaign to eliminate it. Vast sums of money were being earned by prostitutes, although most of it went to procurers, managers and other profiteers, such as pimps, landlords, police, politicians, saloon keepers, madams, and other intermediaries. In large cities, brothel prostitution became even more rationalized and commercialized.[16]

When Earl Warren, later to become governor of California and chief justice of the United States Supreme Court, was elected district attorney of Alameda County, California, in 1926, he tried to shut down Caddy Wells's Parlor House, across the street from his office. He also used the Red Light Abatement Act to attempt to eliminate a whole block of brothels that was a short distance away. There were serious complaints about Warren, not from the syndicate madams but from bankers, real estate interests, retailers, and other influential people who wanted the brothels to remain open. Warren later cited this experience as an example of the entrenched nature of the brothel organization in America.[17]

In large cities, beginning in the Progressive Era and becoming more developed by the late 1920s, the organized criminal groups profiting from prostitution generally were not involved in its daily operations. They made money by blackmail and protection, knowing that a madam was hardly likely to complain to police about an extortion attempt. Another source of revenue was charging a regular fee for legal and bail bonding representation, whether or not it was needed. In many cities, a network of bookers or "bookies" controlled a large number of prostitutes by moving them from house to house on a regular, often weekly basis.[18] "Fresh faces" were important to customers.

The entrance of the United States into World War I led to a major patriotic, national crusade to close the brothels, and every important red-light district in the country was eliminated by the end of 1917. Religious and moral leaders were very concerned about what young soldiers might do in training camps that were far removed from the restraints of hearth and home and where they might feel peer pressure to assert their masculinity. A program of "wholesome" educational and social activities was established by Raymond Fosdick and was the model for the United Service Organizations (USO) and similar programs in every subsequent war through Vietnam.[19]

When the American troops arrived in Europe in 1917, the field commanders, as in every war, imposed few restrictions on troops who could be facing death on the battlefield. Many American soldiers in France frequented brothels that were under the tacit protection of the military authorities, and they returned to the United States with an interest in prostitution.

By the early 1920s, the patriotic antiprostitution momentum had slowed in the United States and the brothels had reopened. The situation reported by Robert S. Lynd and Helen M. Lynd in Middletown, a small Indiana city, in the 1920s was typical: there were more than fifty brothels, and one of the largest was on a square opposite the courthouse.[20] In Middletown as in other cities, a well-developed organization was needed to maintain such a visible and large-scale illegal activity.

When the World War II 1941 May Act made prostitution near a military installation a federal offense and thus subject to FBI investigation, the brothels again closed relatively quickly. The FBI, by the early 1940s, was enjoying enormous visibility and public support. The heavily publicized bureau victories of the 1930s, involving gangsters like John Dillinger, "Machine Gun" Kelly, and "Baby Face" Nelson, and the image of Hoover as the powerful head of a national police force affected the prostitution underworld as well as the public.

Wishing to cooperate with the FBI and the war effort, local governments generally implemented antiprostitution programs. The May Act was continued as a permanent peacetime law in 1946, but it has not been invoked since then. Just as after World War I, the brothels reopened after World War II. But the postwar revival of brothel prostitution that began in 1946 ended soon after the United States entered the Korean War in 1950 and communities were again eager to help the war effort by minimizing prostitution. Because of changing patterns of law enforcement, population redistribution, the rise of the suburbs, and community attitudes, the brothel, with its protection apparatus, never recovered its former prominence in prostitution.

Brothels in New York City

The brothels in New York City in the 1920s and 1930s were typical of those in other large cities and attracted major prosecution attention and subsequent interest from scholars and journalists, because of the prominence of Charles "Lucky" Luciano in organized crime.

Organized prostitution in New York City had been largely dominated by Jewish procurers and madams since the early twentieth century. A widely accepted synonym for procurer was *kaftan*, which was a Yiddish word for the large coats worn by European Jewish procurers. When Prohibition ended in 1932, Luciano is believed to have proposed that the various syndicate groups cooperate in a new reassignment of rackets, with prostitution as his responsibility. He indicated that he would be taking over from the Jewish groups that had largely run prostitution. Luciano, who had become chief of the Unione Siciliana after Al Capone went to prison in 1932, was also a key figure in narcotics, betting parlors, numbers, and a lottery in New York. He lived quietly under an assumed name ("Mr. Ross") in a luxury hotel and kept himself out of the public eye but used threats, intimidation, and violence, as needed.

The syndicate representatives who ran prostitution after 1932 consisted of one Jew and three Italian Americans who reported to Luciano's deputy, Davey Petillo. Luciano seems to have authorized his name to be used but avoided involvement in daily operations. The "combination" paid off the police, who regularly provided advance information about forthcoming raids of brothels. Each house paid a minimum of ten dollars per prostitute and fifteen dollars per madam per week.[21] There was a separate charge for regularly moving the women from house to house. The madams and prostitutes did not know that Luciano was the key figure in the whole enterprise and the ultimate recipient of the largest share of its income.

The houses that refused to cooperate might be demolished, women working in them could be beaten, and pets on the premises could be killed. Most houses agreed to participate with the syndicate after such expressions of racketeer power. The efficiency of the syndicate could be seen in 1935, when over 3,000 women were arrested for prostitution in New York City. Only 175 of the "combination" (the syndicate) women were arrested, and none served any jail time.[22]

Luciano was tried for promoting compulsory prostitution in 1936. Of prosecutor Thomas E. Dewey's sixty-eight witnesses, most were prostitutes and madams. Luciano, testifying in his own defense, denied all the charges but was found guilty and received a sentence of thirty to fifty years. After the trial, three of the key prosecution witnesses recanted their testimony, but Luciano's request for a new trial was denied.

Luciano, who was the first major organized crime figure to serve a prison sentence for promoting prostitution, always maintained that he had been framed by prosecutor Dewey. Nine years later, then governor Dewey commuted Luciano's sentence, presumably because his Mafia connections contributed to the

Allied invasion of Sicily in World War II. Frank Costello replaced Luciano as head of the strongest organized crime family in New York, but its role in prostitution declined somewhat after Luciano went to prison.

Other Communities

A very visible relationship between organized crime and prostitution also existed in Chicago during the 1920s and 1930s. The Chicago crime syndicate, headed by Capone, operated a large number of brothels extending as far west as Seattle. A prostitute would start in Chicago and work her way west, spending two weeks in each place. Capone also owned the Speedway Inn, the country's largest brothel, in the Chicago suburb of Burnham. Fifty women were on duty for each of three shifts, charging two dollars to five dollars, depending on services offered. The customer would go through a turnstile and be assigned to a prostitute. Each woman's efficiency was evaluated regularly, and the less productive women were dismissed.[23]

Another syndicate in Los Angeles controlled that city's brothels during the 1930s. The syndicate paid the vice squad off for every brothel. Any new brothel entrepreneur would have to pay a proportion of profits to the syndicate, or it would receive regular police raids.

In some communities through the 1940s and 1950s, the underworld leaders who ran gambling also controlled brothel prostitution, as in Phenix City, Alabama; Galveston, Texas; Lexington, Kentucky; and Agua Caliente, California. These racketeers profited from the connections between sex and gambling that have been traditional for decades. Prostitutes have long gone to the site of major sports events, like horse races or football games, that feature gambling on the outcome, because men attending such events are good customers for prostitutes. Today, hardly any communities have an organization that controls both gambling and prostitution.

In the decades during which brothels predominated, there were cities in which the brothels were used as hideouts for organized crime figures. A criminal could disappear into the brothel and remain hidden for extended periods of time or move from one to another. Such cities were called "holy cities" by the underworld. Dillinger successfully hid in several brothels in St. Paul during the 1930s. The syndicates that dominated prostitution also protected the brothels from robbery and burglary on the part of other criminals.

Prostitution in Nevada

A special kind of prostitution organization exists in Las Vegas, Nevada, to provide women to the many gamblers who expect that such services will be available as part of the casino offerings.[24] Prostitution is illegal in the city and the county, but the hotel networks are not bothered by law enforcement because of a mutual understanding that has evolved. The "bell girls" or "hotel girls" are referred only to a client who has asked a bellman or bell captain for the service. The women wishing to work on each of the three shifts report their availability to the hotel bell desk. The captain calls the woman to the hotel and refers her to the room of the specific client, where she usually arrives within a few minutes. After her interaction with the guest is completed in his room, the woman will meet the bell representative and give him 40 percent of the fee, which has been traditional for intermediaries for decades. The three bell captains contribute their shares to a kitty that is divided among them at the day's end. If a bellman has contributed to the arrangement, he would get half the captain's share.[25]

This procedure minimizes the possibility of assault, robbery, arrest, public exposure, and venereal disease. The various participants cooperate through their mutual interests, and the police devote their attention to freelance prostitutes who are on the street or not cooperating with the hotel staff.

Las Vegas has approximately 3,000 prostitutes and 650 pimps.[26] Although the role of traditional crime families in the operation of the gambling casinos has been investigated over the years, such families do not seem to directly control the operation of hotel prostitution.

Organized crime also does not appear to have a role in the operation of the brothels that operate legally in fifteen of Nevada's seventeen counties. The leading investigator of the economics of prostitution has noted that if organized crime were involved in the brothels, they would be expanded and improved, receive more publicity, and be more profitable.[27]

Recent Trends in Prostitution

A number of recent trends in prostitution affect its relationship to organized crime. These trends include the geographical mobility of prostitutes, the relationship between prostitution and crime, and changes in organized crime itself.

Geographic Mobility of Prostitutes

In the 1950s, a New York City ring moved women among cities such as Pittsburgh, Cleveland, Chicago, Buffalo, Youngstown, and Fort Worth.[28] Another circuit, headquartered in New Iberia, Louisiana, covered eight southern states. Phenix City, Alabama, was the site of another confederation. These were not tightly controlled operations of a large crime ring but relatively loose affiliations created for the prostitution business. Cities were chosen on the basis of factors like convention dates, weather conditions, payday schedules at large employers, condition of the local economy, and degree of law enforcement. Often the women were moved on a regular schedule, as often as every week.

Individual prostitutes not under the control of a syndicate may also be mobile.[29] A study of Seattle streetwalkers found that over 60 percent of the women moved a minimum of 500 miles every three months, remaining at an address from a few days to several months.[30] Such a "road ho" or "circuit ho" may travel with a pimp and another prostitute, covering as many as ten cities, which on the West Coast may include San Diego, San Francisco, Seattle, and Portland.[31] Another route involves flying from Houston to Miami, working there for a few weeks, and then driving to Atlanta.[32] Where possible, the pimps purchase cocaine in Miami and sell it on their arrival in Atlanta, for an additional source of income.

Prostitution and Crime

It is widely believed by many Americans that prostitution in an area leads to an influx of other kinds of crime. In recent decades, a substantial proportion of urban prostitutes are regular users of illegal drugs, and their ability to work may involve some corruption of criminal justice agencies. There is no necessary connection, however, between traditional street crimes and prostitution, although prostitutes represent a despised group that has sometimes attracted certain kinds of violence. In the last few decades, serial killers have been especially likely to target prostitutes. The most recent such case is that of New York State gardener Joel Rifkin, who confessed in 1993 to killing seventeen prostitutes.[33] The country's lengthiest string of unsolved murders consists of the forty-nine prostitutes whose bodies were dumped along the Green River south of Seattle in the 1980s.

In different states, there have been both informal and formal actions taken by community residents who fear the violence and crime that they associate with massage parlors or street prostitutes and their pimps in the area. In recent years, many such citizen and official actions have been quite successful. A law enforcement task force in New York City's midtown area, for example, in 1991–92 padlocked twenty-six massage parlors, and lap dancing clubs that were used for prostitution were closed. Twenty-nine other premises for prostitution were sued for violation of the nuisance abatement law.[34]

Changes in Organized Crime

A number of field investigations have concluded that organized crime now has little or no role in the control of prostitution.[35] As far back as 1967, the President's Commission on Law Enforcement and the Administration of Justice concluded that prostitution played a small and declining role in organized crime's operations.[36]

The closest approximation to organized crime in prostitution today involves big-city pimps, who sometimes exchange information on degree of law enforcement in different venues.[37] In a particular city, pimps may agree to have their women work only in a specific territory or move the women around on geographical circuits, but this is loosely organized and does not compare to the rationalized structure of many syndicates in the 1930s and the late 1940s.

One reason that organized crime has little interest in prostitution today is that its income is low compared with extortion, selling illegal drugs, labor racketeering, hijacking, loan-sharking, and similar activities. Prostitution's market is segmented among many settings, such as streets, bars, lap and table dancing clubs, call houses, photo studios, physical culture establishments, dance studios, massage parlors, escort services, and apartments. Such a range of formats cannot easily be monitored by criminal entrepreneurs. Standby defense lawyers are less necessary when prostitution statutes are minimally enforced. Paying money for protection is unimportant when competing gangs are nonexistent and it is relatively difficult for police to take bribes.

Large-scale transfers of women from one location to another, on any regular basis, might be detected relatively easily today. Citizens now would be less likely to file a civil complaint and seek an injunction for abatement of prostitution as a public nuisance than they would be to telephone a local television station or themselves videotape any signs of prostitution activity.

Another reason for declining organized crime interest in prostitution after the 1930s was the decline in immigration to the United States, which not only cut down on the supply of women but also led to a sharp drop in the number of transient males in big cities. By 1933, only 23,068 immigrants came to America, compared with an average of 820,000 a year between 1900 and 1909. Now that legal immigration again approximates 800,000 annually, prostitution could attract the attention of organized crime in the future.

In recent years, organized crime has also found prostitution to be a poor investment because of difficulties in controlling the highly individualized customer-prostitute and pimp-prostitute relationships. Larger social trends have also operated to diminish the demand for prostitution, including decreasing segregation of the sexes, equalization of the sex ratio, the women's movement, more effective contraception and liberalized sex attitudes that have reduced the inhibitions to female sexual activity, the concept of crimes without victims, changing priorities in law enforcement, and declining pressures on poor women to enter prostitution.[38]

Prostitution and organized crime have changed, along with the larger society, in a way that makes their three-way interaction different from what it was in previous decades. Prostitution met a range of needs and fulfilled a number of functions that are much less salient today. These relationships are, however, subject to continual change.

ORGANIZED CRIME AND SEXUALLY EXPLICIT MATERIALS

Although organized crime groups have clearly profited from prostitution for generations, the relationship of such groups to the marketing of sexually explicit or oriented materials in the media is relatively recent and more ambiguous. Such materials are often inappropriately called ''adult,'' as if the only content worthy of such settings, such as coin-operated minimovies, peep shows in booths at sex shops, feature-length movies shown in specialized or general theaters, videotapes that can be rented or purchased, telephone services providing individual conversation or recorded messages, books, magazines, pay and cable television services, sex tabloids, photographs, audiotapes, mail order materials, and, most recently, computer networks and subscription services. The income from these activities cannot be fully documented, but unconfirmed and nondatabased estimates of over $10 billion annually have been made.[39]

Pornography, the term that is often used in this context, is difficult to define legally, although U.S. Supreme Court justice Potter Stewart's statement "I know it when I see it" has often been quoted (*Jacobellis v. Ohio*, 378 U.S. 184, 197 [1964]. The two American federal commissions that considered the subject rejected *pornography* as a term to describe their subject matter and used *obscenity* for explicit content that is not legally protected.[40] We refer in this discussion to sexually explicit or oriented materials, erotica, sex media, or the sex media industry.

Sexually oriented and explicit materials are produced for many purposes and media and are constitutionally protected by the First Amendment, unless they are found to meet the criteria for obscenity. The criteria are set forth in state and federal statutes that are interpreted by trial and appellate courts. Only a tiny proportion of explicit materials, regardless of who produces or distributes them, is ever adjudicated to be obscene. Presumably no major, mainstream media or organized crime functionary would have any interest in being indicted and tried for violation of the obscenity laws. Mainstream and other media, in recent decades, have carried so much explicit content that they have been the focus of two presidential commissions, national and local political campaigns, prosecution task forces, and innovative legal approaches and become a significant part of the continuing debate over sex roles. These larger considerations provide a necessary context for any consideration of the role of organized crime in producing, distributing, and profiting from these materials.

Expansion of the Market

A small and relatively outlaw market for "blue" movies, explicit magazines and comic books, and other sex-oriented media always existed and was supplied by nonmainstream sources. Sex shops, which sold such materials, could be found in marginal areas of a number of cities through the 1940s. But in the 1950s and 1960s, there was an unprecedented growth of interest in such content, resulting from a variety of social factors, including responses to war and disaster, the more open attitudes of young people, increases in Americans traveling abroad, the liberating content of rock music, growing American interest in optical lubricity and peeping, and the women's liberation movement. A 1977 article on these trends was called "From Deviant to Normative: Changes in the Social Acceptability of Sexually Explicit Material."[41]

Ever since the 1868 Hicklin Rule, in England, there had been legal restrictions on sexual content in the arts. The modern era of American acceptance of such materials emerged after a series of literary works was found to be not obscene in the courts in the 1950s and 1960s, and movies were found to be entitled to the protection of the First Amendment in 1952.[42] The Earl Warren Supreme

Court, in a series of path-breaking decisions (*U.S. v. Roth*, 1957; *Jacobellis v. Ohio*, 1964; *Memoirs v. Attorney General*, 1966; *Redrup v. New York*, 1967; and *Stanley v. Georgia*, 1969), made prosecution of explicit materials much more difficult. These decisions and the 1970 recommendation of President Lyndon Johnson's Commission on Obscenity and Pornography that obscenity laws affecting adults be repealed were interpreted by many media producers as encouragement to be more explicit.

In spite of the increased quantity and explicitness of sex-oriented movies and printed materials, there was a decline in prosecutions from 1966 to 1973 because of the impact of the liberal Warren Court decisions and the widespread expectation that the appointment of new conservative members to the Supreme Court could contribute to the formulation of a more conservative definition of obscenity. Explicit media producers perceived the prosecutorial hiatus as a window of opportunity.

The sharp drop in federal prosecution for obscenity from 1966 to 1973 also provided a spur to the sexual dimension of mainstream Hollywood movies. In 1970, the X-rated *Midnight Cowboy* won an Academy Award for Best Picture, and in 1973, X-rated *Last Tango in Paris*, starring the country's most celebrated actor, Marlon Brando, was the third most successful film at the box office. Major films with path-breaking sexual content by world-class film directors such as Michelangelo Antonioni's *Blow Up* (1967), Luchino Visconti's *The Damned* (1970), and Luis Buñuel's *Belle de Jour* (1967) were critical and box office triumphs in America.

Two low-budget explicit films made stars of previously unknown actresses and attracted enormous attention and box office revenue. *Deep Throat* (1971), starring Linda Lovelace, was the first humorous explicit film and grossed over $50 million, with only $25,000 in production costs. *Behind the Green Door* (1973), a variant of a locker room folktale starring a mute Marilyn Chambers, whose photograph had previously been on the package of Ivory Snow, was another great financial success that was also reviewed positively in major conventional media.

Such films and the associated expansion of sex content in other media attracted many millions of new customers for explicit materials. As a result, when chief justice Warren Burger's Supreme Court, with its new conservative members Lewis F. Powell and William H. Rehnquist, handed down a more restrictive definition of obscenity (*Miller v. California*, 1973), the decision did not stimulate either more prosecutions or more convictions.[43] Subsequent survey data indicate a strong inclination on the part of American adults to have tolerant and accepting attitudes toward such materials.[44]

Organized Crime Interest

During this period of the 1960s and 1970s, the expansion of the markets and profits for sex in the media appears to have attracted persons affiliated with organized crime or using techniques of organized crime. Extortion approaches were used to obtain the distribution rights to *Deep Throat* from its producer and in attempting to obtain the rights to *Behind the Green Door*.[45] The *Sourcebook on Pornography* summarizes a number of reports and observations from law enforcement agencies citing various relationships between producers and distributors of media sex materials and organized crime.[46]

Perhaps the only dealer in explicit materials who was convicted for crimes that involve traditional organized crime tactics was Michael G. Thevis of Atlanta. He was convicted in 1971 of shipping obscene materials and in 1979 of murder, arson, and extortion, directed against business rivals.[47] Thevis was not a member of any organized crime family.

In 1984, an amendment to the Racketeer Influenced and Corrupt Organizations (RICO) Act included obscene matter as a predicate racketeering activity. A prosecutor would therefore have to prove that (1) the material was obscene in terms of the three prongs of the federal law (patent offensiveness, appeal to prurient interest, and lack of socially redeeming qualities); and (2) there was a pattern of racketeering activity, implemented by at least two predicate offenses.

A special obscenity unit was established by the Criminal Division of the Justice Department in 1987.[48] It has obtained many convictions, some of which involved application of the RICO statute. In none of the RICO cases was there any allegation of organized crime involvement or of the kind of activity associated with organized crime. In a listing of the major organized crime trials during the years from 1985 through 1987, including twenty-one trials with 109 defendants, there were no obscenity-related offenses. None of the many organized crime trials in the federal courts in New York's Southern and Eastern District in the last fifteen years have cited obscenity violations.

Federal Investigative Groups

Two major federal government commissions have had occasion, since 1970, to investigate the relationship between organized crime and the traffic in sexually explicit materials. The two American commissions concerned with these materials, each of which is usually named after the official appointing it, considered the role of organized crime in the creation and distribution of sex media materials and emerged with different conclusions. The Commission on Obscenity and Pornography was established in January 1968 by President Johnson and completed its work in September 1970.[49] Its sixteen members included six lawyers, three sociologists, three religious officials, three professors, and a media executive. The commission chair was Dean William B. Lockhart of the University of Minnesota Law School.

The Attorney General's Commission on Pornography was appointed by Attorney General Edwin Meese in May 1985 and completed its task by July 1986.[50] Its eleven members included four lawyers, a psychiatrist, a psychologist, a radio executive, a marketing researcher, a magazine editor, a Catholic priest, and a child abuse investigator. The commission chair was Henry E. Hudson, a U.S. attorney in Virginia.

The 1970 Johnson Commission felt, after conducting empirical market investigations, that the available data were insufficient to warrant any conclusions about the role of organized crime in the sex media business. No concrete findings supported the existence of a collaboration between organized crime and sex-related media.

Sixteen years later, the Meese Commission came to a contrary conclusion. It found that the machinery for creating and distributing explicit materials is not owned, operated, or controlled by La Cosa Nostra, defined as a highly structured and elaborately subdivided organization involved in a range of criminal activities and consisting of Italian crime families. However, it suggested that major parts of the industry are controlled by organized crime, if one of two other definitions of the latter are used. One definition sees organized crime as a large organized enterprise engaged in criminal activity, with continuity and a defined membership. The second definition adds that the enterprise is likely to use other crimes and methods of corruption, such as extortion, assault, murder, or bribery.

The differences in the findings of the two commissions can be interpreted on several levels: composition, staff, and time and findings available. The Johnson Commission had more social scientists, religious functionaries, and academics than the later group. The Meese Commission had more media officials and more members (six of the eleven) who had previously taken public positions against sexually explicit media.

A social psychologist was staff director of the Johnson Commission, and most of its studies involved empirical social science investigations with surveys, experiments, trend and content analyses, and field data. A prosecutor was staff director of the Meese Commission, and its information derives from existing police investigative reports and its own hearings.

The Johnson Commission spent $1,750,000, and the Meese Commission budget was $500,000. Considering the changing value of the dollar, the 1970 Commission budget was almost sixteen times larger than that of the 1986 group. The Johnson Commission funded a number of new research studies; the Meese Commission conducted no original research but had a large number (208) of witnesses at its public hearings.

The Johnson Commission conducted two empirical studies on the relationship between organized crime and explicit media. One survey reported on interviews with a sample of police and prosecutors in seventeen cities, and a second study examined the traffic in sex-oriented materials in five cities.[51]

Two legal scholars who wrote a book on the role of sexually explicit materials in the American legal system evaluated, among many other aspects of the problem, the differences between the two federal commissions on the issues of the importance of organized crime. Gordon Hawkins and Franklin E. Zimring concluded that the Meese Commission conclusions on organized crime cannot be justified. Hawkins and Zimring, in their assessment of the Meese panel's "cumulative evidence" on organized crime's role, describe the material as "a loosely articulated aggregation of rumors, allegations, and unconfirmed reports."[52] The commission's primary attempt to substantiate the organized crime-sex media link involves the business of Reuben Sturman, operating out of the Cleveland area, with operations throughout the country. He is said in the Meese Report to operate a highly organized enterprise devoted to materials that could probably be determined to be legally obscene. Hawkins and Zimring regard the commission's citation of the role of Sturman's enterprise in organized crime as "entirely vacuous," since the commission offers no empirical evidence of a link. Sturman is currently serving concurrent federal sentences for income tax and obscenity violations and is facing other charges.

There is a relevant discussion in the report of the President's Commission on Organized Crime, chaired by U.S. Second Circuit judge Irving R. Kaufman. This commission, including a congressman, a U.S. senator, and U.S. Supreme Court justice Stewart among its nineteen members, filed its final report on 25 March 1986, shortly before the Meese report was released. None of the several previous analyses by scholars of the income of organized crime cited by the Kaufman Commission list any income from sex-oriented media. The Kaufman group's own listing of the eighteen kinds of crime that are the major sources of income for organized crime does not include such media. The commission states that the anecdotal evidence dealing with the subject cannot be used to develop reasonable estimates of any income that organized crime may derive from sex media.[53]

Director William H. Webster of the FBI, at the request of the Meese Commission, surveyed the bureau's fifty-nine field offices. He reported that "about three fourths of those offices indicated that they have no verifiable information that organized crime was involved either directly or through extortion in the manufacture of pornography. Several offices did, however, report some involvement by members and associates of organized crime."[54]

Thus, there has been significant disagreement with the Meese Commission's linkage of organized crime to the production and distribution of sexually explicit materials. One possibility is that the strong-arm techniques that were sometimes used in the early development of the business, as in the extortion threats reported for *Deep Throat* and *Behind the Green Door*, did reflect organized crime activity at that time. However, such approaches could have become less important as the trickle of material turned into a torrent, many more producers began competing to supply a broader and larger market, and more traditional media expanded their own sexual content. Also, prosecutors became more experienced, and cases were increasingly tried in federal courts, where conviction is more likely than in state courts.

Broadening the Market

Organized crime's ability to profit from an activity declines as the activity becomes more broad-based and available and less furtive. This process is illustrated by developments in the field of explicit movies, sometimes called XXX-rated in order to distinguish them from the few movies that were officially given an X-rating from the motion picture industry's classification office.

In the 1960s, a small number of producers made and distributed a relatively few explicit titles each year. The films, some in 16mm and others in 35mm, were shown at a limited number of theaters in large cities, with tickets usually costing more than admission to conventional movies.

Simultaneously with increasing public interest in explicit movies, the new technology of the videocassette recorder (VCR) emerged in the 1970s. Movies could be put on videotape and viewed in the privacy of the consumer's home. In the first few years after the VCR was introduced, explicit videotapes could not be rented but had to be purchased at sex shops and theaters for prices approximating $100.

The widespread adoption by Americans of the VCR, which was in over half the households by 1989, dramatically changed the situation. The number of movie producers increased so sharply that they established a trade association, which now has 285 members.[55] The number of explicit movies made jumped from less than 100 in 1975 to over 1,700 in 1991. The movies may be bought, often for less than twenty-five dollars, or rented. They are available at over 42 percent of general video retail outlets.[56] A 1986 directory of available explicit videotapes reviews 4,140 titles, and 1991 and 1993 supplements review 1,200 and 1,000 new titles, respectively.[57]

Erotic movies now have their own stars, trade magazines, award ceremonies, critics, agents, and directors and otherwise mimic the marketing apparatus of the Hollywood industry.[58] Also like Hollywood, the XXX-industry has fierce competition for customers. Specialized production organizations, like Candida Royalle's Femme Productions, are making more humanistic sex films for women and other special audience groups. Such films, with minimal stereotypes, less formulaic sex, eroticization of safe sex, narrative development, and couple orientation, are expanding the market and attracting more producers.[59] These trends have made organized crime's ability to profit from the explicit film industry ever more problematic, as the industry becomes more open and competitive.

The expansion of the market for explicit movies is analogous to the huge expansion of the explicit magazine market. There are no reliable estimates of the number of such magazines in the 1960s, but it surely was only a fraction of the 50,000 to 60,000 different titles estimated by a law enforcement officer in 1986.[60] Just as a relatively small number of general interest magazines (e.g., *Look, Collier's*) stopped publication and yielded to a large number of niche magazines targeted to specific subgroups in the general reading population, there has been a vast increase in the number of explicit magazines that are addressed to persons with special sexual interests.[61] As with movies, the surge in competition makes domination of the industry by any closed conspirational group less likely.

Law Enforcement Activity

In addition to the impact of media proliferation and the mainstreaming of sex-related media, there is the cumulative effect of twelve years of vigorous federal prosecutions for obscenity, under Presidents Ronald Reagan and George Bush. They appointed 558 of the 828 federal judges, and their choices tended to be relatively conservative.[62] The new weapons available to federal prosecutors and the prosecutors' growing experience contributed to a large increase in the conviction rate. One 1989 report on the campaign against obscenity described it as "one of the most far-reaching criminal justice crackdowns ever" and concluded that "the war on porn is the biggest success of Ronald Reagan's social agenda."[63]

Practically every single person listed in the *Sourcebook on Pornography* who is alleged to have organized crime affiliations and to have been active in the sex media business has either fled, retired, left the business involuntarily, gone to prison, or died.[64] A number of important distributors, many of whom employed their sons or wives, were forced to leave the business, along with their relatives, either by conviction or plea bargain. Successors to these former producers and distributors do not seem to have emerged.

Another contributor to the decline of the putative role of organized crime in the industry is the declining importance of some media: photofinishers, mail order, 8mm film, XXX feature-length films, explicit/child materials, sex shops, and telephone services.

Sting operations have cut back on photo finishing and mail order operations, 8mm film loops lost popularity because of poor technical quality and lack of sound, and the number of "adults only" theaters have shrunk from 1,100 in 1977 to 700 in 1985 to less than 300 today. A 1984 statute makes possession of explicit child materials illegal, and a 1988 updating of the Criminal Code bars the use of computers to advertise explicit child materials. The U.S. Postal Service has very aggressively pursued producers and users of explicit child media. Sex shops are closing because of prosecution, zoning, and other community changes. A number of regional telephone companies have eliminated "dial-a-porn" services.

Hawkins and Zimring suggest that the patterns of change in the distribution of explicit materials in this country fit the typical scenario of middle-stage decriminalization.[65] This partial decriminalization has expanded the market, and if end-stage decriminalization approaches, we can anticipate that even newer kinds of producers could emerge with newer products. These trends, if confirmed and documented, and the great community tolerance that they imply could make problematic any future role for organized crime in sex media.

In the case of prostitution, the move toward decriminalization has been under way for some decades, because of changing attitudes, a lack of criminal justice resources, and uncertainty over what the courts ought to be doing, in terms of prostitutes or their customers. There is no national voluntary agency to monitor policy. Reflecting the decreasing salience of prostitution as a social problem, a brothel has been the locale for a successful musical movie (*The Best Little Whorehouse in Texas*, 1982), and madams have published best-selling autobiographies and become celebrities who give advice on social and romantic matters.[66] Sympathetic prostitutes have been presented in many popular movies, such as *Klute* (1971), *Pretty Baby* (1978), *Trading Places* (1983), *Night Shift* (1983), and *Pretty Woman* (1990).

In both prostitution and media sex, larger community and social changes have been tilting toward making each of these activities less financially attractive to organized crime. Future changes in the cultural/moral climate, national priorities, leadership in Washington, attitudes toward law enforcement, and composition of the judiciary will contribute to the relationship between organized crime and the two aspects of commercial sex.

NOTES

1. Joel Feinberg, *Offense to Others* (New York: Oxford University Press, 1985).

2. George Kibbe Turner, "The Daughters of the Poor," *McClure's* 34 (November 1909), 45–61.

3. James Wunsch, "Prostitution and Public Policy: From Regulation to Suppression, 1858–1920," Ph.D. diss., University of Chicago, 1976).

4. George J. Kneeland, *Commercialized Prostitution in New York City* (New York: Century, 1913).

5. Richard Gid Powers, *Secrecy and Power: The Life of J. Edgar Hoover* (New York: Free Press, 1978), 134.

6. Frederick K. Grittner, *White Slavery: Myth, Ideology, and American Law* (New York: Garland, 1990), 145–76.

7. Kathleen L. Barry, *Female Sexual Slavery* (New York: New York University Press, 1979, 1985).

8. Grittner, *White Slavery*, 168–72.

9. Ko-lin Chin, *Chinese Subcultures and Criminality* (Westport, CT: Greenwood, 1990), 110–12.

10. "Voyage to Life of Shattered Dreams," *New York Times*, (B1) 23 July 1993, 14.

11. "The Skin Trade," *Time*, 141(25), 21 June 1993, 44–51.

12. Gordon Thomas, *Enslaved* (New York: Pharos, 1991).

13. Charles Winick and Paul Kinsie, *The Lively Commerce: Prostitution and the United States* (New York: New American Library, 1973).

14. Mark T. Connelly, *The Response to Prostitution in the Progressive Era* (Chapel Hill: University of North Carolina Press, 1980).

15. Edwin R. A. Seligman and the Committee of Fifteen, *The Social Evil* (New York: Century, 1902).

16. Ruth Rosen, *The Lost Sisterhood: Prostitution in America 1900–1918* (Baltimore: Johns Hopkins Press, 1982), 69–85.

17. Stephen Fox, *Blood and Power: Organized Crime in Twentieth Century America* (New York: Morrow, 1989), 152–54.

18. Timothy Gilfoyle, *City of Eros: New York City, Prostitution, and the Commercialization of Sex, 1790–1920* (New York: Norton, 1992), 306–15.

19. Winick and Kinsie, *The Lively Commerce*, 215–21.

20. Robert S. Lynd and Helen M. Lynd, *Middletown: A Study in Contemporary American Culture* (New York: Harcourt Brace, 1929), 29, 113.

21. Hickman Powell, *Ninety Times Guilty* (New York: Arno, 1974), 230–32.

22. John M. Murtaugh and Sara Harris, *Cast the First Stone* (New York: McGraw Hill, 1978), 242.

23. Winick and Kinsie, *The Lively Commerce*, 205–6.

24. James H. Frey, Loren R. Reichert, and Kenneth V. Russell, "Prostitution Business and Police: The Maintenance of an Illegal Economy," *Police Journal*, 54 (1981): 239–49.

25. Loren D. Reichert and James H. Frey, "The Organization of Bell Desk Prostitution," *Sociology and Social Research* 69 (1985): 516–26.

26. Helen Reynolds, *The Economics of Prostitution* (Springfield, Illinois: C. C. Thomas, 1986), 126.

27. Ibid.

28. Isabel Drummond, *The Sex Paradox* (New York: Putnam, 1953).

29. Richard Symanski, *The Immoral Landscape: Female Prostitution in Western Societies* (Toronto: Butterworths, 1981).

30. Jennifer James, "Mobility as an Adaptive Strategy," *Urban Anthropology* 4 (1975): 239–664.

31. Jennifer James, "Sweet Cream Ladies: An Introduction to Prostitute Taxonomy," *Western Canadian Journal of Anthropology* 3 (1972): 102–18.

32. Claire Sterk, Georgia State University, personal communication, 8 August 1993.

33. Diano J. Schemo, "Police List Items from Search," *New York Times*, 13 July 1993, B3.

34. Mayor's Office of Midtown Enforcement, *Annual Report Fiscal Years 1991 and 1992* (City of New York: Office of Midtown Enforcement, 1993).

35. Marilyn G. Haft, "Hustling for Rights," *Civil Liberties Review* 1 (1974): 8–26; Bernard Cohen, *Deviant Street Networks: Prostitution in New York City* (Lexington, MA: Lexington Books, 1980), 101–2.

36. President's Commission on Law Enforcement and the Administration of Justice, *Final Report* (Washington, DC: U.S. Government Printing Office, 1967), 189.

37. Francis A. J. Ianni, *Black Mafia: Ethnic Succession in Organized Crime* (New York: Pocket Books, 1975).

38. Ethan A. Nadelmann, "Global Prohibition Regimes: The Evolution of Norms in International Society," *International Organization* 44 (1990): 479–526.

39. Andrea Dworkin, *Pornography: Men Possessing Women* (New York: Putnam, 1981), 201.

40. Commission on Obscenity and Pornography, *Final Report* (Washington, DC: U.S.

Government Printing Office, 1970); Attorney General's Commission on Pornography (Washington, DC: U.S. Government Printing Office, 1986).

41. Charles Winick, "From Deviant to Normative: Changes in the Social Acceptability of Sexually Explicit Material," *Deviance and Social Change*, ed. Edward Sagarin. (Beverly Hills, CA: Sage, 1977), 219–46.

42. Charles Rembar, *The End of Obscenity: The Trials of Lady Chatterley, Tropic of Cancer, and Fanny Hill* (New York: Random House, 1968); Edward De Grazia and Roger K. Newman, *Banned Films: Movies, Censors and the First Amendment* (New York: Bowker, 1982).

43. Obscenity Research Project, "An Empirical Inquiry into the Effects of *Miller v. California* on the Control of Obscenity," *New York University Law Review* 52 (1977): 810–939.

44. Joseph E. Scott, "What Is Obscene? Social Science and the Contemporary Community Standard Test of Obscenity," *International Journal of Law and Psychiatry* 14 (1991): 29–45.

45. Kenneth Turan and Stephen F. Zito, *Sinema: American Pornographic Films and the People Who Make Them* (New York: Praeger, 1974), 154; Attorney General's Commission on Pornography, *Final Report* (Washington, DC: U.S. Government Printing Office, 1986), 1197.

46. Franklin Mark Osanka and Sara Lee Johann, eds., *Sourcebook on Pornography* (Lexington, MA: Lexington Books, 1989, 62–79.

47. Attorney General's Commission, *Final Report*, 1055.

48. "Despite U.S. Campaign, A Boom in Pornography," *New York Times*, July 1993, 20.

48. Jay Albanese, *Organized Crime in America* (Cincinnati: Anderson, 1989), 62–66.

49. Commission on Obscenity and Pornography, *Final Report* (Washington, DC: U.S. Government Printing Office, 1970).

50. Attorney General's Commission on Pornography, *Final Report*.

51. Commission on Obscenity and Pornography, *Technical Report*, Vol. 5 (Washington, DC: U.S. Government Printing Office, 1972), 42–60.

52. Gerald Hawkins and Franklin E. Zimring, *Pornography in a Free Society* (New York: Cambridge University Press, 1988), 66.

53. Commission on Organized Crime, *The Impact: Organized Crime Today* (Washington, DC: U.S. Government Printing Office, 1986), 455.

54. Letter, William H. Webster, Federal Bureau of Investigation to Henry E. Hudson, Chairman, Attorney General's Commission on Pornography, 15 November 1985.

55. "Despite U.S. Campaign."

56. Attorney General's Commission on Pornography, *Final Report*, 1397.

57. Robert H. Rimmer, *The X-Rated Videotape Guide* (New York: Harmony, 1986); Robert H. Rimmer and Patrick Riley, *The X-Rated Videotape Guide II* (Buffalo: Prometheus, 1991); Robert H. Rimmer and Patrick Riley, *The X-Rated Videotape Guide III* (Buffalo: Prometheus, 1993).

58. Gary Indiana, "A Day in the Life of Hollywood's Sex Factory," *Village Voice*, 1993, 24 August 1993, 27.

59. Lisa Katzman, "The Women of Porn," *Village Voice*, 24 August 1993, 31–32.

60. Attorney General's Commission on Pornography, *Final Report*, 1413.

61. Charles Winick, "Content Analysis of Sexually Explicit Magazines Sold in an Adult Bookstore," *Journal of Sex Research* 21 (1985): 206–10.

62. Neil A. Lewis, "Unmaking the G.O.P. Court Legacy," *New York Times*, 23 August 1993, A10.

63. "The Drive to Make America Porn-Free," *U.S. News and World Report*, 6 February 1989, 26.

64. Osanka and Johann, *Sourcebook on Pornography*.

65. Hawkins and Zimring, *Pornography*, 72–73.

66. Sally Stanford, *Lady of the House* (New York: Putnam, 1968); Polly Adler, *A House Is Not a Home* (New York: Rinehart, 1953); Xaviera Hollander, *The Happy Hooker* (New York: Dell, 1979); Sidney B. Barrows and William Novak, *The Mayflower Madam* (New York: Ivy Books, 1990).

13

Turning Black Money into Green:
Money Laundering

*ROBERT J. KELLY, RUFUS SCHATZBERG,
AND KO-LIN CHIN*

In their first *Interim Report*, the President's Commission on Organized Crime defined money laundering as "the process by which one conceals the existence, illegal source, or illegal application of income, and then disguises that income to make it appear legitimate."[1] The fact that the commission chose money laundering as the subject of its first report illustrates the importance of the phenomenon. The term refers to several different, but interrelated processes, all of which meet the basic definition of transforming criminally tainted cash illegally earned into a form that disguises its origins so that it can be used in legitimate commerce as a legally appearing instrument or asset and thus becomes "clean." Recently, the term's meaning has broadened to refer not only to the individual act of laundering but to numerous complex steps used in the illegal asset conversion process, beyond the basic exchange of cash, for less conspicuous and more socially acceptable methods of payment.

Criminal organizations or persons who hide hoards of cash inventories, which may or may not represent assets from an illicit operation, face serious risks of confiscation and punishment when these are discovered. For these organizations or persons to be able to use this money, they must convert it to an alternative medium that is both easier than cash to use in everyday commerce and that also avoids pointing, even indirectly, to the activity that generated it.

While the flagrant uses of offshore and foreign money-laundering havens assume many forms, an analysis of case law[2] reveals that these entities are used to launder illegal proceeds, primarily derived from narcotics trafficking, to facilitate tax evasion or avoidance, and to expedite illegal investments or other frauds.

According to Clifford L. Karchmer, there are several types of laundering.[3] At one end of the spectrum, for someone who wishes to make cash more portable, there is the exchange of small-denomination bills for larger ones. Cash is converted quickly into disposable funds. Another major type of money laundering is more significant because it takes advantage of the vast constellation of investment opportunities available. The more sophisticated processes begin where currency conversions leave off. By multiplying the number of financial transactions through bearer-bonds, through the formation of a maze of boilerplate corporations, sizable sums are transformed into capital, which may be moved into income-producing enterprises and properties: apartment buildings, shopping malls, warehouses, and numerous wholesale and retail businesses. Real estate investments are only half of it. Entire industries may be threatened by infiltration of money controlled by organized criminal networks. Untaxed, illicit dollars provide criminals with enormous leverage, and their cash flow enables them to undermine law-abiding competition.

Laundered money moves about restlessly, as its clean versions do in legitimate business, integrating forward and backward into topless bars, linen supplies, restaurants; it flows from casino skims into travel agencies and transportation, from prostitution into pornography into massage parlors, films, and adult bookstores. In the case of narcotics, large sums of money stream into banks, brokerage firms, and savings and loans banks. As the cocaine frenzy peaked in the United States, Miami emerged as a key transshipment and transfer point for drug cartels.

Miami banks were distinctive among the thirty-seven in the Federal Reserve system in holding a sizable currency surplus.[4] In 1991, Drug Enforcement Administration officials estimated that the monthly gross for some traffickers in New York was between $7 million and $12 million. In small bills, this translates into a logistical nightmare. Before sophisticated international electronic banking became a reality, disposing of bulky cash caches was a serious problem.

The proceeds of a heroin or cocaine sale generally weigh five times more than the drugs themselves. The sheer bulk of illicit profits confronts traffickers with problems. In many instances moving the money is harder than moving the drugs. The accumulation of illicit money before it is laundered has become a tempting target for hijackers. Cottage industries of currency relocation specialists have materialized to handle the problem.

One such currency relocation specialist, Ramon Rodriguez, using a Learjet, regularly flew from Fort Lauderdale to Panama with half-ton loads of currency. Rodriguez was eventually arrested in Fort Lauderdale with $5.4 million in cash. His accounts, computerized on disks, showed he had flown nearly a quarter of a billion dollars to Panama in the previous year.[5]

The electronic rinse cycle operates with perverse efficiency: dirty money, drug money, is mixed in with billions of dollars in legitimate transfers and wired out of the country. The fact that most drug transactions are in cash makes money-laundering processes indispensable to drug-trafficking activities.[6] The U.S. Department of the Treasury estimates that drug traffickers launder $100 billion yearly in this country alone.[7]

Money laundering is not unique to drug dealing. Since the rise of the illicit alcohol syndicates and major gambling enterprises, criminals have sought means to clean and disguise their money. Cash businesses—restaurants, fast-food shops, convenience stores, retail consumer businesses of all sorts—have been used to mingle moneys from legitimate and illegitimate sources. Casinos in Nevada and New Jersey, where cash flows are staggering, have been attractive targets for rinsing and recycling dirty money. Funds are laundered from numerous other crimes, including fraud offenses, securities manipulations, gambling, illegal gun smuggling, and tax evasion. With these offenses aggregated into the comprehensive assessment of the problem, money laundering may run as high as $300 billion annually.[8]

The complexity of the schemes involves cash conversions into cashier's checks, which are easier to handle and difficult to trace since they lack a receiver's name and address. In other scenarios launderers use individuals to convert cash into money orders and cashier's checks that do not specify payers or are made in the name of fictitious persons. These multiple transactions are usually under $10,000, avoiding the need for Currency Transaction Reports (CTR), required by the Bank Secrecy Act, which obliges bankers to file Customs Form 4790 when more than $10,000 in currency or monetary instruments is taken in or out of the United States. One ring operating in New York employed people to launder $100 million a year for the Cali cocaine cartel. The checks were hidden in magazines and shipped to Cali, Colombia; from there, the money was transferred to Panamanian banks.[9]

Another real-life incident of a money-laundering strategy was reported by the Centre for International Documentation of Organised and Economic Crime located in Cambridge, England:

A U.S. organized crime group with a lot of hot cash forms a cozy relationship with the central bank of a British Commonwealth country. Diplomats of the country carry the cash out of the U.S. If it's $10,000 or more, they are supposed to report that to U.S. Customs, but they don't; they *externalize* the cash. It goes into the central bank and then into various dummy companies in different countries in return for shares in those companies. The money is thus *agitated*, so it'll be just about impossible for investigators to follow. Then, to *repatriate* the money, dummy companies in the U.S. sell their worthless shares to investors in Britain—who are in fact in on the scam—and behold, the money is back in the U.S. clean! Now it buys legitimate businesses, banks, political power. An operation like this, involving highly placed officials and businessmen, will cost quite a bit, maybe 35 percent, but once the system is in place, people will want to use it—not only drug profiteers but also arms dealers, terrorist organizations, intelligence agencies. ... A prime haven for such shady customers was BCCI, the Bank of Credit and Commerce International, headquartered in the Cayman Islands and Luxembourg with branches in 72 countries. It is said to have secretly controlled the First American Bank of Washington, D.C. After BCCI collapsed in 1991, having defrauded depositors of several billion dollars, it became known as the Bank of Crooks and Criminals International.[10]

In 1988, the Bank of Commerce and Credit International (BCCI) faced federal charges of laundering $14 million for the Medellin cocaine cartel. Cash from traffickers was put into certificates of deposit in European, Bahamian, Panamanian, and Uruguayan branches. Loans would be created using the certificates as collateral, permitting the traffickers to withdraw the funds through other branches. Loans would be repaid with funds from certificates of deposit.[11] Another investigation into the activities of BCCI showed:

In the summer of 1991 . . . the BCCI was convicted of money laundering in Tampa, Florida. In addition, BCCI has, as part of a global plea agreement, pled guilty in the District of Columbia to conspiracy to commit racketeering acts involving money laundering, fraud, and tax evasion, and in New York to charges of money laundering, fraud, bribery, and theft. . . . The bank has been called *the most pervasive money-laundering operation and financial supermarket ever created, a marathon swindle* and a *steering service for (Colombian) drug traffickers to deposit hundreds of millions of contraband dollars outside the country.* . . . BCCI is only one example of the pervasive, worldwide money laundering industry. . . . Worldwide, people spend as much as $500 billion annually on illegal drugs, with up to $200 billion spent in the United States. . . . According to the U.S. Department of Treasury, drug traffickers launder an estimated $100 billion each year in this country alone.[12]

Because successful criminal ventures generate illicit cash, there is a need to disguise its origins to avoid attracting the attention of other criminals and the government. The simplest and crudest way to hide illegal wealth is to sit on it. By so frustrating enforcement efforts, an audit trail cannot be observed or uncovered, nor can monitoring conspicuous spending that exceeds one's net worth or reports of legally earned income be conducted. Such concealing tactics limit law enforcement investigations but also restrict the criminal's freedom to generate assets with their illegally gained capital.

Given the torrent of dollars flowing into criminal organizations, especially drug-trafficking groups, an illegal industry has developed to serve clientele that includes tax-avoiding corporations and cocaine traffickers. The system depends on the collaboration or often just the negligence of bankers and other moneymen who can use electronic funds networks and the secrecy laws of tax havens to electronically shuffle assets.

Much is at stake as narco-dollars are recycled through the world's financial networks. Drug lords and other organized criminals put some of their money back into criminal enterprises, but most is invested in legitimate businesses. The legitimate sector of the economy affords numerous benefits and opportunities for criminals, especially where the possession of large amounts of cash is not convenient. Investments into legitimate business provide tax exposures so that internal revenue audits can be avoided.

In general, money laundering functions as the scaffolding for criminal penetrations of the legitimate sectors of the economy. With clean assets, cash, and financial instruments, criminals are positioned to initiate investment in a wide range of commercial enterprises.

THE MONEY-LAUNDERING INDUSTRY
AND ITS CLIENTELE

Many of the major drug-trafficking organizations employ the services of specialists familiar with the methods and techniques for handling large sums of cash. Some drug organizations take care of this aspect of their operations internally; many, however, turn to experts. Many launderers function as independent contractors and are not part of drug-trafficking operations. The processes of moving money and cleansing it developed before drug cartels discovered the values inherent in washing and concealing their illicit profits: multinational corporations, for example, that seek to minimize their tax burdens move their profits to tax-free havens. Others faced with stringent controls on their wealth have also resorted to money-laundering schemes.[13]

Modern banking technologies have altered the implementation of these schemes, but the basic procedures remain the same: using drug profits as an example, the first step is to move them offshore. This can be accomplished in several ways—as part of a payment to suppliers or as the initial amount setting in motion the laundering process. Traffickers or their agents may deposit cash in foreign banks routed cleverly through shell corporations and then return it to the United States for investment in various legitimate enterprises or as loans back to the original criminal groups that launched the money on its devious course. Once overseas, cash is easy to funnel into black markets, especially in unstable economies where the dollar is the favored underground currency. Since so many traffickers see America as a safe and profitable haven for their assets, their laundered cash is usually invested back in the United States.

The transfer of funds out of the United States is complex and risky. In many cases it amounts to a smuggling operation. The goal of launderers is to get their money into the maelstrom of global money movements, where the volume is so great that effective regulation and monitoring are virtually impossible. Because of the globalization of the world economy, the flow of trade and currency transfer has exploded. Billions of dollars are moved about internationally every day.

Much of the electronic money zips into a secret banking industry that got its start in Switzerland in the 1930s, when worried Europeans shifted their savings beyond the reach of the totalitarian regimes in Europe and the Soviet Union. With Swiss banking secrecy practices weakened by series of money-laundering cases, other countries have attracted banking business by creating discrete, tax-free havens. In a period of four years, Luxembourg's total bank deposits grew from $40 billion in 1984 to $100 billion in 1988. In the wake of the drug-money scandal involving the Luxembourg-based BCCI, the country has tried to burnish its public image by making money laundering a criminal offense, even while it has fortified its bank secrecy regulations.[14]

The most inventive havens allow investors to set up shell corporations with invisible owners, which means that both legitimate and illegitimate persons can secretly hide money in real estate, corporate stocks, and other assets. From the Isle of Man to Vanua Levu in the South Pacific, tax havens have sprouted up offering tax-free deposits. Drug traffickers launder their dollars in these island banks. But the main business of these tax-free, offshore havens is servicing some of the world's largest multinational corporations.

A technique widely used by corporate giants to minimize their tax burdens is a quasilegal fabrication called reinvoicing, a paper shuffle that enables firms to credit sales and profits to these offshore centers. For example, a legitimate firm may import raw materials through an offshore dummy company, which buys shipments at the lowest possible price and resells the material to the parent firm at a high markup. This dumps profits in the tax-free havens, while the parent U.S.-based company can boost its apparent cost to reduce taxes in the United States. The profits in the offshore entity can then be repatriated in the form of tax-free loans to the U.S.-based parent corporations.

In 1982 the Permanent Subcommittee on Investigations (PSI) began examining the criminal exploitation of offshore tax havens and found them flourishing. A 1983 Joint Economic Committee reported that the U.S. underground economy concealed $222 billion from the Internal Revenue Service (IRS)—7.5 percent of the $150 billion to $600 billion.[15] In a 19 April 1984 letter from the commissioner of the IRS to Senators William Roth and Sam Nunn, the commissioner clearly described the phenomenal growth of the use of haven secrecy laws to hide resources. He stated:

Today, more of our investigations are centered around organized efforts to evade and defeat the payment of taxes. Tax evaders are becoming more sophisticated in their methods and techniques of committing these violations. We are not dealing with tax evasion on an international scale. The current trend is to use the secrecy laws of tax haven countries to facilitate tax evasion. For example during the period 1977 through August 1983, we identified 772 criminal cases which had financial transactions involving some 90 foreign countries. A conservative estimate of unreported income in these 772 cases exceeds $2.6 billion.[16]

Though the IRS tolerates such schemes to a point, the U.S. government has taken a more aggressive stance with criminally bred monies and has tried to choke off the river of drug money flowing through such channels. Yet, laundering hot spots tend to be moving targets. After the U.S. government negotiated new treaties similar to those with Switzerland, Bermuda, and Cayman Islands authorities to allow limited access to banking records in narcotics cases, many of the launderers found new lairs in which to nest their money.[17]

As the international financial center of gravity has shifted toward the Pacific Rim, new tax and secrecy havens have multiplied in Micronesia and the New Hebrides in the western Pacific. Hong Kong, however, remains the preeminent laundering locale in the Pacific.[18]

In the United States, a money-laundering center can be spotted by the huge surplus of cash that flows into the local branch of the Federal Reserve System. Complicating the picture is the fact that both the United States and abroad, financial businesses and even governments are often reluctant to impose regulations to keep out launderers. One reason is that a thriving financial industry creates jobs and income. Perhaps even more appealing is the inflow of foreign capital. Now that a consensus is building that the United States must sort out the legitimate money from drug dollars, the tools at hand, though formidable, have only just begun to be rigorously employed.[19]

FEDERAL EFFORTS AGAINST MONEY LAUNDERING

The emphasis on money laundering reflects another method of combating organized crime. Since Prohibition, it is estimated that organized criminals have amassed substantial, untaxed wealth in narcotics trafficking, illegal gambling, smuggling contraband, and loan-sharking. As part of the federal government's general enforcement strategy, the Justice and Treasury departments' agencies shifted their focus toward retrieving the profits generated by illicit activities.

In 1970, the Bank Secrecy Act was passed. It requires financial institutions to maintain records and to report certain categories of financial transactions to the U.S. Department of the Treasury. The aim of this law and subsequent legislation was made clear by the chairman of the President's Commission of Organized Crime:

Money laundering is the lifeblood of organized crime . . . the recommendations (of the Commission) will arm the financial community and law enforcement authorities with weapons needed to strike at the very heart of the narcotics trade and other activities engaged in by organized criminal groups. The driving force of organized crime is the incentive to earn vast sums of money; without the ability to utilize its ill-gotten gains, the underworld will have been dealt a crippling blow.[20]

From a brief look at prior legislative control efforts it is possible to appreciate the importance of the Bank Secrecy Act of 1970 and the Money Laundering Control Act of 1986. In 1970, a piece of legislation, Title 31 USC, sec. 427, passed that required financial institutions to report unusual currency transactions over $2,500. There were no penalties attached for noncompliance. The law was unfortunately vague and few institutions paid attention to it. Consequently, banking institutions were subjected to substantial criticism for indirectly aiding and abetting criminal efforts to shield their illegal wealth. Two other policy considerations intensified the effort to monitor and identify the movement of illegitimate moneys. As Karchmer points out:

The focus on money laundering represents something on the order of a fourth-level defensive strategy. The problem of channeling billions of illegally earned dollars into the United States would not be nearly so formidable were it not for the failure of both domestic and foreign enforcement activities to reduce opportunities for making illegal profits.[21]

The emphasis has been placed on laundering because of the lack of effective control or reduction of illegitimate activities and because of the inherent threats the process of laundering poses to financial institutions. Will targeting laundering—the penultimate stage in putting illegally earned monies into the legitimate sector—compensate for the inadequacies of other control policies? Probably not, so long as the markets that generate illegal wealth succeed in resisting or circumventing enforcement efforts. However, the laundering process itself may be one of the weaker components in organized criminal activities.

Many criminals share the same financial objectives as law-abiding citizens. It is safe to assume that they seek a return on their investments and that under the cover of legitimacy they wish to use their tainted assets to leverage legitimate transactions and to liquidate assets in order to apply these to financial options that yield income-producing capacities. What cannot be overlooked is the mantle of legitimacy that participation in the upperworld business sector confers on criminals who wish to disguise the criminal origins of their assets.

The propensity to move into the legitimate sector has ramifications—risks, actually—that expose criminal entrepreneurs to enforcement scrutiny that they may have been able to evade in their strictly criminal operations. By investing laundered funds in legitimate institutions, criminals subject themselves to restrictions on their freedom to manipulate assets. The investment of racketeering proceeds in sectors where financial transactions must conform to basic standards that govern the uses to which assets can be put creates a paper trail that opens up accounts and assets to investigative analysis. Further, the placement of laundered funds in banks, real estate investments, securities, and so on means that a degree of discretion must be sacrificed if an illusion of propriety is to be preserved. Monies earned through violence, intimidation, and corruption that are invested in socially useful ventures involve less socially hazardous activities than if they were recycled back into illegal activities. The reasons for laundering money are predicated on shrewd calculations and would seem to have less to do with goodwill, guilt, or the need for a positive image on the part of criminal entrepreneurs than with the need to protect their earnings.

The exigencies of the illegal marketplace play a role that promotes interest in depositing illicit funds in the legitimate sector of the economy despite the risks of confiscation and prosecution. Peter Reuter shows that illegal enterprises are likely to be smaller and more precarious than their legal counterparts. First, criminal enterprises cannot exploit legitimate external credit markets; second, by the very criminal nature of the enterprise, there is a need to constrict knowledge of the enterprise itself and its participants; third, contracts are not enforceable in conventional ways—violence and the threat of it are the principal means of ensuring compliance with agreements. Another negative operational consequence of criminal enterprises is that assets may be seized at any time and the participants arrested and prosecuted. Police intervention and the lack of legally enforceable contracts keep most criminal enterprises fragmented, ephemeral, and localized.[22] For these reasons, placing illegal monies in the legitimate sector becomes attractive.

BANK SECRECY ACT

With the enactment of the Bank Secrecy Act in 1970, Congress attempted to legislate banking policies to disrupt criminal laundering. The act provides that banking institutions must set up a record-keeping system of financial transactions involving three components. The first required activity is IRS Form 4789, which is a Currency Transaction Report that financial institutions are obliged to file when a currency transaction of $10,000 or more occurs with an individual at one time. An institution is also required to report multiple transactions if, for the same depositor, the transaction totals more than $10,000 in a single day.

The Bank Secrecy Act assists authorities in flagging the movement of illegally acquired cash in financial institutions and across international borders. But the very inclusion of a specific dollar amount has provided an obvious way to skirt the law: money launderers could simply make multiple transactions in amounts less than $10,000 (e.g., $9,500). This practice of using structured transactions, also known as smurfing, is now illegal (Title 31 USC, sec. 5324).

The second instrument developed by the act is Customs Form 4790 (CIMR), a currency and monetary report enumerating shipments of more than $10,000 in various monetary forms in or out of the United States.

A third feature of the Bank Secrecy Act is IRS Form 90.22-1, a foreign bank account report that compels individuals to declare the existence of foreign bank accounts if the account exceeds $10,000 in any year.

Under the provisions of the act, individuals can be criminally indicted if they fail to file a report or do so falsely. Initially, enforcement of the law was deferred for five years while questions of its constitutionality were determined. Additional delays were caused by uncertainties over which agencies would be accountable for ensuring compliance. Among the problems that beleaguered enforcement of the act and hindered the detection and prosecution of money launderers, some of which were addressed in subsequent amendments, had been banking institution delinquencies in identifying individuals making currency transactions, and low compliance rates with CTR mandates.[23]

Initially, the banking industry, the object of the legislation, took a defensive posture regarding the provisions of the Secrecy Act. It argued vigorously about government incursion into the privacy of banking transactions and records. However, the pressures the Secrecy Act exerts on banks have occasioned some self-discipline: banks have begun to exercise more internal supervision, prodded by statute tightening in 1986, when money laundering became a specific crime, and in the aftermath of a series of investigations in the 1980s involving some prestigious institutions that were forced to pay hefty fines. Even with increased official vigilance, authorities will need more voluntary support from the financial community if a dent is to be made in the money-laundering trade.[24] Many banks feel terrorized by government agencies relentlessly monitoring their transactions, which are relatively strict in currency reporting compared with those in other nations.

THE MONEY LAUNDERING CONTROL ACT

Before the passage of the Money Laundering Control Act of 1986 (Title 18, USC, sec. 1956, 1957) money laundering itself was not a crime. The law was part of the Anti-Drug Abuse Act. Three significant aspects of this law affect financial institutions and their security departments. The first involves amendments to the Bank Secrecy Act; the second specifies the process of money laundering as a criminal act; and the third entails changes in the Right to Financial Privacy Act.

According to the provisions of the act, people are guilty of money laundering if they attempt to conceal or disguise the nature, source, location, ownership, or control of proceeds that they know derive from some illegal activity. Further, knowingly transporting monetary instruments or funds out of the United States with the intent to promote unlawful activity or to avoid the currency transaction report is a violation of the Money Laundering Act.

Money laundering is now a separate federal offense punishable by a fine of $500,000 or twice the value of the property involved (whichever is greater) and twenty years' imprisonment. Sections 981 and 982 of 18 USC provide for the confiscation of property connected to a money-laundering scheme. The Money Laundering Act consolidates federal statutes that had been used to prosecute money laundering with the objective of increasing prosecution.[25]

Another legal instrument against money laundering is the Money Laundering Prosecution Improvement Act of 1988. It authorizes the Department of the Treasury to require financial institutions to verify the identity of persons who purchase money orders, bank checks or traveler's checks in the amount of $3,000 or more. The act also enables the Department of the Treasury to target certain types of institutions or geographic areas for special reporting requirements (31 USC, sec. 5325-5326).

With respect to changes in the Bank Secrecy Act, under Title 31 USC, sec. 5324, prosecutors may pursue individuals who attempt to corrupt a bank or financial institution. Sections of the legislation directly impinge on banking and

financial institutional operations at comparatively low levels of business interactions. For example, concerning structuring transactions, if an individual plans
to deposit $15,000 in cash and a bank teller informs the depositor that the
customer can avoid transaction report forms by splitting the transaction, say, by
depositing $8,000 one day and $7,000 on another, then the teller is at risk and
may be criminally liable.

Another significant consequence of the legislation has to do with bank discretion in identifying businesses and clients under the reporting exemption
rules.[26] Typically, banking staff are instructed to recognize anomalies in patterns
of transactions and banking activities among customers. Employees and bank
officers are expected to be vigilant and alert bank officers who, in turn, must
inform government officials for evaluation and action of the following types of
behavior:

• Individuals who make large cash deposits when their business account is not known
  to ordinarily generate substantial amounts of cash.

• Persons whose accounts show virtually no normal business-related banking activities
  and who use the accounts primarily as a temporary repository for funds routinely
  transferred to foreign bank accounts.

• Customers who provide information not readily verifiable concerning property own-
  erships, credit history, or sources of income—particularly when such information is
  needed to establish eligibility for credit lines and banking services.

• Individuals who regularly engage in cash transactions in amounts just below the
  $10,000 threshold for completion of Currency Transaction Reports.

• Customer maintenance of large accounts not commensurate with business type or activity.

While these and similar types of transactions may be observed in the context
of legitimate business, they can provide financial institutions with some guidance
on steps that may be taken to discourage money laundering. When customers
of a banking or financial institution wish to be exempted from reporting requirements, financial institutions are required to review applications. Ordinarily, in
order to avoid the hazards of corruption and fraud, a bank committee will be
organized.

The Money Laundering Act has had substantial impact on financial institutions, requiring them to be better informed about their clients and inquire into
transactions that appear suspicious. They must cooperate with, and refer appropriate matters to, law enforcement agencies within the parameters of the Rights
to Financial Privacy Act whenever transactions seem atypical.

The strictures of the money-laundering legislation are not without critics. Until 1988, the act allowed the government to seize attorneys fees if it could be
shown that these derived from unlawful activity. Situations occurred in which
defendants lacked the resources to retain counsel of choice. Defendants were
bereft: they could not freely select attorneys to defend them and often had to

rely on inexperienced legal aid lawyers in complex RICO cases. Though President Ronald Reagan signed the antidrug abuse bill that amended section 1957 of Title 18, exempting defense attorneys' fees from the provisions of the money-laundering act, in 1989 the Supreme Court ruled in a 5 to 4 decision that under the Comprehensive Forfeiture Act, the government could freeze assets of criminal defendants before trial.[27]

In sum, the Money Laundering Act and the Bank Secrecy Act together may present some distasteful consequences for defendants at trial and create some dislocations of business. But more is at risk than these inconveniences and stresses. The repercussion of not vigorously enforcing the money-laundering laws may jeopardize the financial stability and national security of entire countries.

THE EUROPEAN EXPERIENCE WITH MONEY LAUNDERING

As the European community follows through on the Maastricht resolutions, which will loosen restrictions on capital flows and liberate economies from historic constrictions, the movement of capital across national borders will make the continental financial consortiums increasingly attractive as money-laundering sites. Criminal organizations are known to thrive in free market environments. The unfettered flow of capital in Europe and numerous offshore centers will encourage and entice criminal organizations to use Europe's banking system as a washing machine for their money. Thus, what seems necessary is an internationally coordinated response to money laundering. Some discussion forums emerged in 1991 to estimate enforcement and financial institutional needs against financial crimes and money laundering; these are presently constituted by the Group of Seven (G-7), the European Council of Ministers, the Council of Europe, and the European Parliament. Their primary purpose has been to enhance uniform action on currency transaction reports and money-laundering laws and to control organized criminal activities such as drug trafficking.

The G-7 Financial Action Task Force, which represents the United States, the United Kingdom, France, Germany, Italy, Japan, Canada, Sweden, the Netherlands, Belgium, Luxembourg, Switzerland, Austria, and Spain, examined international money laundering and found that it may be described in terms of three basic processes: placement, layering, and integration.

Placement refers to the physical disposal of bulk cash proceeds. It takes many forms, from simple smuggling to the purchase of retail assets. Some of the principal methods include bank complicity in which correspondent bank deposits are used for transfers of deposits; false currency transaction reports; and use of nontraditional financial institutions, such as securities and commodities brokers and currency exchanges for the purposes of disguising illicit funds.

Layering is the creation of complex financial transactions that obscure the audit trail of illicit moneys. The conversion of cash into such monetary instruments such as cashier's checks, letters of credit, stocks, and bonds is among the more common techniques utilized by money launderers.

The third method, integration, describes the technique whereby launderers seek to develop a facade of legitimacy. This means that they attempt to route their money in ways that make it appear as normal business earnings. Real estate sales, the formation of front companies, and false export-import invoices are some of the methods used to divert attention from the stream of illicit money flows.

A survey of countries in Europe shows a spotty record in response to money laundering. The criminal code of Germany has not criminalized money laundering, though it has signed the United Nations (UN) drug convention to improve methods for cooperating in bilateral and multilateral efforts against drug trafficking. France enacted legislation (Law No. 87-1157) that establishes money laundering as a criminal offense. The penalties include imprisonment and fines for those who contribute to the laundering of proceeds from a drug law violation. France has also strengthened its customs laws, making it a crime to conduct financial operations between France and foreign countries involving funds deriving from drug law violations.

In 1975, the Italian government created two legislative requirements that affected financial operations. Law 533/1975 made it obligatory for the banks and government officials to ascertain the identity of anyone performing transactions relating to sums in excess of 20 million lire. Law 152/1975 suspended the right, in certain circumstances, to administer personal assets. In 1989, the Italian banking association's anti-money-laundering codes became operational. Clients of member banks are required to identify themselves for every cash or capital transaction in excess of approximately $7,500.

The most important provision of the United Kingdom's Drug Trafficking Offenses Act, enacted in 1987, are aimed at those who assist drug dealers and benefit from such crimes by laundering the proceeds. Additionally, the Prevention of Terrorism Act of 1989 requires bankers and others to disclose their suspicion about funds or assets that may derive from terrorist sources.[28]

In order to foster a spirit of cooperation, the United States has entered into various types of treaties with foreign governments to facilitate bilateral and multilateral investigations. Mutual legal assistance treaties enable law enforcement authorities to obtain evidence, exchange documents, and make requests for search and seizure and asset forfeitures. Under strictly defined conditions, legal assistance treaties permit the IRS to obtain testimony, financial information, and bank records needed to investigate international money launderers and drug traffickers.

The U.S. government participates in several multilateral programs designed to combat money laundering. Spin-off groups from the G-7 economic summit, in which the United States is an active member, are the Financial Action Task Force, the Gulf Cooperation Council, and the Commission of the European Communities. The task forces have formulated some forty recommendations to assist countries plagued by money-laundering problems by drafting model money-laundering and asset forfeiture statutes.[29]

In the immediate future, the European Community is likely to clarify its currency transactions and money-laundering laws, but not without skirmishes within and among countries over the rights to financial privacy. Currently, not all countries in Europe—Luxembourg is a case in point—are prepared to co-operate with the creation of uniform financial identification and reporting protocols. In the end, however, the threat of a financial crisis brought about by criminal activity and money laundering is likely to produce agreements.

Paradoxically, the enormous success of the drug cartels and other criminal organizations are forcing the community of nations to reexamine the intricate networks of international finance that have developed haphazardly over the past sixty years since Switzerland introduced secret banking. Some nations may still be reluctant to make their banking procedures fully transparent, but some light must be shed on everybody's books. Still, deep-seated reservations persist, and drastic measures are not likely in the immediate future. The inescapable facts are that no country can handle the global scope of money laundering. What appears to be needed is an international effort, but this process will have to be balanced against freedom from unnecessary red tape. Too many controls—which critics of U.S. policies complain about—could constipate financial exchanges. But this very attitude is precisely what has brought the world financial exchange system to its current state, where drug money mingles with the life force of the world economy, like a virus in the bloodstream.

INFILTRATING LEGITIMATE BUSINESSES

Because of shortsighted propriety, the banking institutions' reluctance to vigorously endorse money-laundering controls serves to encourage the mobilization of untaxed, unregulated crime profits into a continuous cash flow, allowing criminals to put law-abiding competitive businesses at serious risk. When organized criminals become involved in legitimate businesses, at least two consequences are likely: a business may be used as a front, disguising not only the true owner of the business but the illegitimate business associated with it. Second, a legitimate liquor business does not use violence to establish itself in the market, but ostensibly independent distributors could if they operated through a front.

When organized criminals move into legitimate business, they do not ordinarily operate it honestly and legally. Scams may be worked that milk the business of its assets. Should criminals wish to sustain and make a business grow, intimidation of competitors may occur so that the criminally infested firm may gain ascendancy and ultimate control of a local market.

To control a business, criminals do not need to actually take it over; all that is required is to control key officers, and the company's assets are at their disposal. By placing funds in a firm or helping to generate business by whatever means, criminals can significantly influence an entire business sector. In the toxic waste industry, simply by destroying the competitive capacities of other firms through overt acts of intimidation and violence, criminals were able to gain control over the waste haulage business in substantial market areas.[30]

So far, organized crime's infiltration of legitimate business seems to be limited to small companies. But given its formidable cash flow and the ceaseless pressure to fund investment outlets, sooner or later larger corporations will be targeted. In moving into legitimate business, organized crime has the advantage of large amounts of venture capital derived primarily from its illicit enterprises.

Most important, in select businesses influenced or operated surreptitiously by criminals, there is a unique edge: cost advantage. In these businesses the cost is low because the criminal firm deals in stolen goods, coercive labor practices, and significant amounts of money derived from purely criminal activities so that competition may be effectively thwarted. To legitimize their illegal money, organized criminal groups look for businesses where the misuse of a company's receipts does not leave paper trails. Gambling casinos, bars, restaurants, vending-machine companies, laundries, and so on are the kinds of businesses used by the underworld operators to launder and obtain needed cash. These types of businesses offer opportunities to their operators to make money through skimming from cash receipts. What matters, however, is that because such businesses deal mainly in cash, their assets are difficult to track. It is virtually impossible for anyone—management, labor, or the government—to be certain of how much money such businesses are actually generating. It is understandable why organized criminals buy or muscle their way into legitimate businesses that generate large amounts of cash.

To be effective against organized crime, a money-laundering deterrent that the government depends on to combat the drain on the country's economy involves the legitimate sector saying no to Mob money. Specifically, the banks and financial institutions stand between the underworld and its capacity to penetrate and exploit upperworld economic institutions. Despite the laws, government efforts lack strength without the cooperation of the financial sector. If banks investigated large or unusual depositors as thoroughly as they do borrowers, many launderers may very well be exposed. If controls on electronic banking are tightened and standard client information on all wire shipments of cash are meticulously monitored, the scope and intensity of laundering may diminish. Moreover, if the government is serious in its determination to target launderers, it must insist on scrutiny abroad. The United States shall have to call on, and demand the cooperation of, foreign financial institutions in identifying the real owners and manipulators of money. This may be considered the price of access to the global payments system that operates in the United States. In the traditional stage, all bankers should make their presence felt. Success in these efforts requires a political will for uniform action worldwide.

NET WORTH ANALYSIS

The Bank Secrecy and the Money Laundering acts are two instruments among several that are designed to cope with abuses of institutional processes by organized criminals. Net worth analysis, on the other hand, is an analytical process that is part of the IRS investigation and prosecutorial apparatus and has been used to confront the organized criminal at the personal level. Perhaps the most famous case involving net worth analysis was that of Al Capone, who was convicted of tax evasion and sentenced to eleven years in a federal penitentiary. Capone's incarceration effectively ended his notorious career.

Organized criminals have been deft at evading taxes by disguising their illegal sources of income. Through its Criminal Investigation Division (CID), the Internal Revenue Service of the Department of the Treasury has developed a methodology known as net worth analysis for uncovering unreported income. Earl Johnson, Jr., describes the procedure:

The government establishes a taxpayer's net worth commencement of the taxing period, deducting that from their net worth at the end of the tax period to prove that the net gain in net worth exceeds the taxpayer's reported income.[31]

By examining individuals' standard of living and comparing it with their reported income, the government is able to determine if they filed an accurate tax return and maintained proper business records; if they filed a false tax return; or if they concealed assets with an intent to defraud. The legal precedents supporting the government's right to conduct such investigations were settled in a Supreme Court decision in 1927 (*United States v. Sullivan*, 274 US 259). The Court denied the claim of a Fifth Amendment violation of self-incrimination as an excuse for failure to file an income tax on illegal earnings; in fact, this decision enabled the government to prosecute Capone and other racketeers.

The basis for tax prosecution of Capone and other organized criminals originated in the case of a bootlegger, Manley Sullivan, who had filed no tax return on the grounds that income from illegal transactions was not taxable and, moreover, that to declare such income would be self-incriminating within the meaning of the Fifth Amendment. The Supreme Court ruled against him, finding no reason that the fact that a business is unlawful should exempt it from paying taxes that, if lawful, it would have to pay. As for self-incrimination, the Court declared that the Fifth Amendment does not authorize citizens to refuse to state the amount of their income because it was earned criminally.

The government chose the Chicago gang lords against whom to test the new legal weapon. The challenge was to find Capone's gross income over $5,000 (the then standard exemption) for years in which he filed no return. This proved formidable because Capone never maintained a bank account or acquired property under his own name, and he endorsed no checks, signed no receipts, and paid cash for everything.[32]

To detect taxpayers who concealed income, the IRS had developed two methods of indirect proof based on circumstantial evidence, the first involving their net worth and the second their net expenditure. According to the first method, taxpayers' scale of living and any outward indications of wealth were analyzed. If commensurate with an income of only a few thousand dollars, Internal Revenue assumed that they had increased their net worth by an unreported amount. This gain it then declared taxable. According to the second method, investigators applied the same yardstick to the taxpayers' running expenses aside from accumulated assets. In Capone's case, both methods were adopted.

The government searched Chicago and Miami for shops, real estate agents, hotels, and establishments of any kind with which Capone might have dealt. They compiled a partial list of his outlay for goods and services during the years 1926–29, together with evaluations of his fixed possessions. IRS agents were able to uncover about $165,000 of taxable income. This evidence was the basis for Capone's conviction for tax evasion.

Since Capone's conviction for tax evasion, most criminals in organized networks report their incomes—at least, that portion of it that they spend and derive from legitimate sources. While the primary role of the IRS is the collection of revenue and ensuring compliance with the tax codes, its criminal investigation units seek evidence of criminal violations for prosecution by the Justice Department.

Based on the case law, the IRS holds that all taxpayers have tax obligations even when their income is derived from illicit sources.

Additional income for criminal purposes is established by both direct and indirect methods. The direct method consists of the identification of specific items of unreported taxable receipts, overstated costs and expenses (such as personal expenses charged to business, diversions of corporate income to office—stockholders, allocation of income or expense to incorrect year in order to lower tax, etc.), and improper claims for credit as exemptions. The advantage of using this method is that the proof involved is easier for jurors and others to understand.[33]

The success of prosecutions for tax violations by organized criminals continues. Coupled with Racketeer Influenced and Corrupt Organizations Act (RICO), Money Laundering and Bank Secrecy instrumentalities, the use of illicit moneys as a tool in the furtherance of criminal enterprises has been constricted; criminal activists and their enterprises are more vulnerable to legal interdiction since the Capone conviction. In many respects, RICO and subsequent legal tactics designed to control the white-collar types of organized crime activity are part of the legacy of control policies dating back to the 1927 Supreme Court decision in *Sullivan*.

CONCLUSION

After illegal funds have been removed from the United States, the money launderers begin legitimizing the income from these illegal sources so that it appears to be the product of legal business or personal transactions. The funds are repatriated back in the United States and invested in businesses and in personal and real property. As money launderers shift operations away from locations that have grown hazardous from enforcement pressure, their laundering operations will follow suit. For example, the Republic of Nauru, an island in the western Pacific, only four miles long and three miles wide, has 1,000 to 2,000 foreign corporations and banks.[34] Though much tax-haven activity is completely aboveboard—some is not—dirty money cries out to be laundered. For the U.S. banking system electronically dealing globally with financial institutions (Cook Islands, Vanuatu in the Pacific, the Turks and Caicos in the Caribbean, Bermuda, the Bahamas, the Cayman Islands, and especially Luxembourg, Switzerland, and Liechtenstein), an emphasis on international money-laundering research is clear. Exploring ways to improve cooperation between law enforcement agencies and financial institutions is vital if the transgressions of laundering black (dirty) money into green are to be contained.

NOTES

The term *black money* (dirty) is part of the criminal argot. It refers to illegally earned cash that, when washed, becomes green or legitimate.

1. President's Commission on Organized Crime (1984), "The Cash Connection: Organized Crime, Financial Institutions, and Money Laundering," *Interim Report to the President and the Attorney General* (Washington, DC: U.S. Government Printing Office, October 1984), 7.

2. U.S. Congress, Senate Committee on Governmental Affairs, *Crime and Secrecy: The Use of Offshore Banks and Companies*, Ninety-ninth Congress, First Session, 1985, Report 99-130, 153–79.

3. Clifford L. Karchmer, "Money Laundering and the Organized Underworld," in *The Politics and Economics of Organized Crime*, ed. Herbert E. Alexander and Gerald E. Caiden (Lexington, MA: Lexington Books).

4. James Cook, "The Invisible Enterprise," *Forbes*, 29 September 1980, 33.

5. James Mills, *The Underground Empire: Where Crime and Governments Embrace* (New York: Doubleday, 1986), 1131.

6. The United States Attorney and the Attorney General of the United States, "Drug Trafficking," *A Report to the President of the United States*, 3 August 1989.

7. National Institute of Justice, Research Plan, "Multijurisdictional Task Force," 1991, 53.

8. U.S. General Accounting Office, "Money Laundering: Treasury's Financial Crimes Enforcement Network," 18 March 1991, 2.

9. Thomas Morgan, "16 Charged in Scheme to Launder Drug Millions," *New York Times*, 14 May 1989, 24.

10. Peter T. White, "The Power of Money," *National Geographic*, January 1993, 105.

11. Mark Potts, N. Kochan, and R. Whitlington, *Dirty Money: BCCI* (Washington, DC: National Press Books, 1992), Chapters 9, 10.

12. National Institute of Justice, *International Money Laundering: Research and Investigation Join Forces*, September 1992, 1.

13. President's Commission, "The Cash Connection."

14. President's Commission on Organized Crime, "Organized Crime and Money Laundering," *Record of Hearing 11*, 14 March 1984, New York, Claire Sterling, *The Octopus: The Long Reach of the International Sicilian Mafia* (New York: W. W. Norton, 1990), Chapters 8-9.

15. Senate Committee of Governmental Affairs, *Crime and Secrecy: The Use of Offshore Banks and Companies*, Ninety-ninth Congress, First Session, 1985, 1-2.

16. Ibid.

17. Ibid. Report lists twenty-nine havens, 33–34. A description of the principal havens as to their banking practices, 53–125.

18. Ibid.; Michael Grace and John Guido, "Hong Kong 1997: Its Impact on Chinese Organized Crime in the United States." Washington, DC: U.S. Department of State, Foreign Service Institute.

19. U.S. Comptroller General, *Bank Secrecy Act: Treasury Can Improve Implementation of the Act* (Washington, DC: U.S. General Accounting Office, 1986).

20. Irving R. Kaufman, "The Cash Connection: Organized Crime, Financial Institutions and Money Laundering," *Interim Report*, President's Commission on Organized Crime (October), U.S. Government Printing Office.

21. Karchmer, "Money Laundering," 42.

22. Peter Reuter, *The Organization of Illegal Markets: An Economic Analysis* (Washington, DC: U.S. Department of Justice, National Institute of Justice, February 1985).

23. John Dombrink and Melodie Melrose, "Following Dirty Money: The Kaufman Commission and Organized Crime," in *Organized Crime in America: Concepts and Controversies*, ed. Timothy S. Bynum (Monsey, NY: Willow Free Press, 1987).

24. Herbert Edelhertz and Thomas D. Overcast, "A Study of Organized Crime Business: Type Activities and Their Implication for Law Enforcement" (Washington, DC: National Institute of Justice).

25. Adam J. Weinstein, "Prosecuting Attorneys for Money Laundering: A New and Questionable Weapon in the War on Crime," *Law and Contemporary Problems* 51 (Winter 1988): 369–86.

26. President's Commission, "Organized Crime."

27. *Caplan and Drysdale v. United States*, No. 87-1729; *United States v. Monsanto*, No. 88-454.

28. George Heavey, "Organized Crime in the Common Market," paper presented at the ASC annual meeting, Baltimore, MD, November 1991, United States Customs Service, Dept. of Treasury.

29. Barbara Webster and Michael S. McCampbell, "International Money Laundering: Research and Investigation Join Forces," *Natural Institute of Justice* (September 1992).

30. Robert J. Kelly, "Dirty Dollars: Organized Crime and Toxic Waste," *Criminal Justice Ethics* 7.1 (Winter/Spring 1988): 47–68.

31. Earl Johnson, Jr., "Organized Crime: Challenge to the American Legal System," *Criminal Law, Criminology and Police Science* 54 (March 1963): 1-29. 17–19.

32. John Kobler, *Capone: The Life and World of Al Capone* (New York: G. P. Putnam's Sons, 1971).

33. Committee on the Office of Attorney General, *Prosecuting Organized Crime* (Raleigh, NC: National Association of Attorneys General, 1974).

34. White, "The Power of Money," 103.

Part IV

Control and Containment: Law Enforcement Strategies

14

A History of Organized Crime Control: Federal Strike Forces

PATRICK J. RYAN

INTRODUCTION

The first law enforcement effort against organized crime in America occurred sixty years before the first Presidential Commission on Law Enforcement was convened in 1967. Lieutenant Joseph Petrosino, commander of the New York City Police Department's Italian Branch since 1905, was frustrated over the refusal of Black Hand extortion victims to identify and testify against the Mano Nero criminals for fear of brutal retaliation. Without victim complainants, Petrosino's efforts to imprison those who preyed on the population of immigrant Italians were stymied.

Petrosino tried a novel tactic: find evidence of criminal records in Italy and Sicily that would make Black Hand members subject to deportation. Before he was able to examine the Sicilian police files, the bad guys learned of the threat to their organization, and Petrosino was assassinated on orders of capo mafioso, Vito Cascioferro, whose alibi could not have been better: at the time the lieutenant was killed, the don was dining with a member of the Italian Parliament.[1] The business of organized crime continued and continues apace, as do the law enforcement efforts to combat it.

For this discussion, however, the pertinent point in this anecdote is not the novel enforcement tactic devised by Petrosino, nor even his tragic death. It is his identification (or definition) of the Black Hand organization as an appropriate target. Petrosino was of Italian descent. Did that fact influence his appointment to head the New York Police Department's (NYPD) Italian Branch? Did his background engender a personal concern for the protection of Italian immigrants? Did that provincialism focus his police activities on a single segment of the criminal world? Was his knowledge of this particular type of criminal activity made known to those in a position to make policy, direct resources, and identify investigative targets? All these questions probably can be answered yes.

Good police work narrows the focus of the investigation and, better yet, assigns the investigation to one who knows the territory, the actors on the scene, and their activities. In practice and of necessity,[2] police—and probably prosecutors—develop a powerful sense of autonomy[3] that operates beyond the usual devices for control.[4] The autonomy of law enforcement personnel is a crucial element in a history of organized crime in America, for in defining the target of investigations, the enforcers, in effect, define the subject matter of their efforts and that becomes the subject matter of the history. Because the definition of organized crime has never enjoyed even the semblance of consensus,[5] efforts to control it have similarly been the ad hoc product of those doing the enforcing.

Asked to define "organized crime," many ordinary citizens would conjure up a vision of Mafia or La Cosa Nostra (LCN), and the popular image is not limited to the public. "The same understanding of organized crime [as a formalized, hierarchical secret society, a corporation of crime] pervaded the thinking of the President's Crime Commission and congressional sponsors of the precursors [proposed laws] of RICO."[6] The focus of the 1967 President's Commission on Law Enforcement is nearly exclusively on the organized crime of Italian Sicilian groups. By 1987, at least in the eyes of federal commission members, that view changed to recognize a broader ethnic makeup of Asians and South and Central Americans.[7] Similarly, traditional presentations of the history of organized crime "as a morality tale," with xenophobic, alien conspiracy undertones of origin and genesis, have given way to countermanding views that common characteristics such as durability, continuity, hierarchy, multiplicity, violence, and corruption better define organized crime than do the more traditional notions.[8] As the government, public, and academic definitions changed, so did the law enforcement response.

How, then, to write a "history" of something as indistinct as prosecutorial discretion or a subject matter that changes over two scant decades from a limited Italian Sicilian organization to one embracing that plus Asians, South and Central Americans, and more by 1987? There would be two different "histories," indeed.

This issue of mutable definition shapes the contours of this chapter and its purpose, which is to draw attention to the fact that the history of control efforts against organized crime is a chronicle of changing definitions of target and that the latter are largely driven by the individual politicking of those involved in the effort. "Federal efforts against organized crime are more the result of individual decisions made at the local level than the result of a national strategy."[9] By 1990, there was no apparent change in strategy, yet the major federal program to combat organized crime was placed under the control of U.S. attorneys.

Squeezed into the "scant" two decades from 1967 to 1987 is the substantive history of organized crime control. Before the work of the 1967 Presidential Commission brought the idea of a nationwide criminal organization to the forefront, discussion of organized crime was limited to popular press accounts,[10] novelistic works,[11] or the rather sensationalistic public displays at congressional hearings and the literature produced from them. In the academic community, early on, W. Lippmann argued that "certain socioeconomic conditions encourage the existence of organized crime,"[12] and R. K. Merton theorized that deviant behavior (of which organized crime is a specimen) ensues when goals for the population at large are closed to a considerable segment.[13] Yet, research on organized crime was then and is still devoid of a comprehensive theory acceptable to practitioner and academic alike.[14] No definition, no adequate theory, and a huge cost to control it, $80 million in 1977[15]—this was the state of organized crime research and interdiction in the mid-1970s.

Indeed, the participants in a symposium on "Major Issues in Organized Crime Control"[16] felt that a search for one single definition of organized crime "misses the mark" because the goals and objectives of agencies involved in the control effort conflict with definitions sought by various researchers in various disciplines. Rather than "waste time trying to reach the ever receding goal of a definition that would satisfy everyone," it was "better" to discuss organized crime in terms of its members' attitudes.[17] Defining crime to suit the goals of a particular investigative agency or office is exactly what the law enforcement community had been doing since concerted efforts at controlling organized crime began in 1967. The practice continues today.

A review of all efforts at controlling organized crime, local, state, and federal, is a huge undertaking, beyond the scope of this presentation. There is, however, one specific law enforcement undertaking that encapsulates most others. Activities of organized crime groups transcend jurisdictional boundaries,[18] and common to most definitions was agreement, even if tacit, that control of organized crime must respond to this broad, diffusive characteristic. The concept of a multiagency investigative body, a group able to cross jurisdictional boundaries to attack a multifarious target, was made real in the formation of federal strike forces. Installed by Attorney General Robert Kennedy in 1967, they were returned (consolidated) into the offices of individual U.S. attorneys general in 1990 during the tenure of Attorney General Robert Thornburgh. The strike forces were criticized, mainly for lack of interagency cooperation among participants, a poor record of sentenced defendants, and a failure to define organized crime or explicate a national strategy to control it. At the same time, they were praised for their operational accomplishments.

This debate over the merger of strike forces into the offices of attorneys general draws together the history of organized crime control at the federal level. The debate is lopsided in favor of leaving the strike forces to operate as autonomous units. That the other side prevailed is inexplicable, given the information available. It is a political decision, perhaps born of Thornburgh's experience with the strike forces in Pittsburgh in the mid-1970s.[19] A retrospective examination of the work of the strike forces, with the knowledge that they were restructured in a way that supporters feel spells their demise, provides insight into the bureaucracy and its intrinsic struggles for power. This is a "turf battle" par excellence. Promise that the effort at control of organized crime will continue as before is found in Paul Vaira's comment that "it's a plan [the merger] that we had back in the 1960's."[20] Circularity, it seems, is a cornerstone of "good" federal-level bureaucracy and so, by the year 2010 or sooner, we may expect to find the strike force concept restored, in altered trappings perhaps, but basically doing the same job it did in its earlier incarnation.

This chapter briefly recalls the six historical highlights of control efforts prior to 1970:

1. the Maranzano purge in 1931
2. the Dewey investigations in the 1940s
3. the 1951 Kefauver hearings
4. the 1957 Apalachin meeting
5. 1963 McClellan congressional hearings
6. the 1967 Presidential Commission on Law Enforcement and the Administration of Justice

For various reasons, each of these events is distorted by the agendas of its interpreters, but collectively they create an image of organized crime that is, at the same time, heroic and vicious, appealing and appalling, clearly described and amorphous. Far from accurate, nonetheless, this image prevails today.

The discussion moves from the primer to the multiple definitions that have served to inform both theoretical and practical approaches to, respectively, the study and interdiction of organized crime. The review of a single federal effort, the strike force program, finds a litany of failings and condemnations enough to cause wonder why the strike forces were allowed to continue operating for some twenty-five years. This "straw man" is then torn down with an equally large collection of accolades from the same public record that causes wonder and consternation as to why they were returned to the offices of the U.S. attorneys general in 1990.

THE EARLY YEARS—A REFRESHER

The Maranzano Purge

Prohibition created an underground free market that needed a large criminal organization. The loosely knit extortionists of the Black Hand operating early in this century developed into a close-knit organization that satisfied a depression era demand for particular goods and services in a way that gave identifiable shape to the emerging groups engaged in this type of criminal activity. The organization that supplied outlawed liquor was eminently positioned to supply access to other illegal goods and services—prostitution, gambling, extortion. This organization was later described in the Kefauver Committee hearings in 1951 as the American Mafia and in 1963 became known as La Cosa Nostra.[21]

Undisputably, "the Cressey model" of the structure of organized crime that developed from his work with the 1967 Presidential Commission helped build the classical working conceptualization[22] that pervaded the field for the next decade or so.

Central to D. Cressey's model is the Maranzano "purge" of 1931. He writes that "the basic framework of the current structure of American organized crime, . . . was established as a result of a gangland war in which an alliance of Italians and Sicilians was victorious."[23] It is one of the "most important issues" in the traditional history of organized crime[24] and is the subject of several historical descriptions epitomizing LCN as organized crime.[25]

A. Block's analysis[26] debunks most of what "made" the syndicate as not much more than an exaggeration of hearsay or misinterpretation of testimony by those who were blinded by their own prior assumptions. For example, the testimony of Joe Valachi before the McClellan Committee that "four or five gang members were killed"[27] during the purge is translated by D. L. Chandler to "sixty victims,"[28] by Cressey to about "forty Italian-Sicilian gang leaders across the country,"[29] by J. R. Davis to "about ninety guineas,"[30] by H. Mesnick's informer, Nicola Gentile, into a "massacre,"[31] and by B. B. Turkus and S. Feder into "some thirty to forty leaders of Mafia's older group all over the United States."[32] Block cites these examples[33] not to deny that some gangsters killed others but to draw attention to "the scholarly attachment to the purge" as a "conspicuous example of the insensitivity to historical methods found all too often in work on organized crime."[34]

If the Maranzano purge was widely believed to be so extensive that it eliminated forty to sixty gangster types, it logically follows that the organization to which they belonged may very well have been national or international in scope. Later, in *Theft of the Nation*,[35] Cressey gave substance and academic credence to a model of a nationwide, hierarchically structured organization.

The Dewey Investigations

After a series of scandals involving politicians and mobsters in the mid-1940s, Thomas Dewey became Manhattan district attorney and prosecuted the de facto leader of LCN, Charles "Lucky" Luciano, and some of his associates. The Luciano case is the most notable of the traditional prosecutions that struck at the leadership but not the body of the organization. Dewey lost his thirst for gangbusting to the lure of the political arena, and when he ran for governor of New York, the enforcement activity against organized crime waned.

Beyond the immediate impact on the particular group Dewey attacked was the nationwide press coverage he enjoyed and the placing of "Mafia" and "organized crime'' in the common lexicon. This marks the beginning of the ''traditional'' imagery of organized crime couched in those terms. They and, later, ''La Cosa Nostra,''[36] added to the popular mystique[37] a ready moniker for ''this thing'' that too few people really understood. ''Mafia'' is neat; it packages those involved into a recognizable entity. The name and the notion were even more strikingly embedded in the popular and professional depictions of the phenomenon after the Kefauver hearings.

Kefauver Committee

In 1951 Estes Kefauver chaired a Special Committee to Investigate Organized Crime in Interstate Commerce.[38] The narrow scope implied by the committee's title was ignored in favor of inquiry into the national scale of organized crime's influence. Kefauver ''worked'' the media and public opinion well. In one year, the committee held public hearings in fourteen states and heard more than 800 witnesses. Many of the hearings, for the first time on the subject of organized crime, were televised.

Sustaining an objection to having his face known to an estimated 20 million viewers, the committee allowed its star witness, Frank Costello, to testify under a hood; and the 20 million ''enjoyed'' extended views of his fingers drumming the table while Chief Counsel Rudolph Halley asked embarrassing questions about his gambling interests and political connections.[39]

More by innuendo and insinuation from committee members than from Costello's testimony, the Mafia mystique grew.

The Apalachin Meeting

Six years later, in 1957, a change of leadership in the New York mob occurred when Albert Anastasia was machine-gunned to death while getting a shave in his favorite hotel. In May of that year, an attempt had been made on the life of Costello. A war was underway. On 11 November 1957, perhaps to calm the waters, a meeting was held in the town of Apalachin, New York, that was to rival Dewey and Kefauver for the national media spotlight.

As reported by P. Shelton,[40] a New York State police officer, Sergeant Edgar Croswell, assigned to the Bureau of Criminal Investigation, had become suspicious of the activities of an Apalachin resident, Joseph Barbara. After learning that Barbara had made arrangements for overnight guests at a local motel and had placed a large order for meat to be delivered to his home on 14 November, Croswell and his partner, Vincent Vasistro, became even more interested. It seems the Federal Bureau of Investigation (FBI) people were not so interested in Croswell's suspicions, and he turned for aid to two U.S. treasury agents, who agreed the case had merit.

The four officers staked out Barbara's home and, after observing a number of high-priced autos, some with out-of-state license plates, decided to get a closer look. They were discovered, and an estimated crowd of sixty organized crime figures fled into the woods. In all, fifty-eight people were taken into custody, and although none were holding weapons, drugs, or incriminating records, collectively, the men were carrying more than $300,000 in cash.[41] The meeting may have been nothing more than a high-stakes card game, but the "organized crime figure" angle played prominently in the news media, and to this day, the real reason for the meeting is speculative.

Again, enter the media's penchant for sensationalism, and the incident receives national coverage. Apalachin is described as a summit meeting of gang bosses from around the country, and, once more, another layer is added to the patina of organized crime as a disciplined, sinister part of the American crime scene. The frenzy about organized crime as a monolith controlled by a "commission" of Sicilian dons (only hinted, at this point) reached its peak with the testimony in 1963 of Valachi before the McClellan Permanent Subcommittee on Investigations in the Senate.

The McClellan Committee

While Valachi was serving a fifteen-year sentence for narcotics trafficking, he murdered another inmate in the yard of the federal penitentiary at Atlanta, Georgia, in June 1962. The murder was provoked by Valachi's belief that a contract on his life had been authorized by Vito Genovese. Speculation is that Valachi believed the dead inmate was about to make good on the contract. Valachi received a life term for the murder. Soon after, he began cooperating with federal law enforcement people.[42]

Valachi testified before McClellan's subcommittee during September and October 1963 that he was a member of a secret criminal organization called "Cosa Nostra." Valachi sated public eagerness for crime stories with a detailed account of his initiation into the LCN. None other than Salvatore Maranzano had presided over the ritual, he said. Valachi's finger was pricked for a few drops of blood; then a piece of paper was burned in his hands while he intoned: "This is the way I burn if I expose this organization."[43]

Valachi described a national organization of twenty-four families ruled by a commission. Each family was headed by a boss, assisted by an underboss and consiglieri. Soldiers report to a capo, and they to the bosses.[44] This is the testimony with which Cressey laid the foundation for his characterization of organized crime as bureaucracy complete with division of labor, discipline, profit motives, and job titles and definitions.[45]

Personalities and the Media

Ten years before the McClellan hearings, Robert F. Kennedy was named as assistant counsel to the Permanent Subcommittee on Investigations, in late 1952. The committee was chaired by Republican Joseph McCarthy. The senior Democrat on the committee was John L. McClellan. By mid-1953, the Democrats on the committee were becoming disenchanted with McCarthy's authoritarian leadership and threatened to leave the committee. A compromise arrangement included the appointment of Kennedy as minority counsel. The elections of 1954 gave the Democrats control of the Senate, and McClellan became chair of the Permanent Subcommittee on Investigations, and Kennedy was named general counsel.[46]

Usually, the general counsel identifies targets for investigation, and Kennedy moved the committee from McCarthy's hunt for red sympathizers to waste and mismanagement in government. The FBI successfully thwarted his probe into illegal wiretapping in Washington, D.C.,[47] but throughout 1955 the committee conducted a series of successful investigations into misconduct in government agencies.

After a short hiatus to serve on the Democratic campaign in 1956, Kennedy returned as general counsel and immediately secured McClellan's authorization to begin an investigation into labor racketeering.[48] Without going into congressional rules and its committee system, the vehicle for the investigation was to take the form of a Select Committee on Improper Activities in the Labor Management Field to be composed of four from each political party, and they equally from the Permanent Subcommittee on Investigation and the Labor Committee. McClellan, Robert Kennedy's committee boss, from the Select Committee and John Kennedy, his brother, from the Labor Committee volunteered to serve. Robert Kennedy was named counsel to the Select Committee.

The work of the Select Committee brought sufficient media and popular attention to McClellan and, especially, Kennedy that both were identified publicly as *the* leaders in the federal efforts to control organized crime. Kennedy was able to organize a team of investigators and accountants that ventured into new areas of identifying and thus defining organized crime. Like Kefauver's, the McClellan Committee attracted public attention by televising the hearings. From his dramatic confrontations with labor leader James Hoffa, International Brotherhood of Teamsters president, Kennedy would emerge as a thorough and able interrogator and tenacious investigator.

For the first time, the nation was presented with an expanded view of organized crime that described traditional criminal types holding sway and influence with leaders in the labor union field. The impression was of a symbiotic relationship of equally criminal participants. Kennedy described Hoffa as a criminal on par with any of the "family" bosses: "First, he [Hoffa] does a favor for them [the bosses], and they'll stick by him; second, by hiring an ex-convict he's doing a favor for another gangster, so then the gangster will do Hoffa a favor; and third, he uses them to move in on a city."[49]

So, even before the celebrated Valachi hearings, Kennedy and McClellan were connected in the fight against organized crime. Arguments have been made that Kennedy's early exposure to organized crime was to later influence his policies and priorities as attorney general in the 1960s. "It was in the Senate that Robert Kennedy learned about organized crime as counsel to Senator McClellan's committee.''[50] As attorney general, Kennedy assigned G. Robert Blakey to a newly expanded Organized Crime and Racketeering Section of the Criminal Division at Justice.[51] Blakey is generally credited with authorship of the Racketeer Influenced and Corrupt Organization Act (RICO) statute; McClellan with its sponsorship. From a reading of RICO and some of the controversy surrounding the law,[52] reasonable inference can be drawn that both Blakey and McClellan were informed by work in the Congress that showed organized crime is not synonymous with LCN, despite its being embraced by, and serving as figurehead for, all organized crime activities. From this and similar experiences in the Congress, the issue of organized crime control gets its impetus. "It was only with the prodding of Congress that in fact an organized crime program started; and it was only with the experience that Attorney General Kennedy had in congress with those hearings before the McClellan committee that in fact anything was done about the issue of organized crime.''[53]

More often than not, the personalities involved, more than the issue itself, drive efforts at control. In 1950, public enemy no. 1 was some poorly defined "red menace" that caught the public's attention mainly because McCarthy chose to take to the television airwaves. By 1960, the no. 1 target had changed to labor racketeering and the mix of traditional "Mafia" and union bosses; the union roles up to then had been perceived as respectable and law-abiding. Was the red menace so much less a threat? How or why labor racketeering and organized crime took the stellar role seems to be a function of the arbitrariness of the power brokers involved. The change of focus would become more palatable were it due only to the competition of one social issue over another for circumscription as a significant "problem." Indeed, Kennedy, McClellan, Blakey, and others might just as readily have reinforced McCarthy's position about the dire threat of Communism to national security or have defined drug distribution or governmental corruption as the major menace. They chose organized crime. This is not error; it merely serves as an interesting example of personal opinion that focuses the public at large on one issue in favor of another.

Yet, Kennedy's expanded definition of the players and their activities still concentrated on criminals of Italian ethnicity when it came to crimes of violence, loan-sharking, or gambling. Apparently there was no compelling reason to correct the record. Indeed, given the state of collected knowledge about organized crime, circa 1955–65, there was no evidence that a correction was necessary. It was believed that the LCN was organized crime and that attacking that group would eliminate its influence and clean the slate. Other criminal groups were ignored, unknown, or subordinated to the Mafia hegemony.

It is not clear whether public attention, the attention paid organized crime by the Congress, the synergism of both, increased knowledge of the workings of the criminal underworld (much of that generated in the academic community), or some combination of all of the above spurred Lyndon Johnson to create a Presidential Commission on Law Enforcement and the Administration of Justice in 1967.

1967 Presidential Commission on Law Enforcement and the Administration of Justice

Singularly, this commission[54] did more to change the face and philosophy of our criminal justice system regarding organized crime than did any other official body—not because it accurately described the phenomenon of organized crime (it did not) but because it elevated the issue to one of national concern and so aroused the Congress that many of its recommendations were enacted as legislation. The commission was divided into task forces to separately study the components of the criminal justice system. One was concerned with organized crime.

The Organized Crime *Task Force Report* found that both state and local law enforcement agencies were inadequately staffed to successfully deal with the problems of attacking organized crime. The report criticized short-term assignments of investigators and prosecutors to units charged with combating this kind of criminality. Its authors stressed the lack of coordination among local authorities and even among the various federal law enforcement agencies similarly involved as a hindrance to successful prosecution.[55]

In the prosecution of organized crime, one of the most tellingly effective tools of the last two decades has been the witness security program that grew out of the task force's recommendations. A "vital component" of effective criminal justice process is the granting of immunity against prosecution, a tool that has been around since 1789.[56] The "matters of proof" needed to prosecute effectively suffered from too few witnesses being willing to testify against organized crime figures, and even those immunized were often yet fearful for their lives and their ability to go about their normal lifestyle after the criminal proceedings ended. The task force recommended:

Enactment of a general witness immunity statute at Federal and state levels, providing immunity sufficiently broad to assure compulsion of testimony. Efforts to coordinate Federal, State and local immunity grants would be made to prevent interference with existing investigations.[57]

The 1967 task force sweetened the attractiveness of testifying in organized crime cases by recommending the establishment of a program of residential facilities, relocation, employment assistance, and anonymity for cooperative witnesses. These recommendations are now embodied in the Federal Witness Protection Program.

Citing the "great majority" of law enforcement officials who felt that electronic surveillance techniques were key to the gathering of evidence in organized crime cases, the task force recommended that Congress enact legislation dealing specifically with wiretapping and bugging. New York County district attorney Frank Hogan said wire monitoring is the "single most valuable weapon" in the fight against organized crime.[58] This specific recommendation is codified in the Omnibus Crime Control and Safe Streets Act of 1968.[59]

The electronic surveillance statute authorizes federal law enforcement agencies to ask the courts to order wiretapping. Requests require the approval of the attorney general at the federal level, and for states that have enacted enabling legislation in compliance with the Omnibus Act, similar authority to access the courts is granted.

A third recommendation resulted in the enactment by Congress in October 1970 of the RICO Act,[60] which has virtually revolutionized the prosecution of organized crime. The major purpose of RICO is to allow, in a single prosecution, a multidefendant criminal group for all of its diverse criminal activities. In the pre-RICO era, guilt was an individualized notion. Rules of criminal procedure were intended to promote fairness for individuals by separately weighing each defendant's behavior. This generally meant that in conspiracy cases a comprehensive picture of all crimes and all involved defendants could not be presented coherently in one prosecution. By law, prosecutors were forced to focus on discrete criminal acts, on criminals for specific acts, or on a group in a single conspiracy.[61] The recommendation of the task force that produced the RICO legislation opened this particular set of prosecutorial handcuffs.

RICO, the Omnibus Crime Control and Safe Streets Act, with its enhanced electronic surveillance provisions, and the Federal Witness Protection Program grew out of the 1967 Presidential Commission's inquiries into the state of law enforcement before 1967. The effort was yeoman's work but still left undefined organized crime.[62]

THE STRIKE FORCES

Chronology

Federal efforts to combat organized crime began in July 1954, when the attorney general established within the Criminal Division of Justice the Organized Crime and Racketeering Section of the Dept. of Justice (OCRS). Its averred purpose was to:

- coordinate enforcement activities against organized crime
- initiate and supervise investigations
- accumulate and correlate intelligence data
- formulate general prosecutorial policies
- assist federal prosecuting attorneys throughout the country.[63]

During the decade of the 1950s, OCRS "was moribund—it did nothing."[64] "Because conventional methods of law enforcement had proven ineffective against organized crime," OCRS established eighteen federal strike forces between January 1967 and April 1971, the first in Buffalo, New York.[65] The strike forces were staffed with justice attorneys and representatives from other federal investigative and law enforcement agencies. As of December 1976 strike forces were operating in Boston, Brooklyn, Chicago, Cleveland, Detroit, Kansas City, Los Angeles, Miami, Newark, Philadelphia, San Francisco, and Washington, D.C.

Strike force operations were terminated in Baltimore in 1974 and by 1976 in Manhattan, New Orleans, Pittsburgh, and St. Louis.[66] In addition to OCRS as overseer, participating agencies included: Bureau/Alcohol, Tobacco and Firearms (BATF); U.S. Customs Service (Customs); Department of Labor (Labor); Drug Enforcement Agency (DEA); Federal Bureau of Investigation (FBI); U.S. Postal Service; Securities and Exchange Commission (SEC); Internal Revenue Service (IRS); Immigration Naturalization Service (INS); U.S. Marshals Service; U.S. Secret Service.[67] As of June 1981, fourteen strike forces were in operation (the thirteen mentioned previously, plus New Orleans), and agency participation remained the same.[68]

In addition to the strike forces, a National Council on Organized Crime (NCOC) was established in 1970 to "formulate a strategy to eliminate organized crime."[69] In November 1976, a National Organized Crime Planning Council (NOCPC) replaced the NCOC. The goals of NOCPC were to facilitate detailed planning and coordination between the strike forces and federal law enforcement agencies and thus facilitate a coordinated approach to the federal efforts to combat organized crime. The NOCPC held its first meeting on 11 January 1977; agencies represented were OCRS, FBI, INS, DEA, BATF, IRS, Treasury, Customs, SEC, Labor, Secret Service, and U.S. Postal Service.

These were later jointed by the Law Enforcement Assistance Administration (LEEA) (March 1977), the International Association of Chiefs of Police (LACP) (August 1977), and, in September 1978, the inspector general of the U.S. Department of Agriculture.[70]

Aside from the fact that the NCOC met only five times between 1970 and June 1971 and never met thereafter,[71] a major difference between it and its successor was the bureaucratic level of participation. NCOC was chaired by the attorney general, and its members were at the assistant secretary level. NOCPC is chaired by the OCRS chief and members are managers from the division branch or section levels.[72] In other words, those doing the enforcement were now in a position to formulate strategy and facilitate interagency cooperation.

The strike force concept received high praise early on: the attorney general stated that "he intended to deal with and eventually eliminate organized crime and that this goal could best be achieved through a national strategy implemented by the strike forces."[73] The pilot program in Buffalo, New York, the forerunner operation, ran so successfully that the attorney general decided to locate strike forces throughout the country. In its first year of operations, the Buffalo strike force:

- identified the power structure of the local organized crime family
- targeted individuals whose removal would most severely damage criminal operations
- initiated prosecutions in areas in which prosecution would be successful and would seriously curtail the activities of the criminal organization.[74]

Operations

Strike forces generally operate in the same manner. Cases are (1) initially investigated by a participating agency, and, if warranted, (2) referred to the strike force for investigation and (3) indictment and prosecution. The participating agencies initiate and determine at which stage of the investigation the case should be brought to the strike force's attention. An agency representative discusses the investigation with a strike force attorney, and the latter decides whether or not it is appropriately a strike force matter.

Once accepted by the strike force, a case is assigned to an attorney who makes recommendations regarding electronic surveillance, wiretaps, and requests for assistance from other agency representatives or Justice. When prosecution is deemed warranted, the case is reviewed by the U.S. attorney and OCRS. The assistant attorney general at the Criminal Division at Justice makes the prosecutorial decision should any conflicts exist. Upon approval, a strike force attorney presents the case before a grand jury. The strike force attorney is assisted in prosecuting a case by the U.S. attorney with special expertise.

As of 1981, strike forces obtained about 83 percent of their case initiations from investigations conducted by the four participating law enforcement agencies (BATF, DEA, FBI, and IRS). The FBI supplies about 55 percent of all cases for prosecution.[75]

U.S. Attorney Oversight—Dispute Resolution

Rules in force since January 1988 governing the relationship between strike force attorneys and the U.S. attorney and OCRS, in effect, a determination of who has the "ultimate authority" in a particular district, say that (1) the U.S. attorney must concur with case openings and sentencing recommendations, requests for electronic surveillance, and search and arrest warrants; (2) disputes over case assignment are resolved initially by the U.S. attorney; final resolution is made by the assistant attorney general at Justice's Criminal Division; and (3) after indictment issues, the U.S. attorney oversees the judicial of the case. Perhaps most important in light of the political nature of the process, "All press releases on the subject of organized crime shall be cleared by the Justice Department's Office of Public Information and issued in the name of the U.S. attorney."[76]

Strike force attorneys can call on OCRS for expert help and intelligence gathered on the national level about particular suspects, groups, and associates.

Justice, through the assistant attorney general, Criminal Division, and OCRS, provides some measure of nationwide direction regarding target selection and also coordinates and facilitates agency interactions (resolves jurisdictional disputes).

Criticism of the Strike Force Program

The strike force program was operational for ten years when its performance was reviewed by the comptroller general in 1977. The report asked, "Why [is it that] organized crime still flourishes, despite 10 years of work by Federal strike forces to combat it."[77]

The report notes the importance of consumer demand for illegal goods and services in providing "billions" of dollars of income to organized crime each year and places the onus for the criminals' continued success on "Federal work" that is not planned, organized, or directed efficiently and an end product (convictions from strike force investigations) that has resulted in many cases closed with no prison sentences or sentences of less than two years.[78]

In the middle of a list of strike force deficiencies found by the comptroller general in 1977 is, once again, the need to define organized crime: "Although the strike forces were created for the special purpose of providing a coordinated national effort to fight organized crime, in practice this effort has been hampered because of definitional confusion."[79]

In summary, the 1977 report showed that (1) there was no national strategy on how to fight organized crime or even agreement on what organized crime was; (2) federal efforts to combat organized crime were hampered because strike forces had no authority over participating agencies; (3) there were no statements of objectives or plans to direct strike force efforts; and (4) Justice had no system for evaluating the effectiveness of the national organized crime effort or of individual strike forces.

In 1981, the comptroller general again examined strike forces in Brooklyn, Chicago, Los Angeles, and Philadelphia for the U.S. Senate and redundantly reported a "need for the Department of Justice to better coordinate the Federal attack against organized crime."[80] Although Justice had written in 1977 that it would work toward a "better planned, organized, executed and directed" federal effort against organized crime, by 1981, these objectives had "not completely" been accomplished.[81]

In 1989, the Government Accounting Office took a look at "issues concerning strike forces,"[82] and despite many prosecutions and convictions of traditional organized crime leaders as a result of federal initiatives (the strike forces included), the review found that all of the "required" mechanisms for planning and coordinating "a unified federal effort" were not being fully used.[83] The unused, "required" mechanisms referred to were strike force-level executive committees that did not function as intended and U.S. attorneys who did not fully comply with a requirement to develop strategic plans.[84]

The Criticism as a Management Issue

The 1989 report to Congress[85] solidifies the criticism surrounding operation of the strike force in terms of a management issue. The failure to form committees or to devise plans, conflicts over prosecutorial jurisdiction between strike forces and U.S. attorneys (turf battles), and a fear of dilution of a national mission all speak to issues that, from a manager's standpoint, may need correcting but say little about the efficacy of investigative protocols. Do field investigators truly need the guidance from a national strategy in the conduct of their investigations in specific jurisdictions? The comptroller general's reports in 1977 and 1981, the hearing in the House in 1981, and the report to the Senate in 1989 find faults in the strike force operations. But is the blame properly placed?

For instance, the 1977 report[86] says there are no national strategy to fight organized crime, no definition of organized crime, no statement of objectives, no evaluation program, an inadequate intelligence-gathering effort, and too few "real time" sentences given in strike force prosecutions. Each deficiency is external to the running of an investigative unit. The only criticism directly related to strike force operations is that the attorneys in charge do not have sufficient authority over the participating agencies to get the job done; this, too, is more a problem of organization and management than an operational one.

The 1981 report faults the strike forces for not establishing executive committees;[87] however, the convening of these committees is a task assigned to the individual U.S. attorneys.[88] The rest of the 1981 report, much like its predecessor in 1977, is concerned with issues such as setting priorities; planning, organizing, executing, and directing the federal effort; reviewing sentences, and an underutilized RICO, none of which address the operating effectiveness of strike forces.

In the 1989 report to the Senate the strike forces were again faulted for not being part of the executive committees (that the U.S. attorneys had not formed),[89] but the review noted that on a case-by-case basis, the strike force attorneys were able to "coordinate" with investigative agencies. Again, this report also spends a good deal of its space on planning for a "unified effort" of national scope that ignores the transjurisdiction and differential character of organized crime groups.

In fairness, the priorities prevent strike force investigators from playing a numbers game, a game of getting on the score sheet with high numbers of cases with low-level criminal charges, and "ground ball" investigations. They concentrate strike force resources on specific areas of organized crime activity, precluding investigations that focus on relatively minor crimes.

The fact still remains that "priorities" are a management decision. They are policy, not application. That "national strategies" and interagency coordination are so much a part of evaluations of strike forces speaks to deficiencies in the upper echelons of management, not weakness at the operational level.

Turf Battles

The 1989 Senate report pays particular attention to a similar issue: "conflicts between strike force and U.S. attorneys."[90] "Turf battles" are a management issue that goes beyond textbook resolution. The personalities of the actors involved are as important, if not more so, than the conflict itself. Where the opposing chiefs cooperate against a common enemy, turf battles are rare.

At the core of the characteristic turf battle is the question of who, which office, will investigate, arrest, and prosecute. The potential for conflict is born of the very nature of criminal activity; much of it transcends jurisdictional boundaries. Criminals do not limit their activities to the geographic divisions created by law enforcers. Turf battles are a way of life in law enforcement, at all levels. Beat cops argue with their opposite number over who will arrest the burglar, just as U.S. attorney Rudy Giuliani "fought tooth and nail" with Robert Morganthau and Mario Merola (respectively, New York and Bronx district attorneys) over who would lock up whom.

Another aspect of turf battles—target selection—complicates the question of whether or not the strike forces are optimally effective against organized crime. Precursory to the 1990 merger of strike forces, the strike force for the Southern District of New York was merged into the U.S. attorney's office in 1976. It is often held as a "shining example" of how effective a U.S. attorney, without a strike force unit, can be in the battle against organized crime.

In 1980 Dominick Amoroso, the attorney in charge of the strike force unit within the U.S. attorney's office for the Southern District of New York, wrote to his superiors in Justice that his unit was lacking in productivity and was not making use of prosecutorial tools such as RICO and electronic surveillance. The U.S. attorneys at the time were "extraordinarily effective," but their priorities were in areas other than organized crime. In 1983, Giuliani was appointed to that office and quickly demonstrated a tremendous impact on organized crime. More than twenty assistant attorneys were assigned to organized crime cases, and several important prosecutions ensued. Amoroso's complaint was laid to rest simply because a new U.S. attorney (Giuliani) decided to make organized crime a priority target.

By 1987, target selection changed. There was some publicity about the demise of the Mob in New York, and Giuliani shifted his focus. The Mob was still operating, but public corruption and business crime became the focus of investigations. The number of attorneys in the organized crime unit was halved. It is probably incidental to the decision to change priorities that the next year Giuliani ran for mayor of New York and left his previous office.

The pertinent points are that the persona of the U.S. attorney can resolve jurisdictional disputes where strike forces coexist with U.S. attorneys' districts and can or cannot focus resources on organized crime investigations when the strike force unit is physically housed in the U.S. attorney's office. In either instance, the "problem" is management technique, not operational effectiveness. In the latter case, organized crime as a target is vulnerable to the capricious demands of resources, clientele, and personal preference.

There is some difficulty in dichotomizing "turf" and "politics." The two are most often hand in glove. When any attorney invests some level of energy fighting for control of a case, be assured that the case has political implications, some aspect that makes its prosecution attractive. It may be a large forfeiture, a big-name defendant, or a sensitive issue. Whatever makes the case worth fighting to keep in the attorney's own turf is the very same thing that is political. Under the penumbra of "political" are found personal ambition, glory, hunger for power, and self-aggrandizement. Turf battles do not occur when people cooperate in what should be a common goal. Absent politics, joint ventures work.

The success of the strike forces in rearranging the hierarchies of organized crime families by imprisoning a large number of the top leaders "is no accident." A crucial difference between investigative units such as the U.S. attorneys' offices, which jurisdictions are limited to a judicial district, and the strike force units is the latter's ability to target the enterprise and eliminate an entire chain of command at one time. The transjurisdictional nature of the strike forces allows pursuit without regard to geographical locations. Pragmatically, this allows one investigative unit to cast a net over areas that otherwise would involve one or several, often competitive U.S. attorneys' jurisdictions. The prosecution of the Patriarca family in New England demonstrates this point.

The strike force was responsible for all of New England. The Patriarca family's activities ranged from Providence, Rhode Island, to Boston, Massachusetts, and into Connecticut. The criminal activity spanned three judicial districts and would have required the coordination of three separate U.S. attorney's offices. "Anyone familiar with multi-jurisdictional investigations knows only too well the bureaucratic infighting among prosecutors' offices for headline-making cases."[91] It is speculative that the Patriarca case would not have been successful without the broad jurisdiction of the strike force. It is a fact that the process went with minimal conflict because of it.

Finally, regarding target selection, the jurisdictions of U.S. attorneys must address the needs of a constituency much broader than those concerned with organized crime. If New York is one of the largest concentrations of organized crime activity, that fact alone cannot dictate the prosecutorial focus of the U.S. attorney in New York. High levels of political corruption, narcotics, violence, securities or savings and loan frauds, and more demand attention and investigative resources. Necessarily, organized crime must take its place in the line of priority cases. Too, U.S. attorneys represent the government in civil matters, a time-consuming task that impacts resource allocation as well as criminal matters.

Just as a longitudinal review of cases brought by any U.S. attorney's office will mirror the priorities of the incumbent U.S. attorney for any given period—Giuliani in New York is an example—the review's results might themselves hide ulterior motives. Those who criticize the selection of a particular target simply believe another target, usually their own, is more important. Target selection, like deviance, is in the eyes of the beholder, and he or she must defend it against charges of misplaced priorities or political motivation. In any event, if investigative units created for the express purpose of controlling a specific criminal segment are to be effective, they should specialize on the named target exclusively. A U.S. attorney's office is not such a unit.

In no way should this discussion be construed as a denigration of the performance of the U.S. attorneys. Multifocus investigations are their bread and butter. It would be an incompetent or ineffectual U.S. attorney who did not address all segments of the constituency. For the immediate discussion however, a priori logic says that organized crime is a phenomenon so threatening to us all that it should be a high-priority target. If the prior assumption is erroneous, we might surrender in the fight against organized crime. The twenty-year funding history of strike forces by Congress evinces the opposite, that the fight is of national concern.[92] The expansive array of matters that must concern U.S. attorneys can only dilute efforts to control organized crime. This leaves, then, the strike forces, whose reason for existence is to control organized crime in whatever apparition it appears or by whatever definition it is identified.

The Debate for Consolidation

A statement prepared by Acting Deputy Attorney General Edward S. G. Dennis for the Subcommittee on Criminal Justice collects the "history of the debate" for putting the strike forces under the control of the individual U.S. attorneys.

1970—Three years after Attorney General Ramsey Clark created the strike force program in 1967, the Presidential Council on Executive Organization (the Ash Council) recommended the merger of the Strike Forces into the U.S. attorneys' offices.

1974—The recommendation for merger was repeated by the Attorney General's Advisory Committee of United States Attorneys.

1987—That Committee repeated the formal recommendation to Attorney General Meese in February 1987.[93]

The issue was again before Congress in 1989 in response to an announcement by Attorney General Thornburgh that the merger was imminent. In 1987, Attorney General Edwin Meese installed new rules to put a halt to the turf battles that had been frustrating the mission of the strike forces. To fears expressed by some in Congress that the parochial interests of U.S. attorneys would lead to a balkanization of the national war on organized crime, proponents of consolidation offered the fact that the program already has (since the 1987 rule changes) a demonstrated track record of the U.S. attorneys' securing approval of case initiations from OCRS for strike forces cases.

According to Dennis, the benefits of consolidation were seen to be

1. an improved utilization of Justice's resources
2. mobilizing the power of the "personal relationships and local clout" of the U.S. attorneys on alliances with local district attorneys and other state and local law enforcement officials
3. stopping "prosecutor shopping" by the investigative agencies
4. eliminating turf battles
5. centralizing accountability for crime in a district
6. consolidating efforts that would encourage U.S. attorneys to dedicate their resources strategically to combat organized crime

The final benefits are economies of scale: there will be no need for two libraries or two telephone systems, and Justice can "expect" that merging "other administrative functions" will similarly save money.

Consolidation risked the potential dissipation of the effort against "traditional elements of organized crime" in favor of "other work" done in the U.S. attorneys' offices. The fact that strike force jurisdictions cross over the boundaries of U.S. attorneys' districts induced misgivings that some areas of the country would be less ably served by the organized crime investigators. To both these concerns, Deputy Attorney General Dennis countered, "I believe that the fear, ... will not be realized" because the U.S. attorneys already approve case initiations by the strike forces and, since that procedure is in effect, there has been "no perceptible change" in the pattern of cases initiated.[94]

A third risk voiced "by some in Congress" assumes that strike force attorneys tend more often to be career prosecutors than do their counterparts on the U.S. attorneys' staffs and the consolidation would drive these career prosecutors to seek other employment. Just the opposite should happen, said Dennis, since there presently exists a salary differential between the two job titles that would be ameliorated when the strike force attorneys gain parity with the U.S. attorneys' assistants in the merger.

The congressional presentation favoring the merger can be construed as an assurance that the strike forces were not to be abolished, merely consolidated and maintained as separate units within U.S. attorneys' offices. The position of the attorney general was supported by the National District Attorneys' Association, which took the same position regarding turf battles, as logistical savings, improved coordination between law enforcement agencies, and a broadened authority for the U.S. attorneys made it easier for them to forge crucial alliances with state and local prosecutors.

The Debate Against Consolidation

The strike forces are credited with busting up the largest mafia families in New York and New England, the casino-related prosecutions in Las Vegas and Kansas City and the convictions of hundreds involved in mob corruption in eastern seaboard ports. After all these victories, I think it's fair to ask, "What is broke that needs fixing?"[95]

Three elements are crucial to successful strike force operations: experience and expertise; dedication and continuity; and independence. The concentration on local prosecutions by the strike forces inevitably develops a group of attorneys experienced by narrow focus. Attorneys in the strike forces generally are viewed as experienced career prosecutors, as opposed to the perception that the political patronage modus operandi of the U.S. attorneys' offices recruits untested lawyers, many of whom use the office as a place to be groomed with trial experience prior to their entry into more lucrative private practice. The average assistant U.S. attorney has about 5 to 6 years' prosecutorial experience while the average strike force attorney has 11.5 years' such exposure. Strike force attorneys in Chicago in 1989, for example, averaged 14 years of prosecutorial experience, with the attorney-in-charge and his two assistants each having served 17 or more years as federal prosecutors. The experience and expertise bred of such longevity are vital factors for successful prosecutions in the area of organized crime.

If only because of the discontinuous personnel practices occasioned by change in U.S. attorneys (and most staffers) with each presidential election, the assistant U.S. attorney positions are considered more political than are like assignments to a strike force staff. As a result, offices that are not faced with a change in leadership every four or so years tend to develop more dedicated personnel. The attorneys remain in position long enough to create a sense of continuity and responsibility that helps to develop a trust with the seasoned investigators upon whom they must rely. Longevity in this instance creates a sense of dedication and mutual trust and a singular purpose that can only benefit the clients being served.

Attorneys (and investigators) who stay in the same place, working on one criminal activity with a somewhat stable cast of characters, develop an "institutional memory" that serves as a repository of the historical sense of organized crime in their regions. A statement interpreted by the tyro investigator as merely passing the time of day may be read by the experienced one as a reference to a mob hit of twenty years past. Only time teaches how to put oblique, seemingly disconnected references into the semblance of an investigation worth pursuing.

Along with dedication, continuity, and issue-specific investigative acumen, long tenure develops a certain sense of independence that encourages new and sometimes innovative inroads in the prosecutorial arena. The apolitical foundation of strike force units enables and encourages such a posture. Strike force attorneys get fired, for sure, just as do assistant U.S. attorneys, yet the former terminations are far more often for cause while the latter are products of the nearly whimsical variegations in the political arena.

The Rationale for Consolidation

The strike forces were merged into the U.S. attorneys' offices in 1990. In view of Attorney General Thornburgh's demonstrated commitment to the fight against organized crime and the success of the strike force program,[96] the consolidation is puzzling.

The consolidation is a management decision. The public debate pits upper-echelon Justice administrators who speak in support of the boss's decision against law enforcement practitioners who fault it. The strike forces were put in place by Attorney General Kennedy by administrative fiat, and it seems appropriate for a successor to prerogatively eliminate them via the same avenue. Thornburgh's expressed reasoning is that the nationwide effort will be enhanced by centralizing command decisions.

Thornburgh's predecessor, Attorney General Meese, had worked out a compromise that gave the U.S. attorneys wider oversight of strike force personnel but still left those units intact. Charles Schumer, charting the Oversight hearings, melded the opinions of all witnesses and made ''so bold'' as to suggest that the status quo, keeping the strike forces as they are but giving the U.S. attorneys responsibility for actual prosecution of the case, might be ''the best solution.'' Indeed, were the decision put to a vote, the testimony is overwhelmingly against consolidation. Opinion appears divided into camps of management types who see productivity returns from the merger and law enforcement types who see organized crime taking a back seat under the restructuring.

For good reason, there were no strike forces against organized crime before 1967. Few had defined it as a ''problem.'' Fewer still had even an inkling of how it truly operated. In the early years of operation, strike forces worked virtually without oversight. By 1976, limited requirements for warrants, electronic surveillance orders, and the like were put in force. The 1987 orders by Meese effectively put operational control in the hands of the U.S. attorneys. By 1990, the strike force was no longer a separate unit.

Thus far, the history of the strike forces (or, at least, oversight of them) may be paved with personal ambitions and desires for power and glory, and the consolidation may be ''a feather in the cap'' of the U.S. attorneys. The consolidation may even be good management. Yet, there remains a large body of dissenting opinion, and dissenting opinions have a history of returning to favor, refurbished with a compelling patina.

CONCLUSION

Whatever lesson this short history tells, one thing is clear: the operations of the federal strike force program had little, if anything, to do with the reasons it was abolished, all disclaimers to the contrary notwithstanding. Every practitioner who spoke publicly in the debate extolled its merits, and one must wonder why it was not left intact.

It would be too easy to characterize the decision to merge the strike forces as raw power politics, the work of egocentric U.S. attorneys looking to bolster individual power bases with the resources held by the strike forces, or, in the same mode, to claim that the decision fulfills a circumscribed view that the program needed fixing held by one who finally arrived at a position to do the fixing (Attorney General Thornburgh). The fact that both "reasons" may be right or wrong is of little importance. Thornburgh made what essentially is a management decision. He must rise or fall on its merits.

Management systems are not management. In this debate, two realities prevail; the philosophy of a government dedicated to deregulation is at odds with the freezing of energies to improve efficiency. Putting the strike forces beneath the canopy of the U.S. attorneys will stifle the energy, professional pride in achievement, and the exercise of initiative heretofore shown by the single-purpose, career investigators who now find themselves responding to a hydra-like mission. Collectively, the comments of those opposing the merger say that operational problems will follow. Inexperienced and uninformed "experts" will be available to assist with local prosecutions and will effectively be ineffective. A cadre of attorneys and investigators experienced exclusively with organized crime will find themselves working on whatever the particular U.S. attorney general they work for decides is a priority issue. The alternative prediction is that these career prosecutors will look for greener pastures. The control of organized crime will be spotty again, due to local priorities. Organized crime activity will most likely ebb and flow with the level of attention its members receive from the offices of U.S. attorneys general.

It is not clear if those in the U.S. attorneys' offices understand the "culture" of the strike forces. Career investigators bring to the task a different bag of talents and need a different kind of recognition than do investigators who are eased in and out of office with political grease. Also unclear is the effect the control mentality implicit in the consolidation will have on the efficiency of the strike force attorneys. On the whole, strike force attorneys have performed well because they see clearly and exactly what their mission is. They develop an expertise that grows and is nurtured by concentrating in a single area of criminality. Will their dedication to fighting crime suffer, having to perform a diverse set of tasks?

America now finds itself without a force of investigative units dedicated solely to the control of organized crime. District U.S. attorneys general are left with the responsibility to target and prosecute who and what they see as organized crime. Each of the ninety-four judicial districts will receive its own brand of organized crime control, and those areas of the country outside these districts must now rely on local law enforcement for the same. Ninety percent of local police departments have less than ten sworn members, a woefully inadequate contingent for this fray.

The arguments against the merger far outweigh those for it. No single organization can perform well a variety of tasks; inevitably, some will be neglected. The turf-conscious executive who stoutly insists on a hands-on approach in a multitask agency is courting disaster. If organized crime control is treated as an "orphan" task now that the dons are in prison, the failure to commit discrete resources to the fight may lead to a political crisis. There is hope, however.

U.S. attorneys general change with each administration. So does the attorney general. Some time in the next two or three administrations, a new attorney general may bring to the debate a preformed opinion that the strike force concept is sound. A management decision will once again change the face of federal efforts to control organized crime. Such a decision will be welcomed by organized crime control advocates and dreaded by organized crime members, just the reverse of the present case.

NOTES

1. T. M. Pitken and F. Cordosco, *The Black Hand: A Chapter in Ethnic Crime* (Totowa, NJ: Littlefield Adams, 1977).

2. P. J. Ryan, "Accountability, Discretion and the First Line Supervisor," paper presented at the annual meeting of the American Society of Criminology, Montreal, 11 November 1987, 2–6, 27; J. A. Mark, "Police Organizations: The Challenges and Dilemma of Change," in *The Ambivalent Force: Perspectives on the Police*, A. Neiderhoffer and A. S. Blumberg, ed. 2nd ed. (Hinsdale, IL: Drydcn, 1976), 356–59.

3. A. J. Reiss, Jr., *The Police and the Public* (New Haven, CT: Yale University Press, 1971), 125.

4. B. Smith, *Police Systems in the United States* (New York: Harper, 1960).

5. See the contribution by M. Maltz, "Defining 'Organized Crime,' " in this volume; P. J. Ryan, "RICO, OCCA, and Defining Organized Crime [Organized Crime Is What Organized Crime Does]," *Criminal Organizations* 5.2 (1990): 18–26.

6. G. E. Lynch, "RICO: The Crime of Being a Criminal, Parts I & II," *Columbia Law Review* 87.4 (1987): 661–764, 685–726; RICO is the Racketeer Influenced and Corrupt Organizations Act, 18 U.S.C. 96 §. 1962–68, 1970.

7. J. Albanese, "Government Perceptions of Organized Crime," *Federal Probation* 51.1 (1988): 62.

8. P. J. Ryan, and R. J. Kelly, "An Analysis of RICO and OCCA: Federal and State Legislative Instruments Against Crime," *Violence, Aggression and Terrorism* 3.1/2 (1989): 58–60, 62–66.

9. R. F. Kipper to the Comptroller General of the United States, *War on Organized Crime Faltering—Federal Strike Forces Not Getting the Job Done* (Washington, DC: General Accounting Office [GGD-77-17, 1977]), 7.

10. J. R. Davis, "Things I Couldn't Tell Till Now," *Collier's*, 5 August 1939, 12–13; R. J. Kennedy, "The Mafia Exposed—What It Means," *Saturday Evening Post*, 10–17 August 1963.

11. B. B. Turkus and S. Feder, *Murder, Inc.: The Story of the Syndicate* (New York: Farrar, Strauss and Young, 1951); W. F. Whyte, *Street Corner Society* (Chicago: University of Chicago Press, 1943); F. Thrasher, *The Gang* (Chicago: University of Chicago Press, 1927).

12. W. Lippmann, "The Underworld as Servant," *Forum* (January/February 1931): 162–72.

13. R. K. Merton, *Social Theory and Social Structure* (New York: Free Press, 1957), 146.

14. P. Reuter, "Methodological and Institutional Problems in Organized Crime Research," in *Major Issues in Organized Crime Control*, ed. H. Edelhertz (Washington, DC: National Institute of Justice, 1987), 171.

15. Kipper, *War*, 1.

16. Edelhertz, *Major Issues*, 192–93.

17. Ibid.

18. C. A. Bowsher to the Comptroller General of the United States, *Stronger Federal Effort in Fight Against Organized Crime* (Washington, DC: General Accounting Office [GGD-82-2], 1981), 135; U.S. Congress, House Subcommittee on Criminal Justice of the Committee on the Judiciary, *Oversight Hearing on Organized Crime Strike Forces*, 101st Congress, First Session, Serial No. 14 (Washington, DC: U.S. Government Printing Office, 1989), 64.

19. U.S. Congress, *Oversight Hearing*, 149.

20. Ibid., 63

21. The term *La Cosa Nostra* was first introduced to an incredulous public in 1963 by Joe Valachi. See U.S. Congress, Senate Special Committee to Investigate Organized Crime in Interstate Commerce, *The Kefauver Committee Report on Organized Crime*, No. 307 (Washington, DC: U.S. Government Printing Office, 1951), 151.

22. J. L. Albini, "Donald Cressey's Contributions to the Study of Organized Crime: An Evaluation," *Crime & Delinquency* 54.5 (1988): 338–54.

23. D. Cressey, "The Functions and Structures of Criminal Syndicates," President's Commission on Law Enforcement and Administrations of Justice, *Task Force Report: Organized Crime* (Washington, DC: U.S. Government Printing Office, 1967), Appendix A, 26.

24. A. Block, "History and the Study of Organized Crime," *Urban Life* 6.4 (1978): 456.

25. See, for example, D. L. Chandler, *Brothers in Blood: The Rise of the Criminal Brotherhoods* (New York: E. P. Dutton, 1975); D. Cressey, *Theft of the Nation: The Structure of Crime in America* (New York: Harper and Row, 1969); Davis, "Things"; H. Messick, *Lansky* (New York: G. P. Putnam's Sons, 1971); Turkus and Feder, *Murder, Inc.*

26. Block, "History."

27. U.S. Congress, Senate Hearings Before a Permanent Subcommittee on Investigations of the Committee on Government Operations, *Organized Crime and Illicit Traffic in Narcotics* (Washington, DC: U.S. Government Printing Office, 1963), 232.

28. Chandler, *Brothers*, 160.

29. Cressey, *Theft*, 44.

30. Davis, "Things," 44.

31. Messick, *Lansky*, 49.

32. Turkus and Feder, *Murder Inc.*, 87.

33. Block, "History," 456–59.

34. Ibid., 464.

35. Cressey, *Theft*.

36. See note 21.

37. D. C. Smith, Jr., *The Mafia Mystique* (New York: Basic Books, 1975).

38. U.S. Congress, *The Kefauver Committee Report*.

39. V. W. Peterson, *The Mob: 200 Years of Organized Crime in New York* (Otawa, IL: Green Hill, 1983), 268.

40. P. Shelton, *History of the New York State Police* (Dallas: Dallas Press, 1987).

41. Ibid., 110–11.

42. H. Abadinsky, *Organized Crime* (Chicago: Nelson Hall, 1990), 473.

43. Peterson, *The Mob*, 364.

44. Ibid., 365.

45. Cressey, *Theft*; Cressey, "The Functions."

46. A. S. Schlessinger, Jr., *Robert Kennedy and His Times* (Boston: Houghton Mifflin, 1978), 105.

47. Ibid., 120–21.

48. Ibid., 124.

49. Ibid., 174.

50. U.S. Congress, *Oversight Hearing*, 130.

51. National Advisory Committee on Criminal Justice Standards and Goals, *Report of the Task Force on Organized Crime* (Washington, DC: Law Enforcement Assistance Administration, 1976), 278.

52. See, for example, P. J. Ryan and R. J. Kelly, "An Analysis of RICO and OCCA: Federal and State Legislative Instruments Against Crime," *Violence, Aggression and Terrorism* 3.1/2 (1989): 81 n. 2, 86–89, Appendix A.

53. U.S. Congress, *Oversight Hearing*, 130.

54. President's Commission on Law Enforcement and the Administration of Justice, *Task Force Report: Organized Crime* (Washington, DC: U.S. Government Printing Office, 1967).

55. Ibid., 14–20.

56. R. L. Thornburgh, "Reconciling Effective Federal Prosecution and the Fifth Amendment: 'Criminal Coddling,' 'The New Torture,' or 'A Rational Accommodation,' " *The Journal of Criminal Law & Criminology* 67.2 (1976): n. 3, 155, citing *Kastigar v. United States*, 406 U.S. 441, 443–447.

57. President's Commission, *Task Force Report*, 19.

58. Ibid.

59. Omnibus Crime Control and Safe Streets Act, U.S.C. 18 § 2510 1968.

60. See n. 6.

61. See Ryan and Kelly, "An Analysis," 71–74, for a discussion of joinder as applied under RICO.

62. Ryan, "RICO," 4.

63. Kipper, 5.

64. U.S. Congress, *Oversight Hearing*, 130.

65. Kipper, 5.

66. Ibid., 5.

67. Ibid., 5–6.

68. Bowsher, 6.

69. Ibid., 3.

70. Ibid., 8.

71. Kipper, 7.

72. Bowsher, 8.

73. Kipper, 7.

74. Ibid., 11–12.

75. Bowsher, 3.

76. U.S. Congress, *Oversight Hearing*, 148.

77. Kipper, Cover.

78. Ibid.

79. Ibid., 14.

80. Bowsher, Cover Letter.

81. Ibid., 6.

82. U.S. Congress, Senate Subcommittee on Investigations, Committee on Governmental Affairs, *Report to the Chairman* (Washington, DC: U.S. Government Printing Office, 1989).

83. Ibid., 3.

84. Ibid., 15–21.

85. See n. 107.

86. Kipper.

87. Bowsher, 14.

88. U.S. Congress, *Report*, 3.

89. Ibid., 16, 20–21, 26.

90. Ibid., 21–24.

91. Ibid., 135.

92. Ibid.

93. Ibid., 18–19.

94. Ibid., 20.

95. Ibid., 1. Remarks of Representative Schumer, Chair of the Subcommittee on Criminal Justice, presiding.

96. For highlights of the strike forces' successes, see Kipper 24–27, 38–43; Bowsher, 1, 15, 28–29, 40–41; U.S. Congress, *Oversight Hearing*, 92–128, 168–70, 180–219, 224–60.

15

Intelligence and Analysis Within the Organized Crime Function

MARILYN B. PETERSON

INTRODUCTION

The need for more sophisticated investigative techniques has been driven, in part, by an ongoing organized crime presence. One of those techniques is known as the intelligence process. The intelligence process, simply, is collecting, analyzing, and disseminating information. This process is found at all levels of law enforcement work but is most often associated with the organized crime function.

As Justin J. Dintino and Frederick T. Martens noted, intelligence as a process remains the only rational means of addressing the problem of organized crime.[1] They later stated that the failure of law enforcement executives to recognize the potential of the intelligence process has resulted in ill-conceived and politically expedient organized crime control policies.[2]

In 1974, Francis A. J. Ianni commented that organizational (i.e., enterprise) intelligence and analysis, rather than individual case development, could dramatically improve the ability of the criminal justice system to study organized crime.[3] Since then, organized crime units have shown that whole organizations can be effectively investigated and prosecuted by using an organizational or network approach.

Key to the intelligence process is analysis. In 1985, the International Association of Chiefs of Police said that the analysis of collected information is critical to the control of organized and sophisticated crime.[4] The use of analysts, particularly at the federal and state levels, grew significantly in the late 1980s and early 1990s.

Complex investigations require the uses of intelligence. As Michael Libonati and Herbert Edelhertz stated,

In order to determine the form of prosecution and to exploit convictions, the existence of an intelligence base that reveals the potential property interests of the subjects of interest is crucial. This knowledge is especially important if criminal and civil remedies, such as a RICO statute, are available. Such intelligence, validated by specific investigations, could determine whether RICO preliminary remedies should be sought and whether criminal or civil remedies, or both, be pursued.[5]

But many law enforcement agencies have still not incorporated intelligence and analysis into their organized crime control function. One reason for this may be the failure of analysts to clearly articulate the concrete uses of intelligence and analysis within the daily operations of the organized crime unit. Another cause may be that management has not maximized its application of analysis due to a reluctance to deviate from the traditional methods of investigation. A reason for not using analysis is the difficulty management may have in evaluating the results of analytical work products.

This chapter provides an overview of tactical (investigative) and strategic (longer-range overview) intelligence and analysis as they are or can be applied to organized crime work. It provides examples of analytical methods and products not only to familiarize readers with intelligence terminology but also to make readers aware of what managers can expect analysts to contribute to their investigation. At its conclusion, some key issues in the intelligence/analysis field are discussed.

The Intelligence Process

Before going into detail on methods and products of analysis, some terms will be defined; a look at the intelligence process will be taken; and a brief history of law enforcement intelligence and analysis in the United States will be offered.

"Intelligence" to an operational officer means a piece of information that has not been corroborated or is not known to be fact. This usage varies significantly from the definitions proffered by experts over the past fifteen years.

Don R. Harris termed it information that has been processed—collected, evaluated, collated, analyzed, and reported.[6] The definition accepted by the U.S. Department of Justice, Bureau of Justice Statistics is "information on identifiable individuals compiled in an effort to anticipate, prevent or monitor possible criminal activity."[7]

One state's laws define intelligence as data on the habits, practice, characteristics, possessions, associations, or financial status of an individual.[8]

Dintino and Martens refer to a concept of intelligence as a process, rather than as a definable product. They state that an intelligence system includes data that are continually manipulated to create an understanding of reality that produces knowledge, defines potential problems, and recommends strategy and policy to impact on the problem.[9]

A definition crafted by the author stated:

Law enforcement intelligence is a product resulting from analyzing past and present activity to predict future activity, and suggesting implementable alternative courses of action that may be taken to interdict or minimize the impact of a threatening crime group or activity.[10]

"Law enforcement analysis" has likewise been defined as:

A process/method used to compile and summarize relevant data, draw conclusions, make specific recommendations of feasible alternatives, and report the results to the decision-makers with a need to know.[11]

Intelligence Cycle

The intelligence process represents the life cycle of data—information needs are determined, data are collected, evaluated, and organized or compiled, varied analytical techniques are applied to them, conclusions are made and recommendations are drawn, and the resultant products are disseminated. Often, the recommendations emanating from an analysis include further data collection needs.

Certain elements are necessary to a successful intelligence process:

1. guidelines and specifically assigned responsibility for determining the kind of information that shall be kept in the files, the method of reviewing the material for continued usefulness and relevance, and the method of disposing material purged from the files considered to be no longer useful or relevant
2. a systematic flow of pertinent and reliable information
3. a uniform procedure for evaluating, cross-indexing, and storing information
4. a system for proper analysis of information
5. a system capable of rapid and efficient retrieval of all information
6. explicit guidelines for disseminating information from the files
7. security procedures[12]

Intelligence Files

While no nationwide standards have been established relative to intelligence files, the prevailing standard is that promulgated by the Bureau of Justice Assistance in 28 Code of Federal Regulations 23. This became the standard because it applies to all information shared by state and local agencies through their participation in the regional information sharing systems (RISS). As of 1991, the RISS network includes over 2,500 agencies.

This model has also been used to develop statewide standards relative to information sharing in states including California and New Jersey (Department of Justice, Bureau of Organized Crime and Criminal Intelligence, 1991; and Department of Law and Public Safety, Statewide Narcotics Task Force, 1988). The standards include criteria for an individual to be placed into a law enforcement file and the types of data that may be maintained. They further require information to be evaluated and designated as to source reliability and content validity prior to filing. Further still, information is classified as to its sensitivity and confidentiality. Dissemination is based on the common standard of need-to-know and right-to-know. File review and purge criteria are also stipulated in the standards.

It is important to note that information systems are not synonymous with intelligence systems. As Dintino and Martens commented, an intelligence system makes use of the agency's information system but goes beyond in its search for relevant data and in its transformation of data into knowledge.[13]

Brief History

A history of police intelligence in the United States shows that its earliest use related to concerns about alien residents, particularly "bomb throwers, German agents and anarchists."[14] In the 1920s, New York City's Radical Squad was broken into three units—the Bomb Squad, the Industrial Squad, and the Gangster Squad.[15] In 1924, the Federal Bureau of Investigation was created within the U.S. Department of Justice.

It was not until the 1950s and the Kefauver hearings on organized crime that the Justice Department, in 1954, formed the Organized Crime and Racketeering Section. In 1956, the Law Enforcement Intelligence Unit (a private organization of intelligence officers from highly screened law enforcement member agencies) was formed.

The 1963 assassination of President John F. Kennedy resulted in some criticism of law enforcement and a call for preventive intelligence systems.[16] The President's Commission on Law Enforcement and the Administration of Justice called for greater information exchange among federal, state, and local agencies and recommended the establishment of regional criminal intelligence information systems.

In the late 1960s and early 1970s, several nascent intelligence systems were dealt a fatal blow. The growing insurgency of the anti–Vietnam War movement caused many departments to collect data on "radicals" that included not only some persons who broke laws but also a number of those who did not (antiwar protesters, radical group members, and so on). When this breach of civil liberty came into the public eye, many systems were effectively shut down or prohibited from collecting and sharing data because of their overzealous approach to data collection and compilation.[17] Twenty years later, some systems were still operating under the strict regulations passed during that time frame.

The late 1970s and early 1980s saw the creation of the federally funded regional information sharing systems predicted in 1967, all of which focused on organized crime and narcotics. These systems operated under strict federal regulations that prohibited collecting material on people's families, businesses, or group associations unless those relationships were shown to be involved in criminal activity (28 Code of Federal Regulations 23). This may have been one result of the overcollection of the 1970s, combined with concern that data collected on organized criminal associations might include a number of persons who were in unwitting relationships with crime figures.

Until the middle to late 1980s, most organized crime units focused on "traditional" organized crime and "traditional" crimes committed by those groups. That is, criminal intelligence was gathered on the members and associates of La Cosa Nostra (the Mafia) who were engaged in gambling, loan-sharking, narcotics, prostitution, pornography, and the like. With the advent of widespread narcotics trafficking, however, a number of new organized crime groups were recognized, and a number of different criminal activities were noted.

Intelligence, however, has generally remained a separate territory within police, being available only to those within the intelligence or organized crime unit. Criminal investigation sections devoted to major crime and organized crime sometimes have little or no access to the intelligence unit's capabilities. It is clear that intelligence function has not yet been integrated into the daily operations of police work.

In some areas, work is under way to remedy this situation. Narcotics units, for example, have been combined with organized crime units in several large departments, for the purpose of shifting the emphasis from "buy-bust" narcotics cases to narcotics enterprise cases.

ANALYTICAL FORMS AND PRODUCTS

The collection and dissemination of information alone are not the workings of an intelligence system. The understanding of organized crime requires critical and thoughtful analysis.[18] Without analysis, there is not intelligence being produced.

Three overall types of analysis are used within law enforcement—crime, tactical, and strategic. Crime analysis uses data from the past and analyzes it in response to a series of crimes committed. The key factors in the crimes—locations, times, victims, weapons, suspect descriptions, and so on—are analyzed to develop a profile or indicators of future occurrences of the same crime by the same group or person.

Tactical or investigative analysis uses current data collected in the course of a case under investigation. It supports both investigations and prosecutions of criminal violations. Strategic analysis uses both past and current data to predict the future of criminal activity and recommend alternatives to intervene in future trends. All three types of analysis assist management in establishing courses for further action.

Crime analysis has been the most widely used methodology within law enforcement, although its applications were limited. The most typical example of a crime analysis would be to study a series of burglaries. Each incident would be reviewed, and key elements of its occurrence would be extracted.

These elements could include the times of day, days of the week (or of the month), the articles stolen, weapons used, methods of entry, locations of entry, types of structures (residences, commercial or industrial buildings, multifamily dwellings, number of stories, etc.), physical description of suspects, geographic locations of offenses, and victims' data (including presence at the time of the occurrence). The perpetrator's ''signature'' on the crime might then be discerned, or the likely time, date, and, possibly, the general location of another crime could be uncovered.

Because it requires the occurrence of a series of criminal actions, analysis is reactive. It can, however, also be proactive, since it may be used to prevent similar crimes. In fact, crime analysis techniques are the basis for much of the profiling work done by agencies such as the Federal Bureau of Investigation. Based on numerous incidents and subjects in their files, they can construct behavioral profiles of perpetrators that can be compared with suspects' behavior in various cases.

Moreover, if an organized group of burglars were involved, certain indicators within the individual acts, when viewed in total, might reveal a conspiracy. Thus, crime analysis can be the first line of awareness relative to the presence of criminal groups.

Investigative analysis is what has been called in the past ''intelligence analysis'' or tactical analysis. It involves taking information collected in the course of an investigation, analyzing that data, and drawing conclusions and recommendations from those data to support the investigation or a prosecution. Tactical intelligence is aimed at providing information regarding an immediate and specific threat of a criminal event.[19] Some of the many applications of tactical or investigative analysis to organized crime are delineated in the following section.

Although strategic intelligence is of a more general nature, it has been viewed as probably the single most important activity in assisting law enforcement executives to plan strategies and resource allocations for the entire organization.[20] Within the organized crime milieu, strategic analysis is crucial in that it provides an overall basis for assessing the threat of particular groups and recommending strategies to combat those groups' activities. Some applications of strategic analysis to organized crime are shown in section five of this chapter.

Tactical Analytical Application in Organized Crime

The nuts and bolts of analytical work is done in support of investigations and tactical efforts, whether in the area of organized crime or in other areas of criminal investigation.

Numerous analytical products are used to support investigations and prosecutions, in particular, organized crime investigations. Some of them include telephone record analysis, association analysis, event flow analysis, net worth analysis, commodity flow analysis, business record analysis, conversation analysis, and visual investigative analysis. It is important to note that any given case may require the use of several analytical methods and may result in a number of analytical products. The conclusions that can be drawn from these products can provide investigative leads and can assist in organizing cases for presentation in court.

Telephone Record Analysis

The most common analytical product used within organized crime investigations is the telephone record analysis. Telephone record analysis is the compilation, review, and analysis of telephone bill or dialed number recorder (DNR) data to determine contacts, patterns, and other information about a subject's telephone usage. Telephone record analysis is usually done on telephone calls made over a period of six moths or more and is generally computerized. Sophisticated databases have been developed that can allow the analyst to compare several subjects' records, into the tens of thousands of telephone calls.

What results from a telephone record analysis are usually

- a listing of "primary" numbers contacted—the numbers called most frequently

- a time-series analysis of calls by hour to determine the hours the phone is most commonly used (this is particularly helpful to determine the needed coverage of later electronic surveillance)

- a time-series analysis of calls by date, day of week, and day of month to determine significant date patterns

- an analysis of the calls by area code, state, or other geographic range

- a listing of unusual calls—those made at odd hours or dates, those lasting significantly longer than others, third-party calls

- a chart depicting the interrelationships of the calls if a multiple subscriber analysis is being done

- an indication of any patterns that have occurred in time or date or in order of calls made

- any conclusions that have been drawn and/or investigative recommendations. The latter usually include getting subscriber information and performing

- criminal history background checks on those persons identified as important contacts;

Figure 15.1
Telephone Record Analysis Chart: Subscribers (215) 555-7321 and (301) 555-0973
Interconnecting and Significant Calls

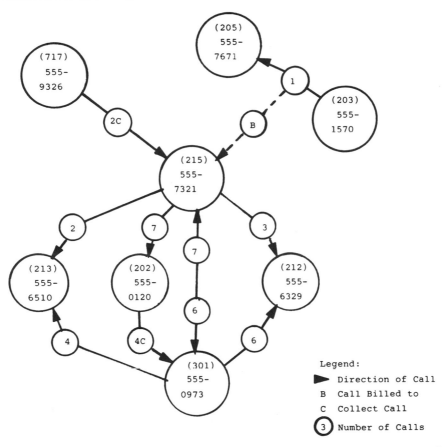

Legend:
▶ Direction of Call
B   Call Billed to
C   Collect Call
③   Number of Calls

the collection of additional sets of telephone records from the key persons contacted is also often suggested.[21]

The types of analytical products associated with telephone record analysis include telephone record matrices, telephone record charts, tables, graphs, and written reports. The analysis of telephone data has become more difficult over the past few years due to the use of beepers, call forwarding, and other technological alterations.

An example of a telephone record analysis chart can be seen in Figure 15.1.

Association Analysis

Association analysis, also called link analysis or network analysis, is the second most common law enforcement intelligence method used in organized crime investigations. This is not the network analysis of the social scientists as employed by Malcolm Sparrow, Ianni, and others. Rather, it is a simplified depiction of relationships among potential criminal actors in graphic and written form.

The information from which association material can be extracted is varied. It can include physical surveillance reports; public records, including deeds, corporate filings, quarterly wage reports, and so on; testimony; electronic surveillance reports; agency files; and others. A thorough association analysis can provide organized crime investigators with

- a graphic presentation of all known participants in a conspiracy
- a depiction of the hierarchy of a criminal organization
- biographical sketches of each person involved in the conspiracy
- business associations of the participants in the conspiracy
- changes in the hierarchy or membership in the criminal organization
- some possible conclusions about the relative strength of the organization, the key participants, which participants could be targeted for prosecution, which participants might be targeted for becoming informants, how easily the group might be infiltrated by an undercover operative, and so on.

The types of analytical products resulting from association analysis can include association matrices, association charts, biographical listings, and written reports.

An example of an association analysis chart can be seen in Figure 15.2.

Event Flow Analysis

Event flow analysis examines a series of events to determine what happened and what they might mean. The known events are placed in chronological order and may require some inferred events to be referenced as well. The benefit of event flow analysis is that it can show the activity or membership of a crime group over time, rather than merely provide a static freeze-frame picture, which an association analysis might show. Moreover, it presents activity as a basis for dynamic connections, rather than just depicting relationships.

Within an organized crime investigation, event flow analysis might reveal

- changes in leadership within a crime group
- realignment of criminal territories
- events leading to a criminal act in which the crime group participated
- other time-based activities

The types of analytical products associated with event flow analysis are event flowcharts and written reports.

An example of an event flow analysis chart can be seen in Figure 15.3.

Figure 15.2
Association Analysis Chart: Known Connections
Between X and Z Crime Families

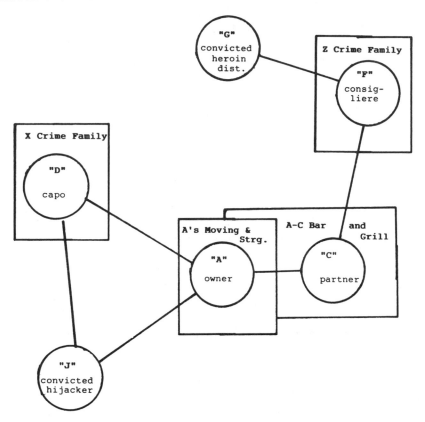

Net Worth Analysis

Net worth analysis is the compilation and review of financial data on an individual to determine if the person had income from illegal sources. This is done by uncovering all legal sources of income, determining expenditures for the years, and ascertaining any significant differences between the two. Net worth analysis is key to many organized crime investigations because it helps to uncover the profits of the crime rather than just focusing on the perpetration of the crime.

Net worth analysis is done in an accounting format developed by the U.S. Department of Treasury, Internal Revenue Service (IRS). The standardized protocols call for information on assets, liabilities, reported income, and yearly

Figure 15.3
**Event Flowchart: Flow of Cocaine from Processing Plant to
New York Distributors**

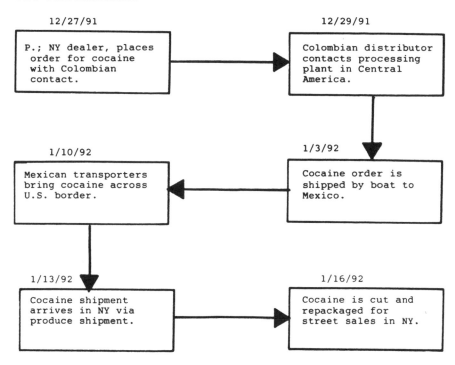

expenses. When the form is tallied, the "bottom line" shows potential illegal income. Charges, including tax evasion, might stem from this type of investigation but are not pursued unless the "bottom line" is large enough to ensure significant advantages in a prosecution.

Because of the confidentiality surrounding financial information as reported to the IRS, most local investigators do not have access to a target's documented reported income but might be able to access such information through other means such as state income records, employer records, credit applications, and so on.

The products associated with net worth analysis are limited to the net worth form. An example of a net worth analysis format is shown in Figure 15.4.

Commodity Flow Analysis

Commodity flow analysis views the movement of goods or services from one person or entity to another and attempts to draw conclusions based on these interactions. Like event flow analysis, it shows activity. But while the event flow analysis shows chronology of activity, commodity flow shows movement be-

Figure 15.4
Net Worth Analysis Format: Net Worth Worksheet for J.B.T.

	6-30-89	6-30-90	6-30-91
Assets			
Residence-Montclair	$749,000	$749,000	$749,000
Residence-Southampton	389,000	389,000	389,000
1990 BMW	-	45,000	45,000
1991 Mitsubishi	-	-	32,000
1988 Honda	16,000	-	-
Jewelry	5,000	20,000	50,000
Furs	-	10,000	30,000
Savings Account	10,000	70,000	150,000
Securities	15,000	50,000	250,000
Total	$1,184,000	$1,333,000	$1,695,000
Liabilities			
Mortgage-Montclair	$650,000	$550,000	$300,000
Mortgage-Southampton	270,000	130,000	-
Total	$920,000	$480,000	$300,000
Net Worth (Assets-Liabilities)	$264,000	$853,000	$1,395,000
Changes in Net Worth	-	+ $589,000	+ 542,000
Living Expenses	-	- 95,000	- 125,000
Total		$684,000	$ 667,000
Reported Income		- $ 70,000	-$ 70,000
Income from Unidentified Sources/Potential Illegal Income		$ 614,000	$ 597,000

tween persons or things, so that it becomes a cross between an event flowchart and an association chart.

In an organized crime environment, commodity flow analysis can be used to demonstrate

- movement of funds through bank accounts
- the movement of drugs and currency
- the movement of stolen property
- the movement of funds through various businesses, including paper corporations, to hide involvement of certain persons
- the steps in money laundering of illegal profits

Figure 15.5
Commodity Flow Analysis: Flow of Business Profits Through Accounts to Individual

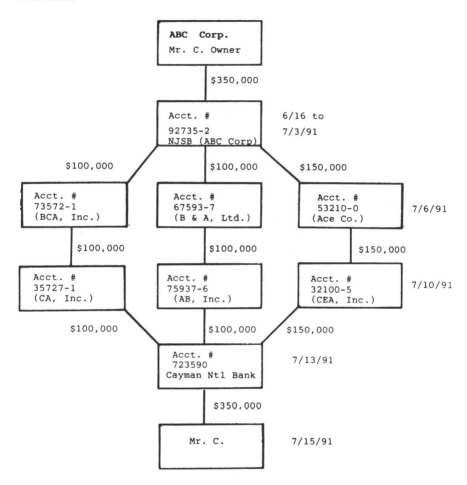

Commodity flow analysis has utility in conjunction with other forms of analysis, particularly business record analysis and bank account analysis. The types of products that result from commodity flow analysis are commodity flowcharts and written reports.

A commodity flow analysis chart is shown in Figure 15.5.

Bank Account Analysis

Bank account analysis compiles, reviews, and analyzes the records of one or more bank accounts to provide information on the financial status of the owner of the account(s). It looks at the overall flow of funds into and out of the account, the specifics of payments, and the resultant financial position of the account holder. It can be used in conjunction with commodity flow analysis or to help ascertain the level of living expenses needed to complete a net worth analysis.

Within an organized crime investigation, bank account analysis might result in information relating to

- money laundering
- the use of corporations and accounts to hide interest or ownership
- potential tax violations
- the presence of illegal income
- the presence of payments for illegal goods or services
- assets owned by the target of the investigation that might be seized as part of a RICO (Racketeer Influenced Corrupt Organization Act) investigation

The types of products that might emerge as part of a bank record analysis include various financial summaries, association charts, and commodity flow-charts.

Business Record Analysis

Business record analysis is an overall term for the analysis of any types of business records to be found. These include sales and order receipt books, journals and ledgers, bank records, employee wage reports, business filings, sales tax filings, and corporate records. Many researchers have noted the involvement of organized crime in business ventures. The analysis of business records to determine criminal activity involvement is at the forefront of many investigations today, particularly those that include forfeiture of assets believed to have been gained through criminal enterprise. Subpoenaing and analyzing business records are the backbone of significant investigative agencies.

Some of the information a thorough analysis of business records may uncover are

- the actual ownership of assets otherwise hidden
- the use of nominees, fronts, and other devices to hide the ownership of businesses or assets
- the actual profits of the business
- the use of business accounts to launder funds received from illegal activities
- the use of business accounts to underwrite personal expenses (and thus avoid taxes)
- the interconnection of businesses seemingly independent
- the use of business funds to provide ''legitimate income'' to persons not actually employed by the business but to whom the owner owes ''tribute''
- the presence of ''silent partners'' in the business whose obvious presence might prohibit the business from being licensed because of their past criminal records

- the presence of vertical or horizontal integration in the industry by organized crime-involved persons

The types of products associated with business record analysis include event flow diagrams, commodity flow diagrams, association charts, financial summaries, and written reports.

Conversation Analysis

Conversation analysis, which is also known as "content analysis," reviews the conversation collected through electronic surveillance, summarizes it, and attempts to determine its meaning. Conversation analysis is one of the most crucial forms of analysis today due to the heavy reliance by investigators and prosecutors on the use of electronic surveillance. In spite of its importance, little on it has been written or taught by persons within the law enforcement analytical field. Experts such as Roger A. Shuy[22] are notably outside the field of law enforcement practitioners, being used by defense attorneys to negate the interpretation of taped material presented by prosecutors.

The use of conversation analysis within the field has been forwarded by agencies including the New York State Organized Crime Task Force. Analysts in that agency review daily tape recordings to catalog the topics in the conversations, to evaluate the accuracy of the information in the conversations, to cull the tapes for emerging criminal schemes that develop, and to assess the meaning of the information.[23]

Some information made available through conversation analysis includes

- the individual(s) that initiates the topics relating to criminal activities
- how the noninitiating person responds—with affirmative interest or with noncommittal comments
- how active a participant in the conversation the suspect was (in a wiretap involving law enforcement or confidential source participants)
- the relative roles in an organization of the persons in the conversation
- the use of euphemisms to mean illicit activity
- knowledge on the part of the conversant with illegal activity
- summaries of the conversation topics
- structure of the conversation
- language functions of conversants

The products associated with conversation analysis are written summaries of the conversation and specific "outtakes" of the conversation highlighting key areas to be proven in court.

Visual Investigative Analysis

Visual investigative analysis is the depiction of activities that have occurred in a chart format to allow for the comprehension of varied and complex activities at a glance. It is used in tracking investigative activities as well as criminal activities and is popular among case managers and persons responsible for overseeing the work of multijurisdictional task force personnel.

The types of data included in a visual investigative analysis chart depend on the use of the chart. If the purpose is to track a complex investigation, it could include

- investigative activities taken
- personnel assigned
- equipment assigned
- results of investigative activity
- leads needed to be followed up
- other pertinent investigative activity

If the purpose is to track illegal activities, it could include

- illegal activities occurring
- persons involved, including identifiers
- locations, vehicles, and so on
- other pertinent criminal activity

The types of products associated with visual investigative analysis (VIA) are VIA charts and written summaries. An example of a VIA chart is shown in Figure 15.6.

Strategic Analytical Application in Organized Crime

Strategic analysis is basically policy analysis. That is, it attempts to define criminal ''problems'' in terms of their political, economic, and social implications and suggests alternative policies that may effectively diminish the negative consequences associated with the particular criminal problem under study.[24]

Strategic analysis is used to compile and summarize relevant data necessary to make assessments, draw conclusions, make predictions, and suggest recommendations for law enforcement policy and action.[25] Peter Lupsha stated that a major problem facing law enforcement is the need for macroanalysis of organized crime operations, rather than enforcement units targeting individuals.[26]

While strategic analysis has been generally described, what has not been apparent is that theoretical strategic research can have practical application to or-

Figure 15.6
Visual Investigative Analysis Chart Fragment: Water Street Homicide Investigation

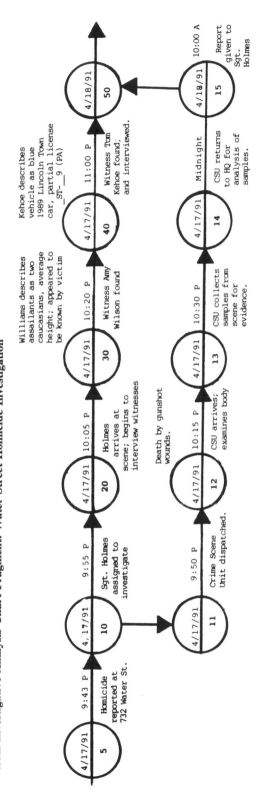

ganized crime investigation. For example, a study of fraudulent transactions over a number of investigations can result in the compilation of indicators listing previously unsuspected or uncovered commonalities. This can then be used to aid investigators in uncovering fraudulent transactions in current investigations. A number of subvarieties of strategic assessment are in use within law enforcement. They include general assessments, threat assessments, vulnerability assessments, market analysis, estimates, premonitories, and indicator analysis. All have application to the organized crime environment.

General Assessment

A general assessment is an overview of a crime group or criminal activity in an area that draws conclusions about the group/activity and recommends alternative ways to deal with the group/activity.

The types of information to be analyzed on a group could include membership, geographic data, hierarchy, criminal activities, legitimate business activities, financial health of group members, connections to other groups, connections to the government structure, previous enforcement efforts toward group, related analyses of group or similar groups, and the social, economic, political, and criminal climate in which the group operates.[27]

Lupsha suggested several criteria on which enforcement agencies should base their decision to prioritize particular organized crime cases.[28] He listed seven areas (level of threat activity/group poses, visibility, community culture, new penetrations, new trends, level of organization, and level of funding) that could be given point values. The organization or activity that received the highest number of points should be accorded the highest priority by the agency.[29]

If an activity were being studied, information including occurrences of crime, geographic range of occurrences, criminal techniques used, known relationship between this and other crime, connections to legitimate business, estimated profits from this crime, market for this criminal service, and other factors could be ascertained.[30]

Within organized crime, general assessments are primarily used to identify group members and illegal activities for future investigation. Libonati and Edelhertz suggest that studying property ownership, for example, to track ownership and control of resources would help predict directions of organized crime activity.[31]

A secondary use of general assessments is the public report function mandated for investigating commissions. One recent publication, *A Decade of Change: 1990 Report*, included overviews of organized criminal activity as well as threat assessments on each criminal group noted.[32] The New Jersey State Commission on Investigation publishes annual reports that include overviews of organized criminal activity within the state. The California Department of Justice, Bureau of Organized Crime and Criminal Intelligence has also published overviews in an annual format.

Threat Assessment

A threat assessment analyzes the potential of danger that may result from the activities of a crime group or criminal activity. Lupsha recommended that strategic analysis efforts within an organization should begin with a threat analysis of the crime groups operating in the enforcement jurisdiction.[33] An organized crime unit must have some starting point in its enforcement program, and such an assessment could provide critical data to help direct that program.

Some questions to be asked in determining where to allocate an organized crime unit's resources could include

- What are the tentative scope and dimensions of the "organized crime problem" to be assessed?
- What resources are currently available to address the problem?
- Are the priorities established consistent with those of the organization?
- What are the apparent social, political, and/or economic implications of the "problem"?
- What will be the projected impact upon the "problem"?[34]

A threat assessment, for example, could be done relative to the predicted upsurge of Asian organized crime in the United States, particularly in light of the upcoming changes in the status of the colony of Hong Kong. In another related arena, threat assessments are conducted on groups that are believed to have potential as terrorist organizations.

Vulnerability Assessment

A vulnerability assessment views the potential danger to a particular event (such as the Olympics) from criminal disturbance; it can determine a crime group's weaknesses in order to decide the best investigative strategy (such as developing informants in the group, electronic surveillance, or direct enforcement), or it can depict a neighborhood's vulnerability of being overrun by a crime group. It is the other side of the coin from a threat assessment in that it focuses on weaknesses, while the threat assessment focuses on strengths.

Vulnerability assessments are also used by corporations with foreign offices that may be concerned about governmental takeovers of foreign corporations or other hostile action toward the company.

Market Analysis

A market analysis looks at the potential demand for criminal goods and services as an indicator of possible organized criminal activity in that area. Examples of market analysis are the recent reports of crystallized methamphetamine, known as "ice," which has been reported on the West Coast and in Hawaii. Once the availability was determined, law enforcement in the East was alerted, as regular methamphetamine users could well create a demand for "ice" in that region. Again, this may also be used in the corporate setting.

Another example is the recent reports of poppies being grown in South America, financed by the cocaine cartels. It is obvious that someone within those cartels has analyzed the drug market in Europe and America and determined that heroin could be competitive with cocaine as a drug of choice in those consumer markets.

Within the field of organized crime research, several market analyses have been done.

Estimates

Estimates are an overview type of strategic assessment commonly done at the federal level. They attempt to give an accurate assessment of the current status of a crime problem and offer predictions on the future status of that problem.

The *NNICC Report* of the National Narcotics Intelligence Consumers Committee, for example, gives an estimate of the supply of illicit drugs available in the United States. It covers smuggling, drug availability, use indicators, source country production, drug prices, and money laundering.[35]

Another example of an overview is the *Organized Crime Committee Report* of the Canadian Association of Chiefs of Police and the Criminal Intelligence Services Canada. This ninety-page report includes descriptive summaries of activities of varied types of organized criminal groups in Canada. Organized crime trends are also reported, with emphasis on the growing problem of Asian organized crime, as well as other forms of criminal syndicate activity.[36]

A less recognized form of estimate was provided in the work published by the President's Commission on Organized Crime. In *The Impact: Organized Crime Today*, the Wharton Econometric Forecasting Associates gathered data in an attempt to estimate the income to organized crime from illegal sources, the number of members and associates of organized crime groups, and the annual income of individual members.[37]

Premonitories

Premonitories are assessments of a crime group that are short-term in nature and form a link between strategic and tactical products. The premonitory looks at a crime group with the intent of gathering as much information on it as possible so that police management can make the determination of whether the group should be a viable candidate for investigation and prosecution.

The data collected for all these forms of strategic analysis can be presented in a variety of analytical formats and products. Several methods used within investigative analysis can be employed, including association analysis, event flow analysis, financial analysis (net worth and business record analysis), and commodity flow analysis. Data can be presented in tables, graphs, biographical listings, charts, or paragraph form (descriptive analysis). Oral briefings are other presentation methods.

Based on this factual information, the analyst can draw conclusions about the potential threat of the organization and its potential weaknesses and may make recommendations to law enforcement management about effective strategies for intervention against the criminal organization.

Indicator Analysis

Indicator analysis consists of assessments about the types of criminal activity or organized crime behavior of a group of individuals that enables one to make hypotheses about patterns of behavior occurring within those activities.

A monograph by Roger W. Davis and Charles H. Rogovin illustrates this technique. Varied indicators of organized crime's impacting on government are examined, such as weak or absent enforcement campaigns, lack of vigor in prosecuting or sentencing, and unusual speed in granting licenses and variances.[38]

Rogovin and Davis looked at indicators of the impact of organized crime in the community (fear of intimidation, reluctance of citizens to report irregularities to authorities, and so on) and the impact of organized crime on the business community, such as the appearance of cash-basis businesses, profit skimming and pressures on business decisions, questionable loans for risky venture, uniformity in display, and price and packaging of pornography.[39]

Current Issues in Organized Crime Analysis

There are several issues under discussion by academics and/or practitioners relative to analysis, particularly as these apply to organized crime investigation. Four of these issues are addressed on the following pages: traditional versus nontraditional models of organized crime; measuring the results of organized crime intelligence; strategic planning within organized crime control; and privacy issues.

Traditional Versus Nontraditional Models of Organized Crime

One major shift in law enforcement during the 1980s was the alteration of focus from the Mafia to "nontraditional" organized crime groups. As Robert J. Kelly commented, the Mafia had been an idée fixe in organized crime control since the Kefauver hearings of 1951.[40]

It has been said that how law enforcement perceives the organized crime problem determines how the problem is defined[41] and, ultimately, determines the solutions used to combat it. This focus on the Mafia, then, led to strategies, legislation, and research models based on the attributes known to exist within Mafia organizations.

An example of a research based on Mafia models is the propensity of intelligence organizations to "structure out" crime groups. Because the Mafia is known to have hierarchical tiers and documented membership, intelligence officers and analysts are determined to collect and report similar data on drug cartels or other organized crime syndicates.

This model of analysis persists despite facts about nontraditional crime groups, particularly those trafficking in narcotics, which include the following:

1. Narcotics trafficking may present opportunities to persons who might be involved in only one or two criminal actions and are not, therefore, part of an ongoing and identifiable organization.
2. Some narcotics groups are known to be decentralized and horizontally "organized," that is, run as independent organizations from a certain midlevel down.
3. Persons from different countries do not organize themselves into crime groups in the same manner as the Mafia or U.S. crime groups.
4. The Mafia model does not translate well onto even U.S.-bred crime groups of different ethnicity.[42]
5. Too little is known by law enforcement investigators and researchers about the culture and beliefs of these nontraditional groups for them to understand the criminal culture of these groups in terms of Mafia/La Cosa Nostra models.
6. Nontraditional crime groups have witnessed the successful investigations and prosecutions of major organized crime groups and the use by investigators of tools such as electronic surveillance and RICO laws. Their future structure and operations may be designed to avoid those traps.[43]

Dintino and Martens observe that organized crime enforcement has been based on limited experiences and poorly analyzed information: "Only when administrators are able to precisely define and discriminate between the exploitive and symbiotic features of organized crime can we hope to evolve a more rational and coherent public policy."[44]

In other words, the models of intelligence gathering and analysis derived from La Cosa Nostra investigation are not necessarily directly applicable to the varied groups and crime situations with which we are now faced. Further, groups per se may not be the focus of organized crime investigation; instead, investigation of criminal activities or potential criminal markets may be the focus.

Analytical tools and methods reflect the focus of the investigation. As new models of organized crime and organized crime investigation evolve, so must the accompanying analytical techniques. A dependence on old models of analysis could prove to be ineffective.

Measuring the Results of Organized Crime Intelligence

A second issue in organized crime analysis is how to measure its results. Analysis will not become commonplace until it is believed to be valuable, but what quantifiable value does it have in an organized crime control effort?

Few organizations have even attempted to quantify the analytical effort. The RISS projects and their evaluator agency, the Institute for Intergovernmental Research (IIR), did attempt assessments of their analytical programs. They looked at the types of analytical methods employed by RISS personnel, counted them, and also broke them down into numbers of products produced (charts, tables, graphs, written reports, and so on). The RISS quarterly reports then reflected those numbers. Thus, the evaluation of their analytical efforts is, to a large degree, based on the numbers of products produced.

The difficulties in using number of products produced as a basis for evaluation include

1. There is no nationally accepted standard for what a particular type of analysis should include. In some areas, an association analysis equals a chart, while in others the chart is just one component of the analysis. In some areas, a telephone record analysis equals a computerized printout of all the numbers contacted by a particular phone.

2. Some products are difficult to quantify fairly. A written report of one page, for example, cannot be fairly equated with a forty-page assessment but is so judged if "written report" covers both extremes.

3. The emphasis is clearly placed on attaining substantial numbers of analytical products, rather than on providing quality analytical products or looking at what results they produce. In other words, it is similar to using street sweeps or buy-busts to inflate narcotics arrest statistics, rather than having longer-term investigations of narcotics organizations with fewer arrests.

4. This does not take into consideration the varying needs of different investigations.

While the RISS/IIR model is more than what is available in most analytical milieus, there are still several possible areas of evaluation that may be more reflective of analytical value in law enforcement.

One way is to evaluate the effectiveness of organized crime intelligence or analysis inside the context of how organized crime control efforts are themselves evaluated. Several alternate measurements of organized crime control evaluation can be referenced, including

1. The body-count measurement—arrests, convictions.

2. Assets that are seized.

3. Changes in the impact of organized crime on community and quality-of-life measures, on licit and illicit business attributes, and on governance.[45]

4. Changes in the number of businesses or industries infiltrated by organized crime.

5. Detailed cost-benefit analysis and postevaluation to assess organized crime control efforts.[46]

6. The impact on organized crime groups, such as the convictions of Mafia leaders leaving vacancies that forced sudden promotions from the less experienced ranks, resulting in unskilled leaders of the groups.[47]

7. Changes in the level of public support for organized crime activities; publicity of organized crime activities may be an effective strategy for its control as it increases public understanding of its operations and increases the risk of exposure for those among the general citizenry participating in the organization's illegal activities.[48]

If one measures organized crime control effort by numbers of arrests and convictions, then value is placed on analytical products that produce those arrests or convictions and on tactical products that can be used to help complete an investigation or present data in court. The number of leads obtained through the analysis, the number of new potential conspirators discovered, or the number and seriousness of the criminal charges supported by analytical products could be measured.

The same is true of the asset seizure measurement under that model, with the addition of the number or value of assets uncovered through financial analysis.

If one measures organized crime control effort by changes in the criminal organization or in the level of public support or organized crime activities, then products that provide an accurate assessment of the crime group or the market for criminal goods and services would be considered valuable. Strategic analysis results to be measured could include the number of crime groups and their members uncovered; the number of trends forecasted; or the number of strategies created that are supported by analysis. A proactive organized crime effort might be measured in community and quality-of-life measures, impact on government, and licit and illicit business attributes.[49]

To employ a "body-count" method is an ineffective yardstick for measuring strategic analytical efforts. Early intervention into crime groups as a result of strategic analysis, however, will not reap the large numbers of arrests and seizures that other methods will. Strategic analysis results in crime prevention measures. A reduction in the numbers of arrests and so on, then, may be the result of an effective program, rather than an ineffective one.

Measures for evaluation of analysis are critical to the use of analysis within organized crime and other law enforcement areas. Analysts must be willing to have their work quantified if they wish it to be valued.

Strategic Planning Within Organized Crime Control

To have significant results, investigations must be part of a general strategy designed to reach more than individuals and individual enterprises, [they] must be based on an informed understanding of the organized crime problem under attack, and [they] must consider the long-range implications of both the particular strategy adopted and the daily operational tactics employed to carry out that strategy.[50]

There is no strategic planning without analysis. There is, at times, the pretense of strategic planning that passes for strategy. Absent quantifiable data on which to base a strategy or focus, the strategy development process may fall captive to the political process.[51]

Edwin Stier and Peter R. Richards view strategic decision making as any that looks beyond an immediate objective of arresting or prosecuting.[52] They point out that many effective organized crime cases result from targets of opportunity, rather than targets of long-range planning.[53] However, some strategy must be in place for people to recognize those opportunities when they occur.

One key to using strategic planning is to adjust and accommodate to new information and ideas within the long-range plan.[54] Strategic plans that are inflexible and immutable are destined for failure. Conversely, strategic analysis in support of potential investigations is done in a short-range paradigm (see the section on premonitories).

Strategic planning need not necessarily be involved, very long-range or complex. Every agency has a strategy relative to organized crime control and a plan by which it intends to carry it out. That strategy may not be articulated or conscious, but it is present. For example, many agencies use a strategy called "have a specialized organized crime unit." They believe that providing dedicated and trained personnel to this focused area of crime will control it. Others use a strategy called "create multiagency task forces." This strategy is thought to produce greater results while reducing duplication of effort. Still others use the strategy called "electronic surveillance." This is a proven strategy that generally results in convictions.

In addition to employing such general strategies, agencies use more specific ones. Most organized crime units, for example, specialize in crime groups that appear to significantly impact their jurisdiction. The emphasis on La Cosa Nostra is an example of this specific strategy.

Strategies are used and are chosen. Seldom are they based on a thorough analysis of the problem. Such analysis is available and should be utilized.

Privacy Issues

There has been considerable attention given to the issue of rights to privacy guaranteed to U.S. citizens through the Constitution. These rights were alleged to be violated by the transgressions of the late 1960s and early 1970s police intelligence departments; for the safeguarding of these rights, several departments' intelligence bureaus were disbanded or severely limited in their scope of operations.

These issues were of primary concern when the federal RISS projects were started in the late 1970s. Strict guidelines and diligence on the part of the federal government have reduced anxiety about breaches of privacy and/or security. During the dozen years since the initial RISS projects began, these fears about constitutional rights violations have abated.

The types of concerns relative to privacy that generally arise relate to either the circumstances under which individuals become part of an intelligence database or the type of information on a person that becomes part of such a database.[55] A secondary concern appears to be the dissemination of the data and their potential derogatory impact on a person's reputation.

These concerns have generally been addressed through the restrictions in 28 *Code of Federal Regulations (CFR)* 23.20, which apply to all information received from, or given to, a RISS project or other federally funded intelligence system. But while these standards apply to thousands of RISS members in relation to RISS data, there is no generally accepted standard that is required to be more broadly applied. That is, the 28 *CFR* 23.20 standard was not designed to apply to state and local systems (except under certain circumstances) and has not been widely copied by state and local agencies.

Moreover, strategic intelligence operations aim to produce information about industrywide or areawide criminal patterns, so strategic files may contain a wide variety of personal information about numerous individuals, many of whom may turn out to be innocent of wrongdoing.[56]

One key to these data is how they are used. If the information is held in intelligence files, safeguarded, and destroyed once no link to criminal activity is found, then there is little danger of improper use. If, however, agencies maintain ''criminal files'' on every name with which they come into contact, then privacy rights may be trampled.

Standards are needed for the proper handling of raw data. Groups such as the International Association of Chiefs of Police have already done preliminary work in this area; that forum could be used to provide consensus for intelligence standards.

Finally, it is important to note that intelligence alone is not used to arrest or convict a person. There is little evidence that intelligence and investigative information are inappropriately disseminated or used. Criminal justice agencies are more often criticized for not sharing or disseminating data[57] than for using them improperly.

CONCLUSIONS

The evolution of law enforcement intelligence and analysis has been closely linked to the rise of organized crime enforcement. It would be impossible to successfully complete an involved organized crime investigation without some form of analysis.

To some, analysis has meant a link chart or a list of names of people discovered through a telephone record analysis. But the varieties of analytical techniques and products are as distinct as the cases for which they are completed. Analysis serves every step of investigations and prosecutions, as well as the longer-range strategic aspect of crime control.

While a number of agencies do not employ analysts in their organizations, investigators and managers may use analytical techniques or concepts on a daily basis. Those who do not use the techniques or analysis may not have been exposed to the value of analysis.

In addition to providing that exposure to some small degree, this chapter has addressed several issues of substance in the analytical field. The areas of privacy, strategic planning, nontraditional organized crime models, and creating evaluations for analysis all bear consideration, further research, and further comment.

NOTES

1. Justin J. Dintino and Frederick T. Martens, *Police Intelligence Systems in Crime Control* (Springfield, IL: Charles C. Thomas, 1983), 5.

2. Ibid., 16.

3. Francis A. J. Ianni, *Black Mafia* (New York: Simon and Schuster, 1974), 331.

4. International Association of Chiefs of Police, *Law Enforcement Policy on the Management of Criminal Intelligence* (Gaithersburg, MD: Author, 1985), 38.

5. Michael Libonati, and Herbert Edelhertz, *Study of Property Ownership and Devolution in the Organized Crime Environment*, prepared under Grant No. 80-IJ-CX-0066 from the U.S. Department of Justice, National Institute of Justice, to the Temple University School of Law (Washington, DC: U.S. Government Printing Office, 1986), 50.

6. Don R. Harris, *Basic Elements of Intelligence* (Washington, DC: Law Enforcement Assistance Administration, 1976).

7. Search Group, Inc., *Intelligence and Investigative Records*, prepared for Bureau of Justice Statistics (Washington, DC: U.S. Government Printing Office, 1984), 9.

8. Ibid., 11.

9. Ibid., 7.

10. Marilyn Peterson Sommers, "Law Enforcement Intelligence: A New Look," *International Journal of Intelligence and Counterintelligence* 1.3 (1986): 25.

11. Ibid., 26.

12. Harris, *Basic Elements*, 16.

13. Ibid., 7.

14. Anthony V. Bouza, *Police Intelligence* (New York: AMS Press, 1976), 24.

15. Ibid.

16. Search, *Intelligence*, 19, quoting from the *Warren Report*.

17. Ibid., 20.

18. Dintino and Martens, *Police Intelligence Systems*, 95.

19. Search, *Intelligence*, 26.

20. International Association of Chiefs of Police, *Law Enforcement*, 6.

21. Marilyn B. Peterson, "Telephone Record Analysis," in *Criminal Intelligence Analysis*, ed. Paul P. Andrews, Jr., and Marilyn B. Peterson (Loomis, CA: Palmer Enterprises, 1990).

22. Roger A. Shuy, "The Analysis of Tape Recorded Conversations," in *Criminal Intelligence Analysis*, ed. Paul P. Andrews and Marilyn B. Peterson (Loomis, CA: Palmer Enterprises, 1990).

23. Joseph DeLuca, "The Need for Intelligence in Organized Crime Narcotics Enforcement," presented to the Organized Crime Narcotics Enforcement Symposium sponsored by the Pennsylvania Crime Commission and the Pennsylvania Commission on Crime and Delinquency, May 1988, 151–58.

24. Dintino and Martens, *Police Intelligence Systems*, 72.

25. Sommers, "Law Enforcement," 31.

26. Peter Lupsha, "Steps Toward a Strategic Analysis of Organized Crime," *Police Chief* (May 1980).

27. Sommers, "Law Enforcement," 34–35.

28. Peter Lupsha, "Some Thoughts on Prioritizing Organized Crime," 1988.

29. Ibid., 2–4.

30. Sommers, "Law Enforcement," 36.

31. Libonati and Edelhertz, *Study of Property*, 52.

32. Pennsylvania Crime Commission, *A Decade of Change: 1990 Report* (Conshohocken: Pennsylvania Crime Commission, 1991).

33. Lupsha, "Steps Toward."

34. Dintino and Martens, *Police Intelligence Systems*, 73–75.

35. National Narcotics Intelligence Consumers Committee, *NNICC Report 1989* (Washington, DC: National Narcotics Intelligence Consumers Committee, June 1990).

36. Criminal Intelligence Services Canada, *Organized Crime Committee Report 1991* (Ottawa, Canada: Criminal Intelligence Services Canada, August 1991), 8–9.

37. Wharton Econometric Forecasting Associates, Inc., *The Impact: Organized Crime Today* (Washington, DC: President's Commission on Organized Crime, April 1986), 45, 60, 71.

38. Roger W. Davis and Charles H. Rogovin, *Indicators of the Impacts of Organized Crime*. Prepared under Grant No. 80-IJ-CX-0066 by the National Institute of Justice, U.S. Department of Justice (Washington, DC: U.S. Government Printing Office, 1986), 15.

39. Ibid., 14, 16.

40. Robert J. Kelly, "The Nature of Organized Crime and Its Operations," in *Major Issues in Organized Crime Control*, ed. Herbert Edelhertz (Washington, DC: National Institute of Justice, 1987), 10–11.

41. Dintino and Martens, *Police Intelligence Systems*, 11.

42. Rufus Schatzberg, "Harlem's Early Black Policy Bankers Were Not Organized Criminals," *Law Enforcement Intelligence Analysis Digest*, 6.1 (Summer 1991): 36–37.

43. Pennsylvania Crime Commission, *A Decade*, 205.

44. Dintino and Martens, *Police Intelligence Systems*, 12, 15.

45. Nicolette Parisi, *Sources of Data That Identify and Measure the Impacts of Organized Crime*, prepared under Grant No. 80-IJ-CX-0066 from the National Institute of Justice, U.S. Department of Justice (Washington, DC: U.S. Government Printing Office, 1986), 2.

46. Dintino and Martens, *Police Intelligence Systems*, 20.

47. General Accounting Office, *Effectiveness of the Government's Attack on La Cosa Nostra*, testimony by David C. Williams before the Permanent Subcommittee on Investigations, Committee on Governmental Affairs, United States Senate (Washington, DC: Author, April 1988), 9.

48. Ibid., 19.

49. Parisi, *Sources*, 3.

50. Ronald Goldstock, "Operational Issues in Organized Crime Control," in *Major Issues in Organized Crime Control*, ed. Herbert Edelhertz (Washington, DC: National Institute of Justice, 1987), 82.

51. Marilyn B. Peterson, "Strategic Intelligence for Law Enforcement," *Law Enforcement Intelligence Analysis Digest*, 6.1 (Winter 1991–92): 18.

52. Edwin Stier and Peter R. Richards, "Strategic Decision Making in Organized Crime Control: The Need for a Broadened Perspective," in *Major Issues in Organized Crime Control*, ed. Herbert Edelhertz (Washington, DC: National Institute of Justice, 1987), as reprinted in *Law Enforcement Intelligence Analysis Digest*, 4.1 (Summer 1989): 15.

53. Ibid., 16.

54. Ibid.
55. Search, *Intelligence*, 35–37.
56. Ibid., 92.
57. Ibid., 93.

16

The Role of Crime Commissions in Organized Crime Control

CHARLES H. ROGOVIN AND
FREDERICK T. MARTENS

In the "war against organized crime," an array of law enforcement approaches have been legislated and implemented. These initiatives, in many respects, represent extraordinary investigative techniques that often require judicial authorization and/or oversight. Electronic surveillance, witness immunity, asset seizure and forfeiture, preventive detention, and anonymous juries require a level of judicial oversight not usually found in society's response to crime. One mechanism that has received little attention but is arguably one of the most useful and valuable is the independent crime commission. This vehicle was recommended by the President's Commission on Law Enforcement and Administration of Justice:

States that have organized crime groups in operation should create and finance organized crime investigation commissions with independent, permanent status, with an adequate staff of investigators, and with subpoena powers. Such commissions should hold hearings and furnish periodic reports to the legislature, governor and law enforcement officials.[1]

COMMISSION TYPOLOGIES

Essentially three types of crime commissions exist in the United States. First are publicly funded crime commissions where powers derive from legislative enactments. Typically these commissions employ investigative agents who are given law enforcement status but lack arrest authority. Further, most such commissions have no prosecutorial authority. The New Jersey, New York, and Pennsylvania crime commissions mirror this model. They are bipartisan in composition, commission members being appointed from the major political parties, and typically, statutory guarantees of political balance promote the independent status of the commissions. Supported by tax revenues, commission budgets remain relatively modest in comparison to other agencies within the criminal justice system.

A second type of crime commission involves a citizens' group usually funded by private contributions from the business community. A citizens' crime commission has no law enforcement authority. The Chicago Crime Commission, formerly headed by the legendary Virgil Petersen, the Citizens' Crime Commission in New York City, and the Citizens' Crime Commission of the Greater Delaware Valley in Pennsylvania are characteristic of this kind of commission.

The third kind of crime commission consists of a temporary group that has been created either by legislation or executive order to investigate—after the fact—a specific incident, event, or phenomenon. The Lilley Commission, charged with the investigation of the Newark riots in 1967, derived its authority from an executive order by former New Jersey governor Richard Hughes. The Knapp Commission created to investigate corruption in the New York City Police Department is another such example. Both were funded with public money, had subpoena power, and could hold both public and private hearings. President Lyndon B. Johnson's executive order created the Kerner Commission in 1968 to investigate the causes of civil disorder in the United States. It, like President Ronald Reagan's 1983 Commission on Organized Crime, was publicly funded, had subpoena power, and could hold both public and private hearings. Once a commission's goal has been achieved or the commission's life has expired, the commission is terminated. These kinds of commissions are analogous to royal commissions in Hong Kong, Japan, Great Britain, and Australia.

All three types of commissions may serve to educate, mobilize, and galvanize the public. They are created to address a specific phenomenon and do not necessarily collect evidence of general criminal activity. However, they are not precluded from providing criminal evidence to law enforcement authorities. The following discussion addresses publicly funded crime commissions such as the Pennsylvania Crime Commission.

POWERS OF PUBLICLY FUNDED CRIME COMMISSIONS

U.S. laws are essentially classified as criminal, civil, or administrative, with each requiring a different standard of proof for implementation. Criminal law requires proof beyond a reasonable doubt, and the rules of evidence are quite exact and restrictive. Civil law utilizes a preponderance-of-the-evidence standard, and procedural rules are often more liberal. Administrative law usually deals with regulatory matters; it utilizes a standard of proof that is clear and convincing—somewhere above preponderance of evidence and proof beyond a reasonable doubt.

Crime commissions such as those in Pennsylvania, New Jersey, and New York have been specifically mandated to expose organized crime and other kinds of public corruption. Their mandate to expose does not carry a requirement that their conclusions be supported by proof beyond a reasonable doubt. In fact, the legislation creating the Pennsylvania Crime Commission and prescribing its duties is silent on the matter of the standard of proof the commission should employ. Traditionally, however, the commission has adopted and utilized the administrative law standard of clear and convincing evidence to make factual determinations. Because crime commissions do not deprive a person of life and/or liberty but can and often do affect reputation, the civil standard of clear and convincing evidence is legally sustainable and appropriate. Operating with a lesser standard than that required for conviction of crime—proof beyond a reasonable doubt—makes somewhat easier the identification and exposure of organized crime conditions and the individuals involved than would be the case if use of the criminal law standard were required. Yet, choice of the clear and convincing standard protects against the possibly cavalier condemnation of persons that a lesser standard might permit or even encourage.

Illustrative are the Pennsylvania Crime Commission's investigation and exposure of racketeering in the state's solid waste industry. The commission gathered information and elicited testimony to demonstrate that New York and New Jersey organized crime groups had invested in Pennsylvania waste corporations. The groups' historic pattern of operation suggested that their entry into waste disposal would result in racketeering in Pennsylvania. The commission recommended regulations to inhibit and prevent such activity from occurring and also provided lead information to federal authorities to pursue criminal prosecutions and civil remedies.

The approach to the organized crime problem used in Pennsylvania allows a crime commission to facilitate and encourage criminal or civil responses by appropriate law enforcement or regulatory agencies. Unrestrained by traditional investigative limitations and evidentiary standard burdens, a crime commission may expose a problem (vis-à-vis arresting individuals) and offer a wider array of remedial options beyond simply a criminal prosecution. A crime commission, employing its law enforcement powers, can collect information and evidence and use both in either a cooperative or an adversarial setting. A commission may thus be far more comprehensive in its response to an organized crime problem than traditional law enforcement. To many traditionalists a crime commission may be seen as an anomaly, that is, an agency where arrest and prosecution are seen as secondary to a primary role of public exposure.

Other powers not found in the traditional law enforcement agency also exist in crime commissions. For example, a witness immunized by the New Jersey Commission of Investigation can be held in contempt and incarcerated for a refusal to testify. Incarceration continues until the recalcitrant witness agrees to testify. The late Angelo Bruno was incarcerated (as were others) for two and a half years for refusing to testify before the New Jersey State Commission of Investigation—the only period of incarceration he ever served.

Another unique authority is the power to subpoena witnesses. This right is usually provided only to grand juries. A subpoenaed witness must appear before a crime commission or grand jury and give testimony. The witness has the right to legal counsel and may exercise Fifth Amendment privileges against self-incrimination. If a witness commits perjury or provides false or misleading information, that witness is subjected to criminal prosecution.

A crime commission is empowered to hold public hearings to present its findings. While it lacks the power to issue indictments or log formal criminal charges, the public hearing serves as a forum where the commission articulates its findings and mobilizes public opinion to encourage institutional responses. A commission's report may be published to provide another means to educate the public about possible remedies. No traditional law enforcement agency in the United States has such authority. Nor does any such agency utilize the public report to expose conditions—other than an occasional presentment by a grand jury—acting at the behest of a prosecutor.

Typically, libel and defamation laws cannot be extended to a crime commission, because its acts are given immunity through its enabling legislation. Unlike traditional law enforcement organizations, which can be sued for false arrest or other civil violations, an aggrieved witness has ordinarily only limited recourse in the face of commission charges.

A FACT-FINDING BODY

Unlike a traditional investigative agency, where arrest and prosecution are the primary goals, crime commissions seek to gather facts and information and ultimately produce intelligence products. The intelligence product or assessment represents the culmination of a complex series of processes—collection, evaluation, collation, and analysis. These are the integral elements of the intelligence process, which is the prerequisite for any effective organized crime control program. Crime commissions are in a most enviable position insofar as they have at their disposal a rich menu of collection avenues, the most valuable, of course, being the subpoena power.

Illustratively, the Pennsylvania Crime Commission engaged in a lengthy investigation of organized crime influence in the city of Chester. Through informants, electronic surveillance, and private hearings (in which witnesses were subpoenaed to testify) the commission was able to assemble a picture of a city that had been systematically looted and plundered and was in fact owned lock, stock, and barrel by "the Mob." Moreover, African American racketeers were shown to have effectively integrated with Italian American mobsters to create an interracial, criminal alliance. The commission further demonstrated how New York organized crime interests had "infiltrated" this rather innocuous little city in southeastern Pennsylvania. The commission's investigation led to the first change in the partisan control of city government in 100 years—an unintended consequence of the commission's fact-finding and public education role.

The power of such commissions to investigate organized crime, in terms of not just individual criminal cases but rather systemic criminal systems, is inherent in their unique role. When a crime commission is most effective, it is seeking institutional change and not criminal prosecution. Its fact-finding can serve to protect a community against the blight of organized crime and alert the citizenry and government to the presence or impending presence of organized crime so that preventive methods can be taken.

ADJUNCTS TO LAW ENFORCEMENT

With their unique collection of powers, crime commissions represent an invaluable adjunct to law enforcement agencies engaged in organized crime control. Seldom do most law enforcement agencies have the time, money, resources, or expertise to investigate organized crime effectively. Public order enforcement tends to be the primary goal of most law enforcement agencies, and vice enforcement—the visible manifestation of organized crime—tends to be nothing more than a "numbers game." If a crime commission is functioning effectively, it is focusing its resources on "the players" who are able to avoid prosecution. Sophisticated racketeers are adept at maintaining the low profile, insulating themselves from the risks associated with crime. In fact, the most successful racketeers maintain a veil of legitimacy yet profit from the crimes of others. To uncover and expose these persons and the criminal syndicates that they direct and operate within, time, resources, and expertise in the law (electronic surveillance, witness immunity, and so on) are essential. An intelligence system that can supply traditional enforcement agencies with the information and analyses critical to successfully investigate and prosecute these criminal enterprises is nothing short of a necessity and is provided by a sophisticated crime commission.

ADJUNCTS TO THE MEDIA

Perhaps no institution is more effective in educating the public than the media. As an institution that has the capacity to create images of reality that certainly affect public policy, the media are, without question, paramount. Crime commissions, because of their unique role within the criminal justice community, are obligated to work closely with the media, in terms of not only enlisting public support but, equally as important, creating intelligent dialogue regarding the public policy issues that address efforts to contain organized crime. For far too long, public policy with respect to organized crime has been wedded to outdated ethnic stereotypes, ill-conceived perceptions of the role of criminal syndicates in society, and control theories that do little more than pander to the "kick-in-the-door" mentality of law enforcement. Seldom do the media attempt to assess the organized crime problem in terms of its systemic (vis-à-vis parasitic) character. Crime commissions can elevate the dialogue to a higher level.

ADJUNCTS TO LEGISLATURES

Similar to congressional committees that investigate various issues, crime commissions serve as adjuncts to their respective state legislatures. Law and public policy is the business of legislatures. To develop law and public policy with respect to organized crime, legislatures need solid, accurate data. They also need the data interpreted so that they make sense in terms of public policy. For example, the Pennsylvania Crime Commission, in its examination of the bingo industry, determined that the law in Pennsylvania did nothing more than entrench racketeers in the bingo industry and, in fact, created the "perfect white collar crime."[2] In this particular instance, passage of the bingo law in 1981 exacerbated the problem of racketeer influence in the bingo industry and impeded law enforcement efforts to prevent infiltration. Had the legislature been given an assessment of the problem before a law was passed, perhaps the current situation could have been prevented. Crime commissions can serve this valuable role.

COMMISSIONS AS AGENTS OF CHANGE

Organized crime control, in many respects, suffers from "intellectual atrophy." That is, most agencies engaged in "the war against organized crime" are consumed with winning battles and neglect either the "bigger picture" or a strategy. Little time or resources can be, or are, allocated to the necessary task of experimentation or pursuing new or unexplored territories. Since the principal (if not only) measure of success is arrests and prosecutions, venturing out into heretofore new and unchartered frontiers raises the probabilities of failure. Certainly no one can argue with the decades of effort put into the "war against La Cosa Nostra." But this "war" was not synonymous with the "war against organized crime." In its pursuit of La Cosa Nostra (LCN), law enforcement essentially ignored other equally compelling forms of organized crime—African American, Cuban, Chinese, and Israeli. Moreover, new groups have entered the marketplace, placing additional burdens on law enforcement. Crime commissions, in the forefront of change, are in a most advantageous position to assess and evaluate new trends and patterns in organized crime. Additionally, new strategies, a concept that often takes a back seat to "fire fights," can be experimented with, absent the fear of failure.

Nothing demonstrates this point more than the Pennsylvania Crime Commission's *1990 Decade Report*. No document, book, or report exists today that provides a comprehensive, multicultural "threat assessment" of organized crime. Not content with theory, this report provides empirical evidence to support its conclusions—empirical evidence that can be obtained only by using extraordinary investigative techniques.

INVESTIGATING POLITICAL CORRUPTION

In many respects, commissions have a unique and enviable role in the investigation of political corruption. They have the authority to make allegations on the basis of evidence that need not meet the standard of persuasiveness necessary in a criminal trial—beyond a reasonable doubt. While a mere preponderance standard—more probably than not—would be sufficient, as in civil litigation, most commissions utilize a standard of clear and convincing evidence; what is typically required to support a factual finding in administrative agency proceedings. They can, and often do, reveal not only the existence of corrupt public officials but the underlying cause(s) of the corruption. Commissions can, and often do, recommend systemic changes to counter corruption—changes that often go to the origin of the corruption. In this respect, crime commissions have a basic responsibility to seek ways to improve political processes or, more simply put, to impact the delivery of resources in society. In this area particularly, it is essential that crime commissions establish an internal working ethos that ensures that such initiatives are carried out in a fair, equitable, and nonpartisan manner.

Fundamental fairness demands a level of internal circumspection to allow and encourage healthy dialogue and debate among commission appointees and executive staff. All possible options and explanations about suspect conduct must be methodically explored. It is clearly inappropriate to issue a conclusory report without having argued the contradictory evidence/explanation for what initially appears as negative information. The role of the "devil's advocate" is no less important in the functioning of a crime commission than to a prosecutor. In fact, it is even more critical, insofar as the "fires of cross-examination" are extinguished in commission hearings. Defense attorneys have no right to test the credibility of witnesses, but crime commissions have almost absolute power over their witnesses.

Judging the credibility of witnesses, testing their truthfulness, and ascribing value to their testimony require deliberate and sharply honed inquiry. Predisposition, while certainly an asset to an adept investigator, is antithetical to the objectivity that crime commissioners should bring to their tasks. Fundamental fairness is essential if crime commission processes are to be regarded as credible.

Equitable treatment involves yet another ethos that must be inculcated into the work of such bodies. A commission must allow the opportunity for those who may be accused by the commission to respond, producing evidence that may refute negative information and/or inferentially challenging the credibility of any witness who has given testimony. Equity demands that a public official whose office is the target of allegations by persons—some of whom may have ill-conceived, misguided, or corrupt motives—be given the opportunity to contravene the charges. While any accused person is entitled to the opportunity to challenge allegations, the issue is particularly sensitive in the case of the public official. Reputation damage is always unfortunate, but in the case of the public official it may also be "career-ending."

Finally, nonpartisan inquiry is essential to the credibility of the process. Anything that smacks of partisan political motivation is certain to undermine the commission's unique role in our system of justice.

Should these prerequisites be applied to all investigations, insofar as all persons enjoy the same right to fair, equitable, and nonpartisan treatment by a commission? The textbook answer is certainly yes. The real-world answer is far more complicated.

Commissions rely on political support for their continued existence. One misstep politically can be lethal. It is not wise to pursue an investigation into political corruption without developing a companion political agenda to deal with what may well be organized political opposition. While there may be good cause for another agency—frequently and preferably a federal agency—to pursue investigation and prosecution, at times such an option is not possible. Proof beyond a reasonable doubt may be lacking and unavailable, yet the indicators of corruption may be obvious. Nevertheless, commission action can be critical. As has been suggested, such action may be life-threatening in the institutional sense, but going forward is the correct action. While there is no formula or exact rule(s) to be applied in deciding whether or not to proceed, the following tests can be helpful in the decision-making process:

- Is the alleged conduct of such a grievous nature that public confidence will be undermined if the official remains in office?
- Is the alleged conduct of such a grievous nature so as not to allow the official still another opportunity or opportunities to continue to engage in such conduct?
- Are the proofs being offered persuasive enough to permit a reasonable inference that the allegation is accurate?
- Has the credibility of the witnesses been sufficiently corroborated with independent evidence?
- Are there other instances of the alleged behavior that can be used to sustain the allegation?
- If the investigation proved "inconclusive," does such a finding warrant a public display of the evidence, if for no other reason than to "clear the air"?
- Could the commission be accused of a cover-up if the evidence and its findings are not revealed?
- Has the investigation developed sufficient media support?
- Has the commission developed a political agenda and enlisted political allies?
- Is the commission sufficiently prepared to "go it alone" if and when political support evaporates?
- Are the commission members unanimous in the decision to proceed, or is there sufficient disagreement that may ultimately impugn the majority's findings?

- What are the implications if "the king" (referring, of course, to the public official) is not slain?
- Could the findings influence the outcome of an election, and if so, does the public have a right to know?

Undertaking and pursuing the investigation of public corruption test the mettle of a crime commission as well as the judgment and values of the commissioners. Too frequently, the investigation of a public official—especially an elected official—arouses a kind of "circle the wagons" defensive response and invites political counterattack. To the extent that an aroused or determined political opposition can be dealt with at all, it is essential that a crime commission's procedures and motivation be credible.

REMEDIES IN POLITICAL CORRUPTION INVESTIGATIONS

Crime commissions are not, and should not be, wedded to the view that criminal prosecution is the only appropriate response to its finding of wrongdoing. As described earlier, its conclusions may be grounded upon proof that is clear and convincing but not provable beyond a reasonable doubt. Further, other remedial actions may be appropriate. However, the evidentiary assessment can, and often should be, made by an independent prosecutorial official. Thus, remedies may include the following.

Referral to prosecuting authorities. Any information developed by a crime commission can be referred for criminal prosecution. For example, witnesses can be subpoenaed before a grand jury, can be used at a criminal trial, or can be used simply to provide additional "lead information" to authorities. Documents that could provide information of a compelling or corroborating nature can be turned over to prosecuting authorities. Under no circumstances, however, should a commission conduct an investigation in tandem with a prosecuting authority. This will more than likely result in a challenge to its subpoena powers, which are solely for fact-finding (vis-à-vis accusatory purposes).

Resignation from office with a promise of cooperation and precluding the official from running for holding public office again. In cooperation with a prosecuting authority, a crime commission can insist that a public official resign from office to avoid criminal prosecution. This can, and should, be accompanied with a promise of cooperation and might include an agreement not to seek future public office.

If the law provides for civil forfeiture of office, proceedings should be initiated. Notwithstanding that a criminal case may not have been established, provisions in the law may allow for a civil forfeiture of a public official's office. Crime commissions can seek such an order, proving the necessary predicate for removal in a civil, as opposed to criminal, proceeding.

If the law provides for impeachment, the process should be initiated. Impeachment may be a remedy available following a crime commission investigation. While a cumbersome process, used by legislatures very rarely, based upon the information provided by a crime commission, impeachment proceedings can be initiated against an elected public official either before or after a criminal prosecution or absent a criminal prosecution. Since the proofs at an impeachment hearing need not be the standard found in a criminal trial, impeachment proceedings, notwithstanding their inherent political implications, represent a viable option.

OBJECTIONS TO CRIME COMMISSIONS

Some critics argue that crime commissions duplicate other law enforcement functions and are unnecessary. Others suggest that crime commissions are "toothless tigers" insofar as they lack prosecutorial powers.[3] Still others view crime commissions as a threat to our concepts of due process. None of these objections can stand the test of logic.

Duplication of Services

The foregoing discussion of crime commission missions and authority have demonstrated the fundamental differences between such a body and the traditional law enforcement agency. The latter lacks subpoena power; it can bring only criminal charges; it has no authority to investigate systemic causes of organized crime; it ordinarily cannot publish its findings; and, absent proof beyond a reasonable doubt, it is precluded from publicly making organized crime charges. In short, the roles of crime commissions and traditional law enforcement agencies are complementary but not duplicative. Most important, they are not, and should not be, viewed as competitive. Police effectiveness and crime commission success are not, and should not be, assessed in the same ways—given the diversity of responsibilities and the disparity in objectives. To lump police agencies and crime commissions together for evaluation purposes misperceives their functions and encourages inappropriate competition for resources.

Commissions as "Toothless Tigers"

"The pen is mightier than the sword" is a phrase that best describes the powers inherent in a crime commission. Not only can a crime commission pursue criminal sanctions, but it has the additional authority to propose institutional remedies. For example, a crime commission that can demonstrate the ineffectiveness of regulation of the solid waste industry or the ineffectual regulation of an element of the gambling industry is of greater value to the citizenry than one that is obligated to react to the problems inherent in a poorly designed and executed regulatory scheme. The opportunity to do so and propose reforms—

legislative or other—extends beyond the address through the imposition of a criminal sanction. A crime commission that shines the light on nefarious criminal elements in the community can certainly have more of an effect than a law enforcement agency that has been co-opted or corrupted or is inept at addressing organized crime.

Due Process Is Violated

The concept of "due process" applies to the criminal justice processes and is a principle of jurisprudence that addresses inequities in the administration of justice. A crime commission is not an accusatory body, nor does it mete out sanctions. Rather, it merely identifies and reports on organized crime conditions, allowing the system of criminal justice to pursue criminal or civil remedies.

A commission functions with the belief that organized crime control remains a public and community responsibility. Community action is the most cost-effective method for controlling organized crime.

PROCEDURAL CONCERNS TO ENSURE FAIRNESS

The powers of a crime commission must be appropriately regulated to ensure that fundamental fairness is protected. Crime commissions, by their very nature, face real civil liberties dilemmas. Because traditional criminal rules of evidence do not apply and they are immune from libel or defamation, crime commissions have the potential for abuse. In the "war against organized crime," crime commissions can become political or ideological battlegrounds for those who are intent on maligning or destroying an opponent's reputation. The Pennsylvania Supreme Court recognized this and concluded:

The nature of the Crime Commission calls for great circumspection in assessing the rights of citizens who may come within its investigative sweep. . . . the magnitude of the infamy. . . . on the mere assemblage of information untested by the fires of due process is enormous.[4]

People in a society, knowing a crime commission can injure or destroy a person's reputation, place considerable trust in a crime commission's reputation for integrity. In a democracy, it is repugnant to basic notions of due process to publicly label an individual as a racketeer, a drug dealer, or a killer in the absence of a conviction in a court. However, proof beyond a reasonable doubt is neither the same as innocence nor synonymous with nonculpability. Truth does not always surface in litigated cases and often becomes obscured. Achieving the delicate balance between a citizen's rights and the prevention of organized crime remains a real challenge and a struggle worth pursuing.

NOTES

1. President's Commission on Law Enforcement and Administration of Justice, *Task Force Report: Organized Crime* (Washington, DC: U.S. Government Printing Office, 1967), 23.

2. *Organized Crime and Racketeering in the Bingo Industry* (Conshohocken: Pennsylvania Crime Commission, 1992).

3. The Federal Bureau of Investigation, Drug Enforcement Administration, state police, and local police agencies lack prosecutorial powers as well.

4. *Organized Crime in Pennsylvania: A Decade of Change* (Conshohocken: Pennsylvania Crime Commission, 1991).

17

Organized Crime and Drug Abuse Control

MARK A. R. KLEIMAN

Organized crime research is both a search for knowledge and a contribution to an ongoing policy-making process. As searchers for knowledge, we want to know what organized crime is, what it does, how it changes over time. We also want to know how it influences, and is influenced by, conditions in the industries, both licit and illicit, where its presence is felt and what enforcement techniques are used against organized crime with what results. As policy analysts, we want to know the consequences of government actions, actual and potential, in order to be able to evaluate current strategies and recommend alternatives.

Organized crime and drug trafficking are linked, both as phenomena and as policy problems. Each is complicated, in description and in action, by the presence of the other. The objective of drug enforcement is to keep drugs away from consumers. The objective of organized crime enforcement is to contain the wealth and power of major criminal organizations and to frustrate their goal of being able to defy the law without paying its price. These two objectives interact where the drug trade affects organized crime or where organized crime affects the drug problem. The illicit drug business can be a major source of power or revenue to organized crime groups. It can also make them unusually vulnerable to enforcement. The capabilities of organized crime groups may make drugs more available to consumers than they would otherwise be.

This chapter examines four critical components that influence organized crime and recommends solutions to consider in dealing with this problem. The four components are (1) What effects does organized crime have on drug trafficking and enforcement? (2) What effects do drug trafficking and enforcement have on organized crime? (3) How should federal agencies engaged in organized crime enforcement adjust their policies to contribute to the objectives of drug policy? and (4) How should federal agencies engaged in drug enforcement adjust their policies to contribute to the objective of organized crime control?

I will lay out what we now know about the topic, identify the key analytic points, and discuss prospects for further research analysis. The term *organized crime* can be defined in at least three distinct ways. First, sometimes it is used merely as an ethnically neutral euphemism for "the Mafia" or "La Cosa Nostra." In this sense, "organized crime" is rather well defined; federal organized crime enforcement officials believe that they can name not only its constituent groups but all of their leaders and most of their individual members.

Second, it may describe a class of criminal organizations whose characteristics make them particularly worthy of law enforcement attention; size, wealth, political power, participation in a variety of criminal activities, and continuity over time have all been suggested as the defining characteristics.[1] Enforcement officials sometimes refer to such non-Mafia groups with Mafia-like characteristics as "emerging" (as opposed to "traditional") organized crime.

While the first approach made the specification of organized crime clear-cut (aside from the problem of "associates"), this second paragraph makes the borders hazier; surely the Hell's Angels qualify, but the Aryan Brotherhood and the El Rukns pose more difficult issues. But one can make a fixed list of organized crime groups, both traditional and emerging, and then have an unambiguous referent for questions such as, To what extent is organized crime involved in the drug business?

The third approach is to define a set of organized crime characteristics and then note to what extent a broad range of criminal organizations shares them. Defining organized crime in terms of its characteristics complicates the analysis, because it treats the set of "organized crime" groups as variable rather than fixed and logically implies a many-valued rather than two-valued classification. Rather than being defined simply as organized crime or nonorganized crime (i.e., on the list or off it), criminal groups will fall along a spectrum of being more or less organized crime-like. This suggests the possibility that drug enforcement activity can increase or decrease the number of drug-dealing organizations with many organized crime characteristics, make existing organized crime-like drug dealers more or less organized crime-like, and give such groups a greater or lesser share of the drug market.

ORGANIZED CRIME AND THE DRUG MARKETS

Organized crime, however defined, can touch the market for any given illicit product or service in one or both of two ways. Organized crime groups may be dealers in that illicit market or suppliers of intermediate goods and services to such dealers (or dealers and service firms in that market may be more or less organized crime-like). Alternatively, organized crime groups may act as extortionists preying on dealers or attempt to organize dealers into a cartel, restricting entry and fixing prices. We can call these two alternative forms of participation "productive" and "parasitic," respectively. "Productive" organized crime involvement will tend to increase the supply of illicit products and thus decrease price and increase the quantity consumed. "Parasitic" involvement, in illicit as in licit trades, will tend to increase prices and decrease the quantity consumed. Since the products and services in question are presumed to be "bads" rather than "goods," productive roles would be undesirable and parasitic ones desirable, from a public policy perspective that examines drug consumption effects alone, rather than taking organized crime as an independent problem category.[2]

In each case, we need to ask what characteristics of the market make it amenable to organized crime participation, whether this means participation by organized crime groups arising outside the market in question or the development of organized crime characteristics by market participants. For example, a reputation for being willing to deliver on threats of violence if debts are not repaid might be of use in the business of financing drug transactions because it would reduce the costs of collection. However, this advantage would be relevant only if drug dealers frequently needed to borrow money and if there were no other arrangements, such as supplier financing, that could offer dealers similar interest rates and less personal risk.

ORGANIZED CRIME AS A DRUG SUPPLY PROBLEM

"Traditional" organized crime—La Cosa Nostra (LCN)—does not now contribute substantially to the drug problem. With the exception of the major role widely, but not universally, believed to have been played in heroin importation by various New York mafiosi, it never has. This is not to say that LCN members and associates do not participate in drug dealing on many levels, but only that heroin importation into the New York area from Europe was their only distinctive contribution to the supply of illicit drugs, and Europe is no longer an important transit point for heroin entering the United States. Nor should this be surprising; much as LCN families might like a share of the $40 billion or so spent at retail on controlled substances, they have no obvious advantages as drug suppliers, aside from their established skill at smuggling heroin from the Mediterranean, and the substantial enforcement attention directed at LCN groups may, in fact, impose substantial competitive disadvantages on them.

As a consequence, as long as organized crime enforcement institutions continue their concentration on "traditional" organized crime groups, they have relatively little to contribute to solving the problem of illicit drug supply. But the concentration on the LCN has been so successful, both in terms of successful cases and in terms of creating and maintaining productive, high-morale enforcement and prosecution institutions, that it seems both unlikely (as a matter of prediction) to be changed and unwise (as a matter of policy analysis) to consider changing.

It may be the case that some "emerging" organized crime groups make distinctive contributions to various parts of the drug supply, so that their disruption would make a special contribution to drug supply control over and above the general effect of enforcement in raising prices by raising the costs and risks of drug trafficking. A large share of the cocaine market is under the control of the cartels based in Peru, Bolivia, and Colombia. American Chinatown-based groups now seem to account for much of the Southeast Asia heroin that is flooding the country. Gangs, based in Los Angeles, known as Crips and Bloods do a thriving business in retail crack distribution. Motorcycle gangs—like Hell's Angels in the West, the Outlaws in the Middle Atlantic region—may be ''least-cost suppliers'' in the distribution of amphetamines. By contrast, neither the importation nor the distribution of marijuana appears to offer the economies of organization that would make breaking up particular trafficking groups a major marijuana enforcement objective; the marijuana trade may be at its most effective as a decentralized set of independent buyers and sellers.

Developing a set of institutions that can appropriately address the role of emerging organized crime groups in the drug markets will require devising organizational incentives and career patterns that support extremely long-term investigations and investments in intelligence (broadly defined) while maintaining a supply-control orientation among agents and prosecutors. This will not be an easy task; there may be lessons to be learned from the Federal Bureau of Narcotics in its approach to LCN heroin dealing.[3]

Evidence about parasitic activities by LCN groups in the drug markets is fragmentary. The Angiulo tapes in Boston reflect that organization's attempts to collect ''street tax'' from the marijuana trade, but the significance or success of that attempt has not yet come out.

THE DRUG MARKETS AS AN ORGANIZED CRIME PROBLEM

The illicit drug traffic contributes to the organized crime problem because of the enormous amounts of money at stake. These potential revenues will both attract and help to sustain existing organized crime groups and call into existence new groups with organized crime characteristics.

LCN families, other ethnically based organizations long in existence, Los Angeles-style street gangs, and outlaw motorcycle gangs may engage in drug dealing as a way to support themselves financially and to take advantage of their organizational abilities in illicit transactions. The opportunities in the drug trade may also allow the development of organizations whose origin is in drug dealing and that may remain specialized in drug dealing, while taking on organized crime characteristics, in particular, organizational continuity and organizational investments in the abilities to use violence and corruption to resist enforcement efforts while remaining prominent in illicit markets.

Drug trafficking is almost certainly the largest source of illegally earned income in the United States, far outstripping the market for illegal gambling or prostitution.[4] Estimates of total revenues from drug sales vary widely[5] and are highly unreliable.[6] It seems unlikely that total annual revenues are much less than $40–50 billion.

Virtually all of this represents rewards for law-breaking; the payments for licit goods and services, lawyers' fees, and the rental or purchase of vehicles and buildings are negligible. On the other hand, relatively little of it represents revenue to large criminal organizations, because so much of the final retail price of illegal drugs consists of the markups of retail dealers and low-level wholesalers. For cocaine, less than one-fifth of the final retail price is collected by the dealer who sells kilogram units.

Organizations with many of the characteristics of organized crime may, however, exist at lower levels of those trades (e.g., the Barnes organization in the Harlem heroin market during the 1960s and 1970s and the Chambers Brothers group in the Detroit crack market of the 1980s).

CONSEQUENCES OF ENFORCEMENT PRESSURE

Whether organized crime characteristics produce a competitive advantage or disadvantage in a given drug market will depend, in part, on the amount of enforcement pressure on that market. One characteristic of organized crime is enforcement resistance: a set of organizational routines and capabilities, including the development of a reputation for using violence against potential witnesses and informants, to reduce the group's vulnerability to investigation and prosecution. It is precisely because organized crime groups are enforcement-resistant that the Federal Bureau of Investigation (FBI) and the strike forces (before their abolition) learned to make such heavy and long-term investments of manpower in order to make LCN cases.

From the perspective of drug dealing, enforcement resistance has costs: customers, suppliers, and employees will all tend to shy away from organizations known to be quick on the trigger. If the level of enforcement losses incident to working in a given drug market is relatively low, the disadvantages of heavily armored organizations in terms of day-to-day dealings will outweigh their advantages in terms of keeping out of the clutches of the law. On the other hand, as the level of enforcement pressure rises, the losses incurred by more loosely organized competitors will make higher and higher levels of investment in enforcement resistance seem worthwhile. Tightened general drug enforcement, as opposed to drug enforcement targeted at organized crime, will tend to give organized crime groups and organized crime-like groups relative competitive advantage, because their capacity for violence and corruption helps protect them against ordinary enforcement actions.[7] This encouragement of the acquisition of organized crime characteristics by drug-dealing organizations must be counted among the costs of increased drug enforcement activity.

The level of drug enforcement activity has another set of effects on the organized crime problem. Assuming that increased enforcement succeeds in raising the costs of drug dealing and, consequently, the price of the drugs at retail, consumption will tend to decrease. Consumption falling as prices rise will cause the total money at stake in the market to rise or fall depending on whether consumption falls faster or slower, in percentage terms, than prices rise.

Tighter enforcement can increase the money to be made in any black market if it succeeds in raising the price of the commodity involved and if consumption decreases less, in percentage terms, than prices rise. (A 50 percent price increase that causes only a 20 percent decrease in volume will create a new market with total revenues $1.5 \times 0.8 = 1.2$ times as large as the revenues in the old market and thus increase the money to be made by 0.2 or 20 percent.) Thus, the sensitivity of consumer demand to retail prices, what economists call the *price elasticity of demand*, becomes an essential number to know.

If the price elasticity of demand is, in absolute value, greater than one (if a given percentage increase in price will cause a larger percentage decrease in volume), then price increases will decrease total revenues. Such goods are said to be ''relatively elastically demanded.'' On the other hand, if the price elasticity of demand is, in absolute value, less than one (if a given percentage change in price will cause a smaller percentage change in volume, as in the previous example), then price increases will increase total revenues. Such goods are said to be ''relatively inelastically demanded.''

In markets where demand is relatively elastic—where consumers will respond to price increases by sharply cutting back consumption—increased enforcement will reduce the money at stake and thus tend to make the markets less lucrative for organized crime. Increasing enforcement where demand is inelastic will increase the money at stake and make the markets more able to support organized crime. Much of the empirical work recommended in this chapter centers on measuring the price elasticity of demand for various drugs.

Unfortunately, the demand for cocaine appears to be relatively inelastic.[8] If this is so, the drift of federal drug enforcement policy over the last ten years to increase total federal drug enforcement combined with a shift in relative emphasis away from heroin and toward cocaine has not been a desirable one from the perspective of organized crime control, though it may have helped limit drug consumption. This is the central tension in organized crime/drug enforcement policy: good drug enforcement may be bad organized crime control.

On the other hand, there is reason to believe that retail-level drug enforcement, particularly retail-level heroin enforcement, will have most of its effects on the number and aggressiveness of retail dealers and thus on the time and risk for the user involved in making a purchase, rather than on price.[9] If that is true, then retail-level enforcement will unambiguously decrease the total revenues of drug dealers and thus make the drug markets less lucrative for organized crime.

PROSPECTS FOR RESEARCH

The previous analysis carries us about as far as the current data sources will support us—some would say, much further. Progress on these issues will rely far more on data gathering than on speculation. We need data on three topics: the drug markets, drug enforcement, and the role of organized crime.

The Drug Markets

From the perspective of organized crime, the drug markets are important principally because of the sums of money involved. Consequently, knowing how large those sums are and how they are allocated among various roles is essential.

Total revenue in any market depends on the prices paid and the quantities purchased. Neither has yet been accurately measured for any of the major drug markets.[10] Estimates of these numbers can be derived either from the knowledge accumulated in the course of enforcement activity or from surveys of drug purchasers (and drug sellers in the limited cases where this is practicable). Survey results are likely to be more useful, particularly in regard to retail prices and quantities consumed. Enforcement-generated "price chain" data can be very informative about market structure and the division of illicit incomes among participants.

The problem with enforcement-derived estimates of drug quantities is that the relationship between enforcement results (e.g., drug seizures) and the overall volumes in the drug markets is unknown and may vary from time to time. Lost in the organizational history of the Federal Bureau of Narcotics is the unsung hero who first proposed the rule of thumb that enforcement agencies capture about 10 percent of the true supply on its way to market. That rule of thumb allows, once the problems with the seizure data are straightened away, a simple calculation of the physical size of the drug markets: take seizures and add a zero. More of the official drug market estimation than anyone would like to admit is still done using some variant of that methodology.

There are two problems with such calculation. First, there was never a period when we had a good measure of the total market to validate 10 percent, or any other number, as the seizure rate. Second, the seizure rate varies from drug to drug and changes over time; increased enforcement pressure will tend to raise it, but adaptation by traffickers will tend to lower it. In fact, if the change in enforcement is great enough to cause shifts in basic smuggling patterns, the result may be a lower overall seizure rate despite a higher level of enforcement. This seems to have been the case for the South Florida Task Force of the early 1980s, which succeeded both in driving drug smugglers away from its territory and in causing many of them to switch from large vessels to smaller, faster vessels.

The same is true of using enforcement measures as estimates of market size. The enforcement success count depends on the size of the market, the vigor and tactics of enforcement, and the countermeasures of traffickers. Without an independent basis for estimating the effect of countermeasures, the success count tells us little even about trends in the size of the market.

Surveys have a different set of problems. First, the survey population may be unrepresentative of the general population in a way that leads to an underestimation of the total quantity consumed. Second, respondents may systematically misrepresent their behavior, either to deceive or because, for psychological reasons, they actually believe that they use cocaine less frequently than they actually do. Third, the population of very heavy users, who account for a large fraction of the total consumption of any drug, may be sufficiently rare so that even a large sample contains too few of them to make accurate measurements.

Finally, the current surveys (of high school seniors by the Institute for Social Research at the University of Michigan and of the general household population by Substance Abuse and Mental Health Services Administration) do not ask directly about some of the topics most relevant to policy-making: purchase habits, personal inventories, drug sharing, quantities purchased, prices paid, how much prices vary over time, what effects those variations have on consumption, whether there are shortages of particular drugs, and how users respond to them.

But all of these problems are surmountable, at least in principle, by changing the current surveys or beginning new ones. We could ask directly about prices and about quantities purchased and consumed; we could work hard on sample representativeness by including the nonhousehold (institutional and homeless) population; we could do validation studies on self-report data; and we could attempt to oversample among populations likely to contain large proportions of heavy users. We could do studies of local markets to determine the extent of geographic variation and local variation over time. In addition, we could supplement one-shot sample surveys with panel studies. These steps would involve various levels of difficulty and expense, but none of them are impossible, and any of them would improve on our current ignorance.

From the enforcement world, we could do more systematic collation of case and informant reports into price chains and create a serious program of retail-level buys to determine prices and drug characteristics (identity, potency, purity).

The combination of data from frequent local surveys and local retail-buy data might allow the contemporaneous measurement of the effects of increased enforcement or changed enforcement tactics on, for example, the marijuana market in eastern Massachusetts. Until we know something about that, any attempt to model the effects of such enforcement changes on organized crime is largely futile.

Drug Enforcement

Our ignorance about the drug markets is attributable largely to the difficulty of observing illegal activity. Our ignorance about drug enforcement is less excusable; it reflects a failure to collate data already in government hands. Three classes of data are of interest here: enforcement inputs, activities, and targets; enforcement outputs; and enforcement effects. What resources are spent on drug enforcement (measured in dollars, agent-hours, prosecutor-hours, cell-years, ship-days, and wiretap orders under Title III), and how are those resources divided among agencies geographically, by target drug, by enforcement technique, and by the trafficking activity (high-seas smuggling, port smuggling, first domestic distribution, wholesaling and middleman activity, retail dealing, money laundering)?

At the federal level alone, something as relatively simple as a unified dollar budget broken out by agency and by drug (e.g., Customs Service expenditures on cocaine cases) is not available. An earlier attempt of mine to estimate the share of marijuana in total federal enforcement illustrates both the limits of current data sources and the conclusions that can be drawn in spite of those limitations.[11]

Assembling meaningful information about inputs in nonmonetary forms (e.g., work-hours) would be a tedious process requiring both access to internal agency reporting systems and an understanding of how those systems represent or misrepresent reality. However, assuming that something resembling the Drug Enforcement Administration's (DEA) annual statistical report[12] is available from the Coast Guard, Customs Service, Internal Revenue Service (IRS), and FBI, it might be possible to assemble a fair picture of federal enforcement activity.

Federal prosecution agencies do not now have the ability to generate statistical profiles of their work that would be useful here. The case-management software system, PROMIS, being installed in the U.S. attorney's offices, may be able to produce estimates of prosecutorial work-hours by case type, though the system may not code enough of the case data (e.g., G-DEP [Grand Jury Depositions] rank of case and defendants) to allow useful analysis.

The Administrative Office of U.S. Courts can produce cases-pending counts by offense. This, though, overestimates drug cases as a proportion of total cases to the extent that drug defendants are more likely than others to default on bail and thus remain as active cases for long periods of time; no estimates are published of the use of judge-days or grand jury days for various kinds of cases. Moreover, since the statute names and numbers attached to a given drug charge (manufacture, distribution, conspiracy, continuing criminal enterprise, and so on) do not vary with drug involved, it is almost impossible to separate the conviction data by drug. From the court data, it is possible to make very crude estimates of federal prison cell utilization by convicted drug dealers. The attempt to work directly from DEA data[13] is frustrated by the fact that the DEA statistical report lists total convictions rather than convictions in federal courts. The lack of a unified set of file numbers for the federal criminal justice agencies or a set of links from one file system to the next (what is called an "Offender-Based Tracking System," or OBTS) makes it nearly impossible to trace a sample of DEA defendants through prosecution and incarceration. Below the federal level, the situation is much worse; there are simply no published figures on drug enforcement spending or activities by state and local police agencies.

The current paucity of enforcement input data would frustrate any attempt to study the effects of changes in enforcement resources on the drug markets, even if adequate price and quantity data were in hand. However, unless the agencies involved have their own reasons for collecting the data, it will be difficult either for "outsiders," even from within the government, to do the job or to persuade the agencies to do it themselves. The situation is similar for state and local enforcement. In the absence of any convenient ways of getting nationwide data, a few studies of individual cities and states might be useful, and the availability of federal research money might be an adequate inducement to local authorities to make the data available.

More sensitive, but even more important from the perspective of organized crime and drugs, is information about how enforcement agencies choose their targets. It was suggested earlier that the general tendency of increased drug enforcement would be to confer competitive advantage on more organized crime-like drug-dealing organizations, because such organizations will tend to be more enforcement-resistant than their competitors. This might not be true if enforcement agency operating procedures were designed to discriminate against enforcement-resistant organizations. How does a reputation for violence compare with a large volume in making a drug-dealing group a target for federal investigation? What incentives exist within enforcement agencies to encourage the long-term investigative techniques that have proven essential in LCN cases?

Outputs

How do those inputs translate into enforcement actions felt by traffickers (arrests, convictions, sentences, time actually served in prison, drug seizures, and asset seizures)? How are those outputs distributed geographically, by drug, by level of the traffic?

These figures are less nebulous than resource and workload data; a man-hour is such stuff as dreams are made of, but an arrest actually happens. Nonetheless, although DEA reports its arrests broken down by almost every possible variable,[14] there is no government-wide collation of all arrest reports. Convictions and prison time, as noted, are simply not available in useful formats.

Even drug seizure data are complicated by the multiplicity of agencies involved; simply adding together agency totals runs the risk of double counting.[15] The Federal Drug Seizure System is supposed to have eliminated that problem, but some agents remain skeptical.

Data on asset seizures are complicated both by interagency (and federal/state/local) cooperation and by the complexity of seizure cases; the appraised value of an asset may be a large multiple of its realized value less the lienholder's equity. The lags in forfeiture actions against seized items, plus the growth in the overall level of seizures, make it difficult to compute seizure-to-forfeiture ratios, because 1992 forfeitures do not correspond to 1992 seizures. Since central responsibility for this area was assigned to the U.S. Marshal Service and the Asset Forfeiture Office of the Criminal Division of the Justice Department, those agencies may now be in a position to provide unified statistics.

Arrests, convictions, seizures, and prison time are basic measures of risk imposed on the illicit drug industry, and it is very hard to plan or evaluate policy in their absence. Unlike most of the input numbers, good output measures can be assembled with only minimal cooperation from the agencies themselves, if someone with authority insists on it.

Below the federal level, the situation is more dismal. Other than the uninformative counts of total drug arrests in the Uniform Crime Reports, no national data are available. It has been almost ten years since the last national study of state prisoners by offense category, and even that study combined all drug offenses into one category. Here again, the best that can be hoped for are a few well-done local studies.

Effects

Enforcement actions impose costs and risks on illicit entrepreneurs and thus tend to increase prices and perhaps to make supplies less reliable. To some extent, the cost-imposition value of a given enforcement action—the imprisonment of a major marijuana importer for an effective term of six years, the seizure of one kilogram of 90 percent pure heroin from a New York City wholesaler—can be calculated. The sum of those imposed costs is then an estimate of the effects of enforcement on the market.[16] These calculations can be useful in policy analysis and evaluation. However, to make them accurately, one needs the right kind of tabulation of enforcement outputs.

The value of any illicit drug grows enormously as it moves down the distribution chain toward the final consumer. A kilogram of heroin that sells for $150,000 is the raw material for street bags of heroin worth more than $600,000. Adding together physical volumes seized at different stages of the traffic is adding apples and oranges; each seizure should be evaluated at its value where and as seized, and then the value should be added together. The "street value" calculations so beloved of reporters resemble calculations of the value of stolen cattle based on the price of a steak dinner in a restaurant. Given estimates of the "price chains," simple rules of thumb based on quantity and location, will give reasonable estimates of the cost imposed on the illicit market by drug seizures.

A similar point applies to imprisonment data. The higher in the trade a trafficker is, the more dollars he would spend to avoid a year in prison, both because he has more dollars and because any given period in prison costs him more in lost earnings.

That willingness to pay per prison-year avoided multiplied by the number of years spent in prison (deterrence measured in dollars) represents the cost imposition effect of imprisonment. In any case, calculating it will require somewhat arbitrary guesses about the willingness to pay of traffickers at different levels. But unless the data on imprisonment are collected by drug and G-DEP violator class, there are no figures with which to calculate.

Organized Crime Participation

What are the drug markets like? We would like to know about the size and durability of the organizations involved, their use of violence in "business" and in resisting enforcement, their involvement with other criminal activities, the barriers to entry by new firms, and so on. These questions and others relating to the mechanics of drug dealing will not be answered by the retail-market data or by the enforcement statistics.

Only two types of people in the world know much about these topics: drug dealers, active and retired, and drug enforcement agents. Asking questions of dealers (in the nature of things, this will usually mean dealers in prison) involves enormous difficulty, but the rewards for success might be equally substantial. Other than that, we have to rely on the knowledge built up by enforcement agents in the course of their work. Unfortunately, the agencies' own attempts to compile these data into a coherent picture of the drug market have been neither systematic nor, when made available, particularly persuasive.

Something about market structure might be inferred from price-chain data if they were reliable and frequently updated. Most of it could be studied only by reviewing the information in case files and agents' minds, information available only to the agencies themselves. But drug enforcement agencies are not in business to collect data or do analysis, they are in business to put drug dealers in jail and seize their assets. Like other agencies, they tend to collect and publish data that will help them do their job better, will persuade someone else to help them do their job better, or will make them look good. Most of the information that would be useful in understanding the effects of drug enforcement on organized crime meets none of those criteria.

This indifference to research and its results, amounting to a conviction that the research activity has no contribution to make to the enforcement mission, is a long-enduring feature of American drug enforcement activity. With exceptions, it is shared by prosecutors as well as investigators. Its consequences for research are far-reaching; in addition to limiting the extent to which research results are used, it frequently means that the research itself cannot be done. The unavailability of qualitative enforcement data forces us back to measuring the markets and the observable enforcement actions.

NOTES

1. Michael D. Maltz, "Toward Defining Organized Crime," in *The Politics and Economics of Organized Crime*, ed. Herbert Alexander and Gerald E. Caiden (Lexington, MA: Lexington Books, 1984); Mark Kleiman, "Drug Enforcement and Organized Crime," in *The Politics and Economics of Organized Crime*, ed. Alexander and Caiden (Lexington, MA: Lexington Books, 1984), 74–75; Mark Kleiman, "Allocating Federal Drug Enforcement Resources: The Case of Marijuana," Ph.D. diss., Harvard University, 161–73.

2. Thomas C. Schelling, "Economics and Criminal Enterprise," *The Public Interest*, no. 7 (Spring 1967), reprinted in Thomas C. Schelling, *Choice and Consequence* (Cambridge: Harvard University Press, 1984); Thomas C. Schelling, "What Is the Business of Organized Crime?" *Journal of Public Law* (now the *Emory Law Journal*) 20 (1971): 71–84, reprinted in Thomas C. Schelling, *Choice and Consequence* (Cambridge: Harvard University Press, 1984); James B. Buchanan, "A Defense of Organized Crime," in *The Economics of Crime & Punishment*, ed. Simon Rottenberg (Washington, DC: American Enterprise Institute, 1973), 119–32.

3. Kleiman, "Allocating," Chapter 8.

4. Ken Carlson et al. *Unreportable Taxable Income from Selected Illegal Activities* (Cambridge, MA: Abt Associates, 1983); Carl Simon and Ann Witte, *Beating the System* (Boston, MA: Auburn House, 1982).

5. Carlson, "Unreportable Taxable Income"; National Narcotics Intelligence Consumers Committee, *Narcotics Intelligence Estimate: The Supply of Drugs to the U.S. Illicit Market from Foreign and Domestic Sources in 1982 (with Projections Through 1983)* (Washington, DC: U.S. Govt. Printing Office, undated); Kleiman, "Allocating"; Peter Reuter and Mark Kleiman, "Risks and Prices: The Economics of Drug Enforcement," in *Crime and Justice: An Annual Review of Research*, ed. Michael H. Tonry and Norval Morris (Chicago: University of Chicago Press, 1986); Office of National Drug Control Policy, "What America's Users Spend on Illicit Drugs," 1992 (Washington, DC: U.S. Govt. Printing Office).

6. Peter Reuter, "The (Continuing) Vitality of Mythical Numbers," *The Public Interest* 75 (Spring 1984); Max Singer, "The Vitality of Mythical Numbers," *The Public Interest* 23 (Spring 1971): 3–9.

7. This is argued at length in Kleiman, "Allocating," Chapters 6–7; and Kleiman, "Drug Enforcement."

8. Reuter and Kleiman, "Risks and Prices."

9. Mark H. Moore, "Policies to Achieve Discrimination on the Effective Price of Heroin," *American Economic Review* 63.2 (May 1973); Michael A. Spence, "A Note on the Effects of Pressure in the Heroin Market," Discussion Paper 588, Cambridge: Harvard Institute of Economic Research, November 1977; Mark A. R. Kleiman, William E. Holland, and Christopher Hayes, "Report to the District Attorney for Essex County: Evaluation of the Lynn Drug Task Force," Harvard University: Program in Criminal Justice Policy and Management, J. F. Kennedy School of Government, 24 October 1984; Mark Kleiman, "Retail Heroin Enforcement and Property Crime," Harvard University: Program in Criminal Justice Policy and Management, J. F. Kennedy School of Government, 15 October 1986.

10. Michael J. Polich et al., *Strategies for Controlling Adolescent Drug Abuse* (Santa Monica, CA: Rand Corporation, February 1984); Carlson, "Unreportable Taxable Income"; National Narcotics Intelligence Consumers Committee, *Narcotics Intelligence Estimate*; Reuter and Kleiman, "Risks and Prices."

11. Kleiman, "Allocating."

12. Drug Enforcement Administration, *Annual Statistical Report, FY 1984* (Washington, DC: Statistical Services Section, Office of Planning and Evaluation, Planning and Inspection Division, 1985).

13. Kleiman, "Allocating," 78–80.

14. Drug Enforcement Administration, *Annual Statistical Report*, 339–93.

15. General Accounting Office, *Federal Drug Interdiction Efforts Need Strong Control Oversight* (Washington, DC: U.S. Govt. Printing Office.: Report GGD-83-52, 1983).

16. Polich et al., *Strategies Controlling Drug Abuse*; Kleiman, ''Allocating,'' 96–101; Reuter and Kleiman, ''Risks and Prices.''

18

Policing Emerging Organized Crime Groups

JOHN DOMBRINK AND
JOHN HUEY-LONG SONG

INTRODUCTION

With the success of federal and state investigations and prosecutions against traditional organized crime groups over the past decade, various observers and analysts have speculated on the future of organized crime in America as the "twilight of the mob."[1] Even skeptical parties have begun to wonder whether the conviction of John Gotti on federal racketeering counts, after several unsuccessful prosecutions, indicates that the final chapter is being written in the federal government's war against traditional organized crime in this country. To some, the end of the Mafia reflects the demise of omerta, a reduction of organizational control and discipline, and the willingness of insiders, such as the Gambino underboss Sammy Gravano, to provide testimony against their colleagues.[2]

Some organized crime experts and law enforcement officials testifying at a special Senate hearing in 1988 took stock of the changes in American organized crime since Joseph Valachi's testimony in 1963. Among these was the testimony of Ralph Salerno, longtime expert and writer on organized crime, who asserted, "It would be a major error to assume that law enforcement will be able to address the non-traditional groups as successfully in the next decade as was the case in the past with the traditionalists."[3] On the issue of violence, Salerno warned that the decrease in Cuban-Colombian violence was not an assuring signal that the prevalence of these groups had declined, but rather that "the criminals are becoming *better* organized, they are learning to cut up the pie peacefully, with profit for all and attracting less attention from the rest of society."[4]

The purpose of this chapter is to examine the ways in which the elements of Asian emerging crime groups challenge the existing capacity of the government to police organized crime. It summarizes certain findings from a two-year National Institute of Justice study of the structure, operation, and control of Asian organized crime in America. The study focused on New York and California and featured interviews with 200 local, state, and federal police and prosecutors and Asian community leaders.

There have been many recent successes in the efforts of local and federal authorities against Asian racketeering. In New York, many substantial cases have been made by the Drug Enforcement Administration (DEA)—also by the Federal Bureau of Investigation (FBI) and the Customs Service—against significant heroin traffickers. Racketeering charges are outstanding against two major New York City criminal groups and their leaders, Born to Kill and the Green Dragons. An unprecedented case has been brought against the national On Leong organizations and some of their chapter leaders in Chicago, New York, and Houston. Alien smuggling rings have been broken and gambling operations disrupted. Against the yakuza, Japanese criminal organizations, the Immigration and Naturalization Service (INS), and customs efforts in Hawaii have utilized visa fraud prosecutions, and investigations of legitimate business involvements are ongoing.

Read against the recent history of the dismantling of the traditional organized crime structures, the challenge of building intelligence, developing informants, monitoring wiretaps, establishing cooperative relationships, managing international joint investigative and prosecutorial undertakings, reaching out to community members, and enlarging all such activities at a time of reduced resources and higher competition for them are a daunting task. While many of the experiences against the La Cosa Nostra (LCN) seem to the lay observer to have come about in the last decade, they are the result of decades of intelligence building and prosecutorial frustration and a relentless federal effort since Robert Kennedy's years as U.S. attorney general in the early 1960s.

In addition, the use of Racketeer Influenced and Corrupt Organizations Act (RICO) and asset forfeiture legal strategies took years to implement and perfect, as case law was established and expertise was built.

In 1979, the University of Southern California sponsored a national conference on organized crime, which brought together many of the country's experts in the prosecution, investigation, and monitoring of organized crime groups. At one general session, a federal organized crime strike force attorney with several years of experience and a string of successes in Kansas City, Las Vegas, and Los Angeles, Michael DeFeo, then a Los Angeles-based organized crime strike force official and later an official of the Organized Crime and Racketeering Section of the the Criminal Division of the U.S. Department of Justice, stood and addressed a response to one of the panel commentators. Organized crime groups in the United States, he stated, have committed themselves to a long effort to achieve profits and power through their various enterprises, and government should ask no less of itself and expect a similar commitment if it is to succeed against determined criminals. It seemed the predictable response of a dedicated government official, but it belied the reality of a crime phenomenon that had eluded legal sanctioning for such a long time and that had acquired a perception of untouchability.

The strategies against Asian racketeering that will be deployed over the next decade should take notice of the steady and committed effort against traditional organized crime by the innovative legal statutes now present and available for use against Asian racketeering groups. Certainly international elements, capitalizing on wire transfers of assets, nonstop air services, facsimile machines and overnight mail, and capital flow in general, make this effort currently a more complex one, requiring greater coordination and cooperation. The demise of traditional organized crime groups—the "twilight of the Mob"—might provide useful examples, helpful encouragement, or merely a vacuum into which Asian racketeering groups move and expand, as they have with heroin. Wherever American investigators and prosecutors follow a timeline comparable to the successful timeline against traditional organized crime, eventual success can best come from the application of traditional methods—greater resources, enhanced cooperation and coordination, and the institutionalization of investigative and prosecutorial expertise.

Here we examine five distinct factors that challenge those who investigate and prosecute Asian organized crime in the United States: properties of the crimes themselves; factors related to the nature of the victims; factors deriving from the organization and behavior of the criminal groups; factors related to the location of the crimes; and factors proceeding from unique investigative and prosecutorial demands.

Many of the recent successes in prosecution of Asian organized crime are reviewed, with recommendations for the deployment of more resources in this area; the recruitment of more Asian agents and police; the encouragement of more interagency, interjurisdiction, and international cooperation in the sanctioning of these groups; the institutionalization of units that currently address this issue; and the simultaneous encouragement of enhanced police-community relations in Asian communities.

CRIME FACTORS

It would be a mistake to believe that Asian crime groups commit only novel crimes. There certainly are some unique crimes—home invasion robberies, for example; crimes that are more prevalent than in other sectors of society, such as business extortion; crimes occurring across societal sectors, but not necessarily in the same way, such as investment in legitimate business; and even some crimes, such as theft of computer chips, that are novel, perhaps because there were fewer opportunities for them in the past.[5] Properties of these groups may make them much more difficult to investigate and prosecute, but the crimes themselves have features that make them difficult, apart from group factors.

For example, heroin trafficking, which is one of the crimes most often cited as a reason to direct more attention to the investigation and prosecution of Asian criminal groups, is by nature conducted between willing partners. Thus, victims and witnesses are not readily available. Certainly we can speak of addicts, neighborhoods, and society in general as victims;[6] and we can even speak of the opportunity for heroin profits being sufficiently attractive to youthful criminals of all sorts—even if it does not involve high-volume heroin trafficking. Law enforcement must have insider information from an informant, either a participant in the network or someone else; it must have an undercover operative, either police or not, initiating a sting operation; it must rely on intercepted telephone calls based on Title III surveillance; or it must intercept the drugs themselves based on suspicion or on some information about their arrival. Even with significant seizures, the threat of long sentences if convicted, and the "flipping" of defendants for purposes of pursuing other crimes or organizations, still the amount of legitimate cargo coming into this country (New York and California particularly) each year from Asia dwarfs the amount of heroin presumably imported and makes detection, arrest, prosecution, and conviction frustrating and cumbersome.

Similarly, with infiltration of legitimate business, the type of legal proof required for an indictment may turn ultimately on the availability of insider information or individuals who have no interest in providing such information.

Clearly, some of the victim factors, discussed in the next section, facilitate the effectiveness of the crime factors. In extortion, for example, victims and witnesses could effectuate the prosecution of offenders. However, cultural restraints within victim groups and criminals' capacities and willingness to use violence make extortion a crime that very often succeeds.

Historically, in gambling and prostitution, the consensual elements of the crime circumscribe investigation and prosecution. In the case of Asian prostitution, certainly there are cases where the prostitutes are brought to the United States against their will and are therefore undocumented persons whose status is used to thwart their cooperation with authorities. Similarly, with gambling, the added element of the low seriousness of crime has been a factor against effective prosecution. Since 1964, America has been engulfed in the "third wave" of legal gambling,[7] and while this has not included legal casinos at a Las Vegas level in any state besides New Jersey and has yet to include sports gambling, the perceived seriousness of gambling as a crime is low, as reflected in government surveys, in the sentences given to convicted illegal gamblers, and in jury reluctance to convict on such charges.[8] Federal officials have the luxury of not needing to police local jurisdictions on the wide range of crime issues that local police must and are not concerned about losing the cooperation of local citizens for being perceived as too vigilant about softer vice "crimes" that are largely tolerated in most communities. John Gardiner[9] found this twenty years ago in his study of "Wincanton," where the public wanted illegal gambling tolerated by police but expressed more negative sentiments toward corruption, a by-product of the first condition. In a survey by the President's

Commission on Organized Crime of federal law enforcement officials in the mid-1980s, the seriousness of illegal gambling was still a significant issue for the respondents.[10] In many government reports on Asian organized crime, gambling is often referred to as a lifeblood of the criminal groups.[11] Profits from it flow into other activities, and it brings together many elements of a community. As gamblers lose, loan-sharking and infiltration of legitimate businesses occur—two crimes involving much more perceived seriousness and community harm. Gambling, the police, and political corruption were the basis of the Chicago prosecution of the national On Leong.

Crimes such as the smuggling of undocumented Fukienese from China similarly have the appearance of involving only those who profit and those who are paying for an illegal service—at exorbitant rates and with little chance of paying off their debt quickly without resorting to crime. This makes the likelihood of a victim's coming forward remote, and the availability of witnesses may depend on whether they have any fear of reprisals against themselves or members of their (extended) family who might be vulnerable to prosecution for participation in smuggling or unrelated crimes, such as tax evasion or labor violations. That such smuggled persons may need to join criminal groups or transport heroin as a way of paying off the debts they might not otherwise meet is more apparent in recent times.

VICTIM FACTORS

In this section, it makes sense to discuss both victims and witnesses. Interview data provided ample evidence that witness/nonvictim participation is very limited in Asian American communities, especially those consisting largely of recent immigrants. Their "blindness" to crime may be a function of cultural attitudes, negative experiences with the law, lack of language facility, or fear of reprisals. That is not an uncommon experience in the criminal justice system in general but is again bounded by the issue of what racketeering entails—a combination of crimes that center on violence, some consensual relationships, and complex financial schemes requiring insider testimony to prosecute effectively.

With victims, there are several issues to consider. First, there is the frightened victim. This is independent of ethnicity, length of time in this country, language facility, and cultural attitudes. Fear of reprisal can be palpable. When one extortion victim participating with the legal system was shot to death in New York City, it reaffirmed the message for many others in the same circumstances that there was a real threat to such cooperation and that police cannot be expected to provide twenty-four-hour protection in such circumstances.[12] In some home invasion robberies, for example, it is clear that the victims are chosen after deliberation, that information about the presence and value of cash, jewelry, gold, or other goods is detailed, often from insider information, and that perpetrators know the family members of the victims, their habits and whereabouts, and can speak very convincingly and in a detailed manner about the manner of reprisal that will occur should the victim choose to cooperate with authorities. Although some law enforcement experts believe that few reprisals actually happen, that may be because the threats are credible, with consequently few cooperating witnesses.

Several interview subjects mentioned aspects of the criminal justice system—bail being the most prominent—that are very confusing for those who come from societies with more punitive approaches to crime and punishment. In the classic example, when a victim summons the strength to testify against a perpetrator, and then the suspect is released on bail, often to return to threaten, taunt, or harm the victim, there is either little understanding of the nature of the American criminal justice process or the belief that an official has been bribed to secure release. Interestingly enough, while police are often vilified for not having enough cultural sensitivity to Asian groups, they are also sometimes criticized (as in the case of Southeast Asian Mien in California's Central Valley) for the system's not being punitive enough with youth or criminals who have been apprehended.[13]

Several of the interview subjects mentioned the "dirty victim," who, if not complicitous in the particular crime under investigation, might be guilty of another infraction—welfare fraud or tax evasion, for example—or might be related to someone who is vulnerable so that the victim is constrained from coming forward as a witness.

Finally, some victims have "access problems"—lack of language facility, lack of time to make a complaint, and lack of understanding about the system itself.

GROUP FACTORS

Several factors have been prominently mentioned over the past decade to explain the strength of Asian racketeering groups, and many of these have been consistent with descriptions of all types of organized crime groups. The use of violence, ability to prevent witnesses from appearing against them in a court of law, and internal rules against participating in government prosecutions against the group are characteristic features.

When one talks about Asian racketeering, it is helpful to distinguish among several types of groups. *Criminal gangs*, such as New York City's Flying Dragons or Ghost Shadows, have been connected to legitimate but suspect self-help organizations (*tongs*) and have been described by various government reports as essentially possessing the longevity, use of violence, and association with certain racketeering crimes to merit definition as organized crime groups. In California, the Wah Ching is considered a sophisticated and powerful *organized crime group*, as its leaders have left behind the street violence and pursued monopolies in legitimate business. *Triads*, which are Chinese in origin and active in Hong Kong (e.g., Wo Group, 14K), may have members who are connected to American criminal groups and gangs, who serve as partners and intermediaries, and who are relocating in the United States before the 1997 transition of Hong Kong to the People's Republic of China. Nonetheless, there is much debate as to whether the triad influence will be significant and redirect the interests of the Asian American groups, cause competition and violence among the American groups, or provide future leaders within the American context.

Yakuza groups are not associated with street crime groups in this country, and Japanese American merchants and community members do not fit the pattern of home invasion robbery victims as do their Chinese or Vietnamese counterparts. However, the financial (and political) sophistication of these groups in their Japanese context and the historical difficulty in tracing such assets make their presence in American commerce a concern, be it in Hawaiian real estate, Las Vegas casinos, or Los Angeles tourist business and commercial development.[14]

Heroin importing groups may be seen as distinct from all previous groups, even if they involve some of their members. This fluidity is often a concern for investigation and poses some problems for the application of conspiracy provisions of the RICO statute.

Federal prosecutors have been consistent in asserting that arrested heroin traffickers have been willing to cooperate by providing information. Perhaps this can be attributed to the length of the sentences for heroin trafficking and the youthful nature of many of the apprehended. It might also be a function of the fluidity of some of these heroin-importing groups, in which profit seeking and "the deal" are paramount, and group cohesion and solidarity are secondary.[15]

Ethnic Vietnamese criminal groups have been historically separated into adult gangs and youth gangs, the former composed of immigrant former military and intelligence officers, whose criminal and extortion activities have had a clearly political function within the immigrant Vietnamese community. Since the fall of Saigon in 1975, the importance of this group as a criminal threat has been supplanted by "youth gangs," whose members range from true juveniles to thirty-year-olds and whose modus operandi includes home invasion robberies and other criminal forms unrelated to the crimes of their elders.[16]

One interview subject, a local police gang intelligence officer, commented that the percentage of crime that was committed by groups or in groups among Asian criminals seemed to be very high (75 percent), which explains some of the disparity between our focus on these crimes and the argument by ecologists like Marcus Felson[17] that crime rates in Asian communities are generally lower than those in non-Asian communities. If the group serves, as the ethnic Vietnamese groups do, to provide safe houses, prepare plans for vulnerable home invasion robbery victims, and constitute a means for criminals to elude capture by creating "circuits" of North American cities with significant Vietnamese populations, then they act in ways that are of direct interest to law enforcement. Their mobility denotes a national network.

Indeed, in the Chinese context especially, the historical parallel of the earlier immigrant organized crime groups to move from street crime to vice to sophisticated infiltration of legitimate business to labor racketeering and political corruption has created the current level of attention. Prosecution seeks to attack the entrenched nature of these criminal groups, especially their ability to threaten significant sectors of their community, as well as their ties to legitimate organizations, but these factors also make prosecution more difficult.

ECOLOGICAL FACTORS

One of the unique features of the scope of Asian racketeering is the fact that such activity includes both crimes in a small, neighborhood, geographic setting and crimes involving multinational movement of drugs, criminals, and cash.

One group of factors relates to the competition for investigative and prosecutorial resources. Most of the locales of Asian criminal groups are themselves cities with other crime problems that occupy all aspects of the criminal justice system. In the case of New York, San Francisco, and Los Angeles, the level of non-Asian gang activity is high. White-collar crime and fraud exist within urban financial centers, and common crime unrelated to organized groups absorbs resources. Fiscal constraints have been significant at the state, county, and municipal level, and police departments have been unable to expend resources as they might wish.

In California, suburbanization of Asian populations has, and will have, significant impact on police departments. Asian victims of means may be living in suburban settings in which police departments are unable to have much of a multilingual staff capacity. With its many jurisdictions, Los Angeles County's Asian criminal group problem calls for a unified response that networks various officers from affected cities. However, one jurisdiction was cut back for a time because it was felt that Asian crime was using resources to provide a clearinghouse and intelligence function for neighboring cities. That decision was reversed, but it points to some of the strains of regional policy. This is not a problem in New York City yet, but even there, the dispersion of the Asian population from the highly centralized Manhattan Chinatown will lead to issues concerning the deployment of scarce resources.

Jurisdictional problems have their own costs, and while the establishment of a strong network of local police around the country on crime investigations and analytical levels has been one of the most positive developments of this area, there are inefficiencies in gathering evidence, merging systems, taking credit, and providing witnesses over multiple jurisdictions. Because of the unique interstate and international quality of some of these crime groups and some of their crimes, these elements will certainly be present much of the time.

When these features are seen at an international level, these issues are even more acute: problems of merging two systems with entirely different intelligence functions and procedures, different expectations of privacy and sharing of information, different constitutional protections and procedural guarantees, language differences, time differences, and the difficulty of establishing relationships of trust and cooperation on delicate matters without being able to meet someone first face-to-face. Then there is the added complication internationally of other vital governmental relationships impinging on the criminal justice matter, whether these are trade concerns, other legal issues, or political matters.

Interjurisdictional overlap has been a prominent feature of the policing or Asian racketeering. Since the country's major Asian populations reside in a relatively small number of cities, the responsibility has been part of the municipal policing functions of those cities, and, even where fairly organized and entrenched crime groups have existed for decades, the problem has been less of a federal concern. Throughout the 1980s, at the same time as they built cases against traditional organized crime, federal law enforcement authorities were building a capability against nontraditional crime groups, but only within the resource constraints of their overall efforts. It has only been recently that Asian racketeering has been separated out as warranting special attention. However, motorcycle gangs, Jamaican posses, prison gangs, and Colombian cocaine importation organizations have drawn their share of attention, depending upon the region where they are most active.

With the more effective use of RICO, there has been a tendency to view federal prosecution as preferable. In certain cases, cross-designated local prosecutors have been utilized to take advantage of the sanctioning features of the federal statute. Still, there is a need to better coordinate, structure rewards, and smooth the way for more effective cooperation between the federal and local levels.

INVESTIGATIVE AND PROSECUTORIAL FACTORS

Many subsets of factors within this category serve to limit the effectiveness of the investigation and prosecution of Asian racketeers, and they can be separated into those that are external, those that are internal, and those that are interactive.

External Factors

Some of the external factors relate to the nature of the crimes, the victims, and the criminal groups. The first of these is, in many ways, the simplest to address and often the most difficult to solve: resources. All of the federal and local policing agencies that are assigned control of Asian racketeering have other pressing priorities they must address. It would be too facile to suggest that the best way to improve the effort against Asian racketeering would be to make it a higher priority in each of these agencies, followed by a redirection of resources. However, each of these agencies has crime concerns of equal and larger magnitude: gang violence and homicides in New York, Los Angeles, San Francisco, and Oakland, for example, are significant. All have seen reductions in their police forces, with an increase in crime rates over the last decade. Both California and New York are experiencing fiscal problems. Homicide trials divert the attention of the district attorneys from less serious crimes. Strategies that would utilize community-oriented policing or the walking of beats would do so at a time when local police forces are trying to make their available force stretch out more efficiently and more effectively over their cities. Policies that would give extra pay for those who are bilingual would run into cost-cutting impulses in general.

At the federal level, agencies have competing demands. For example, the number and severity of savings and loan fraud cases make unprecedented demands on the FBI. Within the category of organized crime, "finishing off" the LCN competes with Asian organized crime. Within the FBI, foreign counter-intelligence priorities create resource conflicts and siphon off prospective Asian agents working in Asian organized crime cases. At the DEA, cocaine is still a competing demand. The INS is both an immigration-processing agency and a criminal investigative agency, a situation that not only puts pressures on conflicting resources but has led to calls for the separation of the two functions.[18] The Customs Service is responsible for monitoring the cargo and persons crossing the border and has money-laundering investigation responsibilities, both of which make significant resource demands on its limited resources.

At the same time, even if agencies were able, or willing, to commit additional resources, the pool of qualified officers who are either Asian or proficient in any of the several languages or dialects relevant to the investigation of Asian racketeering is small.[19] Police work and even the law, to a lesser extent, have not been held out as reputable professions for upwardly mobile Asian Americans in the United States, and recent immigrants, in many cases, bring with them negative attitudes regarding the integrity of legal officials and the utility of pursuing formal legal complaints.[20] In New York City, a detective looking over Asian officers for possible inclusion in a specialized Asian crime unit had to sort through a limited group of available police, some of whom were too junior to have immediate impact, some who did not have the necessary language facility, and most of whom could not go undercover because they would be easily recognized. In addition, many of the skills required for these sorts of investigations develop with experience. There will have to be a maturation period before such police and agents are sufficiently experienced to be effectively employed, and, if these agents are in high demand, it will be difficult for any agency to keep them while they are training them for such duties. Moreover, since the DEA and FBI lawsuits from Spanish-speaking agents have noted the career-limiting prospects of using one's functional abilities, such as language, for a specific investigative goal—listening to wiretaps of drug dealers—there has to be some concern about putting special assignment burdens on police or agents with cultural skills who really yearn for a more generic policing experience. The use of Anglo-Asian-language speakers has been notable in the success of

DEA Group 41 out of New York City, but many activities mandate both language facility and ethnic identity.[21]

State-federal jurisdictional conflicts are an uncomfortable part of many policing endeavors, and intra-agency conflicts at all levels of government are no prettier. With the historical responsibility for the policing of Asian racketeering in local departments, even when the crimes of extortion, assault, gambling, or murder might comprise a federal racketeering case (and before the emergence of Asian heroin importation on a massive scale), local police may be understandably resentful of the increased federal attention to Asian crime and racketeering in their jurisdictions. Some may feel that federal authorities are coming too late and with great fanfare to this topic and tend to exploit local police information without reciprocating. The interagency relationships that exist within any given city were formed and operate quite independently of the issue of Asian racketeering, but the uniqueness of this issue and its impact on intelligence sharing and cooperative efforts bring these conflicts to the forefront.

Internal Factors

An internal factor affecting law enforcement anticrime programs has to do with the reward structure and promotion schedule within the many agencies. A phenomenon we found problematic concerns the reliance upon the goodwill, expertise, established cooperative relationships, and case-making ability of a select number of police in the numerous agencies involved. The other alternative is more formal and more costly: it means building separate units with committed personnel, sizable budgets, training and recruitment strategies, and long-term goals. Many of the committed and successful local police and federal agents have excelled and stayed in this area, even if it meant being passed over for promotion. At the same time, many who have become experts have been promoted and either are lost, in large part, to their previous units or "consult" on an ad hoc basis after their responsibility on paper has ceased. An interview subject noted that, if one looked at seven local police departments, one would find the responsibility for policing of Asian crime and racketeering performed by seven different units—in robbery, in gang details, in special task forces, and so on. It is not certain that uniformity is good or realistic, given the difference in size, scope, tradition, and responsibilities of the various departments involved. If one were to observe the good working relationships and camaraderie that exist among the Asian crime investigators in their regional and national (and international) meetings, work groups, and organizations, one might be less inclined to call for such uniformity. At some point, however, a patchwork of personalistic models might be less workable than a more routinized approach.

However, it is a question whether it is preferable to proceed by utilizing uniform task force models for all American cities affected by Asian racketeering or to build working models around cooperative relationships that do exist. Arguments for the former include the capacity for national planning, intelligence development, and efficiency of effort. Proponents of the latter would point to the pragmatic option of building models around the large and powerful units that have accumulated with years of cooperation and collective knowledge.

Interactive Factors

At the prosecutorial level, many of the interactive issues are less relevant for policy, since there are limited options in the scope of prosecutions. Federal prosecution is often preferable, not because federal prosecutors possess greater skills, insight, or commitment in this area but because federal penalties and procedural advantages are significant. For the majority of cases that are tried as state cases, vertical prosecution (in which police work with the same prosecutor throughout a case and on similar cases) is a necessity, given the sharp learning curve in getting expertise in these groups. At the federal level, the involvement of prosecutors at the earliest investigative opportunity, often used for organized crime and drug investigations, has been a preferable model.

CONCLUSION

The peculiar nature of the issues described is the result of a variety of interesting factors. Comparing Asian crime to early twentieth-century American immigrant examples is of limited value. The shrinking of the world, in terms of communications and transportation technologies, defies comparison with the past. The amount of money involved in organized criminal activity and the intricacies and speed of money-laundering techniques profoundly affect the magnitude of the problem.

Asian racketeering makes demands of local, state, and federal police and prosecutorial resources at the same time that their resources must be allocated in a number of other competing areas.

The federal prosecutorial side has experienced its own changes, some of which may affect this area in years to come. With the absorption of the Department of Justice's organized crime strike force into the various U.S. attorney's offices, the retreat from the use of specialized attorneys with common expertise and years of experience in the organized crime field has taken place. However, with the emphasis on the importance of drug cases, it is conceivable that the shift in federal strategy will de-emphasize criminal organizations that are not identified as drug-trafficking enterprises.

At still another level, the choices are not clear on whether the Asian racketeering issue is best dealt with by regional groups—whether the Regional Intelligence Sharing System (RISS) groups like the Middle Atlantic Great Lakes Organized Crime Enforcement Network—or by task forces, by a national federal agency like the FBI with historic organized crime responsibility, by local police with responsibility for the crimes in these Asian communities, or by some hybrid model. The General Accounting Office's (GAO) report on emerging crime groups was meant to precede a set of hearings by the Permanent Subcommittee on Investigations of the U.S. Senate, which has historically been a group that could assist in formulating organized crime policy.[22] All these choices will take place against a backdrop that is very international and includes liaison with countries such as Japan, Taiwan, the People's Republic of China, Thailand, Hong Kong, Australia, Canada, and others, with which we share extradition treaties and which request a range of working relationships with the United States.

Based on their activities within the last decade, most of the agencies involved in Asian organized crime will find the next decade redefining their roles and capacities, in some cases, resolving problems through more resource allocation while failing to solve the jurisdictional and organizational issues that pertain.

The key consideration that will likely offset how successfully Asian organized crime cases are handled in the near future include

1. To what extent will investigative and prosecutorial agencies commit necessary additional resources to address the issue?

2. To what extent will agencies institutionalize the effort, giving it status in units, with some budgetary autonomy or some sense of continuity?

3. Will the use of the RICO statute, so instrumental in the attack on traditional organized crime, be easily translated to use against these groups, which are elusive because of either their fluidity or the lower level of intelligence against them compared with that developed over years against traditional organized crime?

4. What are the costs of emphasizing "federal" issues and strategies over "local" or "state" issues and strategies?

5. To what extent will agencies recruit the necessary Asian officers, agents, officials, or those who speak the Asian language to provide a full complement of staff able to perform certain necessary operations, such as undercover work, close questioning of monolingual immigrants, and the like?

6. What are the risks of either overemphasizing or ignoring triad membership in American criminal groups?

The following is a selected list of recommendations to those who are conducting and planning for the future of Asian racketeering investigations and prosecutions:

1. Do more of the same—there have been many successful cases developed at the federal level in the past three years, some of them ongoing, spanning a range of groups, criminal activities, and locations.

2. Recruit more Asian officers, but do not depend on them to be operative in sensitive, sophisticated operations until after a few years.

3. Local agencies need to serve the other side of the equation—good police-community relations. The polls that show community fear of gangs and violence are an invitation

for more police involvement, even as some critics complain about the Anglo community and the elite's concern with this topic.

4. Recognize that these are, after all, not entirely new crimes and that the area is not so mysterious that officers must have special language skills, training, or commitment to do any job well. Certainly, undercover operatives are limited by race, for there appears to be little Asian versus non-Asian crime, with the exception of drug sales to Dominican middlemen. Certainly, one cannot listen to wiretaps without language facility, but that is not necessarily driven solely by race, though admittedly it is a high percentage—and nonsworn people can be used in some agencies/instances.

5. Recognize, reward, and prepare to replace and back up the first generation of Asian and non-Asian investigators and prosecutors who have accomplished so much in this area over the past ten years.

6. Invest in these units with line item budgets, higher priorities, and more personnel.

7. Be willing to use a variety of models that take into account the variability of relationships between federal and state agencies and among federal agencies in the cities in which task force operations will be undertaken and built around informal groups that exist.

8. Employ vertical prosecution and encourage its use and funding at the state level, including probation.

9. Invest time, training, personnel, and effort in solving some of the technical translation efforts that limit easy international cooperation among agencies—the standard telegraphic code and the computer program of the type Customs is developing in Honolulu to better identify yakuza members seeking entrance to the United States.

10. Use the existing and hoc international agreements and working relationships that exist to forge a set of Mutual Legal Assistance Treaties (MLATs) and other agreements to make prosecution more efficient and information sharing more common.

11. Be willing to undertake long, quality cases (like infiltration of legitimate business) and difficult cases (extortion) that may not pay off in the short run in lengthy sentences but show the community a commitment to serious law enforcement.

NOTES

1. Frederick T. Martens, "Let's Imagine Winning," *Criminal Organizations* (Vol. VII, No. 2); Ralph F. Salerno, "The Twilight of the Godfathers," *Criminal Organizations* (Vol. VII, No. 2).

2. Ronald Goldstock, Speech of New York Special Assistant Attorney General at a Meeting of the International Association for the Study of Organized Crime, San Diego, CA, November 1985; Ronald Goldstock, Testimony Before the U.S. Senate, Permanent Investigations Subcommittee, Committee on Governmental Affairs, 1988, in PISC, *Twenty Five Years After Valachi* (Washington, DC: U.S. Government Printing Office, 1990); *The Gotti Tapes: Including the Testimony of Salvatore (Sammy the Bull) Gravano* (New York: Times Books, 1992).

3. Ralph F. Salerno, Testimony Before the U.S. Senate, Permanent Investigations Subcommittee, Committee on Governmental Affairs, 1988, in PISC, *Twenty Five Years After Valachi* (Washington, DC: U.S. Government Printing Office, 1990), 1003.

4. Ibid., 1003.

5. Jenna Weissman Joselit, *Our Gang: Jewish Crime and the New York Jewish Community, 1900–1940* (Bloomington: Indiana University Press, 1983); Humbert S. Nelli, *The Business of Crime: Italians and Syndicate Crime in the United States* (New York: Oxford University Press, 1976); James M. O'Kane, *The Crooked Ladder: Gangsters, Ethnicity, and the American Dream* (New Brunswick, NJ: Transaction, 1992); William Foote Whyte, *Street Corner Society: The Social Structure of an Italian Slum* (Chicago: University of Chicago Press, 1943).

6. Michael D. Maltz, *Measuring the Effectiveness of Organized Crime Control Efforts* (Chicago: Office of International Criminal Justice, 1990).

7. John Dombrink and William N. Thompson, *The Last Resort: Success and Failure in Campaigns for Casinos* (Reno: University of Nevada Press, 1990).

8. Thomas W. Mangione et al., "Citizen Views of Gambling Enforcement," in *Gambling in America: Final Report of the Commission on the Review of the National Policy Toward Gambling*, Vol. 1 (Washington, DC: U.S. Government Printing Office, 1976).

9. John Gardiner, *The Politics of Corruption: Organized Crime in an American City* (New York: Russell Sage Foundation, 1970).

10. John Dombrink and James W. Meeker, "Bookies and Bosses: Illegal Gambling and Legalization Efforts," proceedings of the Seventh International Conference on Gambling and Risk Taking, Reno, NE, 1988.

11. This has been argued in the statement of various federal agencies to the President's Commission on Organized Crime in 1984 (in papers reviewed at the National Archives) and was part of the basis for the prosecution of the national On Leong organization in 1991.

12. See James Dao, "Asian Street Gangs Emerging as Violent New Underworld," *New York Times*, 1 April 1992.

13. Lawrence E. Cohen and Tony Waters, *Laotians in the Criminal Justice System* (Davis, CA: 1991). Final report prepared for the California Policy Seminar.

14. Based on interviews with local and federal law enforcement officials, prosecutors, and journalists in Hawaii, California, Washington, DC, and Nevada. See also David E. Kaplan and Alec Dubro, *Yakuza: The Explosive Account of Japan's Criminal Underworld* (Reading, MA: Addison-Wesley, 1986).

15. Based on interviews with FBI and DEA agents and officials in Washington, D.C., and New York and with prosecutors in the two New York federal prosecutors' offices, the Southern District of New York (Manhattan) and the Eastern District of New York (Brooklyn). See also Peter Kwong and Duqsanka Miqsycevic, "The Year of the Horse," *Village Voice*, 17 July 1990.

16. Based on interviews with local, state, and federal law enforcement officials in California and Virginia. See also U.S. General Accounting Office, *Nontraditional Organized Crime: Law Enforcement Officials' Perspectives on Five Criminal Groups* (Washington, DC: September 1989); U.S. Senate, "Staff Statement," Permanent Subcommittee on Investigations, Committee on Governmental Affairs, 5 November 1991; U.S. Senate, *Asian Organized Crime*, Hearing Before the Permanent Subcommittee on Investigations, Committee on Governmental Affairs, 3 October, 5 and 6 November 1991 (Wadsworth Publishing Co., Belmont, CA:.

17. Marcus Felson, "Routine Activities and Crime," University of Southern California, 1992).

18. Recommendations of a recent GAO report, cited in interviews with INS officials.

19. Based on interviews with various federal law enforcement officials in the study sites, including those who have such language facility.

20. John Huey-Long Song, ''No White-Feathered Crows: Chinese Immigrants' and Vietnamese Refugees' Adaptation to American Legal Institutions,'' Ph.D. diss., Program in Social Ecology, University of California, Irvine, 1988.

21. Without racial identity, the function of a bilingual agent who is not Asian is limited in certain undercover settings.

22. U.S. General Accounting Office, *Nontraditional Organized Crime: Law Enforcement Officials' Perspectives on Five Criminal Groups* (Washington, DC: September 1989).

19

The Prosecutor as Problem Solver

RONALD GOLDSTOCK

INTRODUCTION

The primary focus of law enforcement formerly concentrated on discrete street offenses, and the role of the prosecutor was limited to presenting evidence gathered by others (normally the police or the sheriff) to a court and jury. For such purposes, the traditional division between police and prosecutor worked reasonably well. During the 1930s, however, a few prosecutors came to understand that a different approach was required to deal with complex criminal activity— organized crime, labor racketeering, official corruption, and fraud. In such cases there are often no immediate victims, or the victims and witnesses are too frightened to come forward. These cases call for proactive investigation and close cooperation between police and prosecutors. Thus New York's famous racketbuster, Thomas Dewey, found that it was essential to combine the skills of prosecutors, investigators, and even accountants throughout the criminal process. Out of his experience and that of his successor, Frank Hogan, evolved the Rackets Bureau concept. This approach was to spread across the country and ultimately lead to the development of the Organized Crime Section in the Justice Department and the federal strike forces.[1]

The need to merge police and prosecutorial functions grew even more acute as investigations and prosecutions became more sophisticated and the relevant law became more intricate. Legal rules concerning search and seizure, the right to counsel, electronic surveillance, and related issues are now so arcane that police must routinely rely on lawyers to determine what they may and may not do even in the earliest stages of a complex investigation. Moreover, Congress

and state legislatures have formally given attorneys control over the sophisticated investigative techniques used in organized crime, official corruption, narcotics, and labor racketeering cases. Statutory law makes the prosecutor counsel
to the grand jury with the legal responsibility for resolving immunity questions.
Prosecutors are also given the exclusive responsibility for applying for authorization to conduct electronic surveillance and are required to monitor and control
its execution by the police.

But, while the roles played by the prosecutor may have changed over time,
the changes have taken place solely in the context of the criminal process. The
objective of the prosecutor remains the conviction of defendants and the imposition of an appropriate penal sentence. This traditional concern with conviction and punishment of the guilty has multiple justifications. It vindicates the
rule of law, while a just result also serves as society's moral statement concerning the nature of the illegal act; conviction and punishment function together
to satisfy the victim's desire or need for retribution and as a method of inca-
pacitating the dangerous offender and may deter the defendant and others from
future illegal activity.

Yet, to the extent that general deterrence is seen as a goal of the criminal
process, it suggests that the prosecutor's objective might be viewed as including
the reduction of criminal activity in a broader sense. This chapter argues that
affecting criminal activity is, or should be, the primary goal of the prosecutor
and that having a role in the reduction of crime should be viewed as a central
function and not merely as an incidental result of being a case processor who
administers an office in the most efficient manner to produce the greatest number
of just convictions.

Indeed, defining the prosecutor's function as helping to control crime may lead
to an ironic result if that official's appellation is taken literally; for it has not been
uncommon for prosecutions to have served as the vehicle for worsening criminal
problems. For example, corruption has long been pervasive in the Teamsters Union. Historically, the government's response was to prosecute the presidents of the
union. From the exclusive point of view of prosecution, the remedy was successful, with a succession of union leaders investigated and, with the exception of a
couple who died while under investigation or indictment, convicted, and imprisoned. From the point of view of removing organized crime influence from the union, however, it was another story. Deep-seated corruption in the union not only
continued but was clearly facilitated by the changes in leadership. The criminal
process might thus be seen in this instance in a Darwinian sense, as creating a hostile environment in which natural selection removes the lame and weak, allowing
the more corrupt and more powerful to gain control.

Even when it is not counterproductive, prosecution may be ill suited for controlling certain types of systemic criminal activity. The counterfeiting, forging,
and illegitimate use of credit cards, for example, remained largely unaffected
by prosecution but has been minimized to a great degree by the adoption of
holograms and personal identification numbers (PINs). Similarly, hundreds of

thousands of prosecutions of car thieves and joyriders did much less to deter automobile theft than the installation of locking devices on automobile steering columns. Prosecution alone has proven equally ineffective in mob-plagued industries such as construction[2] and carting[3] and has apparently done little to affect burglary, theft, homicide, labor corruption, and even corruption in major police departments.[4]

Why, then, given the availability of other possible remedial action, has the law enforcement response to these problems been limited to investigation, prosecution, and sentencing? Clearly, one answer is that we have given the responsibility for dealing with these "criminal" issues to the police and prosecutors, and investigation and prosecution are the powers that they have historically possessed. But the reason must also have to do with how we conceptualize the problem. The Department of Justice (DOJ), a huge bureaucracy responsible for exercising the legal authority of the U.S. government, has, for the most part, been organized by divisions based on the type of remedy to be utilized; suits for damages are assigned to the Civil Division, while murder on a government installation goes to the Criminal Division. But there are exceptions. Civil rights violations, for example, are rightly viewed as a social problem that ought to be treated with a variety of remedies. Thus, DOJ has established a dedicated Civil Rights Division, which is not confined to either a civil or criminal response. The same is true for antitrust issues. But when it comes to complex criminal problems, the matter is given to the Criminal Division, and, at least until the passage of the Racketeer Influenced and Corrupt Organizations Act (RICO),[5] only criminal remedies were utilized.

The effect of this organizational arbitrariness may be vividly illustrated by analogy to the field of medicine. Suppose medical classifications were arranged by the remedies of surgery, chemotherapy, radiation, and so forth; problems (diseases) would be assigned to one or another, and only that remedy employed. Such an arrangement would make little sense in the context of health and not much more when it comes to law enforcement.

This chapter discusses the feasibility of the prosecutor's evolving from a mere presenter of evidence to a court and jury to a controller of crime, a problem solver. It continues with a description of the rich variety of remedies that have a potential to affect illegal behavior, a methodology by which those remedies may be effectively employed, and a rationale for the prosecutor's assuming the lead in this process.

REMEDIES

The list that follows of remedies that might be employed by law enforcement to reduce and control crime is not meant to be exhaustive; it is merely illustrative of what has not traditionally been considered to be within the province of those given the responsibility of dealing with the social problems we recognize as systemic criminal activity.

Opportunity Blocking

In a sense, every prosecution represents society's failure to prevent a criminal act. If reasonable methods could be designed to reduce vulnerability to criminal activity, they would, of course, be preferable to improved methods for catching and punishing those who would otherwise engage in that criminal activity. One method of reducing such vulnerabilities is by employing techniques referred to as loss prevention or opportunity blocking.

We have already noted that the counterfeiting, forging, and illegitimate use of credit cards have been minimized to a great degree by the adoption of holograms and PIN numbers and that locking devices on automobile steering wheels and columns have probably done much more to deter theft than have the prosecutions of joyriders. Legitimate industries design and implement internal controls designed to prevent loss. Yet there can be no doubt that this remedy is severely underutilized. Every city has stringent fire codes for buildings; how many have regulations relating to the design or use of materials that would inhibit burglars and violent offenders or make them easier to catch?[6]

Forfeiture

Civil forfeiture statutes exist in a number of jurisdictions, permitting suits to be brought to recover instrumentalities, proceeds, and substituted proceeds of crime. These statutes are commonly in rem, brought technically against the property itself. Many of these statutes permit law enforcement agents to obtain provisional relief, such as attachment or a preliminary injunction, to protect against dissipation of assets pending the outcome of the case, a common problem where the assets are accumulated through criminal activity. RICO and its state counterparts also contain potent criminal forfeiture provisions. Defendants convicted of RICO and "little RICO" offenses may, for example, be required to forfeit not only the proceeds of their crimes but their positions or interests in corrupted enterprises. Under these provisions, grand juries are authorized to utilize their subpoena powers to gather evidence, permitting the discovery of assets in a manner more familiar to prosecutors than some civil procedures.

Perhaps no other remedy has the potential of forfeiture to accomplish so many objectives simultaneously. Removal of assets interferes with the criminal activity, weakens the organization engaging in that activity, deters others by making the activity potentially less profitable, punishes the criminal, denies those who would have profited unjust enrichment and the enjoyment of the illegal fruits, satisfies victim claims, and raises revenue for government programs, including law enforcement.

Damages for Monetary Loss or Commercial Injury

Private litigation may also effectively deter criminal activity. Penalties in a criminal driving while intoxicated (DWI) case, for example, may be dwarfed by the potential liability arising out of a civil suit. In recognition of the power of the plaintiff's bar to serve as private attorney's general, RICO provides a private right of action for anyone injured by reason of a RICO violation[7] with the incentive of treble damages, court costs, and attorneys' fees.

When the government is the victim of fraudulent or corrupt activities, it can generally seek monetary compensation for its injury or loss, like any other victim. Where, for example, an investigation uncovers fraud or corruption in the award of public contracts or administration of state or local governmental affairs, damages may often be sought under state or federal law.[8] The federal Qui Tam Act[9] has historically provided a private attorney general mechanism by authorizing suits by private parties on behalf of the government. A portion of the recovery due the government based on a finding of fraud is due the plaintiff as an incentive for bringing the litigation.

The forfeiture of profits on contracts won through fraud or bribery can also be effected through specific contractual provisions. Leaders of the House Armed Services Committee, for example, recently called upon the Pentagon to include such provisions in military procurement contracts as a matter of course. Doing so, these leaders suggested, would increase compliance with existing laws without requiring additional government auditors or new regulations.[10]

Injunctions, Divestitures, Trusteeships, and Receiverships

Certain unions, perhaps because of the nature of their membership and the nature of the industries in which they operate,[11] have historically been dominated by the Mob. While prosecution has failed to remedy the problem of these captive unions, court-ordered trusteeships have been used to reestablish democratic processes and, hence, the possibility of a future free from labor racketeering. The first and most carefully scrutinized of these attempts involved Local 560 of the International Brotherhood of Teamsters in New Jersey.[12] There have been others, including Local 6A of the Cement and Concrete Workers of the Laborers International Union, Local 54 of the Hotel Employees and Restaurant Employees International Union, and Local 1804–1 of the International Longshoremen's Association.

Under RICO, actions for injunctions against defendants and enterprises they control, whether legitimate or illegitimate, may be brought to prevent future misconduct.[13] Courts are empowered to fashion, inter alia, orders requiring defendants to divest themselves of interests in tainted enterprises, imposing restrictions on their future activities, dissolving or reorganizing enterprises, suspending or revoking state or local licenses and permits, and revoking the right of a corporation to conduct business.[14]

Self-Monitoring

Private companies and industries may, in some cases, be willing to impose internal monitoring or, indeed, may be required to subject themselves to outside scrutiny. Banks, for example, have hired private firms to establish and monitor internal mechanisms designed to reduce the likelihood of cash transactions going unreported in violation of the Bank Secrecy Act.[15] Securities and Exchange Commission (SEC) regulations require corporations to hire outside auditors to inspect their books. The New York State Organized Crime Task Force (OCTF), in its report to Governor Mario Cuomo on the New York City construction industry, proposed the creation of a Certified Investigative Auditing Firm (CIAF) Program.[16] CIAFs were defined as licensed, independent private sector firms, having the investigative, auditing, analytic, loss prevention, engineering, and other skills necessary to serve as "private inspectors general" to corporations that hired them. The responsibilities of CIAFs include ensuring compliance with relevant law and regulations and deterring and exposing unethical or illegal conduct. While still in the process of development, the CIAF concept has already been used by OCTF and the New York City School Construction Authority in a variety of industries, including solid waste disposal, construction, and finance.

Regulations, Public Benefit Corporations, Eminent Domain, and Other Means of Fostering Competition

Historically, the Mob has been able to dominate, influence, or monopolize particular industries because it controlled an essential good or service. The state's ability to purchase a critical piece of property, through eminent domain (with just compensation), and allow equal access to it could deprive a syndicate of the instrument by which it extracts monopolistic profits. Similarly, if illicit control is achieved through the supply of essential labor or materials, the establishment of an alternative source may break the monopoly's power. Industries that have historically been the subject of cartels, bid rigging, territorial allocation schemes, or other anticompetitive practices may be affected by the use of public benefit corporations that disrupt such illegal agreements by competing against those who engage in them. OCTF and the Rand Corporation, for example, have recommended the establishment of such a public benefit corporation to reduce collusive behavior by Mob-dominated private sanitation carters.

Regulatory agencies in industries subject to corruption and racketeering—such as garbage collection, construction, liquor, gambling, and the waterfront—may be given a number of powers, including licensing, rate regulation, screening of potential union officials, and investigative or police authority.

Structural Changes

Crimes may be facilitated within certain institutions or industries because of particular organizational or structural attributes. The adoption or imposition of structural changes may therefore be beneficial. Examples of such changes are limits on supervisors' spans of control in police departments, the banning of the "shape-up" on the waterfront,[17] and mandating "one person-one vote" rules in labor unions.

Public Hearings and Reports

Often, public opinion can be mobilized to weaken the resistance to change or at least to isolate those who are opposed to it. Public hearings, the issuance of reports, and public information campaigns are therefore often essential components of the reform process. The Knapp Commission hearings in New York, for example, have been credited by many with playing a key role in reforming the anticorruption practices of the New York City Police Department. Similarly, public information campaigns by anti-DWI and crime victims groups have resulted in significant legislative reforms.

Other Remedial Action

A number of other solutions to "criminal" problems may be more efficacious than prosecution. Several innovative solutions to discrete problems were discussed at the Kennedy School sessions.[18]

An area of one city, for example, was overrun with street prostitutes. The traditional approach, using undercover officers and making arrests, proved ineffective. The police changed their strategy. Uniformed officers began to systematically approach those suspected of being prostitutes or "johns" and sought to question them. Uniformed officers in marked cars also pulled abreast of cars whose occupants engaged prostitutes in conversation. In both situations, the police conspicuously took notes as they did so. This made for a "bad business atmosphere" and was a key factor in virtually eliminating the problem.

Another nontraditional approach was taken by a prosecutor concerned about the quality of life in crime-plagued public housing projects in Florida. With support from local government, she began opening convenience stores in the ghettos' worst areas, hiring people from the projects to work in them, and arranging for day-care and preschool programs. The program was widely hailed. The stores are crime-free, raised people's hopes, and became magnets for other self-improvement projects in their communities.[19]

For certain categories of offenders, resources may be better spent making treatment available rather than in prosecution. One prosecutor helps local agencies apply for grants for treatment programs for juvenile offenders, child abusers, and drug and other offenders. Similarly, a district attorney in another jurisdiction made a conscious decision to reduce juvenile prosecutions by one-third and referred thousands of young offenders to remedial reading programs, truancy programs, work programs, and wilderness programs. Although unsure these programs would work, he was equally unsure of the efficiency of continuing merely to prosecute these offenders.

Another prosecutor set up an "alert" system for local businesses designed to notify them as soon as an identifiable pattern of forgery or fraud in their community was detected. Yet another prosecutor who had obtained convictions against corporate environmental offenders sought and obtained sentences that included a requirement that the companies take out advertisements acknowledging that they had violated the law and had been caught—the corporate equivalent of a stockade. Similarly, some jurisdictions require convicted DWI offenders to display bumper stickers on their cars attesting to their convictions. Applying this idea in a different context, a former prosecutor suggested that certain offenders, instead of being incarcerated, be required to wear "scarlet letter" clothing identifying them as criminals.

ANALYSIS AND STRATEGIC PLANNING

The availability of nontraditional remedies does not guarantee appropriate use. Even if prosecutors were to see their role as controlling crime and to reject the historical limitations caused by exclusive reliance on prosecution, they would need guidance as to what remedy to use in what circumstance. Looking again to a medical analogy, the creation of a sophisticated crime control strategy is much like the search for a cure for a disease. Each requires three sequential steps: first, a recognition and description of the symptoms; second, an analysis and understanding of the mechanisms through which the integrity of the system is compromised; and third, based upon that analysis, the development and implementation of a program of treatment using existing remedies or developing new ones.

This sequence is well understood in the context of medical research, and it has not been totally unrecognized in the field of crime control. Over seventy years ago, the sociologist John Landesco, urged a reasoned approach to systemic criminality:

One reason for the failure of crusades against crime and vice is they . . . are seldom or never based on a study of the problem. What is needed is a program that will deal with the crime problem in detail and consecutively, that is, by analyzing the crime situation into its different elements by taking up each crime situation separately and one by one working out a constructive solution.[20]

The challenge of industrial racketeering is instructive in interpreting and applying the approach recommended by Landesco. Why are some legitimate industries so deeply penetrated by organized crime—such as construction, carting, the waterfront, and the garment trades—while others are not? Why has prosecution failed to achieve reform? One answer to both questions appears to be that some industries provide enormous incentives and opportunities for corruption and exploitation by criminal syndicates. Industries may therefore be profitably studied by examining two related concepts: racketeering susceptibility and racketeering potential.

Racketeering susceptibility is measured by the degree to which an industry's structure and organization create opportunities for racketeers both inside and outside the industry to control or influence critical industry components or to engage in racketeering.

Racketeering potential is measured by the extent to which racketeers can profit from exploitation of an industry's vulnerability and is affected by such factors as the amount of money that industry participants can generate and make available to racketeers, the availability of jobs that can provide legitimate status and income to racketeers and their associates, and the potential of the industry to launder dirty money or generate false business expenses to disguise illicit payments or avoid paying taxes.

Once an industry's racketeering susceptibility and potential are understood, the search for meaningful reform, utilizing remedies designed to reduce those vulnerabilities and incentives, may begin.

Other types of analysis may prove useful in working out constructive ways of combating illegal businesses. Financial analyses of the interrelationship of bookmaking and loan-sharking, for example, suggest the adoption of strategies virtually the reverse of those now employed.[21] Structural analysis of the interrelationship of burglars and fences suggests that reverse stings relating to stolen property (police sales to fences) may be more successful in reducing burglary than traditional sting operations (policy buys from burglars).[22] Historical analysis of heroin importation predicted the rise of ghetto-based minority organized crime groups,[23] and historical analysis of the New York City construction industry made it possible to understand the rationalizing role played by the Mob today and by Tammany Hall at the beginning of the century.[24] Economic analysis of the solid waste pickup industry made possible proposals that, if implemented, would likely reduce the Mob's influence in the carting industry.[25]

Similar analyses and the creation of remedial strategies can be undertaken for virtually all varieties of systemic criminal activity, including the interruption of crack street markets, spousal abuse, illegal possession of weapons, specialty waste disposal, the role of the Mob in the garment industry, fish market, and food industry and on the waterfront, and even the emergence and growth of criminal syndicates and street gangs.

The most modern law enforcement agencies now use attorneys, investigators, accountants, and tactical analysts in conducting investigations and prosecutions. Clearly, the development of sophisticated strategies and the analyses on which they are based require the employment of not only those skilled individuals but also strategic analysts, trained to review broad databases and analyze trends within areas of actual or potential criminal activity, and academics and experts as well. Institutional relationships, rarely existent today, are needed between law enforcement and economists, sociologists, loss prevention specialists, historians, political scientists, and industry specialists. Such relationships will prove critical if law enforcement officials are to be engaged in the creation of social policy.

WHY THE PROSECUTOR?

It is not intuitively obvious that prosecutors, rather than police, criminal justice coordinators, or even the chief governmental officer, should take the lead in developing and implementing strategies for crime control. Certainly, representatives of all four have, to one extent or another, considered themselves to be engaged in problem solving. Indeed, some police departments have explicitly begun to take a problem-oriented approach to crime.[26] A number of successful police programs built on this model, for example, are described in David Anderson's recent study.[27] In two such programs, drug marketplaces were closed down by saturation arrests and other means. In another, an empty lot that had attracted drug users and other disorderly persons was cleaned up, fenced in, and decorated. A fourth program focused on Halloween-night vandalism, which was reduced after the police organized an outdoor party that flooded the streets with celebrants. A fifth involved problems posed by rowdy youths disturbing a residential neighborhood at night. The problem was eliminated when the police, having discovered that the owner of a nearby roller rink provided free transportation to the rink, persuaded him to provide free return rides after the rink closed.

Yet, while police can clearly play an important role in problem solving, the successes listed do not compel the conclusion that they are the best situated to set law enforcement policy. Virtually all of the programs described by Anderson had highly discrete objectives; while some involved nontraditional remedies, none involved the type of broad-based, strategic approach discussed in the previous section. Unfortunately, if predictably, in time most of these programs fell victim to budget cutbacks, changes in department leadership, or swings of the pendulum back to traditional police attitudes favoring apprehension of felons.

Mayors and governors must also be considered. As elected officials with broad mandates, budgetary authority, and powers over a host of criminal justice and regulatory agencies, these chief executives appoint the people in charge of the police, probation, the jails, and other agencies. They are thus arguably best positioned to implement policies that cross agency lines, as many inevitably will. Indeed, some chief governmental officers have established directors or coordinators of criminal justice.

Still, there are a number of reasons prosecutors may be the best fitted to assume the leadership or coordinating role. Many of the potential remedies involve litigation, legislation, or regulation, where legal expertise and the authority to utilize it appropriately are indispensable. All prosecutors are practicing criminal attorneys, and three out of four are explicitly vested with civil responsibilities.[28] Of equal importance, many of the data essential to the analytic effort may be available only to the prosecutor. The prosecutor, for example, is, by legislative mandate, the applicant for electronic surveillance and counsel to the grand jury, and the prosecutor is generally responsible for maintenance and disclosure of the information obtained by those intrusive means of investigation.

Moreover, prosecutorial discretion and plea bargaining often enable the prosecutor to obtain information from knowledgeable defendants willing to cooperate in exchange for leniency. A coordinating role by prosecutors' offices is beginning to emerge in forfeiture and civil damage cases—where the location of criminal proceeds or other assets is sought—while investigations are active.

Prosecutors may, in addition, have special power and authority because of their strategic position between the police and the courts. Their discretion in disposing of cases permits them, in essence, not only to control the traffic but to set the price on crime.

The prosecutor is, in fact, the nearest thing we have to a single, centralized law enforcement official. Most prosecutors have jurisdictions in which there may be a dozen or many dozen different police departments and enforcement agencies. Unlike their counterparts in other Western societies, the vast majority of American prosecutors are independent, elected local officials vested with extraordinarily broad powers and moral responsibilities. As such and especially in a society distrustful of central authority,[29] a level of confidence and heightened expectations attaches to the office not likely to be enjoyed by others involved in anticrime efforts.

Prosecutors, because of their authority and bureaucratic positions, are also likely to have the ears of those in the executive and legislative branches whose assistance and support will be essential. Such access to political support also provides prosecutors opportunities to work quietly, behind the scenes, to influence the direction of policy and gather support for their objectives. To the extent that this new approach will require innovation, prosecutors may also have an advantage over some other candidates for the role. Just as it was once said that only Richard Nixon could go to China, perhaps only prosecutors, generally regarded as conservative, will be given much latitude by the public to propose solutions that may appear unconventional and to experiment with novel programs.

IMPLICATIONS

A number of potential difficulties would flow from casting the prosecutor in an expansive role as problem solver. Some are practical, involving issues of resources, social policy, and political reality. Some of the implications are more theoretical, involving questions of responsibility, accountability, and the preservation of civil liberties. Some relate to legal rules formulated in a different age for a different set of social problems.

Traditional attitudes will persist, and a prosecutor's imagination may fall victim to the expectations of others that only criminal penalties should be pursued. Too often, superiors, public officials, and the press judge success by the number of arrests, indictments, and convictions. Such numbers, of course, are not an appropriate measure of effectiveness in dealing with most crime,[30] and the pressure to produce quantity rather than quality can badly distort tactical and strategic goals. Public impatience may also be a factor. Whatever else may be said about them, criminal investigations and prosecutions are relatively swift, tending normally to require only a year or two until cases are disposed of. More varied and innovative techniques of crime control will require not only political leadership and creativity but considerable time and persistence.

A different concern stems from the prospect of a prosecutor's using intrusive criminal investigative techniques to discover information for analytic purposes. This may lead to the fear that evidence gathered, while insufficient for prosecution, might support a public hearing or report. While this is not an empty fear, concern should not be exaggerated. First, to the extent that problem solving will result in removing incentives for criminal activity, the remedies will tend not to involve actions against individuals. Moreover, it is at least reasonable to suggest that an invasion of privacy that is ultimately used to stop someone from committing a crime has served the public as well as one that is used to sentence someone to a life behind bars in a harsh prison system.

Most important, it is probable that the prosecutor will act more cautiously than other bodies now authorized to engage in nontraditional remedial actions. The prosecutor, institutionally concerned about pretrial publicity and prejudice and bound by the ethical provisions of the Code of Professional Responsibility will likely delay a public hearing or otherwise ensure that it is conducted in a manner designed to minimize prejudice. Moreover, as illustrated recently in the case of Oliver North, the prosecutor, rather than a legislative body, would be most sensitive to the risks involved in granting even "use" immunity.[31]

If prosecutors were empowered to employ a wide variety of remedies in implementing innovative strategies to control "criminal problems," a number of legal rules would have to be functionally reanalyzed. For example, it is ironic that just when prosecutors have come to see the importance of civil forfeiture and injunctive relief in controlling organized crime activities, statutes written without this perspective in mind have increasingly been interpreted to require that a sharp separation of criminal and civil proceedings be maintained. With no clear policy justification, barriers have been erected discouraging the use of grand jury and eavesdropping evidence in civil proceedings instituted by law enforcement agencies for law enforcement purposes. Thus, New York generally does not permit the use of such evidence in civil proceedings. While this restriction is understandable in the context of purely private litigation, it is hard to see why it should apply to civil actions brought on behalf of the state.

So far, the term *prosecutor* has been used in this chapter without differentiation. The existence of prosecutors' offices at the federal, state, and local level itself has implications for the broader approach, as each will have potentially different roles to play in formulating solutions. In traditional prosecution, for example, different roles for law enforcement at the three levels of government have, at least in some areas, begun to emerge. In narcotics enforcement, interdiction and prosecution of the largest-scale conspiracies have, by and large, been assumed by the federal government, while street-level enforcement has been left to local officials. Where statewide units exist, they have tended to assume a role assisting and coordinating the efforts of local officials where problems cross city or county lines, by taking such multicounty cases to their logical conclusion beyond the local prosecutors' areas of geographical jurisdiction.

Similar roles will have to be carved out for prosecutors acting as catalysts for change. Among the relevant factors should be the availability of resources; the existence of expertise, both in their own offices and in agencies at their level of government; and, perhaps most important, the legal and administrative remedies available at each level. Jurisdictional limitations of prosecutors, both geographic and subject matter, may also need to be reevaluated.[32]

It follows that the initial task will be to persuade prosecutors themselves that the approach has merit. This may not be simple, as prosecutors tend to the traditional, and the broader approach requires a type of thinking to which many may be unaccustomed. Assistant prosecutors may be even harder to bring along. Many of them are attracted to prosecution by the lure of trials and courtroom drama—by the television image of what prosecutors do, if not the reality. They may have little taste for analysis or innovation. Even if truancy causes daytime burglary, they will say, the prosecutor's job is to prosecute the burglar, not to deal with the truant.

Some may think it presumptuous for prosecutors to assume the planning and coordinating role. Agencies such as the police, the courts, probation, and parole are generally not within the prosecutor's control,[33] much less agencies involved in education, child welfare, and housing.[34] Even if it is true that cleaning up an overgrown vacant lot will reduce crime, is it not for the sanitation or parks department to decide? If the expansion of community service is desirable, is it not for probation to decide? If interviewing prostitutes' customers will improve the ambience of neighborhoods, is this not for police to determine? Indeed, to the extent that problems involve other institutions, won't the prosecutor be regarded as meddlesome or threatening?[35]

But, it is not at all clear that bureaucratic strife will be a problem of any significant magnitude. Many new initiatives will not be antagonistic to existing programs or agencies at all. Programs are often not adopted merely because no one has considered them or has the time or ability to set them up. Indeed, the more innovative agency heads may see the prosecutor as an ally in aiding them to fortify the social institutions over which they have primary jurisdiction.

There will undoubtedly have to be some changes in the structure of prosecutors' offices and a reallocation of resources. The design and implementation of truly effective strategies against crime, for example, require the application of specialized skills beyond those now normally possessed by prosecutors.[36] A much higher premium will also have to be placed on research. There is already increased demand from prosecutors and other criminal justice professionals for data and research, illustrated by the growth of special units such as the Bureau of Justice Statistics, American Prosecutors Research Institute, and the National Criminal Justice Reference Service. The assumption by the prosecutor of this new role, however, will create a much wider market.[37]

But the ultimate question may be whether or not prosecutors will want to assume the role, responsibilities, and accountability inherent in the role of problem solver. As long as conviction rates remain high and offices scandal-free, prosecutors tend to be secure in their jobs, respected by the public, headlined in the press, and not held responsible for the crime problem. Moreover, prosecutors inundated with an oppressive number of arrests, frustrated by limited resources, and hampered by bureaucratic interference might well reject the notion that they are well situated to take on the problem-solving role. One does not often seek to put oneself in a position where public failure is a realistic possibility.

Yet, prosecutors do have a unique opportunity to orchestrate a more effective set of criminal policies than are currently in place. With the crime problem continuing to grow in gravity and complexity, it may no longer be possible for the prosecutor to remain a case processor; whether manifest destiny, evolution, or mere necessity, the role of the twenty-first-century prosecutor demanded, expected, and deserved by the public may well be that of the problem solver.

APPENDIX A

The operators of most substantial bookmaking businesses are not organized crime figures themselves but independents who have links to organized crime. These links are important because in this business, access to large amounts of cash on short notice is essential. It is, for example, not unusual for gamblers to borrow in excess of $25,000 at 5 percent per week from Mob loan sharks. A brief look at the economics of bookmaking is necessary to explain this unique business practice. A bookmaker accepts bets on sports events, risking $50 to win $55. (Baseball works differently, but the rate return to the bookmaker is not greater.) This $5 difference is the bookmaker's edge or "vigorish." Thus, if he were to maintain an equal dollar amount on each side of a sports event, the bookmaker's gross profit would be 5 percent of the total volume of bets accepted.

Of that 5 percent, half is paid to "runners," individuals who handle the "pay and collect" function and under whose authority the bettors are permitted to place their wagers. Rent, telephones, clerks, figuremen (bookmaking accountants), and so on consume another percent; thus, the bookmaker's net profit is about 1.5 percent. An operation that handles $25,000 in bets per day will show a profit of less than $140,000 per year. From that figure the operator must deduct red figures (runner equity), bad debts, legal expenses, and protection payments.

But bookmakers do not balance their books and accept the "vig." They, like their customers, are gamblers—that is why most of them got into the business—and, hence, they purposefully accept and hold bets to provide themselves the opportunity to win (and the chance of losing) large amounts on individual events. The result is that, despite the long-run 5 percent edge, they are often in need of cash during losing weeks. In order to keep their business, they must pay the winning bettors on time, and that means borrowing at 5 percent per week interest from mob loan sharks.

Since the losses can, and very often do, amount to $20,000–30,000, the interest for a single week may be from $1,000–1,500. Two consecutive losing weeks requires the bookmaker to borrow twice that amount. With the interest at $2,000–3,000, he is now virtually working for the loan shark. The mob is thus able to extract bookmaking profits without having to be in the bookmaking business.

Random gambling raids—the usual policy of many police agencies—create headlines and cause economic harm to bookmakers. However, given the structure of the bookmaking industry, these raids may signify a net gain to organized crime because they force independent bookmakers to turn to organized crime loan sharks who have the ability to finance illicit criminal activities.

The implications for law enforcement activities directed against organized crime's control of bookmaking are clear:

1. Any investigative plan ought to have as its major objective the investigation and prosecution of loan sharks, and resources should be allocated with that in mind.
2. Solvent independent bookmakers should not be driven to Mob loan sharks. If they are to be penalized for violation of the gambling statutes, the penalties imposed should be designated to terminate their businesses, rather than to allow them to continue on borrowed capital.
3. Primary enforcement should be directed against insolvent bookmakers already in debt. Putting such businesses out of operation will cause the Mob to lose its investment and may produce witnesses capable of testifying against organized crime loan sharks.

APPENDIX B

As indicated in Appendix A, an economic principle well known to the organized underworld is that large profits can be extracted from an illicit business by the monopolization of any good or service required to carry on that business. Thus, historically, the entire offtrack betting industry of an area was monopolized not through the cumbersome route of owning every horse parlor but by the simple expedient of controlling the wire service and charging monopolistic prices for the race results. Given potential profits, the bombings and shootings that occurred in the quest for that control during the 1930s and 1940s are quite understandable.

This economic principle was not lost on the Mob when the United States became a lucrative drug market. The time-consuming, risky, and (strangely enough, by underworld standards) immoral factors of distribution could be avoided if one could monopolize another aspect of the business. For a variety of reasons, one such aspect was available to the Mob—importation.

From the 1930s until the late 1960s, the poppy fields of Turkey provided the world's heroin supply. The opium harvested from these fields and converted into morphine could, with minimal hindrance, be smuggled by the Corsican underworld in Marseilles, where the critical morphine-heroin conversion occurred. The drug, destined for the ghettos of North America, could now be purchased and imported by those who had the cupidity, the contacts (for sources, distribution systems, and corruption), and the capital necessary for the undertaking.

At that time and place, one group met those requirements. Cupidity was its raison d'être; prohibition provided the contacts and capital. Thus the Mob entered the narcotics trade through arranging the financing, the smuggling, and the corruption necessary to bring the multikilo loads of white powder into the United States. Mob figures (syndicate members) bought kilo amounts and then parceled out to "quarter-key" or ounce men who arranged for the cutting (dilution), packaging, and sale to distributors. Non-Mob figures entered the scene at the quarter-key level, the point at which the risks substantially increased and the capital requirements were manageable.

The "quarter-key" and ounce men tended to be members of minority groups who were prepared to gain money and power through the sale of heroin in the ghettos they sought to escape. As they worked their trade, the most enterprising, ruthless, and fortunate accumulated considerable supplies of cash and began to put together organizations with distribution, corruption, and enforcement capabilities.

By the late 1960s, the French connection was broken through a number of spectacular cases, increased enforcement by American and French authorities, and U.S. pressure on Turkey to control poppy production. At the same time, two other sources of heroin were gaining in importance. South America and the Golden Triangle of Southeast Asia. For a number of reasons, criminals in minority ethnic groups were in a position to establish contacts with the heroin exporters of those areas. The Hispanics, in particular, had friends, relatives, and common language in South America. At the same time, the Vietnam War took a great number of American blacks into Southeast Asia, where drugs and dealers were readily accessible.

Thus, by the early 1970s, the minority group criminal had the capital, cupidity, and contacts to handle the importation, processing, and distribution of heroin (and other drugs). These were mainly enterprises without a sophisticated structure. The lack of syndication resulted in raiding and stealing from one another. Informing on competitors was commonplace. Yet, certain groups were developing characteristics of their predecessors in organized crime. Affinity based on kinship was replaced by gang participation in both neighborhoods and prisons. Moreover, there appeared the frightening specter of "successful" crime figures being respected and even cheered by the very people on whom they preyed.

Today this type of emerging ethnic crime group is, in many ways, reminiscent of the Chicago Prohibition-era gangs of the 1920s, with drugs replacing liquor as the crucial illicit commodity. It does not require a vivid imagination to foresee what the future holds for the most successful of these groups, especially as other areas of the economic sphere become open to them.

APPENDIX C

The extensive and pervasive corruption and racketeering in the construction industry are a product of that industry's high levels of "racketeering susceptibility" and "racketeering potential."

Many characteristics of New York City's construction industry contribute to racketeering susceptibility. They may be grouped into five categories: labor market, collective bargaining structure, competitive business environment, fragility of the construction process, and high cost of delay. Each of these industry characteristics creates incentives and opportunities that invite and encourage racketeering.

The labor market is dominated by strong labor unions that, to a large extent, control whether union members work and, if so, for whom. Labor racketeers in control of such unions extort money, no-show jobs, and other benefits from builders by threatening labor problems. Likewise, contractors bribe union officials for "waivers" of expensive collective bargaining provisions.

Collective bargaining in the construction industry is marked by specialized craft unions, each claiming exclusive jurisdiction over certain types of work. This leads to conflict and inefficiency and provides an incentive for contractors to seek out racketeers capable of corruptly resolving jurisdictional disputes. The inability of relatively weak employer associations to withstand (or their willingness to accept) the demands of powerful unions has resulted in featherbedding and unjustifiable work rules. Thus, there are additional incentives for contractors to turn to racketeers with the power to grant or impose "waivers" of collective bargaining provisions and to provide other competitive advantages.

Racketeering susceptibility is enhanced by the high costs that construction delays impose on builders. Any delay during the construction process inflates interest costs and imposes unanticipated expenses in reorganizing the complex construction process. Moreover, delays in completing a project result in substantial penalties or costly deferral of revenues. This provides powerful leverage for extortion and strong incentive for bribery. Racketeers with the ability to delay or disrupt a construction project can successfully demand large payoffs. Conversely, contractors can gain substantial advantages by bribing whoever can assure an orderly and stable construction timetable.

A highly competitive business environment also creates incentives for corrupt contractors to reach out to racketeers who can provide a competitive edge, such as membership in cartels, "waivers" of various collective bargaining provisions, and the assurance of a reliable workforce. Furthermore, the industry's fragility—its vulnerability to disruption by so many different actors at so many different levels—makes it particularly susceptible to racketeers who can organize cartels and extract profits with the threat of labor problems or the promise of labor peace.

Racketeering potential is high because of plentiful opportunities to acquire and conceal large cash payoffs. This potential is further increased by the ease of passing on the costs of corruption and racketeering to consumers; a skim of only 1 percent of a construction project can amount to hundreds of thousands, even millions, of dollars. Organized crime racketeers can force contractors to provide their members or associates with high-paying, no-show jobs. They can also use their control over contracting firms to launder money earned in other illicit activities.

The racketeering potential of public works projects is especially high because government builders often have poor supervisory controls over contractors. This frequently leads to shoddy workmanship. New York State's Wicks Law exacerbates this problem by prohibiting government builders from delegating responsibility for overall project supervision to a single experienced contractor.

High levels of racketeering susceptibility and potential contribute to an environment that is extremely attractive to racketeers who can exploit the myriad opportunities to extract money from the industry. The industry's high vulnerability to the depredations of racketeers and the large number of criminals capable of preying upon the industry combine to create unique opportunities for a criminal syndicate. Such a syndicate can use its power over, and networks in, unions, construction companies, and ancillary service firms to provide industry participants with stability and predictability. In exchange for payoffs, it can guarantee that labor problems will not occur. For a fee, it can activate its extensive underworld and "upperworld" connections to establish and police employer cartels or to guarantee a predictable and stable construction process. Thus, the criminal syndicate's ability to organize and control racketeers and to enhance stability in the industry permits it to play a kind of "rationalizing" role. In New York City, in the early part of the century, Robert Brindell and his Tammany Hall allies exploited their ability to act as such a corrupt "rationalizing body." For the last several decades this role has been played by New York's five Cosa Nostra crime families.

Entry into the construction industry by those families dates back to the 1930s. Cosa Nostra members or associates have historically held key union positions in many of these labor organizations and have served as trustees and fiduciaries of worker pension and welfare funds. The Mob has also long been able to control or influence such critical components of the industry as suppliers and contractors.

By virtue of its structure as a criminal syndicate, Cosa Nostra has also had sufficient power to control all or most of the racketeers preying on the industry. Having established itself as the "rationalizing body," Cosa Nostra has created cartels in which companies it controls play dominant roles. The syndicate thus benefits in three ways: by its members' exploitation of racketeering susceptibility and potential, by payments for its "rationalizing" services, and from its interests in businesses selectively favored within its protected cartels.

The implications of Cosa Nostra's domination of the construction industry are profound. During the past five decades, Cosa Nostra has become an entrenched part of the industry. Its presence is, to a large extent, accepted by developers, contractors, and suppliers—in some instances, as a necessary evil providing stability and predictability, and in other instances, as a provider of valuable services. Even those who resent Cosa Nostra's presence in the industry too often believe the government is powerless to remove it. As in the Brindell era, the industry has learned to live with the exploitive activities of a syndicate and, in certain trades, has become dependent upon its rationalizing role.

NOTES

1. See G. Robert Blakey, Ronald Goldstock and Charles Rogovin, *Rackets Bureaus: Investigation and Prosecution of Organized Crime* (Washington, D.C.: National Institute of Justice, 1978), xiii–xiv; G. Robert Blakey, "Organized Crime: Enforcement Strategies," in *Encyclopedia of Crime and Justice*, vol. 3 (N.Y.: Macmillan Co., 1983), 1107–9.

2. *Corruption and Racketeering in the New York Construction Industry (The Final Report of the New York State Organized Crime Task Force)* (New York: New York University Press, 1990).

3. Peter Reuter, *Racketeering in Legitimate Industries: A Study in the Economics of Intimidation*, 81–83 (Santa Monica, CA: Rand Corporation, 1987, report prepared in conjunction with New York State Organized Crime Task Force).

4. During the 1960s, for example, the New York City Police Department was plagued by corruption despite a series of prosecutions throughout its history at every level of the department. See, *People v. Renaghan*, 33 N.Y.2d 991 (1974); *People v. Koutnik*, 44 A.D.2d 48 (N.Y. App. Div., 1st Dept., 1974).

5. The Racketeer Influenced and Corrupt Organizations Act is found in Title 18 of the U.S. Code (sections 1961 et seq.). As such, while it allows for the innovative use of civil remedies, it is assigned to the Criminal Division. This was not happenstance; the authors of the statute designed it to bypass the organizational structure of the department and allow criminal attorneys to utilize civil actions.

6. See, for example, Oscar Newman, *Defensible Space: Crime Prevention Through Urban Design* (New York: Macmillan, 1972).

7. 18 USC 1964(c).

8. Under New York law, where a government contract is obtained by bribery, the vendor can be made to repay all compensation it has received from the government without any allowance for the value of the goods or services it has provided. *S.T. Grand Inc. v. City of New York*, 32 N.Y.2d 300 (1973). Punitive damages can be awarded if the jury finds that defendant's misconduct was malicious and directed at the public generally.

9. Act of 2 March 1863, 12 Stat. 696; *United States ex. rel. Marcus v. Hess*, 317 US 537 (1943). The title of the act is short for "qui tam pro domino rege quam pro se ipso in hac parte sequitur" (who sues on behalf of the king as well as for himself).

10. "Forfeiture of Profit in Pentagon Fraud Cases Urged," *New York Times*, 24 August 1988, A15.

11. See generally Ronald Goldstock, G. Robert Blakey, and Gerald Bradley, *Labor Racketeering: A Simulated Investigation. Teacher's Guide and Background Materials* (Ithaca, N.Y.: Cornell Institute on Organized Crime, 1979).

12. *United States v. Local 560 of International Brotherhood of Teamsters, Chauffeurs, Warehousemen, and Helpers of America*, 780 F.2d 267 (3rd Cir. 1985).

13. 18 USC 1964(a).

14. See *United States v. Cappetto*, 502 F.2d 1351 (7th Cir. 1974), *cert. denied*, 420 U.S. 925 (1975) (suit to enjoin gambling business).

15. The act, codified at 31 U.S.C.A. 5311–5322 and 12 U.S.C.A. 1829b, 1951–59, requires financial institutions to maintain appropriate records and file reports, both of which are useful in criminal, tax, or regulatory investigations and proceedings.

16. *Corruption and Racketeering*, 168, 205 ff.

17. The "shape-up"—the method by which union officials on the New York waterfront selected which stevedores worked each day and which did not—was one method by which organized crime maintained influence over the Longshoreman's Union. Legislation was passed in 1953 permitting the Waterfront Commission of New York Harbor to administer and regulate the distribution of work on the docks.

18. "Summary of the Proceedings: Findings and Discoveries of the Harvard University Executive Session for State and Local Prosecutors at the John F. Kennedy School of Government, 1986–90," research monograph, November 1990.

19. B. Stewart, "Mission Impossible," *Florida Magazine*, 4 October 1987.

20. John Landesco, *Organized Crime in Chicago* (Chicago: University of Chicago Press, 1929).

21. Ronald Goldstock, "Operational Issues in Organized Crime Control," in *Major Issues in Organized Crime Control*, ed. Herbert Edelhertz (1987), 82–83; Ronald Goldstock and Dan Coenen, "Controlling the Contemporary Loanshark: The Law of Illicit Lending and the Problem of Witness Fear," 65 *Cornell Law Review* 127 (1980): Appendix A.

22. See G. Robert Blakey and Michael Goldsmith, "Criminal Redistribution of Stolen Property: The Need for Law Reform," 74 *Michigan Law Review* (1976): 1511.

23. Goldstock, "Operational Issues," 83–85, Appendix B.

24. *Corruption and Racketeering*, 73 ff., Appendix C.

25. Reuter, *Racketeering*, Appendix D.

26. The catalyst for these programs was an article written by Herman Goldstein, "Improving Policing: A Problem Oriented Approach," *Crime and Delinquency* (April 1979). In this article, Goldstein, an advocate of problem-solving approaches, criticized what he

termed a "means over ends" mentality prevalent in police circles, in which administrative competence rather than "results" had become the goal.

27. David C. Anderson, *Crimes of Justice* (New York: Times Books, 1988), 89–158.

28. Joan E. Jacoby, *The American Prosecutor: A Search for Identity* (Lexington, MA: Lexington Books, 1980), xx.

29. See, Anderson, *Crimes of Justice*, 94.

30. See, for example, Michael Maltz, *Measuring the Effectiveness of Organized Crime Control Efforts* (Chicago: The University of Illinois at Chicago, Office of International Criminal Justice, 1990).

31. "Use and derivative use" immunity protects the witness from having the witness's testimony or evidence derived therefrom used against the witness in any criminal proceeding.

32. For example, rational and historical forces combine to create an incredible maze of prosecutors' offices in the New York City metropolitan area: three U.S. attorneys' offices (each of which contains a now-modified organized crime strike force), two state prosecutors' offices, more than fifteen district attorneys, and the Special New York City narcotics prosecutor.

33. But this is not always the case. Perhaps the greatest exception is the Department of Justice, headed by the attorney general and containing the Federal Bureau of Investigation, Bureau of Prisons, and other criminal justice agencies.

34. Thus, under the current system, a criminal problem that affects different agencies and departments might be given to a "czar" so that the institutional barriers can be overcome.

35. Some participants at one Kennedy School meeting characterized this aspect of the proposed role for the prosecutor in phrases that ranged from "nanny to the world" to "vicious intermeddler."

36. While the incorporation of persons with these skills and disciplines into the prosecutor's office may be thought of as a major departure from present practice, that is not actually the case. Again the Department of Justice serves as an example; it has within it prosecutors, civil attorneys, investigative agencies, accountants, analysts, economists, other academics, and specialists in research and report writing.

37. One example of research that had a significant impact on prosecutors was the research undertaken by the Rand Corporation during the 1970s into "career criminals." While criminal justice professionals knew that some offenders committed more crimes than others, the magnitude of the disproportion revealed in the Rand Corporation's research caused most major prosecutors' offices, in little more than a decade, to focus on these career criminals through special programs. That research involved a relatively simple technique—talking to offenders.

20

RICO: The Federal Experience (Criminal and Civil) and an Analysis of Attacks Against the Statute

G. ROBERT BLAKEY

INTRODUCTION

In 1970, Congress enacted the Organized Crime Control Act, Title IX of which is known as the "Racketeer Influenced and Corrupt Organizations Act" (RICO). Congress enacted the 1970 act "to strengthen . . . the legal tools in the evidence gathering process, . . . [to] establish . . . new penal prohibitions, and [to] provide . . . enhanced sanctions and new remedies."[1] RICO covers violence, the provision of illegal goods and services, corruption in labor or management relations, corruption in government, and criminal fraud. Congress found that "the sanctions and remedies available" under the law in 1970 were "unnecessarily limited in scope and impact."[2] It then provided a wide range of new criminal and civil sanctions to control these offenses, including imprisonment, forfeiture, injunctions, and treble damage relief for "person[s] injured" in their "business or property" by violations of the statute.[3] At the time, these sanctions were called for by no less than the president, the President's Commission on Law Enforcement and the Administration of Justice, and the American Bar Association. In response, the Senate passed the bill 73 to 1.[4] The House passed an amended bill 431 to 26. The Senate then passed the House bill after debate, but without objection, and the president signed the legislation on 15 October 1970. Since 1970, twenty-nine states have enacted similar state RICO legislation.[5]

STANDARDS OF UNLAWFUL CONDUCT: CRIMINAL AND CIVIL STANDARDS

RICO sets forth "standards" of "unlawful" conduct, which are enforced through "criminal" and "civil" sanctions. Section 1963 of Title 18 sets out the criminal remedies. Section 1964 of Title 18 sets out the civil remedies. Section 1962 states what is "unlawful," not "criminal." As such, RICO is not, as some believe, "primarily a criminal statute."[6] Accordingly, because the civil scope of RICO is *broader* than its criminal scope, RICO is *not* primarily criminal and punitive, but primarily civil and remedial.[7] RICO's civil remedies, based on a showing of the preponderance of the evidence, are available to the government or other parties.[8]

Congress also directed that RICO be liberally construed to effectuate its remedial purposes. "[T]his is the only substantive federal criminal statute that contains such a directive."[9] The directive is a "mandate."[10] Accordingly, the language of the statute is to be read in the same fashion, whatever the character of the suit.[11]

"Congress was well aware [too] that it was [with RICO] entering into a new domain."[12] The issue was not whether the 1970 act was to apply, but the possible preemption of other sanctions. Congress, however, expressly saved "provision[s] of Federal, State, or other law imposing criminal penalties or affording civil remedies in addition to those provided for" in RICO.[13] "Congress enacted RICO in order to supplement, not supplant, the available remedies, since it thought those remedies offered too little protection for the victims."[14] Such overlap between statutes "is neither unusual nor unfortunate."[15] Cumulative remedies further remedial purposes.[16]

The standards of 18 U.S.C. § 1962(a) embody four essential elements: (1) income derived from a "pattern" of racketeering and (2) the use or investment of the income in the acquisition, establishment, or operation by a defendant (3) of an "enterprise" (4) engaged or affecting interstate commerce.[17]

The standards of 18 U.S.C. § 1962(b) embody three essential elements: (1) the acquisition or maintenance through a "pattern" of racketeering activity by a defendant (2) of an interest in, or control of, an "enterprise" (3) engaged in, or affecting, interstate commerce.[18]

The standards of 18 U.S.C. § 1962(c) embody four essential elements: (1) employment by, or association of a defendant with, (2) an "enterprise" (3) engaged in, or affecting, interstate commerce, (4) the affairs of which are conducted or participated in by a defendant through a "pattern" of racketeering activity.[19]

Section 1962(d) makes it "unlawful for any person to conspire to violate . . . [subsections (a), (b) or (c)]."[20]

The Second Circuit in *Moss v. Morgan Stanley, Inc.*, aptly summarized the substantive elements of RICO:

(1) that the defendant (2) through the commission of two or more acts (3) constituting a "pattern" (4) of "racketeering activity" (5) directly or indirectly invests in, or maintains an interest in, or participates in (6) an "enterprise" (7) the activities of which affect interstate or foreign commerce.[21]

THE CRIMINAL ENFORCEMENT MECHANISM

The criminal enforcement mechanism of RICO provides for imprisonment, fine, and criminal forfeiture. RICO authorizes imprisonment of up to twenty years or life, where the predicate offense authorizes life.[22] Fines are up to $25,000 or, alternatively, up to $250,000 if an individual is convicted or up to $500,000 if an entity is convicted, or twice the gain or loss. Forfeiture is of illicit proceeds, related property, or any interest in an enterprise.[23]

In 1970, Congress also enacted the "Continuing Criminal Enterprise" (CCE) provisions of Title II of the Comprehensive Drug Abuse Prevention and Control Act of 1970.[24] Both RICO and CCE reintroduced the concept of criminal forfeiture into American criminal law and procedure. They are read similarly.[25] Since 1970, Congress has employed the concept in other areas, too.[26]

Federal and state RICO legislation is enforced through a wide range of criminal and civil sanctions. In particular, the legislation embodies criminal and civil forfeiture. They are part of the basic fabric of our law. "Upon this point a page of history is worth a volume of logic."[27]

Federal RICO and related legislation embody criminal forfeiture. Such forfeitures are in personam, not in rem.[28] The criminal indictment must specifically identify the forfeitable property,[29] and the jury must return a special verdict on the extent of the defendant's interest to be forfeited.[30] The court then enters a judgment of forfeiture.[31] As such, the court cannot make an indefinite verdict definite.[32] Nor may it correct a verdict that is not extensive enough.[33]

Most federal and state legislation enacted in the post–Civil War period, however, provided for civil forfeiture. Indeed, a number of other state statutes today embody various kinds of civil, not criminal, forfeitures. While RICO included criminal forfeiture provisions, the 1970 Drug Act included both criminal and civil forfeiture provisions.[34] The civil forfeiture provisions, too, have been upheld against various challenges.[35] Their scope, too, is analogously interpreted to criminal forfeiture.[36] Following the 1970 Drug Act, the National Conference of Commissioners on Uniform State Laws also adopted the Uniform Controlled Substance Act.[37] This act provides for civil forfeitures; the act contains no criminal forfeiture provisions. The civil forfeitures provision is Section 505; it parallels the civil forfeiture provisions of the Federal Drug Act.[38] Forty-six states have adopted the Uniform Act.[39] A majority of the twenty-nine states that have RICO statutes provide for civil forfeiture of property. The provisions parallel the 1970 Drug Act and the Uniform Act.[40]

Both criminal and civil forfeitures have ancient roots. Biblical, Greek, and Roman law knew forms of forfeiture. So, too, did English law. The forfeiture of property is one of the earliest sanctions of Anglo-Saxon law. Three types of forfeitures came to be distinguished: statutory forfeiture, forfeiture consequent to a criminal conviction and attainder, and deodand.

Statutes in England imposed a variety of forfeitures, principally as a means of tax enforcement. In the mid-seventeenth century, Parliament enacted the Navigation Acts, the broadest of the English forfeiture statutes, which required that shipping had to be in English-built, -owned, and -manned vessels, and they provided that violations would result in the forfeiture of the ship and the goods it carried.[41] Suits for these forfeitures were commenced by civil information. They could be brought against a person (in personam) or against the thing to be forfeited (in rem). Typically, they were brought in rem against the vessel and the goods, as the owner could not be located or was beyond the jurisdiction of the court.[42]

Forfeiture consequent to a criminal conviction and attainder was, however, the oldest and best known. It was imposed on traitors and felons, who forfeited all of their personal and real property, as a result not of their conviction, but of their attainder, a pronouncement of legal death.[43]

"Felony" under early English law included any breach of the feudal engagement.[44] As such, it resulted in the forfeiture of the feudal estate to the lord.[45] William Blackstone traces the origins of the word *felony* to the Anglo-Saxon *fee* (estate) and *lon* (price).[46] Chattels went to the king, whose regalian rights included all ownerless property—*bona vacantia*, which is what an outlaw's property was.[47]

Attainder also means corruption of blood; that is, no descendant could ever trace a line of inheritance through the attained ancestor. Forfeiture of lands related back to the time of the commission of the offense, voiding subsequent sales or encumbrances. Forfeiture of goods did not relate back, but transfers collusively made, that is, not bona fide, were not good against the Crown.

Deodands are sometimes spoken of as predecessors of the forfeiture statutes, but the historical evidence indicates that they were atypical.[48] An instrument of death replaced the slayer's kin as the object of vengeance. At first the instrument was taken and sold, and the proceeds were used to buy masses for the victim.[49] Throughout the later Middle Ages, the king received the money, which provided a small but steady source of revenue.

In the American colonies, the extent to which English law and practice should be adopted was a matter of great dispute. Forfeitures did not follow any uniform practice. For example, forfeiture consequent to conviction and attainder was largely abolished in Massachusetts, allowed to fall into disuse in New York, but was fairly widely employed in Pennsylvania and Virginia. The acceptance of deodand presents a cloudier picture, and firm judgments cannot be made on the scope of its adoption. Finally, while the Crown did not insist on most forfeitures, since the proceeds would have gone to the colonial governments, it did insist on the enforcement of the Navigation Acts, which by their terms were applicable to the colonies. They were enforced in the vice-admiralty courts, in effect, not in rem, but in personam, and they were tried by the court without a jury.[50] After independence, criminal forfeitures consequent to conviction and attainder fell into disrepute. The Constitution itself forbade bills of attainder—legislative, not judicial, determinations of guilt.[51] It also limited corruption of blood and forfeitures of estate for treason to life estates.[52] In 1790, Congress abolished by statute both corruption of blood and forfeiture of estate as a consequence of federal criminal prosecutions.[53]

Following the Revolution, a variety of statutes continued the practice of declaring specific forfeitures, which could be imposed in criminal or civil proceedings, either in personam or in rem. How a particular forfeiture was to be treated was a question of legislative intent.[54] So, too, was the time when the forfeiture was to take place, that is, at the time of the offense rather than at the time of the conviction. This rule was described as "settled doctrine" in *United States v. Stowell*.[55] Forfeitures in the federal courts, however, were patterned after the Navigation Acts, and they were imposed in an in rem proceeding. The property could be forfeited without prior criminal conviction.[56] Nevertheless, *Coffey v. United States*[57] held that if an acquittal occurred in a criminal proceeding, no subsequent in rem forfeiture could be had in a civil proceeding. *Coffey* was disapproved of by *United States v. One Assortment of 89 Firearms*.[58] In rem forfeitures were rationalized by the personification fiction. Personal guilt was not implicated. The prosecution was brought not against the owner but the thing itself, and judgment was rendered against the whole world.

The Civil War brought about a major shift in the law of forfeiture. It quickly became evident that traditional treason prosecutions could not be brought against most rebels, for they were safely behind Confederate lines. Their life, liberty, and property—even where their property was not in the South—were beyond the power of northern courts, since in absentia prosecutions were not constitutionally possible. The solution hit on by Congress was civil in rem forfeiture proceedings. The forfeitures were eventually upheld by the Supreme Court. Criminal in personam forfeiture proceedings then largely disappeared from the federal scene. Constitutional attacks on civil in rem forfeitures were again launched when they were used by the Congress during Prohibition to suppress the traffic in illicit alcohol, but the Supreme Court turned them back on the basis of the established precedents of the post–Civil War era.[59] The constitutional validity of the use of in rem civil forfeiture in law enforcement today is, therefore, settled beyond serious question.[60]

THE CIVIL ENFORCEMENT MECHANISM

The civil enforcement mechanism of RICO provides for injunctions, treble damages, and counsel fees. The civil enforcement provisions were modeled on, but are not identical to, the antitrust laws.[61] The antitrust laws have been aptly termed "the Magna Carta of free enterprise"; the antitrust laws "are as important to the preservation of economic freedom and our free enterprise system as the Bill of Rights is to the protection of our fundamental personal freedoms."[62] A private "treble-damages remedy [is needed] . . . precisely for the purpose of encouraging *private* challenges to antitrust violations."[63] Such "private antitrust litigation is one of the surest weapons for effective enforcement of the antitrust laws.''[64] Private suits "provide a significant supplement to the limited resources available to the Department of Justice" to enforce the antitrust statutes.[65]

Like the antitrust laws, RICO creates "a private enforcement mechanism that . . . deter[s] violators and provide[s] ample compensation to the victims.''[66] The private enforcement mechanism is put into force by "private attorney generals.''[67] The antitrust statutes and RICO are well integrated.

ORGANIZED CRIME AND BEYOND

The "legislative history [of RICO] clearly demonstrates that . . . [it] was intended to provide new weapons of unprecedented scope for an assault upon organized crime and its economic roots.''[68] "[T]he major purpose of Title IX . . . [was] to address the infiltration of legitimate business by organized crime.''[69] But "Congress wanted to reach both 'legitimate' and 'illegitimate' enterprises.''[70] "[R]ejected [also has been the] notion [that RICO] applies only to organized crime in the 'classic mobster' sense.''[71] As the Supreme Court observed in its *H.J., Inc. v. Northwestern Bell Telephone Co.* decision:

[The notion that RICO is limited to organized crime] finds no support in the Act's text, and is at odds with the tenor of its legislative history. . . . Congress for cogent reasons chose to enact a more general statute, one which, although it had organized crime as its focus, was not limited in application to organized crime.[72]

The legislative history of the 1970 statute is replete with statements by the bill's sponsors that fully demonstrate that they intend that it apply beyond organized crime. Legitimate businesses, in short, "enjoy neither an inherent incapacity for criminal activity nor immunity from its consequences.''[73] Finally, "the courts [are also] all but unanimous in their refusal to read RICO as prohibiting *only* the infiltration of legitimate business.''[74] As such, RICO fits easily into a consistent pattern of federal legislation enacted as general reform over the past half century or more aimed as a specific target, but drafted without limiting it to the specific target.[75]

IMPLEMENTATION OF PUBLIC CRIMINAL
AND CIVIL RICO

At first, the Department of Justice moved slowly to use RICO criminally. Today, it is the prosecutor's tool of choice in sophisticated forms of crime.[76] The Department of Justice is also moving to implement the civil provisions.[77] Since 1970, criminal RICO has been effectively used against organized crime groups,[78] political corruption prosecutions,[79] white-collar crime-type prosecutions,[80] and violent groups.[81]

IMPLEMENTATION OF PRIVATE CIVIL RICO

The private bar did not begin to bring civil RICO suits until about 1975. When it did, the district courts reacted with hostility and undertook judicially to redraft the statute in an effort to dismiss civil suits in all possible ways.[82] Indeed, before *Sedima*, 61 percent of the reported decisions were dismissed on various motions of the defendants.[83]

The first effort to redraft civil RICO involved reading into it an "organized crime" limitation. Because that limitation has no support in the text of the statute—it was specifically rejected in the legislative debates—the Second, Fifth, Seventh, and Eighth Circuits quickly rejected it.[84] The next effort involved reading a "competitive injury" limitation into the statute. The Seventh and Eighth Circuits quickly turned this effort aside.[85] Then, the district courts hit upon the "racketeering injury" and the criminal conviction limitations. Both limitations, adopted by a sharply divided Second Circuit, were repudiated in *Sedima*.[86]

RICO UNDER ATTACK—THE CRIMINAL MEGATRIAL

Today, RICO is under attack by a wide range of groups. Criminally, the principal focus of the attack is on large trials and pretrial restraints. The recent Report of the National Association of Criminal Defense Lawyers (NACDL) on the so-called RICO megatrial is illustrative of the attacks on criminal RICO.

The NACDL megatrial report recommends:

1. Amendment of the RICO statute to exclude multiple conspiracies;
2. Enactment of a statute limiting the number of defendants that can be tried together or giving judges special directions to sever RICO cases into smaller, less complicated, shorter trials to minimize spillover prejudice and jury confusion;
3. Elimination of forfeiture provisions and substitution of fines on profits;
4. Amendment of the RICO or joinder statutes to preclude joinder of RICO charges with other crimes not charged as predicate offenses;
5. Enactment of limitations on the introduction of enterprise evidence;
6. Endorsement of the use of pretrial evidentiary hearings, at which the government will be required to demonstrate a unifying agreement, to decide the appropriateness of severance;
7. Limitation on charging substantive RICO, which may involve conspiracy predicates, and RICO conspiracy in the same case; and
8. Endorsement of a budget review of megatrials to advance the argument that it is not in the interest of judicial economy for the courts to permit the government to generate massive trials where a massive loss or waste of public funds can be avoided.

Taken together, these recommendations represent an assault on the basic design of RICO, and if they are adopted, they would result in a return to the law that existed before 1970. As such, they merit careful attention, particularly to the character of the reasoning that is offered in justification of them.

The contentions of the NACDL need to be examined and then reviewed in light of the facts and the law. The argumentative tactics used by the NACDL in its attempt to affect public opinion and gain support for its position also need to be highlighted.[87]

First, the NACDL employs language that is designed to persuade the reader on a particular point by emotion, not reason. Such unqualified language is effective rhetoric, yet it ought to be rigorously tested against reality before anyone accepts it as more than mere exhortation.

Second, the NACDL uses its esteemed position, rather than reasoned analysis, in an effort to mold opinion in a particular form. Based on its conceded authority to speak for defendants' rights, the NACDL has apparently decided to use its authority as its method of argument.

[J.] Bentham points out of the danger of arguing from authority: The most fallacious use of authority is in instances where the debaters are capable of forming a correct judgment on the basis of relevant arguments, but in which the opinion, real or supposed, of some person . . . is brought forth in the character of an argument in the place of such relevant arguments as ought to be furnished.[88]

Bentham, too, aptly suggests that "the most rational and desirable course in those branches of useful knowledge would be to substitute decision on the ground of authority for decision on the ground of direct and specific evidence."[89]

Third, the NACDL fails to acknowledge in its report the existence of interests or policies that might compete with its own perspective. Not once in the report are the crime control goals of RICO acknowledged, and not once in the report is the progress toward those goals evaluated or related to RICO. Contrary to the NACDL's depiction of RICO as merely a tool for an overzealous prosecutor, RICO must also be evaluated as an effort by Congress to launch a broad-based attack on the special challenge posed by group crime in our society.

Dean Roscoe Pound said it well:

Civilized society presupposes peace and good order, security of social institutions, security of the general morals, and conservation and intelligent use of social resources. But it demands no less that free individual initiative which is the basis of economic progress, that freedom of criticism without which political progress is impossible, and that free mental activity which is a prerequisite of cultural progress. Above all it demands that the individual be able to live a moral and social life as a human being. These claims, which may be put broadly as a social interest in the individual life, continually trench upon the interest in the security of social institutions, and often, in appearance at least, run counter to the paramount interest in the general security. Compromise of such claims for the purpose of securing as much as we may is peculiarly difficult. [Nevertheless,] . . . in criminal law, as everywhere in law, the problem is one of compromise; of balancing conflicting interests and of securing as much as may be with the least sacrifice of other interests.[90]

Edmond Burke put it another way:

For that which taken singly and by itself may appear to be wrong, when considered with relation to other things may be perfectly right—or at least such as ought to be patiently endorsed as the means of preventing something that is worse.[91].

During the debate over the 1970 act, Senator John L. McClellan, one of its chief Senate sponsors, wrote:

In the long run, [a balancing] approach to criminal legislation will prove more protective of our real civil liberties than a rigid, unthinking rejection of measures to strengthen law enforcement. We must seek that kind of balance now, and achieve a practical reconciliation of the need for effective administration of justice with the need to preserve our substantial rights. [The Organized Crime Control Act] has been written and amended with the intent to make such a reconciliation while there is time and will, on the part of the public, to do so. We must reject the false cries of "wolf" by ... self-appointed shepherds of civil liberties. Crime has a tyranny of its own. Those who love liberty should seek to overthrow this tyrant, too.[92]

Bentham also realized that all policy choices—including those advocated by defense lawyers—inevitably result in some adverse consequences. "[A] minimum of mischief . . . accompanies every change."[93] Yet Bentham also was wary of those who focus in isolation on such mischief in an effort to defeat a reform that is in the best interests of everyone.

He will set up the cry of "Innovation! Innovation!" hoping by this watchword to bring to his aid all whose sinister interests are connected with his own, and which impel them to say, and the unreflecting multitude to believe, that the change in question is one in which the mischief is not outweighed by a preponderant mass of advantage.[94]

Accordingly, the failure to examine the RICO megatrial in relation to RICO's purpose and its success is little more than an attempt to further the interests of a few while sacrificing the safety of the majority.[95]

Finally, the NACDL report suffers from severe overgeneralization. Generally, the reason that people engage in such overgeneralization and strong rhetoric is that "[p]eople who are cautious and tentative are likely to be unimpressive. Moderate statements and half measures seem to indicate weakness and indecision, while bold and forthright assertions suggest strength and vigor."[96] Such hasty generalizations are also usually the result of one of two mistakes: a conclusion based on an insufficient number of instances or a conclusion drawn from unrepresentative, biased, or atypical data.[97] The NACDL report commits both of these errors.

First, the report's broad conclusions are based on an insufficient number of instances. The report cites, for example, only about twenty-seven cases; however, a computer analysis of *all* published RICO cases from 1970 through June 1988, which covers the period of time analyzed in the report, indicates that over 400 RICO decisions were reported since the law was enacted. An analysis of these opinions for data regarding length of the trial, number of defendants, disposition of defendants, motions for severance, and joinder at both district and appellate court levels shows the fundamental defects in the NACDL report.

Such an analysis highlights the second error made by the NACDL: conclusions drawn from an unrepresentative sample. Not only does the NACDL choose a few cases from which to make its point, but it carefully extracts from cases that *affirm* RICO convictions, dicta which, when isolated, seems to support its positions.[98]

Accordingly, because of the selective use of authorities, objective observers are denied access to those facts that might enlighten them to the distorted picture that the report draws.

This section of the NACDL's report forms the basis of the rest of its argument about the evils of RICO. According to the NACDL, because trials are long and complex, defendants experience financial burdens and have their lives disrupted. In short, because dozens of defendants are all joined together in one "mega-trial," they are victims of spill-over prejudice and guilt by association, and jurors are confused and unable to render proper verdicts.

The report, by citing a few cases, makes it sound as if these trials are typical of all RICO trials and atypical of other sorts of trials. Nevertheless, an analysis of reported RICO opinions shows that of the over 400 opinions that provided information regarding trial length, only six trials were found to last more than six months, and only nineteen lasted between three and six months. The vast majority (76.4 percent) were shorter than three months.

One additional conclusion can be drawn from these data: the actual percentage of *all* RICO cases shorter than three months is actually greater than 76.4 percent. This is true for two reasons: (1) those published opinions that did not provide information on trial length in all likelihood did not do so because it was not an issue at the trial and not worth mentioning in the opinion and (2) the large number of RICO cases that go unreported apparently do so because they are resolved quickly, easily, and with little precedential significance. In short, published opinion data can usually be assumed to *overestimate* the problems associated with RICO litigation, since problems receive attention.

These data are corroborated by the general information available from the Administrative Office of the United States Courts. A compilation of data from tables in the *Annual Report* of the director of the Administrative Office of the United States Courts, for years 1972–87, the period of time analyzed in the report, indicates that of all cases classified as "extortion, racketeering, and threats" and tried to a jury, 91.6 percent were concluded in less than twenty days. When judge-tried cases are included, the percentage of cases lasting more than twenty days drops significantly (from 8.4 percent to 5.6 percent). According to these data, this is, in fact, true of *all* kinds of cases.[99] Empirical statistics, in short, do not support the general conclusions made by the NACDL.

On the other hand, it must be conceded that *all* RICO trials are not quickly resolved and that all RICO cases are not resolved more quickly than, or even as quickly as, other types of cases. Nevertheless, the NACDL's attempt to focus solely on RICO trials causes it to misstate the real issue. The more complex an issue in litigation is, either legally or factually, the longer its trial will be. For example, since 1971, of all federal robbery and assault cases tried to a jury, .2 percent lasted longer than twenty days. Likewise, .3 percent of all jury-tried burglary cases were resolved in more than twenty days. In contrast, 1.7 percent of all jury-tried homicide cases lasted more than twenty days.[100] Nothing is "RICO-specific," in short, about complex litigation. Judges, juries, and defendants may experience stress during all types of complex litigation. Civil defendants, too, are required to endure long trials, as are plaintiffs, judges, and juries.

The data on complex litigation lasting more than twenty days are: personal injury—assault, libel, and slander 1.3 percent, trademark 3.3 percent, personal injury—airplane 4.0 percent, securities, commodities, and exchanges 4.5 percent, patent 9.4 percent, and antitrust laws 15.4 percent (or 155 cases total), as compared with 8.4 percent of extortion, racketeering, and threats cases.[101]

These data show two things: (1) it is not only RICO trials that are lengthy and difficult to resolve, and (2) some trials take longer than others because they involve more complex issues and types of evidence. The nature of most complex conspiracy prosecutions (RICO or not) is such that it has the potential for taking substantial periods of time to complete because of the complex nature of the crime and of the evidence involved. But these factors are related to the defendants' *conduct* and not how the prosecution *wants* to try the case. While such trials may result in stress for defendants, juries, and judges (and prosecutors), the alternative would be to rewrite the laws (as the NACDL proposes) so that all or most trials would be limited to simple forms of criminal conduct, the issues relating to which could be resolved swiftly. As such, the real nature of the crime and the criminal would not be treated in the judicial process, and criminals who engage in sophisticated forms of crime would not be appropriately sanctioned for their criminal conduct, since it would be practically impossible to bring to light the real nature of their criminal activity, as it was prior to 1970.[102]

A section of the NACDL's report outlines problems of pretrial detention, violation of defendants' Sixth Amendment rights to a speedy trial and right to counsel of their choice, and violation of defendants' constitutional right to appeal. Regarding these issues, the NACDL cites not one statistic indicating the frequency or extent of any of these assertions.

Pretrial detention, however, is not a problem unique to RICO cases, even though the NACDL attempts to focus on it as such. It is a problem inherent to our entire criminal justice system. As decisions regarding pretrial detention are based on the potential risk of danger to society posed by the defendant and the risk of flight by the defendant, no reason exists to assume that judges do not make equally responsible decisions regarding RICO defendants as they do regarding non-RICO defendants.

Additionally, if any group of criminals is able to employ the assistance of baffling intricate and dangerous networks that can help an offender disappear from a jurisdiction overnight and threaten the safety of many innocent individuals, it is surely those who are engaged in organized crime and similar offenses.

The NACDL bemoans RICO's impact on Sixth Amendment rights. It first insists that defendants' rights to a speedy trial are stretched too far. This generalization, however, hardly holds true in light of the statistics provided earlier regarding trial length. Additionally, the concept of a "speedy trial" must be examined in the appropriate context.

P. Weiss correctly warns of the risk of strictly applying traditional concepts to modern crimes:

A speedy trial in criminal cases is a cardinal constitutional right. No one would minimize its importance. But it has become an easy slogan, blindly applied, without an awareness that newly developed crimes of the contemporary world do not fit the mold of the historic crimes for which the speedy trial safeguard originated.[103]

Weiss was speaking of white-collar crimes, of which RICO prosecutions make up a part. Nevertheless, Weiss argues that investigation in the white-collar area can be in process for months or years before the defendant even learns of it and that the prosecution may well have its case developed and completed before the defendant even gets a chance to begin preparing for trial.[104] As such, a speedy trial may *not* be speedy justice. A similar situation exists with RICO defendants in other areas, whether they are accused of organized crime or violent crimes or a combination of the two. Accordingly, it may actually be to the defendants' *advantage* for the litigation to move at a more deliberate pace.

Judges, of course, possess wide discretion over whether to grant motions and when to schedule hearings and trials, and they can deny those motions that seem only for the purpose of delaying the trial. The criminal justice system has many mechanisms to protect defendants' right to a speedy trial, yet it would be mocking justice to say that criminals who engage in sophisticated forms of crime must go free merely because it takes a relatively long time to try them.

The NACDL also insists that RICO trials, because they are long and expensive, violate defendants' Sixth Amendment right to counsel of their choice. The NACDL provides no proof for this assertion, and since research proves the relative rarity of unduly long trials, the point is not well-taken. Nothing in the text or the jurisprudence of the Sixth Amendment confers upon defendants, moreover, a right to counsel of their unfettered choice.[105]

Such a rule would result in a chaotic system in which thousands of defendants were insisting on a few of the best attorneys in the country. The Sixth Amendment guarantees a right to an attorney, and the appointment of one if one cannot be afforded. Because of these constitutional safeguards, the expense of a RICO trial does not necessarily prevent anyone from getting an effective defense any more than in any other kind of criminal prosecution.

The final argument is that the defendant's right to appeal is violated because the defendant cannot afford an expensive appeal. Nevertheless, the NACDL provides no data on the number of defendants who have, in fact, abandoned their right to appeal. Research, too, indicates that most RICO defendants do not, in fact, encounter particularly long (and therefore expensive) trials, nor is this problem necessarily unique to RICO.

In this section of the report, the NACDL complains about the fact that judges suffer stress and that they, because of megatrials, preside over a one-case court. No one would suggest that the job of a trial judge does not involve stress. While RICO trials (and other complex criminal and civil trials) may be draining, emotionally and physically, on trial judges, it would be inappropriate not to prosecute a particular kind of offender because a particular judge finds that kind of prosecution stressful. Additionally, the NACDL necessarily assumes that it is more stressful to hear a two-month case involving ten defendants than ten six-day trials involving one defendant each. Judges inevitably make decisions regarding the fate of individuals—there is no way stress could be removed from that job. Finally, if society faces the prospect of one-judge courts, the solution is more judges, not freed criminals.

Three separate arguments are taken up in this section. The first is the problem of alleged prejudicial spillover of evidence. The NACDL argues that when many defendants are tried together, juries become confused and use the evidence introduced as to one defendant against another. It argues, in effect, that a defendant who would be found innocent in a separate trial will be found guilty (by association) in a trial with several other, obviously guilty defendants.

On the contrary, it seems just as likely that the typical juror would see the clear distinction between the obviously guilty defendant and one who is not. Indeed, the defendant whose guilt is questionable and who might be found guilty in a separate trial would more likely get off in a joint trial because of the comparisons that would inevitably be made to other, more clearly guilty defendants. When multiple defendants are on trial, it is, in short, at least as likely that "innocence by comparison" rather than "guilt by association" will obtain.

Empirical research does not, moreover, support the NACDL's apparent lack of faith in the good sense of American juries. Research done on the University of Chicago Law School's Jury Project establishes that juries and judges, in the vast majority of cases, come to the same conclusion about guilt or innocence of criminal defendants.[106]

In Harvey Kalven's and Hans Zeisel's study, judges were asked to indicate how they would have decided the cases, when they were, in fact, tried by juries.

In 64 percent of the cases, the judge and jury agreed that the defendant was guilty; in 14 percent they agreed that the defendant should be acquitted (78 percent agreement). The research also indicates that in 19 percent of the remaining cases, in which judge and jury disagreed, the judge would have said guilty, when the jury acquitted. In only 3 percent of the cases that the jury found guilty would the judge have acquitted.[107]

This research establishes, therefore, that judges and juries tend to decide cases alike, and if anything, juries are more lenient on defendants. Additionally, judges were asked to characterize these cases in categories based on whether the evidence was very difficult, somewhat difficult, or easy to understand. Kalven and Zeisel, in fact, found *no* relationship between "evidence difficulty" and judge/jury agreement. Judges and juries agreed just as much in easy cases as in difficult cases.[108]

Empirical research on RICO prosecutions also indicates that juries do not automatically convict defendants. Of reported RICO cases that provided information in the opinion, 12.6 percent of the juries, in fact, acquitted one or more of the defendants on one or more charges.

While a risk is always present in trials with multiple defendants and multiple counts so that the jury may not "individualize" the defendants, that risk can be lessened by various trial techniques, including carefully crafted instructions during and at the end of the trial. The NACDL suggests, however, that explicit instructions given to the jury to apply certain evidence only to certain defendants make no difference in preventing prejudicial spillover. Empirical research demonstrates otherwise.

Myers conducted research on 201 criminal juries in Indianapolis, Indiana, and found that:

[J]uries discriminated between types of evidence. They did depart from the judge's instructions, but only in special circumstances, as for example, when the cases involved a serious offense, a young victim, or an unemployed defendant. However, their departures from the law were limited, and not due to incompetence but rather the jurors' perceptions of what was fair and just.[109]

Another empirical study by Professors Hastie, Penrod, and Pennington (ironically cited by the NACDL) found that while, individually, jurors' memory was not impressive, collectively, it was impressive—90 percent accurate recall regarding the facts and 80 percent correct regarding the law.[110] Accordingly, the empirical evidence establishes that, in fact, juries do, on the whole, listen, remember, and follow the instructions given to them by judges and do discriminate between defendants and between counts as to each defendant.

The NACDL next argues that defendants may use antagonistic defenses against each other in multidefendant trials. This assertion, too, calls into question the competence of jurors to understand evidence and heed judges' instructions not to use some evidence against some defendants. Additionally, research indicates that of reported RICO cases, only in nineteen opinions was it noted that antagonistic defenses were used. The problem hardly is, in fact, pervasive.

The NACDL also ignores the fact that the same people alleging antagonistic defenses might all be called to testify against each other in separate trials, a fact that cannot occur in joint trials. Joint trials may *protect* some defendants from each other.

Finally, the NACDL asserts that the jury may be confused by the introduction under RICO of forfeiture evidence into the trial. The report leads one to the assumption that this problem with forfeiture evidence is widespread. Nevertheless, no statistics are provided for the number of cases in which forfeiture evidence is so complex that it confuses the jury. In fact, empirical research indicates that in only eighteen opinions was it noted that it was necessary to bifurcate the trial to determine guilt and forfeiture separately. Indeed, bifurcation, rather than no trials at all, is preferable. The best solution to the problem regarding commingling of forfeiture evidence with evidence on guilt is, in short, already being employed by the courts when necessary: bifurcation and clear, cautionary instructions to the jury to consider the evidence separately.

The NACDL suggests that judges are reluctant to grant mistrials in RICO megatrials. Here, too, no data are provided indicating the number or percentage of times that judges decide to go on with a case, even though the defendant has suffered prejudice, just because the case has already lasted many months. This dilemma, too, is not specific to RICO. It occurs, if at all, in *any* length criminal or civil proceeding. Fortunately, in the event that a judge would fail to grant a mistrial when one is warranted, a built-in check exists in our system—the appeal.

Empirical research indicates that appellate courts are, in fact, willing to re-examine issues in RICO cases and to reverse lower court decisions if necessary. In 58.5 percent of the reported cases in the relevant time period, the disposition of the defendants was affirmed at the appellate level. But in 11.1 percent, the appeals court reversed and ordered a new trial, in 7.4 percent, the appeals court reversed and found not guilty one or more defendants, and in 9.1 percent, the appeals court remanded the case back to the trial court for additional determinations. These data establish, in short, that if trial courts commit mistakes, for example, by failing to grant a mistrial, appeals courts *are* willing to correct the error.

The NACDL proposes that one solution to this problem of "unendurably mammoth trials" is for judges to grant more or less automatic severances pursuant to Rule 14, Fed. R. Crim. P. The NACDL failed to consider two factors when it discussed the option of severances: (1) the facts and (2) the relative disadvantages of a policy of judges in each case routinely granting severances.

Empirical research indicates little need to grant more severances, certainly not automatically. At least 76.4 percent of all RICO cases are resolved in shorter than three months. Since several defendants can be tried in a relatively short period of time, no need exists automatically to break up the trial and repeat the introduction of the same evidence for each one of those defendants.[111]

The risk of prejudice to any particular defendant will, of course, increase as the number of defendants on trial increases. If it is apparent that a defendant will suffer compelling prejudice (even with clear, cautionary instructions given to the jury), then a severance is justified. Nevertheless, empirical research indicates that RICO trials do not typically involve great numbers of defendants. Out of all reported cases providing data during the relevant period, 53.3 percent of those involved fewer than five defendants; 88.5 percent of those cases involved fewer than fifteen defendants, and in only forty-four cases were more than fifteen defendants on trial together. Even in prosecutions with many defendants, a severance ought not be granted automatically, but only if it is clear that one or more of the defendants would have an unfair trial.

Beyond the goal of saving precious judicial resources, the nature of the sorts of crimes that RICO addresses requires joint trials, if at all feasible.[112] The NACDL, in its effort to protect the rights of the individual, fails to consider the impact that such heinous criminals have on our society through their massive frauds, drug networks, prostitution houses, illegal gambling rings, illegitimate business transactions, coercion of legitimate businesses through threats and extortion, and illegal gun sales to criminals and terrorists.[113]

Independent studies conclude that RICO is effective against sophisticated forms of crime. The President's Commission on Organized Crime had high praise for RICO and recommended that states adopt similar legislation.[114] The General Accounting Office, too, in its study of federal organized crime prosecutions concluded:

Prior to the passage of [RICO], attacking an organized criminal group was an awkward affair. RICO facilitates the prosecution of a criminal group involved in superficially unrelated criminal ventures and enterprises connected only at the usually well-insulated upper levels of the organization's bureaucracy. Before the act, the government's efforts were necessarily piecemeal, attacking isolated segments of the organization as they engaged in single criminal acts. The leaders, when caught, were only penalized for what seemed to be unimportant crimes. The larger meaning of these crimes was lost because the big picture could not be presented in a single criminal prosecution. With the passage of RICO, the entire picture of the organization's criminal behavior and the involvement of its leaders in directing that behavior could be captured and presented.[115]

The NACDL should have dealt with studies of this type in evaluating criminal RICO. That it did not substantially undercuts the soundness of its analysis.

Until the recent investigation, indictment, and conviction of Michael R. Milken, former head of Drexel Burnham Lambert Inc.'s junk bond operations, on ninety-eight counts of RICO and criminal securities fraud for cheating his clients,[116] the public controversy over efforts to modify RICO largely focused on its private civil enforcement mechanism; it now includes its criminal sanctions.

RICO authorizes the criminal forfeiture of ill-gotten gains and the interest of an offender in an enterprise run corruptly.[117] It also authorizes the issuance, on a proper showing, of pretrial restraints or the posting of a bond to prevent the dissipation before verdict of assets subject to forfeiture.[118] Such pretrial remedies are a common feature of civil litigation.[119]

The Milken indictment sought $1.85 billion in forfeitures from Milken and his codefendants.[120] Milken's alleged illegal earnings were exceeded only by those of Al Capone.[121] Milken agreed to post a bond of $700 million in cash and other assets to secure his portion of the forfeiture and to post bail in the amount of $1 million.[122] Drexel itself agreed to plead guilty to securities fraud and pay $650 million in fines and sanctions.[123] While Drexel publicly protested that it was unfairly forced to plead guilty, because of fear that pretrial restraints would put it out of business, it privately told its employees that, if indicted under RICO, it would "have the opportunity to post a bond to forestall any pretrial restraint, [which] will permit us to continue operations."[124] It also informed the U.S. District Court that its plea was "voluntary."[125] Although Milken at first said he would be vindicated at trial, he pleaded guilty, too.

Newspaper columnists decry RICO's pretrial restraints as an unconstitutional interference with the presumption of innocence.[126] In fact, individual defendants, on a proper showing, may be detained in jail before trial consistent with the Constitution.[127] It is doubtful that greater pretrial rights should be afforded property than liberty. Such columnists are also apparently ignorant of the usual features of civil litigation. Nevertheless, those who seek to reform RICO are not moving to alter its criminal provisions.[128]

RICO UNDER ATTACK: CIVIL

Congressman Frederick C. Boucher says: "[T]he federalization of thousands of mere commercial disputes, irrespective of the amount in controversy or the diversity of citizenship of the parties threatens to swamp a Federal judiciary that was never designed to handle these kinds of case."[129]

Until recently, separate data on civil RICO litigation were not kept by the Administrative Office of the United States Courts. The year 1985, however, was typical.[130] Approximately 275,000 civil cases were filed in 1985.[131] Approximately 39,000 criminal prosecutions were brought.[132] Slightly more than 118,000 of the civil cases involved the United States as a plaintiff or defendant; private litigation embraced approximately 160,000 filings, of which 60 percent were federal question and 40 percent were diversity litigation.[133]

The principal areas of litigation were recovery and overpayments and enforcement of judgments (47,000), prisoner petitions (30,000), Social Security (25,000), civil rights (20,000), and labor (11,000).[134] Antitrust included 959 civil filings[135] and 47 criminal cases.[136] Securities, commodities, and exchange-related civil filings made up 3,200 cases[137] and 13 criminal cases.[138] Fraud-related civil filings made up 1,700.[139] In fact, securities and fraud-based RICO litigation, which was initiated pre-*Sedima*, comprised 77 percent of the ABA (American Bar Association) study on civil RICO.[140] Accordingly, if most securities and fraud-related cases were also RICO cases, RICO filings would not exceed 5,000, not more than 2 percent of all federal filings.

How many wholly new pieces of litigation, particularly in the fraud area, RICO will draw into the federal courts cannot be reliably determined. It is doubtful, however, that the number will be relatively high, as most significant commercial litigation is now in the federal courts under other federal statutes or diversity jurisdiction. In fact, the Department of Justice indicated in 1985 that of the approximately 500 civil RICO cases brought pre-*Sedima*, 61 percent of them had an independent basis for federal jurisdiction.[141] More recently, Administrative Office data indicate that approximately 1,000 civil RICO cases are filed each year—not thousands.[142] As such, "the perceived problem of civil RICO case load is exaggerated."[143]

In fact, the decisions have now "calmed down" and "actually present no greater problem than antitrust or complicated securities cases."[144] In fact, too, docket congestion is not everywhere a problem.[145] While the absolute number of general filings has increased by roughly one-half, the average number of cases per federal judge from 1960 to 1980 has stayed about the same.[146] Indeed, from 1900 to 1980, the length of civil cases fell by over one-half.[147] The literature complaining about the litigation explosion, in short, shows "a strong admixture of naive speculation and undocumented assertion."[148]

Dire predictions of an explosion of new federal litigation, moreover, need to be put into perspective. Litigation itself, as the Supreme Court recognized in *Zauderer v. Office of Disciplinary Counsel of the Supreme Court of Ohio*,[149] is not "an evil." "Over the course of centuries," the Court noted, "our society has settled upon civil litigation as a means for redressing grievances, resolving disputes, and vindicating rights when other means fail."[150] "That our citizens have access to their civil court," the Court concluded, "is not an evil to be regretted; rather, it is an attribute of a system of justice in which we ought to take pride." Accordingly, it ought to be recognized that the mere *fact* of RICO suits is *not* a matter to be decried or deplored.

Ray J. Grover, a member of the American Institute of Certified Public Accountants, observed:

[T]he legislative history of the civil RICO confirms that Congress intended to create a weapon in the war against organized crime, but at no time did Congress envision that it was creating a powerful new weapon to be used against legitimate business people in ordinary commercial disputes having nothing whatsoever to do with organized crime.[151]

While RICO was aimed at organized crime, its use "as a weapon against 'white collar crime' is not contrary to the intent of Congress but is in fact one of the 'benefits' Congress saw the Act as providing.''[152] Writing in 1967, the President's Crime Commission, whose studies led to RICO, noted on the question of white-collar crime:

During the last few centuries economic life has become vastly more complex. Individual families or groups of families are not self-sufficient; they rely for the basic necessities of life on thousands or even millions of different people, each with a specialized function, many of whom live hundreds or thousands of miles away.

[W]hite-collar crime [is] [a term] now commonly used to designate those occupational crimes committed in the course of their work by persons of high status and social repute [that] . . . are only rarely dealt with through the full force of criminal sanctions. Serious erosions of morals accompanies [the white-collar offender's violation]. [Those who so] flout the law set an example for other businesses and influence individuals, particularly young people, to commit other kinds of crime on the ground that everybody is taking what he can get.[153]

David Albenda, New York Life Insurance Co., observed, ''The civil liability provisions of RICO were intended by Congress to protect legitimate businesses from infiltration by organized crime.''[154]

''[T]he major purpose of Title IX [was] to address the infiltration of legitimate business by organized crime.''[155] ''[W]e are unpersuaded [, however,] that Congress . . . confined RICO [to] *only* the infiltration of legitimate business.''[156]

Boucher says:

[F]raud allega*'ꞁns are commonly made in contract situations, and all that is needed to convert a simple contract dispute into a civil RICO case is the allegation that there was a contract and the additional allegation that either the mails or the telephones were used more than once in either forming or breaching the contract.[157]

In *H.J., Inc. v. Northwestern Bell Telephone Co.*[158] the Supreme Court made it abundantly clear that RICO does *not* apply to isolated acts. ''RICO is so broad-based that virtually any party that has become embroiled in a commercial dispute becomes a candidate for a civil RICO case. [V]irtually every type of contract dispute has been turned into a RICO case.''[159]

None of RICO's predicate offenses are applicable on a showing of strict liability. Each requires a showing of mens rea, or ''criminal intent.''[160]

N. Minow, reflecting views of Arthur Anderson & Co., says that no effective means exist for controlling frivolous litigation under RICO.[161] *The Report of the Proceedings of the Judicial Conference of the United States, Sept. 21–22, 1983* observes:

Judge Hunter stated that the Subcommittee on Judicial Improvements, at the request of Judge Alfred T. Goodwin, had explored ways and means to reduce frivolous or meritless litigation in the courts and had canvassed the various courts for ideas and suggestions. After consideration of the suggestions received, the Subcommittee concluded, as did many judges, that the existing tools are sufficient, but perhaps not fully understood or utilized.[162]

These tools are not only vigorously enforced, but the district courts are using a RICO Case Statement that requires plaintiffs to provide the court with a statement of what they expect to prove; it is then used to dismiss improper litigation. Rule 56, too, is now extensively used to curtail implausible claims. "[U]pon review . . . RICO abuse is not a serious problem for our legal system so long as counsel and courts appreciate the utility of existing remedial procedures. Accordingly, both Congress and the courts should recognize that abuse arguments are more likely motivated by hostility to the RICO remedy."[163]

Edward I. O'Brien, of the Securities Industry Association, observed: "[H]undreds of years of common law interpretation of state law fraud is completely subverted to RICO." "[The] nation [ought not] . . . abandon well over 200 years of common law development by the states of what fraudulent practices are."[164]

In the eighteenth and nineteenth centuries, state common-law fraud jurisprudence was developed in the context of the then-prevailing philosophies of laissez faire and caveat emptor, which were aptly summed up by Justice Dennison in *Queen v. Jones*: "[W]e are not to indict one man for making a fool of another."[165]

Congress found that sort of jurisprudence inadequate in 1970, when it enacted RICO.[166] Writing in 1967, the President's Crime Commission, whose studies led to RICO, noted in its *The Challenge of Crime in a Free Society*:

Fraud is especially vicious when it attacks, as it so often does, the poor or those who live on the margin of poverty. Expensive nostrums for incurable diseases, home improvement frauds, frauds involving the sale or repair of cars and other criminal schemes create losses which are not only sizable in gross but are also significant and possibly devastating for individual victims.[167]

Since 1970, twenty-nine states have enacted RICO-type legislation, twenty-two of which include the private multiple-damage suit. As such, the law of the eighteenth or nineteenth century can hardly be characterized—simply—as not "inadequate."

Congress, too, enacted legislation in the 1930s to deal with securities fraud, precisely because state fraud law in that area *was* inadequate to deal with "racketeering" on Wall Street.[168]

Voices were also heard in the 1930s that sought to repeal or modify the Securities Act of 1933. It was suggested that the legislation was so "draconian" that it would "dry up the nation's underwriting business and that 'grass' would grow on Wall Street."[169] Justice Frankfurter—then a professor and one of the leading spokesmen for the securities acts—put it well:

The leading financial law firms who have been systematically carrying on a campaign against [the Securities Act of 1933] have been seeking—now that they and their financial clients have come out of their storm cellar of fear—not to improve but to chloroform the Act. They evidently assume that the public is unaware of the sources of the issues that represent the boldest abuses of fiduciary responsibility.[170]

History repeats itself. If anything, the federal law that protects against securities and commodities fraud needs to be strengthened, not weakened.

Grover observed: "It is baseless to assert that the targets of the private Civil RICO cases that private lawyers have brought in the absence of prior convictions would have been prosecuted if only federal and state prosecutors had more resources."[171]

If this myth were true, it would justify the repeal of the antitrust statutes, which also contain a private multiple-damage claim for relief. Congress intended RICO's treble damage action to "provide strong incentives to civil litigants . . . in deterring racketeering."[172] RICO's treble damage provisions were "intended by Congress . . . to encourage private enforcement of the laws on which RICO is predicated."[173] As the antitrust laws seek to maintain economic freedom in the marketplace, so RICO seeks to promote integrity in the marketplace.

Then assistant attorney general, now judge, Steven S. Trott had this to say before the Senate Judiciary Committee about RICO's private enforcement mechanism:

[I]n gauging the overall deterrent value of auxiliary enforcement by private plaintiffs, the deterrence provided by the mere threat of private suits must be added to the deterrence supplied by the suits that are actually filed. Furthermore, as the federal government's enforcement efforts continue to weaken organized crime and dispel the myth of invulnerability that has long surrounded and protected its members, private plaintiffs may become more willing to pursue RICO's attractive civil remedies in organized crime contexts. It should be remembered, too, that civil RICO has significant deterrent potential when used by institutional plaintiffs, such as units of state and local governments, which are not likely to be intimidated at the prospect of suing organized crime members. Finally, civil RICO's utility against continuous large-scale criminality not involving traditional organized crime elements should be kept in mind. These considerations suggest that private civil RICO enforcement in the area of the organized criminality may have had a greater deterrent impact than is commonly recognized, and that both the threat and the actuality of private enforcement might be expected to produce even greater deterrence in the future.[174]

Public enforcement with its principal reliance on the criminal law cannot be relied on to do the whole job of policing fraud. As Justice Jackson observed, "The criminal law has long proved futile to reach the subtler kinds of fraud at all, and able to reach grosser fraud, only rarely."[175] We must, in short, be candid about the limitations of the criminal justice system in the white-collar crime area. Resources available for investigation and prosecution are scarce. The common-law criminal trial is ponderous. The cases are complex. Offenders will be most often treated as "first offenders" even if they actually engaged in a pattern of behavior over a substantial period of time. A few convictions will yield only a minimal deterrent effect.

Public agencies, moreover, will never be funded at adequate levels. The funding of the Securities and Exchange Commission (SEC), for example, has increased since 1979, but its staffing has decreased, and its pending investigations are down. The SEC's annual budget is only $137 million, which is a little less than 25 percent of Milken's 1987 salary and bonuses.[176] Yet the number of shares traded on the New York Stock Exchange has shot up 300 percent since 1977; the number of first-time registrants has increased by 260 percent.[177] Even among legitimate brokerage firms, the incentive structure for commissions encourages a fraud known as "churning," trading stock without regard for investment objectives. Similarly, the futures industry in the United States has grown tremendously in recent years. The 139.9 million futures contracts traded in 1983 represent a level of trading activity fifteen times greater than that reached in 1968. The value of contracts traded exceeds $5 trillion a year. Nevertheless, the resources of the Commodities Futures Trading Commission have remained relatively constant. Its annual budget is only $36.5 million.[178] In 1983, it was suggested that the industry was a scandal waiting to happen, for the commission was thoroughly outgunned in the ongoing battle against commodity fraud.[179] The developments in 1989 in Chicago and New York were that scandal.[180]

The accounting industry, too, once thought to play the role of an outside watchdog, is under heavy competitive pressure to go along with questionable annual reports, and it is increasingly losing its independence, since it also offers management consulting advice.[181] "After a spectacular string of corporate failures and financial scandals in recent years, the industry that is supposed to audit company books and sniff out chicanery" is itself coming under close scrutiny.[182] The General Accounting Office is sharply critical of the accounting profession for its role in failing to uncover the widespread fraud and mismanagement that are contributing to the multibillion savings and loan association scandal.[183] The Federal Home Loan Bank Board is suing ten accounting firms, including Cooper & Lybrand, Grant Thornton, and Touche Ross, which audited failed thrifts.[184] "Some auditors may have been too close to their clients and allowed them to do things that they shouldn't have done. I'm not sure the industry was as independent as it should have been," observes Arthur Bowman, the editor of *Bowman Accounting Report*, an Atlanta-based newsletter.[185] Indeed, the Big Eight, insiders say, are agreeing not to testify against one another.[186] No wonder that the accounting profession is a major contributor to the political campaigns of those in the forefront of the effort to disembowel RICO.[187] Theodore C. Barreaux, vice-president of the American Institute of Certified Public Accountants (AICPA), attributes the Department of Justice's switch in 1988 from opposition to support of the prior criminal conviction limitation on RICO to a series of meetings between AICPA lawyers and department officials.[188] Drexel Burnham Lambert, Inc., too, has put $250,000 into the anti-RICO campaign.[189] The need for a more effective deterrent to fraud in the world of legitimate business is, therefore, manifest.

Charles L. Marinaccio, Securities and Exchange commissioner, observed:

The RICO civil remedy may substantially alter the balance of private and public rights and remedies under the securities law that Congress and the courts have carefully crafted over the last 50 years. . . . It enables plaintiffs to claim treble damages even in cases where Congress has expressly limited recovery under the securities laws to actual damages. [The Securities Acts private claims for relief] have served well with only actual damages as supplements to other enforcement mechanisms.[190]

It is, of course, correct that the Securities Acts provide for only actual damages. It can hardly be contended, however, that they have worked as an adequate compensatory scheme or mechanism for the deterrence of systematic fraudulent practices in light of the recent inside information trading scandals. The *Wall Street Journal* aptly observed:

The abuse of inside information in the take-over game is endemic and has grown systematically over the past half-decade . . . .

Whatever specific numbers come out in the unfolding federal probe, it's probably a safe bet they'll vastly understate the total losses incurred by stock-market investors, as well as many target companies that no longer exist and their acquirers, who doubtless paid too dearly for them.[191]

The need for a strengthened private enforcement mechanism, including multiple damages, is manifest. When Milken was indicted, acting U.S. attorney Benito Romano observed, "The three-year investigation has uncovered substantial fraud in a very significant segment of the American financial community. A serious problem has infected Wall Street."[192] The stock market and the futures market operate well only when people have confidence. Small investors today are avoiding the market.[193] Households today own 58.5 percent of U.S. stocks compared with 82.2 percent in 1968.[194] Wendy Gramm, the chairwoman of the Commodities Futures Trading Commission, put it succinctly, "If customers feel they are being ripped off by an exchange or that the exchange is not vigilant against fraud, they will leave the markets."[195]

The idea of multiple damages for certain kinds of unlawful practices has deep roots. The earliest such provision in English law was the Statute of Gloucester.[196] Modern antitrust statutes had their origin in the Statute Against Monopolies.[197] Parliament recognized that it was "one thing to pass statutes and . . . quite another thing to insure that [they were] actually enforced."[198] Accordingly, "It was a common expedient [in the Middle Ages and beyond] to give the public at large an interest in seeing that a statute was enforced."[199] It was also an idea found in early colonial laws.[200] In turn, the idea of multiple damages for various kinds of wrongs was a characteristic feature of Roman law. The "delict" of theft ran back at least to the Twelve Tables (450 B.C.).[201] "[T]he penalty . . . [was] four times the value of the thing stolen" when the offender was caught in the act; otherwise, it was double.[202] Extortion was remedied by four times the loss.[203] Possession of stolen property was remedied by three times the value of the property.[204] Greek law provided for double damage if stolen property was recovered; tenfold damages otherwise.[205] Biblical law, too, reflected multiple damage recovery.[206]

Modern economic analysis supports the wisdom of this history.[207] Indeed, a number of federal statutes, particularly in the commercial area, contain treble damage provisions.[208] If society authorizes the recovery of only actual damages for deliberate antisocial conduct engaged in for profit, it lets the perpetrator know that if he is caught, he must return the misappropriated sums. If he is not caught, he may keep the money. Even if he is caught and sued, he may be able to defeat part of the damage claim or at least compromise it. In short, the balance of economic risk under traditional single damage recovery provides little economic disincentive to those who would engage in such conduct.[209] In fact, as the court in *Haroco, Inc. v. American National Bank & Trust Co. of Chicago* observed:

It is also true that the delays, expense and uncertainties of litigation often compel plaintiffs to settle completely valid claims for a mere fraction of their value. By adding to the settlement value of such valid claims in certain cases clearly involving criminal conduct, RICO may arguably promote more complete satisfaction of plaintiffs' claims without facilitating indefensible windfalls.[210]

Similarly, studies under the antitrust statute show that most treble damage suits are now settled at close to actual damages. No reason exists to believe that a similar pattern will not develop under RICO, at least in the fraud area. Ironically, it may be necessary to authorize treble damages to assure that deserving victims receive actual damages.

Boucher says:

RICO allows plaintiffs to raise the stakes significantly in . . . [commercial disputes] because a civil RICO claim carries with it the threat of treble damages, attorney's fees, and the opprobrium of being labeled a "racketeer." As Justice Marshall concluded in examining the current situation created by civil RICO: "Many a prudent defendant, facing ruinous exposure, will decide to settle even a case with no merit. It is thus not surprising that civil RICO has been used for extorsive purposes, giving rise to the very evils that it was designed to combat."[211]

Philip A. Feign, assistant securities commissioner, Colorado Division of Securities, and spokesman for the North American Securities Administrators Association before the Senate Judiciary Committee, aptly observed:

Euphemisms like "commercial disputes," "commercial frauds," "garden variety frauds" and "technical violations" . . . are sanitized phrases often used by "legitimate businesses and individuals" to distinguish their frauds from the "real" frauds perpetrated by the "real" crooks. Yet all wilful fraudulent conduct has in common the elements of premeditation, planning, motivation, execution over time, and injury to victims and commerce. And it is all crime.[212]

Indeed, it was persuasively argued in 1934 before the Copeland Committee that it was in part our failure as a society to bring white-collar crime to justice that significantly contributed to the development during Prohibition of what all now concede to be organized crime, a problem that did not end with Prohibition's repeal.

It is simply not true, moreover, that the "racketeer" label results in extortionate settlements. As quoted by Boucher, Justice Marshall suggests that "a prudent defendant, facing ruinous exposure [under RICO], will decide to settle even a case with no merit."[213] Accordingly, civil RICO lends itself, he argued, to the very extortive purpose "it was designed to combat." Justice Marshall cites as authority for this extraordinary proposition the *Ad Hoc Civil RICO Task Force: Corporations, etc.*[214] The Ad Hoc Task Force, in turn, conducted a survey of 3,200 corporate litigation lawyers, of whom only 350 responded. Two factors, however, undermine the scientific credibility of the general results of the survey: (1) the population questioned was unrepresentative of the bar, and (2) the response rate was insufficient to warrant broad generalizations. More to the point here, the survey did *not* ask the respondents a carefully phrased question calling for their opinion or experience with RICO as a settlement weapon. Instead, the opinion relied upon by Marshall was *volunteered* by only 2 of the 350 respondents as grounds for repealing RICO. In fact, it is the experience of a majority of seasoned litigators in the RICO area that adding a RICO claim to a suit does *not* facilitate settlement; it inhibits it, particularly when a legitimate business is involved.[215]

Generally, businesses wrongfully accused of "racketeering" will not settle suits—even those that should be compromised—as long as the racketeer label is in the litigation. Indeed, it is difficult to understand how Marshall or Boucher could believe that a suit with "no merit" faces a defendant with "ruinous exposure." If the plaintiff's suit has *no* merit, his chance of success is zero, and zero multiplied by three (or any other number) is still zero. Before one accepts the task force's, Marshall's, or Boucher's claim, one ought to ask for the name of the defendants and the cases allegedly so settled and then inquire of the plaintiffs what their evidence was. It is doubtful that it will be found that the litigation was meritless. It is doubtful, in short, that responsible corporate or other defendants are paying off strike suits in the RICO—or any other area— at more than their settlement value, no matter what the theory of the complaint is. Neither the racketeer label nor the threat of treble damages will convince prudent managers to surrender lightly scarce resources, merely because another files a suit. No matter how colorfully it is phrased, the claim that such managers act against their own interest is not credible.

Finally, white-collar crime, principally fraud, is no "garden-variety" problem in the United States today. Current estimates put it in the $200 billion range. That figure is similar in dimension to the cost of the drug problem.[216] Commodities investment fraud, for example, costs $200 million.[217] Bank fraud, particularly by insiders, is also deeply disturbing. In the 1980–81 period, the failure of 105 banks and savings and loans cost $1 billion. Roughly one-half of the bank failures and one-quarter of the savings and loan collapses had as a major contributing factor criminal activities by insiders, few of whom, according to the findings of a study by the Bernard Committee, were adequately sanctioned, criminally or civilly. In 1984, the committee noted:

Despite such enormous losses, neither the banking nor the criminal justice systems impose effective sanctions or punishment to deter white-collar bank fraud. The few insiders who are singled out for civil sanctions by the banking agencies are usually either fined de minimis amounts or simply urged to resign. The few who are criminally prosecuted usually serve little, if any, time in prison for thefts that often cost millions of dollars.[218]

Since then, the Federal Deposit Insurance Corporation (FDIC) has reported that bank failures, more than 100 per year, continued to run at postdepression record levels.[219] Most banks, in fact, do not have the financial resources or the expertise to protect themselves from sophisticated schemes to defraud. According to testimony of the FDIC, 97 percent of the federally insured banks have assets of less than $500 million; 84 percent less than $100 million; 66 percent less than $50 million.[220] In 1988, the Bernard Committee reaffirmed and went beyond its basic 1984 findings.[221]

Attorney General Richard Thornberg concurs; he told the Senate Banking Committee on 10 February 1986 that 25 to 30 percent of all thrift failures were attributable to fraud; in 1988 alone, it accounted, he said, for $2 billion in losses. Yet, he reported, only 172 individuals had been convicted, and few received sentences in excess of twelve months, while most received probation and community service.[222] "When [judges] see nicely dressed bankers, it is difficult to send them away for a long time," commented Rosemary Steward, the director of enforcement at the Home Loan Bank Board.[223] The attorney general also lamented, "I think we'd be fooling ourselves to think any substantial portion of those assets are going to be recovered."[224] Finally, criminal and civil RICO is being used by the Department of Justice and the banking agencies in the thrift crisis.[225] Nothing should be done that would undermine the effectiveness of RICO in this crucial area.

The bank and savings and loan crises on the federal level are paralleled at the state level by the collapse of insurance companies. From 1969 through 1983, state guarantee funds assessed healthy insurers only $454 million to cover claims of insolvent members.[226] But in 1987, 234 companies were in liquidation, and

74 companies were in reorganization.[227] State guarantee funds paid out in 1987 a record $909 million to bail out the failures.[228] "Autopsies of several failed insurers across the country have turned up evidence of frauds and inadequate regulations."[229] "[T]he indirect cost to taxpayers already is growing, because insurers deduct from state taxes their rising assessments from guaranty funds."[230] A special report by Arthur Anderson & Co. concluded that "a noticeable number of insurance company insolvencies [would occur] over the next five to seven years."[231] The industry holds a large portion of the "junk bonds" issued by corporate America as well as large portfolios of real estate, each of which is particularly vulnerable to an economic downturn, as in the savings and loan crisis.[232]

The insurance industry is also facing "what may become the biggest financial scandal in the history of Medicare: the misspending of as much as $10 billion in Medicare funds over the past six years."[233] The subjects of the developing investigation by the Department of Justice include some of the nation's biggest insurance companies. During the same period, America's elderly saw their annual deductible in hospital care and doctor care more than double.[234]

Ultimately, most of the costs of fraud are passed on to the rest of society. Indeed, the "insurance crisis" that has led legislatures to rewrite our liability laws to curtail personal injury litigation might be better dealt with by enforcing vigorously our laws against fraud, for the insurance industry loses more than twice as much each year from fraud as it says it lost overall, for example, in 1986 because of the crisis in personal injury litigation. While the cost of vexatious litigation is generally spread throughout society of directors and officers liability insurance, too often the cost of fraud is not shared through various kinds of insurance, and it rests on the shoulders of the victim, who can ill afford to carry or sustain it. Indeed, in light of Ohio's experience with the failure of E.S.M. Government Securities, Inc., including a paid-for false audit report and the repercussions it caused in the savings and loan industry and on the gold market, no one ought seriously to contend that such fraud is a "garden-variety" problem, which may be "weeded out" with business-as-usual legal techniques.[235]

In addition, the collapse of the E.S.M. Company led to the insolvency of Home State Savings Bank in Ohio and the shutdown of sixty-nine privately insured thrift institutions. Subsequently, the accounting firm of Grant Thornton reached a $22.5 million settlement with the American Savings and Loan Association, which lost $55.3 million; it also reached a $50 million settlement with seventeen municipal governments, which sued under RICO.[236] Without RICO, it is doubtful that such a favorable settlement could have been obtained for at least some of the victims.

Judge Milton J. Shadur observed in *P.M.F. Services v. Grady*: "[Civil RICO] was a late edition, spot-welded to an already fully-structured criminal statute."[237]

P.M.F. Services was written by Shadur. His views of the legislative history of civil RICO, which were first expressed in *Kaushal v. State Bank of India*,[238] were followed by the Second Circuit in *Sedima S.P.L.F. v. Imrex Co.*[239] Their "precedential value however, . . . is [now in] considerable doubt . . . [because of] the Supreme Court's total rejection of the conclusions drawn . . . from . . . [Shadur's] historical analysis of . . . RICO" in *Sedima*.[240] They are also plainly wrong.

In 1967, the President's Commission on Law Enforcement and Administration of Justice recommended the adoption of antitrust-type remedies to control sophisticated forms of crime.[241] Bills were introduced in the Senate and House; they included the private enforcement provisions.[242] The American Bar Association testified in the Senate in favor of the treble damage remedy.[243] The president, at that time, added his favorable voice for the treble damage remedy.[244] The Senate passed the bill, of course, with only express government criminal and civil relief, but it is likely a private claim for relief for actual damages would have been implied in the statute based on 1970 jurisprudence.[245] Nevertheless, when the Bar Association testified in the House[246] that the private enforcement mechanism should be added back, it was restored to the bill, accepted by the Senate, and signed by the president. Contrary to Shadur's conclusion in *P.M.F. Services*, RICO is not, in short, a criminal statute with an ill-designed treble damage afterthought.[247] Shadur is just flatly wrong.

Shadur's views on RICO, too, are often reversed or rejected by the Seventh Circuit, which knows his work best.[248] Shadur's single scheme decision on "pattern" was also rejected by the Supreme Court in *H.J. Inc. v. North Western Bell Telephone Co.*[249] Typically, Shadur's analyses are not only wrong but also superficial.

The charges that RICO was being abused in the civil context were, until recently, just that: charges. Now, however, a coalition business group seeking to undermine RICO has produced a list of cases that it terms "abusive."[250] Since the coalition had been in existence for almost five years—and it was richly financed—it is fair to assume that these cases represented the most egregious examples that time and money could find of "litigation abuse" under RICO. As such, the coalition's overall position against civil RICO may be fairly said to stand or fall on the basis of this list. Nevertheless, when it is carefully analyzed and researched, it does not warrant the reforms being proposed to substantially undermine the private civil enforcement mechanism. In fact, the list indicates that little relationship exists between the allegations of abuse and the suggested evisceration of RICO. The allegations of abuse may, therefore, be appropriately termed a smoke screen behind which special interests are seeking to enact laws for their private benefit.

To summarize the coalition's allegations and a careful analysis of them, the coalition has produced a list of fifty-three cases it terms "abusive." The first case was filed in December 1979. The last case was filed in January 1988. Between December 1979 and January 1988, approximately 1,910,520 cases were filed in the federal district courts.[251] Of that number, approximately 2742 were

RICO filings.[252] These "abusive" cases, therefore, constitute only .003 percent of total filings and 1.9 percent of the RICO filings.

Of these fifty-three cases, 53 percent had an independent basis for federal jurisdiction. These cases, as well as the general data,[253] do not establish that RICO filings are of floodgate proportions or are wholly new. Of the fifty-three "abusive" cases, none represented a judgment for money damages. None were brought by government-related entities. Only two were brought by charitable organizations. Only two were against accountants, one of the professions that is a moving force in the coalition. Only four included securities allegations. None was a commodities case.

The charges of litigation abuse totally ignore the presence, in current law, of more than adequate remedies against such abuse, not only under RICO but under other federal statutes and related claims for relief. Indeed, this absent recognition is the most telling point against the civil RICO critics' charges of litigation abuse.

Those who would rewrite civil RICO have the burden of proof to show

1. that a *substantial* number of frivolous or otherwise abusive RICO suits are being filed,

2. that *existing* safeguards against such suits are not adequate to remedy them,

3. that *new* safeguards adequate against such suits *cannot* be designed, and

4. that the detriment from these suits *outweighs* the benefit from legitimate suits.

None of these burdens have been met.

Ethical standards, for example, prohibit the assertion by "a lawyer . . . [of a] position in litigation that is frivolous."[254] It is also subject to sanctions under the Federal Rules of Civil Procedure.[255] Indeed, these sanctions are being employed under RICO in proper circumstances.[256] The high cost of litigation itself erects a substantial barrier, in front of not only frivolous litigation but also meritorious pleas. Contingent fee arrangements mitigate the issue of cost to the poor, but wronged individual; they also act, however, as a screening device employed by counsel, who risk their own funds, to weed out cases where liability is not sure and damages are not high.

The existing system is able to weed out inappropriate cases. Eighty-seven percent of the coalition's "abusive" cases were dismissed in whole or in part on one or more grounds. Thirty-two percent were properly dismissed on "pattern" grounds in such a fashion that they will not be refiled, and similar cases should not appear in the future. Motions for sanctions were made in only 19 percent of the cases; they were granted in 8 percent (or 40 percent of the motions). As such, the defendants themselves apparently did not always believe the cases were frivolous. Many times, the early decisions did not grant the sanctions requested because the courts expressed doubt about the proper construction of the statute. Later cases, however, tend to include the granting of sanctions when they are requested. Ironically, the list of "abusive" cases actually includes a suit against an organized crime figure. In addition, the list includes a suit against a figure who had been charged and convicted for criminal behavior. The cases, moreover, include clear instances of judicial abuse of the statute rather than litigant abuse. In short, the case for RICO "abuse" has not been made. In fact, on careful analysis, the existing system is seen to be working well.

CONCLUSION

When the delegates to the Constitutional Convention met in Philadelphia in that hot summer of 1786, they represented sovereign states, whose preindustrial economics were mainly focused inwardly but in which a substantial element of international trade existed. A key element of the new Constitution that they wrote that summer was the attempt to create a "common market" throughout the new nation, something that it has taken the European democracies 200 years to come to see the benefit of and that will not be realized by them until 1994 or beyond.

The Constitution that the Founders designed and the people, through state conventions, ratified, was not, however, an example of pure federalism. It was, as James Madison put it in *Federalist No. 39*, "in strictness, neither a national nor a federal constitution, but a composition of both."[257] In fact, plenary powers were granted to the federal government, which would operate directly to achieve the ends desired. Other powers were, of course, reserved to the states or to the people. Among the plenary powers granted to the federal government was the power to regulate "commerce."[258]

The hopes of the Founders for a "common market" were realized beyond their highest expectations. At all levels of government, efforts were made to develop the nation's economy.[259]

Today, consumers everywhere realize the benefits of our "common market"—with its economies of scale, which come from its nationwide breadth, and its most fundamental and characteristic feature, free competition, which helps keep prices down and makes diverse choices by consumers possible.

But if the dreams of the late eighteenth and nineteenth centuries are today largely realized in our free enterprise system, the twentieth century has its own problems. National and state laws make possible our free enterprise system with its common market. These laws must now maintain it. Economically, we aspire to "allocative efficiency"; that is, consumers, exercising their "sovereignty," make their individual choices, the aggregate of which controls the allocation of goods and services and marshals the forces of production. When that individual choice is maximized, economic "efficiency" is realized. But "allocative efficiency . . . [is] consistent with the poor starving and the economy's productive activity channelled into the manufacture of . . . luxury items."[260] Justice, too, has its demands. Professor L. Friedman succinctly makes the point:

Legal decisions are by their very nature economic. They allocate scarce goods and services. The legal system is in this sense a rationing system. What it does and what it is reflects the distribution of power in society—who is on top and who is on the bottom; law also sees to it that this social structure stays stable or changes only in approved and patterned ways. The system issues commands, extends benefits, and tells people what they can or cannot do; in each case, the rule of law, if followed, has made some choice about who has or keeps or gets what good. Rules of law reflect past decisions about allocations. Some conflicts or disputes occurred or threatened to occur between people or groups. Inconsistent wants were expressed. Two men fought over one piece of land. Farmers wanted high prices, consumers wanted low. The resulting legal act (rule or decision) chose among possible alternatives. Very likely it was some kind of compromise, but it was surely an allocation. Every function of the law, general or specific, is allocative.[261]

Over the years, Congress and various state legislatures have enacted laws to preserve, strengthen, or modify how our national economy works, seeing to their enforcement through criminal, civil, and regulatory means. They include federal and state antitrust statutes, money and banking statutes, labor legislation (including statutes dealing variously with wages, hours, working conditions, health and safety, and welfare and pension funds), food and drug laws, securities statutes, environmental legislation, and so on. The list is long. RICO legislation, too, fits well into that pattern of twentieth-century economic and social legislation.

Our marketplace must not only be free but also be characterized by integrity—physical, personal, and institutional. Street crime (e.g., murder, rape, robbery, juvenile delinquency) is, and will remain, a problem principally of the legal systems of state and local governments. Organized crime (e.g., narcotics, labor racketeering) and white-collar crime (e.g., price fixing, political corruption, fraud)—each an inevitable incident of our free enterprise system—are, and will remain, problems principally addressed by the legal systems of the federal and state governments.

Criminal RICO prosecutions did not begin until around 1975, but since 1970, they have occurred at the rate of about 125 per year.[262] Roughly 39 percent have been in the organized crime area (not Mafia alone, but also drugs, gambling, labor racketeering, and so on), while 48 percent have been in the white-collar crime area (corruption of government, general fraud in the private sector, securities and commodities fraud, and so on). Thirteen percent fall into other categories (violent groups, including terrorists, white-hate, anti-Semitic, and so on).[263]

Civil RICO litigations did not begin until around 1980, but since 1970, they have occurred at the rate of about eighty-five per month out of 23,000 civil filings; 60 percent of them, too, have an independent basis for federal jurisdiction.

As such, while no one can deny that criminal and civil RICO litigation is, and has been, controversial, the statute's two-track system of public and private enforcement, which was modeled on the antitrust statutes, is today, after an uncertain start, operating largely as it was originally designed. Its impact on organized crime and white-collar crime is, and promises to be, substantial. Federal and state officials and private parties, using alternative criminal and civil sanctions, are forging partnerships to work toward a more just society.

The federal government's experience with RICO, therefore, establishes that it is working well—criminally and civilly—to hold those who misuse power in our society accountable and to keep our markets free and honest.

NOTES

1. 84 Stat. 923 (1970).
2. 84 Stat. 923 (1970).
3. 18 U.S.C. §§ 1963, 1964(c).
4. 116 *Cong. Rec.* 35–37264 (1970).
5. See *Myths* at 988–1011 (chart of state statutes).
6. *In Re Action Industries Tender Offer*, 572 F.Supp. 846, 849 (E.D. Va. 1983). See 116 *Cong. Rec.* 602 (1970) (Statement of Sen. Hruska).
7. *Sedima S.P.R.L. v. Imrex, Inc.*, 473 U.S. 479, 497–98 (1985); *United States v. Turkette*, 452 U.S. 576, 593 (1981).
8. *United States v. Cappetto*, 502 F.2d 1351, 1357 (7th Cir. 1974), *cert. denied*, 420 U.S. 925 (1975); *Wilcox v. First Interstate Bank of Oregon*, 815 F.2d 522, 530–32 (9th Cir. 1987).
9. *Russello v. United States*, 464 U.S. 16, 21 (1983).
10. *Lou v. Belzberg*, 834 F.2d 730, 737 (9th Cir. 1987) (quoting *Sedima*, 473 U.S. at 492 n.10), *cert. denied*, 405 U.S. 993 (1988).
11. *Sedima*, 473 U.S. at 489.
12. *Turkette*, 452 U.S. at 586.
13. 84 Stat. at 947.
14. *Haroco v. American Nat'l Bank and Trust Co. of Chicago*, 747 F.2d 384, 392 (7th Cir. 1984), *aff'd.*; 473 U.S. 6060 (1985).
15. *S.E.C. v. National Securities, Inc.*, 393 U.S. 453, 468 (1969).
16. *Herman & McLean v. Huddleston*, 459 U.S. 375, 386 (1983).
17. *Schreiber Distributing Co. v. Serv-Well Furniture Co.*, 806 F.2d 1393, 1396–98 (9th Cir. 1986).
18. *Medallion Television Enterprises, Inc. v. SelecTV of California, Inc.*, 833 F.2d 1360, 1362 (9th Cir. 1987).
19. *Sun Savings & Loan Ass'n v. Dierdorff*, 825 F.2d 187, 191 (9th Cir. 1987) (citing *Sedima*, 473 U.S. at 496).
20. See "Conspiracy to Violate RICO," *Notre Dame Law Review* 58 (1983): note, 1001.
21. 719 F.2d 5,17 (2d Cir. 1983), *cert. denied*, 465 U.S. 1025 (1984).
22. 18 U.S.C. § 1963. Under the Sentencing Guidelines 2E1.1, the minimum base level of RICO is 19 (30 to 37 months).
23. 18 U.S.C. § 1963.
24. Pub. L. No. 91–513, 84 Stat. 1236 (1970), *codified at*, 21 U.S.C. § 801 et. seq.
25. *United States v. McKeithen*, 822 F.2d 310, 314–315 (2d Cir. 1987).
26. Pub. L. No. 101–73, 103 Stat. 103 (1989).
27. *New York Trust Co. v. Eisner*, 256 U.S. 345, 349 (1921) (Holmes, J.).

28. See, for example, *United States v. Caporale*, 806 F.2d 1487, 1509 (11th Cir. 1986), *cert. denied*, 482 U.S. 913 (1987).

29. Fed. R. Crim. Pro. Rule 7 (c) (2).

30. Id. Rule 31(e).

31. Id. Rule 32 (b) (2).

32. *United States v. Amend*, 791 F.2d 1120, 1127 (4th Cir. 1986).

33. *United States v. McKeithen*, 822 F.2d 310, 312–15 (2d Cir. 1987) (CCE).

34. 21 U.S.C. § 848 (criminal); 21 U.S.C. § 881 (civil).

35. *United States v. One 1978 Mercedes Benz Four-Door Sedan*, 711 F.2d 1297, 1300–03 (5th Cir. 1983).

36. *United States v. One 1980 Rolls Royce*, 905 F.2d 89, 91 (5th Cir. 1990).

37. 9 Uniform Law Annotated 187 (Supp. 1983).

38. Id. at Section 505, 611–14.

39. Id. at 78.

40. See, for example, *Ariz. Rev. Stat. Ann.* § 13–2314 (Supp. 1 1983).

41. L. Harper, *The English Navigation Laws: A Seventeenth-Century Experiment in Social Engineering* at 109, 387–414 (1964).

42. See, for example, III William Blackstone, *Commentaries* (Washington, DC: Washington Law Books Co., 1941) at 262.

43. See, for example, IV William Blackstone, *Commentaries* (Washington, DC: Washington Law Books Co., 1941) at 374–381.

44. M. Radin, *Anglo-American Legal History* at 234 (1936).

45. Id. at 240.

46. IV *Blackstone*, id. at 95–96.

47. Radin, id. *Anglo-American*, at 240.

48. Compare, *Calero-Toledo v. Pearson Yacht Leasing Co.*, 416 U.S. 663, 680–683 (1974) with *Forfeiture* at 771–772.

49. *Calero-Toledo*, 416 U.S. at 681.

50. *American Journal of Legal History* 6 (1962): 250.

51. U.S. Cons. art I, § 9, cl. 3.

52. Id. at art III, § 3, cl. 2.

53. 1 Stat. 117, c. 9, § 24 (1790), *codified at* 18 U.S.C. § 3563.

54. *United States v. 1960 Bags of Coffee*, 12 U.S. 398, 399 (1814).

55. 133 U.S. 1, 16–17 (1890).

56. *The Palmyra*, 25 U.S. (12 Wheat) 1, 15 (1827).

57. 116 U.S. 436, 444–45 (1886).

58. 465 U.S. 354 (1984).

59. *J. W. Goldsmith, Jr.-Grant Co. v. United States*, 254 U.S. 505 (1921).

60. *Calero-Toledo v. Pearson Yacht Leasing Co.*, 416 U.S. 663, (1974).

61. S. Rep. No. 617, 91st Cong., 1st Sess. 81 (1969); H. R. Rep. No. 1549, 91st Cong., 2d Sess. 56–60 (1970).

62. *United States v. Topco Associates*, 405 U.S. 596, 610 (1972).

63. *Reiter v. Sonotone Corp.*, 442 U.S. 330, 344 (1979).

64. *Leh v. General Petroleum Corp.*, 382 U.S. 54, 59 (1965).

65. *Reiter*, 442 U.S. at 344.

66. *Blue Shield of Virginia v. McCready*, 457 U.S. 465, 472 (1982).

67. *Agency Holding v. Mally-Duff & Associates.*, 483 U.S. 143, 151 (1987).

68. *Russello*, 464 U.S. at 26.

69. *Turkette*, 452 U.S. at 591.

70. *Turkette*, 452 U.S. at 590.

71. *United States v. Grande*, 620 F.2d 1026, 1030 (4th Cir.), *cert. denied*, 449 U.S. 919 (1980).

72. 472 U.S. 229, 244–48 (1989).

73. *Sedima*, 473 at 495.

74. *United States v. Altomere*, 625 F.2d 5, 7 (4th Cir. 1980).

75. See, for example, 18 U.S.C. § 1951, (Extortion) held not limited to racketeering in *United States v. Culbert*, 435 U.S. 371, 373–74 (1978); 18 U.S.C. § 1952, (Travel Act) held not limited to organized crime bribery in *Perrin v. United States*, 444 U.S. 37, 46 (1979); 18 U.S.C. § 1953, (lottery tickets) held not limited to organized crime in *United States v. Fabrizio*, 385 U.S. 263, 265–67 (1966); 18 U.S.C. § 2113(b), (bank robbery) held not limited to gangsters in *Bell v. United States*, 462 U.S. 356, 358–62 (1983); 18 U.S.C. § 2421 (1982), (white slave traffic) held not limited to commercial prostitution in *Caminetti v. United States*, 242 U.S. 470, 485–90 (1917). See generally, *Equitable Relief* at 529 n.13 (other cases collected).

76. See *Oversight on Civil RICO Suits, Hearings Before the Senate Committee on the Judiciary*, 99th Cong., 1st Sess., 109–11 (1985) (testimony of Assistant Attorney General Stephen S. Trott) (*Trott*).

77. Id. at 116–17 (litigation against Mob-controlled unions reviewed).

78. *United States v. Brooklier*, 685 F.2d 1208, 1213 (9th Cir. 1982).

79. *United States v. Friedman*, 854 F.2d 535, 541 (2nd Cir. 1988).

80. *United States v. Marubeni America Corp.*, 611 F.2d 763 (9th Cir. 1980).

81. *United States v. Yarbrough*, 852 F.2d 1522 (9th Cir. 1988).

82. See Horn, *Judicial Plague Sweeps United States "Result Orientitis" Infects Civil RICO Decisions*, 5 Nat'l. L.J., May 23, 1983, at 31, col. 1.

83. *Trott* at 127.

84. *Alcorn County Miss. v. U.S. Interstate Supplies*, 731 F.2d 1160, 1167 (5th Cir. 1984) (cases cited).

85. *Schacht v. Brown*, 711 F.2d 1343, 1356–58 (7th Cir.), *cert. denied*.

86. The Second Circuit suggested in *Sedima* that civil RICO suits against "respected and legitimate enterprises" were "extraordinary, if not outrageous." *Sedima S.P.R.L. v. Imrex Co., Inc.*, 741 F.2d 482, 487 (2d Cir. 1984), *rev'd.*, 473 U.S. 479 (1985).

87. *United States v. Hoey*, 131 F.2d 525, 526 (2d Cir. 1942).

88. Jeremy Bentham, *The Handbook of Political Fallacies* 25, ed. Harold Larrabee (New York: Harper & Brothers, 1962).

89. Bentham at 29.

90. See Roscoe Pound, *Criminal Justice in Cleveland* 18–19 (1922).

91. P. Stanlis, *Edmond Burke: Selected Writings and Speeches* 318 (Garden City, NY: Doubleday, 1963).

92. M. McClellan, "The Organized Crime Control Act (S.30) or Its Critics: Which Threaten Civil Liberty," *Notre Dame Law Review* 46 (1970): 57, 200.

93. Bentham, *The Handbook*, at 95.

94. Bentham at 95.

95. Georg Hegel, *Philosophy of History* Part IV, § 3 ch.2 at 537 (New York: American Dome Library, 1903).

96. G. St. Aubyn, *The Art of Argument* 76–77 (1980).

97. T. Damar, *Attacking Faulty Reasoning* 68–69 (1987); D. Huff, *How to Lie With Statistics*, 11–26, 37–52 (NY: Norton 1982); Aubyn, *The Art*, at 83.

98. *United States v. Huber*, 603 F.2d 387, 397 (2d Cir. 1979), *cert. denied*, 444 U.S. 927 (1980).

99. Administrative Office—U.S.C., *Annual Report of the Director of the Administrative Office of the United States Courts*, Table C-7, 1972–1987.

100. Id.

101. Id.

102. *United States v. Elliot*, 571 F.2d 880, 911 (5th Cir.) (cited by the NACDL) *cert. denied*, 439 U.S. 953 (1978).

103. P. Weiss, "The Federal Speedy Trial: Speedy Injustice?" *Connecticut Bar Journal* 56 (1982): 245.

104. Id. at 248.

105. *Morris v. Slappy*, 461 U.S. 1, 13–14 (1983). Studies, too, do not establish a significantly different result between trials conducted by private, as opposed to other, counsel.

106. See the discussion of the empirical data in V. Hans and N. Vidmar, *Judging the Jury*, 116–117 (1986).

107. Id. at 117.

108. Id. at 118.

109. Id. at 120.

110. Id. at 120.

111. *United States v. Kopituk*, 690 F.2d at 1317–1318; *United States v. Castellano*, 610 F.Supp. 1359, 1412 (D.C.N.Y. 1985); *United States v. Dellacroce*, 625 F.Supp. 1387, 1392–1393 (E.D.N.Y. 1986).

112. *United States v. Bernstein*, 533 F.2d at 789.

113. *United States v. Kopituk*, 640 F.2d at 1320–21.

114. *The Report to the President from the President's Commission on Organized Crime* at 133–34 (April 1986) concludes that RICO is one of the most powerful and effective weapons in existence for fighting organized crime.

115. *Effectiveness of the Government's Attack on La Cosa Nostra*, (14 April 1988); *Organized Crime: 25 Years After Valachi*, Hearing before the Senate Permanent Subcommittee on Investigations of the Committee on Governmental Affairs, 100th Cong., 2d Sess. 72 (1988).

116. Benjamin Stein, *Barron's*, 3 April 1989, 24, col. 1, summed up the charges against Milken.

117. *United States v. Porcelli*, 865 F.2d 1352, 1354–66 (2d Cir. 1989).

118. *United States v. Regan*, 858 F.2d 115, 120–22 (2d Cir. 1988).

119. *Republic of Philippines v. Marcos*, 863 F.2d 1355, 1359, 1361 (9th Cir. 1988) (injunction upheld to prevent dissipation of assets).

120. *New York Times*, 30 March 1989, at 1, col. 1.

121. *Wall Street Journal*, 31 March 1989, at 1, col. 4.

122. *New York Times*, 15 April 1989, at 1, col. 1.

123. Id.

124. *Wall Street Journal*, 15 February 1989, at 1, col. 1.

125. *Wall Street Journal*, 31 March 1989, at A4, col. 6.

126. Stephen A. Adler, *Wall Street Journal*, 15 February 1989, p. 1., col. 1.

127. See, for example, *United States v. Salerno*, 481 U.S. 739 (1987).

128. Rep. Boucher, *N.Y. Times*, 12 March 1989, 2C, col. 1.

129. 132 *Cong. Rec.* H. 9371 (7 October 1986, daily ed.).

130. *Annual Report of the Director of the Administrative Office of the United States Courts* (Washington, DC: U.S. Gov't. Printing Office, 1985).

131. Id. at 11.

132. Id. at 16.

133. Id. at 11.

134. Id. at A-12–13.

135. Id. A-12.

136. Id. at A-47.

137. Id. at A-13.

138. Id. at A-46.

139. Id. at A-12.

140. *Ad Hoc Civil RICO Task Force: ABA, Corporations, etc.* 55–56 (1985).

141. *Oversight on Civil RICO Suits*, Hearings Before the Senate Judiciary Committee, 99th Cong., 1st Sess. at 127 (1985).

142. See *Myths* at 1018–19.

143. 2 Civil RICO Report No. 34 at 3, 4 February (1987).

144. Id.

145. *Penvert Development Corp. Ltd. v. Dow Chemical Co.*, 667 F.Supp. 436, 441 (E.D. Mich. 1987).

146. Barbara Clark, ''Adjudication to Administration: A Statistical Analysis of Federal District Courts in the Twentieth Century,'' *Southern California Law Review* 55 (1981): 65, 81–85.

147. Id.

148. Marc Galanter, ''Reading the Legal Landscape of Disputes,'' *UCLA Law Review* 31 (1983): 4, 62.

149. 471 U.S. 626, 643 (1985).

150. Id.

151. See *Oversight* at 241.

152. *Papai v. Cremosnik*, 635 F.Supp. 1402, 1411 (N.D. Ill. 1986); *H.J., Inc. v. Northwestern Bell Telephone Co.*, 492 U.S. 229, 244–48 (1989); *Sedima S.P.R.L. v. Imrex Co., Inc.*, 473 U.S. 479, 495 (1985); *State v. Thompson*, 751 P.2d 805, 815 (Utah App. 1988).

153. *The Challenge of Crime in a Free Society* 47–48 (1967).

154. *Oversight* at 719.

155. *United States v. Turkette*, 452 U.S. 576, 591 (1982).

156. 452 U.S. at 590; Michael Goldsmith, ''RICO and Enterprise Criminality: A Response to Gerald E. Lynch,'' *Colorado Law Review* 88 (1988): 774.

157. 132 *Cong. Rec.* H. 9371 (7 October 1986, daily ed.).

158. 492 U.S. 229 (1989). *Post-H.J. Inc.* litigation establishes that ''pattern'' is a substantial limiting factor in the use of RICO in ordinary commercial litigation. Circuit court opinions indicate that district courts regularly grant dismissals for a failure to show a ''pattern,'' and they are regularly affirmed on appeal; for example, *Arzuaga-Collazo v. Oriental Fed. Sav. Bank*, 913 F.2d 5, 6–7 (1st Cir. 1990).

159. 132 *Cong. Rec.* H. 9371 (7 October 1986, daily ed.).

160. *Durland v. United States* 161 U.S. 306, 314 (1896).

161. *RICO Reform*, Hearings before the House Subcommittee on Criminal Justice, 99th Cong., 1st and 2nd Sess. 177 (1985).

162. Id. at 56.

163. Michael Goldsmith and Keith, "Civil RICO Abuse: The Allegations in Context," *Brigham Young University Law Review* (1986): 55, 103–4.

164. See *Oversight* at 634–35.

165. [1794] Salk 397, 91 Eng. Rep. 330.

166. 84 Stat. 923.

167. Id. at 47–48 (1967).

168. Senator Duncan Fletcher, 77 *Cong. Rec.* 3801 (1933).

169. D. Ratner, *Securities Regulation* 80 (1982).

170. J. Seligman, *The Transformation of Wall Street* 79 (1983).

171. See *Oversight* at 310.

172. *Alcorn County, Miss. v. U.S. Interstate Supplies*, 731 F.2d 1160, 1165 (5th Cir. 1984).

173. Id.

174. *Oversight* at 140–41.

175. R. Jackson, *The Struggle for Judicial Supremacy* 152 (Vintage 1941).

176. *Wall Street Journal*, 31 March 1989, 1, col. 4.

177. "Desperate SEC Seeks More Aid," *National Law Journal* (1 May 1989): 1, col. 3; *Statistics on SEC's Enforcement Program*, GAO Report, 25 March 1985.

178. *USA Today*, 5 April 1989, Sec. B, p. 1, col. 1.

179. S. Rep. No. 97–495, 97th Cong., 2d Sess. 10 (1983).

180. *New York Times*, 24 Feb. 1989, 35, col. 5.

181. John D. Dingle, *New York Times*, 21 February 1985, 46 col. 1.

182. *Time*, 21 April 1986 at 61.

183. *Corporate Crime Reporter* 3, 20 February 1989, 4.

184. *New York Times*, 12 March 1989, Sec. 3, 1, col. 2.

185. Id. at 10, col. 1.

186. Id.

187. "Rolling Back RICO," *National Journal* (6 September 1986): 2114–15.

188. Id. at 2115.

189. *Forbes*, 17 October 1988, 12, col. 1.

190. See *Oversight* at 177–78.

191. 17 February 1987, col. 1, p. 27.

192. *New York Times*, 30 March 1989, 1, col. 1.

193. *New York Times*, 21 April 1989, 30, col. 2.

194. *Wall Street Journal*, 28 March 1989, C1, col. 2.

195. *New York Times*, 26 March 1989, 11, col. 1.

196. 6 Edw. 1, ch. 5 (1278) (treble damages for waste).

197. 21 Jac. 1, ch. 3, § 4 (1624).

198. 4 W. Holdsworth, *A History of English Law* 335 (3d ed. 1945).

199. Id.

200. *The Laws and Liberties of Massachusetts* 5, 24, (1648).

201. The *Institutes of Gaius* (Part I): 217 (1958).

202. A. Watson, *The Law of the Ancient Romans* 76 (1970).

203. Id. at 80.

204. Id. at 77.

205. 5 C. Kennedy, *The Orations of Demosthenes*, app. VI 187 (1909) in J. Wigmore, *Panorama of the World's Legal Systems* 343 (1936).

206. *Exodus 22:1*; *Exodus 22:9, 2 Samuel 12:1–6.*

207. R. Posner, *Economic Analysis of Law* § 7.2 (3rd ed. 1986).

208. 12 U.S.C. § 1464 (1982); 12 U.S.C. § 1975 (1982); 12 U.S.C. § 2607 (1982); 15 U.S.C. § 15 (1982); 15 U.S.C. § 72 (1982); 15 U.S.C. § 1117 (1982); 15 U.S.C. § 1693f (1982); 15 U.S.C. § 1989 (1982).

209. R. Posner, *Antitrust Law: An Economic Perspective* 223 (1976).

210. 747 F.2d 384, 399 n.16 (7th Cir. 1984), *aff'd on other grounds*, 105 S.Ct. 3291 (1985).

211. 132 *Cong. Rec.* E. 3531 (10 October 1986 daily ed.).

212. *Oversight* at 535.

213. *Sedima*, 473 U.S. at 478.

214. Id. at 69.

215. *A Comprehensive Perspective on Civil and Criminal RICO Legislation and Litigation: ABA Criminal Justice Section* 121–23 (1985).

216. Rep. William J. Hughes in Hearings before House Subcommittee on Crime, 99th Cong., 2nd Sess. 1 (1986).

217. S. Rep. No. 495, 97th Cong., 2nd Sess. V (1982).

218. H.R. Rep. No. 1137, 98th Cong., 2d Sess. at 5 (1984).

219. *New York Times*, 5 January 1987, col. 1, 20.

220. *Oversight* at 216.

221. H.R. Rep. No. 100–1088, 100th Cong., 2d Sess. 11 (1988).

222. *New York Times*, 10 February 1989, 29, col. 3.

223. Id.

224. Id. See also *Wall Street Journal*, 10 February 1989, 1, col. 1.

225. Nathan Pusey, ''Fast Money and Fraud,'' *New York Times Magazine*, 23 April 1989, 30.

226. *New York Times*, 5 April 1989, 33, col. 1.

227. *Wall Street Journal*, 8 November 1988, at A.6.

228. Id., 17 February 1989, 1, col. 6.

229. Id.

230. Id.

231. Id.

232. See *New York Times*, 5 April 1989, 33, col. 1.

233. *Wall Street Journal*, 7 April 1989, 1, col. 6.

234. Id.

235. *Chicago Tribune*, 27 January 1987, 2, col. 1.

236. *New York Times*, 17 September 1986, 48, col. 6.

237. 681 F.Supp. 549, 555–86 (N.D. Ill. 1988).

238. 556 F.Supp. 576, 581–84 (N.D. Ill. 1983).

239. 741 F.2d 482, 488–90 (2d Cir. 1984), *rev'd.* 473 U.S. 479 (1985).

240. *Religious Technology Center v. Wollersheim*, 796 F.2d 1076, 1081 (9th Cir. 1986), *cert. denied*, 107 S. Ct. 1336 (1987).

241. *Challenge of Crime in a Free Society*, 208 (1967).

242. See, for example, S.2048, 90th Cong., 1st Sess. (1967); 113 *Cong. Rec.* 17,999 (1967).

243. *Senate Hearing* 259 (statement) 556 report (1969).

244. Id. at 449.

245. *J.I. Case Co. v. Borak*, 377 U.S. 426, 433 (1964); *Merrill Lynch Pierce Fenner & Smith v. Curran*, 456 U.S. 353, 378 (1982).

246. *House Hearings* 543–44.

247. *Iannelli v. United States*, 420 U.S. 770, 786–89 (1975).

248. *United States v. Yonan*, 623 F.Supp. 881, 883–86 (N.D. Ill. 1985), *rev'd.*, 800 F.2d 1964, 167–68 (7th Cir. 1986), *cert. denied*, 479 U.S. 1055 (1987); *Northern Trust Banks/O'Hare v. Inryco*, 615 F.Supp. 828, 831 (N.D. Ill. 1985) *rejected by Morgan v. Bank of Waukegan*, 804 F.2d 970, 973–77 (7th Cir. 1986) (reversing 615 F.Supp. 836) (Shadur, J.).

249. 492 U.S. 229 (1989).

250. See generally, *Myths* at 1021–48.

251. *Ann. Rep. of the Director of the Admin. Off. U.S. Cts.*, 1981–87.

252. Pamela D. Crawford, Civil Program Analyst, Administrative Office of the United States Courts (Personal Communication).

253. See *Equitable Relief* at 535 n.37 (1987).

254. *Model Code of Professional Responsibility* EC 7–4 (1980).

255. Fed. R. Civ. P. 9(b); id. at 11; id. at 12(f); id. at 56.

256. *Farguson v. Bank Houston, N.A.*, 808 F.2d 358, 360 (5th Cir. 1986) (Rule 11: monetary sanctions imposed and injunction granted against further frivolous litigation).

257. *The Federalist Papers* 246 (Mentor Books 1961).

258. It was hoped, too, that the new Constitution would, through its commerce clause, facilitate "intercourse throughout the Union . . . by new improvements," that is, "roads, accommodations for travelers, interior navigation," and so on. Id. at 103 (No. 14).

259. J. Hurst, *Law and the Conditional Freedom in the Nineteenth-Century United States* (1956); O. Handlin and M. Handlin, *Commonwealth: A Study of the Role of Government in the American Economy* (1946).

260. C. Veljanouski in A. Ogus and C. Veljanouski, *Readings in the Economics of Law and Regulation* 22 (1984).

261. L. Friedman, *The Legal System* 20 (1975).

262. See *Wall Street Journal*, 15 February 1989, 1; *Myths* at 1020.

263. Id.

21

Without Fear of Retribution: The Witness Security Program

ROBERT J. KELLY, RUFUS SCHATZBERG, AND KO-LIN CHIN

WITNESS SECURITY PROGRAM

The Federal Witness Security Program (WITSEC) began in the 1960s at a time when efforts against organized crime were meeting with only limited success. The fear of witnesses that they or their families would be murdered if they testified was a serious impediment to prosecutions of organized crime figures.

From 1961 to 1965, the U.S. Department of Justice's Organized Crime Program lost more than twenty-five informants. Hundreds of prosecutions were stymied because witnesses feared murder.[1] It became clear that some precautions had to be devised to keep witnesses alive before, during, and after providing testimony. That consideration led to the 1967 task force recommendation that safe houses be developed with U.S. marshals providing witness protection.

Until 1970, when the Organized Crime Control Act implemented the recommendation of the 1967 President's Task Force Report, the protection of government witnesses was largely left to individual law enforcement agencies. Resources were limited and service inconsistent, and though well intentioned, these efforts were not always successful, as witnesses continued to be tortured and murdered.[2]

THE 1967 TASK FORCE REPORT ON ORGANIZED CRIME

A bench mark in the effort to come to grips with organized criminal activities in the United States, observed that no jurisdiction has made adequate provision for protecting witnesses in organized crime cases from reprisal. The difficulty of obtaining witnesses because of the fear of reprisal could be encountered somewhat if governments had established systems for protecting cooperative witnesses.[3]

The task force recommended that the federal government should establish residential facilities for the protection of witnesses during the litigation of cases in which they are involved. The report also suggested that the government do more than protect witnesses in trial: it urged that the government extend to witnesses its protection beyond trial proceedings and assist them in relocating geographically and reestablishing themselves in new identities, jobs, and life-styles. The purpose was to preserve their anonymity as a defense against repri-sals.

In 1968, pursuant to the authority contained in 28 USC 524, the Department of Justice began to utilize some of its appropriations to complement the protec-tive services of the U.S. Marshal Service in providing for the personal security of prosecution witnesses in organized crime cases. The program was expanded and formalized with the enactment of the Omnibus Crime Bill of 1970, wherein Title 5 of Public Law 91–452 authorized the expenditure of federal funds to protect individuals and members of households of individuals who are witnesses or potential witnesses in legal proceedings against persons engaged in organized crime.[4]

The legislation that authorized the Witness Security Program stipulated the following:

The Attorney General of the United States is authorized to rent, purchase, or remodel housing facilities, and to otherwise offer to provide for the health, safety, and welfare of witnesses and persons intended to be called as Government witnesses in legal proceedings instituted against any person alleged to have participated in an organized crime activity whenever, in his judgment testimony from, or a willingness to testify by, such a witness would place his life or person, or the life or person of a member of his family or household in jeopardy. Any person availing himself of such an offer by the Attorney General to use such facilities may continue to use such facilities for as long as the Attorney General determines the jeopardy to his life or person continues.

The program was placed under the administrative control of the U.S. Marshals Service. The report of the U.S. Senate Permanent Subcommittee on Investigation noted:

Law enforcement officers wanted the protecting and relocating agency to be in the crim-inal justice system but to be as far removed as possible from both investigating agents and prosecution. That way the government could more readily counter the charge that cooperating witnesses were being paid or otherwise unjustifiably compensated in return for their testimony.[5]

Since its formal inception in 1971, more than 5,877 witnesses, as well as 13,000 family members, have entered WITSEC and have been protected, relocated, and provided with new identities by the U.S. Marshals Service.[6]

In 1969, the U.S. Chamber of Commerce alerted the business community to the threats organized crime penetration posed and suggested a plan for collective action to oppose criminal infiltration of legitimate businesses. At the same time, as part of its anticrime program, the 1972 *Deskbook*, published by the Chamber of Commerce, urged the business community to employ protected witnesses.

The National Advisory Committee on Criminal Justice Standards and Goals Report on organized crime in 1976 called for the expansion of witness protection programs. In its recommendations it encouraged state legislatures to enact protective laws and establish procedures, including relocations and new identities for those who cooperate and provide information in organized crime investigations. The Advisory Committee broadened its concept of witness protection. Not only would cooperative witnesses in prosecutions be afforded governmental protection, but this cloak of security would also be extended to key informants whose information might be vital to law enforcement intelligence agencies at the local levels.[7] Finally, in 1984, Congress passed additional legislation, the Comprehensive Crime Control Act, which further defined the parameters of WITSEC and codified the policies and procedures to be instituted by the Marshals Service.

Witness protection can be an expensive operation. Furnishing personnel, family guards, and comprehensive around-the-clock security involves a sizable expenditure of resources and personnel, which may explain why federal recommendations that states develop their own models have not materialized.

OPERATIONAL COMPONENTS OF WITSEC

At the center of witness protection is a network of specially trained witness security inspectors stationed throughout the United States whose primary responsibility is protecting and assisting endangered witnesses (see Figure 21.1). Supporting the inspector staff are deputy U.S. marshals drawn from the ranks of the service. Central control of program field operatives is directed and supervised by the Witness Security Division in Washington, D.C.[8]

In the Marshals Services, working in WITSEC is a prestigious assignment. In addition to the basic training that all marshals receive, deputies recruited into WITSEC undergo six weeks' advanced training in the special skills and technical requirements WITSEC marshals must possess. Every six months, WITSEC deputies receive updated training in the latest technological advances in security and surveillance. Ordinarily, applications for WITSEC assignments are accepted from senior deputies and those with at least three to four years' field experience.[9]

Figure 21.1
Witness Security Program, U.S. Marshals Service

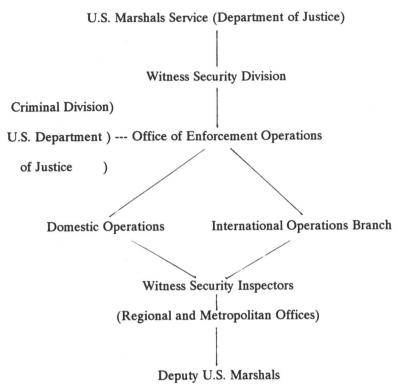

U.S. Marshals Service (Department of Justice)

Witness Security Division

Criminal Division)

U.S. Department) --- Office of Enforcement Operations

of Justice   )

Domestic Operations   International Operations Branch

Witness Security Inspectors

(Regional and Metropolitan Offices)

Deputy U.S. Marshals

Witness Security Inspector Staff

A successful project begins with an inspector's meeting with a potential witness and members of his or her family immediately after the witness's removal from danger to a safe location.

Initiation into the program begins with an orientation about its goals and procedures. It is emphasized strongly and repeatedly that the safety of the witness and family depends primarily on the witness's willingness to comply with security guidelines. During early interviews, inspectors obtain detailed background information that is verified and used to propose safe relocations.

Office of Enforcement Operations

Whether or not an individual is accepted into the Witness Security Program is determined by the Office of Enforcement Operations (OEO) in the Criminal Division of the U.S. Department of Justice. Participation in WITSEC is initiated through application made by federal prosecutors from U.S. attorneys' offices for selected, confidential informants and prospective government witnesses in trial proceedings. Concurrently with the sponsoring agency's application, a case agent makes an assessment of threat and the importance of the witness in the government's case.

After the OEO evaluates the prosecutorial significance of the case and the potential threat posed to the witness, the psychological suitability of the witness in protection is evaluated. The questions the security protection considers here focus on the risk the witness may pose to a relocation community and how well or poorly the witness fits the parameters of the program. The evaluation process is delicate. The value of witness testimony must be weighed against a number of factors, including the ability of the individual to make major readjustments in a new lifestyle. In the majority of cases, witnesses have pursued criminal careers and possess neither the skills nor the determination to profoundly reorder their lives. The protocols that help shape the analysis of the applicant's profile for acceptance also consider the possibility of obtaining similar testimony from other sources and whether providing protection will substantially infringe on the relationship between parents and children who might not be relocated.

The WITSEC program also accepts protection applications from two other sources: the Bureau of Prisons and state prosecutors and local investigative agencies. State applications are submitted to the OEC through the local U.S. attorneys' offices and are reviewed in the same manner as applications from federal prosecutors. Program services extended to state witnesses are identical to those afforded federal witnesses.

Incarcerated witnesses are the responsibility of the U.S. Bureau of Prisons. The designation of a correctional facility for serving a sentence, medical treatment, and inmate services is handled by the Bureau of Prisons. The U.S. marshals are involved only in providing secure transportation between prisons and safe locales and to and from courts during trial proceedings. When prisoner witnesses complete their sentence, they may be sponsored for full services under the WITSEC program. If protection is approved, field inspectors explain the protection program to witnesses and their immediate families in full detail.

Relocation and New Identities

When a witness is accepted into the security program the Marshals Service creates new identities for each family member that break links with the past. In order to begin the process of redocumentation, it is not enough to simply print new Social Security numbers and motor vehicle licenses. These could scarcely stand scrutiny. First, a court-approved name change is processed secretly. Each witness and family member may select names; the only requirement is that they be ethnically compatible and not an alias that may have been used previously or relatives' maiden names. Unlike undercover agents who assume new identities for a limited period of time, a witness and family are redocumented for life. As a result, the Marshals service provides only authentic identity papers for passports, birth certificates, motor vehicle licenses, and Social Security numbers.

Should a document be challenged, it can be verified in a normal fashion. When a witness's documents are questioned, the Marshals Service is notified of such inquiries immediately.

Only documents to which an individual is entitled are provided. For example, a witness who did not graduate from a university will not be given a diploma. In most cases, each participant is provided with a basic portfolio of identity papers. Foreign nationals who are approved through the International Operations Branch (IOB) are usually given Social Security cards, driver's licenses, and immigration papers that allow them to work in the United States. If foreigners have entered the United States legally and have not committed any crimes, most can petition for citizenship upon meeting normal permanent residency requirements. However, those who have entered illegally are allowed to remain and work in the United States indefinitely as long as they abide by the law. Should they break the law, they are subject to the same deportation proceedings as anyone else.

Once witnesses are relocated, the field inspection services assist families in finding permanent housing, enrolling the children in schools, and locating family physicians and in other numerous tasks associated with moving into a new community. The selection of a new community must also be carefully evaluated in terms of the possibility of witness employment opportunities compatible with the individual's background, skills, and former lifestyle, the adequacy of school programs for children, and, most important, the risk of detection of the individual's true identity.

Witnesses and their families are obliged to sever all ties with their previous communities. They can communicate with relatives and friends left behind only through secure mail-forwarding channels administered by the Marshals Service. In cases where a divorced witness enters the program, arrangements are made for visitations between the witness and his or her children who may not accompany the parent into the program. Visits are arranged in safe locales away from both the relocation and danger areas.

Becoming Self-Sufficient

Because participation in WITSEC is a lifetime endeavor, the government helps witnesses become self-supporting through employment. Finding legitimate jobs for witnesses is one of the more significant challenges the marshals face because the majority of those who are federally protected have extensive criminal records and rather limited legitimate job skills. While major drug traffickers may possess formidable managerial abilities, their sordid past lives and criminal orientations may make legitimate work involving executive administrative functions seem less attractive and less lucrative. To those whose illicit earnings far exceeded what they could demand in the legitimate world of work, the comparative modest incomes associated with a straight job may pose a significant psychological problem. Consequently, witnesses must often readjust their expectations profoundly and are encouraged to enroll in training programs or find part-time employment as soon as possible. Until such time as a witness is self-sufficient, he receives a stipend from the Marshals Service. The amount of this allowance is based on the size of the family and the average cost of living in the geographic relocation area.

To facilitate adjustment to the new identity and relocation area, government-vocational psychologists work with witnesses to determine suitable fields of employment. Each witness is given a battery of vocational inventories designed to specify and characterize his interests and intrinsic talents. These preferences, together with the witness' actual experiences, help to locate job opportunities.

For some time, the Witness Security Division has enjoyed the cooperation of more than 300 business firms and corporations throughout the United States and abroad that have agreed to employ witnesses and their family members. In numerous instances, business firms and the Witness Security Division cooperate in training prospective employees for jobs in a company. The rationale from the government's standpoint is prudent and sensible: the sooner the witness is economically self-sufficient and viable, the sooner the government's financial support burdens are reduced.

Psychological Evaluation

Because the majority of witnesses have led criminal lives, the WITSEC Program routinely seeks advice from psychologists as to how to deal with a specific witness's personality and how best to approach recurrent problems associated with readjustment to new lives and new communities. There are emotional traumas connected with forswearing loyalties, family bonds, lifelong friendships, and even the companionship of criminal peers. Uprooting a family is quite stressful and particularly difficult for spouses and children.

To appreciate the stress a witness may encounter, one has only to imagine trying to make friends in a new and strange community while remaining at the same time always vigilant about casual references to one's past and background. Signing one's new, fictitious name—especially for children—is no longer a simple, automatic action but now must be done with concentration to avoid an easy, revealing lapse. Recognizing these stresses and personal demands, the WITSEC Program takes pains to assess the advantages the government accrues with a witness and the deficits it harnesses before making decisions about participation.

Part of the psychological diagnosis entails estimates about a witness's likely future antisocial behavior and criminal dispositions. This enables the program to reject a candidate or impose conditions contingent upon acceptance, including alcohol and drug counseling, or, if the witness is incarcerated, close parole and probation supervision. The program provides counseling and therapy on a twenty-four-hour basis and offers follow-up psychological services, though much of the extended counseling can be done through local therapists in the relocation site.

Keeping secrets is, indeed, a tension-generating process, but what of spilling them? The possibility of repercussions of death and intimidation only exacerbates an already stressful situation. When witnesses are well educated and successful in their former lives, transition to a new lifestyle can be more traumatic. Having more psychic, social, and economic investment in their prior lives, they have presumably more to lose.[10]

International Operations Branch

International fugitive investigations constitute one of the fastest growing responsibilities of the Marshal Service. This is indicative of the global dimensions of organized criminality. Increasingly, criminal activities and networks extend beyond national borders, and criminals themselves have accumulated the resources and developed the habitats that enable them to flee local jurisdictions.[11]

All U.S. Marshals Services' activities in international fugitives' identification and extraditions are coordinated and directed by the IOB of the Office of Enforcement Operations.

IOB acts as clearinghouse, handling requests for international fugitive investigations between the Marshals service and foreign authorities. Its role goes beyond that of the bureaucratic traffic managing of communications. The IOB pursues investigations here and in concert with foreign law enforcement agencies.

When it is determined that a suspect in an investigation might be in another country, the IOB issues through Interpol a lookout bulletin that includes vital information on the fugitive, including physical description, nationality, family background, occupation, criminal history, and suspected location. Domestically, the marshals conduct the vast majority of fugitive investigations requested by foreign governments through Interpol.

Going Astray Again

Only when readjustments go smoothly and efficiently for witnesses do contact and dependency on the Marshals Service diminish. As witnesses settle into communities and begin to lead normal lives, contact with WITSEC occurs only if problems arise. On the other hand, with regard to the program's ability to police witnesses who go astray in their new identities and locations, if a witness becomes a suspect in a criminal investigation, the Marshals Service cooperates fully with the investigating agency even to the extent of assisting in the apprehension of a suspect witness.

The recidivism rate (witnesses with prior criminal history who entered the program and were subsequently arrested and charged with crimes) is less than 23 percent, which is less than half the rate of those released from the nation's prisons. In some respects, the program does have some rehabilitative effects for its participants.

A significant problem is how to ease out certain witnesses—especially those who are older and who never really held a legitimate job. In the early phases of development, most major government witnesses were Mob members whose lives had been jeopardized by their criminal associates. Vowing vengeance for attempts on their lives, individuals such as Joseph Valachi and James Fratianno provided invaluable information on organized crime operations and the structure of its vast rackets in the United States.[12]

Today, associates of organized crime figures in increasing numbers are part of the WITSEC program. Accountants, lawyers, and businesspeople who front for criminals in legitimate enterprises or who conspire with them as partners have turned state's evidence. Their willingness to do so is prompted not only by the stiff Racketeer Influenced and Corrupt Organizations Act (RICO) penalties they confront but by the WITSEC alternatives to incarceration and the opportunity for them and their families to start afresh.

Crippling Organized Crime

The development of powerful legal instruments since Valachi's testimony in the early 1960s, such as RICO and various immunity statutes, has induced many La Cosa Nostra (LCN) members to turn on the organization and enter the Witness Security Program. For younger criminals, it is often nothing more than doing the arithmetic of hard time under RICO, which involves long sentences, compared with witness protection, relocation, and a new life. Arguably, the government is often forced into a Hobson's choice: either provide leniency and immunity to lesser criminals in order to prosecute major criminal figures or continue to arrest, prosecute, and incarcerate minor criminals while the leaders of crime organization evade the law.

If witnesses cannot be protected, then who would trust the government? Another vexing question cannot be ignored: does the justice system, wedded to the likes of admitted career criminals like James Fratianno, Hill, Salvatore Gravano, and others, work? Given the results, the answer must be yes. Federal Bureau of Investigation (FBI) director William Sessions testified that: "the WSP (Witness Security Program) is a necessary program to encourage citizen cooperation and provide for the safety of those individuals who testify at personal risk."[13]

The recent FBI successes would have been greatly diminished had the FBI not found a method to secure testimony from those witnesses and not provided security for them and their families until the lengthy trials concluded.

Interagency Cooperation

With federal and state agencies committing more personnel to investigations, coupled with the enactment of the Witness Security Program of 1984, budgetary and personnel pressures on the FBI mounted, with increasing numbers of witnesses willing to testify against LCN members. In order to thoroughly debrief witnesses and afford them security, it has become necessary to delay witness transfer to the Marshals Service. This entails additional costs for housing, food, and incidental living expenses not only for witnesses but for their family members as well. Resolving coordination problems among agencies that handle witnesses is vitally important if WITSEC is to remain viable as a tactical choice in organized crime control policies.

Containing Organized Crime

WITSEC has been a boon in turning major crime figures into informants and witnesses. Behind the WITSEC program is the legal infrastructure of RICO, the Bank Secrecy Act, the organized crime task forces at all levels of government, electronic surveillance technologies, undercover operations, immunity provisions, and the Bail Reform Act of 1984, which established new guidelines for pretrial detention.[14] As a consequence of the Bail Reform Act, some defendants have pleaded guilty or became cooperative witnesses. Without the legislation defendants would often cause lengthy delays in their trial while free on bail. Further, jailing defendants awaiting trial or pending appeal has effectively disrupted illegal enterprises.

These law enforcement developments have hastened the decay of the LCN. The code of silence is regularly violated and encouraged by WITSEC. The scorecard on WITSEC appears quite favorable: information provided by protected witnesses helped to convict over 89 percent of the defendants they testified against.[15] Not only do witnesses feel safe to speak out against their confederates, but in the majority of cases they go on to live normal, law-abiding lives. This is no small accomplishment when over 97 percent of witnesses come into the program with extensive criminal records. These data should allay fears that justice dependent on career criminals is somehow tarnished. The hard fact is that there is really no other way to win cases against La Cosa Nostra and its associates except to encourage the cooperation of criminals intimately connected to it.

WITSEC is not without its critics. In testimony before the President's Commission on Organized Crime, Fratianno, LCN boss of the Los Angeles family, indicated that WITSEC did not provide sufficient financial support.[16] Other criticisms suggest that the government should demand a criminal's cooperation rather than offering a reduced sentence and a ride in witness protection.[17] In the fourth prosecution of John Gotti, head of the Gambino crime family, the most powerful in the LCN, the government's trump was Salvatore Gravano, underboss of the family and second in command, whose litany of murder, corruption, and violence shocked the public. The gamble in such prosecution is that a jury may focus on the multitude of crimes of government witnesses rather than of those of the defendant and wonder whether a system that tempts unsavory characters into complicity is itself too tainted to protect society.

Experience in understanding organized crime and in refining methods that will diminish its power has led to many improvements. In its earliest days prosecutors and investigations tended to proceed on the assumption that simply incarcerating the top figures in criminal organizations would destroy the groups. Law enforcement has come to understand that despite the removal of leaders from the street environment, groups continue to develop and flourish under new leadership that quickly ascend from the subordinate layers of the organizations or persist under the old leadership capable of transmitting commands and decisions from prison. Consequently, law enforcement agencies came to understand the regenerative character of organized crime—despite temporary setbacks and removal of leaders, groups persist and continue to flourish. Thus, enforcement efforts began to concentrate on the sources of power and influence of organizations and to tailor investigation and prosecutorial efforts to diminish that power.

In recent years, law enforcement has become adept at the deep penetration of organized crime groups through the use of long-term undercover investigations and the development of high-level informant-witnesses.[18] When these techniques are fully exploited, they tend to subvert the group's infrastructure and weaken its ability to sustain itself, rather than merely incapacitate some of its members. Witness protection offers an alternative to those who face long years of imprisonment; it provides opportunities to repudiate the past and start anew. The success of the program in getting convictions and ensuring the safety of its participants who make public disclosure of the inner workings of racketeering groups may sow seeds of doubt and dissension that can lead to the collapse of a crime organization even when its top leaders are not prosecuted.

SUMMARY

WITSEC represents an exit strategy for career criminals. The anecdotal evidence from criminals themselves reinforces the findings of researchers and law enforcement specialists that membership in an organized crime group absorbs most of their time and virtually isolates them from the rest of the society. Their lives are lived through masks, deceptions, and betrayals.[19]

Is there anything the government can do to encourage organized criminals to abandon their way of life? Early on in its struggle against organized crime, the federal government recognized the need for flexible judicial remedies that could facilitate the breaking of the code of silence (omerta) and the fear of retaliation. In order to enhance defection from criminal groups, the government has developed a number of law enforcement instruments—among these RICO and WITSEC. The heavy punitive costs under RICO legislation, coupled with WITSEC, seem to have increased the defections of organized criminals from their way of life. In exchange for renunciation—and testimony—of a criminal way of life, WITSEC provides the criminal with a place in legitimate society.

WITSEC offers the promise of substantial leniency for those facing steep penalties and safety for themselves and their families if they collaborate with law enforcement authorities. Collaboration most frequently takes the form of testifying in criminal proceedings against former associates and providing evidence against them.

WITSEC participation should not be construed as a form of repentance by the criminal; repentance suggests a total rejection of past beliefs and attitudes. In general, WITSEC encourages change: dissociation from the criminal organization and active cooperation with law enforcement do not necessarily imply repentance or contriteness in a moral or psychological sense. The motives driving criminals into WITSEC may be an acknowledgment that they are apprehended and will be successfully prosecuted, convicted, and imprisoned. In this sense, a willingness to enter the program may express realism rather than moral or psychological change. Collaboration, for its part, may result from a cold calculation of possible benefits that would accrue with cooperation. Collaborating with testimony and intelligence does not require a rejection of past ideas— although witnesses who label themselves as such can never return to the criminal life. Without such an option as WITSEC, society has dangerous organized criminals on its hands, either in prison, in hiding, or in a criminal lifestyle. With it, society could benefit from a cohort of persons who must refrain from crime, assist in frustrating its persistence and growth, and contribute usefully to society.

NOTES

1. Gerald Shur, "A Father's Dream Come True," *The Pentacle* 8.1 (Winter 1988).

2. Ibid.

3. The President's Commission on Law Enforcement and Administration of Justice, *Task Force Report: Organized Crime* (Washington, DC: U.S. Government Printing Office, 1967), 19.

4. U.S. Department of Justice/Law Enforcement Assistance Administration, Report of the National Conference of Organized Crime. *Proceedings* (Washington, DC: U.S. Government Printing Office, 1975).

5. U.S. Senate Permanent Subcommittee on Investigation, *Witness Security Program* (Washington, DC: U.S. Government Printing Office, 1981), 59.

6. Howard Safir, "The United States Witness Protection Program," Testimony before the Permanent Subcommittee on Investigation, Committee on Governmental Affairs, U.S. Senate, 1985.

7. Report of the Task Force on Organized Crime, *National Advisory Committee on Criminal Justice Standard and Goals* (Washington, DC: U.S. Government Printing Office, 1976).

8. Shur, "A Father's Dream."

9. Personal communication, U.S. Marshals Service, WITSEC, March 1992.

10. Fred Montanino, "The Federally Protected Witness: Researching Endangered Subjects," *Law Enforcement Intelligence Analysis Digest* (Summer 1988).

11. Robert J. Kelly, "Cooperation Between Italian and American Law Enforcement Agencies: The Fight Against Organized Crime," *Italian Journal* 3.2–3 (September 1989).

12. Ovid Demaris, *The Last Mafioso: The Treacherous World of Jimmy Fratianno*

(New York: Bantam Books, 1981); Peter Maas, *The Valachi Papers* (New York: Bantam Books, 1968).

13. Statement of William S. Sessions, Director, Federal Bureau of Investigation, Committee on Governmental Affairs, Permanent Subcommittee on Investigations, U.S. Senate, 11 April 1988, Hearings, Permanent Subcommittee on Investigation, 100th Congress, Second Session. *Organized Crime: 25 Years After Valachi* (Washington, DC: U.S. Government Printing Office), 286.

14. Statement of David C. Williams, Director, Office of Special Investigations, General Accounting Office, Committee on Governmental Affairs, Permanent Subcommittee on Investigations, U.S. Senate, 11 April 1988, Hearings, Permanent Subcommittee on Investigation, 100th Congress, Second Session. *Organized Crime: 25 Years After Valachi* (Washington, DC: U.S. Government Printing Office), 72.

15. Safir, "The United States."

16. Testimony of James Fratianno, Hearing 11, *Organized Crime and Money Laundering* (14 March 1984), President's Commission on Organized Crime.

17. Michael J. Zuckerman, *Vengeance Is Mine* (New York: Macmillan, 1987).

18. Joseph D. Pistone and Richard Woodley, *Donnie Brasco: My Undercover Life in the Mafia* (New York: New American Library, 1987).

19. Ibid.; Annelise Anderson, *The Business of Organized Crime: A Cosa Nostra Family* (Stanford: Hoover Institute Press, 1979); Francis A. J. Ianni, *A Family Business: Kinship and Social Control in Organized Crime* (New York: Russell Sage Foundation, 1972); Joseph Salerno and Stephen J. Rivele, *The Plumber* (New York: Knightsbridge, 1990).

REFERENCES

Anderson, Annelise. *The Business of Organized Crime: A Cosa Nostra Family*. Stanford, CA: Hoover Institute Press, 1979.

Cantalupo, Joseph, and Thomas C. Renner. *Body Mike*. New York: St. Martin's, 1991.

Chamber of Commerce of the United States. *Deskbook on Organized Crime*. 1972.

Demaris, Ovid. *The Last Mafioso: The Treacherous World of Jimmy Fratianno*. New York: Bantam Books, 1981.

Testimony of James Fratianno, *Record of Hearing 11*, Organized Crime and Money Laundering. (14 March 1988), President's Commission on Organized Crime.

Ianni, Francis A. J. *A Family Business: Kinship and Social Control in Organized Crime*. New York: Russell Sage Foundation, 1972.

Kelly, Robert J. "Cooperation Between Italian and American Law Enforcement Agencies: The Fight Against Organized Crime." *Italian Journal* 3.2–3 (September 1989).

Maas, Peter. *The Valachi Papers*. New York: Bantam Books, 1968.

Montanino, Fred. "The Federally Protected Witness: Researching Endangered Subjects." *Law Enforcement Intelligence Analysis Digest* (Summer 1988).

Pileggi, Nicholas. *Wiseguy: Life in a Mafia Family*. New York: Simon and Schuster, 1985.

Pistone, Joseph D., and Richard Woodley. *Donnie Brasco: My Undercover Life in the Mafia*. New York: New American Library, 1987.

Renner, Thomas C., and Cecil Kirby. *Mafia Enforcer: A True Story of Life and Death in the Mob*. New York: Bantam Books, 1988.

Report of the National Conference of Organized Crime. *Proceedings*, U.S. Department of Justice/Law Enforcement Assistance Administration. Washington, DC: U.S. Government Printing Office, 1975.

Report of the Task Force on Organized Crime. *National Advisory Committee on Criminal Justice Standards and Goals*. Washington, DC: U.S. Government Printing Office, 1976.

Safir, Howard. "The United States Witness Protection Program." *Testimony before the Permanent Subcommittee on Investigation, Committee on Governmental Affairs, United States Senate*. (1985).

Salerno, Joseph, and Stephen J. Rivele. *The Plumber*. New York: Knightsbridge, 1990.

Shur, Gerald. "A Father's Dream Come True." *The Pentacle* 8.1 (Winter 1988).

Statement of William S. Sessions, Committee on Governmental Affairs, Permanent Subcommittee on Investigations, U.S. Senate, 11 April 1988. *Hearings*. Permanent Subcommittee on Investigation, 100th Congress, Second Session, Organized Crime: 25 Years After Valachi, 286.

Statement of David C. Williams, Office of Special Investigations General Accounting Office. *Hearings*. Permanent Subcommittee of Investigations, 100th Congress, Second Session, April 1988.

Task Force Report: Organized Crime. *The President's Commission on Law Enforcement and Administration of Justice*. Washington, DC: U.S. Government Printing Office, 1967.

U.S. Senate Permanent Subcommittee on Investigation. *Witness Security Program*. Washington, DC: U.S. Government Printing Office, 1981.

Zuckerman, Michael J. *Vengeance Is Mine*. New York: Macmillan, 1987.

Epilogue

JOSEPH L. ALBINI

It is a touching moment in my academic career and at the end of this very important work to reflect upon the methodological challenges and the continuing debate concerning issues that have made the study of organized crime one of the most controversial, yet exciting areas in the discipline of criminology. This area of study has called forth research not only in criminology but in anthropology, political science, economics, police science, and other disciplines. Above all, the study of organized crime is, at its very roots, the study of culture. It is the study of social and economic structure. It is the study of social organization and social disorganization. It is the study of social cohesion and social alienation. It is the study of individual needs and how such needs help shape individual definitions of morality. It is the study of risk taking. It is the study of the "cost-benefits" incurred by those willing to gamble with the uncertain odds in the game of providing illegal goods and services in a society that professes an overt homage to morality and the law yet desires and demands the very illegal goods and services it so overtly condemns.

It is a fascinating and captivating arena of study for the creative researcher, and this work is a tribute to the researchers who in the chapters presented here display their innovative ideas and methodologies and set the stage to share their insights with colleagues and students who are interested in continuing the quest for knowledge in this field.

The greatest tribute I can pay to the editor and those who have contributed the chapters in this work is to say how much I wish I had this handbook available to me when I began conducting my research in the 1960s, although I am aware that my pioneering research, along with that of so many others, was necessary to pave the way toward the clarification and focus of those central issues discussed in this work. Many of the issues debated in the past continue to be debated in this work, for they remain controversial, yet generic to the quest for clarification of the theory and concepts employed in the research in this field. That is positive, for controversy and debate are the foundation stones of scientific inquiry.

I have particularly watched, and am gratified by, the movement of researchers in academe and those in law enforcement to view each other as sharing a mutual goal—more clearly understanding and describing the structure and function of organized crime. In this light and knowing that the goals and purpose for the research in these two disciplines differ, this work draws from, and reaches out to, both of these disciplines in a manner that makes for an open and fruitful discussion of the similarities and differences in their perspectives, their data, and their findings.

This handbook is geared toward inviting the student or new researcher into the area of the study of organized crime. But it does more than that; it challenges the thinking of those more seasoned researchers by providing them with thorough and thought-provoking information that will stimulate the exchange of current ideas. The contributors have all brought their expertise to their topics, and each discussion is uniquely thorough and complete.

This work, in the thoroughness and originality of each chapter, forms ultimately a mosaic of interwoven themes. The very nature of our current knowledge concerning new organized crime groups necessitates the discussion of the diversity of theories, definitions, and descriptions that are currently being employed to analyze their structure and function. In this work, the descriptions of these new groups are made more clear and vivid because the authors have carefully and thoroughly discussed the history and development of each group. If there is one basic, essential component of knowledge necessary to the complete understanding of any specific organized crime group and ultimately to the understanding of the phenomenon of organized crime itself, it is the knowledge revealed in the study of the sociocultural history of that group. Organized crime groups or syndicates are not born and do not exist in a social vacuum. They are part of the very culture and social structure in which they operate. Hence, they are part of the historical process, and an analysis of historical factors helps reveal those types of social conditions that lay the breeding grounds for their birth, development, and demise. The chapters in this book are particularly rich in their giving detailed emphasis to the historical roots from which each organized criminal group emerged.

In discussing theory, definitions, and history, the chapters in this book give an appreciation and understanding of the past to better understand the present and give us a more solid basis upon which to formulate hypotheses about the future.

Smith, Reuter, Maltz, Albanese, and Block are to be commended for so carefully and informatively laying the theoretical and historical basis for the information discussed in the chapters that follow.

Kelly, Finckenauer, Dombrink, Song, Chin, Schatzberg, and Lombardo give a new and exciting introduction to the world of the new or nontraditional organized crime groups that have emerged in contemporary American society. These chapters, in themselves, not only give the reader valuable information about the history, organizational structure, and modes of operation of each group but also present new and important data from which comparative studies can emerge and information to develop hypotheses to study ethnic variations in the process of how individuals and groups choose, or are forced into, a life of organized criminality. The phenomenon of networking within and between ethnic groups and individuals needs further study, and the hypotheses of ethnic succession as a process serve at this time in the development of research hypotheses to present more questions than answers. The hypothesis of ethnic succession, as yet, cannot explain why some ethnic and racial groups, more than others, select organized criminality as a means of upward mobility. The chapters in this section help call attention to the fact that, for all the media and other attention that have so desperately sought to argue a uniqueness to the involvement of Sicilians and Italians in American syndicated organized crime, the new groups seem to operate in similar fashion. This illustrates that the manner or method employed by syndicate organized criminals in the United States is more determined by factors inherent in our legal and social system itself than by factors or characteristics found in the ethnic or cultural differences of its participants.

The legal system itself, in terms of the many changes that have taken place within that system in the past two decades, is worthy of notice and attention. In the history of the war against syndicated organized crime in the United States, the changes in the laws enacted to combat organized crime have led the way for law enforcement to take more effective action against this form of criminality.

Law enforcement has for too long taken the brunt and become the scapegoat for a nation and a legal system that, until the 1970s, served only to frustrate law enforcement agencies by not giving them the legal ammunition with which to effectively combat this form of crime. The new approach, involving the enactment and use of RICO statutes, the creation and use of strike forces and the Witness Protection Program, and the resulting improvement of cooperation among the various law enforcement agencies at all levels, has shown its merit.

This merit is given its deserved recognition in the chapters that address the issues of law enforcement and its control of organized crime. Ryan, Goldstock, Blakey, Martens, and Rogovin speak to the specific problems, strategies, and issues that have confronted, and continue to confront, law enforcement in its ongoing battle against organized crime. Again a history of the development and detailed discussion of the various approaches to the resolution of problems inherent in law enforcement's control of organized crime forms the main theme of the chapters in this section.

In total, then, this handbook is a worthy and deeply appreciated endeavor for those seeking to understand the past and current complexities of the phenomenon we call organized crime. Each chapter causes the serious student to reflect upon how complex a phenomenon the social system of syndicated organized crime really is and to appreciate the complexity of the interplay of individuals and social groups as we are made more conscious of the fact that there is, all too often, a very thin line between organized crime and legitimate society. We, as a society, have developed the habit of quickly labeling those who operate organized criminal enterprises as criminals and quickly avoid thinking about those so-called legitimate citizens who provide the necessary legal protection for the continuing existence and operation of such enterprises. So, too, we quickly forget about those average American citizens who willingly demand and buy the illegal goods and services that keep the members of these criminal syndicates in business.

In its total perspective, this work serves another very vital function. At a time when the field of criminology is recognizing the need for cross-cultural studies in crime, this book serves to allow a basis from which organized crime can be better understood in terms of its cross-cultural manifestations. The data and discussions presented here open a discourse for inquiry into the question of what variables, cultural and otherwise, create the conditions for the emergence and continued existence of syndicated organized crime. In this discourse, we search for an answer to the question of whether or not the culture and social system of the country of origin equip some of the migrants who come to America with the necessary knowledge, values, and goals that make for their ability and willingness to enter into the occupation of organized crime. We search for the answer as to whether or not that country of origin itself had or has organized crime enterprises similar to those in the United States. The study of organized crime is, at its very roots, the study of individual cultures as unique social entities. Only after we understand the complexities and differences in cultures and syndicated organized crime itself can we begin to ask whether or not organized crime is a process that can be transported in its original form from its country of origin into other countries. Is syndicated organized crime a phenomenon, irrespective of migration or ethnic influence, that can exist and flourish in a given society only if the social system of that society is structured to allow it to exist? These are questions that are generic to the understanding of the structure and function of syndicated organized crime.

The study of organized crime remains a dynamic area of study. The questions are many, but the road to the answers is an exciting one. This book leads the way.

Bibliographical Essay

GENERAL

This chapter is designed to provide the reader with sources and references for specialized readings. The *Handbook* ranges widely over many areas, and we find it useful to present important books, essays, research monographs, and general accounts of organized crime as these relate to, and supplement, the source material consulted and cited by the authors.

The literature on organized crime is large and growing, and it would be folly to attempt a complete bibliography. Instead, we concentrate on the works we find most useful, most stimulating, or most perverse. In this respect, this is a subjective chapter.

One of the foremost figures in the sociological/criminological literature on organized crime is Donald Cressey. His central work, *Theft of the Nation* (1969), contains a description and analysis of organized crime in the United States that lie at the heart of debates and controversies. Taken together with his papers "Methodological Problems in the Study of Organized Crime as a Social Problem," *Annals* 374 (November 1967), and "The Functions and Structure of Criminal Syndicates," *Task Force Report* (1967), La Cosa Nostra (LCN) model is fully elaborated. Cressey's writings are dependent on government files and Federal Bureau of Investigation (FBI) data, which he openly acknowledges. Nevertheless, they are stimulating and succeeded in providing an impressive account of what has been called the organized crime model that underpins modern law enforcement crime control strategies. Cressey's achievement has been extensively examined in numerous articles and essays.

Perhaps no critique of the effects of Mafia (LCN) on public thinking and expectations has been so widely misunderstood as Dwight Smith's *The Mafia Mystique* (1975, 1991). He looked at the overwhelming dominance of the Mafia paradigm, how it was generated and its images disseminated, and how it eventually became synonymous with organized crime itself.

Mafia/La Cosa Nostra perspectives on organized criminality as developed by Cressey were the results of specific historical circumstances and a database derived primarily from law enforcement files. Alternative views emerged in the same period that challenged the general validity and domain assumptions of the La Cosa Nostra model. Joseph Albini's *American Mafia: Genesis of a Legend* (1971) and Francis A. J. Ianni's *A Family Business: Kinship and Social Control in Organized Crime* (1972) took exception to the bureaucratic model and Italian American dominance of American organized crime. Albini's and Ianni's sharp criticism spurred scholarly interest that is still lively today, more than two decades after the seminal works emerged. It is curious that the debates raging in journals and at conferences treat rather reverentially the works of two scholars claimed by both those committed and those opposed to the Cosa Nostra paradigm that became the more or less official view of the U.S. government. John Landesco's *Organized Crime in Chicago*, Part 3 of the Illinois Crime Survey (1929, 1968), and Thomas C. Schelling's essays, "What Is the Business of Organized Crime?" *American Scholar* 40 (Autumn 1971): 643–52; and "Economic Analysis and Organized Crime," *Appendix D Task Force Report* (1967) avoided the nightmare of ethnicity and focused instead on the market dynamics of racketeering and criminal enterprises. Landesco's work was more sociologically oriented in the tradition of the Chicago school and presented ethnographic data on the role of organized crime and its effects in local communities. Schelling's works encouraged economic analyses of crime as a business activity. However, neither Landesco nor Schelling was much concerned with the bureaucratic structure of crime groups. Consequently, both have avoided sullied reputations.

Among the interesting discussions in Landesco's work is an analysis of the phenomenon of racketeering and the role of violence as the key component in what are otherwise ordinary business associations and transactions. The instrumental use of violence attempts to stabilize illegal commodity markets where no legal jurisdiction exists. Schelling sees organized crime entities as more than mere economic enterprises. His notion includes the latter but also adds another distinctive power dimension—monopoly and tendencies thereto—that distinguishes organized criminal enterprises from legal businesses. It is through monopoly formations that extortion becomes feasible as an operational currency. The underworld government stakes out jurisdictions (territories) and negotiates control of them with other authorities, such as law enforcement, in order to control competition. In this regard, criminal operators themselves become victims, so to speak, in that failure to pay protection inhibits illegal business opportunities. Extortion becomes a major organizing principle and sustaining force in criminal enterprises. Typically, victims (criminal or noncriminal) have little access to the law, and their activities and earnings are fairly easy to monitor. It is expedient in an environment of illegality to pay tribute to ensure a predictable, peaceable work environment. The compensation for informal insurance or rent are the protections offered by criminal groups.

Informative descriptions of modern crime group extortion and vice operations may be found in Mark H. Haller, *Life Under Bruno: The Economics of an Organized Crime Family* (Pennsylvania Crime Commission, 1991); Annelise G. Anderson, *The Business of Organized Crime: A Cosa Nostra Family* (1979); Humbert S. Nelli, *The Business of Crime* (1976); Dwight C. Smith, Jr., "Paragons, Pariahs and Pirates: A Spectrum-Based Theory of Enterprise," *Crime and Delinquency* 26 (July 1982): 358–86. The collection of essays in *Politics and Economics of Organized Crime*, edited by H. E. Alexander and G. E. Caiden (1985) explores the dynamics of criminal linkages with legitimate businesses, money laundering, and the relationships to politics. Various reports of the President's Commission of Organized Crime, *The Edge: Organized Crime, Business and Labor Unions* (October 1985); *The Cash Connection: Organized Crime, Financial Institutions, and Money Laundering* (October 1984) offer detailed discussions on the penetrations of legitimate institutions by organized crime groups.

General treatments of the role of organized criminal activity in society at large are Howard Abadinsky, *Organized Crime* (1991); Jay S. Albanese, *Organized Crime in America* (1989); and Virgil Peterson, *The Mob: 200 Years of Organized Crime in New York* (1983). The focus of some current research efforts steers away from a preoccupation with the organizational structures of Mafia as a generic phenomenon and turns attention to the legal and sociocultural environments in which criminal enterprises operate. Following Schelling, political economists have looked at organized crime as illegal enterprises and employ business models of market organizational structure, supply/demand dynamics, competitive factors affecting costs, prices, and profits, and the technologies utilized by criminal entrepreneurs to sustain their operations. More technical treatments of organized crime as an economic activity may be found in the works of Peter Reuter, *Disorganized Crime* (1983); *Racketeering in Legitimate Industries: A Study in the Economics of Intimidation* (1987); *The Organization of Illegal Markets: An Economic Analysis* (1985); James Buchanan, "A Defense of Organized Crime?" in *The Economics of Crime and Punishment,* ed. Simon Rottenberg and Paul Rubin, "The Economic Theory of the Criminal Firm" (1973); New York State Organized Crime Task Force, *Corruption and Racketeering in the New York City Construction Industry: Final Report* (December 1989); Mark H. Moore, "Organized Crime as a Business Enterprise" in *Major Issues in Organized Crime Control,* ed. H. Edelhertz (National Institute of Justice, September 1987); President's Commission on Organized Crime, *The Edge: Organized Crime, Business and Labor Unions* (March 1986).

HISTORICAL AND NARRATIVE ACCOUNTS

There are many kinds of truth: literary, psychological, economic, cultural, aesthetic, historical. Historians are primarily concerned with historical truth, understood straightforwardly as the question whether or not certain alleged events actually occurred. At the same time there can be much truth in narratives considered as stories. But narrative truth is not the same as historical truth, and it is mistaken to allow one to dissolve into the other. Once it can be established what an author is intending to convey in the question what happened, the issue arises whether or not the account is true. What actually happened is a perilous notion. Several conventional views of organized criminal history are challenged in Alan A. Block's chapter. As may be seen, the issue of what happened is complicated, sometimes extraordinarily so.

Amid a vast literature, the most sensational and emotionally stirring are the numerous personal stories, biographies, and exposés, which are, indeed, subjective, impressionistic, not very rigorous, often a branch of literature, and sometimes an embodiment of a personal vision—or that of a group. Usually narratives lay no serious claim to universal objectivity and prefer to be judged as a particular slant on the past in terms of the demands of the present. Their great appeal is the insider's view, gossip and shocking disclosure, not the sensitive and discriminating (and sometimes tedious) analysis associated with professional academic perspectives. The books by Vincent Teresa (*My Life in the Mafia,* 1973), Ovid Demaris about James Fratianno (1981), and Joseph Bonanno

(*Man of Honor*, 1983) are not meant to scientifically predict but fit their loose and fleeting facts and opinions into a central succession of chronological patterns and enter into the motives and ideas of those identified as the principal actors in dramatic events. To create excitement and interest is a talent that is indispensable to literary artists (and to historians—but not in the same degree), and the writings whose impact on the public is significant tend to be of this type. Occupying an equally prominent status are gangster biographies. Among the most widely known are Peter Maas, *The Valachi Papers* (1969); Vincent Teresa with Thomas C. Renner, *My Life in the Mafia* (1973); Paul Sann, *Kill the Dutchman: The Story of Dutch Schultz* (1971); Nicholas Pileggi, *Wise Guy: Life in a Mafia Family* (1985); Gene Mustain and Jerry Capeci, *Mob Star: The Story of John Gotti* (1988); Paul Meskil, *Don Carlo: Boss of Bosses* (1973); Jack McPhaul, *Johnny Torrio: First of the Gang Lords* (1970); Joseph Bonanno, *A Man of Honor* (1983); Leonard Katz, *Uncle Frank: The Biography of Frank Costello* (1973); Mickey Cohen, *Mickey Cohen: In My Own Words* (1975); Ovid Demaris, *The Last Mafioso: The Treacherous World of Jimmy Fratianno* (1981); Martin Gosch and Richard Hammer, *The Last Testament of Lucky Luciano* (1974); Donald Goddard, *Joey* (1974); John Kobler, *Capone: The Life and World of Al Capone* (1971); George Carpoze, *Bugsy* (1973); Dean Jennings, *We Only Kill Each Other: The Life and Bad Times of Bugsy Siegel* (1967); Robert Lacey, *Little Man: Meyer Lansky and the Gangster Life* (1991); William Broshler, *The Don: The Life and Death of Sam Giancana* (1977).

Within the genre of popular expositions, the works of journalists, attorneys, and law enforcement officials are familiar. Underworld murders and wars, prosecutions and investigations constitute the basis for much of this literature. Because so many of these works are packed with facts, they could hardly help having some uses, and many are sensible and well informed. Books by law enforcement agents and officials describing investigations and trials include Joseph O'Brien and Andris Kurins, *Boss of Bosses: The Fall of the Godfather, the FBI and Paul Castellano* (1991). The book presents details on the secret surveillance of a major Mafia figure and his arrest. Ralph Blumenthal, *Last Days of the Sicilians: At War with the Mafia; The FBI Assault on the Pizza Connection* (1988), and Shana Alexander, *The Pizza Connection: Lawyers, Money, Drugs, Mafia* (1988), are profitable but difficult going. Each is heavily weighted with the humdrum of court proceedings and the eccentricities and antics of defense attorneys. The two journalists inadvertently helped to launch the political career of the chief prosecutor, Rudolph Giuliani, the U.S. attorney in Manhattan, who dramatically declared war on the five families and succeeded in putting most of the important crime family bosses behind bars. Gay Talese, *Honor Thy Father* (1971) is a sympathetic portrait of a powerful Mob figure's son as he struggles with the lures and dangers of underworld celebrity. George Wolf and Joseph DiMora, *Frank Costello Prime Minister of the Underworld* (1974) takes the perspective of a defense attorney representing a major underworld figure whose involvement with big-city and national politics was scandalous.

The activities of law enforcement and government officials in Robert F. Kennedy, *The Enemy Within* (1960); Estes Kefauver, *Crime in America* (1951); John L. McClellan, *Crime Without Punishment* (1962); Burton B. Turkus and Sid Feder, *Murder Inc.* (1953); Charles Siragusa, *The Trail of the Poppy* (1966); Ralph Salerno and John S. Tompkins, *The Crime Confederation* (1969); Joseph Pistone, *Donnie Brasco: My Undercover Life in the Mafia* (1987) illustrate anticrime efforts at various levels in the criminal justice system and give us a glimpse into the ways the problem and operations of police, prosecutors, and politicians concerned with organized crime in the United States since World War II have evolved.

Academic historians have tended to concentrate on major unsettled controversies that serve as a relevant base for a revisionist look at the phenomenon. Professional historians complain long and hard that organized crime is deeper, broader, and more embedded in the local communities where it thrives than formerly believed—a fact often overlooked in the rash of biographies that make up the bulk of media products. The works of serious journalists and investigative reporters such as Jonathan Kwitny, *Vicious Circles: The Mafia in the Market Place* (1979), though not utterly dependent on law enforcement informants and files, tend to be topical and zestful with close attention to myriad details on specific issues but lack the theoretical grip of more scholarly works. Further, popular accounts, no matter how well informed, are constrained by the pressures of media venues for current relevance and mass marketability and are not therefore especially self-conscious about methodologies, and the reliability of evidence and counterevidence or mindful about the need for generalizability. From a law enforcement orientation, historical monographs may add much valuable information on vexing questions, but the enrichment, not matter how persuasive, is dampened by the charge that academic studies, especially those that militantly challenge conventional views, separate head and hand— that is, they ignore or play down law enforcement experiences and knowledge. The alleged disparities in scientific and law enforcement based-work have more to do with emphases and purposes behind the respective activities than negligence or contempt for what others are doing. In brief, the claim is that it is absolutely indispensable that the historian be sensitive to the general structure or pattern of experience, the thick texture of crisscrossing and changing beliefs, circumstances, and behaviors that characterize the subject matter from the law enforcement perspective.

The works of Alan Block, *East Side—West Side: Organizing Crime in New York, 1930–1950* (1985); Mark Haller (various papers); Stephen Fox, *Blood and Power: Organized Crime in Twentieth Century America* (1989); and Marshall B. Clinard, *The Black Market: A Study of White-Collar Crime* (1969) are of particular interest as examples of historical scholarship.

MAFIA AND LA COSA NOSTRA

For all the inexhaustible, at times frightening, outpourings of writings on organized crime, the discussions and analyses of Mafia/La Cosa Nostra have been confined to biographies and largely anecdotal materials of what was believed (and still is among police) to be the major criminal threat in the United States: Mafia. There are some exceptions, and these are fairly recent, sober, and scholarly works on the Mafia in Sicily and the south of Italy. For example, Raimondo Catanzaro, *Men of Respect: A Social History of the Sicilian Mafia* (1992) makes excellent use of the Anti-Mafia Commission Reports to the Italian Parliament and traces the role of the Mafia in politics and in the economy of Italy since World War II. Claire Sterling, *Octopus: The Long Reach of the Sicilian Mafia* (1990) describes the spread and dominance of the Sicilian Mafia's involvement in the heroin trade. Despite its feverish prose, the book contains useful information on the conflicts that raged among Mafia *cosche* for control of vices and the penetration of the legitimate sectors of the Italian economy. Pino Arlacchi's, *Mafia Business: The Mafia Ethic and the Spirit of Capitalism* (1986) is iconoclastic in its formulations and interpretations of the data other scholars consult. Arlacchi sees Mafia resurgence as a function of the response to the institutional disintegration of Italian society that occurred in the stagnation following the furious growth in the economy through the 1960s. Whether the Mafia is a large criminal association much like the American La Cosa Nostra as described by Cressey has been debated among Italian scholars. Henner Hess, *Mafia and Mafiosi: The Structure of Power* (1973), Anton Blok, *The Mafia of a Sicilian Village, 1860–1960; A Study of Violent Peasant Entrepreneurs* (1974), and Christopher Duggan, *Fascism and the Mafia* (1989) argue against the thesis that the Mafia is, in fact, an organizational entity as described by Cressey and others. Among modern scholars, Duggan's view is the most radical in arguing that the idea of the Mafia itself is a fiction constructed out of the cynical political calculations of Fascists who wish to perpetuate the idea for their own purposes. In Duggan's view, the Mafia is not an organized criminal society as ordinarily understood. However, Catanzaro's and Sterling's writings suggest that Mafia *cosche* did develop some structures through which drug trafficking and smuggling could be organized. An early source on Mafia collusion with politicians is Michele Pantaleone, *The Mafia and Politics* (1966).

Anti-Mafia campaigns in Italy have failed repeatedly until fairly recently. Though a bit stodgy, Cesare Mori's, *The Last Struggle with the Mafia* (1933) explains candidly his fruitless efforts to eradicate the elusive phenomenon because it was as much a culturally approved way of life in Sicily as it is criminal behavior.

As with its American counterparts, a confessional literature is emerging in Italy coincident with the collapse of *omerta* (silence) and other values that form the cultural infrastructure of the Mafia. Tim Shawcross and Martin Young, *Men of Honour: The Confessions of Tommaso Buscetta* (1987) is one of the most readable (if questionable) accounts of defection from a criminal way of life.

In the United States, La Cosa Nostra/Mafia, has called forth a sizable literature. While much of it is suggestive and respectable, a reader may rely on a few works for general orientation. One may confidently consult Thomas Monroe Pitken and Francesco Cordasco, *The Black Hand: A Chapter in Ethnic Crime* (1977); Howard Abadinsky, *The Criminal Elite: Professional and Organized Crime* (1983); and Francis Ianni, "Mafia and the Web of Kinship," in *An Inquiry into Organized Crime*, ed. Luciano J. Iorizzo, (New York: The American-Italian Historical Association). Critical views of La Cosa Nostra dominance of American organized crime are numerous; the most trenchant are Gordon Hawkins, "God and the Mafia," *Public Interest* 14 (1969): 24–51; Alan Block, "History and the Study of Organized Crime," *Urban Life* 6 (January 1978): 455–74; Daniel Bell, "The Myth of Cosa Nostra," *New Leader* 46 (December 1963): 12–15; and the studies by Ianni, Albini, and Smith cited previously. The period of history carved out between 1930 and 1980 dramatizes events and conjunctions in American social history that strike many observers of organized crime as decisive.

ETHNIC AND MINORITY ORGANIZED CRIME

Organized crime is perhaps the primary area in criminological and criminal justice studies, where ethnicity, its cultural ethos, and emotional overtones have been mainstays in research. Ethnicity is a major theme of some scholars who subscribe to the view that subcultural values matter in shaping the distinctiveness and character of organized criminal activity among minority groups. A curious aspect of the argument of those who believe that any discussion of organized crime cannot avoid its ethnic aspect concerns the focus on organizational models that do not depend on blood and power and a consciousness of kind but on the quasi-rational legal authority associated with bureaucratic entities. Ironically, La Cosa Nostra, the criminal structure that epitomizes ethnicity in crime, is described in purely bureaucratic terms and concepts. Actually, ethnicity as an organizing principle makes enormously good sense. For Stephen Fox, *Blood and Power* (1989), ethnicity played a significant role in underworld organizational structures, methods, and styles affecting associates and criminal specialties.

Ethnicity as a bonding mechanism effectively suffuses subcultural values through gangs and groups, making it unnecessary to develop elaborate security mechanisms. Organizational integrity can be maintained through shared understanding. An analogy with the British Empire at the zenith of its prestige in the nineteenth century will help to make the point. The ideologies of British hegemonic imperialism served as a substitute for highly articulated centralized control bodies. The English knew what was expected of them no matter where they were; they needed little exhortation or instruction. Similarly, in ethnically homogeneous criminal organizations, collectively shared norms and values facilitate the operations and integrity of criminal enterprises.

The prominence of ethnic groups in organized crime has been debated since the large-scale migration into the United States after the Civil War. A body of literature is tied to alien conspiracy, native reactions, and xenophobia. In the popular accounts of journalists, writers, and law enforcement authorities through 1967, ethnic criminality plagues America. Scientific works on the characteristics and predilections of some ethnic groups for crime may be found in Jenna Joselit, *Our Gang: Jewish Crime and the New York Jewish Community* (1983); Gerald C. Posner, *Warlords of Crime: Chinese Secret Societies—The New Mafia* (1988); Gwen Kinkead, *Chinatown* (1992); Jeremy Bossevain, *Friends of Friends: Networks, Manipulations and Coalitions* (1974). A comprehensive sociohistorical treatment of Chinese crime is presented in Ko-lin Chin, *Chinese Subculture and Criminality: Nontraditional Crime Groups in America* (1990); for a sociological analysis of urban black organized crime in the United States, see Rufus Schatzberg, *Black Organized Crime in Harlem: 1920–1930* (1993). Similar studies examining the structure and dynamics of vice activities in black ghettos are Harold D. Lasswell and Jeremiah B. McKenna, *The Impact of Organized Crime on an Inner-City* (1972); Ivan Light, "The Ethnic Vice Industry; 1880–1944," *American Sociological Review* 42 (June 1977): 464–79; and Frederick T. Martens, "African-American Organized Crime, An Ignored Phenomenon," *Federal Probation* (December 1990): 43–50. A community-wide study focusing on Harlem's blacks and Latino communities that utilized anthropological concepts such as networking to chart the development of incipient organized crime groups in Francis A. J. Ianni, *Black Mafia: Ethnic Succession in Organized Crime* (1975).

Latino gangs and organized criminality are described in James Virgil, *Barrio Gangs* (1988). An interesting comparative analysis using ethnographic data collection techniques of ghetto gangs is utilized in Mercer Sullivan, *Getting Paid: Youth, Crime and Work in the Inner City* (1989). Irish American organized criminality and politics is discussed in Steven P. Erie, *Rainbow's End: Irish-Americans and the Dilemmas of Urban Machine Politics, 1840–1985* (1988); for Italian American participation in urban crime, see Humbert S. Nelli, "Italians and Crime in Chicago," *American Journal of Sociology* 74 (January 1969): 373–91.

For theoretical treatments of ethnic and minority involvement in organized crime, an indispensable article is Daniel Bell, *The End of Ideology* (1964), a popularization of Robert Merton's theory of structurally induced anomie and deviance.

FICTION AND FILM

The world of organized crime in novels and films is, of course, one of commodities but also of representation, and representations—their production, circulation, and interpretation—are the very elements of popular cultural responses. Yet, the thematic content of so many portrayals in writing and film rarely puts organized crime in its full political context, which is primarily corruption. Instead, we have, on one hand, a comparatively isolated criminal sphere, presented as freely and unconditionally available to weightless theoretical speculation and law enforcement investigation, and, on the other, a debased political sphere, alluded to fleetingly, where the real struggle between interests is supposed to occur. To the student of organized crime—scholar, criminal justice practitioner, interested citizen—it would seem that only one sphere is relevant, and, more to the point, it seems widely accepted that politics and crime are separated, whereas the two not only are connected but may be ultimately the same.

A radical falsification has become established in this separation. Construed primarily as a species of ethnic and minority illegal activity, organized crime becomes exonerated of any significant entanglements with power. Yet, while this separation of crime and politics may not be an act of conscious complicity, the choice (accidental or deliberate) disguises, denudes, and purges accounts of it so that a model of organized crime emerges whose principal features are exotic and entertaining. A more embattled model in which the ebb and flow of political intrigue and manipulation would figure centrally might coalesce the discussion and debates more realistically around the continuing struggle over the question of massive, systematic public corruption.

Mario Puzo's *The Godfather* (1969) is the most influential novel written in this century on organized crime, though its focus is limited to a Mafia crime family. The films produced from it, *The Godfather* (1972), *The Godfather, Part II* (1974), and *The Godfather, Part III* (1991), offer a powerfully consolidated vision of the moral and social conflicts informing the activities of the principal characters. Organized crime provides the Corleone family with wealth and sets their dubious social status. The end of this trilogy of ruthlessness and violence offers a sort of redemption for the chief protagonist, the Mafia chief, Michael Corleone, who passes the mantle of leadership to a relative, seeks and achieves personal salvation and reconciliation with the church and his children, and sheds the blemishes of his brutal career through acts of philanthropy. The novel and the films are emblematic of organized crime seen as an organic part of the scramble for wealth, power, and material success in society. Yet, despite their formidable, complex realism, they are distillations, simplifications that are far less messy and mixed up than the reality. It would not be fair to think of them as abstractions, although fictions so elaborately fashioned and so enthralling as these suit the necessities of narrative which, as a result, makes them a highly specialized entry into the discussion of organized crime.

Other contemporary writing and films are unthinkable without the *Godfather* models. *Hoffa* (1992) is a quasi-biographical film about the charismatic labor leader whose stormy career was intertwined with racketeers and corrupt labor leaders. Packed into the plot mechanism are exonerating references to the existing institutions of society and its authority and power. The hero exhibits restless energy and a stubbornness to aspire to the American Dream, but his experiences painfully reveal the limits of legitimacy. As with the *Godfather* theme, the film ends with the death of the hero, who by virtue of his overflowing energy and goodwill does not fit into the orderly scheme of things. It is striking that in many contemporary novels and films about organized crime, including *Bugsy* (1990), the world beyond the gangster is glimpsed as passive and mysterious, as much the victim of criminal activities as its initiator. It is a challenge, then, to see organized crime in this way, not just as antiseptically quarantined from political affiliation but as an extraordinarily varied field of criminal endeavor.

The underworld has dramatically changed since Puzo and Coppola in ways that surprise and often alarm criminal justice experts, scholars, and the public, who must now confront a nonwhite immigrant population in their midst and face an impressive roster of newly empowered criminals. Actually, many nontraditional criminal groups—Chinese, Latinos, African Americans—have been here for some time, but only recently have law enforcement and scholarly and public attention shifted attention to them. Thus, organized crime is no large monolith with La Cosa Nostra at its core. Some melodramatic but nonetheless interesting writings along these lines include Robert Daley, *The Year of the Dragon* (1982), subsequently produced as a film bearing the same title, which focuses on Chinese drug trafficking in New York City's Chinatown; *Malcolm X* (1992), Spike Lee's film based on the *Autobiography of Malcolm X* (1964), in which coauthor Alex Haley describes the Harlem underworld of drugs, prostitution, and vice; Claude Brown *Manchild in the Promised Land* (1965), a sort of great expectations biography in which the protagonist, the author, goes off the rails, enters a life of street crime, and reforms; and Piri Thomas, *Down These Mean Streets* (1965), another autobiography depicting the squalor and violence of Puerto Rican slum life. Most of these books are mechanical recitations of criminal life occasioned by class, oppression, economic deprivation, and racial injustice. Such books do, however, have some value in that they are very much in the history of the social groups and are in some measure shaped by it.

GOVERNMENT REPORTS AND LAW ENFORCEMENT SOURCES

Law enforcement agencies operate within a fairly narrowly constricted environment defined by their specific missions. We do not want to be misunderstood here. Often, too often perhaps, investigative commissions and legislative committees, which are political, exploit formulas and agendas about the causes, prevalence, and structure of organized criminal groups that amount to little more than a conspiracy theory. Alternatively, when lacking preconceived underlying themes or points of view that mold the account by collecting supporting evidence and empirical data, government documents (with rare exceptions) are equivalents of the *Guinness Book of Records*: an exhibition of notable characters, events, and facts deemed to be noteworthy simply because they are widely publicized. The result is a compilation of news clips, anecdotal accounts, or preformed stereotypes masquerading as reliable conclusions based on careful analysis. In short, the problem with many official statements and reports is that they rely on sensational and problematic hypotheses to attract attention.

These caveats might imply that government-generated reports are unreliable or uninformative. Not so. No law enforcement agency product ought to be met with reflexive distrust. Too much skepticism about the integrity of government reports is unfair. What is sorely needed is a comprehensive synthesis of work emerging from numerous agencies at all levels of government.

The most recent major government report on organized crime in the United States is *The Impact: Organized Crime Today*, Report to the President and the Attorney General, President's Commission on Organized Crime (April 1986). Several of the commissions' hearings and reports provide testimony from experts and witnesses on labor racketeering, drug trafficking, money laundering, and so on. Over the past twenty-five years two presidential commissions have focused on organized crime: the 1967 and 1986 reports. Each regarded its primary tasks as developing an agenda assessing (1) the definition of organized crime, (2) the principal areas of activity of organized crime groups, (3) the types and structures of organized criminal groups, (4) their role in private and public corruption, and (5) law enforcement recommendations for control. Also at the federal level, the National Institute of Justice sponsors research on all facets of organized crime through its research programs.

At the state and local levels some organizations, primarily commissions, carry on investigations and hearings. The Pennsylvania Crime Commission, the New York State Task Force on Organized Crime, and the Chicago and New Orleans Crime Commissions are examples of regional and local governmental agencies and bodies. Each possesses investigative resources (in Pennsylvania and New York, commission and task force agents have some law enforcement powers), and each provides a useful public service in alerting the public to problems in specific localities.

The legal authority of citizens and state commissions varies from state to state. The State Commission of Investigation of New Jersey and the New York State Task Force on Organized Crime are authorized to conduct electronic surveillance. Because their main task is to gather information, commissions have proved to be invaluable tools in crime control. See, as an example, *Organized Crime in Pennsylvania: A Decade of Change, 1990 Report*, Pennsylvania Crime Commission; *Corruption and Racketeering in New York City Construction Industry*, Final Report, New York State Organized Crime Task Force (1989).

INVESTIGATIVE AND PROSECUTORIAL
STRATEGIES AND TECHNIQUES

Because organized criminal activity is such that victims are reluctant to come forward or because so much of this crime involves conspiracies of all kinds, traditional reactive police methods are usually ineffective against it. Law enforcement investigations must, therefore, be initiated on the basis of reasonable suspicion or, which is more likely, on intelligence data gathered by specialists and on informants' revelations and disclosures. Most investigations require prolonged searches and undercover surveillance as well as detailed analyses of business records. When sufficient evidence is gathered, arrests, indictments, and prosecutions begin.

The organization of investigative resources is a complex process that analysts and practitioners have developed into models of "rackets bureaus" that pull together and coordinate teams of specialists involving police and prosecutors. See G. Robert Blakey, Ronald Goldstock, and Charles H. Rogovin, *Rackets Bureau: Investigative and Prosecution of Organized Crime* (1978); Herbert Edelhertz, ed., *Major Issues in Organized Crime Control* (September 1987); U.S. Department of Justice, Administrative Office of the United States Courts, *Report on Application for Orders Authorizing or Approving the Intercept of Wire and Oral Communications* (1987).

The scope and power of investigative groups and agencies have dramatically increased since 1967. The sensational committee hearings of various legislative bodies and civil commission reports on organized crime were influential in arousing public support for the Omnibus Crime Control Act of 1970, which provided for use immunity to compel witnesses to testify and for special sentencing of organized criminals. Title IX of the Act (Racketeer Influenced and Corrupt Organizations' Act or RICO) has emerged as one of the most powerful tools to combat organized crime. See U.S. comptroller general, *Drug Investigation: Organized Crime Drug Enforcement Task Force Program's Accomplishments* (1987); Ralph Blumenthal, *Last Days of the Sicilians: At War with the Mafia: The FBI Assault on the Pizza Connection* (1989); Shana Alexander, *The Pizza Connection: Lawyers, Money, Drugs, Mafia* (1988) and *The Gotti Tapes* (1992); Patrick J. Ryan and Robert J. Kelly, "Analysis of RICO and OCCA: Federal and State Legislative Instruments Against Crime," *Violence, Aggression and Terrorism* 3 (1989); U.S. Senate, Committee on Government Affairs, Permanent Subcommittee of Investigation, *Hearings, Organized Crime: 25 Years After Valachi* (1988).

Index

About the Contributors

JAY S. ALBANESE is professor and chair of the Department of Political Science and Criminal Justice at Niagara University. He has recently been elected president of the Academy of Criminal Justice Sciences. He is author of several books on issues of crime and justice, including *Organized Crime in America* (1989), *Crime: A Dozen of America's Existing and Emerging Problems* (with Robert Pursley, 1993), and *Dealing with Delinquency* (1993).

JOSEPH L. ALBINI is visiting professor of Criminal Justice at the University of Nevada, Las Vegas. He has written extensively on organized crime, including his seminal work, *The American Mafia: Genesis of a Legend*.

G. ROBERT BLAKEY is professor of Law in the Notre Dame University Law School. In his distinguished career, he served as chief counsel and staff director of the House Select Committee on Assassinations. His scholarly work on the 1967 President's Task Force on Organized Crime led to the foundation and passage of the federal RICO statute.

ALAN A. BLOCK is professor of the Administration of Justice at Pennsylvania State University. His many studies on organized crime include *The Business of Crime: A Documentary Study of Organized Crime in the American Industrial Economy*, *War on Drugs: Studies in the Failure of U.S. Policy*, and *East Side–West Side: Organizing Crime in New York, 1930–1950*.

KO-LIN CHIN is assistant professor in the Department of Sociology, Anthropology, and Criminal Justice, Rutgers University-Newark. He has conducted research on college students' drug use, alcoholism among Chinese immigrants, crack use and crime, domestic violence in Chinatown, and Chinese street gangs. He is the author of *Chinese Subculture and Criminality: Non-Traditional Crime Groups in America* (Greenwood Press, 1990). His most recent publications include "Out-of-Town Brides: International Marriage and Wife Abuse Among Chinese Immigrant Families" (*Journal of Comparative Families*, forthcoming) and "Triad Societies in Hong Kong" (*Rassegna Italiana de Sociologia*, forthcoming).

WILLIAM J. COOK, JR. is assistant professor in the Criminal Justice Department at Westfield State College. He served as an investigator in the Inspector General's Office of the Board of Education, as well as in the Office of the Deputy Commissioner of Investigation of the City of New York. He has authored a variety of articles and a book (*Security Systems, Layout, and Performance*, 1982).

JOHN DOMBRINK is an associate professor in the Department of Criminology, Law and Society in the School of Social Ecology at the University of California, Irvine. In addition to research on the policing of Asian racketeering, he has published articles and a book on legal gambling, vice and the law, and the use of RICO and other recent laws and strategies against organized crime.

JEFFREY FAGAN is an associate professor in the School of Criminal Justice of Rutgers University, where he also is director of the Center for Research on Urban Violence. He is author, with Joseph Weis, of the forthcoming book, *Drug Use and Delinquency Among Inner City Youth*. He also is editor of the *Journal of Research in Crime and Delinquency*.

JAMES O. FINCKENAUER is a professor of Criminal Justice at the School of Criminal Justice, Rutgers University. His principal current research interests include juvenile delinquency, organized crime, and comparative studies in the Soviet Union. He is the author of *Scared Straight! and the Panacea Phenomenon* (1982). He is the coauthor of *Organized Crime in America* and *The Meaning of Law for American and Soviet Youth: A Comparative Study of Legal Socialization*.

RONALD GOLDSTOCK has been director of the New York State Organized Crime Task Force since 1981. He has designed and developed a law enforcement organization that combines academic research, strategic analysis, and the innovative use of a wide variety of remedies with traditional prosecutorial and investigative efforts. He is also author of a number of law review articles on loan-sharking and extortion, RICO, and labor racketeering. He is on the faculty of the Cornell Law School.

MARK H. HALLER is professor of American History and Criminal Justice at Temple University. He has published extensively on organized crime in urban society and on various aspects of racketeering. His recent works include *Life Under Bruno: The Economics of an Organized Crime Family* (1991) and "Illegal Enterprise: A Theoretical and Historical Interpretation" (*Criminology*, 1990).

FRANCIS A. J. IANNI is professor of anthropology and director of the Horace Mann Institute at Columbia University. Author of many articles and research studies, his books include *The Black Mafia* and *A Family Business: Kinship and Social Control in Organized Crime*, which set in motion new approaches to the study of organized crime in the United States.

ROBERT J. KELLY is Broeklundian professor of Social Science at Brooklyn College, and professor of Criminal Justice in the Graduate School, City University of New York. He has conducted research on organized criminal activities, terrorism, violence in maximum security correctional facilities, and minority students in higher educational institutions. His publications include *Deviance, Dominance and Denigration, Organized Crime: A Global Perspective*, and numerous essays and articles in various journals.

MARK A. R. KLEIMAN is associate professor of Public Policy at the John F. Kennedy School of Government, Harvard University. A former drug policy analyst with the U.S. Department of Justice, he is the author of *Against Excess: Drug Policy for Results* and many articles and research monographs on drug-related issues.

ROBERT M. LOMBARDO is a twenty-five-year veteran of the Chicago Police Department. He is currently a doctoral candidate at University of Illinois at Chicago studying the effects of social structure upon organized crime. He is the former commanding officer of the Chicago Police Asset Forfeiture Unit and has lectured extensively on forfeiture in both the United States and abroad.

MICHAEL D. MALTZ is professor of Criminal Justice and Quantitative Methods at the University of Illinois at Chicago. He is the author of *Recidivism* and numerous articles on organized crime and the problems in defining it.

FREDERICK T. MARTENS is the executive director of the Pennsylvania Crime Commission. He has served as a deputy superintendent in the New Jersey State Police Intelligence Division. He teaches at the Pennsylvania State University. Among his many publications is a book, *Police Intelligence Systems in Crime Control* (with Justin Dintino).

MARILYN B. PETERSON is a management specialist for the Organized Crime Racketeering Task Force within the Division of Criminal Justice, Department of Law and Public Sfety, State of New Jersey, where she now specializes in policy analysis and program development. Her law enforcement career began in 1980 as the chief writer for the Pennsylvania Crime Commission report, *A Decade of Organized Crime*. She coedited the analytical text *Criminal Intelligence Analysis* (1990). Her work has primarily been in the fields of organized crime and narcotics.

PETER REUTER is codirector of the Drug Policy Research Center of the Rand Corporation in Washington, D.C. He is the author of *Disorganized Crime: The Economics of the Visible Hand* and many research monographs on racketeering, gambling, illicit drug markets, and criminal infiltration of the waste disposal industry.

CHARLES H. ROGOVIN is professor of Law, Temple University, president of the International Association for the Study of Organized Crime, and vice-chairman of the Pennsylvania Crime Commission. From 1983 to 1986 he served as a member of the President's Commission on Organized Crime and is a former president of the Police Forum. He has published on racketeering enterprises and crime control strategies.

PATRICK J. RYAN is an assistant professor in the Department of Criminal Justice, Long Island University. He is the executive director of the International Association for the Study of Organized Crime, former editor of *Criminal Organizations*, and director of the Center for Drug Studies, Long Island University, School of Public Service.

RUFUS SCHATZBERG served in the U.S. Navy during World War II (1941–46) as a chief electronic technician. He then served twenty-six years in the New York City Police Department as a detective first class, where he received many awards, including the Department Honorable Mention and the Bronx Grand Jury Medal for Valor. Upon retirement he organized and headed the security forces at Co-op City from its construction stage till five years after completion and fully occupied. He is the author of *Black Organized Crime in Harlem: 1920–1930* (1993) and of numerous articles on terrorism, organized crime, and crime in schools, one of which was recently published in Germany. He is currently writing a book with Robert J. Kelly on the social history of African American organized crime.

DWIGHT C. SMITH, JR., is the author of the *Mafia Mystique* (1975, 1990) and a number of articles and other works concerning organized crime and illicit enterprise. He is currently enrolled in the doctoral program in Organization Studies at the University at Albany/SUNY.

JOHN HUEY-LONG SONG is an assistant professor in the Department of Criminal Justice at the State University College at Buffalo. He received his Ph.D. from the University of California Irvine in 1988. His research interests focus on adoptions of Asian immigrants to the American legal system. He has recently published articles on this topic, on the causes of Asian youth gangs, and on the policing of Asian racketeering.

CHARLES WINICK is professor of Sociology in the Graduate School of the City University of New York. He has published widely and is the author of *The New People, the Lively Commerce* and other books and essays dealing with drugs, prostitution, and social problems. He also serves as editor of the *Journal of Drug Issues*.